AF716638

OXFORD STUDIES IN EUROPEAN LAW

Series Editors

PAUL CRAIG

Professor of English Law at St John's College, Oxford

GRÁINNE DE BÚRCA

Professor of Law at New York University School of Law

Foreign Policy Objectives in European Constitutional Law

OXFORD STUDIES IN EUROPEAN LAW

Series Editors
Paul Craig, Professor of English Law at St John's College, Oxford and
Gráinne de Búrca, Professor of Law at New York University School of Law

The aim of this series is to publish important and original research on EU law. The focus is on scholarly monographs, with a particular emphasis on those which are interdisciplinary in nature. Edited collections of essays will also be included where they are appropriate. The series is wide in scope and aims to cover studies of particular areas of substantive and of institutional law, historical works, theoretical studies, and analyses of current debates, as well as questions of perennial interest such as the relationship between national and EU law and the novel forms of governance emerging in and beyond Europe. The fact that many of the works are interdisciplinary will make the series of interest to all those concerned with the governance and operation of the EU.

OTHER TITLES IN THIS SERIES

Economic Governance in Europe
Comparative Paradoxes and Constitutional Challenges
Federico Fabbrini

Private Regulation and the Internal Market
Sports, Legal Services, and Standard Setting in EU Economic Law
Mislav Mataija

The EU Deep Trade Agenda
Law and Policy
Billy A Melo Araujo

The Human Rights of Migrants and Refugees in European Law
Cathryn Costello

An Ever More Powerful Court?
The Political Constraints of Legal Integration in the European Union
Dorte Sindbjerg Martinsen

The Concept of State Aid under EU Law
From Internal Market to Competition and Beyond
Juan Jorge Piernas López

Justice in the EU
The Emergence of Transnational Solidarity
Floris De Witte

The Euro Area Crisis in Constitutional Perspective
Alicia Hinarejos

The European Fundamental Freedoms
A Contextual Approach
Pedro Caro de Sousa

National Identity in EU Law
Elke Cloots

The Constitutional Foundations of European Contract Law
A Comparative Analysis
Kathleen Gutman

The Criminalization of European Cartel Enforcement
Theoretical, Legal, and Practical Challenges
Peter Whelan

Fundamental Rights in Europe
Challenges and Transformations in Comparative Perspective
Federico Fabbrini

The Principle of Loyalty in EU Law
Marcus Klamert

Constitutional Pluralism in the EU
Klemen Jaklic

EU Consumer Law and Human Rights
Iris Benöhr

The Principle of Mutual Recognition in EU Law
Christine Janssens

The Coherence of EU Free Movement Law
Constitutional Responsibility and the Court of Justice
Niamh Nic Shuibhne

Foreign Policy Objectives in European Constitutional Law

JORIS LARIK

Assistant Professor of Comparative, EU, and International Law, Leiden University; Senior Researcher, The Hague Institute for Global Justice

European University Institute

OXFORD
UNIVERSITY PRESS

OXFORD
UNIVERSITY PRESS

Great Clarendon Street, Oxford, OX2 6DP,
United Kingdom

Oxford University Press is a department of the University of Oxford.
It furthers the University's objective of excellence in research, scholarship, and education by publishing worldwide. Oxford is a registered trade mark of Oxford University Press in the UK and in certain other countries

© J. Larik 2016

The moral rights of the author have been asserted

First Edition Published in 2016

All rights reserved. No part of this publication may be reproduced, stored in a retrieval system, or transmitted, in any form or by any means, without the prior permission in writing of Oxford University Press, or as expressly permitted by law, by licence or under terms agreed with the appropriate reprographics rights organization. Enquiries concerning reproduction outside the scope of the above should be sent to the Rights Department, Oxford University Press, at the address above

You must not circulate this work in any other form
and you must impose this same condition on any acquirer

Crown copyright material is reproduced under Class Licence
Number C01P0000148 with the permission of OPSI
and the Queen's Printer for Scotland

Published in the United States of America by Oxford University Press
198 Madison Avenue, New York, NY 10016, United States of America

British Library Cataloguing in Publication Data
Data available

Library of Congress Control Number: 2015960493

ISBN 978–0–19–873639–4

Links to third party websites are provided by Oxford in good faith and for information only. Oxford disclaims any responsibility for the materials contained in any third party website referenced in this work.

Opgedragen aan mijn ouders Marijke en Joost:
'Voor wie ik liefheb wil ik schrijven'

Series Editors' Preface

This book, which deals with the subject of foreign policy objectives as norms within European constitutional law, comes at a time when the European Union's (EU) global role, and its relationship to the foreign policies of its Member States, is a matter of lively debate. Crises both external and internal to the EU have renewed attention on the EU's effectiveness and character as a global power. Much of the scholarly literature on the topic of the EU's global role has been within the field of political science, and within the sub-field of international relations in particular. This book supplements the international relations literature by focusing on a distinctively legal dimension of the subject, namely an exploration of the significance of enshrining foreign policy objectives as constitutional law.

The book examines both EU foreign policy objectives within the treaties and foreign policy objectives included in the constitutions of other states. The author uses a comparative constitutional methodology—looking at eleven countries outside of Europe, and also surveying the foreign policy objectives across all twenty-eight EU national constitutions—to reflect on the role and function of foreign policy objectives within constitutions, and to derive a 'common vocabulary' from amongst these constitutions. He argues that foreign policy objectives within constitutions focus primarily on the outlook of the political system towards the rest of the world ('dynamic internationalization'), rather than on issues such as rights or separation of powers that are normally found within constitutions. He suggests that they are more like guiding principles than strict rules, and that they are only marginally justiciable.

However, while the early chapters of the book analyse and parse the foreign policy objectives within Member State constitutions and a range of third countries, the predominant focus of the book is on the foreign policy objectives of the EU and on what the inclusion of those objectives as constitutional norms indicate about the EU as an international actor. Ultimately, the author argues that while the EU is certainly not exceptional or even unusual in constitutionalizing foreign policy norms to reflect this kind of dynamic international stance, it is perhaps in the vanguard, having gone further in its rhetoric and verbosity than other political systems and states in this respect.

The last part of the book attempts to bring the substantial international relations literature on the global character of the EU into conversation with the more legally oriented analysis of foreign policy objectives as constitutional norms. The author asks whether the findings of the book's constitutional law analysis are more consistent with one or other international relations theory (constructivism vs realism, for example) and whether constitutional law has anything to offer to international relations scholarship.

In all, the book contains a rich collection of comparative constitutional analysis on a topic which has not been the subject of much legal scholarly inquiry to date.

It makes a distinctive contribution to the literature on the EU as a foreign policy actor, by focusing on the role of foreign policy objectives as constitutional norms. It is a thoughtful and carefully researched book which will be of interest to students and scholars of EU international relations law and EU constitutional law, and to international relations specialists interested in learning more about the role played by European constitutional law in this field.

Paul Craig and Gráinne de Búrca

Acknowledgements

This book is based on my doctoral dissertation, which was defended at the Department of Law of the European University Institute (EUI) in Florence on 3 June 2013. It was subsequently revised and updated in Leuven and The Hague, which—though not under the Tuscan sun—proved to be very inspirational localities as well.

For many reasons, one could say that going to the EUI was one of the best decisions of my life. I spent four fantastic years in Florence, which were both highly formative and extremely enjoyable. It is an extraordinary privilege to be able to gaze at the beauty of the rolling landscape and the Renaissance landmarks while pondering the idea of Europe and the intricacies of the law. This will always be one of my fondest memories.

This decision and the present book in which it culminated would not have come about without the kind help of the right people at the right time. Hence, first of all, I would like to thank Andrés Delgado Casteleiro and Mikko Huttunen for recommending the EUI to me. I am equally grateful to Esa Paasivirta and Jan Wouters for recommending me to the EUI.

The most vocal acknowledgement with regard to this book is certainly owed to Marise Cremona. She has been a formidable supervisor throughout the entirety of this project. She played a crucial part in helping me find, define and refine the topic and in improving each chapter with invaluable feedback, all the while being Head of Department and subsequently President of the EUI. If she is not an academic role model, I would not know who is.

I am very grateful, furthermore, to Loïc Azoulai, Christophe Hillion, and Daniel Thym for having kindly agreed to sit on the jury for the defence of the thesis and for their feedback and support with a view to turning the dissertation into a book. In addition to those already mentioned, and from among the many insightful interlocutors who have enriched the book and the scholarly endeavours that brought it about, I would like to thank in particular Christiane Ahlborn, Eamon Aloyo, Fabian Amtenbrink, Steven Blockmans, Bernhard Blumenau, Piet Eeckhout, Federico Fabbrini, Daniel Halberstam, Christoph Herrmann, Dimitry Kochenov, Panos Koutrakos, Madalina Moraru, Karolina Podstawa, Bart Van Vooren, Pascal Vennesson, and Quentin Weiler.

Beyond being a professional exercise, writing a doctoral dissertation and subsequently transforming it into a monograph also represents close to six years of my life that have been made all the more pleasant by the kindness of many friends, old and new. To name but a few from among the Florentines, I thank Aaron & Maria, Anna, Basia & Matt, Chris, Conor & Constanze, Cornelius, David, Eugenio, Heko & Miluska, Igor G., Igor & Laura, Jannis & Eva, Johanna, Juha & Nathaniah, Keiva, Luísa, Marco, Oliver, Sanne, and Tommaso.

Moreover, this book could not have been written without the proper resources. I therefore acknowledge the privilege of having been able to make use of the excellent libraries of the EUI, the University of Michigan Law School, the University of Passau, the KU Leuven, Leiden University, and the Peace Palace Library in The Hague. I am grateful, furthermore, for the financial subsidy from the EUI to support the publication of this book, as well as for the generous scholarships afforded to me over the years by NUFFIC, the *Studienstiftung des Deutschen Volkes*, and the *Freistaat Bayern*. I am thankful to Erin Jackson for her outstanding editorial support, and to the teams from Oxford University Press, in particular Elinor Shields and the anonymous reviewers of the manuscript, and Newgen for helping to guide the book safely to publication. In addition, I greatly appreciate that both The Hague Institute for Global Justice and Leiden University College, in the face of many projects and commitments, allowed me the time necessary to finalize the book.

Last but certainly not least, I thank Alanna for her love and affection, which—cypress trees and *Duomo* notwithstanding—turned out to be by far the most beautiful aspect of my time in Florence, and continues to be so today as we have come to dwell in the International City of Peace and Justice. She alone is reason enough to keep me writing, if only in the hope of creating something worthwhile that I can dedicate to her.

JL

The Hague
February 2016

Table of Contents

Table of Cases

COURT OF JUSTICE OF THE EUROPEAN UNION

Cases

Opinions

Rulings

AN ARD-CHÚIRT (IRELAND)

BUNDESVERFASSUNGSGERICHT (GERMANY)

CONSEIL CONSTITUTIONNEL (FRANCE)

CORTE COSTITUZIONALE (ITALY)

SUPREME COURT OF INDIA

SUPREME COURT OF THE UNITED STATES

INTERNATIONAL COURT OF JUSTICE

PERMANENT COURT OF INTERNATIONAL JUSTICE

Table of Legislation and Other Documents

EUROPEAN UNION

Treaty on European Union (TEU; consolidated version: [2012] OJ C 326/13)

Treaty on the Functioning of the European Union (TFEU; consolidated version: [2012] OJ C 326/47)

Convention on the Future of Europe

Other EU documents

EU MEMBER STATE DOCUMENTS

Austria

Belgium

UNITED NATIONS DOCUMENTS

OTHER INTERNATIONAL AGREEMENTS AND DOCUMENTS

List of Abbreviations

ACP	African, Caribbean, and Pacific
AFSJ	Area of Freedom, Security and Justice
ASEAN	Association of Southeast Asian Nations
BIT	Bilateral Investment Treaty
BRIC	Brazil, Russia, India, and China
CCP	Common Commercial Policy
CFSP	Common Foreign and Security Policy
CJEU	Court of Justice of the European Union
CSDP	Common Security and Defence Policy
CT	Constitutional Treaty
EAEC/Euratom	European Atomic Energy Community
EBRD	European Bank for Reconstruction and Development
ECHR	European Convention on Human Rights
ECOWAS	Economic Community of West African States
ECSC	European Coal and Steel Community
EDC	European Defence Community
EDF	European Development Fund
EEA	European Economic Area
EEAS	European External Action Service
EEC	European Economic Community
ENP	European Neighbourhood Policy
EP	European Parliament
EPC	European Political Community/European Political Cooperation
ESDP	European Security and Defence Policy
EU	European Union
EUTM Mali	European Union Training Mission in Mali
FAO	Food and Agricultural Organization
GC	General Court
GSP	Generalised System of Preferences
ICC	International Criminal Court
ICJ	International Court of Justice
IGC	Intergovernmental Conference
ILO	International Labour Organization
IO	International Organization
IR	International Relations
JHA	Justice and Home Affairs
Mercosur	Mercado Común del Sur
NATO	North Atlantic Treaty Organization
OECD	Organisation for Economic Co-operation and Development
OEEC	Organization for European Economic Co-operation
OSCE	Organization for Security and Co-operation in Europe
PCIJ	Permanent Court of International Justice
SEA	Single European Act

TEC	Treaty Establishing the European Community
TEU	Treaty on European Union
TFEU	Treaty on the Functioning of the European Union
UDHR	Universal Declaration of Human Rights
UN	United Nations
UNCLOS	United Nations Convention on the Law of the Sea
VCLTIO	Vienna Convention on the Law of Treaties between States and International Organizations or Between International Organizations
VIPs	Values, Images, and Principles
WEU	Western European Union
WTO	World Trade Organization

Introduction

1. Europe's Global Ambitions as a Topic of Constitutional Law

Salus populi suprema lex esto—'the welfare of the people shall be the supreme law'—is probably the most well-known sentence from Marcus Tullius Cicero's *De Legibus*,[1] written during the final years of the Roman Republic before its demise. Many centuries later, a growing number of 'supreme laws', in other words constitutions, do not stop there. They have come to address not only the *salus populi*, but indeed something which Cicero himself might have called the *salus populorum* or *salus mundi*—the 'welfare of peoples' or the 'welfare of the world'. Constitutions today increasingly exhibit a considerable amount of global ambitions. In the vanguard of this trend, we encounter none other than the highest laws of the European Union (EU). With the entry into force of the Lisbon Treaty, the EU has committed itself to a rich catalogue of aims to be pursued on the world stage. At the same time, and not without historical irony, in view of the various and often related financial, sovereign debt, political, and constitutional crises with which the EU is confronted,[2] pessimists may see it too in the final years before its demise.

In order to come to terms with this remarkable development in constitutional design, this book presents a comprehensive account of foreign policy objectives as norms in European constitutional law.[3] It is about norms that have been added to the repertoire of modern constitutional texts only rather recently, but the proliferation of which has become an undeniable fact, with the EU Treaties boasting some of the most wide-ranging ambitions in the world. Codified foreign policy objectives appear weak when compared to individual rights or rules on the allocation of powers, but they promise more than any other kind of norm in constitutional law.

[1] A Dyck, *A Commentary on Cicero, De Legibus* (The University of Michigan Press, 2004) 459, states that the phrase *salus populi* is 'virtually Ciceronian property', having been frequently used by him in different variations in his speeches and writings.

[2] See F Fabbrini, *Economic Governance in Europe: Comparative Paradoxes, Constitutional Challenges* (OUP, 2016); A Hinarejos, *The Euro Area Crisis in Constitutional Perspective* (OUP, 2015); and K Tuori and K Tuori, *The Eurozone Crisis: A Constitutional Analysis* (CUP, 2014).

[3] The terms EU 'external relations', 'foreign policy', and 'external action' are used interchangeably throughout the book. The preference for the expression 'external relations' with regard to the EU is primarily historical in nature: see G de Búrca, 'EU External Relations: The Governance Mode of Foreign Policy' in B Van Vooren, S Blockmans, and J Wouters (eds), *The EU's Role in Global Governance: The Legal Dimension* (OUP, 2013) 43–4.

With the entry into force of the Lisbon Treaty on 1 December 2009, a set of norms became part of the 'basic constitutional charter'[4] of the EU, which mandate it to 'uphold and promote its values and interests and contribute to the protection of its citizens' in its relations with the 'wider world',[5] and which stipulate that its external action 'shall be guided by the principles which have inspired its own creation, development and enlargement'.[6] These include, inter alia, peace, security, sustainable development, free and fair trade, eradication of poverty, protection of human rights, strict observance and development of international law, democracy, and the rule of law.[7] The Union, furthermore, is to 'establish an area of prosperity and good neighbourliness'[8] regionally, and 'build partnerships with third countries, and international, regional or global organisations',[9] while 'promot[ing] an international system based on stronger multilateral cooperation and good global governance'.[10]

Some of the EU Member States match these global ambitions in their respective constitutions. These constitutions call, for instance, for 'the emancipation and progress of humanity'[11] and 'the creation of an international order capable of safeguarding peace and justice in relations between peoples'.[12] Others, however, are more modest. They either remain silent altogether in this respect, or content themselves with terse formulations such as: 'The Grand Duke makes the treaties' (*Le Grand-Duc fait les traités*).[13] The same development can be observed beyond Europe. The constitution of Brazil urges the country to 'seek the economic, political, social and cultural integration of the people of Latin America, with a view towards forming a Latin-American community of nations'.[14] The constitution of the world's youngest country, South Sudan, calls for nothing less than the 'promotion of international cooperation, specially within the United Nations family … for the purposes of consolidating universal peace and security, [and] respect for international law'.[15] By contrast, one of the world's oldest constitutions, that of the United States, makes only a scarce reference to providing 'for the common Defence' against the outside world.[16]

If one were to paraphrase the content of these various provisions in the EU Treaties and the more ambitious national constitutions, the picture of an ideal future world seems to emerge. This is a world in which the values that these respective polities hold dear are upheld; a world characterized not only by the absence of war and poverty, but in which peace in the widest and most positive sense obtains.[17] What the EU Treaties and other constitutions envisage echoes bold

[4] Case 294/83 *Parti écologiste 'Les Verts'*, EU:C:1986:166, para 23.

[5] Art 3(5) TEU. [6] Art 21(1), first subpara TEU.

[7] Arts 3(5) and 21(1), first subpara TEU. [8] Art 8(1) TEU.

[9] Art 21(1), second subpara TEU. [10] Art 21(2)(h) TEU.

[11] Art 7(1) Portuguese constitution. [12] Art 7(2) Portuguese constitution.

[13] Art 37(1) constitution of Luxembourg.

[14] Art 4, sole paragraph Brazilian constitution.

[15] Art 43(a) transitional constitution of the Republic of South Sudan, 7 July 2011, <http://www.wipo.int/wipolex/en/text.jsp?file_id=250715>.

[16] Preamble and Art 1, section 8 United States constitution.

[17] See seminally on the distinction between 'negative' and 'positive' peace J Galtung, 'Violence, Peace and Peace Research' 6 *Journal of Peace Research* 167 (1969).

political pronouncements such as President John F Kennedy's call for 'not a new balance of power, but a new world of law, where the strong are just and the weak secure and the peace preserved',[18] a world in which everyone would indeed be living 'in larger freedom',[19] in short, 'a fairer, safer and more united world'.[20] At the same time, they seem to presuppose that the EU or the state is indeed capable of shaping this kind of future world.

However one may feel about such sentiments, the main question that the present book addresses is the following: What does it mean to codify such lofty objectives into the foundational acts and highest laws of the state and of the European Union? As Chief Justice John Marshall once wrote in a United States Supreme Court decision, 'it is a *constitution* we are expounding'.[21] Accordingly, this book expounds the role and function of such objectives as legal norms contained in the 'basic constitutional charter'[22] of the European Union and in the constitutions of its Member States, and not as part of political speeches, policy documents, or for that matter science fiction, poetry, or scripture.

Some of the reactions which these provisions have triggered from legal scholars, who, it may be surmised, may have applauded such ideas had they been conveyed to them in a speech, exhibited scepticism towards their presence in the EU Treaties. For instance, these Treaty provisions have been called a mere 'wish list for a better world'[23] and 'a political candy box'.[24] They have been ridiculed as 'redolent of motherhood and apple pie',[25] and said to sound 'somewhat utopian'.[26] Conjuring up a rather alarming image, others observe 'an almost epidemic proliferation of objectives of the Union'.[27] One has to wonder, then, whether the inclusion of these objectives in the primary law corroborates the criticism by Bruno De Witte

[18] JF Kennedy, President of the United States, Inaugural Address, Washington DC, 20 January 1961, <http://www.jfklibrary.org/Asset-Viewer/BqXIEM9F4024ntFl7SVAjA.aspx>.

[19] United Nations General Assembly, *In Larger Freedom: Towards Development, Security and Human Rights for All*, Report of the Secretary-General, 21 March 2005, A/59/2005, which refers to and elaborates upon the expression used in the fourth recital of the preamble to the Charter of the United Nations.

[20] European Council, *A Secure Europe in a Better World, European Security Strategy*, 12 December 2003, 14.

[21] *McCulloch v Maryland*, decision of 6 March 1819, 17 US 316 (1819), 407 (emphasis in the original).

[22] *Parti écologiste 'Les Verts'* (n 4) para 23.

[23] In the original: 'Wunschzettel für eine bessere Welt': W Drescher, 'Ziele und Zuständigkeiten' in A Marchetti and C Demesmay (eds), *Der Vertrag von Lissabon: Analyse und Bewertung* (Nomos, 2010) 68.

[24] In the original: 'een politieke snoepdoos': R Barents, *Het Verdrag van Lissabon: Achtergronden en Commentaar* (Kluwer, 2008) 181, referring to the entire Art 3 TEU.

[25] A Dashwood et al., *Wyatt & Dashwood's European Union Law*, 6th edn (Hart Publishing, 2011) 903, referring to Art 21(1) TEU.

[26] S Blockmans, 'Friend or Foe? Reviewing EU Relations with Its Neighbours Post Lisbon' in P Koutrakos (ed), *The European Union's External Relations a Year after Lisbon*, CLEER Working Paper 2011/3, 116, referring to Art 8(1) TEU on the European Neighbourhood Policy.

[27] In the original: 'eine geradezu epidemische Ausbreitung von Unionszielen': J Terhechte, 'Kommentierung zum Art. 3 EUV (Ziele der Union)' in E Grabitz, M Hilf, and M Nettesheim (eds), *Das Recht der Europäischen Union*, loose-leaf, 41st supplement (C.H. Beck, 2010) marginal no 63, arguing in the context of objectives of the Common Foreign and Security Policy.

of what he considers the 'relentless accumulation of constitutional law'[28] resulting in 'too much confusing and unhelpful constitutional law of foreign relations in the EU'.[29] However, the scepticism of these commentators stands in stark contrast to others, who hail these provisions as a 'major innovation' forming the 'spinal column' of EU external action.[30] They are praised for expressing 'the most fundamental statement of Union foreign relations strategy'[31] and reflecting its 'normative power' as an international actor.[32]

On the national level, the same split of opinion can be observed with regard to the codification of constitutional objectives in general. Whereas for critics, such norms amount to nothing more than a 'dustbin of sentiment'[33] or a mere 'political wish list',[34] more enthusiastic commentators regard them as being part of the 'soul, spirit and hope of the Constitution',[35] presenting the codified 'world outlook' of the state,[36] or as providing a sense of direction in the face of a state of 'anomie' in modern society.[37]

The fact that the drafters of the EU Treaties and national constitutions deemed these objectives important enough to be codified should prompt legal scholarship not to dismiss them outright. At the same time, it would be equally misguided to simply assume their legal significance or normative desirability without further scrutiny. Instead, these provisions need to be assessed rigidly and without prejudice as legal norms. However, to date, foreign policy objectives in constitutional law remain under-theorized and under-contextualized. This is particularly so with regard to the EU Treaties and their international ambitions, despite the otherwise flourishing literature on EU external relations law,[38] as well as on EU constitutional

[28] B De Witte, 'Too Much Constitutional Law in the European Union's Foreign Relations' in M Cremona and B De Witte (eds), *EU Foreign Relations Law: Constitutional Fundamentals* (Hart Publishing, 2008) 10.

[29] De Witte (n 28) 12, but acknowledging also that 'values and objectives that must inspire the country's foreign policy' are a common feature in contemporary European constitutions.

[30] C Kaddous, 'External Action under the Lisbon Treaty' in I Pernice and E Tanchev (eds), *Ceci n'est pas une Constitution—Constitutionalisation without a Constitution?* (Nomos, 2009) 178.

[31] M Cremona, 'External Relations and External Competence of the European Union: The Emergence of an Integrated Policy' in P Craig and G de Búrca (eds), *The Evolution of EU Law*, 2nd edn (OUP, 2011) 267.

[32] I Manners, 'Normative Power Europe: A Contradiction in Terms?' (2002) 40 *Journal of Common Market Studies* 235, 241–2.

[33] These were the words used by TT Krishnamachari at the Indian Constituent Assembly on Indian 'directive principles of state policy', as quoted in O Chinnappa Reddy, *The Court and the Constitution of India: Summits and Shallows* (OUP, 2010) 17.

[34] In the original: 'politische[r] Wunschzettel': D Merten, 'Über Staatsziele' (1993) 46 *Die Öffentliche Verwaltung* 368, 376, with regard to objectives of the state in German constitutional law.

[35] B De Villiers, 'Directive Principles of State Policy and Fundamental Rights: The Indian Experience' (1992) 8 *South African Journal on Human Rights* 29, 33–4.

[36] PJ Canelas de Castro, 'Portugal's World Outlook in the Constitution of 1976' (1995) 71 *Boletim da Faculdade de Direito da Universidade de Coimbra* 489.

[37] K-P Sommermann, *Staatsziele und Staatszielbestimmungen* (Mohr Siebeck, 1997) 1.

[38] See as evidence thereof the proliferation of textbooks and edited volumes, eg PJ Kuijper, J Wouters, F Hoffmeister, and T Ramopoulos, *The Law of EU External Relations: Cases, Materials, and Commentary on the EU as an International Legal Actor*, 2nd edn (OUP, 2015); P Koutrakos, *EU International Relations Law*, 2nd edn (Hart Publishing, 2015); B Van Vooren and R Wessel, *EU External Relations Law: Text, Cases and Materials* (CUP, 2014); F Amtenbrink and D Kochenov (eds), *The European Union's Shaping of the International Legal Order* (CUP, 2013); PJ Cardwell (ed), *EU External Relations Law and Policy in the Post-Lisbon Era* (T.M.C. Asser Press, 2012); P Eeckhout,

law, constitutionalism, and pluralism.[39] Therefore, the object of this book is to grasp these objectives as constitutional norms, to discern their legal force and properties, and to situate them in the legal order of the state, the European Union, and the complex European constitutional space.

More particularly, the chapters of the book seek to shed light on the following questions: What is the place of constitutional foreign policy objectives within a given legal order? What is their legal value, their function and substance, and how do they relate to other norm categories of constitutional law? Can the foreign policy objectives enshrined in national constitutions be meaningfully compared with those of the EU Treaties? What are the specific features of the system of external relations of the EU and how do they affect the pursuit of its ambitious set of foreign policy objectives? How are we to perceive the relationship between the objectives of the Member States and those of the Union in which they partake? Beyond these legal considerations, the scrutiny of foreign policy objectives also relates to the wider discussion of the role of the EU in the world. What does it mean for the allegedly distinctive 'normative power' of Europe to entrench specific objectives in a place as prominent as its constitutional law?

2. Foreign Policy Objectives and the Major Trends in European Constitutional Law

This book presents foreign policy objectives codified in both national constitutions and the EU Treaties as part of both the general norm category of constitutional objectives and of the 'foreign affairs constitution'. To make this assertion with regard to the EU would be an easy and straightforward exercise if the analysis could build on a well-established doctrine of constitutional objectives in EU law. However, this is not the case. Objectives play an important role in the case law of the Court of Justice of the EU, not least given its hallmark teleological approach, and in discussions about the *finalité* of European integration. Nonetheless, their role within the legal order has shifted over time, which seems to have thus far prevented a consolidation of a firm constitutional doctrine grasping them as legal

EU External Relations Law, 2nd edn (OUP, 2011); E Neframi, *L'action extérieure de l'Union européenne: fondements, moyens, principes* (L.G.D.J., 2010); M Cremona and B De Witte (eds), *EU Foreign Relations Law: Constitutional Fundamentals* (Hart Publishing, 2008); and G De Baere, *Constitutional Principles of EU External Relations* (OUP, 2008).

[39] See K Jaklic, *Constitutional Pluralism in the EU* (OUP, 2014); G Martinico, *The Tangled Complexity of the EU Constitutional Process: The Frustrating Knot of Europe* (Routledge, 2014); F-X Millet, *L'Union européenne et l'identité constitutionnelle des États membres* (L.G.D.J., 2013); R Schütze, *European Constitutional Law* (CUP, 2012); M Avbelj and J Komárek (eds), *Constitutional Pluralism in the European Union and Beyond* (Hart, 2012); A Rosas and L Armati, *EU Constitutional Law: An Introduction*, 2nd edn (Hart Publishing, 2012); N Walker, J Shaw, and S Tierney (eds), *Europe's Constitutional Mosaic* (Hart Publishing, 2011); G de Búrca and JHH Weiler (eds), *The Worlds of European Constitutionalism* (CUP, 2011); and J Wouters, L Verhey, and P Kiiver (eds), *European Constitutionalism Beyond Lisbon* (Intersentia, 2009).

norms.[40] The initial enthusiasm for the Treaty Establishing a Constitution for Europe, followed by its failure and the subsequent abandonment of the 'constitutional concept'[41] by the European Council, caused confusion instead of bringing more certainty to the debate.

Nevertheless, calls for a constitutional or quasi-constitutional approach to the law of the European Union have been numerous and strong for a long time in scholarship, and were not silenced by these latest developments.[42] The same applies to the law of external relations of the European Union.[43] The essence of these arguments is that while it is recognized that the Union is not a state, its legal order has developed in such a way that it can hardly be characterized as that of an ordinary international organization any longer. Instead, it is captured better in constitutional terms, while taking into account the particular features that the Union retains in comparison to states. In view of the maturity that EU law has acquired today, the insights from comparative constitutional law can indeed provide the basis for the assessment of foreign policy objectives as a trend in both national and EU law. While this debate is concerned with the 'constitutionalization' of EU law,

[40] See the divergent assessments of Union objectives in articles and chapters specifically devoted to this issue, eg C Calliess, 'Kollektive Ziele und Prinzipien im Verfassungsrecht der EU—Bestandsaufnahme, Wirkungen und Perspektiven' (2003) 92 *Archiv für Rechts- und Sozialphilosophie-Beiheft* 85; F Reimer, 'Ziele und Zuständigkeiten: Die Funktionen der Unionszielbestimmungen' [2003] *Europarecht* 992; M Kotzur, 'Die Ziele der Union: Verfassungsidentität und Gemeinschaftsidee' (2005) 58 *Die Öffentliche Verwaltung* 313; F Sorrentino, 'The Purposes of the European Union According to the Constitutional Treaty' in HJ Blanke and S Mangiameli (eds), *Governing Europe under a Constitution: The Hard Road from the European Treaties to a European Constitutional Treaty* (Springer, 2006); Sommermann (n 37) 280–96; B Plecher-Hochstraßer, *Zielbestimmungen im Mehrebenensystem: Die Verzahnung der Staatszielbestimmungen im GG mit den Zielbestimmungen im EUV, EGV, EuratomV und EUVV* (Meidenbauer, 2006) 105–54; J Basedow, 'Zielkonflikte und Zielhierarchien im Vertrag über die europäische Gemeinschaft' in O Due, M Lutter, and J Schwarze (eds), *Festschrift für Ulrich Everling* (Nomos, 1995); and earlier P Pescatore, 'Les objectifs de la Communauté européenne comme principes d'interprétation dans la jurisprudence de la Cour de justice' in *Miscellanea W. J. Ganshof van der Meersch: Studia ab discipulis amicisque in honorem egregii professoris edita* (Bruylant, 1972); as well as in textbooks and commentaries on the EU Treaties such as K Lenaerts and P Van Nuffel, *European Union Law*, 3rd edn (Sweet & Maxwell, 2011) 106–11; M Pechstein, 'Art. 3 (ex-Art. 2 EUV) [Ziele der Union]' in R Streinz (ed), *EUV/AEUV: Vertrag über die Europäische Union und Vertrag über die Arbeitsweise der Europäischen Union*, 2nd edn (C.H. Beck, 2012) 19 (marginal no 3); M Ruffert, 'Art. 3 (ex-Art. 2 EUV) [Ziele der EU]' in C Calliess and M Ruffert (eds), *EUV/AEUV Kommentar*, 4th edn (C.H. Beck, 2011); P-C Müller-Graff, 'Verfassungsziele der EG/EU' in M Dauses (ed), *Handbuch des EU-Wirtschaftsrechts*, loose-leaf, 27th supplement (C.H. Beck, 2010); and earlier notably HP Ipsen, *Europäisches Gemeinschaftsrecht* (Mohr Siebeck, 1972) 545–67.

[41] European Council, Presidency Conclusions of the Brussels European Council 21 and 22 June 2007, 20 July 2007, 11177/1/07 REV 1, Annex I: *IGC Mandate*, para 1.

[42] See eg A von Bogdandy and J Bast, 'The Constitutional Approach to EU Law' in A von Bogdandy and J Bast (eds), *Principles of European Constitutional Law*, 2nd edn (Hart Publishing/C.H. Beck, 2011); P Craig, 'Constitutions, Constitutionalism, and the European Union' (2001) 7 *European Law Journal* 125; JHH Weiler, *The Constitution of Europe: Do the New Clothes Have an Emperor? and Other Essays on European Integration* (CUP, 1999); seminally E Stein, 'Lawyers, Judges, and the Making of a Transnational Constitution' (1981) 75 *American Journal of International Law* 1.

[43] On the constitutional approach specifically in the area of EU external relations law see M Cremona and B De Witte, 'Introduction' in M Cremona and B De Witte (eds), *EU Foreign Relations Law: Constitutional Fundamentals* (Hart Publishing, 2008) xi–xv; Van Vooren and Wessel (n 38) 9–18; and M Cremona and A Thies, 'Introduction' in M Cremona and A Thies (eds), *The European Court of Justice and External Relations Law: Constitutional Challenges* (Hart Publishing, 2014).

the emergence of foreign policy objectives within this constitutional framework can only be explained by taking the wider context into account.

In view of the evolution of constitutional law over the past decades, the appearance of such provisions in constitutional texts is anything but surprising. On the contrary, the presence of these norms in the highest laws of a polity is nothing other than the codified expression of the confluence of three major trends in contemporary constitutional law in Europe: 'dynamization', 'internationalization', and 'Europeanization'. It is this combined stream of constitutional evolution that allows a fuller understanding of foreign policy objectives in European constitutional law and their role in the system of EU external relations.

Regarding the first trend, ever since the writings of German jurist Rudolph von Jhering, the role of objectives in legal reasoning has been a subject of debate.[44] This debate has also reached the highest laws, as constitutionally codified objectives have proliferated in constitutional documents around the world. Such objectives commit a political community to strive towards certain—often ideal—goals, ie something not yet realized or even fully realizable. They represent legal norms emphasizing aspects of the general pursuit of the 'common good' of a political community.[45] The prospect of these goals being pursued was so desirable for the *pouvoir constituant* that it chose to include them in a constitutional document. By virtue of these norms, the constitution sketches out a certain picture of the future that is to be pursued through the constitutional framework. Today, many national constitutions contain explicit goals that the state and its organs must strive for. Karl-Peter Sommermann aptly termed this the *Dynamisierung des Verfassungsrechts*, ie 'dynamization of constitutional law'.[46]

Regarding the second trend, Hans Kelsen noted that the legal system of a country bespeaks a certain 'world outlook'.[47] This has become increasingly apparent in the course of what has been called 'the internationalist fever of the immediate post-war period',[48] as links between the domestic and international legal order have been made explicit in constitutional documents. Today, many national constitutions make ample references to regional or global standards, in particular human rights, and regulate a country's relations with international law and international organizations. This is commonly known as the 'internationalization' of constitutional

[44] First published in 1877 under the title *Der Zweck im Recht* (literally: 'The Purpose in Law'). For an English version, albeit with a somewhat unfortunate translation of the title, see R von Jhering, *Law as a Means to an End*, trans I Husik (The Boston Book Company, 1913).

[45] On the connection between law and the 'common good', one can recall again Cicero's aphorism *salus populi suprema lex esto*, as well as Thomas Aquinas, who posited that 'every law is ordained for the common good': T Aquinas, *Treatise on Law*, trans R Thomas (Hackett Publishing, 2000) 3.

[46] Sommermann (n 37) 374.

[47] H Kelsen, *Essays in Legal and Moral Philosophy* (D. Reidel, 1973) 95–113; see also P Häberle, 'Das "Weltbild" des Verfassungsstaates—eine Textstufenanalyse zur Menschheit als verfassungsstaatlichem und "letztem" Geltungsgrund des Völkerrechts' in B Ziemske, T Langheid, H Wilms, and G Haverkate (eds), *Staatsphilosophie und Rechtspolitik, Festschrift für Martin Kriele* (C.H. Beck, 1997).

[48] In the original: 'la fièvre internationaliste de l'immédiat après-guerre': P De Visscher, 'Les tendances internationales des constitutions modernes' (1952) 1 *Recueil de Cours* 511, 573.

law.[49] Both dynamization and internationalization find their common expression in constitutional provisions that mandate the state to pursue certain objectives on the international stage.

Regarding the third trend, ever since Walter Hallstein, the close relationship between European integration and law has become a common narrative. In Europe, according to Hallstein, '[t]he majesty of law is to achieve what centuries of blood and iron were not capable of'.[50] Thus, in addition to the double trend of the 'dynamic internationalization' of constitutional law, the third major phenomenon emerges: the 'Europeanization' of law, through which European integration has been cast in a legal framework and has matured to the extent that it is regarded by many as 'constitutionalized'. In turn, 'Europeanization' has come to affect both public and private law,[51] as well as international law within the EU Member States[52] and their respective constitutional laws.[53] In addition and beyond the strictly legal, membership in the EU has impacted on various national policy areas,[54] including foreign policy.[55]

In view of these developments, it is still remarkable, but less surprising, that the strongest signs of 'dynamic internationalization' can be found in the 'basic constitutional charter' of the European Union itself. In particular, the post-Lisbon Treaties now boast the boldest and most comprehensive codification of the 'world outlook' of the EU to date, ie the kind of world it mandates the Union, and indirectly the Member States, to strive towards. This is what Fabian Amtenbrink and Dimitry Kochenov have termed the 'active paradigm' in EU external relations,[56] to which these codified objectives testify.

[49] See eg H Tourard, *L'internationalisation des constitutions nationales* (L.D.G.J., 2000); see also J Kokott, 'From Reception and Transplantation to Convergence of Constitutional Models in the Age of Globalization' in C Starck (ed), *Constitutionalism, Universalism and Democracy—a Comparative Analysis: The German Contributions to the Fifth World Congress of the International Association of Constitutional Law* (Nomos, 1999); and T Ginsburg, S Chernykh, and Z Elkins, 'Commitment and Diffusion: How and Why National Constitutions Incorporate International Law' (2008) *University of Illinois Law Review* 201.

[50] In the original: 'Die Majestät des Rechts soll schaffen, was Blut und Eisen in Jahrhunderten nicht vermochten': W Hallstein, *Die Europäische Gemeinschaft*, 5th edn (Econ Verlag, 1979) 53; note in particular also the major *Integration Through Law* project, M Cappelletti, M Seccombe, and JHH Weiler, 'Integration Through Law: Europe and the American Federal Experience—A General Introduction' in M Cappelletti, M Seccombe, and JHH Weiler (eds), *Integration Through Law: Europe and the American Federal Experience. Volume I, Book 1* (Walter de Gruyter, 1986).

[51] See eg F Snyder (ed), *The Europeanisation of Law: The Legal Effects of European Integration* (Hart Publishing, 2000).

[52] J Wouters, A Nollkaemper, and E de Wet (eds), *The Europeanisation of International Law: The Status of International Law in the EU and Its Member States* (T.M.C. Asser Press, 2008).

[53] J Ziller (ed), *L'européanisation des droits constitutionnels à la lumière de la constitution pour l'Europe/The Europeanisation of Constitutional Law in the Light of the Constitution for Europe* (L'Harmattan, 2003).

[54] T Börzel and D Panke, 'Europeanization' in M Cini and N Pérez-Solórzano Borragán (eds), *European Union Politics*, 4th edn (OUP, 2013) on the concept in the social sciences.

[55] R Wong, 'The Europeanization of Foreign Policy' in C Hill and M Smith (eds), *International Relations and the European Union*, 2nd edn (OUP, 2011); and R Wong and C Hill (eds), *National and European Foreign Policy: Towards Europeanization* (Routledge, 2011).

[56] F Amtenbrink and D Kochenov, 'The Active Paradigm of the Study of the EU's Place in the World: An Introduction' in F Amtenbrink and D Kochenov (eds), *The European Union's Shaping of the International Legal Order* (CUP, 2013).

3. Methodological Considerations

This book applies a comparative constitutional law approach in the context of European integration as well as foreign relations, utilizing legal materials including case law and scholarship from different jurisdictions and written in different languages. This merits a number of points on the methodology employed: firstly, as regards the focus on Europe and of the merits of the comparative method in research on European constitutional law; secondly, concerning the selection of third countries and the emphasis on codified constitutional provisions; and thirdly, regarding issues of translation.

As to the focus on the European Union and its Member States, it is the setting of the most deeply integrated regional community in the world which has sparked, in the legal realm, the claims for 'constitutionalization' and the emergence of a European constitutional space. In addition, and with particular regard to foreign affairs, the European Union remains the sole example of sovereign countries pooling their resources in such key areas as trade, while also developing common foreign, security, defence, and other policies, but without giving up their own presence on the international scene.[57]

In order to fully grasp foreign policy objectives as constitutional norms in Europe, a comparative constitutional approach is indispensable. As Monica Claes and Maartje de Visser note, 'the study of constitutional law of the European Union requires a comparative attitude', while at the same time 'the EU context adds additional meaning to comparative research'.[58] Therefore, not only with regard to constitutional values,[59] but also concerning 'objectives', a comparative approach becomes imperative.

On the horizontal level, it is worthwhile enquiring whether there exists a common understanding of foreign policy objectives as legal norms among states. Moreover, similarities and differences regarding the substance of these objectives can be made visible through comparison. Despite general tendencies of convergence, harmonization, or 'Europeanization', constitutions are 'more deeply rooted in a nation's history and culture' and more 'political in nature' than other sources of law,[60] expressing what Joseph Raz called the 'common ideology' of a political community.[61] This also affects their 'world outlook' and the ambitions they impose

[57] See eg F Andreatta, 'The European Union's International Relations: A Theoretical View' in C Hill and M Smith (eds), *International Relations and the European Union*, 2nd edn (OUP, 2011) 22; J Howorth, *Security and Defence Policy in the European Union*, 2nd edn (Palgrave Macmillan, 2014) 1, with specific regard to security and defence policy.

[58] M Claes and M de Visser, 'Reflections on Comparative Method in European Constitutional Law' in M Adams and J Bomhoff (eds), *Practice and Theory in Comparative Law* (CUP, 2012) 143–4.

[59] A von Bogdandy, P Cruz Villalón, and P Huber, 'Vorwort' in A von Bogdandy, P Cruz Villalón, and P Huber (eds), *Handbuch Ius Publicum Europaeum. Volume I: Grundlagen und Grundzüge staatlichen Verfassungsrechts* (C.F. Müller, 2007) v.

[60] Claes and de Visser (n 58) 157.

[61] J Raz, 'On the Authority and Interpretation of Constitutions: Some Preliminaries' in L Alexander (ed), *Constitutionalism: Philosophical Foundations* (CUP, 1998) 154. See also in this

on the state for its actions on the world stage. Comparative research can provide answers to the questions of whether, despite these individual historical trajectories, an abstract legal definition of a 'foreign policy objective' is possible, and whether general patterns begin to emerge in terms of content.

Regarding the European Union, given the absence of a consolidated doctrine of constitutional objectives in EU law, 'comparison of national constitutional laws and traditions provides the basis to further our understanding'[62] also with respect to foreign policy objectives as constitutional norms at the Union level. However, concepts from the national legal sphere cannot be transposed to the EU without further enquiry.[63] Instead, any academic endeavour in this area must 'remain aware of the special features' of the EU and its legal order.[64] Just because both national constitutions and the EU Treaties contain foreign policy objectives does not automatically mean that they operate in the same manner, not least given their different origins. Hence, a central concern of this book is to establish on which grounds the EU legal order can be deemed as 'constitutionalized', and to take account of its peculiar features throughout.

Regarding the vertical legal relationship between the EU and its Member States, the book builds on the idea of a composite European constitutional space, which 'consists of constitutional norms developed at the European level, complemented by national constitutional rules and principles'.[65] This constitutional space is cast in pluralist terms, eschewing strict hierarchies and marked by an overarching theme of maintaining unity while preserving diversity.[66] In addition to constitutional pluralism, the 'the polyphonic nature of the Union's external action'[67] has to be accounted for, ie the fact that both the Member States and the Union remain international actors in their own right. Hence, the book scrutinizes the legal constraints of the Member States' 'venue choice'[68] as to whether they pursue their

respect G Frankenberg, 'Comparative Constitutional Law' in M Bussani and U Mattei (eds), *The Cambridge Companion to Comparative Law* (CUP, 2012) 173.

62 Claes and de Visser (n 58) 161.

63 A von Bogdandy, 'Founding Principles' in A von Bogdandy and J Bast (eds), *Principles of European Constitutional Law*, 2nd edn (Hart Publishing/C.H. Beck, 2011) 24–5; see also N Walker, 'Post-national Constitutionalism and the Problem of Translation' in JHH Weiler and M Wind (eds), *European Constitutionalism Beyond the State* (CUP, 2003).

64 R Streinz, 'European Integration through Constitutional Law' in H-J Blanke and S Mangiameli (eds), *Governing Europe under a Constitution: The Hard Road from the European Treaties to a European Constitutional Treaty* (Springer, 2006) 9.

65 Claes and de Visser (n 58) 149.

66 N Walker, 'The Idea of Constitutional Pluralism' (2002) 68 *Modern Law Review* 317; and M Poiares Maduro, 'Contrapunctual Law: Europe's Constitutional Pluralism in Action' in N Walker (ed), *Sovereignty in Transition* (Hart Publishing, 2003).

67 C Hillion, 'Mixity and Coherence in EU External Relations: The Significance of the "Duty of Cooperation"' in C Hillion and P Koutrakos (eds), *Mixed Agreements Revisited: The EU and Its Member States in the World* (Hart Publishing, 2010) 87.

68 See with regard to lawmaking in general, B De Witte and A Thies, 'Why Choose Europe? The Place of the European Union in the Architecture of International Legal Cooperation' in B Van Vooren, S Blockmans, and J Wouters (eds), *The EU's Role in Global Governance: The Legal Dimension* (OUP, 2013) 24.

own constitutional foreign policy objectives internationally or within the Union framework and through Union external action.

In addition to the choice of the European constitutional space as the focus of the research presented in this book, a number of other selections had to be made. These concern the third countries which are considered alongside the EU and its Member States, the focus on constitutional texts, and the use of three jurisdictions for the establishment of a common understanding of constitutional foreign policy objectives as legal norms.

In order to stress the global scope of the trend of 'dynamic internationalization' of constitutional law, eleven third country constitutions were also taken into account. The selection was made on the basis of power and international or regional clout, as well as geographical balance. This was done to 'ensure that the sample is suitably representative and/or covers in any case the legal systems which are of particular interest for a specific issue'.[69] With this in mind, the selection includes the three non-EU permanent members of the United Nations Security Council, the four 'BRIC' countries (Brazil, Russia, India, and China), as well as Japan and Switzerland as the EU's like-minded, major trading partners.

Together, the EU Treaties, the constitutions of the twenty-eight Member States, and the eleven third-country constitutions represent the entirety of constitutional texts that feed into the analysis. While the inclusion of all the Member States is warranted by their equality under the Treaties,[70] as well as by the aim of providing a comprehensive study of such norms in the European constitutional space, the third countries help to furnish a global context and to avoid 'Eurocentrist' tendencies.

The book deliberately assumes a bird's eye view of constitutional law. The main challenge identified here is the absence of a common understanding of foreign policy objectives as constitutional norms, especially at EU level. While the study of constitutional texts alone—following an admittedly rather 'formalist and positivist path'[71]—certainly does not suffice to gain a full 'understanding of political reality', it remains nonetheless 'a necessary condition of that understanding'.[72] The requirement of codification is employed as a simple but effective filter in order to 'discipline the "explosion of facts" and the textual and contextual richness'.[73] Moreover, as a matter of principle, there is merit in focusing on codified norms. AV Dicey's classic criticism of codification was that beyond confirming the existence of a certain norm, it did not provide any added value.[74] However, in the present case, the confirmation as such of the very existence of an entrenched 'world view' and textual foundations of global ambitions in both national constitutions and the EU Treaties can be regarded as valuable. It serves to highlight the

[69] Claes and de Visser (n 58) 164.

[70] Art 4(2) TEU.

[71] Frankenberg (n 61) 175.

[72] SE Finer, V Bogdanor, and B Rudden, *Comparing Constitutions* (Clarendon Press, 1995) 5.

[73] Frankenberg (n 61) 177.

[74] See AV Dicey, *Introduction to the Study of the Law of the Constitution*, 10th edn (Macmillan, 1961) 207.

expanding scope of the constitution to go beyond merely limiting and organizing governmental powers, and to address issues transcending the borders of the polity that it regulates. Constitutional foreign policy objectives serve as black letter evidence for calls for a globally active state—a *Leistungsstaat* or *État providence* capable of performing and providing in a globalized and interdependent world.

Another issue of selection is the reliance on three settled doctrines for establishing a common 'vocabulary' of constitutional objectives as a norm category, which is subsequently applied to foreign policy objectives as a part of this category. Generally, while the textual research reveals the presence of foreign policy objectives in almost all constitutions that were surveyed, not every jurisdiction can muster a consolidated doctrine outlining their legal properties as norms within a given legal order. Hence, the book draws on the 'repertoire of established doctrines'[75] in this particular context. This by no means denies the existence or future emergence of other doctrines that tackle this issue. Nevertheless, given instances of legal cross-fertilization both between national legal orders and between the EU and its Member States, which the research presented here already reveals, it is likely that other doctrines would be similar, and add to the general validity of the common 'vocabulary'.

Next to the two major doctrines on constitutional objectives hailing from Europe (German *Staatszielbestimmungen* and French *objectifs de valeur constitutionnelle*), the Indian doctrine of *directive principles of state policy* was also used as a key ingredient in establishing this common vocabulary. Relying on these three doctrines, rather than looking through the lens of a single legal system, aims to shield the analysis from 'becoming trapped in the classifications of any one of the national systems under review'.[76] Furthermore, in this narrower sample, it is feasible to move beyond the positive rules laid down in the constitutional documents by assessing the case law and legal academic discourses prevailing in these legal systems. Analysing these materials in their respective original language and drawing on the pre-eminent treatises on the subject from scholars stemming from these jurisdictions facilitated a reflection of 'the local perception of the constitutional system by the local constitutional actors'.[77]

Next to the questions surrounding the operation of foreign policy objectives within a given legal order, they also evoke the global perspective, ie our understanding of the international system and the rules and forces that govern it. This wider context merits 'an attempt at interdisciplinary analysis',[78] especially with respect to the study of international relations. While constitutional foreign policy objectives sketch out a world that constitutional organs are mandated to strive towards, international relations scholars seek to determine what actors, resources, and forces matter on the international stage, and provide diverging assessments on the significance of law, norms, and ideals therein. Hence, a shared 'conceptual space'[79] becomes visible between international relations and constitutional law.

[75] von Bogdandy (n 63) 24. [76] Claes and de Visser (n 58) 165.

[77] Claes and de Visser (n 58) 167. [78] Claes and de Visser (n 58) 167.

[79] A-M Slaughter, 'International Law in a World of Liberal States' (1995) 6 *European Journal of International Law* 503, at 503, with regard to international law and international relations theory.

The book recognizes this and engages in the systematization of the conceptual links between the two spheres.

Lastly, the comparative approach used here raises certain issues with regard to translation.[80] The book draws extensively on constitutional texts, case law, and scholarship from various jurisdictions that are relevant to the analysis of foreign policy objectives. As a consequence, it relies heavily, next to English language sources, on German and French language literature. English being an official language of both India and the European Union, sources from these jurisdictions can be quoted directly. In addition, where appropriate, sources from other languages are also used. Concerning citations from non-English constitutional texts, English language translations from a reliable database were used for the most part.[81] In cases where clarification was needed, the original language was consulted where possible; otherwise the official (albeit not authoritative) English language translations from government websites or other reliable sources were used (such as websites of international organizations).

4. Structure

With these main questions, major developments, and methodological considerations in mind, the structure of the book is as follows. Chapter 1 develops a common understanding of foreign policy objectives as norms of constitutional law. It draws on the German doctrine of *Staatszielbestimmungen*, French *objectifs de valeur constitutionnelle*, and the particularly illuminating Indian doctrine of *directive principles of state policy*. Starting with the origins of each doctrine, it turns to the legal properties of constitutional objectives, and subsequently addresses their application in the field of external relations.

Following the establishment of this common understanding of constitutional foreign policy objectives, Chapter 2 addresses the origins of the EU's foreign policy objectives and their substance in a comparative perspective. It first retraces the drafting history of the foreign policy objectives of the EU Treaties. Subsequently, the chapter presents and organizes evidence of foreign policy objectives in the constitutions of the EU Member States, the EU Treaties, and a selection of third countries, revealing a global trend.

Chapter 3 addresses the constitutional credentials of the EU's foreign policy objectives. It takes into account the Union's peculiar features as a legal order, with its origins as a functional international organization characterized by the 'principle of speciality' serving as the point of departure. It contrasts this with the national

80 This refers to 'the most specific sense of translation', according to which 'theorists and practitioners of European law must translate nationally- and linguistically-specific categories and legal institutions into another language': A Vespaziani, 'Comparison, Translation and the Making of a Common European Constitutional Culture' (2008) 9 *German Law Journal* 547, 570.

81 This refers to 'Oxford Constitutions of the World', <http://oxcon.ouplaw.com/home/OCW>, formerly the Oceana Law® database 'Constitutions of the Countries of the World Online'.

setting, in which the pursuit of the common good is inherent in the notion of statehood. States are hence free to allocate powers with a view to that overall end (*Kompetenz-Kompetenz* in German). The chapter explains that the European Union, through the widening of its goals and powers over time, as well as the 'thickening' of its legal order, has moved far away from being a specialized organization, and can be regarded as having, for all practical purposes, a 'constitutionalized' legal order.

Having addressed the national and EU dimensions of constitutional foreign policy objectives, Chapter 4 tackles the consequences of the fact that the Member States and the Union share a European constitutional space. This combines the sensitive relationship between EU law and Member State constitutional law and the complex legal issues surrounding the parallel existence of the Union and the Member States as actors on the international stage. Despite constitutional pluralism and plurality in international representation, the chapter argues that there is an overarching quest for unity and coherence in the EU polity as regards the pursuit of its international ambitions. In order to manage the quest for international unity while safeguarding internal constitutional diversity or pluralism, it explores a range of legal principles that have emerged, and which can be organized by using a three-dimensional approach to the overall concept of coherence.

Lastly, Chapter 5 highlights and systematizes the various conceptual overlaps between the legal analysis conducted in the preceding chapters and the field of international relations, given the related debate on the kind of power that the EU represents internationally. Views in this respect range from a distinctive 'civilian', 'normative', or 'ethical' power to more critical assessments claiming that the position of the EU is heavily conditioned by its own structural limits as well as the overall power structure of the international system. The chapter accounts for the fact that in the main theoretical strands of international relations, the importance of law and of norms, values, and ideas is appreciated very differently. After briefly recalling the main schools of international relations, the chapter engages in an exercise of reciprocal contextualization of law and IR theory. It explores how each theory contributes to a better understanding of the legal findings elaborated previously.

An overall conclusion sums up the main findings of the book and provides an outlook for future research for which these insights may prove useful. It stresses that while the *salus mundi* has indeed found its way into the highest laws of many states, as well as into the EU Treaties, this is neither a reason for unbridled enthusiasm nor for insuperable scepticism.

1

Understanding Constitutional Foreign Policy Objectives

Insights from Comparative Constitutional Law

1. Introduction

This chapter establishes a common understanding—a common vocabulary—of foreign policy objectives as part of constitutional law, which serves as the theoretical underpinning for appraising them in the European Union's legal order and in the European constitutional space. Firstly, it demonstrates that constitutionally codified objectives are an established norm category of constitutional law, the legal characteristics of which are sufficiently similar across different jurisdictions. Secondly, it shows that foreign policy goals, when codified into a constitutional text, are a part of this norm category. Consequently, the same legal properties pertain to them too, while accounting for the particular features of foreign affairs in constitutional law. In short, the chapter establishes, in general, comparative terms for what such norms can—and cannot—be used, including in particular how they relate to questions of institutional powers and limitations of rights.

It should be underlined at the outset that the purpose is not to rashly transpose any national doctrine to other countries or, a fortiori, to the supranational level. The peculiar characteristics of the EU, its legal order, and system of external relations, as well as the complex European constitutional space are accounted for in Chapters 3 and 4, respectively. Nonetheless, legal practice and thinking, not least in Europe, is quintessentially 'comparative and dependent on the repertoire of established doctrines of viable institutions'.[1] In this spirit, the present chapter draws on the most well-established approaches the European and global repertoires have to offer.

Three doctrinal approaches stand out and will serve here as the basis for establishing this common understanding. Two of them hail from continental Europe and the third from Asia: German *Staatszielbestimmungen*, French *objectifs de valeur constitutionnelle*, and Indian 'directive principles of state policy'. These are three

[1] A von Bogdandy, 'Founding Principles' in A von Bogdandy and J Bast (eds), *Principles of European Constitutional Law*, 2nd edn (Hart Publishing/C.H. Beck, 2011) 24.

different names for the same idea, which will be called here, as a generic term, 'constitutional objectives'. The three jurisdictions have been chosen for four principal reasons: Firstly, each of them has brought forth a specific concept and definition of constitutional objectives, drawing on norms codified in their constitutional documents; secondly, each provides case law from their constitutional courts which grapples with the legal value of such norms; thirdly, each has spawned scholarship debating these norms, elaborating on their role within the constitutional framework; fourthly, and most importantly for the purposes of this book, each doctrine is amenable to foreign policy objectives as part of this norm category.

It is worth emphasizing that this three-pronged approach is not exhaustive. It cannot be excluded that other jurisdictions in the world could provide additional doctrines.[2] Doctrines from other countries and legal orders which at the moment are less well developed in terms of case law and scholarship are likely to mature over the course of time and reach a stage of sophistication comparable to those drawn upon here. Nevertheless, from these three well-established national doctrines, a set of common features can be derived which shows that in comparative constitutional law, codified objectives, including those in the domain of foreign policy, are appraised in a rather uniform way. This is not altogether surprising given that they are the product of a number of instances of constitutional cross-fertilization. The French *Conseil constitutionnel* in all likelihood borrowed from the Court of Justice of the (then) European Communities. The Indians, for their part, borrowed from the Irish, and subsequently further elaborated the doctrine. Overall, these developments show the interwovenness of the grand trends of internationalization and 'dynamization' of constitutional law, and an overall trend of constitutional convergence rather than divergence.

In all three cases, the introduction of the very notion of a constitutional objective was a novelty, which was not readily embraced by scholarship. In both German and French discourse, constitutional objectives were considered by some strange or unusual elements within constitutional law, potentially endangering the supremacy and credibility of the constitution. In India, codification of both rights and objectives constituted a conscious break from the British legal tradition that had characterized the country prior to independence. The scepticism and ridicule directed against codified objectives in all three cases was countered by other voices praising these objectives as substantive core elements of the constitution and attaching great hopes and expectations to them. Crucially, and despite all the claims of 'novelty', the emergence of all three doctrines took place in full awareness of general trends in constitutional law around the world.

Despite the, at times, polemical clamour of both detractors and enthusiasts of these objectives, the judicial and scholarly appraisal of these norms over time yields the legal character common to them. Constitutional objectives are doubtlessly

[2] See for an account of countries with constitutions containing objectives the normativity of which is explicitly distinguished from individual rights, K-P Sommermann, *Staatsziele und Staatszielbestimmungen* (Mohr Siebeck, 1997) 336–47.

weak norms, which is captured well by the French term *normativité limitée*[3] and the Robert Alexy's notion that they represent 'optimization requirements'.[4] They are thus not black-and-white rules, but principles—constitutional aspirations. Their legal force is limited to what can be called the active pursuit of the objective within the bounds of what is legally and materially possible. This acknowledges the necessity to accommodate a variety of political or material constraints (in German captured by the term *Vorbehalt des Möglichen*),[5] and accounts for the fact that constitutional law as a whole frames this pursuit. As regards the different objectives, they are to be seen as of equal importance, unless the constitution specifically says otherwise. Furthermore, and crucially, objectives do not imply, in general, the power to pursue them. Only the state organs with a constitutionally granted competence are called upon to pursue them. For further specification and implementation, this means first and foremost the legislative branch. Their pursuit is qualified by other constitutional restrictions as well, notably the protection of individual rights and the preservation of the basic structural features of the constitutional order. Against this backdrop, courts are rarely able to detect any direct violations of objectives that would be manifest enough to merit judicial intervention.

While true as a general rule, such strict distinctions are not always possible. It is here that the most indisputable legal characteristic of constitutional objectives comes to the fore. Constitutional objectives dispose only of a very low degree of justiciability, which hovers between being marginal (*objectifs de valeur constitutionnelle*), hypothetical (*Staatszielbestimmungen*), and non-existent (directive principles of state policy). However, all three doctrines agree that they serve as an important device for constitutional interpretation. These interpretations can and do produce legal effects which, indirectly, confirm that constitutional objectives have legal force after all. This function highlights that the role of courts is still important in this context, despite the fact that they can hardly enforce them. Herein resides both the potential and the danger of these norms, which is also one of the main causes for both the enthusiasm and scepticism to which they have been subjected. Constitutional objectives are generally seen as dynamic elements with the capacity, through interpretation, to make rigid norms more flexible. For instance, certain individual rights, such as the right to property or free speech, can be abridged with reference to public purposes enshrined in the constitution in the form of objectives. In a similar vein, relying on the need to be able to pursue these objectives effectively can stretch the limits of certain ill-defined competences of the state and its organs. In effect, this merges the interpretive function of objectives with their permissive function. In short, they lend support to allowing the state to do things it would otherwise not have been allowed to do. This emphasizes, in turn, the importance of embedding the objectives into the overall constitutional structure, which they may shape, but not upset. This embedding combined with their limited legal force ought to assuage the critics fearing the abusive potential of

[3] P De Montalivet, *Les objectifs de valeur constitutionnelle* (Dalloz, 2006) 563.

[4] Sommermann (n 2) 360–1. [5] Sommermann (n 2) 224.

constitutional objectives, yet agrees with the enthusiasts that these norms do serve a tangible purpose. In this manner, all parts of the constitution—objectives, rights, competences, or others—are protected from becoming what the Indian Supreme Court called 'a mere rope of sand'.[6]

Turning to the external dimension of constitutional objectives, a few additional common characteristics come to the fore. Firstly, while constitutional objectives in general can be seen as codified aspects of the pursuit of the common good at large, foreign policy objectives are born out of an understanding that the common good of a particular polity is in the modern age intimately intertwined with that of its surroundings, if not with that of the world as a whole. The Indian Supreme Court noted that all constitutional norms have to fit together 'like two wheels of a chariot' and that 'snap one and the other will lose its efficacy'.[7] Similarly, all different parts of today's international order need to fit together, but arguably in an even more complex structure. Instead of a chariot, the image of a clock with a multitude of parts would seem more fitting. If one part breaks or is removed, the consequences may be felt by all. Constitutionally codified foreign policy objectives are a reminder of this.

As to their legal features, foreign policy goals have to be understood not as a category of their own, but as an integral part of constitutional objectives in general. This understanding is most clearly articulated in Indian constitutional law, where foreign policy objectives are located within the part of the constitution that contains all directive principles. At the same time, foreign policy objectives belong to the foreign affairs constitution of a country—its *Außenverfassungsrecht* in German. Their proper place is at the intersection of both. This may explain why in most constitutions containing foreign policy objectives, these are located in the part dealing with foreign affairs. Nonetheless, wherever they may be situated, this does not deprive them of their characteristics as constitutional objectives, while also accounting for the specific features of foreign affairs in constitutional law.

As foreign policy objectives have to be pursued in the framework of competences established elsewhere, their addressees are consequently all organs empowered to conduct the international relations of a country (in German called the *auswärtige Gewalt*). This introduces the executive as the second main addressee of these objectives next to the legislature, given the usual powers of the former as the external representative. Moreover, the 'caveat of possibility' is accentuated in the external domain. This results in decreasing even further the legal force of foreign policy objectives. Their justiciability, already marginal at best, is thus diminished as well.

However, the low level of justiciability should not be equated with an unwillingness of courts to use foreign policy objectives in constitutional interpretation, to the extent that such cases can be litigated within a given jurisdiction. Furthermore, foreign policy objectives can be used by courts to further clarify other constitutional

[6] *Hanif and Others v State of Bihar*, judgment of 23 April 1958, (1959) 1 SCR 629, 648.

[7] *Minerva Mills Ltd v Union of India and Others*, judgment of 31 July 1980, (1981) 1 SCR 206, 255.

norms and resolve constitutional disputes. Coupled with the already wide discretion of the political branches in this domain, they serve to push the boundaries of state action, but can at times also be used to restrain it. Crucially, this means that while the already weak obligatory force of objectives is watered down further when it comes to foreign affairs, their interpretive function remains intact. By virtue of this function they can continue to have permissive (and also, but rarely, prohibitive) effects.

Lastly, there is a general tendency in foreign policy objectives and the discourse surrounding them to extrapolate, or 'translate', internal features to the outside world. Thus, one could say that while domestically constitutional objectives aim at the *perfectionnement de l'ordre social*,[8] in the field of foreign policy they envisage the *perfectionnement de l'ordre mondial* along similar lines as at home.

2. Legal Traditions: A Note on Common Law Countries and Foreign Policy Objectives

While the German and French examples used here hail from the positivist, continental European tradition, a hallmark of which is codification of laws and written constitutions, India belongs to the common law tradition, where one may intuitively not expect norms such as codified objectives, including in the domain of foreign affairs. Hence, in order to fully grasp the Indian 'directive principles of state policy' as legal norms, the nature of common law legal orders and their notion of constitutionalism with regard to the role of constitutional objectives, especially in the field of foreign policy, should first be addressed. This will be done, by way of example, with references to the United Kingdom, the United States, and India.

As is well known in the case of the United Kingdom, a country does not need a document called a 'constitution' in order to have a constitution.[9] Consequently, its 'foreign affairs constitution' is also based rather on unwritten principles of competence allocation (foremost by framing foreign policy historically as a 'royal prerogative')[10] instead of substantive principles. However, in the case of India, it was a sense of suspicion of the government inherited from the colonial past that prompted the framers of the Republic of India to codify its constitution, including sections on individual rights as well as directive principles. The Indian Constituent Assembly rejected the 'British view of rights enunciated by Dicey and subscribed to by others, including the British government',[11] ie that codification of rights has

[8] B Faure, 'Les objectifs de valeur constitutionnelle: une nouvelle catégorie juridique?' (1995) No 21 *Revue française de Droit Constitutionnel* 47, 59–60.

[9] P Leyland, *The Constitution of the United Kingdom: A Contextual Analysis* (Hart Publishing, 2012) 11–14.

[10] See I Loveland, *Constitutional Law, Administrative Law, and Human Rights: A Critical Introduction*, 7th edn (OUP, 2015) 111; and United Kingdom House of Commons Information Office, *Treaties*, Factsheet P14 Procedure Series, revised August 2010.

[11] G Austin, *The Indian Constitution: Cornerstone of a Nation* (Clarendon Press, 1966) 58, referring to AV Dicey and other British constitutional scholars.

little to no added value beyond confirming their 'nominal existence'.[12] For the Indians on the eve of their independence, codification was motivated 'by the suspicion of government engendered by colonial rule'[13] and the anxiety felt by minority communities within Indian society, but foremost by the idea that 'independence meant liberty, that rights expressed this liberty and must, both in their positive and negative forms, be enshrined in the Constitution'.[14]

Similarly, the United States, following its independence, adopted a documentary constitution. The rather succinct American constitution, however, 'appears today to be strangely incomplete'[15] as regards foreign affairs. Concerning foreign policy objectives, the 'purposes of the more perfect union to be established by and pursuant to the Constitution—as set forth in the preamble—barely glance at the foreign relations of the new republic to be'.[16] In contrast, the Indian constitution is considered among the longest national constitutions of the world with over 400 articles and various schedules. It is comparable in length to the two EU Treaties with their combined 413 articles and various attached protocols and declarations.[17] In addition to classic individual rights, it contains social rights as well as foreign policy objectives in the form of the 'directive principles', which are ostensibly missing from the American counterpart.[18] This shows that not only can common law countries have documentary constitutions, but that such documents may well include norms outlining the welfare of the nation as well as foreign policy objectives.

Moreover, in both the United States and the United Kingdom, considerations on the substance and purposes of national foreign policy re-emerge elsewhere. In the case of the United Kingdom, one can consider the attempts, on the policy level, to introduce an 'ethical' foreign policy.[19] In the United States, despite the pre-eminent role of the President in foreign relations,[20] as well as a rather reluctant

[12] See eg AV Dicey, *Introduction to the Study of the Law of the Constitution*, 10th edn (Macmillan, 1961) 207.

[13] Austin (n 11) 58.

[14] Austin (n 11) 58. Austin draws here on Isaiah Berlin's two concepts of liberty, one 'negative' and the other 'positive': see I Berlin, *Liberty: Incorporating Four Essays on Liberty* (OUP, 2002) 166 et seq.

[15] L Henkin, *Constitutionalism, Democracy and Foreign Affairs* (Columbia University Press, 1990) 19.

[16] Henkin (n 15). Note also L Henkin, *The Rights of Man Today* (Stevens, 1979) 31–2, where he notes that the constitution of the United States, given its particular historical circumstances, was primarily concerned with restricting the powers of government.

[17] RS Sarkar, *The Constitution of India* (National Publishing House, 1991) 19, calls it the 'longest and most detailed Constitution known in the world'.

[18] See C Sunstein, 'Why Does the American Constitution Lack Social and Economic Guarantees?' (2005) 56 *Syracuse Law Review* 1. For a critique of the approach of the American judiciary to such social rights see M Tushnet, 'Social Welfare Rights and the Forms of Judicial Review' (2003) 82 *Texas Law Review* 1895.

[19] See in particular the 'mission statement' presented by Robin Cook in 1997: R Cook, British Foreign Secretary, Speech delivered on 12 May 1997, <http://www.guardian.co.uk/world/1997/may/12/indonesia.ethicalforeignpolicy>.

[20] See eg C Bradley and J Goldsmith, *Foreign Relations Law: Cases & Materials*, 4th edn (Wolters Kluwer Law & Business, 2011) 173–80; and L Henkin, *Foreign Affairs and the United States Constitution*, 2nd edn (Clarendon Press, 1996) 31–62.

Supreme Court when it comes to this domain,[21] foreign policy objectives have nonetheless assumed a role of constitutional significance. This is illustrated by the purposes that the President deems legitimate in order to commit the armed forces without the approval of Congress in a situation that does not represent a straightforward war. Accordingly, sets of objectives that would qualify as 'sufficiently important national interests'[22] were drawn up by the executive branch, more precisely the Department of Justice Office of the Legal Counsel. Next to rather self-interested objectives such as the protection of American citizens and assets, these also include more universalist aims such as upholding the United Nations or maintaining regional stability.[23] Thus, here the question of foreign policy objectives creeps into the constitutional discourse on the reconciliation of the respective powers of the President and Congress in foreign relations.

Turning to scholarly appraisals, Anglo-Saxon constitutional theory cannot be considered altogether hostile to the notion of constitutional foreign policy objectives, given that these norms could be well situated within the category of 'constitutional principles', which do not operate on a strictly enforceable basis. The distinction between rules and principles stems from common law jurisprudence itself.[24]

Generally, the theoretical debate on rules and principles concerns the attempts to more accurately define and delineate the discipline of law as a 'system' of rules.[25] HLA Hart's rather strict positivist approach was subsequently criticized, with other theorists emphasizing the role of principles as opposed to rules. The rigidity of rules (ie their absolute character) necessitates a hierarchy and, consequently, the need for an ultimate rule: Hart's famous 'rule of recognition'. The criticism against such a conception of law based exclusively on rigid rules was most prominently articulated by Ronald Dworkin.[26] From this understanding and definition of principles, continental European scholars such as Karl-Peter Sommermann and Christian Calliess derive a link to constitutional objectives. Both principles and objectives, in contrast to rules, do not operate on an all-or-nothing basis, but 'provide reasons for a particular decision'.[27]

Thus, while the collision of two rules requires a rule of conflict or a hierarchy to determine which rule prevails, the collision of two principles requires a weighing

[21] For an extensive criticism see T Franck, *Political Questions/Judicial Answers: Does the Rule of Law Apply to Foreign Affairs?* (Princeton University Press, 1992).

[22] See eg United States Department of Justice, Memorandum Opinion for the Attorney General, 'Authority to Use Military Force in Libya', 1 April 2011, <http://www.justice.gov/sites/default/files/olc/opinions/2011/04/31/authority-military-use-in-libya.pdf>, 10.

[23] United States Department of Justice (n 22) 11–12. On the complex relationship between the President and Congress in foreign affairs in general see Henkin (n 15) 17–43.

[24] R Dworkin, 'The Model of Rules' (1967) 35 *University of Chicago Law Review* 14; see also on the distinction between rules and principles H Ávila, *Theory of Legal Principles* (Springer, 2007) 8–11.

[25] Fundamentally HLA Hart, *The Concept of Law*, 2nd edn (OUP, 1997).

[26] R Dworkin, *Taking Rights Seriously* (Duckworth, 1978).

[27] In the original: '... liefern nur Gründe für eine bestimmte Entscheidung': Sommermann (n 2) 360; similarly C Calliess, 'Kollektive Ziele und Prinzipien im Verfassungsrecht der EU—Bestandsaufnahme, Wirkungen und Perspektiven' (2003) 92 *Archiv für Rechts- und Sozialphilosophie-Beiheft* 85, 86–7.

of the two with regard to the particular facts of the case at hand.[28] For Dworkin, a principle is thus 'a standard that is to be observed, not because it will advance or secure an economic, political, or social situation deemed desirable, but because it is a requirement of justice or fairness or some other dimension of morality'.[29] Dworkin also introduced the category of policies as distinct from both rules and principles. A policy is defined as 'that kind of standard that is to be observed that sets out a goal to be reached, generally an improvement in some economic, political, or social feature of the community (though some goals are negative, in that they stipulate that some present feature is to be protected from adverse change)'.[30] However, he acknowledges that '[t]he distinction can be collapsed by construing a principle as stating a social goal … or by construing a policy as stating a principle … or by adopting the utilitarian thesis that principles of justice are disguised statements of goals'.[31] Constitutional objectives fit well into this overall category of principles as opposed to rules.

With particular regard to the constitutional nature of certain principles, there is a trend in American scholarship framing the constitution in 'aspirational' or 'redemptive' terms. Already Louis Henkin describes constitutions as promises, which indicate 'what a society pretends or aspires to'.[32] According to Jack Balkin, the constitution, as higher law, represents 'an object of political and moral aspiration and offers a potential for redemption' as well as 'a set of principles that critiques present political arrangements and that we must try to realise over time'.[33] This is very much the same language encountered in German and French constitutional thinking, in which constitutions are framed by some scholars as Alexian optimization requirements,[34] an 'alternative plan to social grievances' (*Gegenentwurf der sozialen Mißstände*),[35] and having the overall purpose of 'perfecting the social order' (*le perfectionnement de l'ordre social*),[36] respectively.

As a method of interpretation,[37] 'aspirationalism' competes in the American legal discourse with others, notably 'originalism'.[38] Against this backdrop, constitutional objectives can be understood as a tool to reconcile the two. Where present in the text of a constitution, they can serve as expressions of such aspirations,

[28] Sommermann (n 2) 360. But see Hart's postscript: Hart (n 25) 259–63.

[29] Dworkin (n 26) 22. [30] Dworkin (n 26) 22. [31] Dworkin (n 26) 22–3.

[32] Henkin, *The Rights of Man Today* (n 16) 31.

[33] J Balkin, 'Original Meaning and Constitutional Redemption' (2007) 24 *Constitutional Commentary* 427, 464; see further J Balkin, *Constitutional Redemption: Political Faith in an Unjust World* (Harvard University Press, 2011); also M Dorf, 'The Aspirational Constitution' (2009) 77 *The George Washington Law Review* 1631, 1671, who concludes that '[r]eal constitutions include aspirational rights'.

[34] Sommermann (n 2) 360–1. [35] Sommermann (n 2) 224.

[36] Faure (n 8) 59–60.

[37] See also R West, 'The Aspirational Constitution' (1993) 88 *Northwestern University Law Review* 241.

[38] See on this debate, with an attempt at reconciling originalism and its theoretical antagonist, 'living constitutionalism', R Bennett and L Solum, *Constitutional Originalism: A Debate* (Cornell University Press, 2011). Balkin, as a prominent proponent of the idea of a future-oriented 'redemptive' constitution, describes himself as an adherent to originalism, albeit in a version he labels 'framework originalism': see Balkin, *Constitutional Redemption* (n 33) 226–50.

deemed important enough by the framers of the respective constitution to be codified. Foreign policy objectives, consequently, bear witness that the framers of a particular polity also intended its legal order to facilitate the pursuit of such ambitions on the world stage.

The above considerations show that common law countries and their constitutional interpretations are not categorically opposed to constitutional objectives, including in the domain of foreign policy. On the contrary, ideas such as the distinction between rules and principles, as well as aspirational approaches to constitutional interpretation, which these jurisdictions have brought forth, are indeed useful in the present endeavour to grasp foreign policy objectives as a constitutional norm category. Instead of standing in opposition to the German and French doctrines, they enrich and complete the common understanding of them as constitutional norms, transcending legal traditions.

3. Different Origins: Germany, France, and India

The origins of these established doctrines on constitutional objectives differ significantly. In the German case, it was devised by scholars and is still awaiting explicit endorsement by the constitutional court. In the French case, by contrast, it is a judicial creation. In the case of India, it was termed by the constitutional legislator. However, there are common patterns in the respective discourses of these jurisdictions as to the appraisal of these norms, resulting in different pictures of the same motif.

3.1 *Staatszielbestimmungen*: A scholarly conception

The German concept of *Staatszielbestimmungen*[39] is arguably the most sophisticated approach on constitutional objectives within Europe, making it particularly valuable within what might be called the 'European space of constitutional scholarship'.[40] The term *Staatszielbestimmung* can neither be found in the Basic Law nor in the case law of the German Federal Constitutional Court (*Bundesverfassungsgericht*). Nonetheless, there is a vivid scholarly debate surrounding this concept. Moreover, taking into account not just the federal level of Germany but also its *Länder*, as well as other German-speaking countries, constitutional objectives are also codified. For instance, a number of constitutions of the German *Länder* and Swiss cantons

[39] German scholarship distinguishes further between objectives of the state in general (*Staatsziele*) and constitutional provisions that codify such objectives (*Staatszielbestimmungen*). B Plecher-Hochstraßer, *Zielbestimmungen im Mehrebenensystem: Die Verzahnung der Staatszielbestimmungen im GG mit den Zielbestimmungen im EUV, EGV, EuratomV und EUVV* (Meidenbauer, 2006) 36.

[40] This is a combination of the terms European constitutional space (see Chapter 4 in detail) and the idea of a European research area, as used for instance by A von Bogdandy and J Bast, 'The Constitutional Approach to EU Law' in A von Bogdandy and J Bast (eds), *Principles of European Constitutional Law*, 2nd edn (Hart Publishing/C.H. Beck, 2011) 6.

contain the notion of objectives of the state (*Staatsziele*).[41] For these reasons, the term German will be used widely here, indicating the language area rather than just the federal level of government in Germany.

According to Josef Isensee, 'the academic career' of the modern concept of the *Staatsziel*, ie the objective of the state, starts with the creation of the German Basic Law. The term *Staatsziel* was accordingly coined by Hans Peter Ipsen by defining further the concept of the *soziale Rechtsstaat*[42] found therein (roughly, the 'social state based on the rule of law') as an objective of the state.[43] The concept has since been the subject of lively debate, and experienced renewed interest in the wake of the reunification of Germany. This was prompted by both the amendment of the Basic Law itself and the adoption of constitutions for the new *Länder* that were constituted on the territory of the former German Democratic Republic. In both cases, the introduction or addition of explicit state objectives was a prominent item of discussion.[44]

At one end of the spectrum, harsh critics call constitutions containing state objectives pejoratively a 'political wish list'[45] that harbours 'Trojan dangers'[46] and represents 'long-term time bombs'.[47] Isensee describes the original 'characteristic style' (*Duktus*) of the Basic Law as one 'that abstained from the stipulation of political goals as well as non-justiciable programmatic content in general', which in doing so 'secured political openness for the democratic process within the confines of fundamental rights in view of incalculable future developments'.[48] However, this openness may be at stake when state objectives are codified. The political discretion of the parliament would be fenced in excessively by constitutional law and 'therefore subjected to the ultimate decision of the federal

[41] See eg Art 25 constitution of the Canton Aargau; Arts 15–38 constitution of the Canton Basel-Stadt; Arts 11–19 constitution of Mecklenburg-Vorpommern; and Arts 7–13 constitution of the Freistaat Sachsen.

[42] The term is used in Arts 20 and 28 of the German constitution.

[43] J Isensee, 'Staatsaufgaben' in J Isensee and P Kirchhof (eds), *Handbuch des Staatsrechts der Bundesrepublik Deutschland. Volume IV: Aufgaben des Staates*, 3rd edn (C.F. Müller, 2006) 120; see also Sommermann (n 2) 5.

[44] See D Merten, 'Über Staatsziele' (1993) 46 *Die Öffentliche Verwaltung* 368, 368; also K-P Sommermann, 'Die Diskussion über die Normierung von Staatszielen' (1993) 32 *Der Staat* 430; and in detail for the new Länder PC Fischer, *Staatszielbestimmungen in den Verfassungen und Verfassungsentwürfen der neuen Bundesländer* (VVF, 1994). In addition, in 1983 there was an expert report commissioned by the (West) German ministries for the interior and justice, Bundesministerium des Innern und der Justiz, Staatszielbestimmungen/Gesetzgebungsaufträge, Bericht der Sachverständigenkommission 'Staatszielbestimmugen/Gesetzgebungsaufträge', Bonn, 1983.

[45] In the original: 'politischen Wunschzettel': Merten (n 44) 376, quoting H Klein, 'Staatszielbestimmungen—Die Verfassung als politischer Wunschzettel?' (1992) 29 *Zeitschrift zur politischen Bildung* 78.

[46] In the original: 'Trojanische Gefahren': Merten (n 44) 375.

[47] In the orignal: '… langfristig als Zeitbomben': Merten (n 44) 376.

[48] In the original: '… sich der Festschreibung politischer Ziele wie überhaupt der nichtjustiziablen Programmatik enthielt und so dem demokratischen Prozeß in den Grenzen der Grundrechte die politische Offenheit in der unabsehbaren künftigen Entwicklung sicherte': Isensee (n 43) 144; similarly P Badura, 'Arten der Verfassungsrechtssätze' in J Isensee and P Kirchhof (eds), *Handbuch des Staatsrechts der Bundesrepublik Deutschland. Volume VII: Normativität und Schutz der Verfassung—Internationale Beziehungen* (C.F. Müller, 1992) 46.

constitutional court'.[49] Similarly, Detlef Merten states that, in the extreme, this would turn legislators with originally wide discretion into mere 'executors of state objectives' (*Staatszielvollstreckern*),[50] amounting to a 'shift of competence'[51] (*Kompetenzverschiebung*) away from the parliament and towards the courts.

Moving to the other end of the spectrum, while Hartmut Maurer notes the potential allure of 'constitutional splendour'[52] (*verfassungsrechtlicher Glanz*), he acknowledges with specific regard to social objectives that despite all legal scepticism, constitutional objectives 'are particularly well-suited for highlighting the main problems of the community and the existential concerns of the individual citizen, and to bring them to the attention of the state organs and the population'.[53] More enthusiastically, Sommermann even speaks of constitutional objectives as the response to a general societal 'hunger for values' (*Wertehunger*), providing a sense of direction in view of the 'anomie' created by legal positivism and philosophical relativism.[54] While the formulation of constitutional objectives may question the capacity of constitutional law to deliver (*Leistungsfähigkeit des Verfassungsrechts*),[55] opening a gap between those aspirations and reality, Markus Kotzur stresses the positive side of such looming discrepancy between the two in the case of constitutional references to universal rights and values. He argues that if a state is not adhering to its own constitutional standards, this in fact puts additional pressure on the state to rectify the situation, and contributes to the perception of its shortcomings as a 'scandal', or as a credibility or legitimacy problem. Furthermore, he argues, the 'normative lie of today' retains the potential of becoming actual practice in the future.[56]

However, even before the inception of the Basic Law, the academic interest in state objectives in German scholarship had already formed part of a long tradition in discussing, theorizing, and justifying the existence of the state.[57] Arguably, the most prominent exponent of this is the Austrian public law jurist Georg Jellinek and his 'General Theory of the State' (*Allgemeine Staatslehre*).[58] However, beyond defining statehood per se, these debates dealt with both the question of the abstract *Staatszweck*, the essential *raison d'être* of the state, and the more concrete *Staatsziele*, the specific objectives of the state. According to Isensee, while the former is a

[49] In the original: 'somit dem Letztentscheid des Bundesverfassungsgerichts unterstellt': Isensee (n 43) 144; similarly Badura (n 48) 46.

[50] Merten (n 44) 376.

[51] Merten (n 44) 376.

[52] H Maurer, *Staatsrecht I: Grundlagen, Verfassungsorgane, Staatsfunktionen*, 3rd edn (C.H. Beck, 2002) 180.

[53] In the original: 'daß sie in besonderer Weise geeignet sind, wesentliche Probleme der Gemeinschaft und existentielle Sorgen des einzelnen Bürgers deutlich zu machen und in das Bewußtsein der staatlichen Organe und der Bevölkerung zu rücken': Maurer (n 52) 180.

[54] Sommermann (n 2) 1.

[55] Badura (n 48) 41.

[56] In the original: 'die normative Lüge von heute': M Kotzur, 'Weltrechtliche Bezüge in nationalen Verfassungstexten: Die Rezeption verfassungsrechtlicher Normen durch das Völkerrecht' (2008) 39 *Rechtstheorie* 191, 202.

[57] Isensee put this into a European perspective, arguing that the question of the *Staatszweck* has deep roots in the philosophical traditions of Europe: Isensee (n 43) 120.

[58] G Jellinek, *Allgemeine Staatslehre*, 3rd edn (Hähring, 1914).

matter for the theory and philosophy of the state, the latter is a question of formal public law scholarship.[59]

Instead of a clear-cut distinction, for some scholars the two exist rather on a spectrum. Sommermann argues that on the highest level of abstraction (which seems to coincide with the metaphysical/philosophical), the ultimate purpose of the state is the 'furtherance of the common good' (*Förderung des Gemeinwohls*) as well as, on a subjacent level of abstraction, providing security for the citizens as the most immediate crystallization of the pursuit of the common good.[60] Similarly, Isensee calls the common good 'the most general objective of the state' as well as 'the epitome of all legitimate state objectives'.[61] For others, a more rigid distinction between the realm of law and philosophy is warranted. Roman Herzog, for instance, dismisses any such universalizing statements and emphasizes the very diverse origins of pre-modern statehood in history.[62] This leads him to conclude that there are no 'natural tasks of the state' (*natürliche Staatsaufgaben*) and 'that the tasks of the state cannot be determined in a theoretical-abstract manner, but always only with regard to the concrete state'.[63] For the 'modern state', Herzog identifies from its historical genesis three general tasks, ie protection against external threats, maintaining internal security (taken together meaning security at large), and *Gesellschaftsgestaltug und Sozialstaatlichkeit* (roughly, 'the organization of society and social justice'). He further stresses that those basic tasks are subject to very diverse interpretations.[64] In a similar vein, Isensee notes that it is for the state to engage in this concretization of its objectives, of which a prominent way to do so is putting them in the constitution. He distinguishes *Ziele* from *Zwecke* by the fact that the latter are a given (*vorgegeben*, or one could also say exogenous) for the state, whereas objectives are freely chosen by the state.[65]

These differences of opinion on the existence of universally valid claims explaining the *raison d'être* of the state notwithstanding, there is agreement that the state has as its 'general' objective the common good, an important (albeit very broad) manifestation of which is providing security, both external and internal. For those wanting to steer clear of universal claims and natural law-based discourse, these conclusions are drawn from an examination of the historic picture at large rather than from abstract reasoning. The objectives of the state consequently represent concrete expressions of these general objectives.

[59] Isensee (n 43) 120.

[60] Sommermann (n 2) 3.

[61] In the original: 'Das allgemeinste der Staatsziele' and 'der Inbegriff aller legitimen Staatsziele, das Ziel der Ziele', respectively: J Isensee, 'Gemeinwohl im Verfassungsstaat' in J Isensee and P Kirchhof (eds), *Handbuch des Staatsrechts der Bundesrepublik Deutschland. Volume IV: Aufgaben des Staates*, 3rd edn (C.F. Müller, 2006) 4.

[62] R Herzog, 'Ziele, Vorbehalte und Grenzen der Staatlichkeit' in J Isensee and P Kirchhof (eds), *Handbuch des Staatsrechts der Bundesrepublik Deutschland. Volume IV: Aufgaben des Staates*, 3rd edn (C.F. Müller, 2006) 84–90.

[63] In the original: 'daß die Staatsaufgaben nicht theoretisch-abstrakt, sondern stets nur im Hinblick auf den konkreten Staat bestimmt werden können': Herzog (n 62) 90.

[64] Herzog (n 62) 91–2; for an extensive historical account of the development of objectives of the state see also Sommermann (n 2) 8–198.

[65] Isensee (n 43) 121.

3.2 *Objectifs de valeur constitutionnelle*: A judicial creation

The French counterpart of the German *Staatszielbestimmungen* is known under the name *objectifs de valeur constitutionnelle*. Though this doctrine is younger and in many ways less well established than the German one, the norms forming part of this category are in their legal features very similar to *Staatszielbestimmungen*, forming the second doctrinal pillar within the European space of constitutional scholarship for discerning a general comparative understanding of constitutional objectives. Even though their external dimension has not yet come clearly to the fore, this doctrine would certainly be open to such a development, not least due to the explicit references in the French constitution to external policy and objectives to be pursued, such as the constitutional mandate to maintain the *Francophonie* worldwide.

The French doctrine of *objectifs de valeur constitutionnelle* has a shorter history and different starting point compared to its German counterpart. While it was German scholars who devised the concept of *Staatszielbestimmungen* based on their interpretation of the Basic Law, the French doctrine is a product of the case law of the *Conseil constitutionnel*. The notion of *objectifs de valeur constitutionnelle* was used for the first time by the *Conseil* in its decision of 27 July 1982 concerning a law on the freedom of audio-visual communication. In this decision, the *Conseil* referred explicitly to '*objectifs de valeur constitutionnelle*', in particular safeguarding public order, respect for the freedoms of others, and the preservation of sociocultural pluralism, which the legislator had to reconcile with the freedom of communication as enshrined in Art 11 of the Declaration of the Rights of Man and of the Citizen.[66] A number of additional objectives have been referred to by the *Conseil* ever since. To date, they include the safeguarding of public order, the protection of public health, the search for perpetrators of an offence (*la recherche des auteurs d'infraction*), respect for the liberty of others, combatting fiscal fraud, prevention of encroachment on people's integrity, the provision of decent housing, pluralism,[67] financial transparency, the search for a stable and coherent majority, the financial equilibrium of social security (*l'équilibre financier de la sécurité sociale*), accessibility and intelligibility of the law, equal access of men and women to electoral mandates and functions, and equality among territorial collectivities.[68]

The creation of the concept may well be an instance of legal cross-fertilization. Pierre De Montalivet suggests that the *Conseil* was influenced by the case law of the Court of Justice of the (then) European Communities.[69] He points in particular to

[66] Décision n° 82-141 DC du 27 juillet 1982, *Loi sur la communication audiovisuelle*, Recueil, p 48, para 5. De Montalivet sees some antecedents in the prior case law of the Conseil, before actually using the term: De Montalivet (n 3) 7–9; also B Genevois, *La jurisprudence du Conseil constitutionnel: Principes Directeurs* (STH, 1988) 204–5.

[67] On the different specific aspects of pluralism in this sense, see De Montalivet (n 3) 75–8.

[68] F Luchaire, 'Brèves remarques sur une création du Conseil constitutionnel: l'objectif de valeur constitutionnelle' (2005) No 64 *Revue française de Droit Constitutionnel* 675, 676–7; De Montalivet (n 3) 75–105 (both with references to the corresponding case law).

[69] De Montalivet (n 3) 7; see also Luchaire (n 68) 675.

the landmark *Nold* ruling of 1974, in which the Court of Justice held that restrictions may be applied to fundamental rights when 'justified by the overall objectives pursued by the Community'.[70] Even though the *Conseil* never made explicit reference in its case law to having drawn inspiration from the European Court on this account, De Montalivet strongly suspects that the European Court exerted a certain influence in shaping the creation of the *objectifs* by the *Conseil*. This assumption is based, firstly, on the similar features of the two categories, including use of the term 'objective', references to the general interest, and their function to justify restrictions of rights. Secondly, it is based on the important personal connections between the two courts, not least the fact that Robert Lecourt had been President of the Court of Justice at the time of *Nold* and later was a member of the *Conseil* at the time of the 1982 decision.[71]

The *objectifs* have been criticized in French scholarship, revealing a reflex of aversion towards such norms from a classical constitutional point of view. It has been argued that they may appear at least 'curious' (*insolite*) to the eyes of the average French jurist,[72] that they are furthermore 'unheard of' (*inédit*) and 'foreign' (*étranger*) to the French legal tradition,[73] potentially even risking the 'desecration' (*désacralisation*) of the French constitution.[74] Moreover, the creation of the category of *objectifs* has raised fears in terms of the judicialization of politics, which is captured by the French term *gouvernement des juges*.[75] Equally, however, they have also prompted enthusiasm. Bertrand Faure, for instance, sees them as a contemporary phenomenon and expression of the economically and socially active 'propulsive state' (*État propulsif*).[76] More emphatically, De Montalivet sees them as part of a wider trend of referring to goals in law as the harbinger of 'a post-modern law marked by suppleness and imprecision'[77] yet truly reflective of the welfare state (*État providence*).[78]

3.3 Directive principles of state policy: A codified cornerstone

In the form of German *Staatszielbestimmungen*, there exists a very wide notion of constitutional objectives. However, this is a doctrine entirely driven by scholars,

[70] Case 4/73 *Nold v Commission*, EU:C:1974:51, para 14.

[71] De Montalivet (n 3) 47–53; see also Faure (n 8) 50; and Genevois (n 66) 205–6, who also points to the similarity between the objectifs and the concept of 'objectives pursued by the Community' as established in *Nold*.

[72] Faure (n 8) 48.

[73] C Vimbert, 'L'ordre public dans la jurisprudence du Conseil constitutionnel' (1994) No 3 *Revue du droit public et de la science politique en France et à l'étranger* 693, 712.

[74] P Pactet, 'La désacralisation progressive de la Constitution de 1958' in *La République: Mélanges en l'honneur de Pierre Avril* (Montchrestien, 2001) 389.

[75] See De Montalivet (n 3) 64–9, who eventually rejects that such a judicialization has occurred. Pointing to a similar concern, see also Faure (n 8) 50–1.

[76] Faure (n 8) 48.

[77] In the original: 'un droit post-moderne marqué par la souplesse et l'imprécision': De Montalivet (n 3) 4.

[78] De Montalivet (n 3) 68.

which has not found explicit judicial endorsement. In addition, the German Basic Law itself does not recognize the idea of a constitutional objective (though the constitutions of some *Länder* and Swiss cantons do). On the contrary, the French *objectifs de valeur constitutionnelle* were created by the French constitutional court itself. However, this led to a focus narrowed to only those that have been explicitly pronounced by this court. It is also notable that, in this case, the constitutional text itself does not contain the notion of a constitutional objective.

Given that these are the two most well-established doctrines on constitutional objectives within Europe, it is worthwhile to look beyond this part of the world, and thus beyond the European space of constitutional scholarship in the search for a more complete doctrine. This would ideally contain a constitutional text that itself recognizes the notion of a constitutional objective, including in the field of foreign policy, and is further elaborated by case law and scholarship. Such a doctrine indeed exists, viz in the form of the 'directive principles of state policy' in the constitutional law of India.

The 'directive principles of state policy' of the Indian constitution were inspired by the Irish constitution and its 'directive principles of social policy'.[79] The common struggle of both countries for independence from the British Empire was recognized early in the Indian constitutional discourse.[80] Granville Austin offers two additional influences, one domestic and one foreign. While locating the roots of the directive principles at the 1931 Karachi resolution and the 'two streams of socialist and nationalist sentiment in India that had been flowing ever faster since the late twenties',[81] he also observed that dependence on the government 'for the welfare of the mass of Indians had an even deeper grounding in Indian history'.[82] Apart from affinity with the Irish, he also points to awareness among the drafters of the Indian constitution of general trends in contemporary constitutional law, especially in Germany and Eastern Europe after the First World War, to include objectives of the state and provisions on social welfare in constitutional documents.[83] The Indian constitutional framers were thus well aware of the trend which Sommermann would later term the 'dynamization' of constitutional law.[84]

At the Constituent Assembly for the newly independent nation, the idea to include such principles in the constitutional text was disputed at first. TT Krishnamachari famously decried the directive principles as 'a veritable dustbin of sentiment ... sufficiently resilient as to permit any individual of this House to ride

[79] Art 45 Irish constitution, which does not contain foreign policy objectives. Those can be found primarily in Art 29 Irish constitution. See N Kumar, *Judiciary on Goals of Governance: Directive Principles of State Policy* (Anamika Publishers, 2005) 9.

[80] Austin (n 11) 76 (footnote 7); also J Usman, 'Non-Justiciable Directive Principles: A Constitutional Design Effect' (2007) 15 *Michigan State Journal of International Law* 643, 650–1.

[81] Austin (n 11) 76. [82] Austin (n 11) 76.

[83] Austin (n 11) 76. Note also Austin's quoting of BN Rau, the constitutional advisor of the Constituent Assembly, who noted in a newspaper article of August 1948 that 'Many modern constitutions do contain moral precepts of this kind' (77).

[84] Sommermann (n 2) 374.

his hobby horse into it'.[85] However, in the end the directive principles received large overall support and were introduced as a separate part into the Indian constitution, after the part on fundamental rights.[86]

In India, there is also a spectrum of scholarly appraisal ranging from severe scepticism to unbridled enthusiasm. Scholars such as HM Seervai deem them 'not law at all, much less a part of the supreme law',[87] despite being in the constitutional text, and posit that 'nothing would have happened'[88] if they had not been codified. Others strongly refute such detraction, stressing that the directive principles 'are not a set of new year's resolutions or a political manifesto'.[89] Instead, Austin calls the combined parts on fundamental rights and directive principles taken together 'the conscience of the Constitution'.[90] Similarly, Bertus De Villiers summarizes that following the debates of the Constituent Assembly, '[t]he directive principles and the preamble constitute the soul, spirit and hope of the Constitution',[91] highlighting their dynamic and aspirational nature.[92]

Part IV of the Indian Constitution contains a wide range of objectives in terms of substance, many of which had been introduced through 'scores of amendments'[93] at the Constituent Assembly. This shows a vivid interest in the codification of objectives—not unlike half a century later at the Convention on the Future of Europe (see Chapter 2, section 3.5).[94] These include general directives obliging the state 'to promote the welfare of the people by securing and protecting as effectively as it may a social order in which justice, social, economic and political, shall inform all the institutions of the national life'.[95] Moreover, they contain more specific goals, such as providing work[96] and child care,[97] or even the obligation to pass a uniform civil code for the entire country.[98] Regionally specific and religiously motivated objectives are also present, such as the objective to prohibit the slaughter of cows.[99] Importantly, it also includes a full article on the 'Promotion of international peace and security' as a set of explicit foreign policy objectives.

[85] As quoted in Austin (n 11) 76; also quoted in O Chinnappa Reddy, *The Court and the Constitution of India: Summits and Shallows* (OUP, 2010) 17 (omissions in the original).

[86] See Austin (n 11) 77–83 on the general support for and drafting process of the directive principles; see also B De Villiers, 'Directive Principles of State Policy and Fundamental Rights: The Indian Experience' (1992) 8 *South African Journal on Human Rights* 29, 30–4.

[87] HM Seervai, *Constitutional Law of India: A Critical Commentary. Volume II*, 4th edn (N.M. Tripathi, 1993), 1923.

[88] Seervai (n 87) 1924.

[89] TK Tope, *Constitutional Law of India*, 2nd edn (Eastern Book Company, 1992) 353.

[90] Austin (n 11) 50.

[91] De Villiers (n 86) 33–4.

[92] Also Jawaharlal Nehru pointed out that the 'directive principles represent a dynamic move towards a certain objective'. Quoted in Chinnappa Reddy (n 85) 18.

[93] Austin (n 11) 81.

[94] For a brief commentary on all the individual directive principles see Tope (n 89) 335–52.

[95] Art 38(1) Indian constitution.

[96] Art 41 Indian constitution, which also contains the objectives of providing education and public assistance in certain cases such as old age sickness.

[97] Art 45 Indian constitution.

[98] Art 44 Indian constitution. This could also be seen as a rather ambitious 'legislative command'.

[99] Art 48 Indian constitution on the 'Organisation of agriculture and animal husbandry', which mandates the state, inter alia, to 'take steps for ... prohibiting the slaughter, of cows and calves and other milch and draught cattle'.

In contrast to German and French constitutional law, the notion of a constitutional objective (under the specific label 'directive principle') was present in the drafting process of the constitutional document itself, and was subsequently codified into the same. Hence, foreign policy objectives as a constitutional concept, which German constitutional scholars needed to deduce from the text of the *Grundgesetz* and the case law of the *Bundesverfassungsgericht*, and which the French *Conseil constitutionnel* coined in its own case law interpreting the French constitution, existed in the Indian constitution from its very inception.

4. Constitutional Objectives as a Norm Category

Despite their different origins, the German, French, and Indian doctrines on constitutional objectives exhibit sufficiently similar legal features to speak of a norm category which transcends different jurisdictions. This concerns, in particular, their bindingness, their justiciability, and their relationship with other constitutional norms. In essence, the three doctrines agree that these are norms of constitutional value, that they are binding, and can serve, through interpretation, to justify extending state powers and limited fundamental rights. A difference remains in that while Indian constitutional law is unambiguous as to the lack of direct enforceability of such objectives, German and French constitutional discourse reserve a marginal enforceability for extreme cases. However, this is theoretical variance of little practical import.

4.1 *Staatszielbestimmungen*: Justiciable, in theory

The German Basic Law contains norms that qualify as constitutional objectives. However, since they are not grouped within a specific part of the constitutional document dealing with objectives of the state, their classification as such depends on the view of the reader, especially on constitutional scholars. Nevertheless, this gap in terms of attitude has not impaired the emergence of a consensus on their role within the overall constitutional framework.

The two most prominent definitions of constitutional objectives from German scholarship are arguably that of the 1983 report of the West German expert commission on objectives of the state and that of Sommermann's seminal monograph on the topic. The 1983 report of the expert commission defined constitutional provisions on state objectives as:

> constitutional norms with legally binding effect, which enjoin on public policy [*Staatstätigkeit*] the continuous observance of, or compliance with certain tasks [*Aufgaben*], i.e. objectively delineated objectives.[100]

[100] In the original: 'Verfassungsnormen mit rechtlich bindender Wirkung, die der Staatstätigkeit die fortdauernde Beachtung oder Erfüllung bestimmter Aufgaben—sachlich umschriebener Ziele—vorschreiben': Bundesministerium des Innern und der Justiz (n 44) 21.

According to Barbara Plecher-Hochstraßer, the definition of the West German expert commission on objectives of the state is generally accepted,[101] even though Hartmut Maurer points to the slightly confusing use of both the terms *Aufgabe* ('task') and *Ziel* ('objective').[102] Peter Badura uses a virtually identical definition, but without quoting the expert commission report.[103] He adds that these norms 'sketch a certain public policy programme and consequently are a guideline or directive for state action, but also for the interpretation of laws and other legal rules'.[104] He further states that they do not establish individual rights or obligations.[105]

Sommermann arrives at a similar, yet more precisely worded definition in his 1998 monograph. According to him, *Staatszielbestimmungen* are constitutional provisions stipulating objectives of the state 'which commit the government (the legislative, executive and judicial branch) in a legally binding manner to the pursuit of a certain objective, without granting subjective rights to the citizen'.[106] Overall, these two definitions are compatible and share the same main features.

An examination of these main features reveals the legal effects of this norm category. In German scholarship, there is clear agreement that state objectives are legally binding obligations.[107] In addition, an uncontroversial function of constitutional objectives is that they can be drawn on by courts in interpreting the constitution and other laws.[108]

Concerning the circle of addressees of constitutional objectives, it is emphasized that the objectives bind the entirety of state power (*Staatsgewalt*). This means that the 'government' in the widest sense of the word is the addressee of these obligations, encompassing all branches and levels of government and all state organs.[109] However, it is also generally acknowledged that objectives are primarily addressed to the legislator.[110] It is incumbent upon this branch to both specify and implement the objectives through legislation. The executive, following legislative framing and concretization, will subsequently apply them, even though it is also bound by the objectives as such. The courts, apart from extreme cases, also require legislative acts in order to bring constitutional objectives to bear.[111]

[101] Plecher-Hochstraßer (n 39) 23. [102] Maurer (n 52) 176–7.

[103] Badura (n 48) 41.

[104] In the original: 'Sie umreißen ein bestimmtes Programm der Staatstätigkeit und sind dadurch eine Richtlinie oder Direktive für das Staatliche Handeln, auch für die Auslegung von Gesetzen und sonstigen Rechtsvorschriften': Badura (n 48) 41.

[105] Badura (n 48) 42.

[106] In the original: '... welche die Staatsgewalt (Legislative, Exekutive und Judikative) auf die Verfolgung eines bestimmten Ziels rechtsverbindlich verpflichten, ohne dem Bürger subjektive Rechte zu gewähren': Sommermann (n 2) 5.

[107] See eg Bundesministerium des Innern und der Justiz (n 44) 21; Badura (n 48) 41; Sommermann (n 2) 5 and 326; Merten (n 44) 370.

[108] See eg Badura (n 48) 41; Plecher-Hochstraßer (n 39) 33; K Hesse, *Grundzüge des Verfassungsrechts der Bundesrepublik Deutschland*, 20th edn (C.F. Müller, 1995) 91 (marginal no 208).

[109] In detail see Sommermann (n 2) 383–6; also Isensee (n 43) 122–3; Merten (n 44) 370.

[110] Plecher-Hochstraßer (n 39) 26; and Badura (n 48) 41.

[111] On the prominent role of the legislator and the secondary roles of the other branches of government see Sommermann (n 2) 383–7 and on implementation 427–52. Note in this context in

As to the consequences of the binding nature of these aims, there is agreement that state objectives do not grant individual rights.[112] Moreover, commentators stress that the scope of the obligation is the 'pursuit' of the objective, not its actual attainment.[113] This interpretation is well captured in the reference to state objectives in the constitution of the German *Land* Sachsen-Anhalt, which obligates the *Land* to pursue the state objectives 'to its best endeavours and to orientate its actions accordingly'.[114] The qualification of the scope of the obligation to its pursuit is expressed in the German literature by the term *Vorbehalt des Möglichen*, ie the caveat of what the bounds of possibility allow,[115] which was also used by the *Bundesverfassungsgericht*.[116] In this vein, a notion that is used by a number of German scholars to grasp the legal force of state objectives is Robert Alexy's concept of 'optimization requirements' (*Optimierungsgebote*),[117] ie 'norms that require that something be realised to the greatest extent possible given the legal and factual possibilities'.[118]

This notion of optimization is also useful in defining the relationship between different constitutional objectives and the resolution of conflicts between them. Merten speaks of the 'interpretative argument of the intentional lacuna'.[119] This means that in terms of systematic and teleological interpretation of a constitutional document, the fact that an objective was not included could imply that it matters less than another, thus introducing an element of hierarchy. Merten illustrates this with examples from economic policy, stating that if, for instance, price stability or the social market economic are not elevated to constitutional objectives, they will also not be the focus anymore of those that interpret the constitution.[120]

However, given the broad nature of many constitutional objectives, objectives that were not spelt out could be seen as to a large extent implied in those that are

particular the *Bundesverfassungsgericht* in Decision of 19 October 1983 (*Sozialplan*), BVerfGE 65, 182, para 44.

[112] Sommermann (n 2) 5; Plecher-Hochstraßer (n 39) 24–6; Badura (n 48) 42; Bundesministerium des Innern und der Justiz (n 44) 20.

[113] Isensee (n 43) 121; also Plecher-Hochstraßer (n 39) 32–3.

[114] Art 3(3) constitution of Sachsen-Anhalt: 'Die nachfolgenden Staatsziele verpflichten das Land, sie nach Kräften anzustreben und sein Handeln danach auszurichten.' Similarly, Art 13 constitution of the Freistaat Sachsen. See also Isensee (n 43) 121; Merten (n 44) 370.

[115] Sommermann (n 2) 224, also 415; Maurer (n 52) 179; see also Hesse (n 108) 91–2 (marginal no 208).

[116] In a decision concerning restrictions on the admission to public medical school, the *Bundesverfassungsgericht* stated that a right to access to public facilities 'is qualified by the caveat of what is possible in the sense of what the individual can reasonably claim from society' (in the original: 'stehen sie doch unter dem Vorbehalt des Möglichen im Sinne dessen, was der Einzelne vernünftigerweise von der Gesellschaft beanspruchen kann'), Decision of 3 May 1972 (*numerus clausus I*), BVerfGE 33, 303, para 70.

[117] Sommermann (n 2) 360–1, who calls state objectives optimization requirements 'par excellence' (361); also Isensee (n 43) 126.

[118] R Alexy, *A Theory of Constitutional Rights* (OUP, 2002) 47.

[119] In the original: 'das Interpretationsargument der bewußten Lücke': Merten (n 44) 375–6; similarly Maurer (n 52) 180.

[120] Merten (n 44) 376.

codified. In the above example, both price stability and the social market economy could be seen as part of a wider notion of social justice. Moreover, as long as no direct conflict exists with codified objectives, states would be allowed to pursue any objective they choose in view of their *Kompetenz-Kompetenz*, as well as their general goal to serve the common good. According to Isensee, unless constitutionally prohibited, the state is allowed to act at will.[121] Consequently, the absence of a certain objective from the constitution cannot be interpreted as amounting to the prohibition to pursue that objective. Moreover, as Sommermann rightly points out, the weighing or prioritization of different state objectives is more complex than the issue of whether they are explicitly mentioned.

Among those objectives that are codified, one can examine their position within the constitution. For example, one can look at how prominently they appear in the document or whether stricter rules apply to their modification: Are they part of the 'constitutional identity' of a state or subject to an 'eternity clause'? Moreover, are they specified further in the constitution or linked to other norms on implementation?[122] Plecher-Hochstraßer, who stresses that despite these different criteria all (codified) state objectives are of equal value, favours the application of the German constitutional law concept of 'practical concordance' (*praktische Konkordanz*),[123] ie a case-by-case reconciliation of different objectives with a view to granting the greatest effectiveness possible to each.[124] Given the width of objectives mentioned earlier, 'practical concordance' could also be applied when specific non-codified objectives are 'implied' by virtue of broader general objectives.

With both approaches, it would be possible to respect the choices of the *pouvoir constituant* by factoring in the objectives that were codified, without jumping to rigid conclusions. In any event, the discretion of the political branches in the pursuit of the different constitutional objectives becomes apparent again. Direct judicial scrutiny of whether objectives have been correctly pursued and implemented could therefore be only of a marginal nature.

This leads to the question whether constitutional objectives generally produce hard obligations, the violation of which can be ruled upon by courts, which is a controversial issue. Even though 'the choice of ways and means and the further concretisation of the objectives are left to the state organs',[125] some argue that in extreme cases a court (usually the constitutional court) could in review proceedings find that an organ of the state had breached the obligations flowing from objectives.[126] This would make them justiciable norms. According to Peter Badura, legislation that disregards a constitutional objective would have to be considered unconstitutional.[127] However, the mainstream opinion is also clear in that

[121] Isensee (n 43) 142; see in detail also J Isensee, 'Vorbehalt der Verfassung' in J Isensee and H Lechler (eds), *Freiheit und Eigentum, Festschrift für Walter Leisner* (Duncker & Humblot, 1999) 373 et seq.

[122] Sommermann (n 2) 413–14. However, he dismisses a general *lex specialis* rule.

[123] See Hesse (n 108) 28 (marginal no 72).

[124] Plecher-Hochstraßer (n 39) 93–104.

[125] In the original: 'während die Wahl der Mittel und Wege und die nähere Konkretisierung der Ziele den staatlichen Organen überlassen bleibt': Maurer (n 52) 178.

[126] Sommermann (n 2) 362; Plecher-Hochstraßer (n 39) 33.

[127] Badura (n 48) 42.

such disregard should be manifest and in fact amount to seriously compromising or frustrating the successful pursuit of an objective and not just its neglect.[128]

On this matter, German scholars draw on the case law of the German Federal Constitutional Court. In a case concerning the constitutionality of age limits for orphans' pensions, the *Bundesverfassungsgericht* construed the principle of social justice (*Sozialstaatsprinzip*) as making it one of the 'self-evident duties' of the state to cater to the indigent.[129] Even though the court acknowledges that there is wide discretion in choosing the ways to pursue social justice, the duty to provide for the 'minimum conditions for a dignified life' is of a strict and absolute nature.[130] In a later decision on the tax-free minimum living wage, the court even called this duty 'compelling' (*zwingend*).[131]

German scholarship generally considers constitutional objectives as a category of constitutional law in its own right. Whereas other jurisdictions, such as the French and Indian legal orders, are primarily concerned with the relationship between objectives and individual rights, German scholarship provides for sometimes rather detailed categorizations of constitutional norms.[132] These usually include structural principles (*Strukturprinzipien*), competences, constitutional commands (*Verfassungsaufträge*), and individual rights, which are categories that are also identifiable in the constitutional law of other countries and the EU.

Structural principles can be defined as the formal basic principles enshrined in the constitution on the organization of the state.[133] They are also known as 'the basic choices of constitutional law' (*verfassungsrechtliche Grundentscheidungen*).[134] Austrian constitutional scholarship uses the figurative term of 'building laws of the constitution' (*Baugesetze der Verfassung*).[135] The list of examples for structural principles contained in the Basic Law usually contains republicanism, democracy, social justice (*Sozialstaatlichkeit*), federalism, and the (formal) rule of law (*Rechtsstaatlichkeit*).[136] Unlike state objectives, they establish the basic characteristics of the state, ie of what it is, not what it should strive for.[137] The former are static, to be permanently *preserved*, while the latter are dynamic, and should be constantly *pursued*.[138] Thus, the state would remain the same even in the case of a removal or change of a state objective, but not in the case of a structural

[128] Sommermann (n 2) 429–30 and 436–8; Plecher-Hochstraßer (n 39) 33.

[129] In the original: 'selbstverständlichen Pflichten': Decision of 18 June 1975 (*Waisenrente II*), BVerfGE 40, 121, para 44.

[130] In the original: 'Mindestvoraussetzungen für ein menschenwürdiges Dasein' *Waisenrente II* (n 129) para 44.

[131] Decision of 29 May 1990 (*Steuerfreies Existenzminimum*), BVerfGE 82, 60, para 88.

[132] See Sommermann (n 2) 362; Badura (n 48) 38–9 and the references there respectively; extensively M Sachs, 'Normtypen im deutschen Verfassungsrecht' (1991) 6 *Zeitschrift für Gesetzgebung* 1.

[133] Sommermann (n 2) 373.

[134] See, also for other possible terms, Maurer (n 52) 175.

[135] L Adamovich and B Funk, *Österreichisches Verfassungsrecht*, 3rd edn (Springer, 1985) 98.

[136] These can all be found in Art 20 of the German constitution. Maurer (n 52) 175; Sommermann (n 2) 372–3 (footnote 226); and the references there.

[137] Merten (n 44) 370; and Sommermann (n 2) 373.

[138] Merten (n 44) 370; also Plecher-Hochstraßer (n 39) 44.

principle.[139] They rely on structural principles to provide 'the patterns of action, the modalities of state activity'.[140]

State objectives are to be distinguished furthermore from competence norms. German constitutional law generally distinguishes between vertical (*Verbandskompetenz*, ie between the federation and the *Länder*) and horizontal divisions of competence (*Organkompetenz*, ie between the different branches of government).[141] According to Sommermann, 'whereas competence provisions open up *possibilities* for action, provisions on state objectives impose on the competent state organs *obligations* to act or at any rate to give attention to a certain objective'.[142] In theory, this means that in the absence of competence, a state organ is barred from acting, even in the pursuit of an explicit constitutional objective.[143] However, such a clear-cut distinction cannot always be made. It may be possible to infer an objective from the existence of competence.[144] This interplay can be seen, for instance, in the Swiss constitutional law concept of 'goal-oriented competence allocation' (*zielgerichtete Kompetenzzuweisung*).[145]

Moreover, state objectives do not grant individual rights. In German constitutional scholarship, this is part of the dichotomy of, on the one hand, the law that organizes the state and is able to impose obligations on individuals (*objektives Recht*), and on the other hand, the law that grants individual rights vis-à-vis the state (*subjektives Recht*).[146] The importance of keeping these two apart can be seen, for instance, in the harsh academic criticism the constitution of the *Land* Brandenburg received for putting state objectives and basic rights into the same section,[147] while the clear separation of both in the constitution of Sachsen-Anhalt was lauded.[148] However, somewhat contrary to this critical appraisal of the *Länder* constitutions, scholars generally point out that the relationship between state objectives and individual rights is not at all clear-cut either, but instead rather 'ambivalent'.[149] In particular, while the difference between classic 'defensive rights' requiring state abstention and objectives requiring state action is more evident, German scholars point to the unclear nature of social rights which are not negatively formulated

[139] Maurer (n 52) 177.

[140] In the original: '… die Handlungsmuster, die Modalitäten des Staatshandelns': Sommermann (n 2) 373.

[141] Maurer (n 52) 182.

[142] In the orignal: 'Während die Kompetenzbestimmungen somit Handlungsmöglichkeiten eröffnen, konstituieren die Staatszielbestimmungen Handlungs- oder jedenfalls Befassungspflichten der zuständigen Staatsorgane': Sommermann (n 2) 366.

[143] Sommermann (n 2) 366; see also Isensee (n 43) 127–8; and Merten (n 44) 371.

[144] Isensee (n 43) 128, who speaks of inferring a task (*Aufgabe*) of the state from competence norms.

[145] This was developed with reference to the introduction of environmental protection in the Swiss constitution as a federal goal and competence. See U Breiter, *Staatszielbestimmungen als Problem des schweizerischen Bundesverfassungsrechts* (Schulthess, 1980) 97; and U Häferlin, W Haller, and H Keller, *Schweizerisches Bundesstaatsrecht*, 8th edn (Schulthess, 2012) 57.

[146] Merten (n 44) 370. For a European perspective see M Loughlin, *Foundations of Public Law* (OUP, 2010) 367–72.

[147] Isensee (n 43) 145; Merten (n 44) 375; Sommermann (n 2) 353–5.

[148] Sommermann (n 2) 354.

[149] In the orignal: 'in einem ambivalenten Verhältnis': Sommermann (n 2) 415.

but prompt the state to provide certain goods or services, such as a right to housing or work. These provisions, although they are called 'rights', cannot be invoked unconditionally, and therefore often exhibit characteristics akin to those of state objectives.[150]

A highly contentious issue is the degree to which state objectives can serve to justify limitations of individual rights. Maurer warns that state objectives may increase 'the tendency for the restriction of fundamental rights'.[151] The question of curtailing rights is also of particular historical importance, as calls for sacrifices by the individual for the 'greater good' of the community are reminiscent of authoritarian or totalitarian regimes.[152] Therefore, there is a large amount of anxiety surrounding the potential that state objectives could be perverted by such interpretations. Sommermann stresses that state objectives only play a role within the scope of the derogation from the rights to the extent that such derogations are provided for.[153] This would fit well with the general definition of state objectives. Indeed, within this scope of derogation, Sommermann sees an important role for state objectives, in particular as a factor in assessing the proportionality of the restriction of a right.[154] In the case of social rights or social justice generally, however, objectives and rights cannot be seen as opposing forces, but rather as two sides of the same coin.[155] This is part of the general evolution of individual rights from mere negative rights aimed at prohibiting the state from interfering with individual liberty, towards positive rights through which the provision of certain facilities becomes an obligation of the state.[156]

Another distinction is made between objectives and constitutional commands (*Verfassungsauftrag*). As opposed to state objectives, these are restricted in terms of subject matter and can be achieved through a single measure or set of measures.[157] They require a rather precisely determined action from the state, such as setting up a central bank.[158] A subcategory of this are legislative commands (*Gesetzgebungsaufträge*), ie constitutional commands addressed to the legislature only, obliging it to regulate a certain area.[159]

Within the norm category of state objectives, German scholarship offers a number of typologies.[160] These include the criterion of what is called the 'perfectibility'

[150] Isensee (n 43) 122; Maurer (n 52) 181; and Sommermann (n 2) 223–9.

[151] In the original: 'die Neigung zu Grundrechtsbeschränkungen': Maurer (n 52) 180.

[152] See in detail on the historical aspects Sommermann (n 2) 116–59; also P Häberle, *Europäische Verfassungslehre*, 7th edn (Nomos, 2011) 372.

[153] Merten (n 44) 371. Sommermann (n 2) 422–3. Both refer here also to a decision of the *Bundesverfassungsgericht* on freelancers, in which it ruled that the principle of social justice (*Sozialstaatsprinzip*) cannot restrict fundamental rights without further concretization through law, Decision of 13 January 1982 (*Freie Mitarbeiter*), BVerfGE 59, 231, para 68.

[154] Sommermann (n 2) 423–5, and the (comparative) case law references provided there.

[155] Plecher-Hochstraßer (n 39) 41.

[156] Sommermann (n 2) 1; see also P Häberle, 'Die Verfassungsbewegung in den fünf neuen Bundesländern Deutschlands 1991 bis 1992' (1994) 42 *Jahrbuch des öffentlichen Rechts der Gegenwart* 149, 159, noting a general tendency towards overcoming the strict duality of constitutional objectives and rights in modern constitutional law, while retaining them as separate norm categories.

[157] Isensee (n 43) 127. [158] Art 88 German constitution; Badura (n 48) 39.

[159] Maurer (n 52) 181; and Sommermann (n 2) 362–4.

[160] For other categorizations see Isensee (n 43) 130; and Maurer (n 52) 178.

of objectives and their categorization according to content. Concerning the former, scholars propose to distinguish between 'perfectible' and 'imperfectible' objectives, ie those that can actually be achieved and those that require permanent pursuit, or 'asymptotical'[161] approximation. The classic example for an achievable objective is that of German reunification.[162] Once it is achieved, the objective becomes moot. Other possible examples would be the accession to a supranational organization or the creation of a certain (domestic) institution.[163] In these cases, however, depending on how specific the provision is, one might rather classify it as a constitutional command. Perfectible objectives are seen generally as the exception,[164] while the vast majority of constitutional objectives, such as providing security or protecting the environment, are inherently imperfectible.

State objectives can also be grouped according to their content. A basic categorization has been proposed by Sommermann based on a thorough historical and comparative analysis.[165] At the highest level of abstraction, he identifies the common good. At a somewhat lower level of abstraction, he identifies security as a general purpose of the state.[166] In addition, and at a lower level of abstraction, he identifies five basic state objectives (*Grundstaatsziele*) for the modern democratic constitutional state: The rule of law (*Rechtsstaatlichkeit*, which assumes a particular position), social justice (*Sozialstaatlichkeit*), culture/civilization (*Kulturstaatlichkeit*), peace (*Friedensstaatlichkeit*), and the environment (*Umweltstaatlichkeit*). These basic objectives are only rarely codified as such in the abstract form in constitutional documents. They usually manifest themselves in provisions containing more specific state objectives, ie at an even lower level of abstraction.[167]

Concerning the rule of law, Sommerman considers it Janus-faced, ie it has the character of both a fundamental structural principle as well as that of an objective to be pursued. Sommermann derives this from the distinction between the formal (*formell*) and substantive (*materiell*) meaning of the rule of law.[168] In the formal sense, the rule of law in German constitutional law is comprised of aspects such as the supremacy of the constitution, the separation of powers, and effective judicial protection by an independent judiciary.[169] Concerning the substantive aspect of the rule of law, Sommermann frames it as a state objective. He acknowledges that this interpretation of the rule of law is not generally accepted in German constitutional scholarship.[170] As an objective, it comprises such elements as justice, human dignity, individual freedom/rights, equality/non-discrimination, and judicial guarantees.[171] In the Anglo-Saxon discourse, we also find 'two versions of the rule of

[161] Isensee (n 43) 130. [162] Art 23 German Basic Law in its pre-reunification version.

[163] Sommermann (n 2) 380–1. [164] Isensee (n 43) 130.

[165] Sommermann (n 2) 198–252. [166] See on security also Sommermann (n 2) 203–5.

[167] Sommermann (n 2) 198–9.

[168] E Schmidt-Aßmann, 'Der Rechtsstaat' in J Isensee and P Kirchhof (eds), *Handbuch des Staatsrechts der Bundesrepublik Deutschland. Volume II: Verfassungsstaat*, 3rd edn (C.F. Müller, 2004) 552–3.

[169] Sommermann (n 2) 210.

[170] Sommermann (n 2) 211 (and footnote 555). Plecher-Hochstraßer does not mention the rule of law as one of the objectives of the German Basic Law: Plecher-Hochstraßer (n 39) 46.

[171] Sommermann (n 2) 211–15.

law, a modest version of adhering to the rules and a more lofty ideal that incorporates criteria of justice'.[172] This has also been termed the 'thin' and 'thick' definition of the rule of law.[173] This allows for an understanding of the substantive rule of law as an Alexian 'optimization requirement', ie the constitutional requirement to not just preserve the rule of law as a structural, static element, but also to improve it and develop it. It becomes thus an objective of continuous 'self improvement' of the legal system, ie to be dynamic and to adapt to evolving standards.

Apart from the rule of law, the four remaining basic objectives are less controversial. The objective of social justice (*Sozialstaatlichkeit*) is considered by Sommermann as a call to remedy social grievances.[174] Since there is an obvious tension between the expectations raised and what will actually be feasible, the caveat of the feasibility is of particular importance here. This is also the reason why despite the formulation as 'social rights', in many constitutions social justice and its various manifestations cannot be invoked directly in court, or only under certain conditions.[175] These manifestations would include providing a subsistence level for everyone, the fight against poverty, and more generally, social security and prosperity for all. It would also include the (social) 'right' to work, the 'right' to health, and the 'right' to housing, family protection, and consumer protection.[176]

Concerning culture as a basic objective, it should first be noted that the term *Kultur* in German is wider than the English term 'culture'. It also comprises notions of education and civilization. The cultural state objective (*Kulturstaatlichkeit*) is described by Sommermann as stemming from the ideas of the enlightenment. It links the notion of the autonomous and developable individual to the idea of a state that actively engages in the education of its citizens, ie a state that does not leave this task entirely up to societal actors such as the family or the church.[177] This requires both positive duties such as providing a minimum standard of education to each citizen, as well as negative duties such as not interfering with the freedom of science.

The fourth basic state objective of environmental protection can be seen as a result of the rise of environmental awareness as a policy issue since the 1960s. According to Sommermann, the protection of the environment is present as an objective of the state 'in almost all more recent constitutions'.[178] Aspects of the objective include the protection of natural resources, site preservation, animal protection and the protection of biodiversity, regional planning, waste avoidance and management,

[172] G Fletcher, *Basic Concepts of Legal Thought* (OUP, 1996) 11.

[173] B Tamanaha, 'A Concise Guide to the Rule of Law' in G Palombella and N Walker (eds), *Relocating the Rule of Law* (Hart Publishing, 2009) 4.

[174] Sommermann (n 2) 224.

[175] Sommermann (n 2) 224; see also extensively H Zacher, 'Das soziale Staatsziel' in J Isensee and P Kirchhof (eds), *Handbuch des Staatsrechts der Bundesrepublik Deutschland. Volume IV: Aufgaben des Staates*, 3rd edn (C.F. Müller, 2006) 674–719 on the content of social justice, and 732–4 on the relationship with fundamental rights.

[176] Plecher-Hochstraßer (n 39) 52; Sommermann (n 2) 224–9.

[177] Sommermann (n 2) 230.

[178] In the original: 'in nahezu allen jüngeren Verfassungen': Sommermann (n 2) 249.

and access to environmentally relevant information.[179] Environmental protection also harbours an important inter-generational aspect, which is made explicit in the German Basic Law.[180]

Finally, the objective of peace (*Friedensstaatlichkeit*) is considered by Sommermann as a genuinely externally oriented goal, stating that domestic peace is absorbed in the objectives of the rule of law and social justice, as well as fundamental rights protection.[181] Conceptually, the width of the concept of peace ranges from a narrow, negative definition meaning the absence of war, to the wide, positive notion as '*the ideal condition of international relations*, in which security and justice for all are warranted to the fullest extent'.[182] Aspects of the peace objective include the prohibition of war as a means of politics, the promotion of collective security systems, and 'friendliness towards international law' (*Völkerrechtsfreundlichkeit*), human rights, and integration, as well as international solidarity and development.[183]

4.2 *Objectifs de valeur constitutionnelle*: Marginally enforceable

The French doctrine on the constitutional norm category of *objectifs de valeur constitutionnelle* exhibits essentially the same features as its German counterpart. They, too, are expressions of a constitutionally codified common good. They are addressed at all state organs, with an emphasis on the legislature. They are of a dynamic character, obliging the state to actively pursue these objectives, even when this would entail a non-excessive restriction of individual rights. They do not found subjective rights or competences. They are justiciable before the courts, albeit with a similarly high threshold, which makes detection of a violation of the obligations flowing from objectives themselves rather unlikely. Instead, they can rather be seen as norms helping in the interpretation of limits to fundamental rights and shaping the borders of competence.

The *Conseil constitutionnel* usually seeks to link the *objectifs de valeur constitutionnelle* to a textual foundation in French constitutional law, but sometimes in rather abstract ways.[184] French scholarship deems the *objectifs* a norm category of constitutional law, ie they form part of what is called the *bloc de constitutionnalité*,[185]

[179] Sommermann (n 2) 247–52. [180] Art 20a German constitution.

[181] Sommermann (n 2) 237.

[182] In the orignal: 'Frieden kann den idealen Zustand der internationalen Beziehungen bezeichnen, in dem Sicherheit und Gerechtigkeit für alle in vollem Umfang gewährleistet sind': R Geiger, *Grundgesetz und Völkerrecht: Die Bezüge des Staatsrechts zum Völkerrecht und Europarecht*, 3rd edn (C.H. Beck, 2002) 346 (italics in the original); see also Sommermann (n 2) 238.

[183] Sommermann (n 2) 239–47.

[184] De Montalivet (n 3) 72–89 on cases of implicit textual foundation, 89–98 on instances where the textual foundation is not clarified by the *Conseil*, and 98–105 where it is explicit; also G Drago, *Contentieux constitutionnel français*, 2nd edn (Presses universitaires de France, 2006) 290–1.

[185] See on the concept D Rousseau, *Droit du contentieux constitutionnel*, 8th edn (Montchrestien, 2008) 101–12, who ranks the objectifs as part of the *bloc de constitutionnalité*, but rejects their textual foundation, seeing them purely as a judicial creation (111–12); similarly B Mathieu and M Verpeaux, *Contentieux constitutionnel des droits fondamentaux* (L.G.D.J., 2002) 275–6. Luchaire (n 68) 677–8 derived their constitutional value from the fact that they operationalize constitutional principles.

which encompasses the current French constitution (that of the Fifth Republic), the 1789 Declaration of the Rights of Man and of the Citizen, the fundamental principles recognized by the laws of the Republic (*les principes fondamentaux reconnus par les lois de la République*), the principles contained in the preamble to the constitution of the Fourth Republic, and other principles of constitutional value.[186]

In terms of definition, French scholarship considers as *objectifs de valeur constitutionnelle* those which the *Conseil* has identified as such. This means that it is a rather finite category comprising a number of detailed objectives.[187] Nevertheless, this does not exclude the possibility that, in future cases, new objectives may emerge. However, the strict following of the case law of the *Conseil constitutionnel* by scholars makes it difficult to discern an overarching concept of the objectives as, taken together, expressing a full kaleidoscope of facets of the pursuit of a polity's common good. Rather, the *Conseil* has provided only some insights into what those might be. Nonetheless, they have been described by some as the expression of 'the pursuit of a constitutionally protected general interest'.[188] This dovetails with the idea expressed above in the German context of considering constitutional objectives neither as intimations of a metaphysical and timeless notion of the *bonum commune*, nor as fickle expressions of political self-interest, but as the common good as envisaged by and enshrined in the constitution as a matter of law.

As norms situated within the *bloc de constitutionnalité*, the *objectifs* perform certain legal functions, which are very similar to those of *Staatszielbestimmungen*. Concerning the relation between the different objectives, Bertrand Faure proposes, but ultimately rejects, attempts to classify them according to their degree of concretization.[189] Instead, the *objectifs* all have a priori the same legal value.

For De Montalivet, the *objectifs* are legally binding norms which address the entirety of state power. Among the state organs, the prime addressee is again the legislature as regards the realization of the objectives and conciliation between them as well as with other constitutional norms.[190] He posits that they perform the three basic functions of legal norms, ie they oblige, prohibit, and authorize.[191] In principle, they, too, are justiciable. However, as the case law reveals, the legal

[186] Note that the preamble to the constitution of the Fifth Republic makes reference to the 1789 declaration and the preamble to the constitution of the Fourth Republic, as well as the Environmental Charter (Charte de l'environnement) of 2004. Note in this respect also Décision n° 71-44 DC du 16 juillet 1971, *Loi complétant les dispositions des articles 5 et 7 de la loi du 1er juillet 1901 relative au contrat d'association*, Recueil, p 29.

[187] De Montalivet (n 3) 157; Mathieu and Verpeaux (n 185) 425.

[188] In the original: 'la poursuite d'un intérêt général constitutionnellement protégé': G Drago and N Molfessis, 'Justice constitutionnelle' (1996) No 3 *Justices: Revue générale de droit processuel* 308, 330; also Drago (n 184) 289.

[189] Faure (n 8) 71–2; also De Montalivet (n 3) 417–18, who envisages possible conflicts between objectifs, but speaks of the need to reconcile them with each other rather than proposing a rule of conflict.

[190] De Montalivet (n 3) 459; similarly Mathieu and Verpeaux (n 185) 427–31.

[191] For a discussion of these three functions as the fundamental functions of any norm, see De Montalivet (n 3) 323–31.

force of the *objectifs* is fairly limited.[192] For more critical voices, they represent not actual norms but rather a technique of constitutional interpretation.[193] They do not establish individual rights.[194]

In terms of obligation, the *Conseil constitutionnel* has used language similar to that of the *Bundesverfassungsgericht* by stating, for instance, that 'it is incumbent upon the legislator' to implement the constitutional objective of making decent accommodation available for each person.[195] In other cases, the *Conseil* ruled with regard to the legislature and competent regulatory authorities 'that it is incumbent upon them' to decide on appropriate rules aimed at the 'realization' (*réalisation*) of the objective found in the preamble to the constitution, referring to the duty of the state to provide health protection.[196] However, despite this strong wording (literally, 'to realize' the objective), the scope of the obligation is limited, as objectives cannot be invoked directly by individuals in court, but impose only a 'best endeavours obligation' (*obligation de moyens*) as opposed to obligations of result (*obligation de résultat*).[197]

Closely related to obligation is the function of prohibition. In French doctrine, a law that manifestly disregards a constitutional objective is considered forbidden, which *in extremis* can lead to declaring that law unconstitutional through judicial review.[198] Akin to the often rather general formulations of the *Bundesverfassungsgericht* with regard to social justice or reunification, the *Conseil* also uses language which points to a prohibition to manifestly disregard an objective. For instance, concerning the constitutionality of joining the Schengen Agreement, it ruled that the law approving the agreement 'could not be seen as disregarding the constitutional objective of safeguarding public order'.[199] Concerning an electoral law in French Polynesia, the pursuit of the objective of seeking stable and coherent majorities was deemed by the *Conseil* not to have caused 'a manifestly excessive encroachment' upon other constitutional objectives and principles such as sociocultural pluralism.[200] Furthermore, in a case concerning press legislation, the *Conseil* ruled that the legislator had not committed a manifest error (*erreur manifeste*) with the view of realizing the objective of transparency.[201] These cases show that the *Conseil* recognizes a rather large

[192] De Montalivet (n 3) 561.

[193] H Roussillon, *Le Conseil constitutionnel*, 5th edn (Dalloz, 2004) 82–3.

[194] In detail, De Montalivet (n 3) 470–507.

[195] In the original: 'il appartient au législateur': Décision n° 98-403 DC du 29 juillet 1998, *Loi d'orientation relative à la lutte contre les exclusions*, Recueil, p 276, para 7.

[196] In the original: 'qu'il leur appartient': Décision n° 89-269 DC du 22 janvier 1990, *Loi portant diverses dispositions relatives à la sécurité sociale et à la santé*, Recueil, p 33, para 26; for further case law, see De Montalivet (n 3) 357–64.

[197] De Montalivet (n 3) 561.

[198] De Montalivet (n 3) 528; also Faure (n 8) 67–70.

[199] In the original: 'ne saurait être regardé comme méconnaissant l'objectif de valeur constitutionnelle de sauvegarde de l'ordre public': Décision n° 91-294 DC du 25 juillet 1991, *Loi autorisant l'approbation de la convention d'application de l'accord de Schengen*, Recueil, p 91, para 17.

[200] In the original: 'une atteinte manifestement excessive': Décision n° 2004-490 DC du 12 février 2004, *Loi organique portant statut d'autonomie de la Polynésie française*, Recueil, p 41, para 85.

[201] Décision n° 86-210 DC du 29 juillet 1986, *Loi portant réforme du régime juridique de la presse*, Recueil, p 110, para 18.

scope of discretion for the legislator and consequently sets a high threshold for determining actual violations flowing directly from the pursuit of constitutional objectives. Nevertheless, while in those cases the *Conseil* concluded that such a violation had not occurred,[202] it has ruled in one decision that a contested provision of a law was 'contrary to the objective of the intelligibility and accessibility of the law and inconsistent with the principle of faithfulness to election results' (*principe de loyauté du suffrage*).[203] Thus, the prohibition function of *objectifs*—even though marginal—is not merely a theoretical construct.

As to the permissive function of the *objectifs*, the focus in the French debate is on the extent to which they can justify limitations of individual rights,[204] which leads to framing the relationship between those two norm categories. In this regard, the case law of the *Conseil* is also illuminating. In a decision concerning the objective of public health enshrined in the preamble to the 1946 constitution, the *Conseil* underlined the possibilities for 'limitations to the exercise [of property rights] necessary in the name of the general interest'.[205] Similarly, but in a more straightforward manner, in a decision on the objective to provide decent housing, the *Conseil* ruled that the legislator 'is allowed, to this end, to apply the limitations to the right of property that it deems necessary',[206] as long as it does not undermine the core of that right.[207] The obligation to pursue constitutional objectives thus permits the legislator to limit individual rights to a certain extent.

However, constitutional objectives and rights are not always diametrically opposed. In a number of cases, the *Conseil* prefers to speak of the need to reconcile individual rights with the pursuit of constitutional objectives. This is the case, for instance, between constitutionally guaranteed individual freedoms and the objective of maintaining public order.[208] Furthermore, the *Conseil* has not failed to stress that individual rights and constitutional objectives pursued by the state are also mutually dependent. In the previous example, the *Conseil* added in its decision that in the absence of public order 'the exercise of individual freedoms could

202 See Luchaire (n 68) 678, who concludes that the Conseil has in fact never used a constitutional objective in order to declare a law unconstitutional.

203 In the original: 'contraire tant à l'objectif d'intelligibilité et d'accessibilité de la loi qu'au principe de loyauté du suffrage': Décision n° 2003-475 DC du 24 juillet 2003, *Loi portant réforme de l'élection des sénateurs*, Recueil, p 397, para 26.

204 Faure (n 8) 63; and De Montalivet (n 3) 399.

205 In the original: 'des limitations à son exercice exigées au nom de l'intérêt général': Décision n° 90-283 DC du 08 janvier 1991, *Loi relative à la lutte contre le tabagisme et l'alcoolisme*, Recueil, p 11, para 8; see further De Montalivet (n 3) 401–7.

206 In the original: 'il lui est loisible, à cette fin, d'apporter au droit de propriété les limitations qu'il estime nécessaires': *Loi d'orientation relative à la lutte contre les exclusions* (n 195) para 7.

207 In the words of the *Conseil*, the caveat applies that such restrictions 'are not to be as grave as to distort the meaning and scope of that right' (in the original: 'n'aient pas un caractère de gravité tel que le sens et la portée de ce droit en soient dénaturés'): *Loi d'orientation relative à la lutte contre les exclusions* (n 195) para 7.

208 Décision n° 85-187 DC du 25 janvier 1985, *Loi relative à l'état d'urgence en Nouvelle-Calédonie et dépendances*, Recueil, p 43, para 3.

not be guaranteed'.[209] Faure, who asserts their most obvious function as that of 'conciliation norms' (*normes de conciliation*),[210] sees their emergence as reflective of the evolution of the notion of individual rights, in which they are not set apart but indeed intertwined with the rights of society at large.[211] Against this backdrop, De Montalivet concludes that the most important function, and indeed the very normativity, of the *objectifs* resides not in their limitation of, but instead in their contribution to the effectiveness of individual rights.[212] This understanding is again similar to the German notions of *praktische Konkordanz* as well as Alexian optimization.

Beyond the focus on the interrelationship of objectives and rights, French scholarship also recognizes the distinction between objectives and competence norms. Faure stresses that the objectives do not constitute a source of legislative powers in their own right, ie in addition to those enumerated in Art 34 of the French constitution.[213] The *Conseil* has stressed the limits of competence that apply in the pursuit of constitutional objectives. For instance, the *Conseil* explicitly states that the modalities in the pursuit of public health are to be determined by the state organs (in this case both the legislature and the regulatory authority) 'according to their respective competences'.[214] Nevertheless, as can be seen from the justificatory function of *objectifs* regarding individual rights, they can serve to extend the boundaries of what the competent state organs are allowed to do. While they do not found any competences, they are capable of enhancing them.

In terms of categorizing the *objectifs* as defined by the *Conseil constitutionnel*, they all appear to have an imperfectible character. None of them could be permanently achieved through legislative action. In a similar vein to Sommermann's scheme of classification, and in particular the different degrees of abstraction, Faure proposes to distinguish between first and second order objectives. For Faure, this means that the latter serve, ever more specifically, as a vehicle to realize the former, more general objectives such as public order or pluralism.[215] In addition, and akin to the categorization according to content, Faure identifies several main themes for the *objectifs*: expressions of solidarity (eg public health), liberty (eg pluralism), equality (eg the fight against fiscal fraud), and life in society (eg public order). The main umbrella theme for all, according to Faure, is the perfecting of the social order (*le perfectionnement de l'ordre social*).[216] The notion of *perfectionnement*, together with

[209] In the original: 'l'exercice des libertés ne saurait être assuré': *Loi relative à l'état d'urgence en Nouvelle-Calédonie et dépendances* (n 208) para 3; for further case law see De Montalivet (n 3) 400 et seq.

[210] Faure (n 8) 52.

[211] Faure (n 8) 63–6.

[212] De Montalivet (n 3) 454; also Genevois (n 66) 205.

[213] Faure (n 8) 63; and De Montalivet (n 3) 42, who concludes that the references to certain other types of objectives in that article have to be distinguished from constitutional objectives.

[214] In the original: 'selon leurs compétences respectives': Décision n° 89-269 DC du 22 janvier 1990, *Loi portant diverses dispositions relatives à la sécurité sociale et à la santé*, Recueil, p 33, para 26.

[215] Faure (n 8) 59–60; see also Mathieu and Verpeaux, who propose two categories, one being objectives as different aspects of the general interest, the other being expressions of social and economic rights: Mathieu and Verpeaux (n 185) 425–7.

[216] Faure (n 8) 59–60.

the idea that the *objectifs* sketch out a certain ideal condition—law that is longed for (*droit désiré*)—again serves to underline their dynamic and aspirational character.[217]

Given their limited number and in some cases rather specific character, it is not easy to distribute them along the basic categories established by Sommermann for Germany. Nonetheless, as facets of 'the pursuit of a constitutionally protected general interest',[218] the fundamental state function of providing security would consequently find expression in the objective to safeguard public order. For the five basic objectives according to Sommermann, it is possible to point to expressions of a substantive rule of law in the objectives of identifying perpetrators of offences, respect for another's liberty, the campaign against fiscal fraud, the prevention of encroachments on the integrity of other persons, and the accessibility and intelligibility of the law. The basic social objective is reflected in the protection of public health, the provision of decent housing for every person, and the financial equilibrium of social security. The cultural basic objective could be seen in the preservation of pluralism in the expression of sociocultural currents, albeit with some overlap with the social objective as well the fundamental right of freedom of expression. In terms of the environmental objective, none of the *objectifs* devised by the *Conseil* seem to fit. However, a special instrument, the *Charte de l'environnement*, enjoys constitutional value in France as part of the *bloc de constitutionnalité*.[219] Next to individual rights and duties, it also contains clauses addressing the state in terms of goals. For instance, Art 6 of the *Charte* obliges public policy (*les politiques publiques*) to promote sustainable development.[220] Concerning peace as the umbrella of externally oriented objectives, none of the objectives endorsed by the *Conseil* to date fits explicitly in this category. One objective remains that does not fit easily into any of Sommermann's basic categories, ie the search for stable and coherent majorities. This seems to be rather an expression of a particular vision of democracy, which would be a structural principle at least in German doctrine.[221] Just as the rule of law is viewed, at least by Sommermann, as Janus-faced, French doctrine thus seems to understand democracy, in light of this objective, also in substantive terms and not just as formal structure.

4.3 Directive principles of state policy: 'Not enforceable in any court'

The directive principles of state policy of Indian constitutional law share most of the features of the German *Staatszielbestimmungen* and the French *objectifs*

[217] Faure (n 8) 60–1.

[218] In the original: 'la poursuite d'un intérêt général constitutionnellement protégé': Drago and Molfessis (n 188) 289.

[219] The Charte is referred to in the amended preamble to the French constitution. See further Drago (n 184) 268–70.

[220] Art 6 Charte de l'environnement.

[221] French constitutional scholarship does recognize such a specific concept per se. However, democracy is listed as one of the characteristics of the French Republic: Art 1(1) French constitution.

de valeur constitutionnelle. In addition, and in contrast to the two continental European approaches, two aspects stand out. Firstly, the foreign policy objectives of the Indian constitution are not, as is the case in most constitutions that contain such objectives, situated within the section of the document that deals with foreign policy, but among the other 'directive principles'.[222] Thus, the Indian constitution explicitly recognizes foreign policy objectives as part and parcel of this norm category. Secondly, the definition of the legal effects of the 'directive principles' is provided in the constitutional text itself. By contrast, in Germany and France, in the absence of such codification, it was through scholarship and case law that these had to be defined. Following the codification of the directive principles into the Indian constitution, the Indian courts and legal scholarship grappled with the concept. The application of directive principles, and their delimitation from fundamental rights in particular, remain an issue of intense discussion.

A significant and unique feature of the Indian constitution is that it contains a provision on the legal effects of its directive principles. Art 37 states:

> The provisions contained in this Part shall not be enforceable by any court, but the principles therein laid down are nevertheless fundamental in the governance of the country and it shall be the duty of the State to apply these principles in making laws.[223]

In contrast to the German and French cases, in India the non-justiciability of constitutional objectives is readily acknowledged in the text of the constitution. This separates the directive principles from fundamental rights, which was a deliberate choice of the Constituent Assembly. However, the Independence Movement, which formed the Indian National Congress in 1885, had originally contemplated both as a whole, containing widely defined 'rights'.[224] According to Austin, the first sign of distinction between the two appears only in the 1945 Sapru Report, which identified in its constitutional scheme both justiciable and non-justiciable rights with regard to minority rights.[225] This distinction, also inspired by the Irish constitutional experience, was later taken over more generally by the Constituent Assembly.[226]

In defending the non-justiciable status of the directive principles, their proponents put forward certain non-legal effects which they were bound to produce. For instance, BN Rau spoke of their 'educative value'.[227] Other members of the Assembly pointed out that they may serve as 'a body of doctrines to which public opinion can rally',[228] ie as a benchmark for the electorate to judge the performance of the legislature and the party in power.[229] Nevertheless, the sceptical voices, especially those from a more socialist persuasion, criticized this, stating that if not made justiciable, the directive principles would remain 'pious wishes'.[230] Constitutional

[222] Art 51 Indian constitution, which is the final article of Part IV on the 'Directive Principles on State Policy'.
[223] Art 37 Indian constitution. [224] Austin (n 11) 52. [225] Austin (n 11) 57.
[226] Austin (n 11) 80. [227] As quoted in Austin (n 11) 77.
[228] KM Munshi, as quoted in Austin (n 11) 78. [229] Austin (n 11) 78–9.
[230] KT Shah, as quoted in Austin (n 11) 79.

entrenchment of such objectives was also suggested as beneficial as it puts 'an effective check on the ever-changing pattern of whims of political parties that may be called upon to run the government according to the Constitution'.[231] As Chief Justice Kania stated: 'These principles represent not the temporary will of a majority, but the deliberate wisdom of the nation expressed while settling the paramount and the permanent law of the country'.[232] Against this backdrop, constitutional objectives also came to have a rather weak, but still existent, legal force.

In terms of the addressee of the directive principles, the Indian constitution refers consistently to the 'State' in Part IV. Art 36 points out that 'unless the context otherwise requires, "the State" has the same meaning as in Part III' of the constitution, which deals with fundamental rights. There, it is specified that 'unless the context otherwise requires, "the State" includes the Government and Parliament of India and the Government and the Legislature of each of the States and all local or other authorities within the territory of India or under the control of the Government of India'.[233] Here, too, constitutional objectives address comprehensively all state organs, including 'all three constituents of the state, namely, the legislature, the executive, and the judiciary'.[234] Crucially for a federal entity, the Indian constitution explicitly points out that sub-federal organs are also directly bound. This is in keeping with the rather centrally organized federal structure of India.[235] Nevertheless, from the wording of Art 37 itself, ie the duty 'to apply these principles in making laws', it can also be surmised that it is the legislator which is primarily called upon to pursue them. Directive principles do not establish individual duties,[236] while individual rights are enshrined in the preceding part, distinguishing them as a specific norm category in the constitution.

In order to grasp the scope of the obligation produced by these non-justiciable norms for the state, one has to resolve the seeming contradiction within Art 37 that the directive principles *despite* their non-justiciability are '*nevertheless* fundamental in the governance of the country and it shall be the *duty* of the State to apply these principles in making laws'.[237] Indian constitutional scholarship concludes that this means that the core function of the directive principles is to serve as a means of interpretation.[238] As O Chinnappa Reddy explains, the fact that they are non-justiciable means that 'courts cannot issue directions to the Parliament and the legislatures of the states to make laws'.[239] Critically, it does not mean 'that the court is not bound to take into account the Directive Principles in the discharge of its duties as a court in the matter of interpretation of the constitution and the

231 Tope (n 89) 358.

232 As quoted in Tope (n 89) 358.

233 Art 12 Indian constitution.

234 Chinnappa Reddy (n 85) 73.

235 See on this in detail Chinnappa Reddy (n 85) 221–8.

236 See Part IVA of the Indian constitution, comprising a sole article (Art 51A) on 'fundamental duties' addressed to the citizens of India.

237 Art 37 Indian constitution (emphasis added).

238 See also Tope (n 89) 353; and DK Singh, *V.N. Shukla's Constitution of India*, 6th edn (Eastern Book Company, 1975) 179–80.

239 Chinnappa Reddy (n 85) 73.

laws'.[240] As the Indian Supreme Court noted in one of its decisions: 'The Directive Principles should serve the Courts as a code of interpretation'.[241]

In this respect, Indian scholars largely echo the German and French doctrines, but with the distinction that they accept the non-justiciability of constitutional objectives outright, instead of constructing an extremely high—and largely hypothetical—threshold which would allow for marginal scope for judicial review against consistency with directive principles. Nevertheless, it emerges that the interpretive function of directive principles, or any constitutional objective for that matter, largely coincides with what De Montalivet calls the permissive function of objectives in the French context. Whenever constitutional norms are interpreted in the light of objectives in such a way that they allow state organs to act in a manner that would otherwise have been unconstitutional, such an interpretation in fact amounts to a permission buttressed by the objective.

Beyond their role in court, Indian doctrine recognizes the legally binding nature of directive principles in principle, albeit also with clear limitations. The Indian discourse, from the very outset of the constitutional drafting process, has emphasized the positive obligation inherent in the directive principles. According to SK Hedge, the duties flowing from fundamental rights 'are essentially negative in character' and thus in order to comply with them, 'the State is asked not to do certain things', while the directive principles, as 'positive mandates', oblige the state 'to take certain positive steps for the advancement of society'.[242] Similarly, MS Gurupadaswany noted:

> The sincerity and goodness of this government will be judged by how far they go to implement these Directive Principles. It is easy to stick to Fundamental Rights and appear progressive while doing nothing to reduce class difference.[243]

However, this positive and dynamic obligation has significant limitations. Concerning the first of the principles, the constitution states that '[t]he State shall strive to promote the welfare of the people by securing and protecting *as effectively as it may* a social order in which justice, social, economic and political, shall inform all the institutions of the national life'.[244] The Indian Supreme Court described directive principles in the *Chandra Bhavan* case as being 'deliberately made elastic'.[245] This can be seen as the Indian expression of the caveat of feasibility pertaining to constitutional objectives.

[240] Chinnappa Reddy (n 85) 73.

[241] *Akhil Bharatiya Soshit v Union Of India and Others*, judgment of 14 November 1980, (1981) 2 SCR 185, 257.

[242] SK Hedge, 'Directive Principles of State Policy in the Constitution of India' (1971) 5 *Journal of Constitutional and Parliamentary Studies* 129, 157; also Tope (n 89) 354.

[243] As quoted in Chinnappa Reddy (n 85) 75.

[244] Art 38 Indian constitution (emphasis added). See also Art 41 of the Indian constitution on the right to work, education, and public assistance in certain cases, which contains the qualification for the state to act 'within the limits of its economic capacity'.

[245] *Chandra Bhavan v State of Mysore*, judgment of 29 September 1969, (1970) 2 SCR 600, 612; also Chinnappa Reddy (n 85) 77.

In addition, there is no hierarchy among the directive principles. In the constitutional text the directive principles were simply enumerated. Thus, according to TK Tope, '[p]robably the State has to strive to implement them all'.[246] However, in attempts to strengthen certain directive principles vis-à-vis fundamental rights, constitutional amendments were introduced and later partially struck down by the Supreme Court, which hints at a prioritization between them.

Much like the French discourse on *objectifs de valeur constitutionnelle*, its Indian counterpart on directive principles is predominantly concerned with the relationship between constitutional objectives and fundamental rights. A central function of the former is to interpret, especially with a view to limiting, the latter. The 'dilemma of how to preserve individual freedom while promoting the public good'[247] appears to have been markedly salient in India. Both historic reasons and a strong socialistic influence on the Constituent Assembly, coupled with the reality that India was and remains an enormously populous developing country, meant that the demand for an interventionist government was particularly strong.

In the Constituent Assembly, there were voices calling for a more prominent position and greater legal force for the directive principles. One of their main constitutional architects, BN Rau, believed that sometimes it might be necessary 'for the state to invade private rights in the discharge of one of its fundamental duties'.[248] Others expressly demanded the directive principles to be made justiciable, for instance, after a certain time limit having lapsed lest they become 'window dressing for the social revolution'.[249] The Indian constitution, as it entered into force, however, retained the non-justiciability of the directive principles. The relationship between fundamental rights and directive principles remained ambiguous over the course of time, with shifting attitudes in the Supreme Court and attempts to change the balance between them through constitutional amendments.[250]

In its early cases, the Indian Supreme Court maintained the approach that directive principles 'have to conform and run subsidiary to the chapter on Fundamental Rights'.[251] However, the Supreme Court soon recognized a need for a 'harmonious interpretation':

> the State should certainly implement the directive principles but it must do so in such a way that its laws do not take away or abridge the fundamental rights, for otherwise the protecting provisions of Chapter III [i.e. Part III on fundamental rights] will be 'a mere rope of sand'.[252]

[246] Tope (n 89) 353. [247] Chinnappa Reddy (n 85) 50. [248] Austin (n 11) 77.

[249] This was proposed by KT Shah according to Austin (n 11) 79.

[250] See in detail Chinnappa Reddy (n 85) 76–84; and Tope (n 89) 354–7.

[251] *State of Madras v Champakam Dorairaja*, judgment of 9 April 1951, (1951) 1 SCR 525, 531; see also Chinnappa Reddy (n 85) 76; and Tope (n 89) 355.

[252] *Hanif and Others* (n 6) 648; see also Tope (n 89) 355. Note in this context Art 13(2) Indian constitution: 'The State shall not make any law which takes away or abridges the rights conferred by this Part and any law made in contravention of this clause shall, to the extent of the contravention, be void.'

Subsequently, there was an observable shift over time in the case law concerning the balance between fundamental rights and directive principles.[253] The superiority of fundamental rights was called into question when the Supreme Court ruled that both are 'complementary and supplementary to each other'.[254] Reddy described the subsequent case of *Kesavananda* as 'sea change'[255] in this respect, as it upheld a constitutional amendment[256] which protected laws in the furtherance of a number of directive principles from being invalidated on the grounds of certain fundamental rights arguments.[257]

This shift in emphasis was expressed well in the separate opinion of Justice Chandrachud, who formed part of the majority in the *Kesavananda* judgment. According to him, the non-justiciability of one category in comparison with the other had no bearing on their 'relative importance'.[258] The equal importance of both categories was later affirmed in the *Minerva Mills* case, which concerned, inter alia, the validity of another constitutional amendment aimed at strengthening the position of directive principles, but this time across the board.[259] In this decision, the same Justice Chandrachud, now as author of the judgment, ruled:

> Parts III and IV are like two wheels of a chariot, one no less important than the other. Snap one and the other will lose its efficacy. They are like a twin formula for achieving the social revolution which is the ideal which the visionary founders of the Constitution set before themselves. In other words, the Indian Constitution is founded on the bed-rock of the balance between Parts III and IV. To give absolute primacy to one over the other is to disturb the harmony of the Constitution. This harmony and balance between fundamental rights and directive principles is an essential feature of the basic structure of the Constitution.[260]

However, in that same case, while the bolstering of some directive principles through constitutional amendment was upheld, the Supreme Court was not prepared to accept this for 'all laws made pursuant to any of the Directive Principles' as envisaged by the forty-second amendment to the Indian Constitution.[261] In this particular instance, Justice Chandrachud deemed that this would upset the balance between the two and thus 'destroy an essential element of the basic structure of our constitution'.[262]

This consolidates a distinction in quality between those directive principles which can lend 'immunity' to laws passed in their furtherance and others which

[253] See Singh (n 238) 180; also De Villiers (n 86) 39–49; for further case law and extensive critical commentary, see Seervai (n 87) 1946–2008.

[254] *Chandra Bhavan v State of Mysore* (n 245) 612.

[255] Chinnappa Reddy (n 85) 77.

[256] This was the twenty-fifth amendment introducing Art 31C Indian constitution, aptly entitled 'Saving of laws giving effect to certain directive principles'.

[257] *Kesavananda Bharati v State of Kerala*, judgment of 24 April 1973, (1973) Suppl SCR 1. This concerned Art 39(c) and (d) of the Indian constitution on the distribution of material resources to optimally serve the common good and the avoidance of distribution of wealth to the common detriment, respectively. See also Kumar (n 79) 80 et seq.

[258] *Kesavananda Bharati v State of Kerala*, judgment of 24 April 1973, (1973) Suppl SCR 1, separate opinion of Justice Chandrachud, para 2219.

[259] See further Kumar (n 79) 115 et seq.

[260] *Minerva Mills* (n 7) 208–9.

[261] Chinnappa Reddy (n 85) 79.

[262] *Minerva Mills* (n 7) 209.

cannot.[263] However, the dividing line between the two categories remains fluid, as subsequent cases have at times extended this quality to certain other directive principles.[264]

The Indian Supreme Court has accepted 'that the Fundamental Rights must be construed in the light of the Directive Principles'.[265] For instance, it used directive principles in order to elucidate the term of a legitimate public 'purpose' as found in the part on fundamental rights.[266] Hence, especially in their relation to fundamental rights, the principal function of directive principles as an interpretive tool, which can justify broadening the scope of public powers, is reaffirmed. They bolster the understanding of constitutional objectives as devices shaping the boundaries of legislative and other state powers. Nevertheless, they 'are not the source of legislative power but they presuppose legislative power'.[267]

In addition, next to the norm category of fundamental rights, the *Minerva Mills* decision of the Indian Supreme Court can be linked to the German concept of structural principles as it states that '[t]his harmony and balance between fundamental rights and the directive principles is an essential feature of the basic structure of the Constitution'.[268] This indicates both the existence of the concept of a basic constitutional structure that is to be maintained, and suggests that it may have other features than just the balance between rights and objectives.

In terms of categorizing directive principles, in addition to the distinction between those that have been 'immunized' by constitutional amendment and partially upheld by the Supreme Court, there are also instances of those that can be achieved and those that can never be fully realized. The vast majority of objectives are open-ended. In some cases, however, the objective is attainable, such as that of establishing a 'uniform civil code throughout the territory of India',[269] which could also be described as a legislative command in German constitutional parlance.

Concerning substance, moreover, given the range of principles codified in the Indian constitution, all the levels of abstraction and the five basic categories devised by Sommermann are represented. The 'common good', as the main and most abstract state objective, is explicitly named as such with regard to the ownership and distribution of material resources.[270] Furthermore, as the first principle in the list of Part III, which has been described as expressing the common 'essence' of all directive principles,[271] the constitution stipulates the goal of promoting 'the

263 Chinnappa Reddy (n 85) 81, criticizing this as introducing inconsistency.

264 Chinnappa Reddy (n 85) 81–4.

265 *Unnikrishnan v State of Andhra Pradesh*, judgment of 4 February 1993, (1993) 1 SCR 594, 652; see also *Javed v State of Haryana*, judgment of 30 July 2003, (2003) Suppl SCR 947, para 39, stating that fundamental rights 'have to be read along with the chapter on Directive Principles of State Policy and the Fundamental Duties enshrined in Article 51-A'.

266 *State of Bihar v Kameshwar Singh*, judgment of 27 May 1952, (1952) 1 SCR 889, 997: 'If, therefore, the State is to give effect to these avowed purposes of our Constitution we must regard as a public purpose all that will be calculated to promote the welfare of the people as envisaged in these directive principles of State policy whatever else that expression may mean.' Further, Tope (n 89) 355–6.

267 Seervai (n 87) 1936.

268 *Minerva Mills* (n 7) 255.

269 Art 44 Indian constitution.

270 Art 39(b) Indian constitution.

271 Austin (n 11) 52.

welfare of the people'.[272] The objective of security as the first concretization of the pursuit of the common good is only mentioned with regard to the external sphere ('international peace and *security*'),[273] and not its internal dimension.

Regarding the five basic objectives, the substantive rule of law (*Rechtsstaatlichkeit*) is represented in the directive principles on equal justice and free legal aid,[274] the envisaged uniform civil code,[275] and in the separation of the judiciary from the executive.[276] Social justice is particularly present as a dimension of the directive principles, as can be seen in the cases of promotion of the right to work, education, and public assistance in the event of, for instance, sickness or unemployment.[277] It is also reflected in the objectives of providing humane condition of work as well as maternity relief,[278] ensuring a living wage, ensuring 'a decent standard of life',[279] securing the participation of workers in the management of industries,[280] and raising the level of nutrition and improving public health.[281] The cultural objective is manifested in the securing of the right to education,[282] in particular providing education for children below the age of six,[283] and defining the standard of living, inter alia, as the 'full enjoyment of leisure and social and *cultural* opportunities'.[284] Culture also appears as an objective in its own right in the 'protection of monuments and places and objects of national importance' by the state.[285] The environment is addressed in the objective 'to protect and improve the environment and to safeguard the forests and wild life of the country'.[286] As the last of the directive principles, the objective of promoting international peace and security is a clear example of the externally oriented peace objective.[287] The directive principle to 'organise village panchayats and endow them with such powers and authority as may be necessary to enable them to function as units of self-government',[288] which is a regionally specific form of local self-government, fits rather uneasily with these basic objectives.

As an alternative way of categorizing directive principles, Nalin Kumar and Jeffrey Usman propose to group them according to three ideological categories. These are socialistic principles, liberal intellectualist principles, and Ghandian principles.[289]

[272] Art 38(1) Indian constitution. [273] Art 51(a) Indian constitution.

[274] Art 39A Indian constitution. [275] Art 40 Indian constitution.

[276] Art 50 Indian constitution. Usually, this would rather seem to be a structural principle. Singh (n 238) 188, however, notes that the Indian constitution 'has not indeed recognised the doctrine of separation of powers in its absolute rigidity'.

[277] Art 41 Indian constitution. [278] Art 42 Indian constitution.

[279] Art 43 Indian constitution, which is a similar formulation as employed by the *Bundesverfassungsgericht* in *Waisenrente II* (n 129) para 44 ('Mindestvoraussetzungen für ein menschenwürdiges Dasein').

[280] Art 43A Indian constitution.

[281] Art 47 Indian constitution. See, moreover, Art 46 Indian constitution, emphasizing the state's role towards 'weaker sections of societies' and, as a country-specific feature, towards 'scheduled castes' and tribes.

[282] Art 41 Indian constitution. [283] Art 45 Indian constitution.

[284] Art 43 Indian constitution (emphasis added). [285] Art 49 Indian constitution.

[286] Art 48A Indian constitution. [287] Art 51 Indian constitution.

[288] Art 40 Indian constitution.

[289] Kumar (n 79) 11–12; and Usman (n 80) 643–4; see for a similar categorization De Villiers (n 86) 35–6.

The socialistic principles, as understood by these scholars, coincide with those of the basic objectives of social justice. The liberal intellectualist principles correspond to the objectives of the rule of law, culture, and peace. Meanwhile, Ghandian principles are those that are rather specific to India, such as prohibition of intoxicants, prohibition of cow slaughter, and the organization of village panchayats. Regardless of which categorization one applies, the Indian directive principles exhibit a wide coverage of aspects of the common good, including in the external dimension.

5. The External Dimension

Having analysed the respective origins and common legal features of constitutional objectives in Germany, France, and India in general terms, this section focuses on their external dimension. It shows that foreign policy objectives are part and parcel of the norm category of constitutional objectives, but at the same time belong to a country's 'foreign affairs constitution'. This entails a number of nuances, including a more prominent role of the executive branch as an addressee of these objectives and an even wider margin of discretion for state organs in pursuing these objectives, coupled with a more restrained role of the courts.

5.1 *Staatszielbestimmungen: Außenverfassungsrecht*

German scholarship provides a number of additional features to be taken into account with regard to foreign policy objectives in constitutional law: Firstly, a conceptual widening of the notion of the common good beyond that of the state; secondly, certain nuances in the legal effects of constitutional objectives due to the particular nature of foreign policy; thirdly, more specific categorizations according to content; and fourthly, a general tendency to extrapolate internal features of the legal order to the outside world.

Generally, constitutional objectives can be seen as concrete manifestations of a certain vision of the common good prevalent in a state that has historically grown. When bringing in the external dimension, this historically derived and constitutionally entrenched vision of the common good needs to be revisited. Internally, ie in a closed system, it seems straightforward to talk about the common good of the political community gathered within the system in its entirety, as opposed to the good of the individuals or certain groups of individuals within it. The external dimension, ie looking beyond the closed system, complicates matters. According to Isensee, whereas the idea of a common good within a state functions as the amalgamation of individual interests, 'externally, it presents itself towards other states and international and supranational organisations as national egoism'.[290] However, while this may have been the classic view, Isensee acknowledges that

[290] In the original: '... so stellt sie sich nach außen gegenüber anderen Staaten und supranationalen wie internationalen Organisationen als nationaler Egoismus dar': Isensee (n 61) 9, see also 20–1.

today these national egoisms are 'increasingly integrated into duties of inter-/supranational [*übernational*] solidarity and are relayed to the common good of inter-/supranational [*übernational*] communities'.[291] Furthermore, he stresses that the state increasingly acts as a 'trustee for inter-/supranational tasks' (*Treuhänder für übernationale Aufgaben*), for instance, with regard to environmental and cultural protection, and is committed to universal human rights.[292] This introduces a notion of a *bonum commune* beyond the state. For Isensee, even though the 'prototypical reference figure' (*prototypische Bezugsgröße*) of the common good is the state, it can also be applied, *mutatis mutandis*, to other entities or communities.[293] Therefore, he concludes that the common good should not be restricted to 'an anachronistic concept of introverted, autarkic statehood',[294] but instead should be considered as amenable to inter- and supranational integration. Ultimately, he even sees potential for a global common good or common good of mankind—the '*bonum commune humanitatis*'.[295]

If state objectives are understood as, by definition, being geared towards the pursuit of the common good, this has certain implications. First of all, the pursuit of even the most 'national' objectives must be seen in the context of, and take account of, wider notions of the common good. For instance, the pursuit of national reunification as a constitutional objective also has to be viewed with regard to the objectives of the state to which the territory that is to be reunified with the former state currently belongs. This obviously concerns, first and foremost, its security objectives (a basic and permanent objective in the Sommermann typology), but also the objectives of regional stability and peaceful relations with the international community as a whole. In addition, these considerations reveal the external dimensions of traditionally rather internal objectives. The pursuit of social justice internally is a perfectly legitimate objective, but it may be at odds with the regional or international common good if it is pursued in a way which is detrimental to, for instance, social justice, security, and the environment abroad.

This intertwining of the national and international common good coincides with the notion in German constitutional law of '*offene Staatlichkeit*' (literally,

[291] In the orignal: '… zunehmend eingebunden in übernationale Solidarpflichten und auf das Gemeinwohl übernationaler Gemeinschaften ausgerichtet': Isensee (n 61) 9.

[292] Isensee (n 61) 9. Compare with the notion in EU law of Member States acting as 'trustees' of the Union interest: see Chapter 4, section 5.1.

[293] In German, he uses the very generic term *Verband*: Isensee (n 61) 9. See for an application of the concept of the common good at the European level eg C Calliess, 'Gemeinwohl in der Europäischen Union—Über den Staaten- und Verfassungsverbund zum Gemeinwohlverbund' in W Brugger, S Kirste, and M Anderheiden (eds), *Gemeinwohl in Deutschland, Europa und der Welt* (Nomos, 2002).

[294] In the original: 'ein anachronistisches Konzept introvertierter, autarker Staatlichkeit': Isensee (n 61) 21.

[295] Isensee (n 61) 21, referring to the work of Alfred Verdroß, which is reproduced in A Verdroß, 'Vom Gemeinwohl der Staatsbürger zum Gemeinwohl der Menschheit' in H Kelsen, H Klecatsky, R Marcic, and H Schambeck (eds), *Die Wiener Rechtstheoretische Schule. Volume I* (Europa-Verlag, 2010). Häberle dates this idea back even further to the School of Salamanca and de Vitoria, P Häberle, 'Das "Weltbild" des Verfassungsstaates—eine Textstufenanalyse zur Menschheit als verfassungsstaatlichem und "letztem" Geltungsgrund des Völkerrechts' in B Ziemske, T Langheid, H Wilms, and G Haverkate (eds), *Staatsphilosophie und Rechtspolitik, Festschrift für Martin Kriele* (C.H. Beck, 1997) 1305.

'open statehood'). Germany is therefore frequently defined as an 'open federal state'[296] or 'open constitutional state'.[297] This not only means openness towards international law, but also reflects the fundamental constitutional decision in favour of international cooperation.[298] It dovetails thus with the idea of an 'active paradigm'[299] in the law governing foreign policy. Constitutional foreign policy objectives, in turn, help to clarify along which lines such cooperation, as expressly willed by the constitution, is to be carried out.

Moreover, German scholarship addresses the oft-invoked 'peculiarity' of foreign policy in constitutional law, which results in the executive joining the legislator as primary addressee of external objectives, while the role of the judiciary is limited even further. For Germany, Christian Calliess suggests that the area of foreign policy at least traditionally presupposes an 'exceptional position' (*Sonderstellung*) in the constitutional system.[300] This 'peculiarity' usually means that the executive, as the country's representative in foreign affairs, enjoys wide discretion in order to act in a timely and effective manner and is consequently considered less constrained by parliament and even less so by the judiciary. This wide discretion is warranted by what could be called an 'accentuated caveat of possibility'. This means that the pursuit of foreign policy objectives is also qualified by international law as well as 'the willingness of other states to cooperate'.[301] In addition to the legal requirements, political willingness, and material resources within a state, one has to take into account the legal requirements of the international system, those within other states, the political willingness of other states, and the allocation of resources outside of one's own borders. The increased complexity requires wide executive discretion in the pursuit of its constitutional foreign policy objectives, with the judiciary only stepping in in cases of manifest errors or when the structural principles of the respective constitutional order are being compromised by foreign policy-related acts.[302]

However, German scholarship stresses at the same time that a shift of emphasis towards the executive in foreign policy does not lead to the other constitutional branches ceasing to be addressees of constitutional objectives. While for constitutional objectives the legislature is usually called upon to specify them and provide

[296] B Fassbender, *Der offene Bundesstaat* (Mohr Siebeck, 2007).

[297] C Calliess, 'Auswärtige Gewalt' in J Isensee and P Kirchhof (eds), *Handbuch des Staatsrechts der Bundesrepublik Deutschland. Volume IV: Aufgaben des Staates*, 3rd edn (C.F. Müller, 2006) 597 (marginal no 14).

[298] Fassbender (n 296) 9; Calliess (n 297) 597 (marginal no 14), with further references; fundamentally, K Vogel, *Verfassungsentscheidung des Grundgesetzes für eine internationale Zusammenarbeit* (Mohr Siebeck, 1964).

[299] With regard to the EU, F Amtenbrink and D Kochenov, 'The Active Paradigm of the Study of the EU's Place in the World: An Introduction' in F Amtenbrink and D Kochenov (eds), *The European Union's Shaping of the International Legal Order* (CUP, 2013).

[300] Calliess (n 297) 590.

[301] In the original: '[die] Bereitschaft anderer Staaten zur Zusammenarbeit': Sommermann (n 2) 387.

[302] See Calliess (n 297) 607–8; also J Kokott, 'Kontrolle der Auswärtigen Gewalt' (1996) 111 *Deutsches Verwaltungsblatt* 937.

a legal framework for their implementation,[303] foreign policy puts the emphasis on wide discretion and freedom of scope, resulting in an enhanced role for the executive.[304]

As the overall addressee of constitutional foreign policy objectives, German scholarship uses the term *auswärtige Gewalt* (roughly, 'external state power') to describe the state powers exercised in the domain of foreign policy. For Sommermann, the *auswärtige Gewalt* is the proper addressee for purely external objectives, with a prominent but not exclusive role for the executive branch.[305] Calliess distinguishes two components of the concept: Firstly, the international component relating to international representation; and, secondly, the internal component relating to the internal decision-making processes in the realm of external relations. Therefore, Calliess calls the *auswärtige Gewalt* the 'link between the domestic and the international legal spheres and therefore the subject of international legal and constitutional norms'.[306] Volker Röben, in his extensive monograph devoted to the topic, speaks of *Außenverfassungsrecht* as the legal framework governing the *auswärtige Gewalt*, which he sees as the public power of a constitutionally organized state, including the legislative, executive, and judicial branches, with both external and internal effects.[307] Hence, in terms of situating constitutional foreign policy objectives within the overall constitutional framework, their exact location is at the intersection of both the norm category of constitutional objectives and the domain of *Außenverfassungsrecht* or, otherwise put, the norms pertaining to the 'foreign affairs constitution'.[308]

This finds confirmation in the case law of the *Bundesverfassungsgericht*. In a judgment from 1955, the court stressed that in reviewing the constitutionality of an international agreement, it had to concede to 'the treaty-making organs of the Federal Republic of Germany a large measure of political discretion, especially since the circle of solutions theoretically available to draw up the agreement is in practice narrowed down to what is politically achievable vis-à-vis the respective contractual partner'.[309] This ruling, confirming the idea of an accentuated caveat, does not, however, amount to excluding the courts entirely from foreign policy. In other cases, the *Bundesverfassungsgericht* has interpreted constitutional objectives in a way that impacted on the competence to conclude international agreements by

[303] Badura (n 48) 41–2; and Sommermann (n 2) 427–35.

[304] Eg W Grewe, 'Die Auswärtige Gewalt der Bundesrepublik' (1954) 12 *Veröffentlichungen der Vereinigung der Deutschen Staatsrechtslehrer* 129.

[305] Sommermann (n 2) 387.

[306] In the original: '... ein Bindeglied zwischen staatlicher und völkerrechtlicher Sphäre und damit Gegenstand völkerrechtlicher und verfassungsrechtlicher Normen': Calliess (n 297) 590.

[307] V Röben, *Außenverfassungsrecht* (Mohr Siebeck, 2007) 5.

[308] This is the American term expressing the same idea: see eg R Knowles, 'American Hegemony and the Foreign Affairs Constitution' (2009) 47 *Arizona State Law Journal* 87.

[309] In the original: '... für die vertragschließenden Organe der Bundesrepublik Deutschland ein breiter Bereich politischen Ermessens bestehen muß, zumal der Kreis der an sich zur Wahl stehenden vertraglichen Lösungen sich praktisch auf das dem jeweiligen Vertragspartner gegenüber politisch Erreichbare verengt': Decision of 4 May 1955 (*Saarstatut*), BVerfGE 4, 157, para 37; see similarly the later Decision of 7 July 1975 (*Ostverträge*), BVerfGE 40, 141, para 126.

the Federal Republic. For instance, the court interpreted collective security as mentioned in the German Basic Law[310] as wide enough to include collective defence arrangements, which affirmed Germany's active membership of NATO.[311] Thus, here it is again possible to view the intricate relationship between competences and objectives at work, which through favourable interpretation becomes mutually reinforcing.

Regarding constitutional objectives which are not purely concerned with foreign policy, given the increasing interconnectedness between the internal and external spheres, it is true 'that there is hardly any issue of internal policy conceivable anymore that could not become the subject of international agreements'.[312] Hence, Sommermann derives both a negative and a positive obligation flowing from all state objectives in the conduct of foreign policy. The negative obligation entails that a state and its organs may not commit to obligations in international law that would compromise the pursuit of state objectives internally. The positive obligation entails the use of international means for the pursuit of objectives in the internal sphere, for instance, by concluding international treaties conducive to social justice within a country.[313]

As a third feature, German scholarship provides for more nuanced categorizations of state objectives according to content in the domain of foreign policy. Sommermann distinguishes six main subcategories of the externally oriented basic objective of peace: the prohibition of war, collective security, international law, human rights, integration, and solidarity/development cooperation.[314] All of these subcategories of peace can also be seen as external counterparts to internal objectives. As Röben notes, 'on closer inspection' one discovers 'pairs of equal internal and external target courses [objectives]'.[315]

Regarding the prohibition of war, this can be seen as the constitutional confirmation of the general prohibition of war in international law.[316] Sommermann refers to numerous constitutions that make this prohibition a matter of constitutional law (see also Chapter 2, section 4.2).[317] The German Basic Law even criminalizes conduct that is directed against international peace,[318] which can be seen as a concretization, in the form of a legislative command, of the general objective.

The objective of the 'promotion of collective security systems' is closely related to the prohibition of war, but given its explicit codification in many constitutions, Sommermann ranks it as a separate objective.[319] He stresses the necessity for such provisions in order to enable the accession of states to such systems, which also raises a question of competence to do so under national law, especially with regard

[310] Art 24(2) German constitution.
[311] Decision of 12 July 1994 (*out-of-area-Einsätze*), BVerfGE 90, 286, para 236.
[312] In the original: '… daß nahezu kein innenpolitisches Thema mehr denkbar ist, welches nicht zum Gegenstand völkerrechtlicher Vereinbarungen werden könnte': Sommermann (n 2) 388.
[313] Sommermann (n 2) 388. [314] Sommermann (n 2) 237.
[315] In the original: 'Die Staatszwecke [sic] sind bei näherem Hinsehen Paarungen gleicher innerer und äußerer Zielrichtungen': Röben (n 307) 195.
[316] Art 2(4) Charter of the United Nations. [317] Sommermann (n 2) 239–40.
[318] Art 26(1) German constitution. [319] Sommermann (n 2) 240–1.

to authorizing the limited transfer of sovereign powers to international organizations. At the same time, it elevates the task of ensuring peace to the multilateral level through collectively organized structures, which can be seen as the counterpart to internal security.[320]

The objective to display 'friendliness towards international law' (*Völkerrechtsfreundlichkeit*) concerns both the issue of incorporation of international law into the domestic legal order and the promotion of compliance with international law in general.[321] It is a clear expression of the trend to increasingly refer to international law in national constitutions—the 'internationalization of constitutional law'. It can be understood as the constitutional acknowledgment of the maxim *pacta sunt servanda* in international law. However, given the usual status of international law in the hierarchy of norms in the national legal order as at an echelon below that of the constitution,[322] the pursuit of this objective of domestic compliance is limited by the structural principles of the constitutional order itself. Nonetheless, widely used doctrines of 'harmonious interpretation'[323] of national and international law can be seen as operationalizing the objective of compliance within a given structure. The other aspect concerns urging other states to comply with international law, for instance, by promoting judicial dispute settlement and developing a rules-based international system. Consequently, the rule of law as the Janus-faced structural principle/objective within the state finds its external counterpart in the objective to build rule-based structures internationally and subsequently to abide by their rules. Eventually, the development of the international legal order may become amenable to 'constitutional' paradigms, ie the 'constitutionalization' of the international system itself.[324] These international structures, furthermore, would also serve as a framework for the pursuit of state objectives. In this context, Sommermann observes that all the basic objectives of the state have become objects of international legal instruments as well.[325]

The promotion of human rights could be seen as a subcategory of international law. However, given its prominence in national constitutions, which often refer explicitly to certain human rights related international documents, it assumes a particular role for Sommernann.[326] In addition, the claims of universal validity of core human rights go hand in hand with making them (more) independent from their particular source, be it international or domestic law. For Häberle, in view

[320] Sommermann (n 2) 240–1.

[321] For Sommermann, *Völkerrechtsfreundlichkeit* seems to include only the first aspect: Sommermann (n 2) 241–2.

[322] For a brief overview see M Shaw, *International Law*, 7th edn (CUP, 2014) 98–129.

[323] Sommermann (n 2) 406–8.

[324] See eg B Fassbender, 'Rediscovering a Forgotten Constitution: Notes on the Place of the UN Charter in the International Legal Order' in J Dunhoff and J Trachtman (eds), *Ruling the World? Constitutionalism, International Law, and Global Governance* (CUP, 2009); and S Kadelbach and T Kleinlein, 'Überstaatliches Verfassungsrecht: Zur Konstiutionalisierung im Völkerrecht' (2006) 44 *Archiv des Völkerrechts* 236.

[325] Sommermann (n 2) 259–80.

[326] Sommermann (n 2) 242; Häberle (n 295) 1281–4; and V Vereshchetin, 'New Constitutions and the Old Problem of the Relationship between International Law and National Law' (1996) 7 *European Journal of International Law* 1, 5; for the German context, Röben (n 307) 197.

of the progressing internationalization and universalization of law, mankind itself could even be considered the 'ultimate source of validity' (*letzter Geltungsgrund*) of international law, which in turn would require a fundamental rethinking of the concept of sovereignty and other fundamental precepts of international law (and arguably also constitutional law).[327]

The pursuit of integration (*Integrationsfreundlichkeit*)[328] is considered wider than collective security and the other objectives, both internal and external. It can be used to serve other objectives, for instance, the prevention of war among the members of the integrated community,[329] to provide defence against the outside, or more generally to provide the members with more leverage as a collective actor. Moreover, integration can entail setting common minimum standards for fundamental rights or environmental protection. Therefore, transferring powers to an integrated entity without upsetting the internal structural essence of the national constitutional order (including fundamental rights protection) becomes a sensitive matter. Moreover, it raises questions regarding the pursuit of state objectives within the integrated community of states and the development of autonomous objectives of the community itself vis-à-vis the outside world.

Lastly, development cooperation and international solidarity can be seen as the external counterpart to internal social justice.[330] It would also be covered by a very wide notion of peace, assuming that lasting peace on the global level can only be achieved through a more 'just' allocation of wealth.[331] In addition to socio-economic aspects, an important environmental and cultural dimension should be added to the notion of solidarity in order to preserve global 'common goods' and what is known as 'the common heritage of mankind', including sharing the costs that such preservation entails.

As the fourth particular feature of constitutional objectives in the domain of foreign affairs, German scholarship identifies a tendency to extrapolate certain features of the internal legal order to the outside world, as specifically mandated or implied in the codified foreign policy objectives. In Hans Kelsen's writings, a link was already made between the internal structure of the state and the way in which it conducts its foreign policy.[332] Sommermann speaks of the positive obligation to realize the internally oriented objectives abroad through foreign policy, ie to shape other countries in one's own image. Here, Sommermann again points to the limits set by international law (eg sovereign equality and non-interference) as well as practical considerations.[333] It should be added that this also raises the risk

[327] Häberle (n 295) 1303–5. [328] Sommermann (n 2) 244–6.

[329] Thereby forming what Deutsch termed a 'security community': K Deutsch et al, *Political Community and the North Atlantic Area: International Organization in the Light of Historical Experience* (Princeton University Press, 1957).

[330] See on the idea of justice and transnational solidarity beyond the state F De Witte, *Justice in the EU: The Emergence of Transnational Solidarity* (OUP, 2015) 31–43.

[331] Sommermann (n 2) 246–7.

[332] H Kelsen, *Essays in Legal and Moral Philosophy* (D. Reidel, 1973) 95–113 (a chapter aptly entitled 'State-Form and World Outlook').

[333] Sommermann (n 2) 387–91.

of being seen as normative chauvinism or even neocolonialism by outside actors if the universal appeal of the values that are being promoted is not recognized by the latter (see also Chapter 5, section 5).

Bearing in mind the typology of different categories of constitutional norms, the extroverted character of external objectives leads to what will be called here 'translating' certain norms found in the constitutional order to the international level or other legal orders. Democracy, for instance, does not constitute an objective but a structural principle of a constitutional order. When democracy is mentioned as one of the values to be promoted in a country's foreign policy according to its constitution, then it also becomes an external objective of that state. It is to be presumed that the version of democracy to be 'exported' takes its inspiration from that of the 'exporting' state. This objective, in turn, is perfectible to the extent that, through that country's foreign policy, democracy can take root in other countries or in inter- or supranational settings. Eventually, democracy then becomes a structural element beyond the original state's borders.

5.2 *Objectifs de valeur constitutionnelle*: Waiting for the *Conseil constitutionnel*?

Given the limitation, also within scholarship, of *objectifs de valeur constitutionnelle* to those identified by the *Conseil constitutionnel*, their external dimension is not well developed. Nonetheless, there are no cogent reasons to consider that the French doctrine, which after all emerged three decades after its German counterpart and was likely inspired by the case law of the Court of Justice of the European Union (CJEU), would be categorically opposed to the future elaboration of such an external dimension.

Thus far, the *Conseil* has not pronounced an inherently externally oriented *objectif*. This could be seen either as a denial of their existence, or simply as reflective of the fact that the *Conseil* has not yet had the opportunity to rule on them. It ought to be recalled here that the *Bundesverfassungsgericht* has never adopted the notion of *Staatszielbestimmungen*, referring instead to 'principles' (*Prinzipien*) or simple 'goals' (*Ziele*).[334] Therefore, it was left to academic commentators to theorize about objectives of the state, with German scholars having readily accepted the existence of a wide range of constitutional objectives, including in the field of foreign policy.

To conclude that the French constitutional order and doctrine would be hermetically closed to the idea of constitutional foreign policy objectives is unwarranted. In fact, the *Conseil* has produced decisions in cases with a foreign policy dimension, from which at least an external dimension to the existing *objectifs* may be gleaned. It ruled that the law approving the conclusion of the Schengen Agreement by France was not unconstitutional, since approving that treaty did not

[334] See eg *Waisenrente II* (n 129) para 43. With regard to reunification, it used the term 'command'/ 'imperative' (*Wiedervereinigungsgebot*), Decision of 31 July 1973 (*Grundlagenvertrag*), BVerfGE 36, 1, para 80.

disregard the objective of public order.[335] This means that the pursuit of internal *objectifs* cannot be undermined through international commitments, arguably in the pursuit of implicit external objectives such as international cooperation and integration. In addition, recalling that the *Conseil* derives its *objectifs* from various textual references in the *bloc de constitutionnalité*, French constitutional law would indeed provide numerous provisions upon which to base foreign policy objectives. From the text of the French constitution itself, there are the explicit objectives to develop the international *Francophonie*[336] and to participate in the European Union.[337] The *Charte de l'environnement*, moreover, which forms part of the *bloc de constitutionnalité*, explicitly stipulates that it is to 'inspire the European and international action of France'.[338] Furthermore, the *Conseil* ruled in 1999 that a revision of the French constitution was necessary in order to be able to ratify the Rome Statute of the International Criminal Court.[339] Consequently, the constitution was amended to include a clause stating that '[t]he Republic may recognise the jurisdiction of the International Criminal Court'.[340] This could be seen as establishing a permission in the pursuit of an implicit external objective of international cooperation in the field of international criminal justice, which dovetails with the Swiss notion of a 'goal-oriented competence allocation'. Should the *Conseil* have the occasion in the future to elaborate on *objectifs de valeur constitutionnelle* in the domain of foreign relations, given the prominent role of the president and government in the country's foreign affairs,[341] a shift of emphasis towards the executive branch would also seem plausible.

5.3 Directive principles of state policy: 'International morality' and 'spiritual heritage'

The external dimension of the Indian directive principles of state policy exhibits features similar to the external *Staatszielbestimmungen*. Important added value provided by the Indian experience is the fact that foreign policy objectives are codified in Art 51 and that the Supreme Court and scholarship confirm that it is indeed part and parcel of this norm category.

Unlike in German or French constitutional law, the Indian constitution contains a catalogue of constitutional objectives including explicitly external ones. The external objectives are situated within Part III on directive principles and not, as is the case in many other countries, in the part of the constitution dealing with

[335] *Loi autorisant l'approbation de la convention d'application de l'accord de Schengen* (n 199) para 17. See also De Montalivet (n 3) 460.

[336] Art 87 French constitution. [337] Art 88-1 French constitution.

[338] In the original: 'La présente Charte inspire l'action européenne et internationale de la France': Art 10, Charte de l'environnement.

[339] Décision n° 98-408 DC du 22 janvier 1999, *Traité portant statut de la Cour pénale internationale*, Recueil, p 29.

[340] Art 53-2 French constitution (as amended by the constitutional law of 5 July 1999).

[341] J Gicquel and J-E Gicquel, *Droit constitutionnel et institutions politiques*, 24th edn (Montchrestien, 2010) 603–5.

foreign relations. From this structure, it is evident that the legal properties pertaining to directive principles according to Art 37 of the Indian constitution apply to the external field as well. The objective to promote international peace and security figures last among the list of directive principles. Art 51 reads:

The State shall endeavour to—
(a) promote international peace and security;
(b) maintain just and honourable relations between nations;
(c) foster respect for international law and treaty obligations in the dealings of organised peoples with one another; and
(d) encourage settlement of international disputes by arbitration.[342]

The very origin of this provision is of an international nature. While the directive principles were generally inspired by the Irish directive principles on social policy, the inspiration for Art 51 is to be found in the 1939 Declaration of Havana at the Second Conference of American States Members of the International Labour Organisation.[343] The Declaration contains language which is very close to the formulation which eventually emerged from the drafting process of the Constituent Assembly.[344] Furthermore, the assembly resolved that in addition to the promotion of international peace and security at large, 'it was necessary to specify some method for promoting peace and that the relevant provision should commit India to encouragement of settlement of international disputes by arbitration as a means to avoid war'.[345] Hence, letter (d) to Art 51 was introduced, which emphasizes arbitration as a method of international dispute resolution.

The idea that the Indian common good is closely linked to that of the world is also clearly present. The Constituent Assembly acknowledged, according to Rao, that 'India's pledge to promote international peace and security was necessary, for, if there was no such peace and security, there could be no peace and economic and social progress within the country'.[346] This was unambiguously confirmed in a 2011 Supreme Court judgment, which states that '[b]y recognizing international peace to be sine qua non for India's welfare and security, the framers have charged the State, and all of its organs, with responsibility to endeavour to achieve the goals set forth in Article 51'.[347]

No competences are as such created by Art 51. The allocation of foreign affairs powers is regulated elsewhere in the constitution, ie where this power is bestowed on the Union alone.[348] Chandrasekhara Rao concludes that the foreign policy objectives

[342] Art 51 Indian constitution.

[343] P Chandrasekhara Rao, *The Indian Constitution and International Law* (Martinus Nijhoff/Taxmann, 1994) 3–4.

[344] See Chandrasekhara Rao (n 343) 4–5 for the earlier drafts in assembly. For the Declaration of Havana, see B Shiva Rao, *The Framing of India's Constitution, Select Documents. Volume II* (Indian Institute of Public Administration, 1967) 150.

[345] Chandrasekhara Rao (n 343) 5.

[346] Chandrasekhara Rao (n 343) 5.

[347] *GVK Industries Ltd & Anr. v The Income Tax Officer*, judgment of 1 March 2011, (2011) 3 SCR 366, 416 (para 47).

[348] Arts 73, 245(2), and 253 Indian constitution and 1 and 10-21 Seventh Schedule to the Indian constitution.

'should be taken as a commandment to the Union of India, rather than to its constituent units'.[349] Hence, also in Indian doctrine, it is recognized that foreign policy objectives are addressed to the *auswärtige Gewalt*, ie those organs and levels of government with competence in the field of foreign relations. In this case, these would be the federal legislature and executive, with a marginal role reserved to the courts.

The Indian Supreme Court confirmed that Art 51 contains a genuine 'Directive Principle of State Policy, though not enforceable, nevertheless fundamental in the governance of the country'.[350] To recall, such explicit judicial endorsement of constitutional foreign policy objectives is absent from the case law of the *Bundesverfassungsgericht*, which itself has never even used the term *Staatszielbestimmung*, or the *Conseil constitutionnel*, which in its case law has not elaborated on specifically foreign policy related *objectifs de valeur constitutionnelle*.

Art 51 is used by the Indian Supreme Court as an interpretive device. In the aforementioned *Kesavananda* case, respect for human rights as part of international law, the latter being required by Art 51, was used to point out that constitutional amendment cannot amend rights 'out of existence'.[351] Accordingly, Art 51 was used as a basis for inviting the interpretation of domestic law in accordance with international law, particularly international human rights:

> in view of Article 51 of the directive principles, this Court must interpret language of the Constitution, if not intractable, which is after all a municipal law, in the light of the United Nations Charter and the solemn declaration [i.e. the Universal Declaration of Human Rights] subscribed to by India.[352]

Hence, it serves as a basis for the Indian version of 'friendliness towards international law'.[353] In contrast to the general tension between individual rights and (domestic) objectives in the German and French constitutions, Art 51 serves as an externally bolstered argument to preserve the core of the former.

This function, which could be termed interpretive–prohibitive, as opposed to the usual interpretive–permissive function, reappeared also in the *GVK Industries* case. The case concerned powers of the Indian parliament to pass legislation with extraterritorial effect. Firstly, the court recognized the need for sufficient leeway in international relations for the political branches, much the same way the *Bundesverfassungsgericht* did in its *Saarstatut* decision.[354] The Indian Supreme Court acknowledged that '[h]ow those laws are to be effectuated, and with what degree of force or diplomacy, may very well lie in the domain of pragmatic, and indeed ethical, statecraft that may, though not necessarily always, be left to the discretion of the Executive by Parliament'.[355] Nevertheless, it stressed that this

349 See Chandrasekhara Rao (n 343) 5, also 12–14.
350 *GVK Industries Ltd* (n 347) 414–15 (para 46).
351 *Kesavananda Bharati* (n 257) para 164.
352 *Kesavananda Bharati* (n 257) para 164.
353 See also Seervai (n 87); and Chandrasekhara Rao (n 343) 124–5, stressing that Art 51, too, serves as a code of constitutional interpretation.
354 Saarstatut (n 309) para 37.
355 *GVK Industries Ltd* (n 347) 415 (para 47).

does not mean that this foreign affairs power is unlimited. It used Art 51, among others, to impose a limit on the parliament concerning the power to legislate with extraterritorial effects and insufficient links to India. The authority to do so, that is '[t]o claim the power to legislate for some other territories, even though aspects or causes arising, occurring or existing there have no connection, to India', the Court stresses, 'would be to demolish the very basis on which international peace and security can be premised'.[356] Interpretation thus leads to the restriction of other constitutional powers, ie the legislative competences of the Indian parliament.

Moreover, it is also possible to discern sentiments to extrapolate domestic beliefs externally. As Professor Khardekar noted during the debates of the Constituent Assembly on Indian foreign policy and how it should be framed in the constitution, of which Art 51 was the outcome:

> The part that India is to play is certainly very important because foundations of international morality have to be laid and only a country like India with its spiritual heritage can do it.... Therefore it is in keeping with our history, with our tradition, with our culture, that we are a nation of peace and we are going to see that peace prevails in the World.[357]

This passage was not only quoted by the Supreme Court in *GVK Industries*, but it was used to illustrate the meaning of Art 51. In doing so, the court furthermore stated that 'India's emergence as a free nation, through a non-violent struggle, presaged the emergence of a moral voice'[358] on the international stage.

6. Conclusion: A Common Vocabulary for Foreign Policy Objectives

Grasping foreign policy objectives in European constitutional law as legal norms requires a theoretical foundation that transcends different legal orders and even legal traditions. Drawing on the three well-established doctrines of German *Staatszielbestimmungen*, French *objectifs de valeur constitutionnelle*, and Indian directive principles of state policy, a common understanding of such norms can be discerned. Despite their different origins, ie one devised by scholars, the other by a court, and the last one by the constitutional legislator, they show that constitutional objectives are a norm category in its own right. They highlight, through constitutional codification and interpretation, certain aspects of the common good to be pursued within a polity. Its legal features include according constitutional rank and legal bindingness to these norms, the cardinal role of the legislator to advance and specify them through legislative action within the 'bounds of possibility', marginal—largely theoretical—justiciability in court, and an interpretive

[356] *GVK Industries Ltd* (n 347) 416 (para 47).
[357] *GVK Industries Ltd* (n 347) 432 (para 72), quoting from the official reports of the debates in the Constituent Assembly of India (omissions in the original).
[358] *GVK Industries Ltd* (n 347) 431 (para 72).

function to extend, but at times also to constrain, certain state powers and to justify restrictions of individual rights within the confines of the overall structure of the constitutional framework.

Foreign policy objectives form part of this norm category, and hence exhibit the same legal features. However, they belong at the same time to a country's foreign affairs constitution—its *Außenverfassungsrecht*—which adds a number of nuances. These include the reframing of the national common good in a global context, the emergence of the executive, being a country's external representative, as the co-protagonist in the pursuit of these objectives, and a tendency to radiate ('translate') internal values and principles through foreign policy into the wider world.

Whereas the three doctrines drawn upon here underwrite a general legal understanding of constitutional foreign policy objectives, the 'dynamic internationalization' of constitutional law is a global phenomenon. The constitutions of many more countries around the world—as well as the EU—attest to that.

2

The Substance of Constitutional Foreign Policy Objectives

1. Introduction

The post-Lisbon EU Treaties are amongst the most verbose constitutional documents with regard to foreign policy objectives. The topic was the subject of treaty drafting from the outset of the European integration process and the source of vivid debates at the Convention on the Future of Europe. This chapter shows that foreign policy objectives in constitutional documents are not a rarity at all, nor are they limited to the countries whose respective scholarship has already shown interest in such norms. On the contrary, by comparing the twenty-seven documentary EU Member State constitutions and a sample of eleven third-country constitutions, it emerges that such provisions are pervasive both throughout the EU and the world at large. They represented the codified expression of the double trends of 'dynamization' and 'internationalization' in constitutional design. Therefore, Bruno De Witte's assertion of 'the traditional scarcity of relevant provision that one finds in *national* constitutions and the overabundance of norms in *EU* primary law'[1] must be qualified with regard to foreign policy objectives. Against this backdrop, the foreign policy objectives of the European Union have to be viewed in a different light as well. The present findings challenge the criticism and ridicule which the foreign policy objectives in the EU Treaties received. If a critic speaks of 'an almost epidemic proliferation of [external relations] objectives of the Union',[2] as if this were some kind of disease, one would have to conclude from the comparative evidence that the phenomenon is indeed a 'pandemic' in view of its truly global scale. Moreover, if constitutional legislators all over the world deem it necessary and appropriate nowadays to codify such norms, scholarly criticism should be more profound and ought to be based on the content and

[1] B De Witte, 'Too Much Constitutional Law in the European Union's Foreign Relations' in M Cremona and B De Witte (eds), *EU Foreign Relations Law: Constitutional Fundamentals* (Hart Publishing, 2008) 10 (emphasis in the original).

[2] J Terhechte, 'Kommentierung zum Art. 3 EUV (Ziele der Union)' in E Grabitz, M Hilf, and M Nettesheim (eds), *Das Recht der Europäischen Union*, loose-leaf, 41st supplement (C.H. Beck, 2010) marginal no 63.

legal properties of constitutional foreign policy objectives rather than their mere existence.

In terms of their substance, common themes and emerging patterns can be discerned, including general references to 'global justice', the prohibition of war, international security, respect for international law, human rights, (regional) integration, and solidarity and development cooperation. The degree of detail of those provisions varies considerably both within and outside of the EU. While notions of respect for international law and the desire for international cooperation are generally shared, the devil may be in the detail as to what exact kind of international order these constitutions would conceive as 'just': One that puts human rights or the environment first, one that puts the emphasis on progress and development, or one which stresses non-interference with each other's internal affairs. The EU Treaties have ample evidence for all of these main themes and include, moreover, some additional emphases, ie trade liberalization, the promotion of the rule of law, and democracy.

2. Global Trends in Comparative Constitutional Law: Dynamic Internationalization

The double trend of 'dynamic internationalization' in constitutional design merits a number of preliminary remarks on the current debate as well as the utility of such comparative undertakings, which look primarily at constitutional texts. First of all, regarding the utility of any such exercise, SE Finer, Vernon Bogandor, and Bernard Rudden point to the general criticism of comparative constitutional law that constitutional texts 'are highly incomplete, if not misleading, guides to actual practice'.[3] However, they retort that 'although constitutions are not textbooks on the governance of a particular country, it does not follow that such textbooks should, or even can—without peril—ignore the constitution of that country'.[4] Consequently, to them:

> A constitution resembles a sharp pencil of light which brightly illuminates a limited area of a country's political life before fading into a penumbra where the features are obscured—even if that surrounding darkness may conceal what are the most potent and significant elements of the political process.[5]

Hence, in no case 'does a knowledge of the constitutional text alone equate, even nearly, to an understanding of political reality; but it is a necessary condition of that understanding'.[6] In the same vein, but more assertively, Peter Badura describes

[3] SE Finer, V Bogdanor, and B Rudden, *Comparing Constitutions* (Clarendon Press, 1995) 1.

[4] Finer, Bogdanor, and Rudden (n 3) 2.

[5] Finer, Bogdanor, and Rudden (n 3) 2; see also: 'Just as no one constitution is an entirely complete and realistic description of what actually happens, so very few are entire fictions, bearing no relationship whatsoever to what goes on', 2–3.

[6] Finer, Bogdanor and Rudden (n 3) 5.

a constitution as 'a foundational, programmatic and defining act which aims at bestowing a political community with order, and is intended to provide it with its legal base within a specific historical context'.[7] As the Indian constitutional experience in the previous chapter revealed, by putting the key features of the organization of a polity in writing, they are not only consolidated and perpetuated, but also emphasized, marking a break from the past and a new beginning. For Peter Häberle, the explanatory power of constitutional documents is considerable, 'since contemporary ideas are condensed within them with particular (also conceptual) "exertion" '.[8] They are made plainly visible for everyone, and they are usually difficult to dispose of, given the entrenchment of constitutional law as its distinguishing feature vis-à-vis all other law, and given that it binds the exercise of public power in all its forms, possessing supremacy over the other norms of the legal order.[9] This accords with Joseph Raz's notion of 'thick constitutionalism', which characterizes the constitution, inter alia, as constitutive, enduring, entrenched higher law, which is 'generally held to express the common beliefs of the population about the way their society should be governed'[10] as part of a 'common ideology that governs public life in that country'.[11] Similarly, Markus Kotzur points to the loss of credibility and legitimacy that can result from a government's failure to live up to the standards its *own* constitution imposes upon it.[12] While a mere examination of constitutional documents obviously cannot explain everything, their comparison is indeed capable of yielding conclusions of importance and usefulness, not least when they occupy a shared 'constitutional space' (see Chapter 4).[13]

In addition to this general merit in comparing constitutions, it should be stressed that recent decades have been a heyday of constitutional drafting, which ought to prompt legal scholars to take stock and assess new developments in the overall trajectory of constitutional design. At the national level, Giovanni Sartori, writing in 1997, notes that '[o]f the 170 or so written documents called constitutions in today's world more than half have been written since 1974'.[14] This

[7] In the original: 'ein ordnungstiftender und programmatischer Gründungs- und Gestaltungsakt, der dem Gemeinwesen in einer konkreten geschichtlichen Lage eine rechtliche Grundlage geben will': P Badura, 'Arten der Verfassungsrechtssätze' in J Isensee and P Kirchhof (eds), *Handbuch des Staatsrechts der Bundesrepublik Deutschland. Volume VII: Normativität und Schutz der Verfassung—Internationale Beziehungen* (C.F. Müller, 1992) 34.

[8] In the original: '... weil sich in ihnen in besonderer (auch begrifflicher) "Anstrengungen" Ideen der Zeit verdichten': P Häberle, 'Das "Weltbild" des Verfassungsstaates—eine Textstufenanalyse zur Menschheit als verfassungsstaatlichem und "letztem" Geltungsgrund des Völkerrechts' in B Ziemske, T Langheid, H Wilms, and G Haverkate (eds), *Staatsphilosophie und Rechtspolitik, Festschrift für Martin Kriele* (C.H. Beck, 1997) 1280.

[9] Badura (n 7) 33.

[10] J Raz, 'On the Authority and Interpretation of Constitutions: Some Preliminaries' in L Alexander (ed), *Constitutionalism: Philosophical Foundations* (CUP, 1998) 153–4.

[11] Raz (n 10) 154.

[12] M Kotzur, 'Weltrechtliche Bezüge in nationalen Verfassungstexten: Die Rezeption verfassungsrechtlicher Normen durch das Völkerrecht' (2008) 39 *Rechtstheorie* 191, 202.

[13] See F Mayer, 'Die Bedeutung der Rechts- und Verfassungsvergleichung im Europäischen Verfassungsverbund' in C Calliess (ed), *Verfassungswandel im europäischen Staaten- und Verfassungsverbund* (Mohr Siebeck, 2007).

[14] G Sartori, *Comparative Constitutional Engineering*, 2nd edn (Macmillan Press, 1997) 197.

includes 'the cascade of constitution-making that took place in post-Communist Eastern Europe'.[15] In this regard, it is worth noting that the constitutions of the five youngest states in the world all contain explicit foreign policy objectives.[16]

The constitutions reviewed in this chapter largely share the characteristic of being relatively new. Within the EU, ten out of twenty-seven documentary constitutions (ie excluding the UK) were adopted from 1990 onwards. Nine of these are from the thirteen countries which joined the EU in 2004 or afterwards.[17] Twenty out of twenty-seven were adopted after the end of the Second World War. Within the sample of the eleven third-country constitutions, three were adopted after 1990, while ten out of eleven were adopted after the Second World War. The exception is the constitution of the United States, which was adopted in the late eighteenth century and last amended in 1992. Within this process of innovation two important trends become visible. These are the 'internationalization' of constitutional law and the codification of objectives that the state is to pursue, which has been termed the 'dynamization of constitutional law'.[18]

The issue of the 'internationalization' of national constitutions, as far as it concerns the incorporation of international law and in particular international human rights standards into national constitutional law, has indeed received considerable scholarly attention.[19] Arguably, the first comparative historical account for such internationalization was made by Paul De Visscher in 1952, who coined this phenomenon 'the internationalist fever of the immediate post-war period'.[20] As Robert Wilson formulated it a decade later, 'after each World War of the present century there was a wave of effort to include in national constitutions

[15] D Kommers, 'Comparative Constitutional Law: Its Increasing Relevance' in V Jackson and M Tushnet (eds), *Defining the Field of Comparative Constitutional Law* (Praeger, 2002) 63.

[16] As of August 2015. For practical purposes, this includes Kosovo, notwithstanding of course the controversy surrounding its international recognition. See Arts 16(3), 17, and 20 Kosovar constitution; Art 15 Montenegrin constitution; Art 16(1) Serbian constitution; Art 8 constitution of Timor Leste, also Art 6(a) and (h). An extensive list of foreign policy objectives can be found in Art 43 of the transitional constitution of the Republic of South Sudan, 7 July 2011, <http://www.wipo.int/wipolex/en/text.jsp?file_id=250715>.

[17] The post-Cold War constitutions in Central and Eastern Europe have received particular academic attention, especially with regard to their international (law) aspects. See eg V Vereshchetin, 'New Constitutions and the Old Problem of the Relationship between International Law and National Law' (1996) 7 *European Journal of International Law* 1; and the contributions in R Müllerson, M Fitzmaurice, and M Andenas (eds), *Constitutional Reforms and International Law in Central and Eastern Europe* (Kluwer Law International, 1998).

[18] In the original: 'Dynamisierung des Verfassungsrechts': K-P Sommermann, *Staatsziele und Staatszielbestimmungen* (Mohr Siebeck, 1997) 374; similarly, De Montalivet speaks of 'une conception dynamique du droit': P De Montalivet, *Les objectifs de valeur constitutionnelle* (Dalloz, 2006) 67.

[19] See eg Kotzur (n 12); T Ginsburg, S Chernykh, and Z Elkins, 'Commitment and Diffusion: How and Why National Constitutions Incorporate International Law' (2008) *University of Illinois Law Review* 201; and extensively H Tourard, *L'internationalisation des constitutions nationales* (L.D.G.J., 2000); and J Kokott, 'From Reception and Transplantation to Convergence of Constitutional Models in the Age of Globalization' in C Starck (ed), *Constitutionalism, Universalism and Democracy—a Comparative Analysis: The German Contributions to the Fifth World Congress of the International Association of Constitutional Law* (Nomos, 1999).

[20] In the original: 'la fièvre internationaliste de l'immédiat après-guerre': P De Visscher, 'Les tendances internationales des constitutions modernes' (1952) 1 *Recueil de Cours* 511, 573.

provisions whereby the law of nations would be made a part of municipal law'.[21] Similarly, Vladlen Vereshchetin posits, referring to the developments in the former Soviet bloc:

> The ever-growing interdependence of States and peoples, accompanied by the constant 'intrusion' of international law into many national spheres, including those previously reserved for exclusive domestic regulation (from human rights to economy and defence), and the expansion of the prerogatives of inter-State institutions objectively lead to the de facto affirmation of the primacy of international law and induce States to recognize de jure this primacy.[22]

Going further than the question of mere incorporation, Kotzur detects a clear trend that 'the more modern a constitution is, the more intensely it breathes the spirit of worldwide interconnectedness and the globalization of law, and thus the more naturally it dares to make references to a world beyond the nation state'.[23] Similarly, Volker Röben sees in such references the response to the question of how the modern, open state and its legal order should adapt to the pressures created by globalization and Europeanization as well as their respective lawmaking processes. According to Röben, the answer is for constitutional law to embrace the external dimension by extending the rule of law, democracy, the separation of powers, and the protection of fundamental rights to the international action of the state.[24] From this it may be surmised that 'internationalization' is not only about the role of international law in the domestic legal order, ie about receiving external influences, but also about shaping the international order through the exercise of foreign policy, and giving direction to a state's own input into these influences. This direction, consequently, is codified in the form of objectives, which leads to the second trend.

With regard to 'dynamization', constitutional provisions which mandate the state to pursue certain goals have equally proliferated in constitutional documents around the globe. In doing so, the constitution, in addition to its traditional function of establishing the rules and limits of government for a political community,[25] sketches out a certain future towards which the state should strive through the means provided for within the given constitutional framework. Already in the 1970s, Ulrich Scheuner saw constitutional objectives as reflecting a 'trend of this age towards the socially active polity as well as ... towards transnational

[21] R Wilson, 'International Law in New National Constitutions' (1964) 58 *American Journal of International Law* 432, 432.

[22] Vereshchetin (n 17) 1.

[23] In the original: 'Je moderner eine Verfassung ist, je intensiver sie den Geist weltweiter Vernetzung und einer Globalisierung des Rechts atmet, umso selbstverständlicher wagt sie die Bezugnahme auf eine Welt jenseits des Nationalstaates': Kotzur (n 12) 213.

[24] V Röben, *Außenverfassungsrecht* (Mohr Siebeck, 2007) foreword.

[25] L Henkin, *The Rights of Man Today* (Stevens, 1979) 31–2, points out with regard to the constitution of the United States that given its particular historical circumstances, it was primarily concerned with limiting power. Note also A Marmor, *Law in the Age of Pluralism* (OUP, 2007) 92, who maintains that most constitutions are concerned mainly with 'the basic structure of government with its divisions of political power, and the area of human and civil rights', but also stresses that this is so for historical reasons.

integration'.[26] Thus, for Pierre De Monatlivet, these provisions are nothing less than the expression of 'a post-modernity characterized by complexity, disorder, indetermination and uncertainty'.[27] In view of such uncertainties, and equally emphatically, Karl-Peter Sommermann sees constitutional objectives as a way of allaying a political community's need for orientation and 'hunger for values' (*Wertehunger*).[28] These commentators offer explanations for the fact that constitutions have come to include more recently such aspirational norms which scholars had previously regarded as 'unheard of' (*inédit*)[29] in constitutional law.

Both of these trends converge most visibly in the codification of foreign policy objectives in constitutional documents, attesting to the provident social welfare state in a globalized and interdependent world. As Röben points out, constitutional law in the area of foreign affairs is a means of the modern, 'open' state and its legal order to adapt to the pressures created by globalization and global lawmaking processes.[30] On the one hand, it is clear from this that 'internationalization' is not only about the role of international law in the domestic legal order, but also about the substantive constitutional framework for the exercise of foreign policy. On the other hand, it is evident that constitutional objectives are not to be pursued exclusively internally, but increasingly also through a state's foreign policy.

Hence, constitutional foreign policy objectives indicate that constitutional law not only regulates how external influences are to be received internally, but also provide normative guidance for a state's own input into shaping these influences, reflecting an 'active paradigm' in the law on foreign relations.[31] Taking stock of the expanding evidence of substantive guidance that can be found in constitutions around the world, including within the European constitutional space, becomes imperative for a fuller understanding of foreign policy objectives as constitutional norms, on their own merits as well as for the purpose of grasping the objectives of the European Union as constitutional norms.

3. A Brief History of the Foreign Policy Objectives in the EU Treaties

The EU Treaties outline the quintessential 'foreign policy objectives in *European* constitutional law'. This warrants a look at their origins before turning to the

[26] In the original: 'Trend des Zeitalters zum sozial aktiv tätigen Gemeinwesen, wie übrigens auch ... zu transnationalen Zusammenschlüssen': U Scheuner, *Staatstheorie und Staatsrecht—Gesammelte Schriften* (Duncker & Humblot, 1978) 242.

[27] In the original: 'une post-modernité marquée par la complexité, le désordre, l'indétermination et l'incertitude': De Montalivet (n 18) 571.

[28] Sommermann (n 18) 1.

[29] To use the expression employed with regard to the French *objectifs* by C Vimbert, 'L'ordre public dans la jurisprudence du Conseil constitutionnel' (1994) No 3 *Revue du droit public et de la science politique en France et à l'étranger* 693, 712.

[30] Röben (n 24) foreword.

[31] Referring to the EU, F Amtenbrink and D Kochenov, 'The Active Paradigm of the Study of the EU's Place in the World: An Introduction' in F Amtenbrink and D Kochenov (eds), *The European Union's Shaping of the International Legal Order* (CUP, 2013).

comparative dimension. The evolution of these objectives in the EU Treaties and especially the deliberations at the Convention on the Future of Europe in 2002/03 demonstrate how codification of foreign policy objectives into constitutional documents is a process of condensing and entrenching certain norms, concepts, and ideas, in this case about a particular vision for the international order that the EU is to pursue.

Tracing the development of the codification of the foreign policy objectives of the European Union from the beginning of the integration process to the present day shows that from the very start the external dimension of integration had always been firmly recognized in the founding Treaties. From a vague notion of contributing to 'world peace' and an early focus on trade objectives, over time additional goals were added in various domains, eventually including 'all aspects' of foreign policy.

A leap for the codification of external relations objectives was the drafting process at the Convention on the Future of Europe, where the idea to codify one overall set of goals for EU external relations, while replacing the individual policy area goals, took root. Had this succeeded, a clear analogy between the 'Constitution' of the Union and modern national constitutions would have emerged, as states normally do not distinguish between policy areas in their constitutional foreign policy objectives. Instead, many national constitutions contain one set of principles and objectives by which the foreign policy of a country is to be guided in its entirety.

However, at the end of this latest treaty reform process and due to institutional and political realities, this was only partly achieved. On the one hand, there are now *two* sets of overall foreign policy objectives, Art 3(5) TEU and Art 21 TEU. On the other hand, while some individual policy areas have lost their specific objectives (the Common Foreign and Security Policy (CFSP) and economic, financial, and technical cooperation), others retain objectives of their own (the Common Commercial Policy (CCP), development cooperation, and humanitarian aid). In addition, the shift from the Constitutional Treaty (CT) to Lisbon located the general objectives of the Union, the general external action objectives, and the CFSP in one treaty, while the other policy areas and their objectives can be found in the TFEU. The confusion this may create is mitigated somewhat by the cross-referencing of all the domains to the general external action objectives of Art 21 TEU (but not explicitly Art 3(5) TEU), positioning it as a 'spinal column'[32] of EU external action.

Overall, this partial reform epitomizes the *sui generis* nature of the Union, ie not being a state but more than an ordinary international organization. Akin to most modern national constitutions, it has now codified *general* foreign policy objectives; at the same time, akin to a functional entity of conferred powers, its constitutional documents continue to spell out each specific external policy area in which it can act, attaching in some cases, but no longer in all, *specific* objectives.

[32] C Kaddous, 'External Action under the Lisbon Treaty' in I Pernice and E Tanchev (eds), *Ceci n'est pas une Constitution—Constitutionalisation without a Constitution?* (Nomos, 2009) 178.

The highest laws of the Union are thus clearly marked by the twin trends of internationalization and 'dynamization' of constitutional law. Given the prominence these provisions enjoyed in the history of European integration and especially at the European Convention, the indifference and ridicule among certain EU constitutional law scholars towards external relations objectives (calling them, among other things, 'redolent of motherhood and apple pie')[33] stand in stark contrast to the importance attached to these same objectives by the framers of the Treaties.

3.1 The early beginnings: The ECSC, Euratom, and the EEC

The process of European integration had a strong external dimension and indeed rationale from the very start.[34] For Walter Hallstein, 'internal and external unity are two sides of the same coin'.[35] This external dimension was expressed from the outset in the founding treaties, and later crystallized in the form of codified external relations objectives.

The external orientation of the founding Treaties is already foreshadowed in the 1950 Schuman Declaration, the language of which served as a blueprint for the preamble to the Treaty Establishing the European Coal and Steel Community (ECSC).[36] The 1951 ECSC Treaty starts out in the first recital of its preamble by stating 'that *world peace* can be safeguarded only by creative efforts commensurate with the dangers that threaten it',[37] followed by expressing the conviction of the contracting parties 'that the contribution which an organized and vital Europe can make to civilization is indispensable to the maintenance of peaceful relations'.[38] It was with this in mind that the Coal and Steel Community was set up. In this same vein, the preamble states that the rationale underlying the ECSC, next to fostering economic development and raising living standards, was 'to substitute for age-old rivalries the merging of essential interests' and 'to lay the foundations for institutions which will give direction to a destiny henceforth shared'.[39]

In the operative part, the first elements of external relations objectives become visible in the form of references to international trade. The ECSC is mandated, inter alia, to 'see that the common market [for coal and steel] is regularly supplied, taking account of the needs of third countries'[40] and to 'further the development of international trade and see that equitable limits are observed in prices charged on external markets'.[41]

[33] A Dashwood et al, *Wyatt & Dashwood's European Union Law*, 6th edn (Hart Publishing, 2011) 903.

[34] See D Thym, 'Foreign Affairs' in A von Bogdandy and J Bast (eds), *Principles of European Constitutional Law*, 2nd edn (Hart Publishing/C.H. Beck, 2011) 310.

[35] In the original: 'Innere und äußere Einheit sind die zwei Seiten einer und derselben Münze': W Hallstein, *Die Europäische Gemeinschaft*, 5th edn (Econ Verlag, 1979) 295.

[36] Schuman Declaration, 9 May 1950.

[37] First recital of the preamble, Treaty establishing the European Coal and Steel Community (ECSC Treaty) (original version), Paris, 18 April 1951 (emphasis added).

[38] Second recital of the preamble, ECSC Treaty.

[39] Fifth recital of the preamble, ECSC Treaty.

[40] Art 3(a) ECSC Treaty.

[41] Art 3(f) ECSC Treaty.

As a side note, the failed draft treaties on a European Defence Community (EDC) and a European Political Community (EPC) displayed the same kind of inspiration, and also contained objectives concerning the external relations of these communities. The former refers in the preamble to the maintenance of peace and defence against aggression in the spirit of the Charter of the United Nations.[42] The form of this defence, as is clarified in the operative part, is to take place within the framework of the North Atlantic Treaty Organization (NATO).[43] The Draft EPC Treaty contained among its objectives the coordination of the foreign policies of the Member States as well as a contribution to the pursuit of the objectives of the Council of Europe, the Organization for European Economic Co-operation (OEEC), and NATO.[44]

Turning to the two successfully ratified treaties of 1957, the European Atomic Energy Community Treaty (EAEC, or Euratom) also makes the link to the outside world explicit. Its preamble stresses the desire to associate with other countries as well as 'to cooperate with other international organisations'.[45] In the operative part, these goals appear as part of the 'tasks' of the Community.[46] The Treaty Establishing the European Economic Community (EEC), in its original version of 1957, which would later become the Treaty Establishing the European Community (TEC) and be amended into what is now the Treaty on the Functioning of the European Union (TFEU), displays similar traits. In laying 'the foundations of an ever closer union among the peoples of Europe',[47] as the preamble states, the contracting parties also express their desire to contribute 'to the progressive abolition of restrictions on international trade'[48] through a CCP, their intention 'to confirm the solidarity which binds Europe and the overseas countries', and the aspiration 'to ensure the development of their prosperity, in accordance with the principles of the Charter of the United Nations'.[49]

In addition, the resolve to pool the resources of the Member States is linked to a call 'upon the other peoples of Europe who share their ideal to join their efforts',[50] which can be seen as an early harbinger of enlargement. While the 'task' (singular) of the EEC is focused on the common market,[51] the 'activities' (plural) of the Community include 'the establishment of a common customs tariff and of a

[42] Second recital of the preamble, Treaty instituting the European Defence Community (EDC Treaty), Paris, 27 May 1952.

[43] Art 2(2) EDC Treaty.

[44] Art 2 Draft Treaty embodying the Statute of the European Community adopted by the Ad Hoc Assembly (Draft EPC Treaty; not to be confused with European Political Cooperation), Strasbourg, 10 March 1953; see also Arts 67–74 of Chapter II of the Draft Treaty which covers the international relations of the envisaged Community, specifying further the mechanisms for foreign policy coordination among the Member States.

[45] Fifth recital of the preamble, European Atomic Energy Community Treaty (EAEC Treaty) (original version), Rome, 25 March 1957.

[46] Arts 1(2) and 2(h) EAEC Treaty.

[47] First recital of the preamble, Treaty establishing the European Economic Community (EEC Treaty) (original version), Rome, 25 March 1957.

[48] Sixth recital of the preamble, EEC Treaty.

[49] Seventh recital of the preamble, EEC Treaty.

[50] Eighth recital of the preamble, EEC Treaty.

[51] Art 2 EEC Treaty.

common commercial policy toward third countries'[52] as well as 'the association of overseas countries and territories in order to increase trade and to promote jointly economic and social development'.[53] Furthermore, the CCP, as an unequivocally external policy, is also endowed with specific objectives, ie 'the harmonious development of world trade' and the 'progressive abolition of restriction on international trade and the lowering of customs barriers'.[54] The goals of the association of overseas territories are also restated and elaborated upon in the operative part.[55]

3.2 Enter foreign policy: The Single European Act

Despite the fact that the EDC and EPC Treaties never saw the light of day, in addition to the external relations of the three European Communities, the Member States began to cooperate on an intergovernmental level in matters concerning general foreign policy. This format became known as European Political Cooperation (EPC), which was affirmed and quasi-codified in the Single European Act of 1986 (SEA),[56] foreshadowing the European Union and its CFSP. The SEA also expanded the policies of the EEC into other fields with an external dimension, such as the environment, which included codification of specific objectives for this policy into the TEC.[57]

The Member States of the Community wanted to pursue together certain common goals in the area of foreign policy beyond those enshrined in the TEC. Preceding the SEA (which is a treaty among the Member States),[58] the Solemn Declaration on European Union signed in Stuttgart in 1983 already exhibits this desire of the Member States to cooperate more closely at the European level in matters of foreign policy.[59] In particular, it includes a call for the 'progressive development and definition of common principles and *objectives* as well as the identification of common interests in order to strengthen the possibilities of joint action in the field of foreign policy'.[60] In the preamble to the SEA, subsequently, the then ten Community Member States expressed their awareness

> of the responsibility incumbent upon Europe to aim at speaking ever increasingly with one voice and to act with consistency and solidarity in order more effectively to protect its

[52] Art 3(b) EEC Treaty; see also Arts 18 and 110 EEC Treaty.

[53] Art 3(k) EEC Treaty; see also Arts 131 and 132 EEC Treaty.

[54] Art 110(1) EEC Treaty.

[55] Arts 131 and 132 EEC Treaty, emphasizing the social and economic development of the associated territories.

[56] See Art 1(3) Single European Act (SEA) [1987] OJ L 169/1, stating that political cooperation will be governed by a specific title in the SEA.

[57] Art 25 SEA, introducing what is now Art 191 TFEU. Hereinafter, unless otherwise indicated, 'TEC' will refer to the TEC in the consolidated version following the Nice revision, ie the Treaty establishing the European Community (consolidated text) [2006] OJ C 321E/1. The consolidated text of the TEU post-Nice but pre-Lisbon (Treaty on European Union (consolidated text) [2006] OJ C 321E/1) shall be indicated as 'TEU (Nice version)'.

[58] Art 33 SEA, which requires ratification by all the Member States for the Act to enter into force.

[59] European Council, Solemn Declaration on European Union, Stuttgart 19 June 1983, reproduced from the Bulletin of the European Communities, No 6/1983.

[60] Solemn Declaration on European Union, pt 3.2 (emphasis added).

common interests and independence, in particular to display the principles of democracy and compliance with the law and with human rights to which they are attached, so that together they may make their own contribution to the preservation of international peace and security in accordance with the undertaking entered into by them within the framework of the United Nations Charter ...[61]

From this recital one can glean a number of substantive foreign policy objectives. It represents the prototype of what would later become Art 11 TEU (prior to Lisbon) and eventually Arts 3(5) and 21 TEU (post-Lisbon).

Title III of the SEA deals specifically with cooperation in the area of foreign policy. The Member States pledge to 'endeavour jointly to formulate and implement a European foreign policy',[62] thereby also introducing this term as such into Treaty language. In doing so, they acknowledge in a treaty between the Member States that European integration can cover virtually all aspects of foreign policy and not just some of them, such as international trade. Apart from improving the exchange of information and consultations between them, in the SEA the Member States also vowed to 'ensure that common principles and *objectives* are gradually developed and defined'.[63] The Member States furthermore expressed their readiness to cooperate more closely in the area of security, considering 'that closer co-operation on questions of European security would contribute in an essential way to the development of a European identity in external policy matters'.[64] To this, the caveat is added that '[n]othing in this Title shall impede closer co-operation in the field of security between certain of the High Contracting Parties within the framework of the Western European Union or the Atlantic Alliance',[65] which already highlights the need to accommodate Member State preferences in this sensitive area (see further Chapter 4).

Moreover, it is important to note that Title III (and its sole Art 30) of the SEA on European Political Cooperation are kept neatly separate from the institutions, competences, and procedures of the European Communities.[66] The latter are not to be affected by the former.[67] This cements, at an early stage, a duality of modes for conducting EU external relations, which remains a major characteristic of the system of EU foreign policy today.

3.3 The Union and the pillars: Maastricht, Amsterdam, and Nice

The European Union, which the SEA had envisaged, came into being with the entry into force of the Treaty on European Union (also known as the Maastricht

61 Fifth recital of the preamble, SEA. 62 Art 30(1) SEA.
63 Art 30(2)(c), second indent SEA (emphasis added). 64 Art 30(6)(a) SEA.
65 Art 30(6)(c) SEA.
66 Arts 1 and 31 SEA; see also the second recital of the SEA preamble, which states that the future European Union is to be implemented 'on the basis, firstly, of the Communities operating in accordance with their own rules and, secondly, of European co-operation among the signatory States in the sphere of foreign policy'.
67 Art 32 SEA.

Treaty) in 1993, which was to 'mark a new stage in the process of European integration'.[68] The Treaty introduced the rather complex pillar structure,[69] which was 'opaque to the outside world and posed complex challenges to coherence internally',[70] despite two treaty revision rounds in the following years, resulting in the Amsterdam Treaty of 1997[71] and the Nice Treaty of 2001, respectively.[72] The newly established Union was to be 'founded on the European Communities, supplemented by the policies and forms of cooperation established by this Treaty',[73] with the Communities continuing to exist as one of the three pillars next to the intergovernmental CFSP and Justice and Home Affairs (JHA; narrowed down to Police and Judicial Cooperation in Criminal Matters following the Amsterdam Treaty).

The emergence of the CFSP is a watershed moment in EU external relations law as it legally codifies and institutionalizes European cooperation in this area, including the codification of foreign policy objectives. The importance of this development was also captured in the preamble to the TEU, which expresses that the CFSP is to reinforce 'the European identity and its independence in order to promote peace, security and progress in Europe and in the world'.[74] This is reiterated in the operative part, which contained a general catalogue of 'objectives' of the Union (as opposed to the 'tasks' and 'activities' of the Communities). This included the objective for the Union 'to assert its identity on the international scene, in particular through the implementation of a common foreign and security policy including the eventual framing of a common defence policy'.[75]

What this international identity would entail more specifically for the Union was left open. Nevertheless, Maastricht and subsequent reforms added a number of provisions, both in the TEU and the amended TEC, from which the basic features of such an identity could be assembled. These include the general objectives of Art 2 TEU (Nice version) and the specific objectives of each policy area to the extent that these had an external dimension. The policies which were manifestly external in nature formed the new CFSP, which was spelled out further in the TEU, and the external policies of the Community, which now also comprised,

[68] First recital of the preamble, Treaty on European Union (Maastricht Treaty) [1992] OJ C 191/1; see also Art A(2) TEU (Maastricht Treaty).

[69] See on external relations in particular M Cremona, 'The Common Foreign and Security Policy of the European Union and the External Relations Powers of the European Community' in D O'Keeffe and P Twomey (eds), *Legal Issues of the Maastricht Treaty* (Wiley Chancery, 1994).

[70] M Cremona, 'External Relations and External Competence of the European Union: The Emergence of an Integrated Policy' in P Craig and G de Búrca (eds), *The Evolution of EU Law*, 2nd edn (OUP, 2011) 261; see also C Herrmann, 'Much Ado about Pluto? The "Unity of the Legal Order of the European Union" Revisited' in M Cremona and B De Witte (eds), *EU Foreign Relations Law: Constitutional Fundamentals* (Hart Publishing, 2008), discussing the intricacies of this structure.

[71] Treaty of Amsterdam (Amsterdam Treaty) [1997] OJ C 340/1. See further A Dashwood, 'External Relations Provisions of the Amsterdam Treaty' in D O'Keeffe and P Twomey (eds), *Legal Issues of the Amsterdam Treaty* (Hart Publishing, 1999).

[72] Treaty of Nice (Nice Treaty) [2001] OJ C 80/1.

[73] Art 1(3) TEU (Nice version).

[74] Tenth recital of the preamble, TEU (Nice version).

[75] Art B(1) TEU (Maastricht Treaty) (dash omitted); later Art 2 TEU (Nice version).

next to the traditional CCP, development cooperation[76] and economic, financial, and technical assistance to third countries.[77]

In Art 11(1), the TEU (Nice version) states that the CFSP is to cover 'all areas of foreign and security policy'. As the specific objectives of the CFSP, the article lists:

- to safeguard the common values, fundamental interests, independence and integrity of the Union in conformity with the principles of the United Nations Charter,
- to strengthen the security of the Union in all ways,
- to preserve peace and strengthen international security, in accordance with the principles of the United Nations Charter, as well as the principles of the Helsinki Final Act and the objectives of the Paris Charter, including those on external borders,
- to promote international cooperation,
- to develop and consolidate democracy and the rule of law, and respect for human rights and fundamental freedoms.[78]

Apart from introducing the CFSP, the Maastricht Treaty also substantially amended the TEC.[79] The list of activities of the European Community (with the adjective 'Economic' having been omitted from its name) was extended to now explicitly include development cooperation.[80] This policy area was endowed with its own set of specific objectives, which were to foster:

- the sustainable economic and social development of the developing countries, and more particularly the most disadvantaged among them,
- the smooth and gradual integration of the developing countries into the world economy,
- the campaign against poverty in the developing countries.[81]

Moreover, Community development policy was to 'contribute to the general objective of developing and consolidating democracy and the rule of law, and to that of respecting human rights and fundamental freedoms'.[82] An external source for objectives is added with the statement that, in addition, '[t]he Community and the Member States shall comply with the commitments and take account of the objectives they have approved in the context of the United Nations and other competent international organisations'.[83] Lastly, the amended TEC also obliges the Community to 'take account of the objectives referred to in Article 177 in the policies that it implements which are likely to affect developing countries',[84] which would include internal policies such as the Common Agricultural Policy or the internal market. Similarly, it states that economic, financial, and technical cooperation with third countries is to be carried out in order to 'contribute to the general objective of developing and

[76] Arts 177–81 TEC. The Community had already been pursuing its own development policy before the Maastricht Treaty, but the competence for this had been derived from a broad reading of the provisions on the CCP and association with the Community: see P Eeckhout, *EU External Relations Law*, 2nd edn (OUP, 2011) 127–41.

[77] This policy was codified only by the Nice Treaty (Art 2, pt 16); Art 181a TEC.

[78] Art 11(1) TEU (Nice version).

[79] Art G TEU (Maastricht Treaty).

[80] Art 3(1)(r) TEC.

[81] Art 177(1) TEC.

[82] Art 177(2) TEC.

[83] Art 177(3) TEC.

[84] Art 178 TEC.

consolidating democracy and the rule of law, and to the objective of respecting human rights and fundamental freedoms'.[85]

Through the Maastricht, Amsterdam, and Nice Treaties, EU external relations have undergone significant codification, including through the establishment of the European Union, the introduction of the CFSP, and significant amendments to the TEC. As a result, each major area of external relations has been given a particular set of objectives. The notion that EU external relations, and not just the CFSP, can cover 'all areas of foreign policy and security policy' to include also trade, development, and other related policies, had now been firmly established in the Treaties. However, the objectives remained scattered across different policy areas. A general catalogue of foreign policy objectives for the Union as a whole was yet to come.

3.4 'Responsibilities in the governance of globalisation': The Laeken Declaration

Shortly after the Nice Treaty and with the enlargement of the Union to the east and south already looming, it was decided that another major overhaul of the basic structure of the Union should be considered. This marked the beginning of a decade-long treaty reform process, which reached a climax at the Convention on the Future of Europe, where the failed Treaty Establishing a Constitution for Europe was finalized. At the end of this well-documented and discussed process stands the Lisbon Treaty,[86] which entered into force on 1 December 2009 and carried over many of the changes envisaged by the failed Constitutional Treaty. The treaty reform process too was strongly motivated by the desire not only to bring Europe closer to its citizens but to make it a stronger and more assertive player on the world stage, which resulted in a major expansion and rewriting of the Union's external relations objectives.

The 'beginning started at the end',[87] as Paul Craig puts it, highlighting that after the Nice Treaty had been signed, it was already envisaged that further and more profound treaty reform would be necessary. In a declaration attached to the Nice Treaty on the Future of the Union, this was clearly spelled out, calling 'for a deeper and wider debate about the future of the European Union'.[88] To that end, the Laeken Declaration on the Future of the European Union of December 2001 endorsed the idea of the 'Convention method'. Using a Convention to provide impetus for a subsequent Intergovernmental Conference (IGC) was the result of

[85] Art 181a(1), second subpara TEC (Nice version).

[86] See eg P Berman, 'From Laeken to Lisbon: The Origins and Negotiation of the Lisbon Treaty' in A Biondi, P Eeckhout, and S Ripley (eds), *EU Law after Lisbon* (OUP, 2012); P Craig, *The Lisbon Treaty: Law, Politics, and Treaty Reform* (OUP, 2010) 1–31; J-C Piris, *The Lisbon Treaty: A Legal and Political Analysis* (CUP, 2010) 7–63; and R Streinz, C Ohler, and C Herrmann, *Der Vertrag von Lissabon zur Reform der EU: Einführung mit Synopse*, 3rd edn (C.H. Beck, 2010) 16–36.

[87] Craig (n 86) 1.

[88] Declaration No 23 attached to the Nice Treaty, *Declaration on the Future of the Union*, pt 3.

what could be called 'traditional reform fatigue',[89] ie a feeling that the series of IGCs amending the Treaties had provided unsatisfactory results and had become too detached from the wider public.

As in the Schuman and Stuttgart declarations, the role and goals of Europe in the world assumed a 'central position'[90] and were closely linked to the question of integration at large. In this vein, the Presidency Conclusions to which the Laeken Declaration is attached stress that the declaration 'and the prospects it opens mark a decisive step for the citizen towards a simpler Union, one that is stronger *in the pursuit of its essential objectives* and *more present in the world*'.[91]

The Laeken Declaration represents a rather sweeping statement on the fundamental questions concerning the state of European integration and in which direction it was headed. Evoking 'the dream of a strong, unified Europe',[92] it goes on to set out 'twin challenges'[93] for the Union, one internal and one external. While the internal challenge is about the democratic deficit of the Union, the external one concerns 'Europe's new role in a globalised world'.[94] Asking whether 'Europe [does] not, now that [it] is finally unified, have a leading role to play in a new world order, that of a power able both to play a stabilising role worldwide and to point the way ahead for many countries and peoples',[95] and having recalled some of the historic achievements in European history such as the Magna Carta, the French Revolution, and the fall of the Berlin Wall, it provides an answer to this question itself:

> Now that the Cold War is over and we are living in a globalised, yet also highly fragmented world, Europe needs to shoulder its responsibilities in the governance of globalisation. The role it has to play is that of a power resolutely doing battle against all violence, all terror and all fanaticism, but which also does not turn a blind eye to the world's heartrending injustices. In short, a power wanting to change the course of world affairs in such a way as to benefit not just the rich countries but also the poorest. A power seeking to set globalisation within a moral framework, in other words to anchor it in solidarity and sustainable development.[96]

This is without doubt a rather ambitious statement, enunciating the Union's 'future role in high moral tones'.[97] The declaration urged for a European Union that would be 'more involved in foreign affairs, security and defence, in other

[89] Craig (n 86) 2; also Piris (n 86) 13, and C Closa, 'The Convention Method and the Transformation of EU Constitutional Politics' in E Eriksen, J Fossum, and A Meníndez (eds), *Developing a Constitution for Europe* (Routledge, 2004) 184–5.

[90] P Koutrakos, 'The European Union's External Relations a Year after Lisbon—Introduction' in P Koutrakos (ed), *The European Union's External Relations a Year after Lisbon*, CLEER Working Paper 2011/3, 7.

[91] European Council, Presidency Conclusions, European Council meeting in Laeken 14 and 15 December 2001, SN 300/1/01 REV 1, pt 3 (emphasis added).

[92] European Council, Presidency Conclusions, European Council meeting in Laeken 14 and 15 December 2001, Annex I, *Laeken Declaration on the Future of the European Union*, 19.

[93] *Laeken Declaration* (n 92) 19.

[94] *Laeken Declaration* (n 92) 20.

[95] *Laeken Declaration* (n 92) 20.

[96] *Laeken Declaration* (n 92) 20.

[97] P Norman, *The Accidental Constitution: The Story of the European Convention*, 2nd edn (EuroComment, 2005) 90.

words, greater and better coordinated action to deal with trouble spots in and around Europe and in the rest of the world'.[98] Taken together, the language of the Laeken Declaration represents another leap in terms of global ambition for the EU, now coupling proactive, comprehensive engagement with normativity.

3.5 Constitutionalizing global ambitions: The Convention on the Future of Europe

The Laeken Declaration by no means tasked the Convention on the Future of Europe with drafting a constitution, the latter being only mentioned as a possibility 'in the long run'.[99] Originally, the Convention was launched with the rather vague task 'to consider the key issues arising for the Union's future development and try to identify the various possible responses'.[100] Nonetheless, the Convention ended up doing exactly that. Doing so resulted in an unprecedented reshuffling and expansion of constitutionally codified foreign policy objectives.

The Convention on the Future of Europe started its work in February 2002 and concluded in July 2003 by presenting a complete Draft Treaty Establishing a Constitution for Europe to the President of the European Council.[101] Given the close similarity between the Lisbon Treaty and the Draft Constitutional Treaty, it is 'important to understand the way in which the Constitutional Treaty emerged, and the forces that shaped its content'.[102] Hence, to understand the foreign policy objectives in post-Lisbon primary law, close scrutiny of the work of the Convention is necessary.

The set-up and mode of operation at the Convention can be seen to have led to an ambiguous situation, despite all efforts made for clarification. These were marked in particular by the institutional divide between the Præsidium, which was the 'first-mover' in drafting the general part of the Constitutional Treaty, and Working Group VII, which drafted the provisions on external action. Compared to the wording of the Treaties in the Nice version and before, the Convention has certainly brought about progress in terms of simplification and streamlining.[103] Furthermore, it has been claimed that making a general statement on the values and objectives of the Union at the very beginning of the Treaties has provided the text of the Treaties its spirit or 'breath (of life)' (*souffle*).[104] Nonetheless, a parallelism emerged between the paragraph on the external side of general Union objectives (Art 3(4) Draft CT) and the general objectives of EU external action

[98] *Laeken Declaration* (n 92) 21.
[99] *Laeken Declaration* (n 92) 24.
[100] *Laeken Declaration* (n 92) 24.
[101] For a useful timeline of the work of the Convention see C Church and D Phinnemore, *Understanding the European Constitution: An Introduction to the EU Constitutional Treaty* (Routledge, 2006) 23–4.
[102] Craig (n 86) 6.
[103] See M Cremona, 'The Draft Constitutional Treaty: External Relations and External Action' (2003) 40 *Common Market Law Review* 1347, 1348–9; also A Pilette and E de Poncins, 'Valeurs, objectifs et nature de l'Union' in G Amato, H Bribosia, and B De Witte (eds), *Genesis and Destiny of the European Constitution* (Bruylant, 2007) 309.
[104] Pilette and de Poncins (n 103) 309.

(Art III-193 Draft CT), which do not directly refer to each other. In addition, by using former Art 11 TEU (Nice version) on CFSP objectives as the template for the general article on EU external action, and without replacing it with something else in the section on the CFSP, the latter policy is deprived of its own set of specific objectives, as is the section on economic, financial, and technical aid. In contrast, the external policies on trade and development, as well as the newly codified section on humanitarian aid, all received a set of policy-specific objectives. The Lisbon Treaty did not remedy these ambiguities and asymmetries.

In contrast to IGCs, the Convention was composed of representatives from both the national governments of the Member States as well as their parliaments, in addition to representatives from the European Commission and Parliament. It consisted of 220 members in total (including full members and alternates) and was presided over by former French president Valéry Giscard d'Estaing. It was run by a 'Præsidium' consisting of the Chairman, two Vice-chairmen and ten more members, and assisted by a Secretariat. In addition to plenary sessions, it conducted its work through a division into eleven working groups, of which Group VII on External Action, chaired by former Belgian Prime Minister Jean-Luc Dehaene,[105] is of particular relevance. These institutional divisions within the Convention are of importance in understanding that the TEU post-Lisbon contains not one but two catalogues of overarching external relations objectives, ie Art 3(5) and Art 21 TEU. The former was drawn up within the Præsidium, while the latter stems from deliberations within Working Group VII.

From the outset of the Convention, the external dimension for European integration was clearly present. In Giscard d'Estaing's speech at the inaugural meeting of the Convention, he noted that '[t]he world would feel better if it could count on Europe, a Europe which spoke with a single voice to affirm respect for its alliances, but also to proclaim, whenever necessary, a message of tolerance and moderation, of openness towards difference, and of respect for human rights'.[106] It was also in this speech that Giscard d'Estaing revealed that the Convention might 'open the way towards a Constitution for Europe',[107] provided it could reach the necessary consensus. Remedying the fact that '[t]oday's world lacks a strong, united and peaceful Europe',[108] as Giscard d'Estaing saw it, thus also became a constitutional endeavour.

In the initial 'listening phase' of the Convention and during the subsequent deliberations, Peter Norman stresses the importance accorded to defining the values and objectives of the Union. Spelling out these definitions was 'important if the Convention were to stay true to the goal of producing a constitutional treaty,

[105] Craig (n 86) 6–7.

[106] Secretariat of the European Convention, speeches delivered at the inaugural meeting of the Convention on 28 February 2002, Brussels, 5 March 2002, CONV 4/02, Annex 4: *Introductory Speech by President V Giscard d'Estaing to the Convention on the Future of Europe*, 16.

[107] *Introductory Speech by President V Giscard d'Estaing* (n 106) 20; see also Closa (n 89) 186, stating that 'the most important self-transformational action of the Convention was the subtle modification of its mandate, an action that transformed the initial nature of the Convention itself'.

[108] *Introductory Speech by President V Giscard d'Estaing* (n 106) 15.

which would be easy to understand and so help bridge the gap between the Union and its citizens'.[109] The idea that internal values should also 'translate' into the conduct of the external relations of the Union was emphasized during the general debate at the Convention on external action in July 2002, where '[m]any stressed that the values which were at the heart of the Union were themselves an argument for a greater role globally, and that these values should underpin and inform the Union's external policies'.[110]

Drafting the first and general part of the Constitutional Treaty was a task the Præsidium reserved for itself. This included what would later become Art 3(5) TEU on the general external relations objectives of the EU. Already in October 2002, the Præsidium proposed a preliminary draft constitution,[111] which, even though it lacked substantive content, established the basic structure—the so-called 'skeleton'[112]—of the future Constitutional Treaty. There, a general article on Union objectives, including one with a clear external dimension, was provided in Part One on the 'Constitutional Structure'.[113] On 6 February 2003, the Præsidium circulated the first set of draft articles for the general part. According to the Præsidium, the 'philosophy' underlying the provisions on objectives contained therein was 'to set out the general objectives justifying the very existence of the Union and its action for its citizens in a more cross-sectoral fashion'.[114] Following this, the members of the Convention 'proposed a mass of additional objectives after the Præsidium presented its first draft articles'.[115] The amount of 169 amendment proposals concerning the article on general objectives reveals how contentious the definition of general objectives of the Union was considered to be. Of these 169 amendments,[116] about one-third concerned the substance of the paragraph on the role of the EU in the world. Next to the theme of socio-economic objectives surrounding ideas such as a high level of employment, provision of services of general interest, and competitiveness, the formulation of explicitly external objectives of the Union appears as the most prominent and widely discussed topic in these amendments. The final version of the provision for the Constitutional Treaty stayed close to the basic layout and tone of the formulation of the Præsidum, while also including additions on, for instance, free

[109] Norman (n 97) 65.

[110] Secretariat of the European Convention, Summary Report of the Plenary Session—Brussels, 11 and 12 July 2002, Brussels, 16 July 2002, CONV 200/02, 3 (pt 6).

[111] See Craig (n 86) 10. [112] Norman (n 97) 56–60.

[113] Secretariat of the European Convention, Preliminary draft Constitutional Treaty, Brussels, 28 October 2002, CONV 369/02, Art 3.

[114] Secretariat of the European Convention, Draft of Articles 1 to 16 of the Constitutional Treaty, Brussels, 6 February 2003, CONV 528/03, Annex I: *Draft Text of the Articles of the Treaty Establishing a Constitution for Europe*, 12.

[115] Norman (n 97) 66.

[116] European Convention Website, last updated 28 July 2003, <http://European-convention.europa.eu/EN/amendments/amendments45f5.html?content=3&lang=EN>; see also the summary in Secretariat of the European Convention, Reactions to Draft Articles 1 to 16 of the Constitutional Treaty—Analysis, Brussels, 26 February 2003, CONV 574/1/03 REV 1, 41–3.

and fair trade, strict compliance, and development of international law and the United Nations (UN).[117]

Unlike the general article on Union objectives, the part of the Draft Constitutional Treaty devoted specifically to external action was first discussed and drawn up by Working Group VII on External Action. The group set out the main questions it was to tackle, the first of which was: 'How should the interests of the Union be defined and formulated?'[118] This mandate, however, did not explicitly state that these should be codified in any way in the treaty, which was an idea that emerged only later within the working group.

Already at its first meeting, the working group 'felt that it was important for the EU to think first of the objectives of a common policy before discussing the modalities and institutional aspects' and that a 'common policy could not be an end in itself but needed to be seen and designed in view of the objectives the EU aimed at'.[119] It was stressed that there was a 'need to better define the underlying objectives of EU external action', which, as one member suggested, could be clarified through a 'declaration of principles'.[120] Such a declaration of principles followed in a document presented by Alain Lamassoure, the representative of the European Parliament at the Convention. There, Lamassoure argued that if the Union was to have plenary competence in the area of foreign affairs, it should also specify the objectives and principles that would guide it, both towards its own members as well as to the rest of the world.[121] The working group subsequently confirmed 'the need to define more clearly *in a future Treaty* the underlying objectives of EU external action'.[122] The idea that the overarching objectives for the Union in its external relations should not only be more clearly defined but also codified into the constitutional treaty itself now also had taken root in the Working Group on External Action.

On 16 December 2002, the Final Report of the Working Group on External Action was published, which was presented shortly afterwards to the Convention. The report noted 'a very large consensus in the Group on the need to define in the Treaty the underlying principles and general objectives of EU external action, in a manner that would be clear to the public and the EU's partners'.[123] Moreover, the

[117] Compare Draft Treaty establishing a Constitution for Europe, Brussels, 18 July 2003, CONV 850/03, Art 3(4) with Draft of Articles 1 to 16 of the Constitutional Treaty, Annex I (n 114) 3 (Art 3(4)).

[118] Secretariat of the European Convention, Mandate of Working Group VII on External Action, Brussels, 10 September 2002, CONV 252/02, 2.

[119] Secretariat of the European Convention, Working Group VII on External Action, Summary of the meeting held on 24–25 September 2002, Brussels, 1 October 2002, CONV 307/02, 2.

[120] Secretariat of the European Convention (n 119) 3.

[121] Secretariat of the European Convention, Contribution submitted by Mr Alain Lamassoure, 'Declaration of Principles Underlying the Union's External Relations', Brussels, 3 October 2002, CONV 315/02, 2.

[122] Secretariat of the European Convention, Working Group VII on External Action, Summary of the meeting held on 8 October 2002, Brussels, 11 October 2002, CONV 342/02, 6 (pt 19) (emphasis added).

[123] Secretariat of the European Convention, Working Group VII on External Action, *Final Report of Working Group VII on External Action*, Brussels, 16 December 2002, CONV 459/02, 2.

report stated that the working group had 'reached a very large consensus on a text defining "principles and objectives"'[124] and recommended that it should be included in the future treaty in a section dealing with all aspects of EU external relations.

According to the Convention Secretariat, 'Working Group VII opted for the approach of defining the principles and objectives of all external action in a single Article, therefore deleting the lists of specific objectives of each policy area concerned in existing Articles'.[125] This would have constituted a break in view of how Union policies had been organized in the treaties up to that point. However, this deletion and bundling exercise would only succeed partially. On the one hand, the draft text submitted by the working group to the Convention focused on EU external action and had indeed omitted the individual objectives of the CFSP, ie development cooperation and economic, financial, and technical aid. On the other hand, the CCP had retained objectives of its own and the newly inserted section on humanitarian aid specifically stated to which ends it should be used. In addition, there remained a section on relations with international organizations and third countries, which highlights certain organizations. This situation would be carried over into the Constitutional Treaty and eventually the Lisbon Treaty.

3.6 The new law in force: The Lisbon Treaty

Following a process of 'legal verification', the IGC approved the text of the Treaty establishing a Constitution for Europe in June 2004, which was signed by the Member States in Rome in October of that year.[126] What followed was the well-known story of the failed referendums in France and the Netherlands in 2005, the subsequent 'period of reflection' that led to the drafting of a 'reform treaty' that would not replace the existing treaties and acts but would instead amend them, as the Nice Treaty and the others did before it.[127] The 'constitutional concept', pushed forward by the Convention and its Chairman in particular, was officially abandoned by the Council.[128] However, this is not to be equated with depriving the legal order of the Union of its constitutional features (see Chapter 3, section 2.4).[129] The resulting 'Lisbon Treaty', which had also

[124] *Final Report of Working Group VII on External Action* (n 123) 13.

[125] Secretariat of the European Convention, Draft Articles on external action in the Constitutional Treaty, Brussels, 23 April 2003, CONV 685/03, 25. This approach is at odds with the stance of the Præsidium, as pointed out by Norman (n 97) 66, that the general, broadly defined objectives of the first part of the Constitution would be followed by more detailed, policy-specific ones, unless external relations would be understood as one single policy.

[126] Piris (n 86) 17–19; and Craig (n 86) 16–20; and G de Búrca, *The EU on the Road from the Constitutional Treaty to the Lisbon Treaty*, Jean Monnet Working Paper 03/08.

[127] Treaty of Lisbon amending the Treaty on European Union and the Treaty establishing the European Community, signed at Lisbon, 13 December 2007 (Lisbon Treaty) [2007] OJ C 306/1.

[128] European Council, Presidency Conclusions of the Brussels European Council 21 and 22 June 2007, 20 July 2007, 11177/1/07 REV 1, Annex I: *IGC Mandate*, 15 (pt 1).

[129] See in particular S Griller, 'Is this a Constitution? Remarks on a Contested Concept' in S Griller and J Ziller (eds), *The Lisbon Treaty: EU Constitutionalism without a Constitutional Treaty?* (Springer, 2008).

experienced ratification difficulties with the first failed referendum in Ireland, among other things, entered into force on 1 December 2009.[130]

The Lisbon Treaty has taken over the vast majority of reforms proposed by the Constitutional Treaty, leaving out mostly symbolic provisions such as those on the flag, anthem, motto, or the term 'Union Foreign Minister'. The reformed foreign policy objectives of the Union, by contrast, have not been left behind or cut back in the Lisbon Treaty, thus preserving the expanded body of these objectives as devised by the Convention. Compared to the Constitutional Treaty, there is only one substantive change. In the first sentence of Art 3(5) TEU, there is an addition that next to upholding and promoting its interests, the Union is also to 'contribute to the protection of its citizens'.[131] It has been argued that this was added upon the request of the French government at the Intergovernmental Conference of 2007,[132] in order to stress that the Union is not a 'Trojan horse' of globalization, but indeed protects its citizens from the downsides of globalization.[133]

In terms of the basic structure, which under Lisbon consists of two treaties instead of just one document (the TEU and TFEU), a relocation of the articles on the general objectives of EU external action had taken place. In the Constitutional Treaty (and its draft version), this article was put at the top of Title V of Part III on Union External Action (Art III-292 CT), which also contained all of the external policies of the Union. Under the Lisbon Treaty, by contrast, this article was moved into the TEU (corresponding with Part I of the Constitutional Treaty) and is situated at the start of its Title V on 'General Provisions on the Union's External Action and Specific Provisions on the Common Foreign and Security Policy' (Art 21 TEU). This title contains only the external policy area of the CFSP while the others, already located in the TEC before, are to be found now in Part V of the TFEU on 'External Action by the Union'.[134] This separation highlights the two basic modes for the conduct of EU external relations. Nonetheless, Art 205 TFEU, which introduces this part, refers back to Art 21 TEU. Separating the CFSP from the other areas of EU external action in the Lisbon Treaty was, according to Javier Solana, 'important conceptually' to the United Kingdom.[135] In spite of this, the House of Commons concluded that 'the insertion of principles and objectives for all EU external action into the Treaty on European Union is a sensible way of encouraging greater EU policy coherence while two main EU Treaties

[130] See Piris (n 86) 23–63; and Craig (n 86) 20–5.

[131] This did not appear in the Constitutional Treaty (Art I-3(4) CT). See F-X Priollaud and D Siritzky, *Le Traité de Lisbonne: Texte et commentaire article par article des nouveaux traités Européens (TUE-TFUE)* (La Documentation Française, 2008) 36.

[132] E de Poncins, *Le traité de Lisbonne en 27 clés* (Lignes de repères, 2008) 75–6.

[133] J-L Sauron, *Comprendre le Traité de Lisbonne: Texte consolidé intégral des traités* (Gualino, 2007) 30.

[134] See also Craig (n 86) 380–3.

[135] Cited from the evidence presented by Mr Solana before the British House of Commons, House of Commons Foreign Affairs Committee, *Foreign Policy Aspects of the Lisbon Treaty*, Third Report of Session 2007–8 (The Stationery Office, 2008) 31; see also J Wouters, D Coppens, and B De Meester, 'The European Union's External Relations after the Lisbon Treaty' in S Griller and J Ziller (eds), *The Lisbon Treaty: EU Constitutionalism without a Constitutional Treaty?* (Springer, 2008) 146–9.

remain in place'.[136] Furthermore, the European Neighbourhood Policy (ENP), which was to be found in Part I, Art I-57 CT, remains after the Lisbon Treaty separate from external action, being grouped with the 'Common Provisions' of Title I of the TEU (Art 8 TEU).[137]

4. Emerging Patterns in Europe and the World

In the course of the history of European integration, global ambitions have increased and eventually found their way into the EU Treaties, which today exhibit a wealth of both general and sector-specific objectives in the area of foreign policy. In order to put this development into a comparative context, it is important to set the EU Treaties against the texts of the twenty-seven documentary EU Member State constitutions (ie excluding the UK) as well as a representative set of third-country constitutions.[138] This includes both the operative text as well as the preambles to these constitutional texts.[139] The Indian constitution is one of the few examples where foreign policy objectives have been located in the section on constitutional objectives (see Chapter 1, section 5.3). In most other cases, they are normally part of the section in the constitution dealing with a country's international relations, or they may be scattered throughout the text. The focus here will be on constitutional objectives with an explicit reference to the outside world and some discernible dynamic elements. The fact that some of these objectives have their origins in the internal sphere and then extrapolate internal values externally is not considered a reason to exclude them. On the contrary, such extrapolations will be considered as evidence for the 'translation function' that foreign policy objectives can exhibit (Chapter 1, section 5).

This chapter shows that foreign policy objectives abound in contemporary constitutional law. They are not the exception, but rather the rule, both within and outside of the EU. They vary starkly, however, in terms of the degree of detail that is provided. Four indicative categories can be distinguished: Firstly, the constitutions

[136] House of Commons Foreign Affairs Committee (135) 31.

[137] See also S Blockmans, 'Friend or Foe? Reviewing EU Relations with its Neighbours Post Lisbon' P Koutrakos (ed), *The European Union's External Relations a Year after Lisbon*, CLEER Working Paper 2011/3, 115–16, who criticizes that the ENP is kept separate from both the CFSP and the TFEU instruments found elsewhere in the Treaties.

[138] For the quotes used here, the English language translations of the Oceana Law® database 'Constitutions of the Countries of the World Online' have been used for the most part, which is now 'Oxford Constitutions of the World', <http://oxcon.ouplaw.com/home/OCW>. In case of doubts, the original language was consulted where possible in terms of language skills, otherwise the official (albeit not authoritative) English language translations from government websites were used. Where this was not the case, the source is specified in the footnotes.

[139] For Kotzur, it is especially the preamble which serves as a 'site for self-reassurance and identity of the constitutional state' (in the original: 'Ort verfassungsstaatlicher Selbstvergewisserung und Identitätsfindung'): Kotzur (n 12) 196. Moreover, while preambles usually do not contain enforceable rights or competence norms, they do serve as an interpretive lens shaping other constitutional norms.

that are virtually silent in this regard;[140] secondly, minimalist constitutions which include only a generic pledge to international law and/or scarce generic statements concerning being part of a wider community, supporting international cooperation or fostering historic ties;[141] thirdly, intermediate cases of constitutions, which develop these normative statements on what the international order *should* look like, or to which kind of international order the respective country *should* contribute through its foreign policy, but remain short of containing an actual 'list' of concrete objectives and guiding principles;[142] and, fourthly, extensive cases where constitutions provide an entire list of objectives, values, and principles for a country's foreign policy.[143] The EU Treaties would squarely fall into the extensive category. More than half of the constitutions scrutinized here fall either into the intermediate or extensive category as regards foreign policy objectives. Among the EU Member State constitutions, also half fall into these two categories. Only three Member State constitutions are silent on the matter, including the UK's 'unwritten' constitution (see Figure 2.1).

In order to organize the foreign policy objectives from these various constitutions and with a view to comparing them to the EU Treaties, this section follows the categories devised by Sommermann. This includes general references to a 'global' common good, instances for both 'perfectible' and 'imperfectible' foreign policy objectives, and examples for each of the substantive foreign policy categories: prohibition of war, international/collective security, international law, human rights, integration, and international solidarity and development.[144] As the section demonstrates, the EU Treaties contain codified objectives for each of these categories.

A comparative analysis of constitutional foreign policy objectives reveals that these too are mostly 'imperfectible', ie they require constant effort and can never be entirely achieved (Chapter 1, section 4.1). However, there are a number of instances where objectives could indeed be achieved. Those concern mostly national unity or reunification and the accession to certain specified treaties or international organizations. Regarding independence and unity, the classic example comes from the

[140] Following this typology, the Belgian and Swedish constitutions rank as those not including any explicit external objectives. The non-documentary constitution of the UK could also be placed within the silent category, as the aspects of the British foreign policy that are constitutionally relevant are of a procedural character, such as treaty-making. See eg I Loveland, *Constitutional Law, Administrative Law, and Human Rights: A Critical Introduction*, 7th edn (OUP, 2015) 111. Among the third country constitutions considered, only the constitution of the United States is silent on foreign policy objectives.

[141] A minimalist approach can be found in eleven of the EU Member State constitutions: Austria, Denmark, Estonia, the Czech Republic, Finland, France, Greece, Latvia, Luxembourg, Poland, and Spain. Of the third-country constitutions, the Turkish, Egyptian, and Indonesian constitutions can be considered as minimalist.

[142] Among the EU Member State constitutions, eleven could be qualified as intermediate: Bulgaria, Croatia, Cyprus, Hungary, Italy, Lithuania, Malta, the Netherlands, Romania, Slovakia, and Slovenia. Of the third-country constitutions, intermediate constitutions would be those of Japan, Russia, and South Africa.

[143] Three EU Member State constitutions could be described as extensive: Germany, Ireland, and Portugal. Extensive third-country constitutions include the constitutions of China, Brazil, India, and Switzerland, ie three of the four BRIC countries.

[144] Sommermann (n 18) 237.

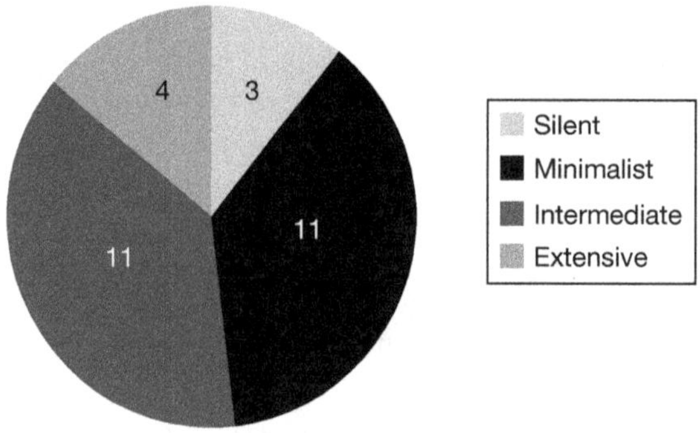

Figure 2.1 Foreign Policy Objectives in the EU Treaties and the Twenty-eight EU Member State Constitutions

German context, as reunification was both an issue of foreign policy and constitutional importance.[145] Before the amendment in the wake of reunification, the preamble to the Basic Law stated that '[t]he entire German people is called upon to accomplish, by free self-determination, the unity and freedom of Germany'.[146] In its current version, the post-reunification Basic Law states that unification was 'achieved'.[147] In other cases, unity has not yet been achieved and thus remains a pertinent issue of foreign policy. For instance, the preamble to the Irish constitution stresses the intention to seek 'the unity of our country restored'.[148] The goal of reunification is stated afterwards in a straightforward way:

> It is the firm will of the Irish nation, in harmony and friendship, to unite all the people who share the territory of the island of Ireland, in all the diversity of their identities and traditions, recognizing that a united Ireland shall be brought about only by peaceful means with the consent of a majority of the people, democratically expressed, in both jurisdictions in the Island.[149]

Even though this formulation might arguably amount to one EU Member State claiming territory currently belonging to another, it expresses at the same time respect for the modern and internationally recognized definition of the right to self-determination, ie the need to be exercised in a non-violent and democratic manner.[150] Among the third countries, a similar case is encountered with China regarding the status of Taiwan. With regard to national unity, the Chinese constitution states that 'Taiwan is part of the sacred territory of the People's Republic of China' and that '[i]t is the lofty duty of the entire Chinese people,

[145] See Röben (n 24) 192–5. [146] Preamble, German constitution (pre-reunification).
[147] Preamble, German constitution (post-reunification).
[148] Preamble, Irish constitution. [149] Art 3(1) Irish constitution.
[150] See eg United Nations General Assembly, Resolution 1514 (XV) (1960), 14 December 1960, *Declaration on the Granting of Independence to Colonial Countries and Peoples.*

including our compatriots in Taiwan, to accomplish the great task of reunifying the motherland'.[151]

Concerning international treaties and organizations, an example would be the reference in the Romanian constitution to NATO membership.[152] Even though it states that a parliamentary majority is necessary to join NATO, it can be seen as an underlying state objective to seek NATO membership. Given that Romania joined NATO in 2004, this particular objective can then be deemed achieved. Similarly, the Croatian constitution presupposes EU membership, which has now been achieved, with its various references to the EU.[153] Furthermore, in the case of the EU, the mandate to accede to the European Convention on Human Rights can be seen as a perfectible foreign policy objective.[154]

4.1 References to the global 'common good'

Internationally expanded understandings of the common good, for instance, towards a regional community or even a global *bonum commune humanitatis*, can be found in numerous constitutions today. These developments indicate that the common good of a given polity is increasingly linked to outside factors, and that wider notions of the common good exceeding national borders are constitutionally acknowledged.

The strongest universalist call can arguably be found in the first article of the German Basic Law. Following the declaration of inviolability of human dignity in the preceding paragraph, it states that '[t]he German people therefore acknowledge inviolable and inalienable human rights *as the foundation of every community, of peace and justice in the world*'.[155] This amounts to an assertion of the universal status of such rights and the establishment of a nexus between them and global peace and justice.

Other European constitutions also explicitly refer to a wider common good. The preamble to the Irish constitution speaks of 'concord ... with other nations'.[156] In addition, in the operative part, 'Ireland affirms its devotion to the ideal of peace and friendly co-operation amongst nations founded on international justice and morality',[157] thereby introducing morality next to the idea of global justice.

The idea of furthering global justice, which can also be seen as the external expression of the substantive notion of the rule of law (Chapter 1, section 4.1), can be found in other constitutions too. The Portuguese constitution, which arguably

151 Preamble, Chinese constitution.
152 Art 149 Romanian constitution.
153 Arts 143–6 Croatian constitution.
154 Art 6(2) TEU.
155 Art 1(2) German constitution (emphasis added). See also Häberle (n 8) 1281, who notes the similar expression found in the preamble to the European Convention on Human Rights: 'Reaffirming their profound belief in those Fundamental Freedoms which are the foundation of justice and peace in the world'.
156 Preamble, Irish constitution.
157 Art 29(1) Irish constitution; see further on the foreign policy objectives contained in Art 29 Irish constitution G Hogan and G Whyte, *J.M. Kelly: The Irish Constitution*, 4th edn (LexisNexis, 2003) 491–506.

provides the most detailed catalogue of foreign policy principles among all the EU Member States, states that Portugal's international relations will be governed, inter alia, by the overarching objectives of 'the emancipation and progress of humanity'[158] and 'the creation of an international order capable of safeguarding peace and justice in relations between peoples'.[159] The Greek constitution stipulates that Greece 'pursues the strengthening of peace and of justice, and the fostering of friendly relations between peoples and States'.[160] The Bulgarian constitution contains explicit objectives in the operative part concerning not only 'national security and independence of the country, the well-being and the fundamental rights and freedoms of the Bulgarian citizens' but also, crucially, 'the promotion of a just international order'.[161] The Lithuanian constitution further stipulates the foreign policy objective that the country 'shall contribute to the creation of the international order based on law and justice'.[162] Sometimes, the image of the 'family' is used to describe a sense of togetherness beyond the state. This includes the Polish constitution, which in its preamble, next to 'universal human values', refers to the awareness 'of the need for cooperation with all countries for the good of the Human Family'.[163] Similarly, the preamble to the Czech constitution states that the country sees itself as 'a member of the family of European and World democracies'.[164]

More generic expressions of being part of a wider community are present in numerous other constitutions. They usually refer to notions such as peace and international cooperation. The Spanish constitution, in its preamble, expresses the nation's will to '[c]ooperate in the strengthening of peaceful relations and effective cooperation among all the peoples of the earth'.[165] Similarly, the Finnish constitution states in its first article that 'Finland participates in international co-operation for the protection of peace and human rights and for the development of society'.[166]

Among the selected third countries, similar expressions of the wider common good can be detected. The constitution of the People's Republic of China, in its long and verbose preamble, states that 'China's achievements in revolution and construction are inseparable from support by the people of the world' and that '[t]he future of China is closely linked with that of the whole world'.[167] The Egyptian constitution states early on in its preamble that 'the Arab nation of Egypt is the heart of the whole world'.[168] In addition, the first article states that 'Egypt is

[158] Art 7(1) Portuguese constitution; see further on Portuguese constitutional foreign policy objectives in this provision PJ Canelas de Castro, 'Portugal's World Outlook in the Constitution of 1976' (1995) 71 *Boletim da Faculdade de Direito da Universidade de Coimbra* 489, who assesses them in essentially the same manner as the doctrines of Chapter 1, and also gives examples from practice showing their implementation by the Portuguese state.

[159] Art 7(2) Portuguese constitution.

[160] Art 2(2) Greek constitution.

[161] Art 24(2) Bulgarian constitution.

[162] Art 135(1) Lithuanian constitution.

[163] Preamble, Polish constitution.

[164] Preamble, Czech constitution.

[165] Preamble, Spanish constitution.

[166] Art 1(3) Finnish constitution; see also Art Q Hungarian constitution.

[167] Preamble, Chinese constitution.

[168] Preamble, Egyptian constitution. This refers to the version adopted in 2014, which replaced the previous version devised under the now ousted President Morsi in 2012, which for its part succeeded the pre-revolutionary version of 1971.

part of the Arab nation and enhances its integration and unity' and that, furthermore, it 'is part of the Muslim world, belongs to the African continent, is proud of its Asian dimension, and contributes to building human civilization',[169] thus highlighting regional, religious and global allegiances.

Moreover, the Japanese constitution contains a number of noteworthy references regarding the wider common good. It expresses the people's determination to 'secure for ourselves and our posterity the fruits of peaceful cooperation with all nations'.[170] Next to the global dimension, the reference to 'posterity' introduces an inter-temporal element. Furthermore, the determination 'to preserve our security and existence, trusting in the justice and faith of the peace-loving peoples of the world' is expressed, as is the belief 'that no nation is responsible to itself alone, but that laws of political morality are universal; and that obedience to such laws is incumbent upon all nations who would sustain their own sovereignty and justify their sovereign relationship with other nations'.[171] Similarly, the Indonesian constitution expresses the objective 'to participate toward the establishment of a world order based on freedom, perpetual peace and social justice' as well as the belief in 'just and civilised humanity'.[172]

The Swiss constitution, in its preamble, stipulates the aim 'to strengthen freedom and democracy, independence and peace in solidarity and openness toward the world'.[173] In the operative part, it states among the goals of the confederation that it 'commits itself to an enduring conservation of the natural resources and to a peaceful and just international order'.[174]

The constitution of Brazil sets out in its Title I on 'fundamental principles' a list of principles governing the international relations of Brazil, which next to 'national independence' features 'cooperation among people for the progress of humanity'.[175] Similarly, the Indian constitution contains as a directive principle of state policy the goal to 'maintain just and honourable relations between nations'.[176]

In the preamble to the Turkish constitution, it is again possible to identify the notion of 'family' in the determination 'to attain the standards of contemporary civilization as an honourable member with equal rights of the family of world nations'.[177] It also refers to 'the desire for and belief in "Peace at home, peace in the world"',[178] which is Turkey's national motto and a generic reminder of the interdependence between the international and external spheres. Similarly, the South African constitution, in its preamble, expresses the intention to '[b]uild a united and democratic South Africa able to take its rightful place as a sovereign state in

[169] Art 1(1) Egyptian constitution. [170] Preamble, Japanese constitution.
[171] Preamble, Japanese constitution. [172] Preamble, Indonesian constitution.
[173] Preamble, Swiss constitution. [174] Art 2(4) Swiss constitution.
[175] Art 4 Brazilian constitution. See on the 'dirigiste', one could also say programmatic or aspirational, features of the Brazilian constitution in general, L Tupiassu, 'Le droit constitutionnel: Les institutions politiques' in D Païva de Almeida (ed), *Introduction au droit brésilien* (Harmattan, 2006) 18.
[176] Art 51(b) Indian constitution. [177] Preamble, Turkish constitution.
[178] Preamble, Turkish constitution. Art 2 Turkish constitution reiterates that the state is 'based on the fundamental tenets set forth in the Preamble'.

the family of nations'.[179] The constitution of the Russian Federation, also in the preamble, expresses consciousness 'that we are part of the world community'.[180]

The many references in national constitutions to a more 'just' international (legal) order or notions of 'international community' are echoed in the EU Treaties, which make explicit references to the global context and to the contours of a 'global common good'. The drafting history discussed in section 3 of this chapter showed that the links between the European common good and the outside world have been present from the very beginning of European integration. These ambitions have been made explicit in the primary law in the form of the enumeration of principles the EU 'seeks to advance in the wider world'.[181] The most obvious evocation of a 'global common good' (or *bonum commune humanitatis*)[182] is to be found in the objective to 'promote an international system based on stronger multilateral cooperation and good global governance'.[183] Taken together, these objectives on the external action of the EU represent not only an acknowledgement of a global common good closely intertwined with the Union's own, but also set out the contours of this common good and highlight specific aspects of it.

4.2 The prohibition of war

The constitutional prohibition of war can be seen as a manifestation of the general objective of peace, as well as the answer of constitutional law to the prohibition to use force in international law. Several constitutions utter such an answer. Among the European constitutions, the German Basic Law not only refers in its preamble to the 'will to promote world peace as an equal partner in a united Europe',[184] but also operationalizes this objective through an operative provision declaring as unconstitutional '[a]cts tending to and undertaken with the intent of disturbing the peaceful relations between nations, especially to prepare for a war of aggression'.[185] Moreover, the Basic Law orders such acts (through a legislative command) to 'be made a punishable offence'.[186] Similarly, but without further elaboration, the Italian constitution prohibits war. It includes an article according to which 'Italy rejects war as an instrument of aggression against the freedoms of other peoples and as a means for settling international controversies'.[187]

179 Preamble, South African constitution.

180 Preamble, Russian constitution.

181 Art 21(1), first subpara TEU.

182 J Isensee, 'Gemeinwohl im Verfassungsstaat' in J Isensee and P Kirchhof (eds), *Handbuch des Staatsrechts der Bundesrepublik Deutschland. Volume IV: Aufgaben des Staates*, 3rd edn (C.F. Müller, 2006) 21.

183 Art 21(2)(h) TEU.

184 Preamble, German constitution.

185 Art 26(1) German constitution.

186 Art 26(1) German constitution.

187 Art 11 Italian constitution. The Hungarian constitution in its pre-2011 version contained a similar renunciation of war in Art 6(1), which was not taken over into the current, post-2011 version. For a critical assessment of constitutional reform and trends in Hungary, see R Uitz, 'Can You Tell when an Illiberal Democracy is in the Making? An Appeal to Comparative Constitutional Scholarship from Hungary' (2015) 13 *International Journal of Constitutional Law* 279.

Less categorical in their renunciation of war are the Portuguese and the Slovenian constitutions. Short of prohibiting the use of force in its own foreign policy, and instead suggesting several means of banishing the use of force from international relations, the Portuguese constitution 'advocates ... the achievement of simultaneous and controlled general disarmament, the dissolution of political-military blocs and the establishment of a collective security system, with a view to the creation of an international order capable of safeguarding peace and justice in relations between peoples'.[188] Meanwhile, the Slovenian constitution limits itself to stating that '[i]n the maintenance of security the state proceeds principally from a policy of peace, and an ethic of peace and non-aggression'.[189]

The most famous and most strongly worded constitutional renunciation of war is found among the third-country constitutions. The Japanese constitution provides that '[a]spiring sincerely to an international peace based on justice and order, the Japanese people forever renounce war as a sovereign right of the nation and the threat or use of force as means of settling international disputes'.[190] The term 'forever' elevates this commitment to a meta-constitutional level.[191] This renunciation is operationalized through the commitment that 'land, sea, and air forces, as well as other war potential, will never be maintained'.[192] All the same, and while the renunciation of war is deemed a 'fundamental principle of the Constitution',[193] this does not mean that Japan renounces its right of self-defence. The Japanese government contends that these provisions are not incompatible with 'the maintenance of a "minimum necessary force" for defence'.[194] This reflects the flexibility inherent in constitutional foreign policy objectives, as well as the importance of the basic goal of the state to provide security, which is construed here as allowing derogations from the renunciation of war.

As for the EU, historically, the process of European integration itself can be seen as an enterprise to make war in Europe, as the Schuman Declaration put it, 'not merely unthinkable, but materially impossible'.[195] According to Walter Hallstein, the 'desire for peace' is paramount among the motives for European unification.[196] However, unlike the constitutions of Italy or Japan, the EU Treaties do not contain an outright constitutional renunciation of war. Nonetheless, like in many other constitutions, the Treaties contain elements that suggest restraining the use of force by the European Union and in international relations at large. Above all, the references to the 'strict observance' of international law and the principles of

[188] Art 7(2) Portuguese constitution. [189] Art 124(3) Slovenian constitution.

[190] Art 9 Japanese constitution. Fisler Damrosch, referring to both Germany and Japan, highlights 'the intense Allied efforts to transform these states into demilitarized constitutional democracies'. L Fisler Damrosch, 'Constitutional Control of Military Actions: A Comparative Dimension' (1991) 85 *American Journal of International Law* 92, 99; also Sommermann (n 18) 380–1.

[191] Akin to the 'eternity clause' (*Ewigkeitsklausel*) of Art 79(3) of the German constitution.

[192] Art 9 Japanese constitution. [193] H Oda, *Japanese Law*, 2nd edn (OUP, 1999) 37.

[194] Oda (n 193) 38. See further also C Aoi 'Asserting Civilian Power or Risking Irrelevance? Japan's Post-Cold War Policy Concerning the Use of Force' in S Katada, H Maull, and T Inoguchi (eds), *Global Governance: Germany and Japan in the International System* (Ashgate, 2004).

[195] Schuman Declaration (n 36).

[196] In the original: 'Verlangen nach Frieden': Hallstein (n 35) 68.

the UN Charter (Art 3(5) TEU) and later to the 'respect for the principles of the United Nations Charter and international law' (Art 21(1) TFEU) would include, as a cornerstone of the UN Charter and contemporary international law, the prohibition to use force in international relations. Despite not being a member of the UN, the EU thus commits unilaterally through its constitutional framework to this principle of the Charter, which is also part of customary international law.[197]

Moreover, the prohibition of war, understood as a narrow definition of international peace, is implied in the many and prominent references to 'peace' in the Treaties. Apart from preambular language,[198] the promotion of peace figures prominently as the first aim to be pursued by the Union in the first paragraph of Art 3 TEU. Paragraph five then mandates the Union to 'contribute to peace' in its relations with the wider world. Art 8 TEU on neighbourhood policy further pledges 'to establish an area of prosperity and good neighbourliness ... characterised by close and *peaceful relations* based on cooperation'.[199] In Art 21(1) TEU, 'peace', curiously, is not listed among 'the principles which have inspired [the Union's] own creation, development and enlargement', but appears in the catalogue of external action objectives in the following paragraph as the goal to 'preserve peace'.[200]

It ought to be added that a 'common defence' has not yet been established within the Union.[201] Currently, it would clearly be beyond the powers and means of the EU per se to wage wars in the first place.[202] The means which the Common Security and Defence Policy (CSDP) provides to the Union in the framework of the Petersberg tasks do not include this high end of the spectrum of military confrontation (Art 43(1) TEU). They do, however, include contributions to the maintenance of international peace.

4.3 Collective security and defence

Next to the outright prohibition of war, systems of collective security and defence can be seen as a feature of contemporary international relations providing a second-best option in the absence of a monopoly of force on the international level to effectively cater to the general objective of peace. As constitutional foreign policy objectives, they can be understood as an external expression of the overall objective of providing security as the foremost manifestation of the pursuit of the

[197] Art 2(4) UN Charter; stating that this is part of customary international law, see the ruling of the International Court of Justice in *Military and Paramilitary Activities in and against Nicaragua (Nicaragua v United States of America)* (Merits) [1986] ICJ Rep 14, para 181.

[198] Eleventh recital of the preamble, TEU: 'RESOLVED to implement a common foreign and security policy ... in order to promote peace, security and progress in Europe and in the world'.

[199] Art 8(1) TEU (emphasis added).

[200] Art 21(2)(c) TEU.

[201] Art 42(2), first subpara TEU, stating that a common defence will only be established 'when the European Council, acting unanimously, so decides', following which '[i]t shall in that case recommend to the Member States the adoption of such a decision in accordance with their respective constitutional requirements'.

[202] Note in this regard also Art 347 TFEU which refers in the context of ensuring the proper functioning of the internal market, among other things, to 'war' with regard to the Member States, not the Union, and measures they might be prompted to take.

common good. Several constitutions explicitly refer to collective security organizations. These references can be both of a positive or negative nature in that they either call for or prohibit the accession to such an arrangement.

Considering the positive manifestations, in the German Basic Law, in the article governing the transfer of sovereign powers to international organizations, it is stated that '[w]ith a view to maintaining peace, the Federation may enter into a system of mutual collective security; in doing so it consents to such limitations upon its sovereign powers as will bring about and secure a lasting peace in Europe and among the nations of the world'.[203] The combination of a competence norm ('the Federation may') with goal-oriented elements ('[w]ith a view to maintaining peace' and 'as will bring about and secure') serve as an illustration of a goal-oriented competence allocation (Chapter 1, section 4.1).

Membership of the United Nations would certainly qualify as being part of a system of collective security, where enforcement action can be taken against any member of the organization. However, these examples raise the question of whether joining a collective defence arrangement would also be covered, ie a common commitment to assist each other against outside aggression.[204] At least in the German context, this question has been answered in the affirmative. The *Bundesverfassungsgericht* confirmed in its decision concerning so-called 'out-of-area operations', that it was irrelevant whether the system concerned exclusively its own circle of members or also committed members to a 'mutual defence against external threats'.[205]

Similar provisions can be found in the Italian and Romanian constitutions. In the Italian constitution, following its renunciation of war, it is stated that the country 'agrees, on conditions of parity with other states, to the limitations of sovereignty necessary for an order that ensures peace and justice among Nations' and 'promotes and encourages international organisations having such ends in view'.[206] More explicitly, the Romanian constitution mentions NATO membership, stating that 'Romania's accession to the North Atlantic Treaty shall be decided by a law adopted by the Chamber of Deputies and the Senate in joint session'.[207] Even though this is neither the explicit language of command or objective, it privileges this organization by the reference itself and establishes a clear constitutional competence to join that organization. NATO membership appears as a constitutional desideratum.

There are also mixed examples, which, on the one hand, endorse collective security, but on the other, reject collective defence. For instance, a provision in the Portuguese constitution calls for 'the dissolution of political-military blocs and the establishment of a collective security system, with a view to the creation of an international order capable of safeguarding peace and justice in relations between

[203] Art 24(2) German constitution.

[204] On this distinction, see P Robinson, *Dictionary of International Security* (Polity Press, 2008) 40.

[205] Decision of 12 July 1994 (*out-of-area-Einsätze*), BVerfGE 90, 286, para 236; see also Sommermann (n 18) 240–1.

[206] Art 11 Italian constitution.

[207] Art 149 Romanian constitution.

peoples'.[208] However, this is rather puzzling since Portugal itself is a member of the 'political-military bloc' of NATO, and recalls the weak prohibitive force of such norms.

Similarly, the constitution of Malta, while being generally elliptical and vague on external affairs, provides rather extensive guidance in terms of safeguarding the country's neutrality. It stipulates that 'Malta is a neutral state actively pursuing peace, security and social progress among all nations by adhering to a policy of non-alignment and refusing to participate in any military alliance'.[209] This entails restricting the presence of foreign military forces and facilities in Malta. An exception is made with regard to 'the exercise of the inherent right of self-defence ... or in pursuance of measures or actions decided by the Security Council of the United Nations'.[210] From these provisions it follows that Malta is only prepared to participate in collective security within the framework of the UN, but not any other arrangement. In addition, in a now anachronistic way, this provision also denies the use of Malta's shipyards 'in accordance with the principles of non-alignment ... to the military vessels of the two superpowers'.[211]

Another mixed, if not a priori contradictory, case is Austria. With a view to safeguarding neutrality within its 'comprehensive national defence', the Austrian constitution states the aim 'to safeguard its independence toward the outside and the unity of the Federal territory, especially for the maintenance and defence of the permanent neutrality'.[212] Neutrality is considered to be among the constitutional objectives (*Staatszielbestimmungen*) of Austrian law.[213] This would entail a clear rejection of collective defence systems. However, the Austrian constitution states in a later provision that the country shall participate in the EU's CSDP,[214] which includes a commitment to mutual assistance in case of armed aggression (Art 42(7) TEU) (see further Chapter 4, section 3.1).

Among the third countries, there is arguably the world's most famous neutral state—Switzerland. In the Swiss federal constitution, it is stated as the task of both the federal legislature and executive to safeguard 'the external security, the independence, and the neutrality of Switzerland'.[215] This does not exclude joining collective security arrangements such as the one established by the United Nations, which the Confederation joined in 2002. However, 'the entry into organizations for collective security or into supranational communities'[216] requires approval

[208] Art 7(2) Portuguese constitution.
[209] Art 1(3) Maltese constitution.
[210] Art 1(3)(b)(i) Maltese constitution.
[211] Art 1(3)(e) Maltese constitution.
[212] Art 9a(1) Austrian constitution read together with Austrian constitutional law (ie having constitutional rank but is not incorporated into the main constitutional document) of 26 October 1955, the so called 'neutrality law' (*Neutralitätsgesetz*). See further R Walter and H Mayer, *Grundriß des österreichischen Bundesverfassungsrechts*, 9th edn (Manz, 2000) 83–5.
[213] T Öhlinger, *Verfassungsrecht*, 9th edn (Facultas, 2012) 73–4.
[214] Art 23j(1) Austrian constitution.
[215] Arts 173(1)(a) and 185(1) Swiss constitution. Further on the neutrality principle, as well as the challenges it faces in the contemporary international security environment, U Häferlin, W Haller, and H Keller, *Schweizerisches Bundesstaatsrecht*, 8th edn (Schulthess, 2012) 64–6.
[216] Art 140(1)(b) Swiss constitution. Note, however, that the Swiss accession to the United Nations was not based on this provision, but was brought about through a people's initiative (*Volksinitiative*) for

through an obligatory popular referendum. In this way, the Swiss constitution links two of the country's hallmark structural elements with the pursuit of security: neutrality and direct democracy.

Turning to the EU, by preventing war *among* its Member States, the Union can be seen as a 'security community' in the sense of Karl Deutsch.[217] By contrast, the Union and its predecessors never constituted a collective security arrangement. In addition, the Union is not a member of the UN or other collective security organizations. Concerning the Union as such, there are neither obligations nor prohibitions concerning joining collective security organizations in the Treaties, in contrast to the ones contained, for instance, in the constitutions of Germany, Romania, or Malta.

The Lisbon Treaty introduced a mutual assistance clause, following the 'absorption' of the Western European Union (WEU) by the European Union,[218] which makes the Union a collective defence arrangement (Art 42(7) TEU).[219] However, this duty for mutual assistance does not involve the Union as such. Whereas the Solidarity Clause of Art 222 TFEU, in the event of a terrorist attack or a disaster, addresses both the Member States and the Union, the mutual assistance clause establishes only an obligation between Member States.

In spite of this, many of the objectives found in the Treaties encourage contributions by the Union to international security writ large, ie measures addressing threats to international security that do not reach the threshold of armed aggression among states.[220] The notion of international security appears, firstly, in the eleventh recital of the TEU preamble, as well as among the various contributions to be made by the EU in its external action under Art 3(5). It figures twice in Art 21 TEU, with a general reference (Art 21(2)(a) TEU) and a more specific objective of the Union to 'prevent conflicts and strengthen international security' (Art 21(2)(c) TEU). Within

the partial revision of the constitution (Art 139(5) Swiss constitution), which led to Art 197(1) Swiss constitution specifically allowing accession to the UN. See Häferlin, Haller, and Keller (n 215) 313.

217 See eg P Tsakaloyannis, *The European Union as a Security Community: Problems and Prospects* (Nomos, 1996); for the concept see K Deutsch et al, *Political Community and the North Atlantic Area: International Organization in the Light of Historical Experience* (Princeton University Press, 1957).

218 A statement of the Presidency of the Permanent Council of the WEU of 31 March 2010 makes explicit reference to Art 42 TEU, and concludes that the WEU now has 'accomplished its historical role' and will cease its activities by June 2011: see Statement of the Presidency of the Permanent Council of the WEU on behalf of the High Contracting Parties to the Modified Brussels Treaty, 31 March 2010; see also R Wessel, 'The EU as Black Widow: Devouring the WEU to Give Birth to a European Security and Defence Policy' in V Kronenberger (ed), *The EU and the International Legal Order: Discord or Harmony?* (T.M.C. Asser Press, 2001).

219 The wording of Art 42(7) TEU is akin to that of Art V North Atlantic Treaty (NAT) and Art V WEU Treaty; see further P Koutrakos, 'The Role of Law in Common Security and Defence Policy: Functions, Limitations and Perceptions' in P Koutrakos (ed), *European Foreign Policy: Legal and Political Perspectives* (Edward Elgar, 2011) 237–40; and A Marchetti, 'Die Gemeinsame Sicherheits- und Verteidigungspolitik' in A Marchetti and C Demesmay (eds), *Der Vertrag von Lissabon: Analyse und Bewertung* (Nomos, 2010) 262–3.

220 Note also E Regelsberger and D Kugelmann, 'Art 21 EUV' in R Streinz (ed), *EUV/AEUV: Vertrag über die Europäische Union und Vertrag über die Arbeitsweise der Europäischen Union*, 2nd edn (C.H. Beck, 2012) 237 (marginal no 5), who stress that in Art 21(2) TEU, apart from the self-referred letter (a), all other objectives, including the preservation of peace, are aimed at the outside world.

the Union's external action, it is the CFSP which focuses on international security, operationalized militarily through the CSDP. In the framework of the latter, the Union may use Member State assets 'on missions outside the Union for peace-keeping, conflict prevention and strengthening international security in accordance with the principles of the United Nations Charter' (Art 42(1) TEU), ie for the Petersberg tasks as laid down in Art 43 TEU.[221] However, this does not mean that the Union's notion of security is focused on such tasks alone. As was already made clear in the European Security Strategy of 2003[222] and in its 2008 Implementation Report,[223] the Union has a comprehensive understanding of security. It recognizes that 'internal and external aspects of security are indissolubly linked',[224] that responses to security threats require the use of all policy tools with an emphasis on multilateral solutions, and are aimed at addressing the root causes of threats and finding sustainable solutions.[225]

In practice, this understanding has been confirmed by the rapid development of the CSDP, as the EU has conducted over twenty missions since 1999, either of a military, civilian, or combined character, involving next to more traditional peace-keeping also rule of law missions, security sector reform, and the securing of elections.[226] The Union furthermore contributes to regional security arrangements elsewhere, such as to the African Peace Facility.[227]

4.4 International law

The promotion of international law as a foreign policy objective has mostly been discussed in terms of the status of international law within the domestic legal order.[228] However, this objective goes further than the mere reception of international law. It can also encompass fostering compliance with international law in

[221] Art 43(1) TEU. These now include joint disarmament operations, humanitarian and rescue tasks, military advice and assistance tasks, conflict prevention and peacekeeping tasks, tasks of combat forces in crisis management, including peacemaking and post-conflict stabilization, and may contribute to the fight against terrorism.

[222] European Council, *A Secure Europe in a Better World, European Security Strategy*, 12 December 2003.

[223] European Council, *Report on the Implementation of the European Security Strategy: Providing Security in a Changing World*, S407/08, Brussels, 11 December 2008.

[224] *European Security Strategy* (n 222) 2.

[225] Joint Communication to the European Parliament and the Council, *The EU's Comprehensive Approach to External Conflict and Crises*, Brussels, 11 December 2013 JOIN(2013) 30 final; see further S Biscop, 'The European Security Strategy in Context: A Comprehensive Trend' in S Biscop and J Andersson (eds), *The EU and the European Security Strategy: Forging a Global Europe* (Routledge, 2008).

[226] See for an overview, M Webber, 'The Common Security and Defence Policy in a Multilateral World' in P Koutrakos (ed), *European Foreign Policy: Legal and Political Perspectives* (Edward Elgar, 2011); and in detail G Grevi, D Helly, and D Keohane (eds), *European Security and Defence Policy: The First 10 Years (1999–2009)* (EUISS, 2009); also J Howorth, *Security and Defence Policy in the European Union*, 2nd edn (Palgrave Macmillan 2014) 144–89.

[227] See M Brosig, 'The Emerging Peace and Security Regime in Africa: The Role of the EU' (2011) 16 *European Foreign Affairs Review* 107.

[228] See eg Sommermann (n 18) 241–2 and the references there; Vereshchetin (n 17) 6–8; and Kotzur (n 12) 213–14.

general (ie also by others) and committing to the observance of international law in the conduct of a country's foreign policy, also with a view to developing further the international legal order. There is empirical evidence in modern constitutions for these different manifestations.

Several constitutions contain general pledges to respect international law, often in addition to more specific provisions on its implementation at home. Examples would be the Czech constitution, which states that '[t]he Czech Republic shall observe its obligations under international law',[229] or the Polish constitution, which stipulates that the country 'respects international law binding upon it'.[230] An interesting nuance is contained in the Romanian constitution, which provides that '[t]he Romanian state pledges to fulfil to the letter and in good faith the obligations resulting from the treaties to which it is a party'.[231] The reference 'to the letter' (or 'exactly', *întocmai* in Romanian) suggests a special effort on the part of that country to comply, but also raises the question of whether there exist various degrees of compliance with international law. This is analogous to the wording of 'strict compliance' in Art 3(5) TEU.

On the status of international law in the domestic legal order, Sommermann concludes that most European constitutions provide both for the incorporation of international treaties as well as compliance with customary international law. Some constitutions explicitly grant precedence to international law over ordinary domestic legislation.[232] As an example of such an open constitutional stance on international law, the German Basic Law stipulates that 'the general rules of international law shall be an integral part of federal law' and 'shall take precedence over the laws and directly create rights and duties for the inhabitants of the federal territory'.[233] Similarly, the Greek constitution states that '[t]he generally recognized rules of international law, as well as international conventions as of the time they are ratified by statute and become operative according to their respective conditions, shall be an integral part of domestic Greek law and shall prevail over any contrary provision of the law'.[234] The Estonian constitution even calls the '[g]enerally recognized principles and rules of international law ... an inseparable part of the Estonian legal system'.[235]

One constitution which is particularly open towards international law is that of the Netherlands, which grants primacy to international law over national law in general: 'Within the Kingdom, legal regulations in force shall not be applicable if such application is incompatible with provisions of treaties that are binding on all persons or of resolutions by international organizations.'[236] This includes not only agreements but also acts of international organizations. In addition, the

229 Art 1(2) Czech constitution.

230 Art 9 Polish constitution; see also Art 1(2) Slovakian constitution.

231 Art 11(1) Romanian constitution.

232 Sommermann (n 18) 242.

233 Art 25 German constitution.

234 Art 28(1) Greek constitution; see also Art 8 Slovenian constitution.

235 Art 3(1) Estonian constitution; see also to that effect Art 10(1) Italian constitution; Art 9(1) Austrian constitution; Art 8(1) Portuguese constitution; and Art 141 Croatian constitution.

236 Art 94 Netherlands constitution.

Netherlands may even conclude treaties which conflict with the constitution, without the need for prior constitutional amendment, instead requiring a parliamentary supermajority.[237] Somewhat less open, in the sense that reference is only made to international treaties but not to customary international law, are, for instance, the French, Czech, Bulgarian, and Romanian constitutions.[238] The Finnish constitution makes its limit to such openness explicit, stating that '[a]n international obligation shall not endanger the democratic foundations of the Constitution'.[239] Compliance as an objective, therefore, must be pursued within the framework of the fundamental constitutional structures.

Apart from questions concerning the domestic status of international law, one can also find constitutional objectives stating that international law should guide foreign policy in several European constitutions.[240] The Irish constitution pledges that 'Ireland accepts the generally recognised principles of international law *as its rule of conduct in its relations with other States*'.[241] This makes clear that there are other concerns beyond the question of domestic implementation of international law. The Bulgarian constitution, in an article devoted to foreign policy, provides that the country 'shall conduct its foreign policy in accordance with the principles and norms of international law'.[242] Similarly, the Lithuanian constitution provides that '[i]n implementing its foreign policy the Republic of Lithuania shall follow the universally recognised principles and norms of international law'.[243] The Romanian constitution, in the same vein, states that the country bases its 'relations of good neighbourliness ... on the principles and generally accepted norms of international law'.[244]

Moreover, certain constitutions emphasize the role of judicial dispute settlement in international law. The German Basic Law, for one, provides that 'the Federation shall accede to agreements providing for general, comprehensive, and compulsory international arbitration'.[245] This is, strictly speaking, a constitutional command, but with clear undertones of the objective of promoting international law. By the same token, yet in a more general fashion, the Irish constitution provides that 'Ireland affirms its adherence to the principle of the pacific settlement of international disputes by international arbitration or judicial determination'.[246]

Regarding the promotion of international law not just in static but also dynamic terms, a particularly pertinent provision exists in the constitution of the Netherlands. It contains the concise statement that '[t]he Government promotes the development of

[237] Art 91(3) Netherlands constitution. See further C Kortmann and P Bovend'Eert, *Constitutional Law of the Netherlands: An Introduction* (Kluwer Law International, 2007) 163–6.

[238] Art 55 French constitution; Art 10 Czech constitution; Art 5(4) Bulgarian constitution; and Art 11(2) Romanian constitution.

[239] Art 94(3) Finnish constitution.

[240] See also Vereshchetin (n 17) 11–13, with additional examples.

[241] Art 29(3) Irish constitution (emphasis added).

[242] Art 24(1) Bulgarian constitution.

[243] Art 135(1) Lithuanian constitution.

[244] Art 10 Romanian constitution.

[245] Art 24(3) German constitution.

[246] Art 29(2) Irish constitution.

the international legal order'.[247] The notion of 'development' bolsters the character of this norm as an objective and the external dimension of the rule of law in general. It shows that the promotion of international law is not just about compliance with the *lex lata*, but also about active participation *de lege ferenda*. In addition, the armed forces are relied upon, as the constitution of the Netherlands provides that their purpose is not only to defend the country and protect its interests, but also 'to maintain and promote the international legal order'.[248]

Among third countries, general pledges of compliance with international law can also be found. The Japanese constitution states that '[t]he treaties concluded by Japan and established laws of nations shall be faithfully observed'.[249] A more general compliance objective can be found in the Indian constitution, which includes, as a guiding principle, 'to foster respect for international law and treaty obligations in the dealings of organized peoples with one another'.[250]

In terms of domestic status, the constitution of the United States, which is in general rather taciturn regarding foreign policy, sweepingly states that 'all Treaties made, or which shall be made, under the Authority of the United States, shall be the supreme Law of the Land'.[251] The more recent constitution of the Russian Federation is more extensive, as it provides that '[g]enerally recognized principles and norms of international law as well as international agreements of the Russian Federation shall be a constituent part of its legal system', and that '[i]f an international agreement of the Russian Federation establishes rules which differ from those stipulated by law the rules of the international agreement shall apply'.[252]

The Swiss constitution, in addition to a general commitment to 'respect International Law',[253] contains an explicit reference to *ius cogens*. It stipulates that a popular initiative for the partial revision of the constitution shall be declared invalid by the federal legislature if it violates peremptory norms of international law.[254] Moreover, in a total revision of the constitution, *ius cogens* may not be violated.[255] This could be seen as acknowledging the superiority of *ius cogens* over constitutional law as well as the democratically expressed will of the people.[256]

In terms of international law as the benchmark of foreign policy, the preamble to the Chinese constitution provides that:

> China adheres to an independent foreign policy as well as to the five principles of mutual respect for sovereignty and territorial integrity, mutual non-aggression, non-interference in each other's internal affairs, equality and mutual benefit, and peaceful coexistence in developing diplomatic relations and economic and cultural exchanges with other countries.[257]

[247] Art 90 Netherlands constitution. Note, however, that the addressee here is the government, and not the state as a whole, which emphasizes again the prominent role of the executive in foreign policy.

[248] Art 97(1) Netherlands constitution.

[249] Art 98(2) Japanese constitution.

[250] Art 51(c) Indian constitution.

[251] Art 6(2) United States constitution.

[252] Art 15(4) Russian constitution; see also Art 231(4) and (5) South African constitution.

[253] Art 5(4) Swiss constitution.

[254] Art 139(3) Swiss constitution; see also Art 194(2) Swiss constitution.

[255] Art 193(4) Swiss constitution.

[256] See Häferlin, Haller, and Keller (n 215) 564.

[257] Preamble, Chinese constitution. However, the lack of thick 'constitutionalism' in the Chinese legal order, for instance, the lack of judicial review and 'constitutionalism' in general, may well qualify

Thus, what is outlined is a list of rather classic international law concepts that the Chinese constitution highlights in the context of its external relations.[258]

The South African constitution, next to a general rule of harmonious interpretation for the courts,[259] stresses international law as a benchmark for national security policy, as '[n]ational security must be pursued in compliance with the law, including international law'.[260] This represents a pledge to international law in a sensitive area, which can be operationalized to a certain extent through the provision that the national security services (ie the armed forces, the police, and the intelligence service)[261] 'must act, and must teach and require their members to act, in accordance with the Constitution and the law, including customary international law and international agreements binding on the Republic'.[262]

Regarding international adjudication, the preamble to the constitution of Brazil contains the commitment 'in the domestic and international orders, to the peaceful solution of disputes'.[263] The endeavour to 'encourage settlement of international disputes by arbitration' is also part of the directive principles of the foreign relations of India.[264]

For the EU, compliance with international legal obligations as well as the fostering of compliance and the development of international law in general is a highly significant goal, given that it is itself a creature of international law. This significance is also reflected in its primary law. Art 3(5) TEU contains the objective to contribute to 'the strict observance and the development of international law, including respect for the principles of the United Nations Charter'. This is taken up in Art 21 TEU, which includes 'respect for the principles of the United Nations Charter and international law' among the guiding principles of EU external action (Art 21(1) TEU) as well as the consolidation of 'principles of international law' among the objectives listed (Art 21(2)(b) TEU). In addition, both the CSDP and the development of the overseas countries of the Member States are to be carried out 'in accordance with the principles' of the UN Charter.[265] Similarly, with regard to humanitarian aid, it is made explicit that Union operations are to be 'conducted in compliance with the principles of international law' (Art 214(2) TFEU).

the importance of the text of its constitution: see Q Zhang, 'A Constitution without Constitutionalism? The Paths of Constitutional Development in China' (2010) 8 *International Journal of Constitutional Law* 950. This would apply of course also to other countries of which the constitutional credentials are questionable. Nevertheless, the fact that a codification of foreign policy objectives has taken place remains significant as a visible benchmark: see Kotzur (n 12) 202.

258 The 'five principles' have their origin in an international agreement between China and India from 1954 and have since been an essential part of Chinese foreign policy. See A Bradford and E Posner, 'Universal Exceptionalism in International Law' (2011) 52 *Harvard International Law Journal* 3, 26.

259 Art 233 South African constitution.

260 Art 198(c) South African constitution.

261 Art 199(1) South African constitution.

262 Art 199(5) South African constitution; see also Art 200(2) stating that '[t]he primary object of the defence force is to defend and protect the Republic, its territorial integrity and its people in accordance with the Constitution and the principles of international law regulating the use of force'.

263 Preamble, Brazilian constitution.

264 Art 51(d) Indian constitution.

265 Art 42(1) TEU and sixth recital of the preamble, TFEU, respectively.

These references to 'international law' constitute a novelty introduced by the Draft Constitutional Treaty. Neither the pre-Lisbon TEU nor the TEC explicitly mentioned 'international law' as such. They contained provisions only stating that agreements concluded by the Union (and the former Community) were binding.[266] Post-Lisbon, international law is mentioned no fewer than five times in the Treaties.[267] A stronger emphasis is also put on the UN Charter, as the pre-Lisbon TEU only spoke of the CFSP being conducted 'in conformity' and 'in accordance' with the Charter.[268] Now, Art 3(5) TEU calls for the 'strict observance of',[269] and Art 21(1) calls for 'respect' for, the principles of the UN Charter.

It has been argued that the new formulation was adopted at the Convention against the backdrop of the Iraq War in 2003.[270] This is plausible, given that the early drafts of the Constitutional Treaty did not contain a specific reference to the UN Charter,[271] and that there were amendment proposals calling for the distancing of the EU Treaties from any endorsement of the 'Bush doctrine'.[272] This is confirmed further by the European Security Strategy, which was adopted in 2003 as a step towards reuniting the EU after internal division over the Iraq War.[273]

Given that the legal order of the EU itself is a creation of international law (see further Chapter 3, section 2.1), the very success of the Union legal order itself, or what Hallstein calls the 'majesty of law',[274] could be seen as a case of strict observance, and, more importantly, as an unprecedented development of international law by interweaving it with the national legal orders of the Member States.[275]

[266] See Art 24(6) TEU (Nice version) on agreements under the former second pillar: 'Agreements concluded under the conditions set out by this Article shall be binding on the institutions of the Union'; Art 38 TEU (Nice version), referring to Art 24 TEU (Nice version) on agreements under the former third pillar; Art 300(7) TEC on Community agreements: 'Agreements concluded under the conditions set out in this Article shall be binding on the institutions of the Community and on Member States.'

[267] Art 3(5) TEU; Art 21(1), first subpara TEU; Art 21(2)(b) TEU; Art 77(4) TFEU; Art 214(2) TFEU.

[268] Art 11(1) TEU (Nice version).

[269] The term strict observance appeared during the Convention in an amendment proposal: Secretariat of the European Convention, Suggestion for amendment of Article 3 by Dr Sylvia-Yvonne Kaufmann, <http://european-convention.europa.eu/docs/Treaty/pdf/3/Art3%20Kaufmann.pdf>, calling for the inclusion of the formulation 'strikte[n] Einhaltung des Völkerrechts' ('strict observance of international law') (bold omitted).

[270] R Barents, *Het Verdrag van Lissabon: Achtergronden en commentaar* (Kluwer, 2008) 189.

[271] Art 3(4) *Draft Text of the Articles of the Treaty Establishing a Constitution for Europe* (n 114).

[272] See the explanatory note in Secretariat of the European Convention, Proposition d'amendement à l'Article 3 déposée par M Caspar Einem, <http://european-convention.europa.eu/Docs/Treaty/pdf/3/Art%203%20Einem.pdf>.

[273] J Howorth, *Security and Defence Policy in the European Union*, 1st edn (Palgrave Macmillan, 2007) 199–200; and G García-Dobarco González, 'Unión Europea, política exterior y Constitución. Apuntas de un viaje a Itaca' in E Álvarez Conde and V Garrido Mayol (eds), *Comentarios a la Constitución Europea. Libro III* (Tirant lo Blanch, 2004) 1311–12.

[274] In the original: 'Die Majestät des Rechts': Hallstein (n 35) 53.

[275] See eg N Walker, 'Late Sovereignty in the European Union' in N Walker (ed), *Sovereignty in Transition* (Hart Publishing, 2003); JHH Weiler, *The Constitution of Europe: 'Do the New Clothes Have an Emperor?' and Other Essays on European Integration* (CUP, 1999) 10–101.

From this perspective, the rule of law, after having been successfully established within the EU, is translated into the objective to further it at the international level. This finds confirmation in Art 21 TEU, which lists among the principles to guide the Union's action on the international scene, after having guided its own creation development and enlargement, both 'the rule of law' and 'respect for the principles of the United Nations Charter and international law'.[276]

In terms of practice, the Union has established itself as a forerunner in the promotion of international law and its further development through practice, treaty-making, and participation in international organizations.[277] Prominent examples include the efforts to universalize certain norms, such as the prohibition of the death penalty[278] or the EU's vocal support for the International Criminal Court (ICC).[279] The Union also uses various tools in order to induce others to respect international law. These include measures of positive and negative conditionality, as well as economic sanctions against countries. The international law norms the EU would like to have respected coincide with the substantive values and norms referred to in Art 3(5) TEU. A good illustration of this is the GSP+ (GSP standing for Generalised System of Preferences) mechanism, which offers developing countries additional trade preferences on condition that they ratify and effectively implement twenty-seven international conventions relating to core human rights and labour standards, and environmental and good governance principles.[280]

Concerning the question of the status of international law within the Union legal order, a topic that has received considerable academic attention,[281] the new

[276] Art 21(1), first subpara TEU.

[277] See extensively F Hoffmeister, 'The Contribution of EU Practice to International Law' in M Cremona (ed), *Developments in EU External Relations Law* (OUP, 2008).

[278] See eg Council of the European Union, Declaration by the Presidency on behalf of the European Union on the occasion of the 20th anniversary of the adoption of the Second Optional Protocol to the ICCPR aiming at the abolition of the death penalty, Brussels, 15 December 2009, 17525/09 (Presse 377); and EU Guidelines on the Death Penalty: revised and updated version, <http://www.consilium.europa.eu/uedocs/cmsUpload/10015.en08.pdf>. See also I Manners, 'Normative Power Europe: A Contradiction in Terms?' (2002) 40 *Journal of Common Market Studies* 235, 245–52, who uses this as a case study for the 'normative power' of the EU (see further Chapter 5, section 5.2).

[279] See eg Council of the European Union, Common Position 2003/444/CFSP of 16 June 2003 on the International Criminal Court [2003] OJ L 150/67. Further J Wouters and S Basu, 'The Creation of a Global Criminal Justice System: The European Union and the International Criminal Court' in C Ryngaert (ed), *The Effectiveness of International Criminal Justice* (Intersentia, 2009).

[280] See Regulation (EU) 512/2011 of the European Parliament and of the Council of 11 May 2011 amending Council Regulation (EC) No 732/2008 applying a scheme of generalised tariff preferences for the period from 1 January 2009 to 31 December 2011 [2011] OJ L 145/28; and Council Regulation (EC) No 732/2008 of 22 July 2008 applying a scheme of generalised tariff preferences for the period from 1 January 2009 to 31 December 2011 [2008] OJ L 211/1, Art 8 together with Annex III, Part A.

[281] For a recent account see the various contributions in E Cannizzaro, P Palchetti, and R Wessel (eds), *International Law as Law of the European Union* (Martinus Nijhoff, 2012); and Eeckhout (n 76) 323–436; also C Tietje, 'The Status of International Law in the European Legal Order: The Case of International Treaties and Non-Binding International Agreements' in J Wouters, A Nollkaemper, and E de Wet (eds), *The Europeanisation of International Law: The Status of International Law in the EU and Its Member States* (T.M.C. Asser Press, 2008).

notion of 'strict observance of international law' gives a broader textual reference for the EU being bound by international law, and not just by international agreements. The more general reference to international law codifies the case law of the CJEU stipulating that other forms of international law, such as customary international law, are also binding on the Union.[282] Following the Lisbon reform, the Court can now point to Art 3(5) TEU as the point of departure for the EU's commitment to international law in general.[283]

However, the case law of the CJEU clearly shows that a contribution to the 'strict observance' of international law does not mean always according direct effect to it,[284] or using it as a standard of review in annulment actions (which are both determined by internal criteria).[285] Furthermore, it does not suggest that international law—including the UN Charter—is superior to EU primary law, including its general principles containing fundamental rights.[286] Rather, what it means is that the EU, including its judiciary, will take measures short of upsetting the internal constitutional order and hierarchy of norms of the Union in order to avoid putting the Union in a position of non-compliance with its international legal obligations. This includes the 'harmonious interpretation' of Union measures with international law,[287] and a 'muted dialogue' with other international bodies such as the WTO Appellate Body,[288] and arguably the UN Security Council.[289]

[282] Case C-162/96 *Racke GmbH & Co. v Hauptzollamt Mainz*, EU:C:1998:293, para 49. See also for decisions of international bodies, PJ Kuijper, 'Customary International Law, Decisions of International Organisations and Other Techniques for Ensuring Respect for International Legal Rules in European Community Law' in J Wouters, A Nollkaemper, and E de Wet (eds), *The Europeanisation of International Law: The Status of International Law in the EU and Its Member States* (T.M.C. Asser Press, 2008).

[283] Case C-366/10 *Air Transport Association of America*, EU:C:2011:864, para 101.

[284] See in detail F Jacobs, 'Direct Effect and Interpretation of International Agreements in the Recent Case Law of the European Court of Justice' in A Dashwood and M Maresceau (eds), *Law and Practice of EU External Relations: Salient Features in a Changing Landscape* (CUP, 2008); on the approach of the CJEU to WTO law see M Bronckers and PJ Kuijper, 'WTO Law in the European Court of Justice' (2005) 42 *Common Market Law Review* 1313.

[285] The CJEU ruled that it could examine 'the validity of Community legislation in the light of an international treaty only where the nature and the broad logic of the latter do not preclude this and, in addition, the treaty's provisions appear, as regards their content, to be unconditional and sufficiently precise': Case C-308/06 *Intertanko*, EU:C:2008:312, para 45. Further J Wouters, 'The Tormented Relationship between International Law and EU Law' in P Bekker, R Dolzer, and M Waibel (eds), *Making Transnational Law Work in the Global Economy: Essays in Honour of Detlev Vagts* (CUP, 2010) 218–20.

[286] Joined Cases C-402/05 P and C-415/05 P *Kadi and Al Barakaat*, EU:C:2008:461, para 285.

[287] See eg Case C-89/99 *Schieving Nijstad*, EU:C:2001:438; and Joined Cases C-300/98 and C-392/98 *Parfums Christian Dior*, EU:C:2000:688; further F Casolari, 'Giving Indirect Effect to International Law within the EU Legal Order: The Doctrine of Consistent Interpretation' in E Cannizzaro, P Palchetti, and R Wessel (eds), *International Law as Law of the European Union* (Martinus Nijhoff, 2012).

[288] M Bronckers, 'From "Direct Effect" to "Muted Dialogue"' (2008) 11 *Journal of International Economic Law* 885.

[289] Using Bronckers' term with regard to the UN Security Council, J Larik, 'Two Ships in the Night or in the Same Boat Together: How the ECJ Squared the Circle and Foreshadowed Lisbon in its Kadi Judgment' (2010) 13 *Yearbook of Polish European Studies* 149, 167.

4.5 Human rights

An aspect of the promotion of the rule of law of particular importance is that of human rights. Numerous national constitutions recognize their special significance, some even attesting to their universal validity. Next to integrating them into the national legal order, ie pursuit of the objective through compliance, human rights promotion is in several cases also made an explicit foreign policy objective.

As a strong expression of the universalist claim, one can recall the famous starting line of the German Basic Law that '[h]uman dignity shall be inviolable'[290] and that '[t]he German people therefore acknowledge inviolable and inalienable human rights as the foundation of every community, of peace and justice in the world'.[291] The Latvian constitution, in the same vein, provides that '[t]he State shall recognize and protect fundamental human rights in accordance with this Constitution, laws and international agreements binding upon Latvia'.[292]

Concerning status within domestic law, one can distinguish between constitutional requirements of interpretation and application of domestic law in conformity with human rights, on the one hand, and the approach of allocating a particular position within the hierarchy of norms to international human rights, on the other.[293]

Within the category of harmonious interpretation, the Spanish constitution states that those fundamental rights 'recognized by the Constitution shall be construed in conformity with the Universal Declaration of Human Rights and international treaties and agreements thereon ratified by Spain'.[294] The Portuguese and Romanian constitutions too call for interpretation and application of national law (including constitutional law) in conformity with the Universal Declaration of Human Rights.[295] Furthermore, these two constitutions explicitly consider themselves as a minimum standard and not a ceiling concerning individual rights.[296]

For direct incorporation, the Slovakian constitution provides that:

> International treaties on human rights and fundamental freedoms, international treaties whose execution does not require a law and international treaties which directly establish rights or obligations of natural persons or legal persons and which were ratified and promulgated in a manner laid down by law shall have primacy over the laws.[297]

In the Swedish constitution, there is a special reference to the European Convention on Human Rights (ECHR), stating that '[n]o act of law or other provision may be adopted which contravenes Sweden's undertakings under the European Convention for the Protection of Human Rights and Fundamental Freedoms'.[298] With a view to restrictions on human rights in a state of emergency, the Finnish

[290] Art 1(1) German constitution. [291] Art 1(2) German constitution.
[292] Art 89 Latvian constitution. [293] Sommermann (n 18) 242–3.
[294] Art 10(2) Spanish constitution.
[295] Art 16(2) Portuguese constitution; Art 20(1) Romanian constitution.
[296] Art 16(1) Portuguese constitution; Art 20(2) Romanian constitution.
[297] Art 7(5) Slovakian constitution. [298] Chapter 2, Art 19 Swedish constitution.

constitution states that these restrictions must be 'compatible with Finland's international obligations concerning human rights'.[299]

The Polish constitution makes special references to minority rights and labour unions. In stating that Polish is the official language, it adds that this 'does not infringe upon national minority rights resulting from ratified international agreements'.[300] Regarding the historically motivated provision on trade unions and employers' organizations, it is stated that the scope of their freedom of association 'may only be subject to such legal limitations as are permissible in accordance with international agreements to which the Republic of Poland is a party'.[301]

As a foreign policy objective, the promotion of human rights features prominently in the Finnish constitution, which states in its first article that 'Finland participates in international co-operation for the protection of peace and human rights and for the development of society'.[302] One can also point to the emphasis that the Italian constitution puts on labour rights, as it is framed as an external objective, according to which Italy 'promotes and encourages international agreements and organizations whose aim is to affirm and regulate labour rights'.[303]

Among the third-country constitutions, examples for these different manifestations of the human rights objective can be identified. The concept of human dignity features, for instance, in the Egyptian constitution. Following several references to this concept in the preamble, dignity appears first in the part on rights, freedoms, and duties.[304]

The South African constitution is a clear case of constitutionally mandated harmonious interpretation of ordinary domestic law. Accordingly, '[w]hen interpreting any legislation, every court must prefer any reasonable interpretation of the legislation that is consistent with international law over any alternative interpretation that is inconsistent with international law'.[305] The human rights dimension becomes evident in view of the special reference to the national bill of rights, for the interpretation of which courts '*must* consider international law',[306] and 'may consider foreign law'.[307]

Concerning the incorporation of human rights, the text of the Russian constitution can be considered as 'markedly international law-friendly'.[308] It provides that '[i]n the Russian Federation human and civil rights and freedoms shall be recognized and guaranteed according to the generally recognized principles and

[299] Art 23 Finnish constitution.

[300] Art 27 Polish constitution. Note also the preamble to the Croatian constitution, which states that national minorities exercise 'their national rights in compliance with the democratic norms of the United Nations and the countries of the free world'.

[301] Art 59(4) Polish constitution. [302] Art 1(3) Finnish constitution.

[303] Art 35(3) Italian constitution. [304] Art 51 Egyptian constitution.

[305] Art 233 South African constitution.

[306] Art 39(1)(b) South African constitution (emphasis added).

[307] Art 39(1)(c) South African constitution. Further H Klug, *The Constitution of South Africa: A Contextual Analysis* (Hart Publishing, 2010) 46, stating that '[t]his imperative recognises past linkages and propels future constitutional struggles to always embrace the international'.

[308] In the original: 'ausgesprochen völkerrechtsfreundlich': Kotzur (n 12) 67.

norms of international law and this Constitution'.[309] Moreover, it is asserted that '[e]veryone shall have the right in accordance with international treaties of the Russian Federation to appeal to interstate bodies for the protection of human rights and freedoms if all available internal means of legal protection have been exhausted'.[310] This refers in the first place to the ECHR and its court, and can also be considered as an implementing measure in terms of international adjudication. Furthermore, the constitution understands itself as a minimum standard, given that '[t]he enumeration in the Constitution of the Russian Federation of the basic rights and freedoms should not be interpreted as a denial or diminution of other universally recognized human and civil rights and freedoms'.[311] Lastly, the constitution states that '[t]he Russian Federation shall guarantee the rights of indigenous small peoples in accordance with the generally recognized principles and norms of international law and international treaties of the Russian Federation'.[312]

The Brazilian constitution also clarifies that it is not an obstacle to more far-reaching human rights protection. It stipulates that '[t]he rights and guarantees established in this Constitution do not exclude others derived from the regime and principles adopted by it, or from international treaties to which the Federative Republic of Brazil is a party'.[313] In terms of rank, it provides that '[i]nternational treaties and conventions on human rights approved by both houses of the National Congress ... shall be equivalent to Constitutional Amendments'.[314] Moreover, human rights promotion features as a foreign policy objective in the constitution of Brazil, as the 'prevalence of human rights' is among the principles that govern the international relations of the country.[315] The Swiss constitution similarly mandates the Confederation to contribute 'to the respect for human rights'.[316]

The promotion of human rights is at least as prominent a theme in the external relations objectives of the EU as it is in many national constitutions. According to Piet Eeckhout, human rights 'are not only ever more central to the EU's internal constitutional development, they are equally vital for the EU's external action'.[317]

The external promotion of human rights is clearly present in the first part of the TEU, starting with a reference in the preamble to the inspiration drawn from the 'cultural, religious and humanist inheritance of Europe, from which have developed the universal values of the inviolable and inalienable rights of the human person'.[318] Human rights figure prominently among the values of the EU in Art 2

[309] Art 17(1) Russian constitution.

[310] Art 46(3) Russian constitution.

[311] Art 55(1) Russian constitution.

[312] Art 69 Russian constitution. Further on human rights and Russian constitutional law, J Henderson, *The Constitution of the Russian Federation* (Hart Publishing, 2011) 91–3 and 228–53.

[313] Art 5(2) Brazilian constitution.

[314] Art 5(3) Brazilian constitution. See also Art 90(5) Turkish constitution, which grants international human rights treaties primacy over national legislation.

[315] Art 4 Brazilian constitution.

[316] Art 54(1) Swiss constitution.

[317] Eeckhout (n 76) 96.

[318] Second recital of the preamble, TEU; see also fourth recital of the preamble, TEU and second recital of the preamble, Charter of Fundamental Rights of the EU.

TEU,[319] which are to be upheld and promoted according to Art 3(5) TEU in its relations with the wider world, and upon which its neighbourhood policy is to be 'founded' (Art 8(1) TEU). Art 3(5) TEU states furthermore that the Union 'shall contribute to', inter alia, 'the protection of human rights, in particular the rights of the child'. The Treaties now also explicitly mandate the Union to accede to the ECHR (Art 6(2) TEU).[320] Similarly, the first subparagraph of Art 21(1) TEU names 'the universality and indivisibility of human rights and fundamental freedoms, [and] respect for human dignity' among the internal principles that the Union 'seeks to advance in the wider world'. This means that cooperation with third countries and international organizations is premised, inter alia, on the respect for human rights.[321] Lastly, consolidating and supporting human rights is listed among the objectives that follow in the same article (Art 21(2)(b) TEU). From both the 'value' link between Arts 2 and 3(5) TEU and the guiding principles that stem from the Union's own history according to Art 21 TEU, the 'translation' of an internal feature into an external objective is evident.

In practice, the EU has long been actively promoting human rights externally in a variety of ways.[322] Next to diplomatic efforts in the form of *démarches* and dialogues, these include incentives such as trade benefits for ratifying and implementing international human rights treaties through GSP+, imposing sanctions on third countries for violations of human rights,[323] and inserting human rights-related 'essential clauses' into agreements with third countries.[324]

4.6 Integration

Just as the universalization of human rights challenges the classic conceptions of sovereignty, so too does integration by pooling sovereign rights or by transferring

[319] Those being 'respect for human dignity', 'freedom', 'equality', 'the rule of law and respect for human rights, including the rights of persons belonging to minorities', and 'non-discrimination', 'tolerance', 'justice', 'solidarity and equality between women and men', Art 2 TEU.

[320] Despite this new language, the CJEU puts in place a high threshold for the EU's accession to the ECHR to be legal, Opinion 2/13 *(ECHR II)*, EU:C:2014:2454.

[321] Art 21(1), second subpara TEU, which states that these third countries and organizations with which the Union is to cooperate 'share the principles referred to in the first subparagraph'.

[322] For an overview see European External Action Service, *Human Rights and Democracy in the World: Report on EU Action in 2011*, June 2012; also K Podstawa, *EU External Human Rights Policy in Search for a Framework of Evaluation*, PhD Thesis defended at the European University Institute (September 2014).

[323] See eg Council Decision 2011/782/CFSP of 1 December 2011 concerning restrictive measures against Syria and repealing Decision 2011/273/CFSP [2011] OJ L 319/56; and Council of the European Union, Common Position 2006/276/CFSP of 10 April 2006 concerning restrictive measures against certain officials of Belarus and repealing Common Position 2004/661/CFSP [2006] OJ L 101/5.

[324] See eg Partnership and Cooperation Agreement establishing a partnership between the European Communities and their Member States, of the one part, and the Republic of Tajikistan, of the other part [2009] OJ L 350/3, Art 2; see for extensive accounts L Bartels, *Human Rights Conditionality in the EU's International Agreements* (OUP, 2005); and F Hoffmeister, *Menschenrechts- und Demokratieklauseln in den vertraglichen Aussenbeziehungen der Europäischen Gemeinschaft* (Springer, 1998).

them to international organizations.[325] The most advanced case of such sovereignty sharing remains the European Union. The constitutional provisions of its Member States regarding EU membership will be discussed later in terms of the European constitutional space (Chapter 4). This subsection will deal with constitutional foreign policy objectives aimed at regional integration and institutionalized international cooperation in general. Next to provisions encouraging such integration, often with certain conditions and guidelines attached, there are also examples that forbid certain kinds of integration.

Concerning European integration as an objective, the German Basic Law stipulates:

> With a view to establishing a United Europe, the Federal Republic of Germany shall participate in the development of the European Union that is committed to democratic, social and federal principles, to the rule of law, and to the principle of subsidiarity, and that guarantees a level of protection of basic rights essentially comparable to that afforded by this Basic Law.[326]

It is evident here that the Basic Law provides guidance of the kind of European integration it envisages (and consequently is prepared to accommodate). This list of normative principles is comparable to, and links up with, the EU's own constitutional basic principles. It can thus also be seen as an example of 'translation' of national constitutional values to the supranational level.

In the Portuguese constitution a similar Europe clause can be found. Firstly, there is a commitment to European integration in general, but it is also linked to a certain normative direction, viz 'the reinforcement of the European identity and to the strengthening of the commitment of the States of Europe to democracy, peace, economic progress and justice in the relations between their peoples'.[327] Later on, EU membership is addressed directly, but also with a number of normative guidelines, those being 'respect for the fundamental principles of a democratic state based on the rule of law and for the principle of subsidiarity'.[328]

The French constitution provides that '[t]he Republic shall participate in the European Union constituted by States which have freely chosen, by virtue of the Treaty on European Union and the Treaty on the Functioning of the European Union as they result from the treaty signed in Lisbon on 13 December 2007, to exercise some of their powers in common'.[329] In all three cases, these provisions are objectives as well as competence-related norms. The pursuit of European integration appears here as a 'goal-oriented competence'.

The Irish constitution also contains an affirmation to the country's 'commitment to the European Union within which the Member States of that Union work together to promote peace, shared values and the well-being of their peoples'.[330] Similarly, the Hungarian constitution stipulates that 'to enhance the liberty,

325 Sommermann (n 18) 245.
326 Art 23(1) German constitution.
327 Art 7(5) Portuguese constitution.
328 Art 7(6) Portuguese constitution.
329 Art 88-1 French constitution.
330 Art 29(4) No 4 Irish constitution.

well-being and security of the people of Europe, Hungary shall contribute to the creation of European unity'.[331] In these cases, provisions authorizing the transfer of competences are kept separate.[332]

Apart from the EU and its rather unique brand of wide-ranging and deep integration, the transfer of sovereign powers to international organizations is also mentioned in national constitutions in connection with certain objectives, which can be pursued through power transfers through global or regional bodies. These can take a very general form or refer to a specific organization. For instance, the Danish constitution contains a blanket reference regarding the transfer of powers to international organizations, which is to be done 'for the promotion of international rules of law and co-operation'.[333] In the same way, the Latvian constitution, in the context of transferring powers, states that this is to be done 'with the purpose of strengthening democracy'.[334] The Slovenian constitution states that such a transfer can only be carried out with regard to organizations 'which are based on respect for human rights and fundamental freedoms, democracy and the principles of the rule of law'.[335] In these cases, the constitutional authorization to carry out such transfers is qualified by one or several other objectives to be pursued internationally. Therefore, one could also question whether international cooperation, as well as integration, are ends in themselves or instead means to other, substantive, ends (see also Chapter 3, section 2.6).

An international organization to which numerous explicit references can be found is the ICC, arguably because cooperation with it (in the sensitive field of criminal justice) requires express constitutional authorization. The Irish constitution provides that '[t]he State may ratify the Rome Statute of the International Criminal Court',[336] while the French constitution states in Art 53-2 that France 'may recognize the jurisdiction of the International Criminal Court as provided for by the Treaty signed on 18 July 1998'. The constitution of Luxembourg, in the same vein, contains a statement that '[t]he provisions of the Constitution do not constitute an obstacle to the approval of the Statute of the International Criminal Court … and to the execution of the obligations resulting under the conditions referred to by the aforementioned Statute'.[337] Whereas these are provisions authorizing these countries to accede to the Rome Statute and ensure that cooperation with the Court is constitutional, any objectives pursued by these means have to be implied or found elsewhere. To the contrary, the Portuguese constitution links explicit objectives to the authorization:

> Portugal may, in view of the realization of an international justice that promotes respect for the rights of the human person, and of peoples, accept the jurisdiction of the International Criminal Court, under conditions of complementarity and also under the terms established in the [Rome Statute].[338]

[331] Art E(1) Hungarian constitution; see also Art 143(1) Croatian constitution.

[332] See also Art 143(1) Croatian constitution stating the objective, and Art 143(2) stating the authorization.

[333] Art 20(1) Danish constitution.

[334] Art 68(3) Latvian constitution; see also Art 28(2) and (3) Greek constitution.

[335] Art 3a(1) Slovenian constitution.

[336] Art 29(9) Irish constitution.

[337] Art 118 Luxembourg constitution.

[338] Art 7(7) Portuguese constitution.

Among the EU Member State constitutions, it is further possible to find examples of prohibitions to certain kinds of integration. Part of the constitution of Lithuania are two constitutional acts, one on EU accession and the other 'On the Non-Alignment of the Republic of Lithuania to Post-Soviet Eastern Unions' of 8 June 1992.[339] The latter provides that Lithuania shall 'never join in any form any new political, military, economic or other unions or commonwealths of states formed on the basis of the former USSR'.[340] A similar provision with regard to the former Yugoslavia can be found in the Croatian constitution, which prohibits 'a renewal of a South Slavic state union or … any form of consolidated Balkan state'.[341] Similarly, the Treaty of Guarantee (between Cyprus, Greece, Turkey, and the UK), which has constitutional status for Cyprus,[342] stipulates that Cyprus 'undertakes not to participate, in whole or in part, in any political or economic union with any State whatsoever' and that '[i]t accordingly declares prohibited any activity likely to promote, directly or indirectly, either union with any other State or partition of the Island'.[343] This prohibition is aimed at preventing (part of) Cyprus merging with either Greece or Turkey. It does not prohibit joining international organizations, as this is specifically provided for in the constitution.[344] The fact that these examples are rare again highlights the generally positive, dynamic, and permissive character of constitutional objectives, but also the fact that at times they can exercise an interpretive–prohibitive function.

Among the third countries, similar cases can be found. Regarding calls for regional integration outside of the European context, the Brazilian constitution states that '[t]he Federative Republic of Brazil shall seek the economic, political, social and cultural integration of the people of Latin America, with a view towards forming a Latin-American community of nations'.[345] The Brazilian constitution also includes a reference to the ICC, which is formulated in terms of an obligation of jurisdiction, not an option: 'Brazil submits itself to the jurisdiction of the International Criminal Tribunal to whose creation it has adhered.'[346] On the surface, this is a constitutional command, but can also be seen as implying the objective to participate in such forms of international adjudication.

As was already mentioned, the Swiss constitution provides for an obligatory referendum to take place to decide on 'the entry into organizations for collective security or into supranational communities'.[347] Integration is made conditional on direct democratic procedures. Otherwise put, the constitution prohibits the pursuit of integration without popular approval. Similarly, the Russian constitution allows the Federation to 'participate in interstate associations and transfer some of

[339] Art 150 Lithuanian constitution.

[340] Constitutional Act 'On the Non-Alignment of the Republic of Lithuania to Post-Soviet Eastern Unions' of 8 June 1992, Art 1.

[341] Art 142(2) Croatian constitution.

[342] Art 181 Cypriot constitution.

[343] Art 1(2) Treaty of Guarantee between Cyprus, Greece, Turkey and the United Kingdom, Nicosia, 16 August 1960.

[344] Art 169 Cypriot constitution.

[345] Art 4, sole paragraph Brazilian constitution.

[346] Art 5(4) Brazilian constitution.

[347] Art 140(1)(b) Swiss constitution; see also Art 141(d) No 2 Swiss constitution on optional referendums on certain treaties.

its powers to those associations in accordance with international treaties',[348] adding the caveat that this should not 'entail restrictions on human and civil rights and freedoms and does not conflict with the basic principles of the constitutional order of the Russian Federation'.[349]

In sum, many constitutions today advocate international cooperation, notably by allowing the transfer of sovereign powers to regional or global bodies. Of course, the EU itself is a product of integration in that it derives its existence from the transfer of powers to it by its Member States. The Union can pursue the objective of integration and other forms of regional or international cooperation itself with a view to furthering its own constitutional objectives, both internal and external. According to the Treaties, it is even mandated to do so.

Five provisions point in this direction. Firstly, Art 21(1) TEU states that the Union 'shall seek to develop relations and build partnerships with third countries, and international, regional or global organizations which share the principles referred to in the first subparagraph' and that it 'shall promote multilateral solutions to common problems, in particular in the framework of the United Nations'.[350] Secondly, the general external relations objectives include the aim to 'promote an international system based on stronger multilateral cooperation and good global governance'.[351] Thirdly, Art 220 TFEU calls upon the EU to establish cooperative relations with international organizations, among which are specifically named the UN system, the Council of Europe, the Organization for Security and Co-operation in Europe (OSCE), and the Organisation for Economic Co-operation and Development (OECD). Fourthly, there is the command to accede to the ECHR, including its institutionalized adjudicatory system, in Art 6(2) TEU. Finally, there is the possibility for the Union to conclude association agreements with third countries or international organizations (Art 217 TFEU).[352] Affiliation with the Union can result in the extension of important features of the internal Union legal order to the associated countries and their citizens.[353]

However, apart from the notion of an 'ever closer union among the peoples of Europe',[354] the Treaties do not explicitly state the promotion of integration and regionalism as a goal. In view of the Union itself being a product of regional integration, the ensemble of principles that have inspired its creation, development, and enlargement could be summed up in such terms. Hence, integration as an external objective can also be seen as the 'translation' of an internal feature of the Union.

348 Art 79 Russian constitution.

349 Art 79 Russian constitution.

350 Art 21(1), second subpara TEU.

351 Art 21(2)(h) TEU.

352 See also numerous provisions mandating the Union and its Member States to 'cooperate with third countries and with the competent international organisations' in various areas, including Art 191(4) TFEU in the area of environmental policy; Art 167(3) TFEU concerning culture; Art 168(4) TFEU concerning public health; Art 211 TFEU concerning development cooperation; Art 212(3) TFEU concerning economic, financial, and technical assistance; and Art 214(7) TFEU concerning humanitarian aid.

353 Note, for instance, that the association with Turkey led to provisions of the agreement on the free movement of workers being accorded direct effect: see Case C-192/89 *Sevince*, EU:C:1990:322.

354 Thirteenth recital of the preamble, TEU; Art 1(2) TEU; and first recital of the preamble, TFEU.

In terms of practice, it was already mentioned with regard to the prohibition of war that the Union promotes its own model of integration in other parts of the world. Indeed, 'regionalism' has become a global phenomenon of which the Union has been considered the 'world champion'.[355] In addition to promoting integration elsewhere, the Union also engages in cooperating and integrating with these new regional organizations, for instance, through Economic Partnership Agreements[356] or by negotiating free trade agreements with Mercosur[357] and ASEAN.[358] Association furthermore plays an important role as a preparatory step for future membership (recalling the Europe agreements of the 1990s) or as an alternative to membership.[359] Beyond (inter-)regional integration, the European Union is a member of, and active participant in, a number of international organizations of global scope, such as the Food and Agricultural Organization (FAO), the European Bank for Reconstruction and Development (EBRD), and the Codex Alimentarius Commission.[360] It is a founding member of the World Trade Organization (WTO).[361] This practice has led Gráinne de Búrca to conclude that the EU employs a distinctive 'governance mode' to foreign policy, ie it has 'a preference for the creation of stable, long-term, institutionalized relationships with other states and entities, and frequent use of regulatory frameworks involving common articulated goals and broad participation to regulate and coordinate policy externally'.[362]

The pursuit of this objective, however, is restricted by the extent of the powers conferred upon the Union, as well as the preservation of the structural principles of the Union's legal order. The Court has confirmed this on various occasions, including two rulings that the Union could not join the ECHR,[363] and in a ruling concerning the creation of a pan-European patent litigation system through

[355] F Söderbaum, 'African Regionalism and EU-African Interregionalism' in M Telò (ed), *European Union and New Regionalism: Regional Actors and Global Governance in a Post-Hegemonic Era*, 2nd edn (Ashgate, 2007) 197.

[356] See eg Economic Partnership Agreement between the CARIFORUM States, of the one part, and the European Community and its Member States, of the other part [2008] OJ L 289/3. Further Bartels (n 324) 166–9.

[357] See the Interregional Framework Cooperation Agreement between the European Community and its Member States, of the one part, and the Southern Common Market and its Party States, of the other part [1996] OJ L 69/4. Further A Vasconcelos, 'European Union and MERCOSUR' in M Telò (ed), *European Union and New Regionalism: Regional Actors and Global Governance in a Post-Hegemonic Era*, 2nd edn (Ashgate, 2007).

[358] See Joint Communication to the European Parliament and the Council, *The EU and ASEAN: A Partnership with a Strategic Purpose*, Brussels, 18 May 2015, JOIN(2015) 22 final, 5, which mentions 'an ambitious region-to-region FTA' as a long-term goal.

[359] See Eeckhout (n 76) 124–7.

[360] See F Hoffmeister, 'Outsider or Frontrunner? Recent Developments under International and European Law on the Status of the European Union in International Organizations and Treaty Bodies' (2007) 44 *Common Market Law Review* 41.

[361] Marrakech Agreement Establishing the WTO, Art XI(1).

[362] G de Búrca, 'EU External Relations: The Governance Mode of Foreign Policy' in B Van Vooren, S Blockmans, and J Wouters (eds), *The EU's Role in Global Governance: The Legal Dimension* (OUP, 2013) 56–7.

[363] Opinion 2/94 *(ECHR)*, EU:C:1996:140; Opinion 2/13 *(ECHR II)* (n 320); see also Opinion 1/91 *(EEA)*, EU:C:1991:490.

an international agreement.[364] The pursuit of this objective is furthermore limited by the legal conditions for membership of the international organizations and the willingness of its members to accept the Union. This is exacerbated by the fact that the EU is a rather unusual international actor, which creates certain difficulties, for instance, with regard to voting rights within the international organization.[365] The EU has thus far not been able to join the International Labour Organization (ILO) or the UN as a full member.

4.7 Solidarity and development cooperation

As the global counterpart to social justice in a domestic setting, expressions of solidarity with economically weaker or less developed countries are also a rather common feature in modern constitutions.[366] To a certain extent, such solidarity already finds expression in notions of a global common good and calls for a more 'just' international order, or the rejection of 'colonialism' or 'imperialism' (see section 4.1). More explicit references can be found as well, which are often linked to historical (post-colonial) ties. However, in some cases solidarity is expressed not to other countries but to a state's own citizens or ethnic minorities abroad.

Among the EU Member States, the Spanish constitution contains a special reference to 'the nations of [Spain's] historical community', in relation to which the King of Spain will represent the country.[367] Similarly, the Portuguese constitution contains a reference to special historical ties among the *Lusofonia*, as 'Portugal maintains privileged bonds of friendship and cooperation with those countries that are Portuguese-speaking'.[368] The French constitution also contains language on the development of special historic ties. The *Francophonie* occupies a title of its own in the constitution (Title XIV). The French constitution stipulates that '[t]he Republic shall take part in the development of solidarity and cooperation between States and peoples sharing the French language'.[369] As an operationalization of such cooperation, it provides furthermore that '[t]he Republic may enter into agreements with States which wish to associate with it in order to develop their civilizations'.[370]

While these former colonial powers display solidarity with their erstwhile dominions, among the newer EU Member States from Central and Eastern Europe, one can find solidarity rather with expatriates and ethnic minorities abroad. For instance, the preamble to the Polish constitution expresses the country's sense of being 'bound in community with [its] compatriots dispersed throughout the

[364] Opinion 1/09 (*European and Community Patents Court*), EU:C:2011:123.

[365] See in detail and with case studies Eeckhout (n 76) 222–41; and I Govaere, J Capiau, and A Vermeersch, 'In-Between Seats: the Participation of the European Union in International Organizations' (2004) 9 *European Foreign Affairs Review* 155.

[366] Sommermann (n 18) 246–7.

[367] Art 56(1) Spanish constitution.

[368] Art 7(4) Portuguese constitution; note also Art 9(f) on the 'international dissemination of the Portuguese language'. Similarly, Art 33(3) Romanian constitution states that 'Romania's cultural and artistic values are promoted throughout the world'.

[369] Art 87 French constitution.

[370] Art 88 French constitution.

world'.[371] Similarly, the Hungarian constitution asserts that the country 'shall bear responsibility for the fate of Hungarians living beyond its borders, shall facilitate the survival and development of their communities ... and shall promote their cooperation with each other and with Hungary'.[372] The Slovakian constitution too makes clear that '[t]he Slovak Republic supports the national awareness and cultural identity of the Slovaks living abroad; it supports their institutions established to achieve this purpose and their relations with the mother country'.[373] In these three cases, it is not entirely apparent whether this refers to citizens, or rather to people of Polish, Hungarian, or Slovakian ethnicity. More explicit in this regard is the Croatian constitution, which provides that '[t]he Republic of Croatia shall safeguard the rights and interests of its citizens living or residing abroad, and shall promote their ties to their homeland'[374] and furthermore 'shall guarantee particular care and protection to those portions of the Croatian nation in other countries'.[375] Thus, while states vow in their constitutions to protect national minorities in accordance with international law at home, which is an aspect of promoting international law at large, the external counterpart of this is an active duty, made incumbent upon the state in its constitution, to protect its own nationals abroad and ensure that their rights are respected.

Among the third-country constitutions, a call for solidarity with developing countries can be seen in the external objective of the Swiss constitution to contribute 'to the alleviation of need and poverty in the world'.[376] A general call for solidarity (from a developing country's perspective) features in the preamble to the Indonesian constitution, which, inter alia, mandates the government 'to participate toward the establishment of a world order based on ... social justice'.[377]

In addition, one can find expressions of solidarity with expatriates. According to the Turkish constitution, the country 'shall take the necessary measures to ensure ... the social security of Turkish nationals working abroad, and shall take the necessary measures to safeguard their ties with the home country and to help them on their return home'.[378] Similarly, the Chinese constitution provides that the State Council (government) has, inter alia, the task '[t]o protect the legitimate rights and interests of Chinese nationals residing abroad and protect the lawful rights and interests of returned overseas Chinese and of the family members of Chinese nationals residing abroad'.[379]

In the EU Treaties, general expressions of solidarity are clearly present and include its socio-economic, environmental, and cultural aspects. First, the general promotion of the Union's values extrapolates elements from Art 2 TEU such as 'justice' and 'solidarity' into its external action. In Art 3(5) TEU, there are explicit references to 'the sustainable development of the Earth, solidarity and mutual

[371] Preamble, Polish constitution.
[372] Art D Hungarian constitution.
[373] Art 7a Slovakian constitution.
[374] Art 10(1) Croatian constitution.
[375] Art 10(2) Croatian constitution.
[376] Art 54(2) Swiss constitution.
[377] Preamble, Indonesian constitution.
[378] Art 62 Turkish constitution.
[379] Art 89 No 12 Chinese constitution.

respect among peoples' and the 'eradication of poverty'. A number of unequivocal objectives pertaining to this category are echoed in Art 21 TEU. Among the guiding principles of EU external action appears 'solidarity',[380] while among the listed objectives there is the goal to 'foster the sustainable economic, social and environmental development of developing countries, with the primary aim of eradicating poverty'.[381] In addition, the objectives 'to encourage the integration of all countries into the world economy',[382] to 'help develop international measures to preserve and improve the quality of the environment and the sustainable management of global natural resources, in order to ensure sustainable development',[383] and to 'assist populations, countries and regions confronting natural or man-made disasters'[384] equally fall into this category.

Furthermore, references pertaining to this theme appear in the provisions on particular external Union policies. The aim 'to establish an area of prosperity and good neighbourliness' in the EU's vicinity can be seen as an expression of wider regional solidarity (Art 8(1) TEU). The section on Union development policy stresses that the EU's 'primary objective' is 'the reduction and, in the long term, the eradication of poverty',[385] and that both the Union and the Member States 'shall comply with the commitments and take account of the objectives they have approved in the context of the United Nations and other competent international organisations'.[386] Similarly, the provisions on humanitarian aid state that action in this domain is to be carried out 'in order to meet humanitarian needs'.[387] The notion of 'solidarity'[388] is also explicitly evoked with regard to the association of overseas territories, which 'shall serve primarily to further the interests and prosperity of the inhabitants of these countries and territories in order to lead them to the economic, social and cultural development to which they aspire'.[389]

The translation dimension of these objectives is clearly evident. Internally, the concepts of justice and solidarity of Art 2 TEU on the Union's values, and more particularly 'the sustainable development of Europe', and promoting, among other things, 'social justice' and 'economic, social and territorial cohesion, and solidarity among Member States' (Art 3(3) TEU) are mirrored by the external objective to contribute to 'the sustainable development of the Earth, solidarity and mutual respect among peoples' in Art 3(5) TEU.

In practice, development cooperation is an area in which the Union has been ambitious and active over the past decades.[390] The Union's policy in this regard was elaborated upon notably in the 2005 European Consensus on Development.[391]

380 Art 21(1), first subpara TEU. 381 Art 21(2)(d) TEU.

382 Art 21(2)(e) TEU. To this one might add 'the harmonious development of world trade' from Art 206 TFEU on the CCP.

383 Art 21(2)(f) TEU. 384 Art 21(2)(g) TEU.

385 Art 208(1), second subpara TFEU. 386 Art 208(2) TFEU.

387 Art 214(1) TFEU. 388 Seventh recital of the preamble, TFEU.

389 Art 198(3) TFEU. 390 *Laeken Declaration* (n 92) 20.

391 Joint statement by the Council and the representatives of the governments of the Member States meeting within the Council, the European Parliament and the Commission on European Union Development Policy: 'The European Consensus' [2006] OJ C 46/1.

The Union often prides itself on being, together with the Member States, the world's largest contributor of development aid.[392]

As shown above, certain national constitutions express their solidarity, on the one hand, specifically towards a certain group of countries or, on the other hand, towards their own citizens and ethnic minorities abroad. Concerning the former, the post-Maastricht TEC contained a reference to the African, Caribbean, and Pacific (ACP) countries, cooperation with which should not be affected by the overall development policy of the Community (Art 179(3) TEC). The ACP largely represented former colonies of the Member States, and thus could be seen as an amalgam of historically rooted special relationships that linked Europe to former colonies.[393] However, following the 'budgetization' of the European Development Fund (EDF), the reference was removed during the drafting of the Constitutional Treaty, and subsequently remained absent from the post-Lisbon EU Treaties.[394] While the constitutional reference to this special inter-regional relationship has vanished, another appeared with the entry into force of the Lisbon Treaty, ie the ENP. According to this provision, which was also first devised at the European Convention, the EU 'shall develop a special relationship with neighbouring countries, aiming to establish an area of prosperity and good neighbourliness, founded on the values of the Union and characterised by close and peaceful relations based on cooperation'.[395] While this codifies into the Treaty 'a core foreign policy'[396] which had already been practised by the Union for years,[397] this change in Treaty language also represents a shift in geographical emphasis. Also within the ENP, which has the explicit translation element of being 'founded on the values of the Union', the various substantive constitutional objectives of the Union are to be pursued.

Lastly, concerning solidarity with citizens living abroad, with the entry into force of the Lisbon Treaty, EU primary law now contains the explicit objective to contribute in its external relations 'to the protection of its citizens'.[398] Before

[392] See eg European Union, *President Barroso at the UN High Level Summit on Millennium Development Goals to push for a global commitment and shared responsibility in the fight against poverty*, press release, IP/10/1137, Brussels, 16 September 2010, with the following quote from the Commission President: 'In 2009 the European Union and its Member States gave a total of €49 billion in development aid, which globally makes the EU by far the largest donor, representing 56% of global aid.'

[393] See L Bartels, 'Trade and Development Policy of the European Union' in M Cremona (ed), *Developments in EU External Relations Law* (OUP, 2008).

[394] See also R Streinz and T Kruis, 'Art. 209 AEUV' in R Streinz (ed), *EUV/AEUV: Vertrag über die Europäische Union und Vertrag über die Arbeitsweise der Europäischen Union*, 2nd edn (C.H. Beck, 2012) 2010 (marginal no 43).

[395] Art 8(1) TEU.

[396] Council of the European Union, Conclusions on Strengthening the European Neighbourhood Policy, Brussels, 19 June 2007, 11016/07, 4.

[397] See eg M Cremona, 'The European Neighbourhood Policy: More than a Partnership?' in M Cremona (ed), *Developments in EU External Relations Law* (OUP, 2008); and C Hillion, 'The EU's Neighbourhood Policy towards Eastern Europe' in A Dashwood and M Maresceau (eds), *Law and Practice of EU External Relations: Salient Features in a Changing Landscape* (CUP, 2008).

[398] Art 3(5) TEU; note also the formulations 'its citizens', who are identified in Art 20(1) TFEU as '[e]very person holding the nationality of a Member State'.

the Lisbon Treaty, the idea of protecting Union citizens abroad was already visible in the provision introduced by the Maastricht Treaty according to which the Member States were to provide consular and diplomatic protection to all Union citizens where their respective country of nationality was not represented in a third country.[399] This has been formalized through secondary measures,[400] but overall the Union's rules on protecting EU citizens abroad remain 'not well developed'.[401] It serves as an illustration of the accentuated caveat of feasibility, which the Union faces as a peculiar actor on the international stage. The fact that the Union is not a state creates additional difficulties in applying international law, devised by and for states in this domain, to the EU.[402] While Union citizenship serves internally as a status, which entails legal rights invokable by individuals and enforceable by courts,[403] in the external domain the protection of citizens remains an aspiration which is not always honoured.[404]

5. Additional Emphases in the EU Treaties

Given the abundance of external relations objectives in the post-Lisbon EU Treaties, a number of objectives remain which do not easily fit into the six main categories devised for national constitutions. They reflect the historical origins of the EU as an economic community, but also its global ambition as well as a degree of innovation vis-à-vis most national constitutions. These additional emphases present in the Treaties can be grouped into three themes: trade liberalization, the promotion of democracy, and the rule of law.

International trade liberalization is not common as a national constitutional objective.[405] For the Union, however, it is not a new goal, but was among the first

[399] Art 20 TEC; now Art 23 TFEU; also Art 46 Charter of Fundamental Rights of the EU. The external dimension of EU citizenship had already been discussed as early as 1985 by the so-called 'Adonnino Committee': see A Ianniello Saliceti, 'The Protection of EU Citizens Abroad: Accountability, Rule of Law, Role of Consular and Diplomatic Services' (2011) 17 *European Public Law* 91, 92.

[400] Decision 95/553/EC of the Representatives of the Governments of the Member States meeting within the Council of 19 December 1995 regarding protection for citizens of the European Union by diplomatic and consular representations [1995] OJ L 314/73.

[401] Ianniello Saliceti (n 399) 97; see also M Moraru, 'Protection of EU Citizens Abroad: A Legal Assessment of the EU Citizen's Right to Consular and Diplomatic Protection' (2011) 3 *Perspectives on Federalism* 67.

[402] See P Vigni, 'The Protection of EU Citizens: The Perspective of International Law' in J Larik and M Moraru (eds), *Ever-Closer in Brussels—Ever-Closer in the World? EU External Action after the Lisbon Treaty*, EUI Working Paper Law 2011/10.

[403] See eg the landmark cases Case C-200/02 *Chen*, EU:C:2004:639; and Case C-34/09 *Zambrano*, EU:C:2011:124. See further L Azoulai, '"Euro-Bonds" The Ruiz Zambrano judgment or the Real Invention of EU Citizenship' (2011) 3 *Perspectives on Federalism* 31; and D Kochenov, 'The Essence of EU Citizenship Emerging from the Last Ten Years of Academic Debate: Beyond the Cherry Blossoms and The Moon?' (2013) 62 *International & Comparative Law Quarterly* 97.

[404] Turning from diplomatic and consular protection to the CFSP, the call *civis Europaeus sum* seems to fall on deaf ears thus far: J Larik, 'Operation Atalanta and Protection of EU citizens: Civis Europaeus Unheeded?' (2011) 3 *Perspectives on Federalism* 40.

[405] Not directly aimed at liberalization, the Swiss constitution enshrines as an objective of the Confederation to safeguard 'the interests of the Swiss economy abroad', Art 101(1) Swiss constitution.

policy-specific external relations objectives codified in the ECSC and the EEC Treaties (see *supra* section 3.1). These objectives are still clearly present in the primary law. Among the goals of Art 3(5) TEU appears 'free and fair trade' and the goal to 'encourage the integration of all countries into the world economy, including through the progressive abolition of restrictions on international trade' is listed in Art 21(2)(e) TEU, which are elaborated upon further in the specific provisions of the CCP (Art 206 TFEU and Art 207(1) TFEU). Even though trade liberalization does not feature among the values or guiding principles that are to be advanced in the world, the link between the internal market, which requires a common trade policy, is evident. In various ways, the Union's considerable trade power 'can be used to attain other, non-economic objectives',[406] which cover all six categories outlined above.[407] These include both measures advancing free trade and measures restricting trade (eg economic sanctions or environmental standards).[408] This reflects that under the Treaties post-Lisbon, sector-specific objectives need to take account of the general canon of EU external relations objectives, to which trade is no exception.[409] Nevertheless, the Treaties also continue to put an emphasis on free trade as an end in its own right, which has even been upgraded to a general objective by virtue of the Lisbon reform.

While trade liberalization can be seen as historically rooted in the EU Treaties, the emphases on democracy promotion and the rule of law are more recent,[410] and also fairly uncommon in national constitutions, at least in this wide formulation.[411] For the EU, democracy ranks among the values of Art 2 TEU to be promoted externally under Art 3(5) TEU, and appears explicitly among the guiding principles and listed external action objectives of Art 21 TEU.[412] Despite the

[406] M Cremona, 'The Union's External Action: Constitutional Perspectives' in G Amato, H Bribosia, and B De Witte (eds), *Genesis and Destiny of the European Constitution* (Bruylant, 2007) 1213, pointing also to case law of the CJEU which highlights the wide scope of the CCP: see eg Case 45/86 *Commission v Council (Generalized tariff preferences)*, EU:C:1987:163.

[407] See S Meunier and K Nicolaïdis, 'The European Union as a Trade Power' in C Hill and M Smith (eds), *International Relations and the European Union*, 2nd edn (OUP, 2011).

[408] Case C-94/03 *Commission v Council (Rotterdam Convention)*, EU:C:2006:2, para 49 and the case law cited there.

[409] Art 207(1) TFEU: 'The common commercial policy shall be conducted in the context of the principles and objectives of the Union's external action.' Further A Dimopoulos, 'The Effects of the Lisbon Treaty on the Principles and Objectives of the Common Commercial Policy' (2010) 15 *European Foreign Affairs Review* 153.

[410] They were first introduced as objectives of Community development cooperation policy by the Maastricht Treaty: see Art 177(2) TEC in the Nice version. For a translation into policy, see Council of the European Union, *EU Strategic Framework and Action Plan on Human Rights and Democracy*, Luxembourg, 25 June 2012 11855/12, 1: 'Sustainable peace, development and prosperity are possible only when grounded upon respect for human rights, democracy and the rule of law.'

[411] The closest to that is again the Swiss constitution, which mandates the Confederation to contribute to 'democracy' in the world: Art 54(2) Swiss constitution. More narrowly, the Portuguese constitution pledges 'to the strengthening of the commitment of the States of Europe to democracy': Art 7(5) Portuguese constitution. The German constitution premises Germany's participation in the European Union on the commitment to democratic principles: Art 23(1) German constitution. The Latvian constitution combines the transfer of powers to international organizations on 'the purpose of strengthening democracy': Art 68(2) Latvian constitution.

[412] Art 21(1), first subpara and Art 21(2)(b) TEU.

oft-criticized internal 'democratic deficit' of the Union,[413] democracy promotion has figured prominently in the practice of EU external action,[414] revealing the active pursuit of this objective by the Union.

Promoting the rule of law is also not a foreign policy objective common among national constitutions.[415] In the EU Treaties, as is the case with democracy, the rule of law is found among the values of Art 2 TEU, which are to be promoted and upheld in the relations of the Union with the wider world. It appears explicitly among the guiding principles of Art 21(1) TEU and as a listed objective in Art 21(2)(b) TEU. The internal feature of a 'community based on the rule of law'[416] is thus clearly being translated into an external objective. To a certain extent, the external promotion of the rule of law is covered by the general objective of promoting international law. However, it also goes beyond that, addressing the state of affairs *within* third countries. This is borne out by practice, as the Union has also actively promoted the rule of law on the national level in third countries, for instance, through rule of law-oriented CSDP missions[417] and a wide range of other instruments.[418]

6. Conclusion: In the Vanguard of a Global Trend

Having situated the foreign policy objectives of the EU both in the historical and comparative context as regards their substance, the following conclusions can be drawn. Firstly, the goals of EU external relations have, from the very beginning, occupied a prominent place in the founding Treaties, and have expanded

[413] See Piris (n 86) 112, who describes the quest for more democratic legitimacy of the EU as a persistent '*leitmotiv*'. With particular regard to democracy and accountability in EU external relations (pre-Lisbon), see G De Baere, *Constitutional Principles of EU External Relations* (OUP, 2008) 161–76; and D Thym, 'Parliamentary Involvement in European International Relations' in M Cremona and B De Witte (eds), *EU Foreign Relations Law: Constitutional Fundamentals* (Hart Publishing, 2008); and post-Lisbon, note in particular Case C-658/11 *Parliament v Council (EU-Mauritius Agreement)*, EU:C:2014:2025; and K Raube, 'Democratic Accountability and EU Diplomacy: The EEAS and the Role of the European Parliament' in D Spencea and J Batora (eds), *The European External Action Service: European Diplomacy Post-Westphalia* (Palgrave Macmillan, 2015).

[414] See eg A Wetzel and J Orbie, 'Promoting Embedded Democracy? Researching the Substance of EU Democracy Promotion' (2011) 16 *European Foreign Affairs Review* 565, as well as the other articles in the same special issue; and P Kotzian, M Knodt, and S Urdze, 'Instruments of the EU's External Democracy Promotion' (2011) 49 *Journal of Common Market Studies* 995.

[415] While not positing the rule of law as an external objective in its own right, as with democracy, the German constitution premises the participation of Germany in the EU also on the commitment to the rule of law: Art 23(1) German constitution. Similarly, the Slovenian constitution premises the transfer of powers to international organizations on respect for the rule of law: Art 3a Slovenian constitution. In the same vein, Art 7(6) Portuguese constitution.

[416] Case 294/83 *Parti écologiste 'Les Verts'*, EU:C:1986:166, para 23; see further L Pech, '"A Union Founded on the Rule of Law": Meaning and Reality of the Rule of Law as a Constitutional Principle of EU Law' (2010) 6 *European Constitutional Law Review* 359.

[417] See eg Council of the European Union, Joint Action 2004/523/CFSP of 28 June 2004 on the European Union Rule of Law Mission in Georgia, EUJUST THEMIS [2004] OJ L 228/21.

[418] See L Pech, *Rule of Law as a Guiding Principle of the European Union's External Action*, CLEER Working Paper 2012/03, 14–22.

significantly through the treaty reform process culminating in the Lisbon Treaty. However, the EU Treaties are not exceptional or unusual on account of their containing a wide range of objectives pertaining to its external action. The vast majority of constitutions of its Member States, but also outside of the EU, contain similar norms. The degree of detail and the emphases that constitutions put on the goals of their respective foreign policies by virtue of constitutional codification varies greatly. General patterns of subject matter emerge, but only a few national constitutions contain language on all or most of them. It is in this regard that the EU Treaties can be considered special. They are in the vanguard of a global trend. Without doubt, they are among the most verbose in terms of foreign policy objectives, covering all main substantive areas outlined here, and furthermore putting forward additional emphases not usually found in national constitutions. On the one hand, these less common goals are due to the EU's historical point of departure as a regional economic organization. On the other hand, they are the result of more recent leaps in its structure and nature as a political community. These two positions also open up a spectrum as to the nature of the EU as a legal order—at the outset a functional international organization, and subsequently transformed into a 'constitutionalized' entity with broad normative foundations. This changing nature affects the operation of constitutional objectives as legal norms, including in the area of foreign policy, and is the subject of the following chapter.

3

Foreign Policy Objectives as Norms of EU Constitutional Law

1. Introduction

In the previous two chapters, it was shown that foreign policy objectives are purposeful norms in a legal order and that they figure increasingly prominently in the constitutional documents of numerous states in Europe and beyond. Drawing on the common vocabulary for understanding them as constitutional norms, which was inspired by the most sophisticated doctrinal approaches, it could be concluded that foreign policy objectives are to be recognized as a subcategory of constitutional objectives as well as part of a country's 'foreign affairs constitution'. As codified specifications of the external aspects of the 'common good', they serve primarily as an interpretive device to enhance public powers.

The purpose of this chapter is to situate the objectives found in the EU Treaties within the Union's legal order and to analyse the ways in which they operate therein. The European Union, its legal order, and system of foreign relations distinguish themselves from states by several peculiar features. The Union is neither a state nor can it be ranked among 'ordinary' or 'classic' international organizations.[1] Correspondingly, its law is neither that of a traditional domestic legal order of a state, nor does it fit easily with public international law. It is often seen as something of its own genre (*sui generis*). This necessitates

[1] The term 'ordinary' or 'classic' international organization is used here to refer to functionally rather narrowly defined organizations. At the same time, it is acknowledged that certain other international organizations have rather far-reaching and all-encompassing objectives as well, such as historically the League of Nations (see preamble, Covenant of the League of Nations), today the United Nations (see Arts 1 and 2 Charter of the United Nations), or regional organizations such as the Association of Southeast Asian Nations (ASEAN) (see Arts 1 and 2 ASEAN Charter). To what extent these would still fit the paradigms of general international institutional law in terms of 'functionality' is debatable, as is the question to what extent the legal regimes they have established have 'thickened' sufficiently to merit the term 'constitutional'. See also E Klein, 'Die Internationalen und die Supranationalen Organisationen' in W Graf Vitzthum (ed), *Völkerrecht*, 5th edn (De Gruyter, 2010) 381–2; P Manin, *Droit constitutionnel de l'Union européenne* (Pedone, 2004) 70–1, who both distinguish the EU from other international or regional organizations; and C Barnard, 'Introduction: The Constitutional Treaty, the Constitutional Debate and the Constitutional Process' in C Barnard (ed), *The Fundamentals of EU Law Revisited: Assessing the Impact of the Constitutional Debate* (OUP, 2007) 3.

a careful assessment of these peculiarities in order to be able to meaningfully compare its primary law with national constitutions. To this end, this chapter will approach the foreign policy objectives of the EU as part of this *sui generis* legal order.

This is done in three main steps. Firstly, it is established that Union objectives are amenable to comparison with national constitutional objectives. Despite the different point of departure for the EU as an international organization characterized by functionality, and thus having an existential need for objectives, its legal order has evolved in such a way as to develop sufficient 'constitutional' traits which allow for its general comparability with national constitutional orders. During the course of its evolution, the goals of the Union have moved away from specific purposes and have come to cover all of the main goals normally associated with states. Following this transformation, moreover, Union objectives no longer serve as an autonomous source of competences. Instead, they have evolved into a norm category of their own, related to but distinct from competence norms. Hence, for both the EU and states, constitutional objectives represent the constitutionally codified specific expressions of how the polity is to serve its most basic objective—furthering the common good. Deepening integration further, by contrast, raises the question of the Union's *finalité*. However, the latter is to be seen as another expression of the need for 'optimization' in terms of competence allocation rather than as an objective in its own right.

Secondly, this chapter shows that beyond overall comparability, the constitutional objectives of the EU exhibit characteristics and assume a place within the Union legal order that is very similar to that of national constitutional objectives. They, too, are legally binding norms of constitutional rank, which commit a priori all Union organs to actively pursue these objectives within the limits of their competence and within the bounds of what is materially possible. They are thus marked by an obligation to optimize, a wide margin of discretion, and a need to prioritize between different objectives while maintaining overall coherence. Hence, while they are in principle justiciable by the courts, the EU judiciary recognizes their fairly weak legal force. The most tangible role of objectives in adjudicative processes resides in their function as interpretive devices. By virtue of this interpretive function, within the Union legal order, constitutional objectives relate to the other main categories of constitutional law in ways very similar to national constitutional objectives. While they may not be pursued in a way that will undermine the structural foundations of the legal order, objectives serve to clarify the scope and nature of Union competences as well as the limits of individual rights protected under Union law.

Thirdly, the foreign policy objectives of the Union are part and parcel of the norm category of EU constitutional objectives, while also belonging to the Union's foreign affairs constitution. In its case law, the Court of Justice of the EU has shown that they exhibit generally the same functions as internally oriented objectives. The criticisms directed specifically towards these objectives as a subset are hence unwarranted.

2. The Constitutionalization of the Union and Its Objectives

In order to situate objectives codified in national constitutions in a meaningful relationship with those found in the EU Treaties, one important issue needs to be addressed at the outset lest any further enquiry become an exercise in futility. The automatic transferability of national law concepts to the supranational level cannot and should not be simply assumed.[2] The 'constitutional' nature of Union law in general, and of its objectives in particular, need to be established on firm ground. If the EU were to be regarded as an ordinary international organization, it would indeed be a case of comparing apples and oranges when looking at their respective codified objectives. In order to shed light on this issue, the notion of the 'functionality' of international organizations will serve as a point of departure for the subsequent assessment of the widening scope of the tasks and objectives of the Union (and its predecessors) over time. The latter is a matter closely related to the changing nature of the Union from an international organization to an autonomous legal order with 'thickening' constitutional qualities. However, the Union is still to be regarded as an unfinished project, ie the question of its *finalité* remains. This unfinished state notwithstanding, *finalité* or the pursuit of an 'ever closer Union' has to be distinguished from the duty to pursue the EU's consolidated constitutional objectives.[3]

2.1 Tasks, functions, and powers in the law of international organizations

To begin the enquiry into the nature of the Union and its objectives, it is worth recalling that international organizations (IOs) are seen as derivative subjects in the international legal order with only partial powers, as opposed to states, which are considered original and complete subjects of international law.[4] IOs are commonly

[2] A von Bogdandy, 'Zur Übertragbarkeit staatsrechtlicher Figuren auf die Europäische Union' in M Brenner, P Huber, and M Möstl (eds), *Der Staat des Grundgesetzes—Kontinuität und Wandel. Festschrift für Peter Badura zum siebzigsten Geburtstag* (Mohr Siebeck, 2004); and A von Bogdandy, 'Founding Principles' in A von Bogdandy and J Bast (eds), *Principles of European Constitutional Law*, 2nd edn (Hart Publishing/C.H. Beck, 2011) 24–5; also M Avbelj, 'Questioning EU Constitutionalisms' (2008) 9 *German Law Journal* 1, 26, who cautions against 'constitutional labelling' without further reflection; and R Streinz, 'European Integration through Constitutional Law' in H-J Blanke and S Mangiameli (eds), *Governing Europe under a Constitution: The Hard Road from the European Treaties to a European Constitutional Treaty* (Springer, 2006) 9, who rightly cautions that even when applying a broad definition of the term 'constitution' we ought to 'remain aware of the special features of the EC/EU'.

[3] The changing role of Union objectives in the context of 'constitutionalization' is also discussed in J Larik, 'From Speciality to a Constitutional Sense of Purpose: On the Changing Role of the Objectives of the European Union' (2014) 63 *International & Comparative Law Quarterly* 935.

[4] See eg M Shaw, *International Law*, 7th edn (CUP, 2014) 143, 946; N Quoc Dinh et al, *Droit International Public*, 8th edn (L.G.D.J. 2009) 644; V Epping, 'Völkerrechtssubjekte' in K Ipsen (ed), *Völkerrecht*, 6th edn (C.H. Beck, 2014) 49 and 197; M Bossuyt and J Wouters, *Grondlijnen van internationaal recht* (Intersentia, 2005) 177.

defined as being based on an international agreement and governed by international law, with states and/or other IOs as members and equipped with at least one organ with a will of its own.[5] In contrast to states, which have the ability to establish their own competences (in German known as *Kompetenz-Kompetenz*),[6] the powers of IOs are confined to those assigned to them by their creators. This defining feature of limited or attributed powers of IOs accords special importance to the objectives that the organization is mandated to pursue. IOs are therefore inherently 'functional', ie they have 'no unlimited power unconnected to the pursuance of specific objectives—and that their competences stretch far enough to include all acts indispensable for the performance of the functions of the organization'.[7]

This contrast was already highlighted in the 1927 Opinion of the Permanent Court of International Justice (PCIJ) on the *Jurisdiction of the European Commission of the Danube*:

> As the European Commission is not a State, but an international institution with a special purpose, it only has the functions bestowed upon it by the Definitive Statute with a view to the fulfilment of that purpose, but it has power to exercise these functions to their full extent, in so far as the Statute does not impose restrictions upon it.[8]

Later, the International Court of Justice (ICJ) reiterated this point in similar terms when it ruled in its 1996 Opinion on the *Legality of the Threat or Use of Nuclear Weapons/WHO*:

> The Court need hardly point out that international organizations are subjects of international law which do not, unlike States, possess a general competence. International organizations are governed by the 'principle of speciality', that is to say, they are invested by the States which create them with powers, the limits of which are a function of the common interests whose promotion those States entrust to them.[9]

[5] H Schermers and N Blokker, *International Institutional Law*, 5th edn (Martinus Nijhoff, 2011) 36–47, who add that an IO 'is usually created as a legal person' (44); see also P Sands and P Klein, *Bowett's Law of International Institutions*, 6th edn (Sweet & Maxwell, 2009) 15–16, who add that an IO 'must be capable of adopting norms (in the broadest sense) addressed to its members' (16).

[6] In Klein's words, IOs do not have the 'competence to invent new tasks for themselves' (*Aufgabenerfindungszuständigkeit*): Klein (n 1) 276. Note also F Sorrentino, 'The Purposes of the European Union According to the Constitutional Treaty' in HJ Blanke and S Mangiameli (eds), *Governing Europe under a Constitution: The Hard Road from the European Treaties to a European Constitutional Treaty* (Springer, 2006) 123: 'For in the case of a state, the problem of its "purposes" is never an issue, because we take for granted that a state is an entity with general purpose.'

[7] Sorrentino (n 6) 158; also Klein (n 1) 276; and Shaw (n 4) 946–8.

[8] *Jurisdiction of the European Commission of the Danube* (Advisory Opinion) PCIJ Rep Series B No 14 (1927), 64; see also A Campbell, 'The Limits of the Powers of International Organisations' (1983) 32 *International & Comparative Law Quarterly* 532. However, note also De Witte, who points out that the European Commission of the Danube had 'very extensive powers' for an IO at that time in history: B De Witte, 'The European Union as an International Legal Experiment' in G de Búrca and JHH Weiler (eds), *The Worlds of European Constitutionalism* (CUP, 2011) 23.

[9] *Legality of the Use by a State of Nuclear Weapons in Armed Conflict* (Advisory Opinion) [1996] ICJ Rep 66, para 25; note also from para 19: 'But the constituent instruments of international organizations are also treaties of a particular type; their object is to create new subjects of law endowed with a certain autonomy, to which the parties entrust the task of realizing common goals.' See earlier also *Reparation for Injuries Suffered in the Service of the United Nations* (Advisory Opinion) [1949] ICJ Rep 174, 180: 'Whereas a State possesses the totality of international rights and duties recognized

Consequently, the objectives of the organization become important for determining which actions would be *ultra vires*. As the ICJ ruled in its 1962 *Certain Expenses* opinion, an action 'which warrants the assertion that it was appropriate for the fulfilment of one of the stated purposes of the United Nations, the presumption is that such action is not *ultra vires* the Organization'.[10] This is important in regard to their interaction with the outside world, for example, in bringing international claims or concluding international agreements with external partners.[11] Henry Schermers and Niels Blokker conclude from this that '[u]sually, the definition of the objectives of the organization forms the only constitutional limit on the scope of operational activities'.[12] By contrast, as was concluded in Chapter 1, national constitutional law separates objectives from competence norms more strictly. While the former may help to clarify the latter, objectives do not establish competences as such.

When looking at the beginnings of the European integration process and the predecessors of the current EU, the same situation as with classical IOs seems to prevail, at least at first glance. The European Coal and Steel Community (ECSC), the European Atomic Energy Community (EAEC, also known as Euratom), and the later European Economic Community (EEC) were set up by states through international agreements. These agreements were governed by international law. They created organs with a distinct will from the Member States in order to pursue certain tasks and perform activities as specified in these agreements. As Pierre Pescatore noted in 1972, the founding treaties of the Communities are 'completely imbued with teleology' and 'entirely founded upon the idea of objectives to be attained'.[13] However, over time it became apparent that with deepening integration the Communities evolved in certain respects away from ordinary international organizations, with repercussions for the nature of their legal order as well as their objectives. Pescatore did not fail to underline that behind the more technical

by international law, the rights and duties of an entity such as the Organization must depend upon its purposes and functions as specified or implied in its constituent documents and developed in practice.'

[10] *Certain Expenses of the United Nations* (Advisory Opinion) [1962] ICJ Rep 151, 168 (italics in the original); see also earlier *Effect of Awards of Compensation Made by the UN Administrative Tribunal* (Advisory Opinion) [1954] ICJ Rep 47, 57, in which the Court ruled that the General Assembly had the power to establish an administrative tribunal in view of the 'expressed aim of the Charter to promote freedom and justice for individuals' and which 'arises by necessary intendment out of the UN Charter'.

[11] The first was at issue in *Reparation for Injuries* (n 9); concerning treaty-making powers, note the preamble to the Vienna Convention on the Law of Treaties between States and International Organizations or Between International Organizations, Vienna, 21 March 1986, not in force (VCLTIO): 'international organisations possess the capacity to conclude treaties which is necessary for the exercise of their functions and the fulfilment of their purposes'.

[12] Schermers and Blokker (n 5) 766.

[13] In the original: 'entièrement pétris de téléologie' and 'entièrement fondés sur la notion d'objectifs à atteindre', respectively: P Pescatore, 'Les objectifs de la Communauté européenne comme principes d'interprétation dans la jurisprudence de la Cour de justice' in *Miscellanea W. J. Ganshof van der Meersch: Studia ab discipulis amicisque in honorem egregii professoris edita* (Bruylant, 1972) 327.

objectives (above all the establishment of the common market) 'looms a more distant *finalité*, that of political union'.[14]

This is also reflected in the use of the term 'functional' in the influential integration theory of (neo)functionalism,[15] which has to be distinguished from the use of that term in international institutional law. In the latter case, it is employed to capture the limited, derivative nature of IOs as opposed to states, which are seen as a given of the international legal order and which are by contrast not confined to any particular 'function' or 'task'. The theory of neofunctionalism sought to theoretically grasp the so-called 'Monnet method'. It viewed the original objectives of the Communities, thought to be uncontroversial due to their largely technical and economic nature, as enabling further European integration as the pursuit of these only seemingly specific and circumscribed functions would ultimately require deeper integration in other (more political) areas. In short, neofunctionalism argues that 'spill-overs' would occur and that the form of the Communities is prone to change ultimately according to these expanding functions (see further Chapter 5, section 2).[16]

Whether one adheres to this theory or not, in terms of legal appreciation the question arises to which extent the objectives of the Union can still be seen through the lens of strict functionality and 'speciality' of international organizations given the progressing and deepening, yet still unfinished, process of integration.

2.2 The widening scope of Union objectives and competences

By revisiting the evolution of the objectives and powers that the founding treaties accorded to the EU and its predecessors over time, and how these relate to each other and the Union's legal order at large, the changing nature of the Union and evolving role of its objectives become visible.[17] The derivative and functional characteristics of international organizations are apparent in the 1951 Treaty Establishing the European Coal and Steel Community (ECSC Treaty), in which the first article states that '[b]y the present Treaty the HIGH CONTRACTING PARTIES institute among themselves a EUROPEAN COAL AND STEEL COMMUNITY, based on a common market, *common objectives*, and common institutions'.[18] It identifies the Member States as 'Masters of the Treaty', which establish an IO for specific purposes.

[14] In the original: 'se profile une finalité plus lointaine, celle de l'unité politique': Pescatore (13) 327; see also De Witte (n 8) 21–8.

[15] See seminally E Haas, *The Uniting of Europe: Political, Social, and Economic Forces 1950–1957* (Stanford University Press, 1968); also W Sandholtz and A Stone Sweet, 'Neofunctionalism and Supranational Governance' in E Jones, A Menon, and S Weatherill (eds), *The Oxford Handbook of the European Union* (OUP, 2012); and B Rosamond, *Theories of European Integration* (Macmillan, 2000) 31–42 on functionalism and 50–73 on neofunctionalism.

[16] Rosamond (n 15) 59–65.

[17] See for a historic overview also H-J Glaesner, 'Les objectifs de la Communauté économique européenne: origine et développements' in *L'Europe et le droit: Mélanges en hommage à Jean Boulouis* (Dalloz, 1991).

[18] Art 1 ECSC Treaty.

The 'mission' of the ECSC is spelled out in Art 2 of its founding treaty: 'to contribute to economic expansion, the development of employment and the improvement of the standard of living in the participating countries through the institution, in harmony with the general economy of the member States, of a common market'.[19] This is subsequently linked to more specific 'tasks' in Art 3 ECSC.[20] Similarly, the Euratom Treaty of 1957 starts out with general and more specific 'tasks' in its first two articles. The former is 'to contribute to the raising of the standard of living in the Member States and to the development of relations with the other countries by creating the conditions necessary for the speedy establishment and growth of nuclear industries',[21] while the latter again consists of a list of more specific tasks.[22]

Both of these communities are clearly functionally circumscribed in terms of subject matter. However, there are early allusions to a wider and more ambitious project, particularly in the ECSC Treaty. In the preamble to this treaty, next to references to fostering peace and prosperity, there is also the expression of the will to use the Coal and Steel Community as the starting point for a more far-ranging integration project.[23] It recognizes 'the fact that Europe can be built only by concrete actions which create a real solidarity and by the establishment of common bases for economic development'.[24] This echoes the 1950 Schuman Declaration[25] and represents an illustration of the (neo)functionalist approach in the sense of integration theory. The preamble to the ECSC Treaty points to a future based on 'a broader and deeper community among peoples long divided by bloody conflicts' endowed with 'institutions which will give direction to a destiny henceforth shared'.[26] As discussed in Chapter 2, it also includes a hint of the external dimension of European integration as it refers to 'the contribution which an organized and vital Europe can make to civilization' and its indispensability for 'peaceful relations' at large.[27]

The 1957 Treaty Establishing the European Economic Community (EEC Treaty), with the latter being conceived of as an organization created for a specific purpose, ie economic integration through the common market, represented the next step in the integration project and opened up new areas of cooperation. While Art 1 TEC highlights that an international treaty is the basis of this community,

[19] Art 2(1) ECSC Treaty.
[20] See also P-C Müller-Graff, 'Verfassungsziele der EG/EU' in M Dauses (ed), *Handbuch des EU-Wirtschaftsrechts*, loose-leaf, 27th supplement (C.H. Beck, 2010) marginal nos 107–11.
[21] Art 1(2) EAEC Treaty; Art 1(1) EAEC Treaty refers to the establishment of the Community by the contracting parties by means of the treaty.
[22] Art 2 EAEC. These relate primarily to information sharing, supplies, and security measures. See further Müller-Graff (n 20) marginal nos 160–5.
[23] Fifth recital of the preamble, ECSC Treaty; see also Müller-Graff (n 20) marginal nos 103–6.
[24] Third recital of the preamble, ECSC Treaty.
[25] Schuman Declaration, 9 May 1950. In the original French version: 'L'Europe ne se fera pas d'un coup, ni dans une construction d'ensemble: elle se fera par des réalisations concrètes créant d'abord des solidarités de fait.' Much of the preamble to the ECSC Treaty has been inspired by this declaration.
[26] Fifth recital of the preamble, ECSC Treaty.
[27] Second recital of the preamble, ECSC Treaty.

Art 2 sets out its general 'task',[28] while Art 3 contains a list of related activities. However, in the original 1957 version of the EEC Treaty there is already evidence that the integration project is meant to evolve further, evoking in the preamble the idea of 'an ever closer union among the European peoples'.[29]

In the course of the different Treaty revisions, the provisions on the tasks and activities of the Community expanded significantly in scope. This resulted in a growing domain of Community competences and deepening integration. Whereas the main objective set out in Art 2 of the EEC Treaty of 1957 still focused largely on the common market and economic integration, the same provision in the version of the Nice Treaty makes this widening and deepening apparent by referring, in addition to economic aspects of integration, to monetary union, sustainability, social aspects, gender equality, solidarity, and environmental protection.[30] The same is reflected in the longer list of activities and more varied policies of the Community. While Art 3 EEC of the Rome Treaty listed eleven such activities, almost all of an economic character,[31] the article as it appears after the Nice reform catalogues no fewer than twenty-one activities and policies, which include environmental, health, and energy policies.[32]

To what used to be called the 'first pillar', ie the European Community, one needs to add the objectives of the second and third pillars, ie the Common Foreign and Security Policy (CFSP) and the Justice and Home Affairs (later Police and Judicial Cooperation in Criminal Matters following the 1997 Amsterdam Treaty). While Art 1 TEU (pre-Lisbon) expresses the international treaty basis of the Union, it adds that the 'task' of the Union 'shall be to organise, in a manner demonstrating consistency and solidarity, relations between the Member States and between their peoples'.[33] This task is much broader and goes beyond the strictly economic sphere.

Subsequently, Art 2 TEU (pre-Lisbon) lists the 'objectives' the Union sets itself, which serve as an overview of the wide range of policy domains the EU was mandated to engage in by that time. Accordingly, those objectives are:

[28] This task is related to the common market: 'The Community shall have as its task, by establishing a common market and progressively approximating the economic policies of the Member States, to promote throughout the Community a harmonious development of economic activities, a continuous and balanced expansion, an increase in stability, an accelerated raising of the standard of living and closer relations between the States belonging to it.' See also Müller-Graff (n 20) marginal no 123.

[29] First recital of the preamble, EEC Treaty (original version); even clearer in terms of continuous evolution is the French version ('union sans cesse plus étroite'); also Müller-Graff (n 20) marginal no 113, who points out that the idea of an overarching community appears here as the paramount consideration, in contrast with the ECSC Treaty, where this was still peace.

[30] Art 2 TEC.

[31] But note Art 3(i) and (k) EEC (original version) on the establishment of a European Social Fund and cooperation with overseas countries (also in terms of social development), respectively.

[32] Art 3 TEC. For the expansion of Community powers beyond the Treaty text, also taking into account its interpretation by the institutions, see D Wyatt, 'Is the European Union an Organization of Limited Powers?' in A Arnull et al (eds), *A Constitutional Order of States? Essays in EU Law in Honour of Alan Dashwood* (Hart Publishing, 2011).

[33] Art 1(3) TEU (Nice version).

- to promote economic and social progress and a high level of employment and to achieve balanced and sustainable development, in particular through the creation of an area without internal frontiers, through the strengthening of economic and social cohesion and through the establishment of economic and monetary union, ultimately including a single currency in accordance with the provisions of this Treaty,
- to assert its identity on the international scene, in particular through the implementation of a common foreign and security policy including the progressive framing of a common defence policy, which might lead to a common defence, in accordance with the provisions of Article 17,
- to strengthen the protection of the rights and interests of the nationals of its Member States through the introduction of a citizenship of the Union,
- to maintain and develop the Union as an area of freedom, security and justice, in which the free movement of persons is assured in conjunction with appropriate measures with respect to external border controls, asylum, immigration and the prevention and combating of crime,
- to maintain in full the acquis communautaire and build on it with a view to considering to what extent the policies and forms of cooperation introduced by this Treaty may need to be revised with the aim of ensuring the effectiveness of the mechanisms and the institutions of the Community.[34]

These objectives are complemented by more specific goals of the second and third pillars. The specific objectives of the CFSP were listed as:

- to safeguard the common values, fundamental interests, independence and integrity of the Union in conformity with the principles of the United Nations Charter,
- to strengthen the security of the Union in all ways,
- to preserve peace and strengthen international security, in accordance with the principles of the United Nations Charter, as well as the principles of the Helsinki Final Act and the objectives of the Paris Charter, including those on external borders,
- to promote international cooperation,
- to develop and consolidate democracy and the rule of law, and respect for human rights and fundamental freedoms.[35]

In addition, the objectives of Police and Judicial Cooperation in Criminal Matters are defined as providing 'citizens with a high level of safety within an area of freedom, security and justice by developing common action among the Member States in the fields of police and judicial cooperation in criminal matters and by preventing and combating racism and xenophobia'.[36] More specifically, the objectives include 'preventing and combating crime, organized or otherwise, in particular terrorism, trafficking in persons and offences against children, illicit drug trafficking and illicit arms trafficking, corruption and fraud'.[37] The addition of these objectives, which were not intimately linked to the common market, changed the previously predominantly economic character of the Treaty objectives.[38]

[34] Art 2 TEU (Nice version). [35] Art 11 TEU (Nice version).

[36] Art 29(1) TEU (Nice version). [37] Art 29(2) TEU (Nice version).

[38] See C Calliess, 'Kollektive Ziele und Prinzipien im Verfassungsrecht der EU—Bestandsaufnahme, Wirkungen und Perspektiven' (2003) 92 *Archiv für Rechts- und Sozialphilosophie-Beiheft* 85, 90.

However, by no means do the Treaties represent the Union as the final step in the integration process. The preamble to the TEU (pre-Lisbon) states that the Union constitutes 'a new stage in the process of European integration'. At the same time it expresses the resolve 'to continue the process of creating an ever closer union among the peoples of Europe' and points to 'further steps to be taken in order to advance European integration'.[39]

The latest step in this widening of the objectives of the Union is the Lisbon Treaty, which entered into force on 1 December 2009. Following the failure of the Draft Treaty Establishing a Constitution for Europe, the Lisbon Treaty incorporates many of the changes envisaged by the Constitutional Treaty, including the objectives (see also Chapter 2, section 3.6). The Community has been absorbed into the single legal personality of the Union.[40] The latter now represents an integrated structure, having abandoned the confusing pillar structure erected by Maastricht, though it is still based on a set of treaties instead of one constitutional document.[41] Even though at the outset their operative parts still reflect the persisting fact that the TEU and TFEU are international treaties,[42] for the first time the values on which the Union is founded have been placed before its objectives.[43] Of course, the order of articles does not determine their legal weight. Nevertheless, it intimates a shift in perspective from a legal entity, which exists primarily to pursue certain aims, to one that exhibits what it stands for in the first place.

However, the notion of objectives is added to Art 1, stating that the Union is not simply established (as the previous versions stated),[44] but that the Member States confer competences on it 'to attain objectives they have in common'.[45] Positioning this notion at the very top of the operative part and referring to objectives shared by the Member States rather than Union objectives (which follow in Art 3 TEU) can be seen as harking back to the principle of speciality of international organizations. It also recalls the central role of the Member States in the integration project, and arguably their continued importance, not least in EU external relations.

This latest episode of treaty reform has not only led to a further expansion, but also to the streamlining and bundling of the objectives of the Union. The main expression of these can now be found in Art 3 TEU, which clearly shows the wide ambit of the Union's activities post-Lisbon:

[39] Thirteenth recital of the preamble TEU (Nice version).

[40] Art 1(3) TEU (Lisbon version).

[41] However, certain special rules in the area of the CFSP remain: Art 24(1), second subpara TEU. Moreover, the EAEC Treaty also continues to exist alongside the TEU and TFEU. See M Cremona, 'The Two (or Three) Treaty Solution: The New Treaty Structure of the EU' in A Biondi, P Eeckhout, and S Ripley (eds), *EU Law after Lisbon* (OUP, 2012); and P Van Elsuwege, 'EU External Action after the Collapse of the Pillar Structure: In Search of a New Balance between Delimitation and Consistency' (2010) 47 *Common Market Law Review* 987.

[42] Art 1(1) TEU and Art 1 TFEU; see also M Pechstein, 'Art. 1 (ex-Art. 1 EUV) [Gründung der Europäischen Union; Grundlagen]' in R Streinz (ed), *EUV/AEUV: Vertrag über die Europäische Union und Vertrag über die Arbeitsweise der Europäischen Union*, 2nd edn (C.H. Beck, 2012) 11 (marginal no 6).

[43] Art 2 TEU; see previously Art 6 TEU (Nice version).

[44] Compare Art 1 TEC and Art 1(1) TEU (Nice version).

[45] Art 1(1) TEU.

1. The Union's aim is to promote peace, its values and the well-being of its peoples.
2. The Union shall offer its citizens an area of freedom, security and justice without internal frontiers, in which the free movement of persons is ensured in conjunction with appropriate measures with respect to external border controls, asylum, immigration and the prevention and combating of crime.
3. The Union shall establish an internal market. It shall work for the sustainable development of Europe based on balanced economic growth and price stability, a highly competitive social market economy, aiming at full employment and social progress, and a high level of protection and improvement of the quality of the environment. It shall promote scientific and technological advance.

   It shall combat social exclusion and discrimination, and shall promote social justice and protection, equality between women and men, solidarity between generations and protection of the rights of the child.

   It shall promote economic, social and territorial cohesion, and solidarity among Member States.

   It shall respect its rich cultural and linguistic diversity, and shall ensure that Europe's cultural heritage is safeguarded and enhanced.
4. The Union shall establish an economic and monetary union whose currency is the euro.
5. In its relations with the wider world, the Union shall uphold and promote its values and interests and contribute to the protection of its citizens. It shall contribute to peace, security, the sustainable development of the Earth, solidarity and mutual respect among peoples, free and fair trade, eradication of poverty and the protection of human rights, in particular the rights of the child, as well as to the strict observance and the development of international law, including respect for the principles of the United Nations Charter.

The turn away from the preponderance of economic goals to a wider set of objectives is undeniable here, as 'the new list focusses on non-economic goals to a far greater extent than the EC Treaty'.[46] As was already the case before the Lisbon reform, these general objectives of the Union are complemented by numerous objectives related to specific policy areas and sub-areas. Art 21 TEU now sets out an additional comprehensive list of objectives for the external action of the Union. Subsequently, Art 206 and Art 208 TFEU indicate specific objectives for trade policy and development cooperation, respectively. Other examples include the aims of environmental policies (Art 191(1) TFEU) and energy policies (Art 194(1) TFEU).

Hence, as a preliminary conclusion, objectives have always figured prominently in the primary law of the Union and its predecessor organizations. However, while they were initially rather limited and focused on specific areas, they have since expanded in the ongoing course of deeper integration, enshrined in the primary law notion of the emblematic 'ever closer Union'. While integration started, as Gráinne de Búrca notes, 'as a kind of pilot project of limited economic integration with a view to securing greater peace and prosperity for the Member States, the EU

[46] K Lenaerts and P Van Nuffel, *European Union Law*, 3rd edn (Sweet & Maxwell, 2011) 107; also M Ruffert, 'Art. 3 (ex-Art. 2 EUV) [Ziele der EU]' in C Calliess and M Ruffert (eds), *EUV/AEUV Kommentar*, 4th edn (C.H. Beck, 2011) 44 (marginal no 6); and W Drescher, 'Ziele und Zuständigkeiten' in A Marchetti and C Demesmay (eds), *Der Vertrag von Lissabon: Analyse und Bewertung* (Nomos, 2010) 67.

has evolved into something much larger, more complex and more ambitious'.[47] Thus, whereas it was still plausible to situate the ECSC, Euratom, and the original EEC among classic international organizations marked by functionality and specificity, this has become an increasingly inapplicable label over time.

2.3 Covering all basic objectives of states

In view of the widening of the Union's objectives over time, the Union has come to address all goals that states are usually mandated by their constitutions to pursue. Regarding the content of Union objectives, Karl-Peter Sommermann's distinction of the five basic state objectives (see Chapter 1, section 4.1), into which the most abstract notion of the pursuit of the common good (and the guarantee of security) can be broken down,[48] can be applied by analogy. Beyond similarities in the patterns of specifically externally oriented objectives (Chapter 2, section 4), this will not only systematize the overall objectives of the Union, but also further bolster the claim that objectives of the European Union can indeed be compared with the constitutional objectives of states rather than those of classic international organizations. In the post-Lisbon TEU, there are codifications of all these levels of abstraction as well as the five basic functions.[49]

The very first among the general objectives of the Union is 'to promote peace, its values and the well-being of its peoples' (Art 3(1) TEU). The notion of 'well-being of its peoples' comes close to the notion of a European common good. It recalls the seminal pronouncement of the Court of Justice of the European Union (CJEU) in *van Gend en Loos* that the subjects of what is now the Union 'comprise not only Member States but also their nationals'.[50] Even though the predominance of the economic dimension of European integration has diminished over time, references to economic well-being are also still clearly present. These would include foremost the objective of advancing 'the sustainable development of Europe based on balanced economic growth and price stability, a highly competitive social market economy, aiming at full employment and social progress' (Art 3(3) TEU).[51]

The evocation of peace, in addition, indicates the wish for security, which is developed further externally through the CFSP and internally through 'an area of freedom, security and justice without internal frontiers' that is to be offered to the

[47] G de Búrca, 'Europe's *raison d'être*' in D Kochenov and F Amtenbrink (eds), *The European Union's Shaping of the International Legal Order* (CUP, 2013) 21.

[48] K-P Sommermann, *Staatsziele und Staatszielbestimmungen* (Mohr Siebeck, 1997) 198 et seq.

[49] See also M Kotzur, 'Die Ziele der Union: Verfassungsidentität und Gemeinschaftsidee' (2005) 58 *Die Öffentliche Verwaltung* 313, 316, who distinguishes for the objectives of the Union the themes community of peace, rule of law, values and responsibility, economics, welfare and solidarity, precaution and development, and culture; see further for a detailed and historical breakdown of Union/Community objectives in terms of content, Müller-Graff (n 20) marginal nos 99–175.

[50] Case 26/62 *van Gend & Loos*, EU:C:1963:1, para 10; the Court also makes reference to the 'ever closer union among the peoples of Europe' that figures in the preamble to the EEC Treaty (para 9). In the post-Lisbon TEU, this notion appears in addition to the preamble in Art 1(2) TEU.

[51] See also Ruffert (n 46) marginal no 21, who argues that 'well-being' is to be understood primarily in the economic sense.

citizens of the Union (Art 3(2) TEU).[52] However, as providing security is one of the most fundamental objectives of the state, the Member States of the EU have been circumspect in endowing the Union with powers for pursuing this objective. According to the TEU, the Union is to respect the Member States' 'essential State functions, including ensuring the territorial integrity of the State, maintaining law and order and safeguarding national security', stressing that '[i]n particular, national security remains the sole responsibility of each Member State'.[53] Thus, even though the Union can contribute to ensuring a secure environment, the Member States have not been deprived of the power to pursue this fundamental objective, for which they retain the 'ultimate responsibility' (*Letztverantwortung*).[54]

Turning to the five basic state objectives, ie the rule of law, social justice, culture, environment, and peace, there is ample evidence in the primary law of the EU that makes them explicit as Union objectives. While some authors regard 'integration' as such as an objective (see section 2.6 below), it is not regarded here as a constitutional and substantive objective. This is because it represents a means to an end, ie it concerns the question of whether further integration is necessary to better pursue the constitutional objectives of the Union.

Firstly, the rule of law, while primarily a structural principle, also exhibits aspirational characteristics. This is no different in the EU legal order. The rule of law already manifests itself in the very existence of the Union and its predecessors as, to cite Walter Hallstein, 'a phenomenon of law'.[55] This has been one of the key arguments of the 'integration through law' theorists of European integration, ie that European integration is mainly driven and safeguarded by embedding states in a legal–institutional framework where they can be held accountable, and in which national courts and citizens are also active participants.[56] As Hallstein noted rather solemnly: 'The majesty of law is to achieve what blood and iron were not capable of for centuries.'[57]

As an objective closely related to that of pacification within Europe, the rule of law can be regarded as largely consolidated today. Illustrative of this is that it ranks

[52] Note also Art 67 TFEU on the objectives of the Area of Freedom, Security and Justice (AFSJ).

[53] Art 4(2) TEU; also Arts 72 and 73 TFEU. However, note that according to the CJEU, Member State actions must still be consistent with obligations under EU law: Case C-284/05 *Commission v Finland*, EU:C:2009:778, para 45 and case law cited therein (see also Chapter 4, section 3.1).

[54] R Streinz, 'Art. 4 [Beziehungen zwischen der Union und den Mitgliedstaaten]' in R Streinz (ed), *EUV/AEUV: Vertrag über die Europäische Union und Vertrag über die Arbeitsweise der Europäischen Union*, 2nd edn (C.H. Beck, 2012) 29 (marginal no 17); see also on the state objective of internal security and the AFSJ, V Götz, 'Innere Sicherheit' in J Isensee and P Kirchhof (eds), *Handbuch des Staatsrechts der Bundesrepublik Deutschland. Volume IV: Aufgaben des Staates*, 3rd edn (C.F. Müller, 2006) 696–8.

[55] In the original: 'ein Phänomen des Rechts': W Hallstein, *Die Europäische Gemeinschaft*, 5th edn (Econ Verlag, 1979) 53.

[56] See seminally JHH Weiler, 'The Transformation of Europe' (1991) 100 *Yale Law Journal* 2403; and E Stein, 'Lawyers, Judges, and the Making of a Transnational Constitution' (1981) 75 *American Journal of International Law* 1; note also *van Gend & Loos* (n 50) para 16, where the court underlines the importance of the decentralized 'vigilance of individuals'.

[57] In the original: 'Die Majestät des Rechts soll schaffen, was Blut und Eisen in Jahrhunderten nicht vermochten': Hallstein (n 55) 53.

among the values of the Union in Art 2 TEU. In that 'formal' sense, within the legal system of the European Union, the rule of law can foremost be understood now as a structural principle.[58] However, as a substantive principle akin to that of justice,[59] there is still scope to view it also as an objective.[60] It commits the Union institutions to making a continuous effort to ensure that the legal system of the EU and its policies are effective and comply with a general notion of justice and fairness.

Secondly, with regard to social justice, there are reflections of this general objective in Treaty provisions evoking 'a highly competitive social market economy',[61] 'social progress',[62] 'social justice',[63] and 'economic, social and territorial cohesion, and solidarity among Member States'.[64] Moreover, explicit reference is made to 'fundamental social rights as defined in the European Social Charter ... and in the 1989 Community Charter of the Fundamental Social Rights of Workers'.[65] Within the area of social policy, more specific objectives are added.[66] This is significant in the historic development of the Union, in the sense that the predominance of economic objectives, especially with regard to liberalization in the framework of the common market, has diminished and that the economic activity of the Union is seen rather as a means of providing greater prosperity for its citizens.[67]

Thirdly, culture first appears as a source of inspiration in the preamble to the TEU, together with the 'religious and humanist inheritance of Europe from which have developed the universal values of the inviolable and inalienable rights of the human person, freedom, democracy, equality and the rule of law'.[68] The TEU thus situates culture as the extra-legal source for the European integration process. It also serves as an objective, albeit in a rather negative sense.[69] In the preamble to the TEU, the desire of the Member States 'to deepen the solidarity between their

[58] See L Pech, '"A Union Founded on the Rule of Law": Meaning and Reality of the Rule of Law as a Constitutional Principle of EU Law' (2010) 6 *European Constitutional Law Review* 359; see further for a discussion of the rule of law in the EU context, N Walker, 'The Rule of Law and the EU: Necessity's Mixed Virtue' in G Palombella and N Walker (eds), *Relocating the Rule of Law* (Hart Publishing, 2009).

[59] The term 'justice' is present in the Treaties as well: As a value (Art 2 TEU), in the notion of the 'area of freedom, security and justice' (Art 3(2) TEU), and as 'social justice' (Art 3(3), second subpara TEU).

[60] In this sense also Kotzur (n 49) 317; and on the various functions of the rule of law in the EU, Walker (n 58) 125–32.

[61] Art 3(3), first subpara TEU.

[62] Art 3(3), first subpara TEU.

[63] Art 3(3), second subpara TEU.

[64] Art 3(3), third subpara TEU; note also Drescher (n 46) 68, who states that Art 3 TEU appears almost 'overloaded' (*überladen*) with language pertaining to social welfare.

[65] Fifth recital of the preamble, TEU; and Art 151(1) TFEU.

[66] Art 151(1) TFEU: those being 'the promotion of employment, improved living and working conditions, so as to make possible their harmonisation while the improvement is being maintained, proper social protection, dialogue between management and labour, the development of human resources with a view to lasting high employment and the combating of exclusion'.

[67] Kotzur (n 49) 320; also Müller-Graff (n 20) marginal no 118.

[68] Second recital of the preamble, TEU.

[69] But see Kotzur (n 49) 321, who is more positive about the Union's role in cultural matters, evoking the image of a 'community of culture' (*Kulturgemeinschaft*). However, he also acknowledges that culture as a unifying factor is more self-evident for nation states.

peoples *while* respecting their history, their culture and their traditions' already becomes evident.[70] This means that solidarity cannot go so far as to undermine the cultural diversity among the different Member States. In this vein, among the general objectives of the Union, there is the stipulation that it 'shall respect its rich cultural and linguistic diversity, and shall ensure that Europe's cultural heritage is safeguarded and enhanced'.[71] This means that Union institutions are to refrain from encroaching upon cultural diversity.[72] This diversity concerns the 'cultures of the Member States'[73] or the 'culture and history of the European peoples'.[74] No reference is made to a notion of culture that pertains to the Union as such (eg 'culture of the European Union'), but only to a common European 'inheritance' (preamble to the TEU), 'common cultural heritage',[75] or 'cultural heritage of European significance'.[76] This represents another feature that sets the Union apart from the (nation) state. Its objective is not to protect and promote *its* culture, but that of the Member States individually or a shared European cultural patrimony that largely predates the process of European integration. However, the EU has a competence in the area of culture, as shown for instance by the conclusion by the (then) European Community of the Convention on the Protection and Promotion of the Diversity of Cultural Expressions (better known as the 'UNESCO Convention') in 2006.[77]

Fourthly, the basic constitutional objective of environmental protection is well codified in the Treaties. The preamble to the TEU already links the internal market with notions of sustainable development and environmental protection.[78] This connection is reiterated in the general objectives of the Union, according to which the Union 'shall work for the *sustainable development of Europe* based on balanced economic growth and price stability, … and *a high level of protection and improvement of the quality of the environment*'.[79] Environmental protection furthermore appears in a horizontal clause, requiring the Union to take it into account in all its policies and activities.[80] More specific environmental objectives are subsequently set out in the provisions concerning the Union's environmental policy.[81]

70 Sixth recital of the preamble, TEU (emphasis added).

71 Art 3(3), fourth subpara TEU.

72 See also Art 167 TFEU, in which the preservation of cultural diversity is also a very present element.

73 Art 167(1) TFEU. 74 Art 167(2) TFEU. 75 Art 167(1) TFEU.

76 Art 167(2) TFEU.

77 Council Decision 2006/515/EC of 18 May 2006 on the conclusion of the Convention on the Protection and Promotion of the Diversity of Cultural Expressions [2006] OJ L 201/15. The Council Decision identifies as legal basis, next to trade, international cooperation in the field of development, and economic, financial and technical cooperation, also Art 151 TEC (now Art 167(4) TFEU) on culture.

78 Ninth recital of the preamble, TEU.

79 Art 3(3), first subpara TEU (emphasis added). See in detail, but in the pre-Lisbon context, L Krämer, *EC Environmental Law*, 6th edn (Sweet & Maxwell, 2007) 8–14 on environmental objectives.

80 Art 11 TFEU. In this vein, both Müller-Graff and Kotzur contextualize environmental protection in terms of the improvement of the quality of life and the principle of precaution, respectively, Müller-Graff (n 20) marginal no 118; Kotzur (n 49) 321.

81 Art 191(1) TFEU: those being 'preserving, protecting and improving the quality of the environment', 'protecting human health', 'prudent and rational utilisation of natural resources', and

Finally, the objective of peace has a fundamental internal as well as external dimension for the Union. It appears as the first among the Union's general objectives.[82] Matthias Ruffert calls it the 'intrinsic' (*ureigentlich*) goal of the process of European integration.[83] Similarly, Markus Kotzur deems it the 'main goal' (*Hauptziel*) of the Union, but stresses that ensuring peace is to be seen as the overarching, legitimacy-creating paradigm of any legal order.[84] Historically, it reaches back to the very beginnings of European integration, with the Coal and Steel Community being set up first and foremost to make war between France and Germany materially impossible.[85] Today, internally, it largely coincides with the general objectives of prosperity and security to be provided within the Union. As a positive and wide notion of peace, it links to and indeed encapsulates the other main objectives.[86] As an external objective of the Union, peace also figures prominently in the Treaties.[87] This constitutional mandate to promote a positive and widely defined notion of peace highlights that the constitutional objectives of EU external action go far beyond trade or protecting the EU and its Member States from external threats (see Chapter 2, sections 4 and 5).[88]

This overview of the constitutional objectives of the Union underlines once more the degree of comprehensiveness they have reached, which can hardly be compared with the strict functionality of a traditional international organization. These objectives of the EU can be reorganized easily into the five basic categories proposed by Sommermann for state objectives. In terms of content, this bears testimony to the overall comparability of Union and national constitutional law, while keeping in mind the structural need of the Union for objectives. This last point can also be gleaned from the fact that unlike national constitutions, which usually contain rather specific objectives reflecting an implied general objective, Union primary law actually spells out all of the basic objectives as well as the most abstract ones such as security and well-being. For a state to codify in its constitution that it exists for the 'well-being' of its citizens, by contrast, may appear superfluous. However, as the example of Indian directive principles of state policy shows, national constitutions can also contain provisions on every basic category of state objectives (see Chapter 1, section 4.3). There are, moreover, national examples where the common good is explicitly evoked, albeit only in preambles. These include the preambles to the constitutions of Spain, Russia, and Brazil, which all evoke the notion of the 'well-being' of their peoples as a general purpose. The preamble to the constitution of Ireland, moreover, states the intention 'to promote the common good'.

'promoting measures at international level to deal with regional or worldwide environmental problems, and in particular combating climate change'.

82 Art 3(1) TEU.
83 Ruffert (n 46) marginal no 15.
84 Kotzur (n 49) 316.
85 Müller-Graff (n 20) 104; see also Hallstein (n 55) 66–7.
86 Müller-Graff (n 20) marginal no 115; Kotzur (n 49) 316.
87 Eleventh recital of the preamble, TEU; Arts 3(5) and 21(2)(c) TEU; further Kotzur (n 49) 316.
88 Ruffert (n 46) marginal nos 16–18.

2.4 The contested nature of the Union

As integration has progressed, the objectives of the EU have been expanded significantly from rather narrow, economic ones to a large variety of areas, covering what could be termed a 'European common good'. Contemplating this in isolation, however, would merely amount to an international organization with an extraordinarily large catalogue of tasks and functions.[89] However, representing one of the most prominent topics in European legal scholarship, the nature of the Union itself is often understood as having transformed.[90] Into what exactly the Union and its legal order have changed is a source of controversy and debate, with opinions ranging from merely an enhanced international organization to a quasi-federal entity with its own constitution.[91] Moreover, as an ongoing process, the end point of integration, ie what the 'end stage' of the Union should be, also remains a contentious issue after the Lisbon reform. This is the question of *finalité* of the Union, which has to be distinguished from the general objectives of the Union.

The CJEU usually appears as the main protagonist of effecting and elaborating upon these changes.[92] It famously declared the Treaties and the legal order they established as representing 'a *new* legal order of international law'.[93] In the following paragraphs, this story of transformation will be revisited with a particular regard to the objectives enshrined in the Treaties as legal norms within this new legal order. To recall the classic distinction: States, given their all-encompassing *Kompetenz-Kompetenz*, do not need objectives. As shown in Chapter 1, constitutional objectives do not establish any competences in the national legal order. The ends do not justify *eo ipso* the accompanying powers. These are provided for elsewhere in the constitution. Nonetheless, it was also revealed from a comparative perspective that states increasingly choose to include objectives in their constitutional documents, which in turn can help to interpret other constitutional norms, including those on the allocation of powers. In contrast, international organizations, as derivative subjects of international law and created to perform certain functions, exist only by virtue of their very functionality. Against this backdrop, it is essential to enquire how the transformation of the EU to something 'more than an international organization (as reflected by the judicially recognized doctrines of supremacy, direct effect etc.) but less than a federal state (no welfare state, insufficient resources, no army etc.)'[94] affects the role of its objectives as legal norms.

[89] See Klein (n 1) 276, who stresses that however broadly defined the functions of either an international or supranational organization may be, they remain entities of attributed powers lacking a *Komptenz-Kompetenz*.

[90] See Weiler (n 56).

[91] For an overview of some of the more prominent labels used to describe the Union and its legal order, see N Walker and S Tierney, 'Introduction: A Constitutional Mosaic? Exploring the New Frontiers of Europe's Constitutionalism' in N Walker, J Shaw, and S Tierney (eds), *Europe's Constitutional Mosaic* (Hart Publishing, 2011) 7–8; and N Walker, 'The Place of European Law' in G de Búrca and JHH Weiler (eds), *The Worlds of European Constitutionalism* (CUP, 2011) 78–9.

[92] See in particular Stein (n 56).

[93] *van Gend & Loos* (n 50) para 10 (emphasis added).

[94] Barnard (n 1) 3.

At the outset, the European Communities were dependent upon objectives, which reflects their original conception as international organizations. Hans Peter Ipsen aptly coined the term '*Zielbedarf*', ie the 'need for objectives', as a defining feature of the Communities.[95] The existential importance of the objectives also becomes apparent in the judgment of the CJEU of 1987 in *Gímenez Zaera*. The Court ruled there that 'Article 2 of the Treaty describes the task of the European Economic Community' and that 'the aims laid down in that provision are concerned with the *existence* and functioning of the Community'.[96]

The objectives contained in the Treaties have played a significant role in the legal process of integration, including within the distinctly teleological interpretation employed by the Court aimed at ensuring the greatest practical effectiveness of EU law (the *effet utile*).[97] In the *van Gend & Loos* judgment, the CJEU had already referred to the 'objective of the EEC Treaty, which is to establish a Common Market, the functioning of which is of direct concern to interested parties in the Community'.[98] This objective, coupled with the observation that sovereign rights had been transferred to the Community institutions, led the Court to conclude that the EEC Treaty was 'more than an agreement which merely creates mutual obligations between the Contracting States'.[99] It is thus apparent that the Treaty objective itself—or rather the interpretation of the objective provided by the Court—established the point of departure for distinguishing the EEC Treaty from traditional international agreements and the Community from ordinary international organizations.

In the subsequent case law of the Court, the objectives codified in the Treaties continued to play a prominent role. The CJEU stressed that former Art 2 TEC 'is placed at the head of the general principles which govern [the Treaty]'.[100] The Court established that whenever a more specific provision refers back to the 'objectives of the Treaty, it means the provisions of articles 2 and 3',[101] ie the codified objectives. Therefore, despite the distinction between 'tasks' and 'activities', Arts 2 and 3 TEC can both be seen as expressing the 'objectives' of the Community.[102] With the entry into force of the Lisbon Treaty, this distinction has become moot, as both have been merged into the 'objectives' of current Art 3 TEU.

In the milestones in the case law of the Court relevant to the transformation thesis, other norms and features come to the fore, which qualify the importance of, and the need to rely on, Treaty objectives. In its landmark judgment of *Les*

[95] HP Ipsen, *Europäisches Gemeinschaftsrecht* (Mohr Siebeck, 1972) 995.

[96] Case 126/86 *Giménez Zaera*, EU:C:1987:395, para 10 (emphasis added).

[97] Calliess (n 38) 85; and Pescatore (13) 327; also M Pollack, *The Engines of European Integration: Delegation, Agency, and Agenda Setting in the EU* (OUP, 2003) 189.

[98] *van Gend & Loos* (n 50) para 9.

[99] *van Gend & Loos* (n 50) para 9.

[100] Case 167/73 *Commission v France*, EU:C:1974:35, para 18.

[101] *Commission v France* (n 100) para 23.

[102] The 'activities' are thus more specific expressions of the 'tasks'. See Case 32/65 *Italy v Council and Commission*, EU:C:1966:42, 405; and Case 249/81 *Commission v Ireland*, EU:C:1982:402, para 28, which refers to 'the aims of the Community as set out in Article 2 and enlarged upon in Article 3 of the Treaty'.

Verts in 1986, the CJEU emphasized that 'the European Economic Community is a Community based on the rule of law' with a 'basic constitutional charter, the Treaty'.[103] In *Opinion 1/91*, the Court reiterated the constitutional claim and expressly distinguished the (then) Community from international organizations: 'In contrast, the EEC Treaty, *albeit* concluded in the form of an international agreement, none the less constitutes the constitutional charter of a Community based on the rule of law'.[104] It also highlighted primacy and direct effect as 'essential characteristics of the Community legal order'.[105] Subsequently, in *Opinion 2/13*, the Court noted that the Union is equipped with 'a new kind of legal order, the nature of which is peculiar to the EU, its own constitutional framework and founding principles',[106] highlighting again primacy, direct effect, conferral, common values, and fundamental rights.[107]

The latter two types of principles hark back to the much-discussed judicial 'discovery' of fundamental rights as general principles of Community law by the CJEU.[108] This was subsequently (partially) codified in Art 6 TEU (pre-Lisbon), which stated the values on which the Union was founded.[109] This development took place against the backdrop of challenges from national constitutional courts, most famously the *Bundesverfassungsgericht*, which claimed the power to review the validity of Community acts against the standard of fundamental rights protection enshrined in national constitutions.[110] Introducing fundamental rights as general principles of (then) Community law is generally seen as a response to these challenges, which was answered by an overall acceptance of the primacy of Community and later Union law by the national constitutional courts.[111]

This development, arguably more than any other, signifies the departure from a functional association governed by public international law towards what in German is known as an *objektive Wertordnung*, ie 'an objective order of values'.[112] In Joseph Raz's terminology, one could speak of a 'thickening' constitutionalism in the Union legal order.[113] At the same time, this marks the emergence of the

[103] Case 294/83 *Parti écologiste 'Les Verts'*, EU:C:1986:166, para 23.

[104] Opinion 1/91 *(EEA)*, EU:C:1991:490, para 21 (emphasis added).

[105] Opinion 1/91 *(EEA)* (n 104) para 21. See also A Rosas and L Armati, *EU Constitutional Law: An Introduction*, 2nd edn (Hart Publishing, 2012) 66–85.

[106] Opinion 2/13 *(ECHR II)*, EU:C:2014:2454, para 158.

[107] Opinion 2/13 *(ECHR II)* (n 106) paras 165–9.

[108] See for the first time Case 29/69 *Stauder*, EU:C:1969:52; generally and for further case law see eg S Douglas-Scott, *Constitutional Law of the European Union* (Longman, 2002) 431–50.

[109] Art 6(1) TEU (Nice version).

[110] Starting with the so-called *Solange I* decision of the *Bundesverfassungsgericht*, Decision of 29 May 1974 (*Solange I*), BVerfGE 37, 271; note also the *controlimiti* doctrine of the Italian *Corte costituzionale*, in particular Decision of 18 December 1973 (*Frontini*), Sentenza N 183/1973. See further on the latter A Tizzano, 'Der italienische Verfassungsgerichtshof (Corte costituzionale) und der Gerichtshof der Europäischen Union' (2010) 37 *Europäische Grundrechte Zeitschrift* 1.

[111] See eg for Germany Decision of 22 October 1986 (*Solange II*), BVerfGE 73, 339; and for Italy Decision of 5 June 1984 (*Granital*), Sentenza N 170/1984. Further J Kühling, 'Fundamental Rights' in von Bogdandy and Bast (eds), *Principles of European Constitutional Law* (n 2) 48.

[112] The term was introduced in the *Lüth* decision of the *Bundesverfassungsgericht*, Decision of 15 January 1958 (*Lüth*), BVerfGE 7, 198, 205, para 27.

[113] J Raz, 'On the Authority and Interpretation of Constitutions: Some Preliminaries' in L Alexander (ed), *Constitutionalism: Philosophical Foundations* (CUP, 1998) 153–4.

European constitutional space, given that the constitutionalization of the EU legal order cannot be viewed in isolation from the existing constitutional orders of the Member States (see Chapter 4, section 2.1). The Court, after all, drew on the 'constitutional traditions common to the Member States'[114] as its first source of inspiration for its fundamental rights case law.

This 'thickening' of the Union legal order then led to changes in the role of objectives within this order, which is neatly illustrated by the advent of fundamental rights. As the Court asserted in *Internationale Handelsgesellschaft*, the protection of such rights would henceforth have to 'be ensured within the framework of the structure and *objectives* of the Community'.[115] Thus, as the legal order is 'constitutionalizing', objectives have to be contextualized with other emerging norms.

The assessment of whether the Union legal order has developed—or thickened—to such an extent that one could properly speak of a constitutional order depends on the definition and criteria applied to the notion of 'constitution'. If this was inextricably linked to the state, or made the presence of a single 'people' a prerequisite, the EU would clearly fail the test.[116] However, as soon as one accepts that entities other than states can have constitutions as well,[117] and that a state-centred *demos* is not an indispensability,[118] there is indeed scope to qualify Union primary law (including the general principles) as its 'constitution'.[119] On the basis of this, it can be argued that EU primary law within the European Union exercises most of the central functions that a constitution fulfils in the legal order of a state.[120] In any event, the combined elements, or 'partial constitutions' (in

[114] Case 11/70 *Internationale Handelsgesellschaft*, EU:C:1970:114, para 4. This was later supplemented by international sources, in particular the ECHR: see Case 4/73 *Nold v Commission*, EU:C:1974:51, para 13.

[115] *Internationale Handelsgesellschaft* (n 114) para 4 (emphasis added); reiterated also in Opinion 2/13 *(ECHR II)* (n 106) para 170.

[116] For references to this literature see Streinz (n 2) 9 (footnote 65).

[117] For historical examples see E Tanchev, 'The Lisbon Treaty within and without Constitutional Orthodoxy' in I Pernice and E Tanchev (eds), *Ceci n'est pas une Constitution—Constitutionalisation without a Constitution?* (Nomos, 2009); for further historical contextualization see L Besselink, 'The Notion and Nature of the European Constitution after the Lisbon Treaty' in J Wouters, L Verhey, and P Kiiver (eds), *European Constitutionalism Beyond Lisbon* (Intersentia, 2009); and S Griller, 'The Reform's Typology: Treaty or Constitution?' in I Pernice and E Tanchev (eds), *Ceci n'est pas une Constitution—Constitutionalisation without a Constitution?* (Nomos, 2009) 47.

[118] See Müller-Graff (n 20) marginal no 84, who refutes this requirement. Note also G Frankenberg, 'Comparative Constitutional Law' in M Bussani and U Mattei (eds), *The Cambridge Companion to Comparative Law* (CUP, 2012) 179, who describes the EU Treaties as a revival of the constitutional archetype of the 'contract'. In its famous *Maastricht* judgment, the *Bundesverfassungsgericht* had ruled that the membership of Germany in the EU, which did not have a people of its own, was constitutionally valid, but stressed the importance of legitimation through national democratic processes, Decision of 12 October 1993 (*Maastricht*), BVerfGE 89, 155, para 100. Further on the so-called 'no demos' debate JHH Weiler, 'Does Europe Need a Constitution? Demos, Telos and the German Maastricht Decision' (1995) 1 *European Law Journal* 219.

[119] See eg Paul Craig, who applies Raz's concept of 'thick constitutionalism' to the EU: P Craig, 'Constitutions, Constitutionalism, and the European Union' (2001) 7 *European Law Journal* 125, 126–35.

[120] C Calliess, 'Art. 1 (ex-Art. 1 EUV) [Gründung der Europäischen Union; Grundlagen]' in C Calliess and M Ruffert (eds), *EUV/AEUV Kommentar*, 4th edn (C.H. Beck, 2011) 22 (marginal no 55); also D Grimm, 'Ursprung und Wandel der Verfassung' in J Isensee and P Kirchhof (eds), *Handbuch des Staatsrechts der Bundesrepublik Deutschland. Volume I: Historische Grundlagen*, 3rd edn

German *Teilverfassungen*),[121] of the European constitutional space, including national, supranational, and also certain international elements, could certainly not fail to meet this standard. Otherwise, any notion of constitutionalism would have to be deemed lost somewhere along the path of the integration process.[122]

Furthermore, from this point of view, the use of the term 'constitutional' to describe the nature of the EU Treaties remains accurate regardless of the fact that the ostensibly constitutional Treaty Establishing a Constitution for Europe never entered into force and that the European Council subsequently claimed to have abandoned the 'constitutional concept'.[123] The same applies to the upheavals surrounding the financial crisis and the Eurozone, which in fact are framed by many scholars as 'constitutional' issues.[124] In that sense, the term 'constitution', while accounting for the fact that the EU is not a state and that it is part of a wider 'constitutional space', is also applied here to the EU Treaties and other primary law.

2.5 The changing position of objectives in the EU's legal order

What does the constitutionalization of the EU's legal order entail for the role of Union objectives? In addition to features such as direct effect and supremacy, this turn from functionality to overarching goals, far-reaching competences, and the emergence of normative foundations, in particular fundamental rights, was a sign of the constitutionalization of the Union for certain scholars.[125] For Armin von Bogdandy, the rise of such founding principles goes hand in hand with a declining importance of objectives. He argues that only initially were the objectives enshrined

(C.F. Müller, 2003) 41; and R Streinz, C Ohler, and C Herrmann, *Der Vertrag von Lissabon zur Reform der EU: Einführung mit Synopse*, 3rd edn (C.H. Beck, 2010) 16.

[121] As coined by C Tomuschat, 'Der Verfassungsstaat im Geflecht der internationalen Beziehungen' (1978) *Veröffentlichungen der Vereinigung deutscher Staatsrechtslehrer* 7, 52 et seq.

[122] M Claes and M de Visser, 'Reflection on Comparative Method in European Constitutional Law' in M Adams and J Bomhoff (eds), *Practice and Theory in Comparative Law* (CUP, 2012) 149, who note that this composite of constitutional norms performs 'the function which in a national legal system is fulfilled by constitutional law'. Similarly, Grimm (n 120) 40–2 stresses the intertwined nature of the legal orders of the Member States and of the EU and concludes that the latter is indeed 'capable of having a constitution' (*konstitutionsfähig*) akin to the federal level in a federal state.

[123] European Council, Presidency Conclusions of the Brussels European Council 21 and 22 June 2007, 20 July 2007, 11177/1/07 REV 1, Annex I: *IGC Mandate*, 15 (pt 1). Discounting this 'proclamation' for the debate on the constitutional approach are eg Griller (n 117) 52–5; and A von Bogdandy and J Bast, 'The Constitutional Approach to EU Law' in A von Bogdandy and J Bast (eds), *Principles of European Constitutional Law*, 2nd edn (Hart Publishing/C.H. Beck, 2011) 1–3. Also, Lenaerts and Van Nuffel (n 46) 819, still maintain the constitutional nature of the EU Treaties, together with fundamental rights and general principles in EU law.

[124] K Tuori and K Tuori, *The Eurozone Crisis: A Constitutional Analysis* (CUP, 2014); and E Chiti and PG Teixeira, 'The Constitutional Implications of the European Responses to the Financial and Public Debt Crisis' (2013) 50 *Common Market Law Review* 683.

[125] See A von Bogdandy, 'Founding Principles of EU Law: A Theoretical and Doctrinal Sketch' (2009) 16 *European Law Journal* 95; also J d'Aspremont and F Dopagne, 'Two Constitutionalisms in Europe: Pursuing an Articulation of the European and International Legal Orders' (2008) 68 *Zeitschrift für ausländisches öffentliches Recht und Völkerrecht* 939, 943–50, who distinguish between 'substantive', ie value-based, and 'systemic', eg direct effect and primacy, constitutionalism.

in the Treaties 'at the centre of efforts to develop an "overarching conception"'.[126] Subsequently, he concludes that due to the 'multiplication of these objectives this approach, however, lost its persuasiveness'.[127] Even more strongly, Franz Reimer contends that the idea of *Zielbedarf* put forward by Ipsen, which served both as the 'vanishing point and source of legitimacy for all Community action while at the same time a sign for the lacking *Kompetenz-Kompetenz* of the Communities', has disappeared.[128] He argues that as a unitary legal person aiming to be understood as a 'community of destiny and values', the Union is defined by catalogues of values and fundamental rights rather than provisions on objectives.[129] Moreover, in view of the competence catalogues which the Constitutional Treaty was to establish, and which the Lisbon Treaty did establish, he argues that objectives have lost their 'competence-enabling function' (*zuständigkeitseröffnende Funktion*), which he considers a veritable paradigm shift.[130]

However, this shift in importance of objectives in the course of progressing 'constitutionalization' should not be confused with the complete sidelining of the Union objectives as legal norms. It is not mutually exclusive to assert the 'constitutional' character of the Union while at the same time acknowledging the remaining, albeit diminished, importance for objectives within the EU legal order. Peter-Christian Müller-Graff, for instance, still defines the Union as a 'sui generis goal-oriented transnational polity [*Gemeinwesen*]'.[131]

The fact remains, even after Lisbon, that the Union does not possess a *Kompetenz-Kompetenz*, but is still an entity of conferred powers. Now, the crucial difference is that the objectives do not act anymore, as they do with international organizations, as the primary source of, and boundary to, the powers of the organization.[132] Instead, they have become goals which shape the exercise of powers defined elsewhere and embedded in a more sophisticated, 'thickened', legal order, in the same vein as constitutional objectives found in national legal orders.

In this manner, one can point to the evolution of Treaty language over time, which captures this move away from the functional international organization and towards national constitutional orders with regard to the role of objectives therein. Prior to the Lisbon Treaty reform, there was no unified competence catalogue in the Treaties, as there is now in Arts 2 to 6 TFEU.[133] Instead, the 1957 EEC Treaty

[126] von Bogdandy (n 125) 99; see also Ipsen (n 95) 128 et seq.

[127] von Bogdandy (n 125) 99. He sees the replacement of the former 'specific objectives' of Arts 2 and 3 TEC by current Art 3 TEU as evidence for this.

[128] In the original: 'Fluchtpunkt und Legitimationstitel allen Gemeinschaftshandelns, zugleich Ausdruck fehlender Kompetenz-Kompetenz der Gemeinschaften': F Reimer, 'Ziele und Zuständigkeiten: Die Funktionen der Unionszielbestimmungen' [2003] *Europarecht* 992, 992. He writes with regard to the (then) looming Constitutional Treaty. His findings can, overall, be transferred to the advent of the Lisbon Treaty.

[129] In the original: 'Schicksals- und Wertegemeinschaft': Reimer (n 128) 992.

[130] Reimer (n 128) 993, also 1009.

[131] In the original: 'zielbezogenes transnationales Gemeinwesen eigener Art': Müller-Graff (n 20) marginal no 73.

[132] Larik (n 3) 962.

[133] The clarification of competences, until then provided by rather scattered Treaty provisions and through CJEU case law, had been a major issue on the agenda ever since the Nice Treaty. To which

contained 'aims' (Art 2) and 'activities' (Art 3), but did not explicitly mention conferral of competences. In the later TEC, as amended by Nice, the principle of conferral was codified in the terms that '[t]he Community shall act within the limits of the powers conferred upon it by this Treaty *and* of the objectives assigned to it therein'.[134] Using this formulation, the competences of the Community were circumscribed by *both* conferred powers *and* objectives. In the post-Lisbon version, it is stated that 'the Union shall act only *within the limits of the competences* conferred upon it by the Member States in the Treaties *to attain the objectives set out therein*'.[135] As Loïc Azoulai rightly notes, '[t]his clearly indicates a change of perspective',[136] seeing that 'objectives are made subject to the competences listed in the Treaties post-Lisbon'.[137] Hence, objectives are no longer the only or even one of the sources for delimiting the powers of the Union.[138] Competences and objectives are set apart. Union competences, now catalogued elsewhere, have to be exercised with a view to pursuing the objectives. This is confirmed by another provision in the Treaties, viz that '[t]he Union shall pursue its objectives by appropriate means *commensurate with the competences* which are conferred upon it in the Treaties'.[139] Objectives and competences now appear, next to others, as two related yet distinct constitutional norm categories (see also section 3.3 below). While keeping in mind that EU competences are still conferred and not inherently comprehensive, this mirrors the position of objectives in the national constitutional order as presented in Chapter 1.

With regard to the principle of conferral, it should be considered that in view of the wide scope of Union competences, while it still applies in theory,[140] its de facto significance has diminished. As a matter of principle, the TEU now makes clear that '[c]ompetences not conferred upon the Union in the Treaties remain with the

extent this cataloguing in the TFEU was a success is, however, debatable. See J-C Piris, *The Lisbon Treaty: A Legal and Political Analysis* (CUP, 2010) 74–8; and rather sceptically R Schütze, 'Lisbon and the Federal Order of Competences: A Prospective Analysis' (2008) 33 *European Law Review* 709.

[134] Art 5(1) TEC (emphasis added). Note also Art 5(3) TEC: 'Any action by the Community shall not go beyond what is necessary to achieve the objectives of this Treaty.'

[135] Art 5(2) TEU (emphasis added).

[136] L Azoulai, 'Introduction: The Question of Competence' in L Azoulai (ed), *The Question of Competence in the European Union* (OUP, 2014) 11.

[137] Azoulai (n 136) 12.

[138] This conclusion would challenge the position maintained by some others that acts beyond the objectives of the Union would have to be considered *ultra vires*, rather than looking at competence norms. See Müller-Graff (n 20) marginal no 178; similarly Reimer (n 128) 992–3; but see P Craig, 'The ECJ and ultra vires Action: A Conceptual Analysis' (2011) 48 *Common Market Law Review* 495, who defines EU action *ultra vires* in terms of competences rather than objectives.

[139] Art 3(6) TEU (emphasis added). Note also in this regard Art 13(2) TEU, which distinguishes between limits imposed by powers and a conformity requirement of objectives: 'Each institution shall act within the *limits* of the *powers* conferred on it in the Treaties, and *in conformity* with the procedures, conditions and *objectives* set out in them' (emphasis added).

[140] Note in this regard also Declaration No 24 annexed to the final Act of the Intergovernmental Conference which adopted the Treaty of Lisbon concerning the legal personality of the European Union, which stresses that granting legal personality to the EU 'will not in any way authorise the Union to legislate or to act beyond the competences conferred upon it by the Member States in the Treaties'. See also Declaration No 18 in relation to the delimitation of competences.

Member States'.[141] Accordingly, objectives cannot be pursued in the absence of corresponding powers provided by the Treaties.[142] However, in view of the scope of competences, it has become rather difficult to pinpoint areas where the Union would clearly not be competent. Thus, despite the 'axiomatic' principle of conferral, defining the powers of the Union 'so as to impose meaningful limits' has become a rather difficult exercise.[143] Instead, questions concerning the nature of the competence and identification of the proper legal basis become relevant, rather than considerations of the existence of competence per se.

Special attention should be paid in this context to the 'flexibility clause' now found in Art 352 TFEU (ex-Art 308 TEC), which provides a link between competences and objectives, with a potential for blurring the two. In a case where Union action becomes necessary 'within the framework of the policies defined in the Treaties, to attain one of the objectives set out in the Treaties, and the Treaties have not provided the necessary powers', such powers can be created following a special procedure, which requires unanimity in the Council and the consent of the Parliament.[144] This provision has been used generously in the past, which was sanctioned by its wide interpretation by the CJEU.[145] Pre-Lisbon, this interpretation already 'meant that it would become virtually impossible to find an activity which could not be brought within the objectives of the Treaty'.[146] However, one cannot consider this an indication of the functionality of the EU legal order or of the function of objectives to establish competences. In this regard, it is the extreme width of Union objectives, providing a kaleidoscope of the 'European common good', which has enabled the flexibility clause to be relied upon for various purposes. Had the objectives remained narrow and specific, this would have weighed against the wide use of this mechanism. Moreover, it is not the objectives

[141] Art 5(2) TEU.

[142] This follows *a contrario* from Art 3(6) TEU and subject to Art 352 TFEU where its procedure is used successfully.

[143] P Craig and G de Búrca, *EU Law: Text, Cases and Materials*, 4th edn (OUP, 2008) 107; the newer edition of the book focuses on the Lisbon reform with a view to clarifying Union competences: P Craig and G de Búrca, *EU Law: Text, Cases and Materials*, 6th edn (OUP, 2015) 74–5 (note: subsequent references refer to this edition); see also S Prechal, S de Vries, and H van Eijken, 'The Principle of Attributed Powers and the "Scope of EU Law"' in L Besselink, F Pennings, and S Perchal (eds), *The Eclipse of the Legality Principle in the European Union* (Kluwer Law International, 2011); U Di Fabio, 'Some Remarks on the Allocation of Competences Between the EU and its Member States' (2002) 39 *Common Market Law Review* 1289, 1296, questioning 'whether a clear delimitation of competences is possible at all'; and generally Wyatt (n 32). Note Case C-74/99 *Imperial Tobacco Ltd and Other*, EU:C:2000:547, as the exceptional case in which a directive was actually annulled for lack of internal competence; see further Douglas-Scott (n 108) 168–9.

[144] Note, however, also Declaration Nos 41 and 42 on Article 352 of the Treaty on the Functioning of the European Union attached to the Lisbon Treaty.

[145] See eg Case 8/73 *Massey-Ferguson*, EU:C:1973:90, para 4; Case 242/87 *Commission v Council (Erasmus)*, EU:C:1989:217; Joined Cases C-402/05 P and C-415/05 P *Kadi and Al Barakaat*, EU:C:2008:461, para 235. See further Douglas-Scott (n 108) 155–63; Lenaerts and Van Nuffel (n 46) 122–4; and Craig and de Búrca (n 143) 90–3.

[146] Weiler (n 56) 2446; for post-Lisbon, see Rosas and Armati (n 105) 26, who similarly state that 'the breadth of these objectives make [sic] it difficult to imagine areas where the Union clearly has no authority to go'.

that found competences here, but the special procedure established in the Treaties. Hence, it confirms the general observation that *constitutional* objectives, while not an independent source of powers, serve to clarify and round off public powers for their proper and effective exercise.

It can be concluded that the Union remains in a state of limbo, being neither a state nor a classic international organization. Does this mean that the enquiry is stuck with the famous 'unsatisfying shrug'[147] while applying the *sui generis* label? With regard to the importance of objectives, this is certainly not the case. The bottom line of the discussions concerning the nature of the European Union and its legal order is that the EU has ventured far from what can be termed a purely technical, *functional* international organization.[148] To draw on the example employed at the start of this section, the European Union today is radically different from the European Commission of the Danube, with regard to which the PCIJ underlined that it was 'an international institution with a special purpose' and with 'functions bestowed upon it by the Definitive Statute with a view to the fulfilment of that purpose'.[149] Looking at the objectives contained in the EU Treaties today, it is impossible to discern any one 'special purpose' or even a discrete set of objectives pertaining to a particular policy area.[150] Instead, the overall purpose of the Union, as the post-Lisbon TEU states, is 'to promote peace, its values and the well-being of its peoples'.[151] This purpose may be interpreted as the fostering of a European 'common good',[152] which is then crystallized further through a range of more specific objectives. As shown in Chapter 1, this corresponds with the abstract definition of the main objective (or even the *raison d'être*) of the state, which is formalized through the insertion of objectives into its constitutional law.

Nonetheless, the EU is not a state, and a dividing line remains between states and the Union even after the Lisbon reform.[153] In the absence of a formal *Kompetenz-Kompetenz*, the Union still has theoretical *Zielbedarf*—a need for objectives. However, even though states have no existential need for objectives,

[147] P Hay, *Federalism and Supranational Organisations: Patterns for New Legal Structures* (University of Illinois Press, 1966) 44.

[148] See Rosas and Armati (n 105) 15–19 on the state-like and non-state like features of the Union; see also Douglas-Scott (n 108) 260, who concludes that 'even if the EEC did conform to the status of international organization in its early days (which is unlikely) it has now moved well beyond that'. Similarly Klein (n 1) 381.

[149] *Jurisdiction of the European Commission of the Danube* (n 8) 64.

[150] See also, commenting on the general objectives of the failed Constitutional Treaty, L Azoulai, 'Article I-3' in L Burgorgue-Larsen, A Levade, and F Picod (eds), *Traité établissant une Constitution pour l'Europe. Volume I* (Bruyalt, 2007) 62.

[151] Art 3(1) TEU.

[152] Piris (n 133) 73 states that the post-Lisbon Art 3 TEU objectives, 'when compared with the past Treaties, go in the direction of respecting human values and caring for the well-being of the people'. On the notion of a European common good, see further C Calliess, 'Gemeinwohl in der Europäischen Union—Über den Staaten- und Verfassungsverbund zum Gemeinwohlverbund' in W Brugger, S Kirste, and M Anderheiden (eds), *Gemeinwohl in Deutschland, Europa und der Welt* (Nomos, 2002) 172–214.

[153] Ruffert (n 46) marginal no 3.

the comparative analysis reveals that they increasingly *choose* to integrate objectives into their constitutional documents. Thus, to draw on Ipsen's term (and to make use of the nuances of the German language), one could say that states have an increasing *Zielbedürfnis*, ie a perceived need or desire to state their objectives in a constitutional document. At the same time, the evolution and thickening of the Union legal order has led to diminishing its *Zielbedarf*. It is here that the 'constitutionalization' of the dynamic, goal-oriented European Union and the overall 'dynamization' of national constitutions of the all-competent state result in the conceptual rapprochement of the two. Hence, the objectives which have emerged in the highest laws of both the national and EU legal orders are indeed similar as legal norms, and can be compared as a matter of comparative *constitutional* law.

2.6 *Finalité*: The open future of the Union

Having concluded that the current state of the Union legal order and objectives are generally amenable to comparison with national constitutions, it should be clarified that the original *Zielbedarf* and the 'dynamization' of EU primary law must be distinguished from its *finalité (politique)*, ie the final form or the ultimate objective of the integration process. *Finalité* has been a prominent topic in EU scholarship,[154] especially when linked to the constitutionalization debate in the EU and particularly within the context of the failed project of the Treaty Establishing a Constitution for Europe.[155]

To a certain degree, the different concepts of *Zielbefarf*, 'dynamization', and *finalité* overlap. Ruffert, for instance, goes as far as calling Art 3 TEU on the objectives of the Union the 'basic norm of the programme of integration'.[156] He argues that even though Union objectives are very closely related to national constitutional objectives, within the Union legal order they have a more important role to play in that they point the integration process in a particular direction.[157] Similarly, Christian Calliess observes that objectives, forming this basic norm of the integration programme, impose a 'standstill' command that prohibits the progress achieved in the pursuit of the objectives from being undone.[158] For him, integration is a one-way process in which the pursuit of Union objectives requires, if anything, more integration. He also points to the teleological interpretation by the CJEU as a way to use objectives to advance integration, which arguably represents

[154] See eg C Joerges, Y Meny, and JHH Weiler (eds), *What Kind of Constitution for What Kind of Polity? Responses to Joschka Fischer* (EUI, 2000).

[155] See N Walker, 'After Finalité? The Future of the European Constitutional Idea' in G Amato, H Bribosia, B De Witte (eds), *Genesis and Destiny of the European Constitution* (Bruylant, 2007); also Walker (n 91) 100; and A Follesdal, 'Towards a Stable *finalité* with Federal Features? The Balancing Acts of the Constitutional Treaty for Europe' (2005) 12 *Journal of European Public Policy* 572.

[156] In the original: 'Grundnorm des Integrationsprogramms': Ruffert (n 46) marginal no 1, using a formulation with clear Kelsian undertones.

[157] Ruffert (n 46) marginal no 2.

[158] Calliess (n 38) 91, referring to Joined Cases 80 and 81/77 *Société Les Commissionnaires Réunis SARL v Receveur des douanes*, EU:C:1978:87, para 36.

the most significant linkage between objectives and *finalité*.[159] Furthermore, the CJEU seems to link objectives to the integration process. In *Opinion 2/13*, the Court notes:

> The pursuit of the EU's objectives, as set out in Article 3 TEU, is entrusted to a series of fundamental provisions, such as those providing for the free movement of goods, services, capital and persons, citizenship of the Union, the area of freedom, security and justice, and competition policy. Those provisions, which are part of the framework of a system that is specific to the EU, are structured in such a way as to contribute—each within its specific field and with its own particular characteristics—to the implementation of the process of integration that is the *raison d'être* of the EU itself.[160]

However, this perspective blurs, on the one hand, the pursuit of Union objectives and, on the other, the changing structure and nature of the Union, as well as the allocation of competences between the Union and Member States. It misconstrues the role of objectives as part of the constitutional law of the Union. Union objectives do not exhaust their function in creating a momentum towards deepening integration. Their dynamic character refers primarily to the establishment of a continuous obligation to actively pursue a certain substantive goal. As to the 'need for objectives' characteristic of international organizations, whether this *Zielbedarf* will become obsolete depends on reaching an end point, a terminus of integration. It would not, however, abrogate the *constitutional duty* to pursue Union objectives within whatever kind of 'final' framework the Union would be consolidated.

On the one hand, if one employs the term *finalité* as 'a negative check on any further integration',[161] then the Union would retain certain core characteristics of an international organization, including those of attributed powers. Nevertheless, even in a state of arrested integration, the Union would still be bound to the objectives already present in primary law. Consequently, it would remain obliged to pursue them, albeit in a way that would not lead to further integration, but still respectful of the characteristic features which have already developed in the Union legal order. On the other hand, if one proposes this end point to be a (federal) state, the existential need for objectives would vanish.

Regardless, it was demonstrated that national constitutional law experiences an increasing shift towards codifying objectives, putting a constitutional obligation on state organs to pursue these goals. In terms of its nature, the Union would have crossed the line demarcating statehood, but even in that case, it would remain bound to pursue its constitutional objectives in much the same way. The important difference here is that the Union would be equipped with a *Kompetenz-Kompetenz*, ie in theory it could allocate competences freely so as to optimize the effective pursuit of its objectives. Nevertheless, as in any federal state (assuming the EU would

[159] See eg Calliess (n 38) 85, who refers to the preservation and coherent further development of European integration as the overarching goal of the EU, on which the teleological interpretation of the CJEU draws.

[160] Opinion 2/13 *(ECHR II)* (n 106) para 172.

[161] Walker (n 155) 1253, who points out the rather diverse positions that have been connected to *finalité*.

not become a centralized state), competences would remain divided between the federal level and the sub-units and constitutional rules would exist governing the division of competences.[162] As Neil Walker rightly underlines, what both those arguing for more and those arguing for less integration share is 'a somewhat static view of the political community',[163] which also sits uneasily with the evidence of a more dynamic understanding of constitutional law expounded here. Even in an allegedly 'final' politico-legal construct, a constant duty to optimize the pursuit of the common good persists.

A more nuanced and accurate approach to the issue of *finalité* and the study of Union objectives would require a distinction between proper 'integration objectives' and other constitutional objectives, and the recognition of an integrative capacity present in 'ordinary' constitutional objectives of the Union. Müller-Graff, for instance, identified specific 'integration objectives' (*integrationspolitische Ziele*) in the pre-Lisbon primary law.[164] For him, these were the evocation of 'economic and social cohesion and solidarity among Member States'[165] and the task of the Union 'to organise, in a manner demonstrating consistency and solidarity, relations between the Member States and between their peoples',[166] which has to be viewed in conjunction with the notion of the 'ever closer union among the peoples of Europe'.[167]

This view suggests that further integration would be necessary for the 'effective' pursuit of Union objectives. However, this entails integration *tout court* not being an end in itself. As Ruffert rightly underlines, the goal is not integration as such, but the achievement of certain objectives *through* integration.[168] Thus, integration should be understood rather as a *means* to pursue substantive constitutional objectives. Crucially, it is *one* means and not the only means, as not all Union objectives have to be pursued through deeper integration at all times. This consequently remains a question of competence allocation and the use of existing Union competences as 'governed by the principles of subsidiarity and proportionality',[169] which raises questions concerning which level of government offers the best platform for the pursuit of objectives. Using the terminology of Robert Alexy, integration can be perceived as one way of 'optimizing' competence allocation with a view to the most effective pursuit of constitutional objectives.[170] Only in the case where the

[162] Note Rosas and Armati (n 105) 19, who stress that the principle of conferral 'is not unknown in the constitutions of certain federal states and it is therefore open to debate whether the principle of conferral amounts to a state or a non-state feature'.

[163] Walker (n 155) 1254.

[164] Müller-Graff (n 20) marginal no 119; but see P Dollat, *Droit européen et droit de l'Union européenne*, 3rd edn (Sirey, 2010) 113 on the vagueness and openness of these 'objectifs politiques internes de l'intégration de l'Union'.

[165] Art 2 TEC. Note that Art 3(3), third subpara TEU uses a slightly different formulation ('economic, social and territorial cohesion, and solidarity among Member States').

[166] Art 1(3) TEC; this formulation is not reiterated in the post-Lisbon Treaties.

[167] First recital of the preamble, TEC; in the Lisbon version, it is referred to in the preambles to both the TEU and TFEU, as well as in the operative part in Art 1(2) TEU.

[168] Ruffert (n 46) marginal no 3.

[169] Art 5(1) TEU.

[170] R Alexy, *A Theory of Constitutional Rights* (OUP, 2002) 47.

Union level would be deemed preferable, yet competences are absent, would questions of further conferral and of further integration arise. This, however, would require sufficient political will to make use of the flexibility clause (Art 352 TFEU) or to amend the Treaties (Art 48 TEU).

In sum, and in view of the dynamic understanding of constitutional law maintained in this book, the usefulness of the concept of *finalité* resides in it being a concept that evokes major shifts in the allocation of competence between the Union and the Member States in favour of the former. This would have consequences for the pursuit of both Union and Member State constitutional objectives, including in the sphere of foreign policy. Apart from that, the Union legal order, similar to national legal orders, is also under constant pressure to adapt to forces and developments from both within and without in living up to its constitutional objectives.

3. Union Objectives as a Constitutional Norm Category

Having addressed the question of the nature of Union objectives as stemming from a *sui generis* legal order, which exhibits constitutional features, the legal properties of these objectives can be addressed, including an assessment of how they fit as a norm category in the overall scheme of EU constitutional law. To this end, their legal effects will be determined, followed by their contextualization with other main categories of Union law and their categorization according to content. Moving first to the basic legal features of Union objectives, ie their legally binding nature, their relationship *inter se*, their circle of addressees, and their justiciability, it becomes evident that they are 'very closely related' to constitutional objectives at the national level.[171]

As this section demonstrates, Union objectives can be defined as norms of constitutional rank within the Union legal order which address a priori all Union organs and commit them to the active and balanced (coherent) pursuit of these objectives within the bounds of what is materially feasible. The entirety of Union law and actions by Union organs is to be interpreted in light of Union objectives. However, Union objectives as such neither found competence nor establish rights or obligations for individuals. Hence, despite the peculiar nature of the Union, they operate as veritable constitutional objectives as defined in Chapter 1.

Union objectives have their direct source in the Treaties in which they are codified. This is similar to the Indian 'directive principles', but in contrast to the French *objectifs de valeur constitutionnelle*, and to a lesser degree also the German *Staatszielbestimmungen*. Unlike in the German scholarly debate, for the EU certain principles (such as the social welfare state) do not have to be interpreted by scholars to reveal their nature as objectives. In contrast to the French situation, there is no need for a court to 'discover' that certain constitutional provisions and principles

[171] In the original: 'aufs engste verwandt': Ruffert (n 46) marginal no 2.

represent objectives. They are not a type of norm that was introduced into the legal discourse and viewed as a strange and unorthodox addition to the constitutional law at first, as was the case in France and Germany. Unlike the case of India, the codification of objectives did not constitute a break with the colonial common law tradition, but came rather naturally with the original functionality of an international organization.

In both case law and scholarship, the objectives in the Treaties have been generally accorded quite lofty titles, unlike some of the commentary on the post-Lisbon foreign policy objectives. The CJEU itself recognized Treaty objectives as standing 'at the head of the general principles which govern [the Treaty, here the TEC]'.[172] Scholars from Germany have called them the 'basic norm of the integration programme',[173] 'vanishing points of action',[174] or described them as an 'overarching *Leitmotiv*'.[175] Others have also highlighted their importance. According to Jean-Claude Piris, Art 3 TEU 'tries to give answers to two basic questions: why has the EU been established? What is it aimed at?'[176] For Alain Pilette and Etienne de Poncins, referring to the Constitutional Treaty, the article on Union objectives 'expresses notably the grand political visions which are at the heart of European integration'.[177]

3.1 Legal bindingness and addressees

Legal scholarship addressing the nature of EU constitutional objectives is virtually unanimous in stating that they are legally binding norms to be distinguished from non-binding guidelines and phrases.[178]

The view on the constitutional character and legal force of objectives is underpinned by the case law of the CJEU. In its early judgment in *Groupement des hauts fourneaux et aciéries belges*, the Court ruled that the ECSC High Authority was

[172] Case 167/73 *Commission v France*, EU:C:1974:35, para 18.

[173] In the original: 'Grundnorm des Integrationsprogramms': Ruffert (n 46) marginal no 1, and the references there (footnote 1).

[174] In the original: 'Fluchtpunkte eines Handelns': Reimer (n 128) 996.

[175] In the original: 'übergreifende[s] Leitmotiv': H-J Blanke, 'Art. 2 (ex-Art. B)' in C Calliess and M Ruffert (eds), *EUV/EGV: Das Verfassungsrecht der Europäischen Union mit Europäischer Grundrechtecharta*, 3rd edn (C.H. Beck, 2007) 28, speaking in the pre-Lisbon context of the three pillars.

[176] Piris (n 133) 72.

[177] In the original: 'énonce notamment les grandes visions politiques qui sont au cœur de la construction européenne': A Pilette and E de Poncins, 'Valeurs, objectifs et nature de l'Union' in G Amato, H Bribosia, and B De Witte (eds), *Genesis and Destiny of the European Constitution* (Bruylant, 2007) 302.

[178] M Pechstein, 'Art. 3 (ex-Art. 2 EUV) [Ziele der Union]' in R Streinz (ed), *EUV/AEUV: Vertrag über die Europäische Union und Vertrag über die Arbeitsweise der Europäischen Union*, 2nd edn (C.H. Beck, 2012) 19 (marginal no 3); Müller-Graff (n 20) marginal no 176; Blanke (n 175) 29; Ruffert (n 46) marginal no 4; B Plecher-Hochstraßer, *Zielbestimmungen im Mehrebenensystem: Die Verzahnung der Staatszielbestimmungen im GG mit den Zielbestimmungen im EUV, EGV, EuratomV und EUVV* (Meidenbauer, 2006) 113; C Blumann, 'Objectifs et principes en droit communautaire' in *Le droit de l'Union européenne en principes: Liber amicorum en l'honneur de Jean Raux* (Apogée, 2006) 52; and Drescher (n 46) 60; Calliess (n 38) 90; Reimer (n 128) 997; and Ipsen (n 95) 558.

under a 'duty to observe the other Articles of the [ECSC] Treaty and in particular Articles 2, 4 and 5 which, together with Article 3, must always be observed because they establish the fundamental objectives of the community'.[179] Furthermore, the Court stressed that these 'provisions are *binding* and must be read together if they are to be properly applied'.[180] In its subsequent judgment in *Continental Can*, which concerned former Art 3(f) EEC on ensuring competition as a Community task, the Court ruled that the 'argument that this provision merely contains a general programme devoid of legal effect, ignores the fact that Article 3 considers the pursuit of the objective which it lays down to be indispensable for the achievement of the Community's tasks'.[181]

The addressees of Union objectives include a priori all Union organs. They have to respect Union objectives when legislating or adopting other acts and measures. This would make the co-legislators Council and Parliament the natural addressees.[182] However, in the specific EU context, the Commission, with its sole power to propose legislation[183] as well as its broad regulatory competences and task to 'promote the general interest of the Union',[184] is equally called upon to pursue the objectives of the Treaties in exercising these functions. By virtue of the Lisbon Treaty, the distinction between the Community and the Union disappeared,[185] making a differentiation between Union and Community objectives now a moot question as the Treaties provide for general and more specific *Union* objectives.

The issue of the Member States as addressees of Union objectives is more complex and controversial. With regard to Art 2 TEC (on the tasks of the former Community), the CJEU ruled that '[t]hose aims, on which the establishment of the Community is based … cannot have the effect … of imposing legal obligations on the Member States'.[186] Member States are bound by Union law, but they are more than mere 'Union organs', retaining the leeway to act and legislate in areas where they hold competences, not least in the field of foreign policy.[187] They are, however, indirectly bound to Union objectives by virtue of the 'duty of sincere

[179] Case 8/57 *Groupement des hauts fourneaux et aciéries belges*, EU:C:1958:9, para 8.

[180] *Groupement des hauts fourneaux et aciéries belges* (n 179) para 8 (emphasis added).

[181] Case 6/72 *Continental Can*, EU:C:1973:22, para 23. See also *Giménez Zaera* (n 96) para 10, concerning the objectives of Art 2 TEC of establishing the common market and approximating the economic policies of the Member States.

[182] Arts 14(1) and 16(1) TEU. [183] Art 17(2) TEU.

[184] Art 17(1) TEU; see further Craig and de Búrca (n 143) 36–8. [185] Art 1(3) TEU.

[186] Case C-339/89 *Alsthom Atlantique*, EU:C:1991:28, para 9; also Case C-181/06 *Deutsche Lufthansa*, EU:C:2007:412, para 31: 'It is sufficient to state that Articles 3 and 4 EC specify the fields and objectives to which the activities of the European Community are to relate, and do not lay down obligations on Member States or public or private bodies'; see also Lenaerts and Van Nuffel (n 46) 111; and A Hatje, 'Artikel 2 [Gemeinschaftsaufgabe]' in J Schwarze (ed), *EU-Kommentar*, 2nd edn (Nomos, 2008) 263 (marginal no 5). But note Case C-137/00 *Milk Marque*, EU:C:2003:429, para 92, where the CJEU seems to conflate a duty not to undermine the effectiveness of secondary Union legislation with a duty on the part of the Member States to comply directly with Union objectives, *in casu* of the Common Agricultural Policy. Confusion, however, can be avoided by regarding this as an implicit reference to the duty of loyal cooperation.

[187] Note in this context Declaration Nos 13 and 14 annexed to the Lisbon Treaty concerning the common foreign and security policy.

cooperation', which states that '[t]he Member States shall facilitate the achievement of the Union's *tasks* and refrain from any measure which could jeopardise the attainment of the Union's *objectives*'.[188] This complex relationship will be elaborated upon with regard to the European constitutional space (see Chapter 4, section 5.1).

With regard to other possible addressees, Union objectives are not directed at any other legal persons or individuals. They do not establish individual rights. The CJEU made this clear in the *Giménez Zaera* judgment, where it ruled that the objective of raising the standard of living, even though it constitutes 'one of the aims which inspired the creation of the European Economic Community', given its 'general terms and its systematic dependence on the establishment of the Common Market and progressive approximation of economic policies, cannot ... confer rights on individuals'.[189] Neither do these objectives impose obligations on individuals,[190] or more precisely on Union citizens, to pursue them.

3.2 Functions and justiciability

Before turning to the legal functions proper, one can point to the extra-legal functions that Union objectives fulfil, which are strongly reminiscent of those put forward by members of the Indian Constituent Assembly (see Chapter 1, section 3.3). Franz Reimer calls these the information and integration functions. Linked to the earlier discussion on the changing nature of the Union, he stresses that in view of the widening objectives and competences of the Union, it is not the existence of the Union itself that is to be justified. Instead, Union objectives reflect what the EU strives for as a matter of substance and what outputs it is to produce (drawing on the notion of 'output legitimacy', see also Chapter 5, section 5.3).[191] A similar function has been proposed by von Bogdandy, who refers to the 'manifesto function' of a constitution.[192] He does this with reference to the values of the Union, but it may also be applied to its objectives, given that one of the overall objectives of the Union is to promote these same values.[193]

Turning to the legal functions of Union objectives that result from their binding nature, their primary function resides in being an interpretive tool. Apart from that, Union objectives can be seen, in theory, as marginally justiciable in

[188] Art 4(3), third subpara TEU (emphasis added). See also Müller-Graff (n 20) marginal no 177; and Plecher-Hochstraßer (n 178) 114–19.

[189] *Giménez Zaera* (n 96) para 11; see also *Alsthom Atlantique* (n 186) para 9; further Lenaerts and Van Nuffel (n 46) 111; Hatje (n 186) 263 (marginal no 5); and Plecher-Hochstraßer (n 178) 112.

[190] *Deutsche Lufthansa* (n 186) para 3.

[191] Reimer (n 128) 999–1001. He refers here also to 'output legitimacy' as opposed to 'input legitimacy' through democratic procedures; see in this vein also F-X Priollaud and D Siritzky, *Le Traité de Lisbonne: Texte et commentaire article par article des nouveaux traités Européens (TUE-TFUE)* (La Documentation Française, 2008) 35.

[192] A von Bogdandy, 'The European Constitution and European Identity: Text and Subtext of the Treaty Establishing a Constitution for Europe' (2005) 3 *International Journal of Constitutional Law* 295, 308.

[193] Art 3(1) TEU.

court. They impose a constant duty to pursue the objectives within the margins of feasibility.

The imposition of a duty of continuous pursuit of the EU's constitutional objectives stems from their 'imperfectible' nature, as they cannot be entirely achieved. Instead, they require a continuous 'optimizing' effort. However, sometimes there are exceptions, such as (historical) reunification objectives, other rather specific goals (eg joining a particular international organization), or negative objectives (eg not merging with a particular country). These goals, which can be fully realized, could also be classified as constitutional commands (see section 3.3 below). Nevertheless, they can always be subsumed under a wider 'imperfectible' objective such as international cooperation, security, or the 'common good'. The same also applies for the Union and its manifold objectives.

An example of a realizable objective within the Union would be its original task, ie the establishment of the common market of Art 2 TEC and some of the more specific measures this entails. This includes, for example, the 'elimination' of customs duties and quantitative restrictions between the Member States[194] or the establishment of a common customs tariff.[195] The achievement of these specific goals is illustrated by the subsequent amendment of the Treaty, which replaced 'elimination' of customs duties with their 'prohibition' and the deletion of a reference to the common customs tariff from the list of the 'activities' of the Community.[196] Nevertheless, the common—or rather now the internal—market[197] as such will remain a 'work in progress' for the time being due to the need for constant adjustment and adaptation.[198] This finds expression in the Treaties too, as they do not only mandate the Union to 'adopt measures with the aim of establishing' this market, but also of 'ensuring the functioning of the internal market'.[199] Furthermore, as the Eurozone crisis has shown, the same applies to the seemingly perfectible objective of establishing 'an economic and monetary union whose currency is the euro'.[200] In this regard, the questions of further integration and consequently the *finalité* of the Union come to the surface once more.[201]

[194] Art 3(a) EEC Treaty (original version). [195] Art 3(b) EEC Treaty (original version).

[196] Art 3(1)(a) TEC (Nice version); note also Art 23 TEC and now Art 28 TFEU, where the customs union remains as part of the structure of the Union coupled with individually enforceable market freedoms.

[197] Art 3(3) TEU.

[198] See eg the 2010 Monti Report, which addresses the challenges facing the Single Market and states that '[t]he Single Market is Europe's original idea and unfinished business': M Monti, *A New Strategy for the Single Market—At the Service of Europe's Economy and Society*, Report to the President of the European Commission José Manuel Barroso, 9 May 2010, <http://ec.europa.eu/internal_market/strategy/docs/monti_report_final_10_05_2010_en.pdf>, 37.

[199] Art 26(1) TFEU. [200] Art 3(4) TEU.

[201] See, for instance, the amendment of the TFEU using the simplified procedure (Art 48(6) TEU) to allow for a stability mechanism to be established for the Eurozone countries: European Council Decision 2011/199/EU of 25 March 2011 amending Article 136 of the Treaty on the Functioning of the European Union with regard to a stability mechanism for Member States whose currency is the euro [2011] OJ L 91/1; and the ensuing litigation resulting in a reference to the CJEU: Case C-370/12 *Pringle*, EU:C:2012:756.

A perfectible objective (which could also be understood as a constitutional command) introduced by the Lisbon Treaty is the accession of the EU to the European Convention on Human Rights.[202] Once the inter-institutional issues have been resolved and the EU has actually acceded to the Convention, that particular objective can be deemed as fulfilled. However, it will then require 'strict compliance'[203] with Convention obligations as well as good faith participation within the Convention framework by the Union,[204] which can be subsumed under the general objectives of fostering international cooperation, extending the international rule of law, and fostering respect for human rights both at home and abroad.[205]

Turning to the legal functions this entails for the EU's constitutional objectives, the interpretive function is arguably the most important, and certainly the least controversial aim.[206] Recalling Pierre De Montalivet's approach to *objectifs de valuer constitutionnelle* (Chapter 1, section 4.2), the permissive function of constitutional objectives becomes evident through this capacity for interpretation. Given their prominent place and span, Union objectives loom large over the entirety of EU law and its interpretation.[207] For Koen Lenaerts and Piet Van Nuffel, the legal function of Treaty objectives is indeed 'limited to guiding the interpretation of Union Law'.[208] Alan Dashwood and others stress that objectives, while not establishing competences as such, 'obviously perform an important and sometimes even decisive role when it comes to interpreting the nature and limits of the powers vested in the Union institutions'.[209]

These assessments are firmly anchored in the case law of the CJEU. In 1974, Advocate General Reischl opined with regard to Community tasks and objectives that their 'significance for the interpretation of the Treaty can scarcely be overestimated'.[210] In *Gaston Schul Douane Expediteur*, the Court stressed 'the need to take account of the objectives of the Treaty' when interpreting it.[211] In *Istituto Chemioterapico Italiano*, the Court ruled that EU law needs to 'be interpreted and applied in the light of' the Treaty objectives.[212] Indeed, the hallmark teleological approach to interpretation employed by the CJEU would be unthinkable without

[202] Art 6(2) TEU. [203] Art 3(5) TEU.

[204] R Uerpmann-Wittzack, 'Rechtsfragen und Rechtsfolgen des Beitritts der Europäischen Union zur EMRK' [2012] *Europarecht (Beiheft 2)* 167, who notes that acceding to the Convention next to its Member States makes it a 'mixed agreement' for the EU (183–4).

[205] Art 21(2)(b) TEU.

[206] Stressing the importance of the interpretive function Calliess (n 38) 91; A Dashwood et al, *Wyatt & Dashwood's European Union Law*, 6th edn (Hart Publishing, 2011) 24; Streinz, Ohler, and Herrmann (n 120) 80–1; Drescher (n 46) 60; and Lenaerts and Van Nuffel (n 46) 111.

[207] In this sense Pescatore (13) 327; see also Azoulai (n 150) 72–3; and Reimer (n 128) 103–4.

[208] Lenaerts and Van Nuffel (n 46) 111.

[209] Dashwood et al (n 206) 24; also Dollat (n 164) 108–14.

[210] Case 27/74 *Demag AG v Finanzamt Duisburg-Süd*, Opinion of Advocate General Reischl, EU:C:1974:94, 1056.

[211] Case 15/81 *Gaston Schul*, EU:C:1982:135, para 33; and see later Case 299/86 *Criminal proceedings against Rainer Drexl*, EU:C:1988:103, para 24.

[212] Joined Cases 6 and 7/73 *Istituto Chemioterapico Italiano*, EU:C:1974:18, para 32; and Case 85/76 *Hoffmann-La Roche*, EU:C:1979:36, para 125; also Case 53/81 *Levin*, EU:C:1982:105, para 15.

recourse to objectives.[213] In particular, and akin to national constitutional objectives, the objectives of the Union have played an important role in framing fundamental rights protection (and justifying exceptions to rights) as well as in shaping the borders of competences of the Union institutions.

Beyond the importance of objectives for the interpretation of EU law, the question of their justiciability as such is more contested. Some commentators posit that they are 'in principle justiciable legal norms'.[214] Others, to the contrary, deny their justiciability, at least with regard to the objectives of the pre-Lisbon TEU.[215]

With particular regard to the pre-Lisbon TEU objectives, it can be recalled that it was ambiguous whether the jurisdiction of the Court extended over the objectives of the TEU, as opposed to the objectives and tasks of the Community as codified in the TEC. In a 1995 order, the Court ruled that due to the exclusion of Court jurisdiction (then Art L TEU), 'a national court may not refer to the Court a question on Article B [on EU objectives] of the Treaty on European Union'[216] within the framework of a preliminary reference procedure. In the post-Lisbon setting, this qualification of ex-Art L TEU has disappeared, as today there is a single set of Union objectives. However, a degree of ambiguity remains given that CFSP objectives have disappeared as a separate set within the Treaty text, while certain Treaty provisions refer to 'objectives pertaining to the common foreign and security policy' (Art 352(4) TFEU) (see also Chapter 4, section 4.2).

Analogous to *Staatszielbestimmungen* and *objectifs de valuer constitutionnelle*, in theory, Union objectives are considered justiciable. Here it is also possible to discern from the case law of the Court the basic functions to oblige, to forbid, and to authorize. With regard to the function of obligation, the CJEU has explicitly pointed out the 'obligatory force'[217] of Treaty objectives. Moreover, it ruled that the stipulation of objectives in the TEC '*requires* the Community' to take them into account in its various policy fields.[218] The CJEU has held furthermore that the discretionary powers of the Union organs are to be exercised 'in accordance with the objectives of the [then] Community'.[219] Regarding the scope of such an obligation, as is the case with national constitutional objectives, the caveat of possibility also applies here. The legal obligation always extends only to the active pursuit of the objective. In this vein, the

[213] See Calliess (n 38) 92, who calls ex-Art 2 TEC the 'central benchmark norm for the teleological interpretation that is typical for EC law' (in the original: 'zentralen Maßstabsnorm bei der für das EG-Recht typischen telologischen Auslegung'); also Douglas-Scott (n 108) 209–10; and Dashwood et al (n 206) 24.

[214] In the original: 'im Grundsatz justiziable Rechtsnormen': Reimer (n 128) 1000; also Plecher-Hochstraßer (n 178) 112; Müller-Graff (n 20) marginal no 176. Streinz, Ohler, and Herrmann (n 120) 80 stress that objectives would only be marginally operable as concrete calls for action.

[215] C Stumpf, 'Artikel 2 [Ziele]' in J Schwarze (ed), *EU-Kommentar*, 2nd edn (Nomos, 2008) 75 (marginal no 19).

[216] Case C-167/94 *Criminal proceedings against Juan Carlos Grau Gomis and others*, Order of the Court, EU:C:1995:113, para 6.

[217] *Continental Can* (n 181) para 25.

[218] Case C-268/94 *Portugal v Council*, EU:C:1996:461, para 23 (emphasis added); see also Case C-166/07 *Council v Parliament (International Fund for Ireland)*, EU:C:2009:499, para 45.

[219] Case 1/69 *Italy v Commission*, EU:C:1969:34, para 5; also Case 24/62 *Germany v Commission*, EU:C:1963:14, para 7. See further Calliess (n 38) 92; and Reimer (n 128) 1004.

Court employed the terms 'duty to observe'[220] and 'pursuit of the objective'[221] rather than stressing any duty to realize the objective to the fullest. In *Groupement des hauts fourneaux et aciéries belges*, it explicitly acknowledged that:

> In practice it will always be necessary to reconcile to a certain degree the various objectives of Article 3 [TEC] since it is clearly impossible to attain them all fully and simultaneously as those objectives constitute general principles which must be observed and harmonized as far as possible ...[222]

In *Milk Marque*, furthermore, the CJEU speaks of a 'permanent duty to reconcile' different objectives on the part of the Union institutions.[223] In a similar vein, the Court ruled in a later judgment that 'those are broad objectives in the sense that it must be possible for the measures required for their pursuit to concern a variety of specific matters'.[224]

The weak legal force of Union objectives also becomes visible in their prohibitive function.[225] Especially where several objectives are at stake, the CJEU has underlined the limited prohibitive function and awarded wide discretion to the institutions. In *Milk Marque*, the Court stressed 'that no single aim may be pursued in isolation in such a way as to make the achievement of the others impossible', but also noted that giving 'temporary priority' to one of them is permissible if the circumstances so require.[226] Moreover, with regard to objectives of the Common Commercial Policy (CCP), the Court ruled in another case that the:

> 'aim to contribute, in the common interest, to the harmonious development of world trade, the progressive abolition of restrictions on international trade ...', cannot be interpreted as prohibiting the Community from enacting, upon pain of committing an infringement of the Treaty, any measure liable to affect trade ...[227]

This meant that trade constraining measures at stake in this case, which were in the interest of the Common Agricultural Policy, could be validly enacted. Arguably, only the protracted and manifest disregard of an objective could be deemed a violation that the CJEU could determine.[228] However, the notion of prohibition appears

220 *Groupement des hauts fourneaux et aciéries belges* (n 179) para 8.

221 *Continental Can* (n 181) para 23. Note that while the Court refers to the 'achievement of the Community's tasks', it is the 'pursuit of the objectives' which it deems 'indispensable', not their achievement.

222 *Groupement des hauts fourneaux et aciéries belges* (n 179) para 8.

223 *Milk Marque* (n 186) para 91.

224 *Portugal v Council* (n 218) para 37; see also Lenaerts and Van Nuffel (n 46) 111.

225 This is to be distinguished from the general rule prohibiting the misuse of powers (*abus de pouvoir*) in EU law, which is a ground for review of Union acts under Art 263(2) TFEU. Misuse of powers is not only concerned with Treaty objectives, but concerns any discrepancy between the stated goal of a measure of an EU institution on the one hand, and its actual purpose on the other. See Craig and de Búrca (n 143) 576.

226 *Milk Marque* (n 186) para 91.

227 Case 112/80 *Dürbeck*, EU:C:1981:94, para 44.

228 The language used in the *Racke* decision employing the notion of 'manifest error' in assessing the application by the Council of the international law of treaties may be illustrative not only of the wide discretion of political institutions in this area, but also of the existence of this limited standard of review for the Court, which could well be applied by analogy to assessing compliance with the obligations flowing from external relations-related Treaty objectives: Case C-162/96 *Racke GmbH & Co. v Hauptzollamt Mainz*, EU:C:1998:293, para 56. See also J Wouters, 'The Tormented Relationship between International

more rigid and judicially enforceable when coupled with the duty of cooperation and addressed at the acts of the Member States. Sincere cooperation according to Art 4(3) TEU requires both 'special duties of action and abstention'.[229] The case law of the Court of Justice reveals that it is often Member States that are condemned for having acted when this duty obliged them to 'refrain from any measure which could jeopardise the attainment of the Union's objectives',[230] not least in the area of external relations (see further Chapter 4, section 5.1).[231]

The choice of words by the Court reveals this similarity between Union objectives and national constitutional objectives in that their legal function is captured best not by strict enforceability but rather by constant pursuit. In this vein, Markus Kotzur's definition of Union objectives draws once more on the Alexy's notion of 'optimization'.[232] Generally, it emerges that the caveat of possibility and the Alexian notion of 'optimization' are basic characteristics that all constitutional objectives have in common, whether national or supranational.

Importantly, harmonizing and optimizing a variety of different objectives also leads to the issue of the relationship among the different objectives *inter se*. In the national setting, constitutional objectives have a priori the same legal value and all need to be pursued within the bounds of feasibility, unless the constitution explicitly provides otherwise. The same would seem to apply to the EU. However, given the wealth of objectives, as well as the presence of both general and specific objectives, the question can be raised whether there is a hierarchy among them. Writing in the pre-Lisbon context, Christian Calliess proposes a 'hierarchy of objectives' (*Zielhierarchie*), according to which legitimate (then) Community action would cascade from the overall objectives (Art 2 TEC) to more concrete Community tasks and means, then to a specific policy (in his example, environmental policy), subsequently to a competence norm for this specific policy as clarified by the policy-specific objectives, and finally to secondary law and other measures adopted accordingly.[233] Thus, all Union action, to be in conformity with the constitutional objectives, would have to be retraceable to the general objectives of the Union.[234] Although Calliess calls it a 'hierarchy', this appears rather as a coherence requirement as it does not presuppose conflict.[235] Coherence, much like the idea

Law and EU Law' in P Bekker, R Dolzer, and M Waibel (eds), *Making Transnational Law Work in the Global Economy: Essays in Honour of Detlev Vagts* (CUP, 2010) 210.

[229] Case C-246/07 *Commission v Sweden (PFOS)*, EU:C:2010:203, para 74, and the further cases cited therein.

[230] Art 4(3), third subpara TEU.

[231] See further A Delgado Casteleiro and J Larik, 'The Duty to Remain Silent: Limitless Loyalty in EU External Relations?' (2011) 36 *European Law Review* 522, and the cases cited therein.

[232] Kotzur (n 49) 315: 'Objectives are the general, superior mandates for action, appeals for action or constitutional expectations, which common action [*Gemeinschaftshandeln*] ... has to live up to through optimizing approximation' (in the original: 'Ziele sind die allgemeinen, übergeordneten Handlungsaufträge, Handlungsappelle oder Verfassungserwartungen, denen das ... Gemeinschaftshandeln im Sinne optimierender Annäherung gerecht werden soll.'). See also Azoulai (n 150) 75.

[233] Calliess (n 38) 90. [234] See also Pechstein (n 178) 19 (marginal no 2).

[235] In the post-Lisbon version, Art 13(1) TEU and Art 7 TFEU; and Art 21(3), second subpara TEU on coherence between internal and external policies. See Calliess (n 38) 87. In this sense one can

of *praktische Konkordanz* as reconciliation between different norms,[236] is the more apt way of characterizing the interrelationship between the different constitutional objectives in EU law.

3.3 Delimitation from other norm categories

Following the general definition of Union objectives and their legal features, the question needs to be answered how, as a norm category, they relate to the other major categories of EU constitutional law. These include, in analogy to Chapter 1, section 4, structural principles, competences, constitutional commands, and individual rights. While the specific features of the Union are accounted for, a similar picture to that of the national context emerges.

Structural principles, defined as the formal basic principles set out in the constitution on the organization of a polity, can also be found in the constitutional law of the EU.[237] In contrast to objectives, which state what the Union strives for, they define what the Union *is* and what it stands for.[238] The introduction of foundational values into the Treaties was considered an important sign for the 'constitutionalization' of Union law. However, next to being founded on values, Art 1 TEU still makes clear that the EU is also 'founded' on the Treaties as international agreements between the Member States.[239] In the post-Lisbon framework, the foundational values can be found in Art 2 TEU, which states:

> The Union is founded on the values of respect for human dignity, freedom, democracy, equality, the rule of law and respect for human rights, including the rights of persons belonging to minorities. These values are common to the Member States in a society in which pluralism, non-discrimination, tolerance, justice, solidarity and equality between women and men prevail.[240]

Even though there is a degree of overlap, the legal term 'structural principles' is not equivalent to that of 'values'. The latter are 'normative convictions of a highly abstract order and are part of the social identity of the individual'.[241] However, by codifying them in the highest laws of the Union, they become legal concepts, and serve as a source for the interpretation of Union law.[242] Crucially, these legal

also understand the early assessment of J Basedow, 'Zielkonflikte und Zielhierarchien im Vertrag über die europäische Gemeinschaft' in O Due, M Lutter, J Schwarze (eds), *Festschrift für Ulrich Everling* (Nomos, 1995).

[236] Plecher-Hochstraßer (n 178) 93–104.

[237] See von Bogdandy (n 2) 21; also, Kotzur (n 49) 314; and in detail C Calliess, 'Art. 2 [Die Werte der Union]' in C Calliess and M Ruffert (eds), *EUV/AEUV Kommentar*, 4th edn (C.H. Beck, 2011) 32 (marginal no 8).

[238] von Bogdandy (n 2) 23. [239] Art 1(3) TEU. [240] Art 2 TEU.

[241] von Bogdandy (n 192) 308.

[242] M Cremona, 'Values in EU Foreign Policy' in M Evans and P Koutrakos (eds), *Beyond the Established Legal Orders: Policy Interconnections Between the EU and the Rest of the World* (Hart Publishing, 2011) 283–5; see sceptically and with regard to the Draft Constitutional Treaty F Reimer, 'Wertegemeinschaft durch Wertenormierung? Die Grundwerteklausel im europäischen Verfassungsvertrag' (2003) 18 *Zeitschrift für Gesetzgebung* 208.

concepts can be considered as 'having a normative founding function for the whole of the Union's legal order', which are needed 'to justify the exercise of public authority'.[243] To these, it is essential to add other core norms as well, especially such central tenets of the Union legal order as the principles of conferred powers, subsidiarity, proportionality, loyal cooperation, *effet utile*,[244] and the institutional balance.[245]

Even before the entry into force of the Lisbon Treaty, the CJEU had spoken in its case law of 'the very foundations of the Community'.[246] Moreover, the terms 'fundamental provisions of the Community legal order' of *Opinion 1/91* or 'fundamental institutional implications for the Community and for the Member States ... of constitutional significance'[247] of *Opinion 2/94* can be seen as a defence of structural principles.

As an interpretive device, structural principles of the Union at first glance appear very similar to Union objectives. However, given their static and preserving nature, they exercise a prohibitive rather than permissive function. Should a measure upset these structural principles, it is unconstitutional and is therefore to be voided by the Court.[248] This difference can be illustrated by the references to values in the context of accession to the EU and the suspension of rights of a Member State. Concerning accession, a state can only join the EU if it 'respects the values referred to in Article 2 [TEU] and is committed to promoting them'.[249] This means the state must, at the moment when it accedes, be in compliance with these values. Commitment to respect them at some point in the future, which would be the case with objectives, does not suffice. Regarding the second example, in cases in which the European Council has determined 'a serious and persistent breach by a Member State of the values referred to in Article 2 [TEU]',[250] the Council may suspend certain rights of the Member State in question, including voting rights in the Council.[251] Consequently, in order to be a part of the Union, and in order to exercise their prerogatives within its institutions, Member States are obliged to respect the Union's values at all times. The same does not apply to the pursuit of Union objectives.

Thus, in their mutual relationship, as with national constitutional objectives, Union objectives cannot be pursued in a way that would be inconsistent

[243] von Bogdandy (n 2) 21; note also Pilette and de Poncins (n 177) 302–3, who stress also the integrative power of the values.

[244] von Bogdandy (n 125) 105–7; see also later von Bogdandy (n 2) 21–3.

[245] C Calliess, 'Art. 13 [Die Organe der Union]' in C Calliess and M Ruffert (eds), *EUV/AEUV Kommentar*, 4th edn (C.H. Beck, 2011) 217 (marginal no 18).

[246] Joined Cases C-402/05 P and C-415/05 P *Kadi and Al Barakaat*, EU:C:2008:461, para 282; Case C-459/03 *Commission v Ireland (Mox Plant)*, EU:C:2006:345, para 169.

[247] Respectively, Opinion 1/91 (*EEA*), EU:C:1991:490, para 41; and Opinion 2/94 *(ECHR)*, EU:C:1996:140, para 35.

[248] See eg with regard to institutional balance Case 138/79 *Roquette Frères*, EU:C:1980:249, para 33: 'due consultation of the Parliament in the cases provided for by the Treaty therefore constitutes an esential [sic] formality disregard of which means that the measure concerned is void'. See also Case C-658/11 *Parliament v Council (EU-Mauritius Agreement)*, EU:C:2014:2025, paras 80–6.

[249] Art 49(1) TEU. [250] Art 7(2) TEU. [251] Art 7(3) TEU.

with, or undermine, the structural principles of the Union. Joining the ECHR, as a way to pursue the (constitutional) objective of human rights protection,[252] was considered by the CJEU as capable of upsetting the constitutional 'building laws'[253] (*Baugesetze*) of the EU, in particular the conferral of powers and the institutional architecture of the Union. The same can be said for the *Kadi* case,[254] where the pursuit of measures in the area of international security was at odds with fundamental rights protection and the rule of law as structural principles of the Union.

The principle of conferral, which has been codified in the primary law, forms an important structural principle governing the Union.[255] As an entity lacking the *Kompetenz-Kompetenz* of a state, the Union only possesses those competences attributed to it by its Member States, a feature it shares with international organizations. By contrast, and akin to a national constitutional order, competences and objectives today form distinct norm categories within the Union legal order. This means, firstly, that objectives are not an independent source of power. In the absence of a legal basis indicating competence, the Union is not allowed to act. Secondly, however, objectives play an important role in clarifying the boundaries of Union competence and in identifying the proper legal basis. In addition, once competence is established, its exercise is guided by the objectives of the Union, though for all practical purposes direct judicial enforcement is limited in this respect.

Union objectives cannot, as such, create competences.[256] This is made explicit in the Treaties, where Art 3 TEU states in its last paragraph that '[t]he Union shall pursue its objectives by appropriate means commensurate with the competences which are conferred upon it in the Treaties'.[257] Nevertheless, as an interpretive tool, Union objectives are a crucial element in clarifying the scope of Union competences.[258] According to Lenaerts and Van Nuffel, 'competence is often inferred from specific Treaty provisions read together with the "objectives of the Union" or, before the Treaty of Lisbon entered into force, the "requirements of the common market" enshrined in Article 3 EC'.[259] Moreover, objectives can help to establish the proper legal basis where this is contested. This is

[252] Opinion 2/94 *(ECHR)* (n 247) para 32.

[253] L Adamovich and B Funk, *Österreichisches Verfassungsrecht*, 3rd edn (Springer, 1985) 98.

[254] *Kadi and Al Barakaat* (n 246).

[255] See in detail H-P Kraußer, *Das Prinzip begrenzter Ermächtigung im Gemeinschaftsrecht als Strukturprinzip des EWG-Vertrages* (Duncker & Humblot, 1991).

[256] See eg Dashwood et al (n 206) 24; Müller-Graff (n 20) marginal no 180; Hatje (n 186) 263 (marginal no 7); Ruffert (n 46) marginal no 12; and Ipsen (n 95) 559–60; the exception being Reimer (n 128) 993, also 1009.

[257] Art 3(6) TEU; see also Art 5(2) TEU. See further C Calliess, 'Art. 5 (ex-Art. 5 EGV) [Grundsatz der begrenzten Einzelermächtigung, Subsidiarität und Verhältnismäßigkeit]' in C Calliess and M Ruffert (eds), *EUV/AEUV Kommentar*, 4th edn (C.H. Beck, 2011) 118 (marginal no 8).

[258] See Dashwood et al (n 206) 24; Müller-Graff (n 20) marginal nos 180–3; Blumann (n 178) 48–9; and Reimer (n 128) 1001–2.

[259] Lenaerts and Van Nuffel (n 46) 111. For an example using the formulation 'requirements of the market' enshrined in Art 3 TEC, see Case 97/78 *Schumalla*, EU:C:1978:211, para 6.

important in view of the type of competence that is involved, which in turn has institutional and procedural consequences. In order to determine the applicable legal basis, particular attention has been paid by the Court to the objectives pursued by the measure and to which Treaty objectives it can be linked.[260] Furthermore, the necessity of the pursuit of objectives can, under certain circumstances, be used to grant additional powers to the Union in accordance with the flexibility clause of Art 352 TFEU.

The Lisbon reform introduced a number of changes in the scope of this provision that should be highlighted. Former Art 308 TEC referred only to attainment of Community objectives 'in the course of the operation of the common market'. By contrast, post-Lisbon Art 352(1) TFEU refers more widely to 'the framework of the policies defined in the Treaties' to attain 'one of the objectives set out in the Treaties',[261] but now also requires the consent of the Parliament. In addition, an ambiguous exception for the CFSP is carved out.[262] Declarations No 41 and 42 on Art 352 of the TFEU attached to the Lisbon Treaty roll back further the scope of the article. The former states that the Treaty objectives mentioned in Art 352(1) TFEU only refer to Art 3(2), 3(3), and 3(5) TEU with regard to external action under the TFEU (ie not the CFSP). In doing so, Declaration No 41 aims to prevent that 'an action based on Article 352 of the Treaty on the Functioning of the European Union would only pursue objectives set out in Article 3(1) of the Treaty on European Union'. This provision, which amounts to a quasi-evocation of the 'common good' as the overall Union objective, hence cannot serve as a basis for additional competences alone. Declaration No 42 essentially states that Art 352 TFEU 'cannot be used as a basis for the adoption of provisions whose effect would, in substance, be to amend the Treaties without following the procedure which they provide for that purpose'. This could also be seen as preserving the basic structural features by preventing the bypassing of the amendment procedure.

A distinction can furthermore be made between Union objectives and constitutional commands. The latter oblige the Union to realize something rather concrete through the adoption of a single measure or set of measures. For instance, the Treaties oblige the Council to adopt measures ensuring administrative cooperation between the departments of the Member States responsible with regard to the Area of Freedom, Security and Justice (AFSJ).[263] As an example from the external domain, by virtue of the Lisbon reform, the Treaties mandate the Council to set up the organization and functioning of the new European External Action Service

[260] Case 45/86 *Commission v Council (Generalized tariff preferences)*, EU:C:1987:163, para 19 referring specifically to Common Commercial Policy (CCP) objectives. See further Douglas-Scott (n 108) 163–9.

[261] However, the CJEU had already maintained a wide interpretation of this provision before the Lisbon reform 'as if the reference to the common market was not there', Piris (n 133) 121 (footnote 17); see further P Craig, *The Lisbon Treaty: Law, Politics, and Treaty Reform* (OUP, 2010) 182–4.

[262] Art 352(4) TFEU, which prohibits deriving powers from the flexibility clause in the area of the CFSP, which highlights the still 'special' character of this policy area (see also Chapter 4, section 4.2).

[263] Art 74 TFEU.

to assist the High Representative.[264] Furthermore, the accession of the EU to the European Convention on Human Rights can be seen in terms of a legislative command requiring international legal measures, including the successful adoption of an accession agreement.[265] As in the national constitutional setting, these tasks are consumed once such measures have been enacted. However, a duty remains to maintain and adapt them, linking the commands and objectives. The way in which this task is carried out is framed by the parameters of the objectives, as is any action undertaken with a view to maintaining and adapting the measures thus enacted or institutions thus created.

In national constitutional law, among the different norm categories, the relationship between objectives and individual rights usually receives the most attention. Union objectives do not create individual rights.[266] While objectives, in their interpretive–permissive function, are generally seen as a device employed for justifying measures that restrict fundamental rights, others have also argued that they help to enhance the effectiveness of rights (see Chapter 1, section 4). The same applies to Union objectives.

In terms of restrictions of rights, the French doctrine of *objectifs de valeur constitutionnelle* was likely inspired by the case law of the CJEU (Chapter 1, section 3.2). This concerned cases in which the CJEU dealt with the issue to which extent restrictions of fundamental rights can be justified. In *Nold*, the Court ruled that fundamental rights may 'be subject to certain limits justified by the *overall objectives pursued by the Community*, on the condition that the substance of these rights is left untouched'.[267] Already in the earlier decision in *Internationale Handelsgesellschaft*, the Court hinted at the link to the (then) Community objectives when it stated that the protection of fundamental rights, 'whilst inspired by the constitutional traditions common to the Member States, must be ensured within the framework of the structures and *objectives of the Community*'.[268] In its subsequent settled case law the Court established that fundamental rights 'are not absolute … but must be considered in relation to their social function'.[269] Therefore, according to the CJEU:

> restrictions may be imposed on the exercise of those rights … provided that those restrictions in fact correspond *to objectives of general interest pursued by the Community* and do not constitute, with regard to the aim pursued, a disproportionate and intolerable interference, impairing the very substance of those rights.[270]

[264] Art 27(3) TEU. This was subsequently done by Council Decision 2010/427/EU of 26 July 2010 establishing the organization and functioning of the European External Action Service [2010] OJ L 201/30.

[265] Art 6(2) TEU.

[266] *Giménez Zaera* (n 96) para 11.

[267] *Nold v Commission* (n 114) para 14 (emphasis added).

[268] *Internationale Handelsgesellschaft* (n 114) para 4 (emphasis added). See also P De Montalivet, *Les objectifs de valeur constitutionnelle* (Dalloz, 2006) 432–4.

[269] Case 5/88 *Wachauf*, EU:C:1989:321, para 18.

[270] *Wachauf* (n 269) (emphasis added); see also Case C-84/95 *Bosphorus*, EU:C:1996:312, para 21 and the cases cited therein.

However, the Court does not consistently refer back to the objectives as codified in the Treaties. At times, the Court makes explicit reference to particular provisions in the Treaties containing objectives or generally to 'objectives of the Community'. In other instances, it merely speaks of 'objectives of general interest pursued by the Community' or, as in *Bosphorus*, of 'objective of general interest so fundamental for the international community'.[271] This lack of consistent referencing to the text of the primary law indicates that the concept of Union objective or aim of general interest is wider than the set of objectives codified in the Treaties. Reminiscent of German and French doctrines, is it thus worthwhile to keep in mind that beyond the codified objectives, other objectives of constitutional impact can be 'discovered' by courts. By contrast, the Indian Supreme Court has stayed closer to the constitutional text, having used the codified directive principles for defining the 'public purposes' which are able to justify the restriction of individual rights under Indian constitutional law (Chapter 1, section 4.3).[272]

Correspondingly, effective fundamental rights protection, which as a whole can also be counted among the structural principles of the Union, serves as a bar to the pursuit of Union objectives. This was a central issue in the *Kadi* case, in which the pursuit of the objectives of contributing to international measures in the area of counterterrorism and compliance with international law risked undermining the Union's internal standard of fundamental rights protection. With regard to the right to property, the Court found that 'an objective of general interest as fundamental to the international community as the fight by all means, in accordance with the Charter of the United Nations, against the threats to international peace and security posed by acts of terrorism' in fact allowed for the restriction of that right.[273] However, with regard to procedural guarantees and effective judicial protection, the Court found that the measures in question, which were indeed pursuing this fundamental objective, fell short of the fundamental rights standard of the Union and were thus to be annulled.[274]

Beyond an adversarial relationship between rights and objectives, the Court of Justice also establishes a clear link between individual rights (also as market freedoms), the effectiveness of EU law, and Treaty objectives. In its *Levin* judgment, for example, the CJEU pointed out that by limiting the application of the freedom of movement of workers both 'the effectiveness of Community Law would be impaired and the achievement of the objectives of the Treaty would be jeopardized'.[275] In the *Viking* case, the Court found that given the scope of the tasks and activities of the (then) Community according to Arts 2 and 3 TEC,[276] 'the Community has thus not only an economic but also a social purpose',[277]

[271] *Bosphorus* (n 270) para 26.
[272] *State of Bihar v Kameshwar Singh*, judgment of 27 May 1952, (1952) 1 SCR 889, 997.
[273] *Kadi and Al Barakaat* (n 246) para 363.
[274] *Kadi and Al Barakaat* (n 246) para 372.
[275] Case 53/81 *Levin*, EU:C:1982:105, para 15.
[276] Case C-438/05 *Viking*, EU:C:2007:772, para 78.
[277] *Viking* (n 276) para 79; see also Case C-341/05 *Laval*, EU:C:2007:809, para 105.

which requires consequently that market freedoms 'must be balanced against the objectives pursued by social policy, which include … inter alia, improved living and working conditions, so as to make possible their harmonisation'.[278] In other words, the balanced pursuit of these different objectives also necessitates balancing the different rights related to them. Hence, akin to the appraisal of *objectifs de valeur constitutionnelle* by De Montalivet (Chapter 1, section 4.2), in this instance there is also an interrelated and mutually reinforcing relationship between rights and objectives.

4. EU Foreign Policy Objectives as Constitutional Norms

Foreign policy objectives form a subcategory of the EU's constitutional objectives. In terms of legal effects, subject to the important intricacies of the European constitutional space (Chapter 4), the same picture emerges as with the national constitutional objectives pertaining to foreign policy. They, too, are binding norms of constitutional rank, serving primarily as an interpretive device employed to enhance the powers of Union organs called upon to pursue these objectives in the conduct of EU external action. They do not establish competences or grant individual rights, and have to be pursued within the bounds of what is—internationally—feasible, in a manner consistent with the structural principles of the EU legal order.

This similarity between EU foreign policy objectives and their national counterparts exists despite their different origins. The divergent starting points of national and Union constitutional objectives in the area of foreign policy become evident from the ways in which they have been received by scholarship. The codification of objectives in national constitutions was at first regarded as something foreign to the original 'style' of constitutional law (Chapter 1, section 3). By contrast, given the origins of the European Union as a functional international organization with *Zielbedarf*, it was seen as a matter of course that its foundational document should include objectives.

However, the picture with foreign policy objectives is the inverse one. Once national constitutional scholarship came to terms with the codification of objectives, foreign policy-related ones were not singled out for further criticism. With regard to the European Union, however, the codification of more wide-ranging foreign policy objectives that go beyond those closely connected to the external dimension of the common market has spawned numerous criticisms. These include calling the external objectives in the EU Treaties a mere 'wish list for a better world',[279] 'redolent of motherhood and apple pie',[280] and the observation of 'an almost epidemic proliferation of objectives of the Union' in the area of the

[278] *Laval* (n 277) para 105.
[279] In the original: 'Wunschzettel für eine bessere Welt': Drescher (n 46) 68.
[280] Dashwood et al (n 206) 903, referring to Art 21(1) TEU.

CFSP.[281] It appears that European Union law scholarship still has to fully accept the codification of objectives beyond those that could be considered of existential importance for the original function of the EU and its predecessors.

Similarly, the EU Courts also seem to have gone through a phase of adjusting themselves to the reformed Treaties in this respect. For instance, the General Court (GC; former Court of First Instance) in its 2010 *Kadi* decision made a rather obscure reference to the external action objectives of the Union as contained in the TEU. The GC referred to 'certain doubts [that] may have been voiced in legal circles as to whether the judgment of the Court of Justice in *Kadi* is wholly consistent' with requirements of international law, as well as a number of provisions from EU primary law, including among others Arts 3(5) and 21(1) and (2) TEU.[282] In 2011, Advocate General Kokott made explicit reference to the Union objective of 'strict observance' of international law (Art 3(5) TEU) in her opinion in *The Air Transport Association of America*,[283] which was picked up by the Court in its judgment.[284] In 2012, the listed external action objectives of Art 21(2) TEU were referred to by both Advocate General Bot and the Court in a dispute concerning the correct legal basis for restrictive measures post-Lisbon.[285]

In any event, there are no cogent reasons to single out external relations-related objectives from the constitutional law of the European Union or to deny their legal significance. According to Art 3(5) TEU, the 'Union shall uphold and promote its values and interests and contribute to the protection of its citizens' and it 'shall contribute' to a number of specified objectives. The language used in Art 21(3) TEU is even clearer, as it makes explicit the link between the objectives and the different policies and competences at the disposal of the Union to pursue them:

> The Union shall respect the principles and pursue the objectives set out in paragraphs 1 and 2 in the development and implementation of the different areas of the Union's external action covered by this Title and by Part Five of the Treaty on the Functioning of the European Union, and of the external aspects of its other policies.[286]

As in the national setting, the external objectives of the Union form part of the norm category of constitutional objectives as well as of the foreign affairs constitution of the Union.[287] This has a number of important implications. Generally, it entails the

[281] In the original: 'eine geradezu epidemische Ausbreitung von Unionszielen': J Terhechte, 'Kommentierung zum Art. 3 EUV (Ziele der Union)' in E Grabitz, M Hilf, and M Nettesheim (eds), *Das Recht der Europäischen Union*, loose-leaf, 41st supplement (C.H. Beck, 2010) marginal no 63.

[282] Case T-85/09 *Kadi v Commission*, EU:T:2010:418, para 115.

[283] Case C-366/10 *The Air Transport Association of America*, Opinion of Advocate General Kokott, EU:C:2011:637, paras 43, 75, and 108; see also Joined Cases C-103/12 and C-165/12 *Parliament and Commission v Council*, Opinion of Advocate General Sharpston, EU:C:2014:334, paras 3 and 68 (footnote 30); and Case C-285/12 *Diakité*, Opinion of Advocate General Mengozzi, EU:C:2013:500, para 23.

[284] Case C-366/10 *The Air Transport Association of America*, EU:C:2011:864, para 101.

[285] Case C-130/10 *Parliament v Council (Al-Qaeda Sanctions)*, Opinion of Advocate General Bot, EU:C:2012:50, paras 62–4; and Case C-130/10 *Parliament v Council (Al-Qaeda Sanctions)*, EU:C:2012:472, para 62.

[286] Art 21(3), first subpara TEU.

[287] Stressing the constitutional quality of EU primary law relating to external relations, D Thym, 'Foreign Affairs' in A von Bogdandy and J Bast (eds), *Principles of European Constitutional Law*,

responsible organs being awarded rather wide discretion in the pursuit of the objectives. It should not lead to the conclusion, however, that the constitutional organs of the Union become completely unbound by external relations objectives or that their actions are removed entirely from judicial scrutiny with regard to the latter.

In its case law, the Court of Justice availed itself of references to external relations objectives in a variety of cases. In *Portugal v Council*, the Court ruled that the presence of Treaty objectives 'requires the Community to take account of the objective of respect for human rights when it adopts measures in the field of development cooperation'.[288] This can be seen as confirmation of their binding nature in the external field. The term 'requires' furthermore evokes the functions of obligation and prohibition that apply in the external domain as well.

With regard to external relations objectives of the Union, there is the duty to pursue the objectives actively within the bounds of possibility, which necessitates a commensurate measure of discretion.[289] As the CJEU put it, 'those are broad objectives in the sense that it must be possible for the measures required for their pursuit to concern a variety of specific matters'.[290] Furthermore, even though there would arguably be a prohibition to manifestly disregard an external objective,[291] when several objectives, internal or external, are at stake, the Court acknowledged in *Dürbeck* that they cannot all be pursued at the same time and that priorities must be set by the responsible organs.[292] This also raises the question of the 'coherence' between all policies of the Union and their respective objectives, both internal and external (see Chapter 4).[293]

2nd edn (Hart Publishing/C.H. Beck, 2011) 310–16; and M Cremona and B De Witte, 'Introduction' in M Cremona and B De Witte (eds), *EU Foreign Relations Law: Constitutional Fundamentals* (Hart Publishing, 2008) xi–xv. This includes also the CFSP: see D Thym, 'The Intergovernmental Constitution of the EU's Foreign, Security & Defence Executive' (2011) 7 *European Constitutional Law Review* 453, 477–8.

288 *Portugal v Council* (n 218) para 23.

289 See also PJ Kuijper, 'The Case Law of the Court of Justice of the EU and the Allocation of External Relations Powers: Whither the Traditional Role of the Executive in EU Foreign Relations?' in M Cremona and A Thies (eds), *The European Court of Justice and External Relations Law: Constitutional Challenges* (Hart Publishing, 2014).

290 *Portugal v Council* (n 218) para 37.

291 As was stated earlier, the Court has not ruled specifically in this regard. It might employ, by analogy, a marginal review standard such as that used in *Racke* (n 228) para 56.

292 *Dürbeck* (n 227) para 44, concerning objectives of the CCP and of the Common Agricultural Policy; also later Case C-150/94 *United Kingdom v Council*, EU:C:1998:547, paras 67–8. See also R Holdgaard, *External Relations Law of the European Community: Legal Reasoning and Legal Discourses* (Kluwer Law International, 2008) 70–2. Note further A Dashwood, 'Article 47 TEU and the Relationship between First and Second Pillar Competences' in A Dashwood and M Maresceau (eds), *Law and Practice of EU External Relations: Salient Features of a Changing Landscape* (CUP, 2008) 103, who concludes from the language of post-Lisbon Art 21(3) TEU that '[w]hatever the external competence in question, therefore, all of the listed objectives are capable in principle of bearing some degree of relevance to its exercise. Though not, of course, the *same* degree of relevance' (emphasis in the original).

293 See C Hillion, '*Tous pour un, un pour tous!* Coherence in the External Relations of the European Union' in M Cremona (ed), *Developments in EU External Relations Law* (OUP, 2008). Note though that coherence as a concept is wider than just reconciliation between objectives: see M Cremona, 'Coherence in European Union Foreign Relations Law' in P Koutrakos (ed), *European Foreign Policy: Legal and Political Perspectives* (Edward Elgar, 2011).

With regard to the interpretative function of objectives in their external relations domain, the Court emphasized that Treaty objectives represent 'an important factor, in particular for the interpretation of [then] Community law'.[294] As Chapter 4, section 4 explains in detail, Union objectives, in cases such as *ERTA* and *Kadi*, play an important role in justifying and shaping Union competences in the area of external relations. Also, with regard to delimiting different externally oriented Union competences by identifying the proper legal basis, Union objectives become an important factor.[295] Hence, also in the foreign affairs domain, the interpretive function of objectives is used for the enhancement of powers of the constitutional organs, ie for an *arrondissement* of otherwise unclear competences, but within the confines of the overall constitutional structure.

A special reference should be made to the first instance in which the CJEU used Art 3(5) TEU, which was in the judgment on *The Air Transport Association of America*. There, a foreign policy objective was used as a textual basis to argue that the Union is bound, and thus its political branches restricted in their behaviour, by customary international law. The Court found that the objective of 'strict observance and development of international law' meant that the Union is bound by customary international law.[296] On the one hand, this is reflective of an interpretive–prohibitive dimension of foreign policy objectives. On the other, it can be seen as enhancing the powers of the Court, as the latter can point to a Treaty provision in order to justify its own power to review secondary Union law on the basis of (its own interpretation of) rules of customary international law.[297]

In the external domain, Union objectives do not grant individual rights either, ie they cannot be invoked directly by individuals in court. On the contrary, external relations objectives can serve to bolster the legality of measures that have the effect of curtailing individual rights. For instance, the right to property can be restricted through economic sanctions. When these measures were challenged on the basis of fundamental rights violations, the CJEU ruled in *Bosphorus* that the measure restricting property rights in question was not to be regarded as disproportionate since it was adopted in view of 'an objective of general interest so fundamental

[294] Case C-149/96 *Portugal v Council*, EU:C:1999:574, para 86.

[295] See eg Case C-94/03 *Commission v Council (Rotterdam Convention)*, EU:C:2006:2, which concerned trade and environmental policy; Case C-91/05 *Commission v Council (Small arms and light weapons)*, EU:C:2008:288, concerning development policy and the CFSP; and *Parliament v Council (Al-Qaeda Sanctions)* (n 285), concerning the AFSJ and the CFSP.

[296] *The Air Transport Association of America* (n 284) para 101: 'Under Article 3(5) TEU, the European Union is to contribute to the strict observance and the development of international law. *Consequently*, when it adopts an act, it is bound to observe international law in its entirety, including customary international law, which is binding upon the institutions of the European Union' (emphasis added).

[297] In previous case law, it had already drawn the same conclusion, but without an explicit basis in the Treaties. Compare, for instance, *Racke* (n 228) para 45: 'It should be noted in that respect that, as is demonstrated by the Court's judgment in Case C-286/90 *Poulsen and Diva Navigation*, EU:C:1992:453, para 9, the European Community must respect international law in the exercise of its powers. It is *therefore* required to comply with the rules of customary international law when adopting a regulation suspending the trade concessions granted by, or by virtue of, an agreement which it has concluded with a non-member country' (emphasis added).

for the international community, which consists in putting an end to the state of war in the region and to the massive violations of human rights and humanitarian international law in the Republic of Bosnia-Herzegovina'.[298]

However, the structural principles of the Union, including its system of fundamental rights protection viewed in its entirety, also set limits on the ability to pursue external objectives.[299] In this respect, it is important to recall the *Kadi II* ruling of the General Court, in which it adhered to the judgment of the CJEU in *Kadi*, discarded objections based, inter alia, on Arts 3(5) and 21 TEU, and ruled that derogations from primary law cannot be allowed when 'principles that form part of the very foundations of the Community legal order, one of which is the protection of fundamental rights' are at stake.[300]

5. Conclusion: Expounding Constitutional Objectives

This chapter established the constitutional credentials of the objectives of the EU as stipulated in the Treaties in general, and of its foreign policy objectives in particular, building on the comparative findings from the previous two chapters. It did so by retracing the origins of the Union in functional international organizations, the widening scope of the goals and domains of activity of the EU and its predecessor organizations, and contextualizing this with the transformation of its legal order into one with 'thick' constitutional features. Moreover, it situated Union objectives within the overall legal framework of the Union as it currently stands, including their binding legal nature, addressees, and relation to the other main norm categories of EU constitutional law.

Scrutinizing these different features yielded a general definition of Union objectives as norms of constitutional rank that bind all Union organs, committing them to the active and coherent pursuit of these objectives within the bounds of what is materially feasible. Whereas Union objectives neither establish competences nor individual rights, the entirety of Union law is to be interpreted in light of these

[298] *Bosphorus* (n 270) para 26. Again, however, the Court does not make an explicit link to a codified Union objective. See also *Kadi and Al Barakaat* (n 246) para 355 and the case law cited therein.

[299] See *Kadi and Al Barakaat* (n 246) especially para 303. However, it should be stressed that the Court in *Kadi* nonetheless maintained the effects of the measures with a view to avoiding 'seriously and irreversibly prejudicing the effectiveness of the restrictive measures' and thus de facto maintained compliance with international obligations of the Member States (para 373). Note also the successful appeal in Case C-376/10 P *Tay Za*, EU:C:2012:138, in which the Court annuls the contested measures since it considers the legal basis of former Arts 60 and 301 TEC insufficient for restrictive measures against family members of people associated with a government which commits widespread human rights violations.

[300] *Kadi v Commission* (n 282) para 119, quoting *Kadi and Al Barakaat* (n 246) para 304; in the unsuccessful appeal, Joined Cases C-584/10 P, C-593/10 P, and C-595/10 P *Commission v Kadi*, EU:C:2013:518, the CJEU referred in para 31 to Arts 3(5) and 21 TEU and stressed in para 131 that 'judicial review is indispensable to ensure a fair balance between the maintenance of international peace and security and the protection of the fundamental rights and freedoms of the person concerned'.

objectives. Such interpretations serve primarily to clarify the outer boundaries of Union powers, relations between EU institutions, or in restricting fundamental rights. However, the pursuit of Union objectives must always be consistent with the structural foundations of the EU's legal order. Following this general definition, foreign policy objectives of the Union were identified as a subcategory of the EU's constitutional objectives, which shares the principal characteristics of their counterparts found in national constitutions. Accordingly, the institutions of the Union are bound, within their respective sphere of competence, to pursue these foreign policy objectives actively, without encroaching upon the basic constitutional structure of the Union. As legal norms, they too serve primarily as an interpretive device for EU law as a whole. From this, the analysis can move forward to the questions surrounding their operation within the pluralist European constitutional space and the polyphonic system of external relations of the Union and its Member States.

4

E pluribus cohaerente

Foreign Policy Objectives in the European Constitutional Space

1. Introduction

The present chapter examines the third trend that guides the enquiry of this book—'Europeanization'—and builds on the preceding chapters on the constitutional credentials of EU objectives and their substance, which match trends in national constitutional law as it relates to the foreign policy domain. It sheds light on how constitutional foreign policy objectives operate in the European constitutional space, where the pursuit of such objectives of both the Union and the Member States is framed by two conditions that are not usually encountered within states. These are, firstly, the multiple claims to ultimate supremacy and adjudicative authority in the legal hierarchy; and, secondly, the parallel existence of the Union and its Member States as actors on the international stage coupled with the peculiarities of the system of external relations of the Union. This chapter addresses the role that constitutional foreign policy objectives play in bringing about a cohesive foreign policy, ie a *coherent* message to the rest of the world, while maintaining the *pluralism* and *diversity* inherent in the European legal order and its way of interacting with the outside world.

Within the European constitutional space, the pursuit of foreign policy objectives finds its limit not only in the preservation of structural principles of the legal order to which they belong, the EU also has to respect the constitutional identity of its Member States. Although narrowly defined, at least to a limited degree foreign policy objectives fall within this category. Statehood per se, and with it international actorness, are part of such identity and consequently 'immune to integration' (*integrationsfest*).[1] However, in many cases it is the constitutional objectives of the Member States regarding (European) integration which have helped to constitutionally justify the transfer of powers to the supranational level and to intertwine the different legal orders. This pooling of sovereign powers has

[1] This is the term used by the *Bundesverfassungsgericht*, Decision of 30 June 2009 (*Lissabon*), BVerfGE 123, 267, para 239. See extensively, F-X Millet, *L'Union européenne et l'identité constitutionnelle des États membres* (L.G.D.J., 2013).

translated into numerous constraints on the Member States, also with respect to the pursuit of their own constitutional objectives, including those relating to foreign policy.

To a large extent, salient issues such as neutrality and other security and defence policy preferences of the Member States have been mutually accommodated within the constitutional space. The Member States have made sure that in more sovereignty sensitive areas, where a Schmittian rather than an Arendtian understanding of the political community prevails,[2] they retain a strong voice within the EU 'agora' as well as larger autonomy externally. Nonetheless, the Member States have to respect not only the structural principles of their respective national legal order in the pursuit of their foreign policy objectives, but also have to act in a manner consistent with all obligations that EU membership entails. This includes above all the faithful application of all EU law, which they helped to adopt, in their national legal order. Apart from the protection of constitutional identity, constitutional provisions at Member State level, including their own constitutional foreign policy objectives, cannot serve as an excuse for not complying with membership obligations. In short, the EU is free to act within its competences, as long as it does not infringe upon the narrow boundaries of the constitutional identity of any of its Member States. For its part, each Member State is free to 'contribute to the creation of the international order based on law and justice',[3] to use the wording of the Lithuanian constitution, as long as it does so in a manner consistent with EU law at large.

Both the Union and the Member States remain competent to act internationally in meaningful ways. Neither is completely overshadowed by the other. This means that both are in principle entitled, and constitutionally mandated, to pursue their respective foreign policy goals at the international level. This requires a division of tasks with a view to safeguarding coherence despite the multiplicity of actors on the international stage. The principle of conferral and the ensuing division of competences among them means that, in some cases, only the Union can act; in others, both can play a role internationally, and, at least in theory, in yet other cases the Member States remain solely responsible. Where the Member States are no longer competent to act at the international level, either due to exclusive Union powers or through pre-emption, they can (and *must* from the point of view of their own legal order) pursue their constitutional objectives *within* the Union 'agora' instead of in the international arena, lest they undo internal commitments which would undermine the trust underlying the EU as a polity. In these cases, their constitutional foreign policy objectives have become fully 'Europeanized'. Moreover, among the EU's organs, its 'foreign affairs power' (*auswärtige Gewalt*) is pluralistic. Consequently, the organs called upon to pursue the objectives and the procedures to be followed depend on the policy area involved, and in particular whether the

[2] Drawing on R Post, 'Constructing the European Polity: ERTA and the Open Skies Judgments' in M Poiares Maduro and L Azoulai (eds), *The Past and Future of EU Law: The Classics of EU Law Revisited on the 50th Anniversary of the Rome Treaty* (Hart Publishing, 2010).

[3] Taking the examples of Art 135(1) Lithuanian constitution.

CFSP or other areas of external action are concerned. The foreign policy objectives of the EU play an important role in making such determinations.

Lastly, beyond mutual accommodation and respect, as well as the division of tasks, both the Union and Member States are to act loyally towards each other in a complementary fashion in order to produce synergy between their various actions. This means that regardless of the particular policy area or procedure concerned, they are to act towards common purposes. Crucially, the legal expression of such common purposes is to be found in the foreign policy objectives of the EU Treaties, not at Member State level. The foreign policy objectives of the EU Treaties can be regarded as the supreme legal norms guiding the external action of the Union as well as that of the Member States, which is operationalized mainly through the duty of sincere cooperation.

This duty can extend as far as mandating Member States to abstain from acting at all, or to act not in the pursuit of their own interests, but in pursuit of those of the Union alone. Hence, also in their international action, the Member States can be regarded as partially 'Europeanized'. Following the reasoning of the Court of Justice of the EU (CJEU), this serves to protect not only the 'unity in the international representation' of the Union and its members, but also the viability of the European polity, within which the Member States remain free to pursue their own interests. Consequently, pluralism and coherence are by no means contradictory. On the contrary, it is the maintenance of the internal political space, of which pluralism is an inherent feature, which is to be safeguarded by virtue of 'unity in external affairs'.[4] Nonetheless, here the distinction between CFSP and non-CFSP becomes crucial again, where the constraining effects of the duty of sincere cooperation are heavily curtailed through the exclusion of jurisdiction by the CJEU. Instead, it highlights the fundamental nature of security as a *state* objective.

Regardless of the presence or absence of legal constraints to do so, it may be more opportune for the Member States, despite all assertions of constitutional identity, international actorness, and the limits of conferral, to pursue their global ambitions collectively through the Union since it widens the bounds of what is materially possible for them. EU external action can amplify their voice on the international stage, and can lend more credence to their internationally entrenched foreign policy goals than their acting unilaterally. The peculiarity of the Union and its dependence on the Member States, as the other side of the coin, as well as the rules of contemporary international law limit the bounds of what is internationally feasible for the Union. This highlights the importance of coherence as positive synergy. Both the set-up of the European constitutional space and the international legal order frequently do not allow for a single European voice to be heard. However, the message Europe conveys to the world as a political community, formulated through its institutions as guided by the foreign policy objectives of the Treaties, can nonetheless be coherent, regardless of who utters it.

[4] Post (n 2) 239.

2. Diversity and Unity in the European Constitutional Space

Constitutionally codified foreign policy objectives evoke two essential features of the European Union, which reflect the diversity that is inherent in its nature. On the one hand, as constitutional norms, they have to be understood within the context of the complex relationship between EU law and the constitutional law of the Member States. On the other, as part of the 'foreign affairs constitution' of the Union, they operate in the multifaceted and multi-actor system of EU external relations.

Both aspects stem from the fact that the Union is more than an international organization, yet not conceived of as a state (Chapter 3, section 2). It remains an entity of conferred powers. These powers, even though far-reaching, are limited and the Member States retain collective control over their distribution. The latter remain the 'Masters of the Treaties' as well as the bearers of *Kompetenz-Kompetenz.*[5] In addition, and regardless of the international presence of the Union, the Member States all remain subjects of international law and players on the international scene in their own right.

Despite their continued presence and activity on the international stage, the Member States are bound by the entirety of obligations flowing from their membership of the EU, which conditions their scope of manoeuvre in conducting their respective foreign policies. The existence of the EU thus leads to both a diversity of sources of supreme law as well as a multiplicity of foreign policy actors. These additional complexities serve as the background against which one must assess the role of foreign policy objectives in this composite constitutional construction and its non-unitary external representation.

The diversity and complexity present in the constitutional arrangement and external relations system of the European Union, however, do not automatically lead to a chaotic situation fraught with haphazardness and uncertainty. By contrast, there is a strong pull towards unity, both of the legal orders in general and the external action of the Union and its Member States in particular. Robert Post argues with a view to the EU, drawing on both Hannah Arendt and Carl Schmitt's work, that '[i]f politics within an agora creates power through promises and mutual pledges, this power would quickly dissipate if participants were free separately to engage with those outside the agora in ways that were inconsistent with their mutual commitment'.[6] Hence, external unity is not an end in itself. Rather, it is the maintenance of a viable internal political space, or 'agora', which requires such external unity since otherwise 'the trust necessary for internal politics could be fatally undermined'.[7] This also applies to the European constitutional space and the pursuit of constitutional foreign policy objectives. Neither the objectives of the

[5] The Treaties cannot be amended without approval of the Member States 'in accordance with their respective constitutional requirements': Art 48(4), second subpara and (6), second subpara TEU.

[6] Post (n 2) 238.

[7] Post (n 2) 238.

Member States nor of the Union are to be pursued in a way that would undermine this mutual trust. In some cases, this may mean that the Union can pursue certain objectives internationally only in a limited fashion, requiring the united political will of the Member States. In other cases, it means that the Member States cannot pursue their objectives on the international stage where this would undermine internal commitments or where they have lost their power to act. In any case, they always have the choice of pursuing them internally, ie *within* the EU 'agora', and subsequently *through* EU external action internationally.

2.1 Multiple constitutional sources

As a starting point, having concluded that the EU has indeed acquired a form of 'thick' constitutionalism, the relationship between its constitutional foreign policy objectives and those of the Member States needs to be scrutinized. To varying degrees, one can find constitutional 'heterarchy' and 'pluralism' also in national federal systems or between the national and international legal orders.[8] In the case of the European Union, the questions of constitutional supremacy and the final word in constitutional adjudication remain unresolved and therefore the object of high-profile judicial decisions and scholarly debate.[9] While the EU can no longer be classified as an ordinary international organization, and consequently its law is no longer considered as ordinary public international law, it is ostensibly not a state, even though it has acquired a quasi-federal structure.[10] Within this structure, however, there is no clear hierarchy subjugating the Member States and their powers unconditionally to those of the Union. In particular, the relationship of the constitutional law of the Member States with the law of the Union remains a contentious issue, which is significant for foreign policy objectives as constitutional norms on the level of both the Member States and EU. In the absence of unconditional supremacy, in order to understand the relationship between constitutional foreign policy objectives from these different sources within the European constitutional space, the basic parameters of the overall relationship between the EU Treaties and Member State constitutions need to be clarified.

In terms of scholarship, this situation characterized by competing claims of ultimate primacy and the final word in constitutional adjudication has spawned multiple concepts. Most prominently, these include that of 'constitutional pluralism'[11]

[8] For an elaborate challenge against equating constitutionalism with hierarchy and closure, see D Halberstam, 'Systems Pluralism and Institutional Pluralism in Constitutional Law: National, Supranational and Global Governance' in M Avbelj and J Komárek (eds), *Constitutional Pluralism in the European Union and Beyond* (Hart Publishing, 2012).

[9] See from the more recent past *Lissabon* (n 1).

[10] See, eg A von Bogdandy and J Bast, 'The Federal Order of Competences' in A von Bogdandy and J Bast (eds), *Principles of European Constitutional Law*, 2nd edn (Hart Publishing/C.H. Beck, 2011); and R Schütze, *From Dual to Cooperative Federalism: The Changing Structure of European Law* (OUP, 2009).

[11] See for a history of the concept and its different meanings M Avbelj and J Komárek, 'Introduction' in M Avbelj and J Komárek (eds), *Constitutional Pluralism in the European Union and Beyond* (Hart Publishing, 2012); earlier seminally N Walker, 'The Idea of Constitutional Pluralism'

or related theories such as 'multilevel' or 'composite constitutionalism'.[12] However, any normative claims of constitutional pluralism are not the object of the present enquiry, taking as a starting point only its empirical claim, ie the existence of 'a plurality of constitutional sources and claims of final authority which create a context for potential conflicts that are not hierarchically regulated' within the European Union.[13] Despite this plurality and potential conflict, these constitutional sources and actors form part of an overarching whole, which is encapsulated in the English language by the term 'European constitutional space',[14] which will be used here to denote the construct, which is proverbially 'united in diversity', and within which constitutional foreign policy objectives operate.

As is well known in EU legal scholarship, the first claim to primacy of (then) European Community law over national law was made in the famous *Costa v ENEL* judgment of 1964. There, the Court of Justice of the EU ruled that 'the law stemming from the treaty, an independent source of law, could not, because of its special and original nature, be overridden by domestic legal provisions, however framed'.[15] This does not entail inconsistent national law becoming void, but 'only' its disapplication in the presence of contrary Union law.[16] The finding also applied to the constitutional law of the Member States, as the Court later clarified.[17]

(2002) 68 *Modern Law Review* 317; M Poiares Maduro, 'Contrapunctual Law: Europe's Constitutional Pluralism in Action' in N Walker (ed), *Sovereignty in Transition* (Hart Publishing, 2003); and K Jaklic, *Constitutional Pluralism in the EU* (OUP, 2014).

[12] This is largely an issue of translating the German term *Verbund*, which came to prominence in the *Maastricht* judgment of the *Bundesverfassungsgericht* in the form of the composite 'Staatenverbund' as a description of the EU, Decision of 12 October 1993 (*Maastricht*), BVerfGE 89, 155, para 90. Pernice stressed the constitutional features of this *Verbund*, coining the term 'Verfassungsverbund': see I Pernice, 'Theorie und Praxis des europäischen Verfassungsverbundes' in C Calliess (ed), *Verfassungswandel im europäischen Staaten- und Verfassungsverbund* (Mohr Siebeck, 2007). While Pernice translates his own concept of the *Verfassungsverbund* into English as 'multilevel constitutionalism' (I Pernice, 'The Treaty of Lisbon: Multilevel Constitutionalism in Action' (2009) 15 *Columbia Journal of European Law* 349), others prefer the term 'composite' (see A von Bogdandy and S Schill, 'Overcoming Absolute Primacy: Respect for National Identity under the Lisbon Treaty' (2011) 48 *Common Market Law Review* 1417, 1421 (footnote 12)). See also F Mayer and M Wendel, 'Multilevel Constitutionalism and Constitutional Pluralism: Querelle Allemande or Querelle d'Allemand?' in M Avbelj and J Komárek (eds), *Constitutional Pluralism in the European Union and Beyond* (Hart Publishing, 2012) 151, concluding that constitutional pluralism and multilevel constitutionalism 'display significant similarities in terms of theoretical foundations, without merging into a single concept'.

[13] M Poiares Maduro, 'Three Claims of Constitutional Pluralism' in M Avbelj and J Komárek (eds), *Constitutional Pluralism in the European Union and Beyond* (Hart Publishing, 2012) 69–70.

[14] A von Bogdandy, 'Constitutional Principles for Europe' in E Riedel and R Wolfrum (eds), *Recent Trends in German and European Constitutional Law* (Springer, 2006) 3; note also R Bieber and P Widmer (eds), *L'espace constitutionnel europeen/Der Europäische Verfassungsraum/The European constitutional area* (Schulthess, 1995).

[15] Case 6/64 *Costa v ENEL*, EU:C:1964:66, para 13.

[16] See eg Case C-184/89 *Nimz*, EU:C:1991:50, para 19; building on Case 106/77 *Simmenthal*, EU:C:1978:49, para 24. Further B De Witte, 'Direct Effect, Primacy, and the Nature of the Legal Order' in P Craig and G de Búrca (eds), *The Evolution of EU Law*, 2nd edn (OUP, 2011) 341.

[17] Case 11/70 *Internationale Handelsgesellschaft*, EU:C:1970:114, para 3; later confirmed, among others, in Case C-213/07 *Michaniki*, EU:C:2008:731.

A principle of primacy, however, has never been codified in the Treaties. A provision to this end was foreseen in the Constitutional Treaty,[18] but dropped from the Lisbon Treaty.[19] Instead, the Member States opted to attach a Declaration in which they recall the case law of the Court, according to which 'the Treaties and the law adopted by the Union on the basis of the Treaties have primacy over the law of Member States, under the conditions laid down by the said case law'.[20]

The understanding of primacy as devised by the CJEU was not shared unconditionally and immediately by the courts of the Member States. Most notably, the Italian and German constitutional courts challenged the notion of such 'absolute primacy' extending over national constitutional law and attached certain limits to it. While the *Corte costituzionale* developed the idea of certain 'counterlimits' (*controlimiti*) to primacy,[21] the *Bundesfervassungsgericht* developed the notion of constitutional principles that are 'immune to integration' (*integrationsfest*).[22] In other Member States, courts developed similar doctrines, amounting to what may be called a '"counterlimits" consensus'.[23] Armin von Bogdandy and Stephan Schill summarize the substance of this protected core of national constitutional law, which frequently forms part of the particularly entrenched provisions of the Member States' constitutions, as comprising of 'the statehood of Member States, key requirements of the rule of law, the principle of democracy, the essential core of fundamental rights, and, in federal systems, the principle of federalism'.[24] Moreover, national constitutional courts have underlined the importance of national parliaments in this context as principal addressees of their constitutional integration objectives. As the German Federal Constitutional Court observed, the parliament has a distinct responsibility for integration (*Integrationsverantwortung*), of which it cannot be deprived by the process of integration itself.[25]

It is within this pluralist context of diverse sources of supreme laws that constitutional foreign policy objectives are situated, which has consequences for their operation as legal norms. On the one hand, foreign policy objectives of the Union codified in the Treaties do not enjoy unconditional primacy. Hence, they do not automatically trump the objectives enshrined in Member State constitutions. Their pursuit is conditioned by the limits imposed by Member State constitutional law. On the other hand, to the extent that the primacy of EU law over national constitutional law is accepted, the duty to pursue foreign policy objectives under national constitutional law is conditioned by the respect for EU law in general.

[18] Art I-6 CT.

[19] See J-C Piris, *The Lisbon Treaty: A Legal and Political Analysis* (CUP, 2010) 79–82.

[20] Declaration No 17 concerning primacy attached to the Lisbon Treaty.

[21] Starting with Decision of 18 December 1973 (*Frontini*), Sentenza N 183/1973.

[22] This is the term used in *Lissabon* (n 1) para 239. The starting point of this case law is the *Solange I* judgment, Decision of 25 May 1974 (*Solange I*), BVerfGE 37, 271.

[23] De Witte (n 16) 356, for the pertinent case law from these countries see 352–6.

[24] von Bogdandy and Schill (n 12) 1436.

[25] *Lissabon* (n 1) para 236.

2.2 Multiple foreign policy actors

Next to the relationship between legal orders within the European constitutional space, there are a number of additional considerations to be taken into account regarding the system of external relations of the European Union.[26] The complexities and peculiarities of this system, when compared to the national setting, stem from the *sui generis* nature of the Union.

The method of conducting external relations by the EU is rather unique in the world. While it is true that a number of countries also exhibit different varieties of foreign affairs federalism or non-unitary external representation,[27] the constituent units in a national federal system, when granted a measure of power in foreign affairs by the constitution, are by no means as active on the international stage as the Member States of the EU. This is particularly true for the political and security domains. In the traditional approach to foreign affairs, despite internal diversity and fragmented sovereignty, the 'nation' is represented externally by a 'sole organ', ie the national or federal executive.[28] By contrast, Eric Stein's finding in 1986 that 'there is no evidence that an organ equipped with centralized diplomacy and other requisite instrumentalities will emerge in the foreseeable future in Europe' still holds true today.[29] In this external sphere, as aptly put by Enzo Cannizzaro, neither the Union nor its Member States possess 'the plenitude of the foreign relations power, which is instead deeply segmented in a plurality of actors, objectives and decision-making procedures'.[30] The Union remains an international actor of conferred powers across different policy areas, but the Member States also retain 'only limited capacity to act on the international plane because of the European integration system in which they take part'.[31] Consequently, to borrow Bruno De

[26] The choice of the terms 'order' and 'system' is deliberate. It recognizes the existence of different autonomous legal orders, which are also part of, and routinely applied in, a wider whole. Here, the focus is on a part of this 'European legal system', viz the reproduction of legal norms and practices in the external relations domain. This draws on Poiares Maduro (n 13) 70. This term 'system' is also used in international relations to describe the composite of EU and Member State foreign policies: see C Hill and M Smith, 'International Relations and the European Union: Themes and Issues' in C Hill and M Smith (eds), *International Relations and the European Union*, 2nd edn (OUP, 2011) 6–7.

[27] Examples for this would include federal states such as Germany, Belgium, or Switzerland, where the subnational units have certain powers to act internationally, albeit in rather limited ways. See E Cannizzaro, 'Unity and Pluralism in the EU's Foreign Relations Power' in C Barnard (ed), *The Fundamentals of EU Law Revisited: Assessing the Impact of the Constitutional Debate* (OUP, 2007) 195–201; and R Schütze, 'Federalism and Foreign Affairs: Mixity as an (Inter)national Phenomenon' in C Hillion and P Koutrakos (eds), *Mixed Agreements Revisited: The EU and Its Member States in the World* (Hart Publishing, 2010).

[28] See Henkin (n 341) 41–5, who attributes the term 'sole organ' to Chief Justice Marshall in a statement to the House of Representatives.

[29] E Stein, 'Towards a European Foreign Policy? The European Foreign Affairs System from the Perspective of the United States Constitution' in M Cappelletti, M Seccombe, and JHH Weiler (eds), *Integration Through Law: Europe and the American Federal Experience. Volume I, Book 3* (Walter de Gruyter, 1986) 82.

[30] Cannizzaro (n 27) 194.

[31] B De Witte, 'The Emergence of a European System of Public International Law: The EU and its Member States as Strange Subjects' in J Wouters, A Nollkaemper, and E de Wet (eds), *The Europeanisation of International Law: The Status of International Law in the EU and Its Member States* (T.M.C. Asser Press, 2008) 39.

Witte's expression, both the Union and the Member States have become 'strange subjects' of international law.[32]

On the contrary, hardly anybody would consider Germany a 'strange subject' of international law in view of the fact that its *Länder* assume a role in the making of certain treaties concluded by the federation or even enter into certain international agreements with other countries.[33] After all, this practice remains limited. It is Germany, not the Free State of Bavaria or the city-state of Hamburg in its capacity as 'intermediary between all continents and peoples of the world',[34] that is represented at the United Nations and NATO,[35] or which sends troops on international peace and security missions.[36] Instead, what makes Germany and the other Member States 'strange' is the fact of being a member of the EU.

The downsides of this fragmented international representation and lack of a 'sole' European voice in the world have long been recognized, not least since the Single European Act. Calls for a more visible, more assertive Union, whose different external policies are coherent, and whose external action as a whole is in harmony with that of its Member States, have been made throughout the years. It was one of the main concerns of the Laeken Declaration and the Convention on the Future of Europe and resulted, inter alia, in the streamlined catalogues of goals for EU external action in the Treaties today (Chapter 2, section 3).

However, the situation that has evolved over time remains complex. On the one hand, the Member States, as 'Masters of the Treaties', have ensured that the Union does not eclipse them entirely as international actors. On the other, the Treaties, as interpreted by the CJEU, provide for numerous legal and institutional devices to minimize adverse consequences for the Union caused by Member State action, including on the international scene.

A hallmark of this 'mixed sovereignty'[37]is the different types of competence for the Union to act internationally, as well as the different ways for establishing such competence. Next to expressing external competences found in the Treaties, the Union can also acquire 'implied' competences by virtue of internal rules or the necessity for external action to effectively pursue internal objectives.[38] Whether

[32] De Witte (n 31) 39.

[33] See Art 32(3) and Art 24(1a) German constitution. See further, C Calliess, 'Auswärtige Gewalt' in J Isensee and P Kirchhof (eds), *Handbuch des Staatsrechts der Bundesrepublik Deutschland. Volume IV: Aufgaben des Staates*, 3rd edn (C.F. Müller, 2006) 620–6. According to an understanding between the federation and the *Länder* of 1957, the *Lindauer Abkommen*, the federation can also conclude treaties touching on the legislative powers of the *Länder* while providing for the involvement of the *Länder* in the negotiations and after obtaining their consent.

[34] First recital of the preamble, Hamburg constitution.

[35] U Fastenrath, *Kompetenzverteilung im Bereich der ausgewärtigen Gewalt* (C.H. Beck, 1986) 153, noting that politically significant organizations usually cover matters going beyond the legislative powers of the *Länder* and thus require federal action.

[36] See F Kirchhof, 'Verteidigung und Bundeswehr' in J Isensee and P Kirchhof (eds), *Handbuch des Staatsrechts der Bundesrepublik Deutschland. Volume IV: Aufgaben des Staates*, 3rd edn (C.F. Müller, 2006) 649–60.

[37] De Witte (n 31) 49.

[38] In detail M Cremona, 'External Relations and External Competence of the European Union: The Emergence of an Integrated Policy' in P Craig and G de Búrca (eds), *The Evolution of EU Law*, 2nd edn (OUP, 2011).

these competences are exclusive to the Union or shared with the Member States has important legal consequences. As Allan Rosas and Lorna Armati summarize the situation:

the type of competence will determine whether it is the Union alone, the Union together with its Member States (in the context of shared competence) or in parallel with them (parallel competence), or the Member States alone which take part in international discussions and negotiations, conclude international agreements, are members of international organisations, and so on.[39]

Furthermore, the institutional framework of EU external relations can hardly be compared to that of a state. It includes various policy-making, implementing, and representative institutions, including the European Commission, the President of the European Council, and the High Representative for Foreign and Security Policy, assisted by the European External Action Service (EEAS). Moreover, the decision-making procedures, the allocation of tasks and distribution of powers, as well as the standards of parliamentary oversight and judicial review, shift according to the policy area involved. A 'bipolarity'[40] continues to exist between the external policies found in the TFEU and the Common Foreign and Security Policy (CFSP), which is located in the TEU. Generally speaking, in the case of the former, which comprises the former Community policies and the 'third pillar' under the Maastricht architecture, the Commission, Parliament, and Court of Justice play a more important role than in the latter case, where the European Council and the Council of Ministers assume a predominant position.

Hence, in addition to the multiple sources of constitutional law, 'the polyphonic nature of the Union's external action'[41] and the complex legal–institutional framework of EU external relations also have an impact on the pursuit of all the constitutional foreign policy objectives present in the European constitutional space. Taken together, these features condition the leeway and sites for the Member States to pursue the foreign policy objectives enshrined in their respective constitutions. At the same time, these same features frame the ability of, and modalities for, the Union and its organs to pursue the objectives of EU external action as codified in the Treaties.

2.3 Overall substantive convergence and possible tensions

Despite the diversity of constitutional sources and actors in the European constitutional space, there is ample common ground in terms of substance, although tensions remain in particular areas. When looking at the legal orders of the EU

[39] A Rosas and L Armati, *EU Constitutional Law: An Introduction*, 2nd edn (Hart Publishing, 2012) 244.

[40] A Dashwood, 'The Continuing Bipolarity of EU External Action' in I Govaere et al (eds), *The European Union in the World: Essays in Honour of Marc Maresceau* (Martinus Nijhoff, 2014).

[41] C Hillion, 'Mixity and Coherence in EU External Relations: The Significance of the "Duty of Cooperation"' in C Hillion and P Koutrakos (eds), *Mixed Agreements Revisited: The EU and Its Member States in the World* (Hart Publishing, 2010) 87.

and the Member States in general, von Bogdandy and Schill conclude that both 'share a common legal and politico-ideological framework that legitimizes and limits the exercise of public power'.[42] As Art 2 TEU states, the Union is founded on values 'common to the Member States'. Moreover, in order to join the Union in the first place, states need to respect these values and be 'committed to promoting them'.[43] In other words, these are the common foundations of the EU as a 'polity' or 'agora'. Hence, it is plausible to subscribe to the view that 'conflict will be exceptional because of the far-reaching convergence between the principles of domestic constitutional law enjoying specific protection and the constitutional principles of the EU'.[44] This exceptionality of conflict applies to constitutional foreign policy objectives as well.

Such objectives can only be pursued within the framework of the respective overall constitutional structure. However, European integration itself figures as a codified objective in many Member State constitutions (Chapter 2, section 4.6). From the perspective of Member State constitutional law, including both clear-cut regional integration objectives and general international cooperation objectives, these clauses have been used to justify further integration and the transfer of more powers to the Union. At the same time, many of them stress the need for conformity with the structural principles of the respective national legal order.[45] For instance, the Swedish constitution succinctly stipulates: 'Within the framework of European Union cooperation, the Riksdag [Parliament] may transfer decision-making authority which does not affect the basic principles by which Sweden is governed'.[46] More proactively, the German Basic Law mandates the Federal Republic to:

> participate in the development of the European Union that is committed to democratic, social and federal principles, to the rule of law, and to the principle of subsidiarity, and that guarantees a level of protection of basic rights essentially comparable to that afforded by this Basic Law.[47]

These are instances where internal structural features are being translated into the object of foreign policy objectives (Chapter 1, section 5). The more they are achieved outside of their own polity, the more they approximate structural features of their target, in this case the EU itself. Constitutional integration clauses are even used as a national constitutional basis to justify the primacy of EU law over national (secondary) legislation.[48] Therefore, foreign policy objectives of the

[42] von Bogdandy and Schill (n 12) 1432.
[43] Art 49(1) TEU.
[44] von Bogdandy and Schill (n 12) 1433.
[45] See C Grabenwarter, 'National Constitutional Law Relating to the European Union' in A von Bogdandy and J Bast (eds), *Principles of European Constitutional Law*, 2nd edn (Hart Publishing/C.H. Beck, 2011) 95–102, who distinguishes between clauses on the transfer of sovereignty or sovereign rights and structural safeguard clauses.
[46] Chapter 10, Art 6(1) Swedish constitution.
[47] Art 23(1) German constitution; and similarly Art 7(6) Portuguese constitution.
[48] See in the case of Germany, for example, the ruling of the *Bundesverfassungsgericht* in Decision of 9 June 1971 (*Milchpulver*), BVerfGE 31, 145, para 95. Further J Wouters, 'National Constitutions and the European Union' (2000) 27 *Legal Issues of Economic Integration* 25, 72–3.

Member States serve as an essential building block of the joint European constitutional space. In other words, the Union itself can be seen as the product of the active pursuit by Member States of their constitutional objectives for integration and regional or international cooperation, insofar as their constitutions so provide. The fruits of these constitutionally mandated endeavours, ie the transfer of powers and the pooling of sovereignty, have shaped the very structure of this constitutional space.

This common pursuit of integration has yielded a set of external action objectives of the EU that cover the same substantive areas as national constitutions, albeit with certain specific emphases (Chapter 2, sections 4 and 5). Hence, any direct conflict between constitutional foreign policy objectives, or generally between the objectives of one legal order with the structures of another, is unlikely.

However, the complexities of the European constitutional space and the EU system of foreign relations reveal that Member States are at the same time adamant to preserve the protections afforded by their national constitutions as well as a certain leeway in the conduct of their foreign policies. The refusal to put the principle of primacy into the Treaties, the emphasis on conferral and preservation of constitutional identity by national constitutional courts, and the intergovernmental nature of the CFSP all account for this.

Furthermore, despite overall convergence, a degree of constitutional diversity between the Member States remains. As von Bogdandy and Schill summarize:

> we find republics and monarchies, parliamentary and semi-presidential systems, strong and weak parliaments, democracies based on competition and those based on consensus, unitary and federal structures of government, strong and weak systems of constitutional adjudication, and considerable differences regarding the scope and impact of fundamental rights.[49]

This is no different in the domain of foreign policy. Next to members of NATO, there are neutral Member States, nuclear haves and have-nots, countries with large military forces and others with rather modest capabilities, and former colonial powers and former colonies. Of course, not all of this is of constitutional value, but some of it was deemed of such fundamental importance that it found its way into the Member State constitutions. For instance, whereas the constitutions of Malta and Austria declare these countries to be neutral, the Romanian constitution has a provision regulating, and thus anticipating, NATO membership, while the German Basic Law specifically allows the Federal Republic to participate in a system of collective security. Similarly, while the French and Portuguese constitutions mandate the constitutional organs to reach out to other countries sharing their respective languages (the *Francophonie* and *Lusofonia*), Lithuanian and Croatian constitutional law prohibits these countries from engaging in any international association based on the former USSR and Yugoslavia, respectively (Chapter 2, section 4.6).

[49] von Bogdandy and Schill (n 12) 1426.

2.4 Making ends meet in the constitutional space: Coherence in EU external relations

Given the pluralistic nature of the European constitutional space and the polyphonic quality of the system of EU external relations, ie 'within a diversified structure, with multiple players and different voices, with different competences and powers',[50] there is no 'sole organ', and not even a single 'federal level' to single-handedly conduct the Union's foreign relations. Instead, the quest for 'harmony'[51] between legal orders, as well as in the external action of the Union and its Member States, is a source of trials and tribulations. The following sections show how the pursuit of constitutional foreign policy objectives is conditioned by these additional complexities, but also demonstrates how these objectives contribute to fostering harmony in the external relations of the European polity.

The approach employed here builds on Bart Van Vooren's contextualization of external relations coherence and constitutional pluralism. He rightly asserts that 'the pluralist construction of the EU legal order informs the application of the principle of coherence in concrete contexts of legal conflict and synergy'.[52] This dovetails with Daniel Thym's observation that:

> Coherence and complementarity of national and European foreign affairs constitute the external dimension of the European system of multilevel constitutionalism that is being built upon the non-hierarchical relations between national and European constitutional norms and emphasises the various linkages and interdependences within the European constitutional sphere.[53]

Echoing Robert Post's conception of internal politics of the EU as an 'agora', both concepts urge breaking with strict hierarchies and dichotomies, and promote working instead through mutual respect, adjustment, and accommodation towards a more unified whole.[54] Constitutional pluralism, drawing on Miguel Maduro's definition of 'contrapunctual law', is characterized by mutual concessions and accommodation between legal orders. On the one hand, the national identity of the Members States will not be encroached upon by the Union. On the other, the latter will loyally contribute to the uniform application of EU law. This entails the justification of decisions, concerning both the substance and the

[50] Cremona (n 38) 91.

[51] This musical metaphor is popular both in the literature on constitutional pluralism and EU external relations. For instance, drawing on Poiares Maduro's idea of 'Contrapunctual Law', Komárek and Avbelj label this particular brand of pluralism 'harmonious–discursive constitutionalism': J Komárek and M Avbelj, *Four Visions of Constitutional Pluralism*, EUI Working Paper Law 2008/21, 3, while Hillion stresses 'the polyphonic nature of the Union's external action whose audibility ultimately depends on the degree of harmony achieved among its key players': Hillion (n 41) 87.

[52] B Van Vooren, *EU External Relations Law and the European Neighbourhood Policy: A Paradigm for Coherence* (Routledge, 2012) 65.

[53] D Thym, 'Foreign Affairs' in A von Bogdandy and J Bast (eds), *Principles of European Constitutional Law*, 2nd edn (Hart Publishing/C.H. Beck, 2011) 338.

[54] This is so despite the range of 'sometimes also very different' understandings of pluralism: see Avbelj and Komárek (n 11) 4.

institutional choice, based on commonly accepted principles.[55] Evident expressions of such principles are the 'identity protection' clause in Art 4(2) TEU and the 'integration clauses' found in the constitutions of various Member States. These allow the mutual 'permeability' of the legal orders within the constitutional space of the European polity.[56]

In the foreign relations domain, principles such as pre-emption, the duty of sincere cooperation, or the unity in the international representation of the EU emerge with a view to safeguarding this internal cohesion from external erosion. Despite a focus on the pluralism discourse on constitutional adjudication,[57] pluralist considerations are applicable to all actors within the legal system. Critically, one such key consideration is that of institutional choice, which does not refer only to a selection between different levels of governance regarding the same branch (the judiciary), but can equally involve other branches across different levels.[58] Thus, the reduced role of courts and judicial review in the area of foreign affairs and the 'executive character'[59] of the CFSP do not exclude a constitutional pluralist perspective. It is thus possible to identify intertwined legal orders forming a composite 'foreign affairs constitution', involving a variety of constitutional organs, the actions of which require coordination in the absence of clear-cut hierarchy and uniformity.

This brings to the fore the framing concept of 'coherence' in the external relations of the EU and its Member States. The idea of coherence originates from the need to harmonize the two basic modes of external relations of the EU, but has since acquired a larger meaning. The Single European Act first called for the external policies pursued in the framework of the Community and those within European Political Cooperation (EPC) to be 'consistent'.[60] In other language versions, the corresponding term 'coherent' was used (such as *cohérent* or *kohärent* in French and German, respectively). However, there remains a degree of ambiguity between 'coherence' and 'consistency'. Both are regarded as partially interchangeable, with the former being the broader concept.[61] Here, too, 'coherence' will be used as the overall concept and 'consistency' as one of its dimensions.

[55] Poiares Maduro (n 11) 527–9.
[56] Mayer and Wendel (n 12) 138–9.

[57] See M Poiares Maduro, 'Courts and Pluralism: Essay on a Theory of Judicial Adjudication in the Context of Legal and Constitutional Pluralism' in J Dunoff and J Trachtman (eds), *Ruling the World: Constitutionalism, International Law, and Global Governance* (CUP, 2009).

[58] N Komesar, *Imperfect Alternatives—Choosing Institutions in Law, Economics and Public Policy* (Chicago University Press, 1994), whose theory of institutional choice, and on which Poiares Maduro draws, includes choices between different branches of government. However, the focus of the present enquiry is on what institutions are legally called upon to pursue (or are barred from pursuing) constitutional objectives in the conduct of foreign policy, and not the question which institution is best suited, according to this model, to address a particular problem.

[59] D Thym, 'The Intergovernmental Constitution of the EU's Foreign, Security & Defence Executive' (2011) 7 *European Constitutional Law Review* 453, 463.

[60] Art 30(5) SEA.

[61] M Cremona, 'Coherence in European Union Foreign Relations Law' in P Koutrakos (ed), *European Foreign Policy: Legal and Political Perspectives* (Edward Elgar, 2011) 59–60; and further on the different language versions C Hillion, '*Tous pour un, un pour tous!* Coherence in the External Relations of the European Union' in M Cremona (ed), *Developments in EU External Relations Law* (OUP, 2008) 12–17.

The concept of coherence later found expression in Art 3 TEU (Nice version), but has since been 'dissected and dispersed over a number of new Lisbon provisions',[62] while at the same time elevating it 'more than ever to the constitutional level'.[63] In the post-Lisbon Treaties, Art 13(1) TEU addresses the institutional framework of the Union, mandating it to 'ensure the consistency, effectiveness and continuity of its policies and actions'. Art 7 TFEU reiterates this, stating, '[t]he Union shall ensure consistency between its policies and activities, taking all of its objectives into account and in accordance with the principle of conferral of powers'. The principle appears again in the part of the TEU dealing with EU external action in general. According to Art 21(3) TEU, the 'Union shall ensure consistency between the different areas of its external action and between these and its other policies'.[64]

Ever since the term entered into the primary law of the Union, it has attracted sustained interest in the legal discourse regarding EU external relations.[65] In order to break down the different aspects of consistency, traditionally a distinction between horizontal and vertical coherence has been employed, ie between the different policies or actors at the Union level on the one hand, and between the policies of the Union and the Member States on the other.[66]

The approach devised by Marise Cremona and applied by Van Vooren adds more nuance by identifying three levels of coherence, which are applicable to both the horizontal and vertical dimensions: Firstly, coherence as legal consistency, ie the avoidance and resolution of conflict through hierarchy; secondly, coherence as delimitation, ie the effective allocation of tasks between actors and instruments; and, thirdly, coherence as synergy between actors, norms, and instruments, achieved through cooperation and complementarity.[67] These considerations dovetail with the idea of creating harmony in the sense of constitutional pluralism, and represent precisely 'the external dimension of the European system of multilevel constitutionalism'.[68] Coherence, it would seem, is the Union's shorthand for the quest of achieving external unity with a view to maintaining the essential characteristics of the EU as a pluralistic polity.

[62] P Van Elsuwege and H Merket, 'The Role of the Court of Justice in Ensuring the Unity of the EU's External Representation' in S Blockmans and R Wessel (eds), *Principles and Practices of EU External Representation*, CLEER Working Paper 2012/5, 41.

[63] Van Elsuwege and Merket (n 62) 40–1.

[64] Art 21(3), second subpara TEU.

[65] For an account of the literature see Van Vooren (n 52) 59; for a (pre-Lisbon) monograph devoted to the issue see I Bosse-Platière, *L'article 3 TEU: Recherche sur une exigence de cohérence de l'action extérieure de l'Union européenne* (Bruylant, 2009).

[66] S Nuttall, 'Coherence and Consistency' in C Hill and M Smith (eds), *International Relations and the European Union*, 1st edn (OUP, 2005); Hillion (n 61) 17–18. Note also G De Baere, *Constitutional Principles of EU External Relations* (OUP, 2008) 231–303, who distinguishes the legal 'management' of the vertical and horizontal axes in EU external relations.

[67] Cremona (n 61) 60–1; applied to the European Neighbourhood Policy by Van Vooren (n 52) 57–72.

[68] Thym (n 53) 338.

Coherence is an inherently goal-oriented concept,[69] which makes constitutional foreign policy objectives vital ingredients for operating the different legal principles driving the quest for harmony and unity in a pluralistic context. As a common denominator of the scholarship regarding coherence, Cremona identifies 'its dynamic nature, involving balance and an incremental approach: a goal that is strived towards'.[70] However, just like external unity, and much like the *finalité* of integration, coherence is not a goal in itself. This becomes apparent in Van Vooren's general definition of coherence in EU external relations:

> To attain coherence between norms, actors and instruments *towards a common objective*, between them conflicts should be avoided and resolved (first level), tasks should be allocated effectively (second level), and positive synergy should be achieved (third level).[71]

This 'common objective' is not to be understood as any single one found in the constitutional law of the EU, but as all of them taken together. Van Vooren speaks of Art 21 TEU as the 'core expression of coherent EU external relations'.[72] This view can be subscribed to, while adding Art 3(5) TEU as well. The following three sections revisit the three levels of coherence from the point of view of the role of constitutional foreign policy objectives in fostering such coherence. For each level, both the vertical and horizontal levels is assessed.

3. Consistency in Diversity: EU Membership and National Identity

On the first level, coherence can be defined as the resolution between norm conflicts, ie coherence as 'consistency'. This may well be described as the most Kelsian dimension of coherence as it evokes a hierarchical relationship. At first sight, this may appear incompatible with a pluralist perspective. However, it is the large degree of mutual constitutional accommodation and the explicit protection of core constitutional principles by the Member States that brings the pluralist dimension of consistency to the fore.

3.1 Consistency in the vertical relationship

European integration, including a common European foreign policy, is to be consistent with the national identity of the Member States and, unsurprisingly, has largely been framed in such a way by the Member States in their capacity as 'Masters of the Treaties'. For the pursuit of foreign policy objectives, this has two

69 Coherence and goal-orientedness are also hallmarks of multilevel constitutionalism. Mayer and Wendel (n 12) 139 stress the importance of unity 'in a *functional* sense' (italics in the original) in multilevel constitutionalism. However, note that they see the 'accentuation of coherence, mutual stabilisation and functional unity' (151) as the factors that *distinguish* the latter concept from pluralism.

70 Cremona (n 61) 60.

71 Van Vooren (n 52) 69 (emphasis added).

72 Van Vooren (n 52) 69.

important, albeit asymmetrical, consequences. Firstly, Member State objectives have to be pursued in a manner consistent with their own structural principles *as well as* with all of their obligations under EU law. Secondly, EU external objectives have to be pursued in a manner consistent with EU structural principles *as well as* with the constitutional identity of the Member States.

Despite the substantive convergence addressed above, conflicts may still arise with regard to the pursuit of foreign policy objectives. However, such possible tensions have been accommodated to a large extent in both Member State constitutions and the EU Treaties. This concerns, in particular, the sensitivities of the Member States regarding their actorness on the international stage and their autonomy in the area of security and defence policy. Regarding the latter, constitutionally, the issues of neutrality and collective defence stand out.

This accommodation is reflected in a number of specific provisions and documents. Declarations No 13 and No 14 attached to the Lisbon Treaty concerning the CFSP express the concerns of the Member States in these policy areas most clearly. Declaration No 13 stresses that Treaty provisions on the CFSP 'do not affect the responsibilities of the Member States, as they currently exist, for the formulation and conduct of their foreign policy nor of their national representation in third countries and international organisations' and that 'the provisions governing the Common Security and Defence Policy do not prejudice the specific character of the security and defence policy of the Member States'. Moreover, it states that the Union and the Member States 'remain bound by the provisions of the Charter of the United Nations and, in particular, by the primary responsibility of the Security Council and of its Members for the maintenance of international peace and security'.[73] Declaration No 14 adds that the CFSP:

> will not affect the existing legal basis, responsibilities, and powers of each Member State in relation to the formulation and conduct of its foreign policy, its national diplomatic service, relations with third countries and participation in international organisations, including a Member State's membership of the Security Council of the United Nations.

Furthermore, it stresses that the provisions on the CFSP under the Lisbon Treaty will 'not give new powers to the Commission to initiate decisions nor do they increase the role of the European Parliament'. In short, the Declarations affirm that despite progressing European integration, the autonomy of the Member States as international actors as well as their prerogatives in security and defence policy (such as neutrality, collective security, or collective defence) are to be safeguarded.

This accommodation of sensitivities in the field of security and defence is also reflected in the Treaties, which state that the Common Security and Defence Policy (CSDP):

> shall not prejudice the specific character of the security and defence policy of certain Member States and shall respect the obligations of certain Member States, which see their

[73] The idea that the EU 'remain[s]' bound by the UN Charter, being an agreement which it has not concluded, is controversial: see P Eeckhout, *EU External Relations Law*, 2nd edn (OUP, 2011) 401–21.

common defence realised in the North Atlantic Treaty Organisation (NATO), under the North Atlantic Treaty and be compatible with the common security and defence policy established within that framework.[74]

In other words, the pursuit of external security through the CFSP/CSDP has to be consistent with these preferences of the Member States. The two basic manifestations of such preferences are neutrality and collective defence through NATO.

Apart from Austria, Cyprus, Finland, Ireland, Malta, and Sweden, all EU Member States are also members of the North Atlantic Treaty Organization. The others have in the past pursued foreign policies labelled 'neutral'.[75] However, Sweden and Finland have abolished this in favour of the political label 'alliance-free'.[76] Cypriot foreign policy is not strictly tied to neutrality in any rigid sense either.[77] While political neutrality might pose an 'integration dilemma'[78] for all neutral Member States, it only becomes a multilevel constitutional dilemma for those where it is part of their constitutional law. This distinction becomes clear in the case of Ireland, the constitution of which is silent on neutrality. As the Irish High Court (*An Ard-Chúirt*) ruled in *Horgan v An Taoiseach*:

Despite the great historic value attached by Ireland to the concept of neutrality, that status is nowhere reflected in Bunreacht na hÉireann [the Irish Constitution], or elsewhere in any domestic legislation. It is effectively a matter of government policy only, albeit a policy to which, traditionally at least, considerable importance was attached.

Ireland is thus in a different position than certain other States, who have incorporated a permanent status of neutrality in their domestic laws.[79]

Nevertheless, it is noteworthy that the neutrality caveat in the Maastricht Treaty, stating that the CFSP 'shall not prejudice the specific character of the security and defence policy of certain Member States'[80] was introduced by the Irish delegation.[81] Even though it is not part of Irish constitutional law, the Treaties came to legally accommodate the political sensitivity of Irish foreign policy.

In contrast to Ireland, neutrality is a constitutional matter in both Austria and Malta. In the case of Austria, its constitutional law contains the concept of 'permanent neutrality'.[82] With a view to implementing the Amsterdam Treaty,

[74] Art 42(2), second subpara TEU.

[75] See for case studies on neutrality as a policy, G Lysén, 'Some Views on Neutrality and Membership of the European Communities: The Case of Sweden' (1992) 29 *Common Market Law Review* 229; R Doherty, *Ireland, Neutrality and European Security Integration* (Ashgate, 2002); N Alecu de Flers, *EU Foreign Policy and the Europeanization of Neutral States: Comparing Irish and Austrian Foreign Policy* (Routledge, 2012).

[76] Alecu de Flers (n 75) 12.

[77] Note that Cyprus left the Non-Aligned Movement, of which it was a founding member, upon joining the EU in 2004: Alecu de Flers (n 75) 129; see also M Reichard, *The EU-NATO Relationship: A Legal and Political Perspective* (Ashgate, 2006) 212–13.

[78] A Wivel, 'The Security Challenge of Small EU Member States: Interests, Identity and the Development of the EU as a Security Actor' (2005) 43 *Journal of Common Market Studies* 393.

[79] *Horgan v An Taoiseach*, judgment of 28 April 2003, ILDC 486 (IE 2003), paras 120–1.

[80] Art 17(1), second subpara TEU (Nice version).

[81] Alecu de Flers (n 75) 50.

[82] Art 9a(1) Austrian constitution; together with the constitutional law on neutrality (*Neutralitätsgetz*).

a provision was added which explicitly allows Austria to take part in the CFSP, including CSDP missions as outlined by the Petersberg tasks.[83] This provision, in its current form, makes an explicit reference to the external relations objectives of the Treaties, ie Arts 3(5) and 21(1) TEU.[84] It also underlines that in the case of Austrian participation in CSDP missions entailing the deployment of personnel abroad, Austria can only consent to decisions in this regard at the EU level on condition that the procedure authorizing such deployments under national constitutional law be respected.[85] This can be seen as an instance of reconciling the pursuit of the combined external objectives of European integration and international security with the basic tenets of Austrian constitutional law. At the same time, this has been interpreted in scholarship as effectively narrowing the constitutional understanding of Austrian neutrality.[86] Consequently, Austrian constitutional law has been amended to the extent that its concept of neutrality is made unambiguously consistent with its EU membership, and particularly participation in the CFSP/CSDP and vice versa. In practice, this interpretation manifests itself by Austrian contributions to EU Battle Groups and CSDP missions.[87]

By contrast, in the case of Malta, the constitution was not amended to accommodate its participation in the CFSP/CSDP in view of its neutrality.[88] Instead, a declaration on Maltese neutrality is contained in the Final Act of the Accession Treaty of the 2004 enlargement, by which Malta became an EU member. The declaration states, on the one hand, that 'Malta affirms its commitment to the common foreign and security policy of the European Union as set out in the Treaty on European Union'. On the other hand, it notes that:

> Malta confirms that its participation in the European Union's common foreign and security policy does not prejudice its neutrality. The Treaty on European Union specifies that any decision by the Union to move to a common defence would have to be taken by unanimous decision of the European Council adopted by the Member States in accordance with their respective constitutional requirements.[89]

Whereas substantive inconsistency between Maltese neutrality and the CFSP is ruled out *tout court*, the declaration highlights the institutional mechanisms at the

[83] Now Art 23j Austrian constitution. [84] Art 23j(1) Austrian constitution.

[85] Art 23j(4) Austrian constitution. See also G Lienbacher, 'Ausgewählte Rechtsfragen der Anwendung des Vertrages von Lissabon in Österreich' in W Hummer and W Obwexer (eds), *Der Vertrag von Lissabon* (Nomos, 2009) 437.

[86] See T Öhlinger, *Verfassungsrecht*, 9th edn (Facultas, 2012) 74, who describes this as a shift from an 'integral' towards a 'differential' notion of neutrality; similarly M Stelzer, *The Constitution of the Republic of Austria: A Contextual Analysis* (Hart Publishing, 2011) 16.

[87] Alecu de Flers (n 75) 97–9.

[88] Art 1(3) Maltese constitution, which declares Malta to be a 'neutral state' and contains a number of applications of this status. For instance, no foreign military bases are allowed on its territory: Art 1(3)(a). However, collective security measures under the UN Charter allow for exceptions for foreign forces to use military facilities in Malta, provided the government consents: Art 1(3)(b)(i).

[89] Treaty of Accession of the Czech Republic, Estonia, Cyprus, Latvia, Lithuania, Hungary, Malta, Poland, Slovenia and Slovakia [2003] OJ L 236/1, Final Act, Declaration by the Republic of Malta on Neutrality, 982. Further J Redmond and R Pace, 'European Security in the 1990s and Beyond: The Implications of the Accession of Cyprus and Malta to the European Union' (1996) 17 *Contemporary Security Policy* 430.

EU level which ensure such consistency, viz the unanimity rule and consequently a veto option for Malta. In this way, the EU Treaties put the decision to move towards greater unity in defence matters in the hands of the Member States. If Malta agreed to this, its constitutional notion of neutrality would also be altered. As long as such a unanimous decision is required, diversity in the security and defence policies of the Member States is safeguarded.

As opposed to neutrality, some Member State constitutions contain specific provisions regarding the participation in systems of collective security and defence. The Romanian constitution provides explicitly for the accession of the country to NATO,[90] while the German Basic Law mandates the country to participate in a system of international collective security, which the *Bundesverfassungsgericht* also interpreted as covering collective defence within the framework of NATO.[91] These constitutionalized preferences are accommodated by the latter part of the second subparagraph of Art 42(2) TEU by expressing respect for Member States 'which see their common defence realised in the North Atlantic Treaty Organisation (NATO)'.[92] Otherwise put, the pursuit of the objectives of peace and security by the EU through the CSDP cannot lead to eroding these constitutionally enshrined preferences of certain Member States.

Generally, both the North Atlantic Treaty and the UN Charter can also find cover under Art 351 TFEU, which provides that agreements concluded by the Member States before the founding of or accession to the EU are not affected.[93] In this regard, Declaration No 13 on the CFSP may be highlighted, which emphasizes that the obligations of the Member States under the UN Charter are not to be affected. However, Member States are duty-bound to eliminate incompatibilities stemming from these prior agreements with their obligations flowing from EU membership.[94]

To a large extent, the potential conflict that could result from the pursuit of foreign policy objectives of either EU or Member State constitutional law is eliminated through mutual accommodation. This is not surprising, since the Member States, as masters over their respective constitutions as well as, collectively, over the EU Treaties, had ample opportunity to frame the law in such a way. Thus, the sensitivity that can be discerned with regard to security and defence policy reflects the fundamental nature of this objective for the *state*. In this respect, Post notes a difference in the conception of the 'political space' by Schmitt and Arendt. While for the latter, according to Post, it represents a 'metaphoric space' or 'constructed framework',[95] for Schmitt it has clear territorial and existential elements, involving 'the inescapable question of "what ultimately matters for man", "the life-and-death quarrel" that divided "humanity into friends and enemies"'.[96] When touching on

[90] Art 149 Romanian constitution. [91] Art 24(2) German constitution.

[92] Art 42(2), second subpara TEU.

[93] Art 351(1) TFEU. Note also Art 355 TFEU, which specifically accommodates the Benelux regional union.

[94] Art 351(2) TFEU. [95] Post (n 2) 237.

[96] Post (n 2) 237, quoting from Leo Strauss' notes on Schmitt contained in the edition C Schmitt, *The Concept of the Political*, trans G Schwab (University of Chicago Press, 2007) 101–3.

such existential questions in the domain of security and defence policy, the 'political space' tends to shrink from the 'constructed' European constitutional space to the level of the Schmittian political community of the state. Consequently, whatever aspirations the EU has in this domain, their pursuit needs to be consistent with the basic preferences of the Member States as expressed in their constitutions or which are otherwise of 'ultimate' significance to them.

Aside from the specific provisions that serve to reconcile possible tensions in the area of foreign, security, and defence policy, the Lisbon reform has also introduced a general provision accommodating the limits that Member State constitutional law imposes on compliance with obligations resulting from Union membership.[97] The new 'national identity' clause of Art 4(2) TEU reads:

> The Union shall respect the equality of Member States before the Treaties as well as their national identities, inherent in their fundamental structures, political and constitutional, inclusive of regional and local self-government. It shall respect their essential State functions, including ensuring the territorial integrity of the State, maintaining law and order and safeguarding national security. In particular, national security remains the sole responsibility of each Member State.

An overlap with the previous issue exists to the extent that the provision restates that territorial integrity and national security, which reflect the general constitutional objective of providing security, remain within the ambit of Member State competence. Thus, the EU cannot encroach upon the pursuit of these objectives. The jurisdiction of the CJEU extends over this provision. Invoking 'national identity' can aid in the justification of proportionate restrictions of an individual right (also under EU law) in the pursuit of policies that are aimed at preserving this identity.[98]

In view of this clause, the general observation that the pursuit of constitutional objectives is conditioned by respect for the fundamental constitutional principles of that same legal order receives a nuance in the pluralistic context of the European constitutional space. The pursuit of the constitutional objectives of the European Union, internal and external, has to be consistent with both its own constitutional structures *and* the constitutional identity of its Member States, the latter being a special mechanism to preserve the diverse nature of the 'political space' within the Union.

There is no simple way to determine the extent to which constitutional objectives of the Member States represent a part of their respective constitutional identity. According to von Bogdandy and Schill, a strong indicator for being part of the latter category is the additional entrenchment of certain norms within the constitution, such as the so-called 'eternity clause' (*Ewigkeitsklausel*) in the German Basic Law (Art 79(3)) or Art 168 of the Spanish constitution, which imposes a

[97] Prior to Lisbon, Art 6(3) TEU (Nice version) had included a provision stating merely that '[t]he Union shall respect the national identities of its Member States'.

[98] Case C-208/09 *Sayn-Wittgenstein*, EU:C:2010:806; further von Bogdandy and Schill (n 12) 1422–5.

particularly burdensome procedure in instances where certain parts of the constitution were to be affected by amendment. Among these norms, which include provisions on the form of government, state sovereignty, or the rule of law, von Bogdandy and Schill also rank 'State aims'.[99]

However, it would be inaccurate to consider all constitutional objectives as part of the 'constitutional identity' of a country without further enquiry as to deeper entrenchment. Such a qualification will require a case-by-case analysis. In Germany, for instance, the 'eternity clause' covers only Arts 1 and 10 of the Basic Law. By contrast, Art 23 on European integration and Art 24 on international cooperation are not protected by it. Art 1(2) of the Basic Law, however, which states the universal validity of human dignity and its indispensability for world peace, is covered. To the extent that this can be viewed as an (implicit) external objective, the latter provision could be deemed a part of the constitutional identity of Germany. Consequently, Germany would be 'eternally' mandated by its constitution to promote human dignity in its foreign relations, a feature that the EU would have to act in consistency with and respect.

In the case of Spain, Art 168 of the Spanish constitution covers Art 56(1) and its reference to 'the nations of [Spain's] historical community', in relation to which the King of Spain will represent the country.[100] Following this benchmark, this provision, too, is part of Spanish constitutional identity and commands respect from the European Union. By contrast, Arts 10(2) and 39(4) of the Spanish constitution, which link fundamental rights protection to internationally agreed standards (also as an implied reference to the respect for international law: see Chapter 2, sections 4.4 and 4.5), are not covered by Art 168.[101]

Austrian neutrality, to give another example, is deemed in the literature as not representing a 'leading constitutional principle' (*leitendes Verfassungsprinzip*), since it has not been introduced by referendum and can be dropped without the need for such.[102] This would militate against considering it as part of Austrian constitutional identity and therefore as a ground for derogation from obligations under EU law. The same would seem to apply to the many foreign policy objectives of Art 7 of the Portuguese constitution, given that they are not protected from constitutional amendment.[103] Hence, not every constitutional foreign policy objective in Member State constitutional law is automatically a part of that country's national identity, and consequently 'immune to integration'.

[99] von Bogdandy and Schill (n 12) 1432. Note also that Kotzur regards Union objectives as the very expression of the constitutional identity of the Union: M Kotzur, 'Die Ziele der Union: Verfassungsidentität und Gemeinschaftsidee' (2005) 58 *Die Öffentliche Verwaltung* 313, 315, and 322, but distinguishes them from the constitutional principles of the Union (314), which creates ambiguity.

[100] Art 56(1) Spanish constitution.

[101] However, Art 168(1) Spanish constitution does cover the 'Fundamental Rights and Public Freedoms' (Arts 15–29 Spanish constitution).

[102] Öhlinger (n 86) 74; also Lienbacher (n 85) 435–8.

[103] Note Art 288 Portuguese constitution, which lists substantive limits to constitutional revision, and does not cover the foreign policy objectives of Art 7.

Turning to the obligations incumbent upon the Member States, the duty to comply with the entire spectrum of obligations of EU membership rests on them, to the extent that this does not intrude on the exceptional limits that were addressed in the preceding paragraphs. This means, first of all, uniform compliance with, and application of, EU law (primary and secondary) across all Member States. Except for the limits of national identity, as well as any others that national constitutional courts might proffer, primacy is accepted in practice, ie under non-exceptional circumstances. Otherwise put, to use the famous term of the *Bundesverfassungsgericht*, 'as long as' (*solange*) there is an assumption that certain core constitutional principles such as fundamental rights are being duly respected at the European level, constitutional courts will refrain from reviewing the constitutionality of EU law on a case-by-case basis.[104] For instance, legislation adopted within the EU, also in the pursuit of foreign policy objectives, is to be applied throughout the Union. As the *Bananenmarktordnung* dispute in Germany showed, challenges to EU legislation that had a clear external rationale, based on alleged violations of the Basic Law, were dismissed.[105]

Consequently, Member States cannot use the duty to pursue their own constitutional objectives, internal or external, as an excuse to deviate from their obligations under EU law, primary or secondary. The scope of the latter is wide and includes international agreements concluded by the Union as an 'integral part' of Union law.[106] Whereas, in principle, the autonomy of the Member States as international actors is affirmed, which is the basis of the external relations polyphony of the European constitutional space, they cannot use a 'foreign policy' dimension to deviate from such obligations. The Court of Justice made this clear in the *Centro-Com* judgment. It acknowledged that 'Member States have indeed retained their competence in the field of foreign and security policy'.[107] Nonetheless, the CJEU observed that 'the powers retained by the Member States must be exercised in a manner *consistent* with Community law'.[108] Of course, this presupposes that Member States are still competent to act at all, which is not the case where the EU has exclusive competences (see section 4.1 below).

Respect for international law, which is a rather common constitutional foreign policy objective (Chapter 2, section 4.4), serves as an excuse for Member States only in rather narrow circumstances. According to the CJEU, the uniform application of EU law is not to be upset by international agreements concluded by the latter.[109] A limited exception to this is provided by Art 351 TFEU, which

[104] Decision of 22 October 1986 (*Solange II*), BVerfGE 73, 339, para 132.

[105] Decision of 7 June 2000 (*Bananenmarktordnung*), BVerfGE 102, 147.

[106] See Case 104/81 *Kupferberg*, EU:C:1982:362, para 13; also Case 181/73 *Haegeman*, EU:C:1974:41; and Art 216(2) TFEU, which states: 'Agreements concluded by the Union are binding upon the institutions of the Union and on its Member States.'

[107] Case C-124/95 *Centro-Com*, EU:C:1997:8, para 24; building on the earlier Case C-70/94 *Werner*, EU:C:1995:328, para 10 on the scope of the CCP.

[108] *Centro-Com* (n 107), para 25 (emphasis added). Further Cremona (n 61) 63; and Eeckhout (n 73) 537.

[109] See the *Open Skies* cases eg Case C-476/98 *Commission v Germany (Open Skies)*, EU:C:2002:631; or bilateral investment treaties (BITs) concluded by the Member States, eg Case C-205/06 *Commission v*

applies to agreements concluded by states before they became EU (or formerly Community) members. As the Court of Justice clarified, this provision intends to protect the rights of third countries under these agreements rather than those of the Member States that concluded them.[110] At the same time, this protection imposes a duty on the Member States to eliminate inconsistencies between the agreement and their EU obligations,[111] which may include terminating the agreement with the third country.[112]

From the perspective of pluralism, a mutual obligation to respect the 'identity' of each legal order is clearly discernible, also with regard to the externally oriented aspects of such identity. Accordingly, the pursuit of constitutional foreign policy objectives of one legal order may not invade the constitutional core of another legal order within the constitutional space. However, the obligations of the Member States towards the EU do not stop there, resulting in a stark asymmetry of obligations on the vertical axis. This favours the pursuit of Union objectives and severely limits the pursuit of Member State objectives, including in the area of foreign policy. On the one hand, this means legislative and other measures can, and have to be, adopted by the Union in pursuit of its own foreign policy objectives as long as this is consistent with the narrowly defined constitutional identity of the Member States. On the other hand, Member States can only adopt measures, even if they further their national constitutional foreign policy objectives, to the extent that these are consistent with the entire body of EU law.

Hence, the considerable constraints on the external action of the Member States, as observed by De Witte,[113] apply to the pursuit of their constitutional objectives. For all practical purposes, it is true that at this level coherence is sustained 'by giving priority in the case of conflict to the Treaties themselves and to Union-created norms over national law'.[114] Nevertheless, in theory, where a constitutional foreign policy objective also forms part of the constitutional identity of a Member State, this could arguably serve as a limit to the primacy of EU law. However, given the degree of substantive convergence, the narrow scope of constitutional identity, a large degree of mutual accommodation, and the institutional set-up of EU external relations, such a conflict is rather unlikely to occur.

3.2 Consistency in the horizontal relationship

On the horizontal level, ie within the EU legal order and among its institutions, Cremona points to the Treaty objectives and various cross-references between

Austria (BITs), EU:C:2009:118. Note that in the former case, a violation of the duty of cooperation was detected as well, while this was not the case in the latter judgment.

[110] Case 10/61 *Commission v Italy*, EU:C:1962:2, 10-11; Case 812/79 *Burgoa*, EU:C:1980:231. Further Eeckhout (n 73) 421–34; and M Cremona, 'Defending the Community Interest: The Duties of Cooperation and Compliance' in M Cremona and B De Witte (eds), *EU Foreign Relations Law: Constitutional Fundamentals* (Hart Publishing, 2008) 131–5.

[111] Art 351(2) TFEU.

[112] Case C-62/98 *Commission v Portugal*, EU:C:2000:358.

[113] De Witte (n 31) 41–5.

[114] Cremona (n 61) 66.

foreign policy objectives and other treaty norms as a focal point for consistency. In the area of external relations, these indicate a certain hierarchy in favour of the general objectives of Arts 3(5) and 21 TEU over the sector-specific objectives and policies, as the latter stress that these are to be conducted in the framework or context of 'the principles and objectives of the Union's external action'.[115] Furthermore, there is a hierarchy between different kinds of Union law and other (non-legislative) measures. Here, it is worthwhile recalling Christian Calliess' model for the application of Union objectives, which cascade from the constitutionally entrenched Treaty objective to the policy field, to the competence, and finally on to secondary law and other acts (see Chapter 3, section 3.2).[116]

While Calliess used the field of environmental protection as an example, such a cascade can also be followed for virtually every measure of EU external action, including the CFSP. The Treaties situate the external relations objectives as the focal point. It is on their basis (Art 21 TEU) that 'the European Council shall identify the strategic interests and objectives of the Union'.[117] Subsequently, the 'Council shall frame the common foreign and security policy and take the decisions necessary for defining and implementing it'.[118] In the case of the CFSP, however, there are no legislative acts and the jurisdiction of the Court is generally excluded.[119]

A specific example among the general objectives of EU external action is international security. More precisely, the Union is to 'preserve peace, prevent conflicts and strengthen international security' according to Art 21(2)(c) TEU.[120] With reference to the policy field, the CFSP is to be conducted '[w]ithin the framework of the principles and objectives of [EU] external action'[121] and covers, as a field of competence, 'all areas of foreign policy and all questions relating to the Union's security'.[122] Heeding the guidance provided by the European Council, the CSDP, being 'an integral part' of the CFSP, can be used to execute the 'Petersberg tasks', one of which is 'military advice and assistance'.[123] Based on these treaty provisions, a Council Decision can be adopted creating a military operation 'relating to' such tasks.[124] This was done, for instance, in January 2013 by virtue of Council Decision 2013/34/CFSP on an EU military mission to help train the Malian Armed Forces (EUTM Mali).[125] The Decision indicates Arts 42(4) and

[115] Art 207(1) TFEU on the CCP; also Art 208(1), first subpara TFEU on development cooperation; Art 212(1) TFEU on economic, technical, and financial cooperation; Art 214(1) TFEU on humanitarian aid; and Arts 23 and 24(2) TEU on the CFSP.

[116] C Calliess, 'Kollektive Ziele und Prinzipien im Verfassungsrecht der EU—Bestandsaufnahme, Wirkungen und Perspektiven' (2003) 92 *Archiv für Rechts- und Sozialphilosophie-Beiheft* 85, 90. It should be stressed that such inferior law not only includes EU legislation but also international law binding on the Union.

[117] Art 22(1), first subpara TEU; and Art 26(1), first subpara TEU for the CFSP in particular.

[118] Art 26(2), first subpara TEU.

[119] Art 24(1), second subpara TEU. See sections 4 and 5 below on these issues.

[120] Note that peace and security also appear as external objectives in Art 3(5) TEU.

[121] Art 24(2) TEU; also Art 23 TEU.

[122] Art 24(1), first subpara TEU.

[123] Art 43(1) TEU; see also Art 42(1) TEU.

[124] Art 43(2) TEU; see also Art 42(4) TEU and Art 28(1) TEU.

[125] Council Decision 2013/34/CFSP of 17 January 2013 on a European Union military mission to contribute to the training of the Malian Armed Forces (EUTM Mali) [2013] OJ L 14/19.

43(2) TEU as the legal basis. As this example shows, the Treaties and their procedural architecture link all of these different stages of the implementation process, ensuring that the end product, in this case a CSDP operation, is consistent with the relevant constitutional objectives of the Union.

4. Delimitation of Tasks

In a pluralist setting, it is accepted that several legal orders coexist with their own set of institutions, which retain powers of their own, ie they do not become mere agents or organs of the overarching order. At this second level of EU foreign policy coherence, unity is thus sought by means of 'an effective allocation of tasks between actors and instruments'.[126] This obviously affects the pursuit of constitutional foreign policy objectives as they are the codified 'tasks' of the Union and its Member States, and their respective organs, on the international stage. In the execution of these tasks by the various actors, unity of the European Union as a polity is to be maintained. Constitutional objectives become a prime instrument in the framing, and legal contestation of the delimitation of tasks in the external relations of the European constitutional space.

Some but not all powers in the field of external relations have been conferred upon the EU, a selection of which are exclusive to it, while others are shared with the Member States. There are a number of competences the Union does not have. The dividing lines between these competences are not static, but instead rather fluid. This complicates another basic finding regarding the operation of constitutional foreign policy objectives. In a national setting, constitutional objectives are to be pursued by all constitutional organs within the sphere of competence as allocated by their respective legal order. Generally, the legislative body is the main addressee to ensure that these objectives are being advanced. In the domain of foreign affairs, the executive assumes the role of co-protagonist in the pursuit of foreign policy objectives. Both internally and externally, the role of the judiciary is limited in this regard due to the restricted legal force of objectives.

In the case of the European constitutional space, the mechanisms to determine the existence and nature of Union competence have to be accounted for in order to ascertain which entity is called upon to pursue which set of objectives, both in the relationship between the Union and the Member States and among Union institutions. The Member States play a 'dual role' here, ie 'on the one hand they form part, through the Council and its Working Groups, of the EU's decision-making machinery'.[127] In other words, they partake in the 'internal agora' of the Union. On the other hand, they retain 'their own autonomous foreign policy agendas'.[128] In the pluralist context, Member States can pursue their constitutional foreign policy objectives both through the Union or internationally in their own right. However, in the interest of unity, in the latter case, the international

[126] Cremona (n 61) 66. [127] Cremona (n 61) 73. [128] Cremona (n 61) 73.

pursuit of Member State objectives is conditioned in various ways depending on the extent and nature of external Union competence. In the former case, the role of the Member States *within* the Union also depends strongly on the type of Union policy at hand and the procedures to be followed in its implementation. In both cases constitutional foreign policy objectives play a role in shaping this vertical and horizontal allocation of tasks. It is especially in Union external relations that the interpretive–permissive function of constitutional objectives becomes evident.

4.1 Task allocation in the vertical relationship

The Union remains an entity of conferred powers. It has only the powers 'conferred upon it by the Member States in the Treaties to attain the objectives set out therein' (Art 5(2) TEU). As the Treaties make clear, '[c]ompetences not conferred upon the Union in the Treaties remain with the Member States'.[129] EU external relations are no exception to this fundamental rule. The question of competence in external relations has been one of the most prominent issues in litigation before the CJEU and has been widely discussed by scholars.[130] The foreign policy objectives of the EU are an important factor in shaping the Union's external competence. At the same time, the nature and extent of Union competence determine the modalities through which the Member States can pursue their own respective objectives.

The Lisbon Treaty introduced a catalogue of Union competences in the TFEU comprising different types (exclusive, shared, parallel, and supporting) in an attempt to codify and clarify the case law of the CJEU (Arts 2 to 6 TFEU).[131] Areas of shared competences continue to represent after the Lisbon reform 'a significant part'[132] of Union external competence.[133] Consequently, coexistence of Member States and the Union on the international scene is certainly not the exception, confirming that international actorness is a core constitutional feature of the Member States. Against this backdrop, it first must be determined whether the Union has external competence at all, and subsequently what kind of competence is at hand. Secondly, it is important to further clarify the way in which these powers are to be exercised with regard to the Member States as concurrent international actors in consideration of their ability to pursue their own foreign policy objectives. Through the implied powers doctrine and the flexibility clause of Art

[129] Art 5(2) TEU; also Art 4(1) TEU.

[130] See, eg Cremona (n 38); A Dashwood et al, *Wyatt & Dashwood's European Union Law*, 6th edn (Hart Publishing, 2011) 909–36; Rosas and Armati (n 39) 244–50; and D O'Keeffe, 'Exclusive, Concurrent and Shared Competence' in A Dashwood and C Hillion (eds), *The General Law of E.C. External Relations* (Sweet & Maxwell, 2000).

[131] See also Art 216(1) TFEU as an attempted codification of the 'implied powers' doctrine with regard to the conclusion of international agreements; also Art 3(2) TFEU. But see the critique by R Schütze, 'Lisbon and the Federal Order of Competences: A Prospective Analysis' (2008) 33 *European Law Review* 709.

[132] P Craig and G de Búrca, *EU Law: Text, Cases, and Materials*, 6th edn (OUP, 2015) 333.

[133] See on the different kinds of shared competence, Craig and de Búrca (n 132) 333–4; O'Keeffe (n 130) 192–9.

352 TFEU, Union objectives, both internal and external, play an important role in the moulding of external Union competence.

Generally, EU external competence can be founded on express Treaty provisions or on so-called 'implied powers'. Considering express powers, historically, the Treaties conferred external powers to the (then) EEC only 'in limited areas',[134] most notably the Common Commercial Policy (CCP), the conclusion of association agreements, and the maintenance of relations with certain international organizations. The CCP provided the first set of explicit external relations objectives in the Treaties. This is not simply a historic constitutional anomaly, recalling that national constitutions normally do not address trade policy among their foreign policy objectives (Chapter 2, section 5). The combination of a broadly defined CCP linked to the notion of exclusivity had important consequences for the role of Member States on the international stage.[135] The CCP, as defined in the Treaties at the time, was interpreted by the Court as the exclusive domain of the Community. The CJEU viewed it 'in the context of the operation of the Common Market, for the defence of the common interests of the Community, within which the particular interests of the Member States must endeavour to adapt to each other'.[136] Consequently, it ruled that:

> this conception is incompatible with the freedom to which the Member States could lay claim by invoking a concurrent power, so as to ensure that their own interests were separately satisfied in external relations, at the risk of compromising the effective defence of the common interests of the Community.[137]

Given the emphasis on the 'effective defence of the common interests', this is a starkly teleological reasoning. Union objectives, in turn, are nothing other than the codified expression of the 'common interest', or the 'common good', of the Union. In this sense, the idea that the Union needed to execute effectively its basic tasks, ie both the common market and its external dimension, helped give birth to the notion of exclusive external relations competence. Today, the entirety of the CCP is explicitly acknowledged as exclusive in the Treaties as amended by Lisbon, next to a number of other policy areas.[138] Exclusivity, following its definition in the TFEU, means that 'only the Union may legislate and adopt legally binding acts, the Member States being able to do so themselves only if so empowered by the Union or for the implementation of Union acts'.[139]

[134] O'Keeffe (n 130) 180; also Cannizzaro (n 27) 203–7.

[135] See in detail, P Koutrakos, *EU International Relations Law*, 2nd edn (Oxford: Hart Publishing, 2015) 17–74.

[136] Opinion 1/75 *(Local Cost Standard)*, EU:C:1975:145, 1363–4.

[137] Opinion 1/75 *(Local Cost Standard)* (n 136) 1364.

[138] Art 3(1)(e) TFEU. The other areas are the customs union, competition rules necessary for the functioning of the internal market, monetary policy for the Member States whose currency is the euro, and conservation of marine biological resources under the common fisheries policy (Art 3(1) TFEU). On the exclusive nature and widened scope of the CCP post-Lisbon, see Case C-414/11 *Daiichi Sankyo*, EU:C:2013:520; and Case C-137/12 *Commission v Council (European Convention on the legal protection of services based on, or consisting of, conditional access)*, EU:C:2013:675.

[139] Art 2(1) TFEU.

In terms of the pursuit of foreign policy objectives, Member States can no longer pursue their own aims autonomously from the moment they come under the scope of the CCP or other areas of exclusive Union competence. Instead, they are dependent in their international action on Union 'empowerment'. In other words, there cannot be polyphony in these cases, but either a solo performance by the Union or at best external relations conducted in unison as guided by the foreign policy objectives of the EU Treaties. Only in their actions within the Union framework would the Member States still be free to pursue their own objectives (for instance, in the Council or the Trade Policy Committee). If a Member State would, for instance, like to pursue its basic objective of preserving its culture, especially from foreign interference, it could do so by virtue of its voting rights in the Council, but not through international action in the area of trade. A degree of mutual accommodation can be detected here, above all in the switch from qualified majority voting to unanimity in the case of international agreement in sensitive commercial areas including trade in 'cultural and audiovisual services'.[140] External monophony is thus compensated by internal unanimity requirements where sensitive issues are at stake, giving the Member States a strong voice within the Union.

In other cases, however, it was already accepted at an early stage, also by the CJEU, that it was necessary for the Union and the Member States to act in concert. This means that wherever there is no exclusive competence, external relations polyphony persists and other mechanisms to foster unity must be relied upon. A prominent expression of this is the phenomenon of mixed agreements, ie agreements of which both the Union and the Member States become parties. Other express Union competences, such as development cooperation or environmental protection, were only added later and were 'explicitly labelled as concurrent'.[141] The Treaties state that in the areas of development cooperation and humanitarian aid, the existence of Union competence 'shall not result in Member States being prevented from exercising theirs'.[142] Furthermore, Union competence in the areas of development cooperation and economic, financial, and technical cooperation and humanitarian aid 'shall be without prejudice to Member States' competence to negotiate in international bodies and to conclude agreements'.[143] With regard to the former two policy areas, the TFEU also speaks of the 'respective sphere of competence' of the Union and the Member States in these areas.[144]

Following the TFEU's definition of shared competence, both 'the Union and the Member States may legislate and adopt legally binding acts in that area'.[145] Furthermore, '[t]he Member States shall exercise their competence to the extent that the Union has not exercised its competence' and may even re-exercise it in

[140] Art 207(4) TFEU. [141] Cannizzaro (n 27) 206. [142] Art 4(4) TFEU.

[143] Respectively, Art 209(2), second subpara TFEU; Art 212(3), second subpara TFEU; and Art 214(4), second subpara TFEU.

[144] Respectively, Art 211 TFEU and Art 212(3), first subpara TFEU. This reference is—somewhat curiously—missing from the provisions on humanitarian aid.

[145] Art 2(2) TFEU.

the event that the Union ceases to exercise its competence.[146] In these spheres, consequently, there remains a scope for the international pursuit of the foreign policy objectives of the Member States. However, as the section below on the third level of coherence shows, their pursuit must still be coordinated with the Union institutions.

In addition to such expressly provided external competences of the Union, the latter can also derive external powers by virtue of internal rules and the necessity to achieve Union objectives effectively. This concerns the 'implied powers' doctrine originating from the *ERTA* judgment.[147] According to Craig and de Búrca, the 'logic underpinning' this doctrine was to bolster 'a sufficiently strong international presence'[148] of the Union beyond its explicitly codified external powers. This, too, has important consequences for the delimitation of spheres within which Union and Member States can pursue their respective constitutional foreign policy objectives.

As Cremona summarizes, in the pertinent case law, in particular the clarifying *Opinion 1/03*,[149] there are 'two traditional bases for implied powers: the existence of legislation … and second, the existence of a Union objective for the attainment of which Treaty-based internal powers may be complemented by external powers'.[150] The first avenue pre-empts Member State action on the international plane since the Union, proverbially, has occupied the field.[151] As the Court ruled as early as the *ERTA* decision:

> each time the Community, with a view to implementing a common policy envisaged by the Treaty, adopted provisions laying down common rules, whatever form these may take, the Member States no longer have the right, acting individually or even collectively, to undertake obligations with third countries which affect those rules.[152]

As the Court indicated in other cases, it is not just the current EU legislation that can lead to pre-emption. The risk of interference with future rules at Union level can also have that effect,[153] clearly going beyond consistency with existing legislation as described in the previous section.

Consequently, Member States are pre-empted from using their international actions, even if they are clearly in pursuit of their own constitutional foreign policy objectives, if these risk 'affecting' such common rules. External relations polyphony is forbidden here, as it would disturb the internal unity of EU law. However, this is compensated by the very fact that the Member States play an

[146] Art 2(2) TFEU. [147] Case 22/70 *Commission v Council (ERTA)*, EU:C:1971:32.

[148] Craig and de Búrca (n 132) 324.

[149] Opinion 1/03 *(Lugano Convention)*, EU:C:2006:81, para 114.

[150] Cremona (n 38) 221. [151] Cannizzaro (n 27) 210.

[152] *Commission v Council (ERTA)* (n 147) para 17. Note that the Court highlighted in this context also that a common transport policy was 'specifically mentioned among the *objectives* of the Community' (para 20) as well as the duty of cooperation incumbent upon the Member States, obliging them 'to abstain from any measure which might jeopardize the attainment of the *objectives* of the Treaty' (para 21) (emphasis added).

[153] See eg *Commission v Germany (Open Skies)* (n 109) para 127.

important part in the internal legislative process of the Union, which brings forth these common rules in the first place. In Post's words, the CJEU relied in *ERTA* 'upon power created within the internal agora to authorise the Community to engage in external politics to defend the exercise of that power'.[154] At the same time, in the internal process of legislation the Member States remain free (from the EU point of view) to honour their obligations (from the point of view of their national constitutions) to pursue their own constitutional objectives, including in the area of foreign policy.

In the second case, when establishing non-pre-emptive implied powers, there is a specific 'emphasis on Treaty objectives'.[155] Here, it is EU constitutional objectives themselves, and more precisely the external dimension of internal or general Union objectives, which help to shape the contours of Union competence, revealing their interpretive–permissive function. According to the CJEU in *Opinion 1/76*:

> whenever Community law has created for the institutions of the Community powers within its internal system for the purpose of attaining a specific objective, the Community has authority to enter into the international commitments necessary for the attainment of that objective even in the absence of an express provision in that connexion.[156]

Even though the presence of the objective does not establish competence as such—*in casu*, competence to establish internal 'common rules' in the area of transport already existed—the Court reasoned that it would be 'impossible fully to attain the objective pursued by means of the establishment of common rules'[157] alone. This competence, consequently, must also exist externally lest the objective be deprived of its effectiveness—its *effet utile*.[158] This concerns Treaty objectives in general, which underlines that not just the expressly external objectives of the Union are relevant, but all of its objectives as soon as they reveal an external dimension. Taken together, they play an important role in shaping the scope of external competence of the Union. This competence shaping function is now also reflected in the primary law. According to Art 216(1) TFEU one of the avenues for establishing treaty-making competence for the Union is the necessity 'in order to achieve, within the framework of the Union's policies, one of the objectives referred to in the Treaties'.

These competences are of a concurrent nature, ie they do not pre-empt Member State action.[159] Whereas constitutional objectives serve here to enlarge the ambit of external competences of the Union, the non-pre-emptive nature of

[154] Post (n 2) 243. [155] Cremona (n 38) 222.

[156] Opinion 1/76 *(European Laying-up Fund for Inland Waterway Vessels)*, EU:C:1977:63, para 3; see also Joined Cases 3, 4, and 6/76 *Kramer*, EU:C:1976:114.

[157] Opinion 1/76 *(European Laying-up Fund for Inland Waterway Vessels)* (n 156) para 2; also later Opinion 2/92 *(Third Revised Decision of the OECD on national treatment)*, EU:C:1995:83, para V-4.

[158] Cremona (n 38) 221. Van Vooren also points to the potential of *effet utile* as a possible additional contrapunctual principle for connecting 'different spheres of authority' in the domain of external relations: Van Vooren (n 52) 66. See also the link the Court established between pre-emption and *effet utile* of Union law: Opinion 1/03 *(Lugano Convention)* (n 149) para 128.

[159] Cannizzaro (n 27) 218.

competence-by-necessity allows both the Union and its Member States to pursue their constitutional foreign policy objectives internationally. It is a mechanism to add the voice of the Union to the polyphony of the Member States so that it, too, can act internationally where such action is necessary for the effective pursuit of its constitutional objectives.

With regard to the CFSP, it represents a case apart in the catalogue of Union competences. In the Treaties, it is separated from the other types of competence.[160] While the nature of CFSP competence is not further specified, its scope is extremely wide, encompassing 'all areas of foreign policy and all questions relating to the Union's security, including the progressive framing of a common defence policy that might lead to a common defence'.[161] From practice and academic opinion, it can be concluded that CFSP competence is of a strictly non-exclusive,[162] non-pre-emptive nature.[163] Here, Member States retain their ability to pursue their own foreign policy objectives to a very large extent. They are under no legal obligation to act through the Union. This is not surprising given the fundamental nature of security as a state objective, which more easily trumps the quest for unity in an integrated Europe than other less existential functions of the state. However, there are legal mechanisms to ensure that no measures are adopted under the CFSP when their proper legal basis resides in another policy area and vice versa.

In sum, in the vertical delimitation of tasks between the Union and the Member States, there are various mechanisms to extend the external powers of the former. Wherever such powers can be established, either by express codification or by implication, they have to be pursued in a way that furthers the constitutional objectives of the Union. In addition, Union objectives and their external dimension can even be drawn upon to justify the emergence of 'implied' external powers in the first place. As regards the Member States, whenever exclusive competences or cases of pre-emption arise, they are barred from pursuing their respective constitutional foreign policy objectives internationally. Here, there is no polyphony but unison. Whereas primacy of any Union rules usually renders Member State law, including national constitutional objectives, inapplicable, the existence or even prospect of common rules also pre-empts them from pursuing their constitutional

[160] Art 2(4) TFEU simply states: 'The Union shall have competence, in accordance with the provisions of the Treaty on European Union, to define and implement a common foreign and security policy, including the progressive framing of a common defence policy.'

[161] Art 24(1), first subpara TEU. [162] Eeckhout (n 73) 171.

[163] Note also Declarations No 13 and No 14 attached to the Lisbon Treaty concerning common foreign and security policy, which emphasize the retained powers of the Member States in this area. M Cremona, 'Defining Competence in EU External Relations: Lessons from the Treaty Reform Process' in A Dashwood and M Maresceau (eds), *Law and Practice of EU External Relations: Salient Features of a Changing Landscape* (CUP, 2008) 65 describes CFSP competence as 'a type of sui generis competence that shares characteristics of both shared and complementary competences'. See further R Streinz, C Ohler, and C Herrmann, *Der Vertrag von Lissabon zur Reform der EU: Einführung mit Synopse*, 3rd edn (C.H. Beck, 2010) 137–8; A Sari, 'Between Legalization and Organizational Development: Explaining the Evolution of EU Competence in the Field of Foreign Policy' in PJ Cardwell (ed), *EU External Relations Law and Policy in the Post-Lisbon Era* (T.M.C. Asser Press, 2012); and De Baere (n 66) 108–12.

objectives externally. This is reflective again of the asymmetry in the European constitutional space and of a push for unity, both internal and external. Instead, the Member States can pursue their own constitutional objectives within the Union 'agora'. As Van Vooren puts it, 'the "vertical" interests of the Member States will be felt horizontally through the Council',[164] which includes the constitutionally entrenched ones.

4.2 Task allocation in the horizontal relationship

In contrast to states, the external relations of the Union are characterized not only by the coexistence of the Union and its Member States on the international scene, but also by a number of peculiar features in the horizontal relationship. Here, external relations coherence is complicated by the different procedures to be followed in making and implementing different Union policies, especially between the two basic modes of conducting EU external relations, as well as the complex institutional set-up of EU external action, including as regards external representation. Even within the Union, there exists a plurality of voices and a need to foster a coherent message, not least through mechanisms for the proper allocation of tasks. As will be shown, foreign policy objectives perform important functions in these mechanisms. This allocation, in turn, determines which institution is called upon to pursue the foreign policy objectives of the Union.

As a preliminary point, it should be noted that the situation following the Lisbon reform represents a step forward in terms of simplification. After Maastricht and pre-Lisbon, the EU was divided into three pillars, one of which was the already existing Community and another, the CFSP. This created a situation rife with legal uncertainties. It raised questions about the legal personality of the Union as such, the legal nature of the second pillar, and the relationship between the pillars.[165] External relations had already been conducted within the framework of the supranational Community, and then faced an intergovernmental 'second' pillar that had emerged from the previously entirely diplomatic European Political Cooperation (EPC). As De Witte observed, 'the pillar structure was simply a *mal nécessaire*, a condition for allowing a deal to be struck in Maastricht and for allowing European integration to move forward'.[166] In other words, more diversity and complexity, and less unity, were accepted with a view to advancing integration in foreign affairs.

164 Van Vooren (n 52) 71.

165 See eg J Klabbers, 'Presumptive Personality: The European Union in International Law' in M Koskenniemi (ed), *International Law Aspects of the European Union* (Kluwer Law International, 1998); and C Herrmann, 'Much Ado about Pluto? The "Unity of the Legal Order of the European Union" Revisited' in M Cremona and B De Witte (eds), *EU Foreign Relations Law: Constitutional Fundamentals* (Hart Publishing, 2008).

166 B De Witte, 'The Pillar Structure and the Nature of the European Union: Greek Temple or French Gothic Cathedral' in T Heukels, N Blokker, and M Brus (eds), *The European Union after Amsterdam: A Legal Analysis* (Kluwer Law International, 1998) 51.

By virtue of the Lisbon Treaty, there is now but one European Union (Art 1(3) TEU) with one single international legal personality (Art 47 TEU).[167] The pillar structure has formally disappeared. However, traces of what Piet Eeckhout termed the 'original sin of EU external action'[168] remain in the form of the 'special rules and procedures'[169] that apply to the CFSP, which have institutional implications.[170] These, in turn, affect the circle of addressees called upon to pursue the Union's various external relations objectives. Institutionally, one is confronted with a variety of different actors that do not correspond to the classic branches of government and which have varying stakes in the external action of the Union.[171] In principle, all EU organs are addressees of the foreign policy objectives found in the Treaties. However, the extent to which they can pursue them and in what capacity is contingent upon the kind of policy at hand.

Hence, whereas the Treaty language pertaining to 'institutional balance' and task allocation is combined with references to Union objectives,[172] it is important to discern which institution is obliged to pursue these objectives, firstly through policy-making, and secondly, through policy implementation and external representation.

With regard to policy-making, the first institution called upon in the Treaties to act on the codified foreign policy objectives of the Union is the European Council. According to Art 22 TEU, it shall '[o]n the basis of the principles and objectives set out in Article 21 ... identify the strategic interests and objectives of the Union'.[173] These cut across the CFSP/non-CFSP divide, as the decisions of the European Council 'relate to the common foreign and security policy and to other areas of the external action of the Union'.[174] However, the European Council acts, by unanimity, only upon recommendation by the Council, which the latter adopts 'under the arrangements laid down for each area'.[175] Furthermore, the decisions adopted by the European Council 'shall be implemented in accordance with the procedures provided for in the Treaties'.[176] A procedural differentiation along different policy areas emerges.[177] Subsequently, the 'Foreign Affairs Council shall elaborate the Union's external action on the basis of strategic guidelines laid down by the

[167] Note also Declaration No 24 attached to the Lisbon Treaty concerning the legal personality of the European Union; further Streinz, Ohler, and Herrmann (n 163) 49–51 and 132; and Piris (n 19) 86–8 and 259–60 regarding the conclusion of international agreements.

[168] Eeckhout (n 73) 172.

[169] Art 24(1), second subpara TEU.

[170] P Van Elsuwege, 'EU External Action after the Collapse of the Pillar Structure: In Search of a New Balance between Delimitation and Consistency' (2010) 47 *Common Market Law Review* 987; also Dashwood et al (n 130) 905–7.

[171] Of course, the Union in general does not 'conform to any rigid separation-of-powers principle of the sort that has shaped some national systems': Craig and de Búrca (n 132) 30.

[172] See Arts 13(1) and (2) TEU.

[173] Art 22(1), first subpara TEU. Note though the absence of a reference to Art 3(5) TEU.

[174] Art 22(1), second subpara TEU.

[175] Art 22(1), third subpara TEU.

[176] Art 22(1), third subpara TEU.

[177] Note also in this vein that the 'High Representative of the Union for Foreign Affairs and Security Policy, for the area of common foreign and security policy, and the Commission, for other areas of external action, may submit joint proposals to the Council': Art 22(2) TEU.

European Council'.[178] With regard to the CFSP, the policy-guiding role of the European Council, as well as the elaborating function of the Council, are reiterated in the chapter in the TEU on the CFSP.[179] The European Council is thus the primary addressee in terms of formalizing constitutional foreign policy objectives into actual foreign policy guidance.

In terms of policy implementation and external representation of the Union, the divide between actors and policies becomes even clearer. There is obviously 'no dearth of actors who may represent the EU externally'.[180] Outside of the CFSP, the Commission as the 'guardian of the Treaties' serves important functions in the conduct of EU external relations, in many ways similar to that of a national executive.[181] According to the Treaties, '[w]ith the exception of the common foreign and security policy, and other cases provided for in the Treaties, it shall ensure the Union's external representation'.[182] This includes the former Community policies that can now be found in the TFEU (the CCP, development policy, humanitarian aid, etc, as well as the external aspects of other former Community policies) and the earlier third pillar, now the Area of Freedom, Security and Justice (AFSJ). The Commission is usually the negotiator on behalf of the Union for international agreements falling into these domains.[183] Consequently, in terms of representing the Union and negotiating international agreements in these areas, the Commission can be seen as the main addressee of the Union's external relations objectives. However, internally, the Council, in which the Member State representatives are united, and the European Parliament (EP) exercise important functions as well. In many cases, the European Parliament needs to consent to the conclusion of such agreements or at least needs to be consulted.[184] The Council, for its part, authorizes the opening of negotiations and the signing of agreements and has the power to issue negotiating directives to the Union negotiator.[185] Moreover, the Council concludes the agreement on behalf of the Union.[186] In performing these functions, the Council and Parliament are committed to the furtherance of Union objectives.

The CFSP remains the important exception to this rule. The most peculiar aspect of this, when compared to states, is the substitution of the Commission

[178] Art 16(6), third subpara TEU.

[179] Respectively, Art 26(1) TEU and Art 26(2) TEU.

[180] Eeckhout (n 73) 486.

[181] On executive functions of the EU in external relations see N Nugent, *The Government and Politics of the European Union*, 7th edn (Palgrave Macmillan, 2010) 133–4.

[182] Art 17(1) TEU.

[183] Art 218(3) TFEU.

[184] Parliamentary consent is required for the conclusion of association agreements, the accession of the EU to the ECHR, agreements 'establishing a specific institutional framework by organising cooperation procedures', agreements with 'important budgetary implications for the Union', and, importantly, agreements in fields to which internally either the ordinary legislative procedure is applicable, or the special legislative procedure where consent of the EP is required: Art 218(6), second subpara (a) TFEU. This includes now notably also trade agreements (Art 207(2) TFEU). In other cases, the EP only needs to be consulted (Art 218(6), second subpara (b) TFEU). See also R Mögele, 'Art. 218 (ex-Art. 300 EGV) [Vertragsabschlussverfahren; Gutachten des EuGH]' in R Streinz (ed), *EUV/AEUV: Vertrag über die Europäische Union und Vertrag über die Arbeitsweise der Europäischen Union*, 2nd edn (C.H. Beck, 2012) 2079–80.

[185] Art 218(2)–(5) TFEU.

[186] Art 218(6), first subpara TFEU.

by the Council and Member States as the protagonists. According to the TEU, the CFSP 'shall be defined and implemented by the European Council and the Council acting unanimously, except where the Treaties provide otherwise' and 'shall be put into effect by the High Representative of the Union for Foreign Affairs and Security Policy and by Member States'.[187] It is the Council that 'shall frame the common foreign and security policy and take the decisions necessary for defining and implementing it'.[188] Finally, the CFSP 'shall be put into effect by the High Representative and by the Member States, using national and Union resources'.[189]

Hence, the Council, as the institution that usually operates as the co-*legislator* of the Union together with the European Parliament,[190] becomes its main *executive* organ in the area of the CFSP. The Commission and Parliament, for their part, are sidelined.[191] Next to the autonomy they retain to act internationally in this area, the Member States retain, through their representation in the European Council and the Council of the EU, a high degree of internal control given the prevalence of unanimity in voting procedures.[192] This provides them with a strong intra-EU mechanism to ensure the pursuit of their own respective foreign policy objectives. Here, international action of the Union in the framework of the CFSP, in the pursuit of the EU's objectives, can only occur when there is, as *a sine qua non*, unity among the Member States.

In terms of representation in CFSP matters, the High Representative and the President of the European Council come to the fore. The President of the European Council shall, 'at his level and in that capacity, ensure the external representation of the Union on issues concerning its common foreign and security policy, without prejudice to the powers of the High Representative'.[193] According to Art 27(2) TEU, '[t]he High Representative shall represent the Union for matters relating to the common foreign and security policy' and shall 'conduct political dialogue with third parties on the Union's behalf and shall express the Union's position in international organizations and at international conferences'. In doing so, both are to be guided by the Union's foreign policy objectives.

This 'bipolarity'[194] also persists with regard to the conclusion of international agreements despite the now single Treaty provision on Union treaty-making.[195] Art 218(3) TFEU sets apart agreements related 'exclusively or principally to the common foreign and security policy', in which case the High Representative is

[187] Art 24(1), second subpara TEU. [188] Art 26(2), first subpara TEU.

[189] Art 26(3) TEU.

[190] Arts 14(1) and 15(1) TEU. See further Nugent (n 181) 139–41 on the legislative powers of the Council.

[191] In this vein, D Curtin and I Dekker, 'The European Union from Maastricht to Lisbon: Institutional and Legal Unity out of the Shadows' in P Craig and G de Búrca (eds), *The Evolution of EU Law*, 2nd edn (OUP, 2011) 172; Piris (n 19) 260–3; and Rosas and Armati (n 39) 242–3. Generally on the role of the European Parliament in external relations, D Thym, 'Parliamentary Involvement in European International Relations' in M Cremona and B De Witte (eds), *EU Foreign Relations Law: Constitutional Fundamentals* (Hart Publishing, 2008).

[192] Art 24(1), second subpara TEU and Art 31 TEU. [193] Art 15(6) TEU.

[194] Dashwood (n 40).

[195] See also Van Elsuwege (n 170) 993; and Streinz, Ohler, and Herrmann (n 163) 133–6.

to replace the Commission as the Union negotiator. In addition, the role of the Parliament, already not an external relations protagonist, is rolled back further in the area of the CFSP as 'the result of the choice made by the framers of the Treaty of Lisbon'.[196] Generally, its powers are limited to being consulted and informed (Art 36 TEU). Its consent is not required for agreements related 'exclusively to the common foreign and security policy' (Art 218(6) TEU), though the Parliament is to be 'immediately and fully informed at all stages' of the negotiation and conclusion of international agreements, including in the area of the CFSP.[197] In a similar fashion, the role of the CJEU is limited due to the fact that its jurisdiction is largely excluded.[198] Hence, the Council and the High Representative become the main addressees of the constitutional foreign policy objectives of the Union when Union external action takes place within the framework of the CFSP.

The crucial element in the management of this divide, and consequently in the determination of the institutions called upon to pursue Union objectives, is the identification of the proper legal basis of a Union measure, which determines whether it falls within the ambit of the CFSP or of another Union policy such as development cooperation or environmental protection. In the words of the CJEU, the legal basis of Union acts 'is relevant in determining the type of act that may be adopted and the procedures to be followed, for example the role of the European Parliament and voting procedure in the Council'.[199] According to the Court, this has 'constitutional significance'.[200] Since this involves judicial interpretation, constitutional objectives, including in the area of foreign policy, have come to play an important role.

The CJEU, with a view to determining the legal basis of distinctly external measures, established in its case law that the choice of the legal basis, 'including one adopted with a view to conclusion of an international agreement, must be based on objective factors which are amenable to judicial review and include in particular the aim and content of the measure'.[201] These factors are then linked to the corresponding Treaty objectives and competences in order to establish where the proverbial 'centre of gravity' of the measure lies. A particular challenge is posed

[196] Case C-130/10 *Parliament v Council (Al-Qaeda Sanctions)*, EU:C:2012:472, para 82.

[197] Art 218(10) TFEU, which is a justiciable obligation, Case C-658/11 *Parliament v Council (EU-Mauritius Agreement)*, EU:C:2014:2025, paras 69–74.

[198] Art 24(1) second subpara TEU together with Art 275 TFEU. See C Kaddous, 'External Action under the Lisbon Treaty' in I Pernice and E Tanchev (eds), *Ceci n'est pas une Constitution—Constitutionalisation without a Constitution?* (Nomos, 2009) 181; Streinz, Ohler, and Herrmann (n 163) 145–6; and M Brkan, 'The Role of the European Court of Justice in the Field of Common Foreign Security Policy after the Treaty of Lisbon: New Challenges for the Future' in A Dashwood and M Maresceau (eds), *Law and Practice of EU External Relations: Salient Features of a Changing Landscape* (CUP, 2008).

[199] Cremona (n 38) 83. In detail on this question, P Koutrakos, 'Legal Basis and Delimitation of Competence in EU External Relations' in M Cremona and B De Witte (eds), *EU Foreign Relations Law: Constitutional Fundamentals* (Hart Publishing, 2008).

[200] Opinion 2/00 *(Cartagena Protocol)*, EU:C:2001:664, para 5.

[201] Case C-94/03 *Commission v Council (Rotterdam Convention)*, EU:C:2006:2, para 34.

by the requirement that the implementation of the CFSP and other Union policies are not to affect each other according to Art 40 TEU.

The *Small arms* case, a pre-Lisbon decision, serves as a clear illustration of the important interpretive function of foreign policy objectives in such disputes. Both sides to the dispute relied in their reasoning on the foreign policy objectives of the Union and the former Community. The Commission and the Parliament challenged a measure adopted by the Council with a CFSP legal basis concerning a Union contribution to a disarmament programme conducted by the Economic Community of West African States (ECOWAS).[202] They argued that this encroached upon the competences of the (then) Community, in particular its development cooperation policy, 'thus infringing Article 47 [TEU (Nice version)]',[203] which is the predecessor of what is now Art 40 TEU. The applicants considered the programme in question an 'indispensable means of achieving the objectives of development cooperation policy'.[204] The Council contested this assertion, arguing that '[n]either the combating of the proliferation of small arms and light weapons, nor the more general objectives of preserving peace and strengthening security, appear among the objectives of the Community'.[205] Instead, it pointed to the fact that, 'according to Article 177(1) [TEC], the main aim of Community development cooperation policy is the reduction of poverty'.[206]

The CJEU, too, relied on foreign policy objectives in its reasoning, making explicit reference to the Treaty provisions codifying them, referring in particular to the wider aims of development policy, including 'the development and consolidation of democracy and the rule of law, as well as to respect for human rights and fundamental freedoms',[207] as well as to objectives of the CFSP relating to peace, security, and international cooperation.[208] The Court concluded that in view of the aims as well as the content of the measure, it could fall within both the CFSP and development cooperation policy, but that in view of the non-encroachment provision of Art 47 TEU (Nice version), the proper legal basis should have been with the latter and not the former.[209]

As this case shows, foreign policy objectives play a crucial role in legal basis determinations. Both sides relied on them to make their case, and the CJEU drew on them in order to come to a conclusion. This recalls the significance of such objectives in interpretation. Furthermore, it highlights the importance of the

[202] Council Decision 2004/833/CFSP of 2 December 2004 implementing Joint Action 2002/589/CFSP with a view to a European Union contribution to ECOWAS in the framework of the Moratorium on Small Arms and Light Weapons [2004] OJ L 359/65.

[203] Case C-91/05 *Commission v Council (Small arms and light weapons)*, EU:C:2008:288, para 35.

[204] *Small arms and light weapons* (n 203) para 37.

[205] *Small arms and light weapons* (n 203) para 46, referring to Arts 2 and 3 TEC.

[206] *Small arms and light weapons* (n 203) para 46; see now Art 208(1), second subpara TFEU for the reference on poverty eradication.

[207] *Small arms and light weapons* (n 203) para 65, referring to Arts 177–181 TEC. Note that post-Lisbon, instead of directly referencing democracy, the rule of law, and human rights in the provisions on EU development cooperation, Art 208(1), first subpara TFEU now simply links back to 'the framework of the principles and objectives of the Union's external action'.

[208] *Small arms and light weapons* (n 203) para 105, referring to Art 11(1) TEU (Nice version).

[209] *Small arms and light weapons* (n 203) paras 108–9.

peculiar structure of the Union's foreign affairs constitution within which these objectives are to be pursued.

However, to what extent the findings in *Small arms* retain their validity after the entry into force of the Lisbon Treaty is unclear, especially as regards delimiting the CFSP from the other external policies of the Union. Whereas Art 47 TEU (Nice version) stipulated that nothing in the TEU 'shall affect the Treaties establishing the European Communities',[210] its successor, the post-Lisbon Art 40 TEU, is worded in a reciprocal fashion. While implementation of the CFSP 'shall not affect the application of the procedures and the extent of the powers of the institutions' in other policy areas of the Union, '[s]imilarly, the implementation of the policies listed in those Articles shall not affect the application of the procedures and the extent of the powers of the institutions' of the CFSP.[211] An a priori tilt towards non-CFSP policies thus seems no longer warranted.

Moreover, streamlining external relations objectives under Lisbon raises the question of whether they can still be regarded as useful in determining the appropriate legal basis. This may continue to be the case where the Treaties still provide policy-specific objectives such as in trade and development policy. The exception to this is the post-Lisbon CFSP, which has been deprived of its own set of objectives.

This may suggest, from a strictly textual point of view, that pursuing international security, for instance, may no longer tilt the 'centre of gravity' towards CFSP, as this is an objective situated among the general goals of EU external action, as laid down in Arts 3(5) and 21 TEU. However, post-Lisbon case law suggests that the CJEU continues 'to apply a form of aim and content test based on a pre-Lisbon understanding of the scope of the CFSP'.[212] For instance, the CJEU judgment *Parliament v Council (Al-Qaeda Sanctions)* of July 2012 concerned the proper legal basis post-Lisbon for restrictive measures in the fight against terrorism. The Parliament argued that this would now have to be found in the provisions concerning the AFSJ (more precisely Art 75 TFEU) and not the CFSP (and Art 215 TFEU).[213] The Advocate General and the Court disagreed. In his reasoning, Advocate General Bot in particular relied on a historical understanding of CFSP objectives, pointing out that 'the objectives defined in Art 21(2)(a) to (c) TEU are in essence the same as those assigned to the CFSP under Art 11(1) [T]EU [pre-Lisbon]'.[214] The Court, more cautiously, stated that preserving international security is a general objective of EU external action.[215] But given the fact that terrorism

[210] Art 47 TEU (Nice version).

[211] Art 40 TEU. Van Vooren regards Art 40 TEU as a matter of first-level coherence, ie as a way to avoid conflicts: Van Vooren (n 52) 70. Given the post-Lisbon formulation of the clause, which requires *mutual* non-affection, and given the present focus on the identification of the addressees of foreign policy objectives and the procedures to be followed to pursue them, here it is regarded as pertaining to second-level coherence, ie as a matter of the delimitation of tasks.

[212] Cremona (n 61) 87.

[213] *Parliament v Council Al-Qaeda Sanctions* (n 196) paras 12–16. Note also the reference to Art 3(2) TEU on AFSJ objectives in para 31.

[214] Case C-130/10 *Parliament v Council (Al-Qaeda Sanctions)*, Opinion of Advocate General Bot, EU:C:2012:50, para 63.

[215] *Parliament v Council Al-Qaeda Sanctions* (n 196) para 62.

represents a threat to international security and considering the wide scope of the CFSP (Art 24(1) TEU), including the explicit reference to using the CSDP in the fight against terrorism (Art 43(1) TEU), it found that the CFSP could represent a possible legal basis for the contested measures.[216] In view of the particular circumstances of the case, ie the 'international dimension of the threat' at hand, it deemed the CFSP the correct legal basis, as opposed to the AFSJ, and consequently dismissed the complaint of the Parliament.[217]

The lack of CFSP objectives sits uneasily with other important treaty provisions. With regard to the flexibility clause of Art 352 TFEU, this provision can provide an additional legal basis when 'the Treaties have not provided the necessary powers' but where 'action by the Union should prove necessary, within the framework of the policies defined in the Treaties, to attain one of the *objectives* set out in the Treaties'.[218] In the *Kadi* case, for instance, it served to help establish a legal basis for restrictive measures against individuals, which could not be found at the time in any explicit form in either the pre-Lisbon TEU or the TEC.[219]

However, Art 352 TFEU cannot be used to grant necessary additional powers to the Union 'for attaining objectives pertaining to the common foreign and security policy'.[220] This is reflective again of the reluctance of the Member States to accord too much power to the EU in this area.[221] From a legal–structural point of view, this is a rather curious formulation given that following the Lisbon reform the 'main substantive novelty'[222] regarding external relations objectives is the very fact that there are no more specific CFSP objectives.[223] Art 23 TEU merely states that EU action in the framework of the CFSP 'shall be guided by the principles, shall pursue the objectives of, and be conducted in accordance with, the general provisions laid down in Chapter 1', ie the objectives set out in Art 21 TEU. This requires reconsideration of what is meant by Art 352(4) TFEU when it refers to 'objectives pertaining to the common foreign and security policy'. According to Declaration No 41 on Article 352 of the TFEU:

[216] *Parliament v Council Al-Qaeda Sanctions* (n 196) paras 63–5.

[217] *Parliament v Council Al-Qaeda Sanctions* (n 196) para 78. Note also Case T-190/12 *Johannes Tomana*, EU:T:2015:222, para 106, where the General Court ruled that it is 'legitimate and compatible with the objectives of the CFSP' to adopt restrictive measures which aim at encouraging targeted individuals to 'reject policies that lead to the suppression of human rights, of the freedom of expression and of good governance'.

[218] Art 352(1) TFEU (emphasis added).

[219] Joined Cases C-402/05 P and C-415/05 P *Kadi and Al Barakaat*, EU:C:2008:461, paras 179–236. For criticism see D Halberstam and E Stein, 'The United Nations, the European Union, and the King of Sweden: Economic Sanctions and Individual Rights in a Plural World Order' (2009) 46 *Common Market Law Review* 13, 39–42.

[220] Art 352(4) TFEU.

[221] But note that no use can be made of this provision without unanimity in the Council, which acts upon a proposal from the Commission and after having obtained the consent of the Parliament: Art 352(1) TFEU.

[222] Cannizzaro (n 27) 229, referring to the Constitutional Treaty establishing 'a common set of aims'; also M Cremona, 'The Draft Constitutional Treaty: External Relations and External Action' (2003) 40 *Common Market Law Review* 1347, 1348.

[223] Streinz, Ohler, and Herrmann (n 163) 139–40; making this observation with regard to the Constitutional Treaty, Cremona (n 222) 1348–50.

the reference in Article 352(1) of the Treaty on the Functioning of the European Union to objectives of the Union refers to the objectives as set out in Article 3(2) and (3) of the Treaty on European Union and to the objectives of Article 3(5) of the said Treaty with respect to external action under Part Five of the Treaty on the Functioning of the European Union.

This formulation boils down to restating that the CFSP is excluded, but still sheds no light on what is meant exactly by a 'CFSP objective'. For Advocate General Bot, they are those which are 'in essence the same as those assigned to the CFSP' before the Lisbon reform.[224] In *Ahmed Abdelaziz Ezz*, the CJEU highlighted 'the broad scope of the aims and objectives of the CFSP, as expressed in Articles 3(5) TEU and 21 TEU'.[225] It did not clarify which parts of these provisions would be CFSP-specific, but noted that the General Court, in the judgment under appeal, considered that the contested decision is lawfully based on the CFSP, in particular Art 29 TEU, 'and satisfies the objectives referred to in Article 21(2)(b) and (d) TEU'.[226] These provisions refer to democracy, the rule of law, human rights, and sustainable economic, social, and environmental development of developing countries, respectively. Alan Dashwood, to whom the Advocate General refers in his Opinion in *Parliament v Council (Al-Qaeda Sanctions)*,[227] argues in the same vein. Despite the generality of objectives applicable to the CFSP, it would be reasonable to assume that the objectives found in Art 21 TEU which were taken over from pre-Lisbon Art 11(1) TEU (Nice version) on CFSP objectives remain specifically directed at the CFSP.[228] Cremona, by contrast, argues for a rather restrictive interpretation of the scope of the CFSP, pointing out, firstly, that policy-specific objectives found elsewhere represent *lex specialis*,[229] and that the preservation of the *acquis communautaire* remains imperative.[230] This would seem to entail a rather restrictive reading of what can still be considered CFSP-specific objectives, but may amount at the same time to a historical reading of Art 40 TEU.

At the same time, as *Parliament v Council (Al-Qaeda Sanctions)* shows, there is a diminished need to rely on the 'flexibility clause' post-Lisbon, also with regard to the CFSP. Art 352 was no longer needed to buttress the competence of the Union to adopt the contested restrictive measures,[231] and the CJEU explicitly

[224] *Parliament v Council Al-Qaeda Sanctions*, Opinion of Advocate General Bot (n 214) para 63.

[225] Case C-220/14 P *Ahmed Abdelaziz Ezz*, EU:C:2015:147, para 46.

[226] *Ahmed Abdelaziz Ezz* (n 225) para 43. Art 29 TEU concerns 'decisions which shall define the approach of the Union to a particular matter of a geographical or thematic nature'.

[227] *Parliament v Council Al-Qaeda Sanctions*, Opinion of Advocate General Bot (n 214) para 63 (footnote 19).

[228] This would seem to be the case for Art 21(2)(c) TEU which contains the objective to 'preserve peace, prevent conflicts and strengthen international security, in accordance with the purposes and principles of the United Nations Charter', but Dashwood also mentions (a) and (b) in this regard as 'broadly political objectives': A Dashwood, 'Article 47 TEU and the relationship between first and second pillar competences' in A Dashwood and M Maresceau (eds), *Law and Practice of EU External Relations: Salient Features of a Changing Landscape* (CUP, 2008) 103.

[229] Note that Advocate General Bot explicitly rejects such a *lex specialis* reasoning: *Parliament v Council Al-Qaeda Sanctions*, Opinion of Advocate General Bot (n 214) para 69.

[230] Cremona (n 163) 46; see also Cremona (n 61) 87.

[231] Council Regulation (EU) No 1286/2009 of 22 December 2009 amending Regulation (EC) No 881/2002 imposing certain specific restrictive measures directed against certain persons and entities associated with Usama bin Laden, the Al-Qaeda network and the Taliban [2009] OJ 2009 L 346/42, which is based solely on Art 215(2) TFEU.

acknowledged the broad nature of the CFSP as covering 'all areas of foreign policy and all questions relating to the Union's security'.[232]

A similar problem presents itself with the procedure to be followed for negotiating and concluding international agreements. In the absence of specific CFSP objectives, the Court is deprived of an important textual basis that will help to establish when such an envisaged agreement relates 'exclusively or principally to the common foreign and security policy'.[233] Thus, while the streamlining of foreign policy objectives creates more coherence in the sense of the first and third levels (see below section 5), a side effect may be that the elimination of specific CFSP objectives makes task allocation in the sense of second-level coherence more difficult, at least where measures are aimed at purposes broader than 'international security'.

Lastly, regarding the justiciability of foreign policy objectives, the delimitation of competences and tasks in the EU system of external relations complicates the general findings as well. In the doctrinal approaches used in Chapter 1, as well as the general approach to Union objectives, in particular former Community objectives (Chapter 3), it emerged that constitutional courts can draw on foreign policy objectives as constitutional norms, and that they use them principally as an interpretive device rather than as strictly enforceable norms.

In the case of EU external relations, the boundaries of the jurisdiction of the Court of Justice shift depending on whether it is concerned with CFSP or non-CFSP matters. Outside of the CFSP, or within matters pertaining to the constructed Arendtian polity, the Court has full jurisdiction over external relations matters, which it has been willing to exercise, as its case law demonstrates. In particular, the CJEU has been adamant in preserving its jurisdiction, and with it the autonomy and uniform application of Union law, from external interference. It has ruled on international agreements that would subject the Union to an external judicial mechanism, concluding repeatedly that this was incompatible with EU law.[234] For the Union, preservation of what has been called 'the very foundations'[235] of Union law conditions the pursuit of its own foreign policy objectives. It has also rejected not only the direct effect of WTO law in the Union legal order, but also reliance on WTO law to challenge the legality of Union acts or reliance on UN Security Council Resolutions to bar judicial review within the Union.[236]

[232] *Parliament v Council Al-Qaeda Sanctions* (n 196) para 62, referring to Art 24(1), first subpara TEU.

[233] Art 218(3) TFEU.

[234] See Opinion 1/09 *(European and Community Patents Court)*, EU:C:2011:123; on the European Economic Area (EEA), Opinion 1/91 *(EEA)*, EU:C:1991:490; but later the Court accepted the revised set-up of the EEA in Opinion 1/92 *(EEA II)*, EU:C:1992:189; on the ECHR, Opinion 2/94 *(ECHR)*, EU:C:1996:140, and Opinion 2/13 *(ECHR II)*, EU:C:2014:2454. Further B De Witte, 'A Selfish Court? The Court of Justice and the Design of International Dispute Settlement beyond the European Union' in M Cremona and A Thies (eds), *The European Court of Justice and External Relations Law: Constitutional Challenges* (Hart Publishing, 2014).

[235] *Kadi and Al Barakaat* (n 219) para 282; Opinion 1/91 *(EEA)* (n 234) para 71.

[236] See Case C-280/93 *Germany v Council*, EU:C:1994:367; *Kadi and Al Barakaat* (n 219) paras 278–330; see further N Lavranos, 'Protecting European Law from International Law' (2010) 15 *European Foreign Affairs Review* 265.

Furthermore, it ruled that Member States could not avail themselves of external dispute settlement when this would touch upon EU law.[237]

This last point also affects the pursuit of national constitutional foreign policy objectives such as respect for international law, fostering international dispute settlement, and cooperation. Member States whose constitutions contain such objectives, in view of their EU membership and the case law of the CJEU, can only pursue these objectives in a limited manner. The *Mox Plant* judgment is a case in point in this respect. The constitution of the defendant in that case, Ireland, expressly underlines the country's 'adherence to the principle of the pacific settlement of international disputes by international arbitration or judicial determination'.[238] While being faithful to its own constitutional goal, Ireland was found to be in breach of its obligations under the EU Treaties for 'instituting dispute-settlement proceedings' against the United Kingdom under the United Nations Convention on the Law of the Sea (UNCLOS).[239] This harks back to the earlier finding regarding the vertical relationship that the pursuit of national foreign policy objectives in the European constitutional space must be consistent with EU law in general (see section 3.1 above). However, it is the variable delimitation of the jurisdiction of the Court that makes these consistency requirements judicially enforceable within the Union legal order only outside of the CFSP domain.

With regard to the CFSP, in the rather Schmittian domain of politics, this is a priori not the case. According to Art 24 TEU, in the area of the CFSP, the Court of Justice 'shall not have jurisdiction with respect to these provisions' with the exception of monitoring compliance with Art 40 and the review of legality of restrictive measures against natural and legal persons.[240] Hence, the polyphony in external relations is shielded from judicial interference. This may, at first sight, seem to indicate the exclusion of jurisdiction over CFSP objectives as well. However, as was indicated above, it is unclear what CFSP objectives are under the post-Lisbon Treaties. The reference to 'these provisions' in the sentence excluding Court jurisdiction in the area of the CFSP is equally elusive. However, it seems improbable to exclude jurisdiction over objectives that are situated in the general parts of the Treaties, ie Arts 3(5) and 21 TEU. In any event, as an interpretive device, especially in order to ascertain the limits and types of Union competence with a view to allocating tasks between the different institutions, they can certainly be drawn upon by the Court. Nonetheless, when a matter falls with the scope of the CFSP, the Court is barred from exercising its jurisdiction, leaving the Member States at greater ease to pursue their own objectives through the Union or autonomously. Where such matters are at stake, the pull towards unity is less strong, a fact that is also sanctioned by the Treaties.

[237] Case C-459/03 *Commission v Ireland (Mox Plant)*, EU:C:2006:345.

[238] Art 29(2) Irish constitution.

[239] *Mox Plant* (n 237), operative part.

[240] Art 24(1) second subpara TEU together with Art 275 TFEU.

5. Synergy through Loyalty

The preceding two sections discussed in which ways constitutional foreign policy objectives play a role in framing rules of hierarchy and in allocating tasks in EU external relations. Once these rules are established, the objectives have to be pursued in accordance with the framework established by these rules. These create situations where the Member States or certain Union institutions are barred or heavily constrained in their actions. However, in many cases, Member States and Union institutions continue to act in parallel on the international stage. Hence, coherence also needs to be understood as finding a common purpose, a set of common goals towards which all actors can strive, beyond divisions based on rules on hierarchy and different policy areas and institutions.

A pluralist perspective, despite its different varieties, has 'a crucial common point of departure, namely the recognition that there is something valuable, appealing and justified in legal and political plurality in the European legal order'.[241] This plurality extends to the external sphere, with different sources of constitutional foreign policy objectives and a multitude of actors to pursue them. The first and second levels of coherence accommodate and cement such plurality. To draw on Poiares Maduro's terminology, 'foundational' pluralism is ensured through respect for the constitutional identity of the Member States,[242] which includes their actorness on the international scene and retaining the power to pursue core state objectives such as defence policy. A 'participative' dimension is added in the sense that Member States and all Union institutions have their allocated place and role in the system of external relations, with none being transformed into mere instruments at the disposal of the other.[243]

Nevertheless, this diversity is contained within a framework of the 'unitary character' of the polity.[244] This in turn produces a pull towards unity in spite of diversity, including vis-à-vis the outside world. This represents the third level of coherence, which Cremona terms 'complementarity'[245] and Van Vooren calls 'positive synergy'.[246] Critically, this complementarity or synergy is not an end in itself, but is inherently goal-oriented. For Van Vooren, 'the core expression'[247] of EU external relations coherence is Art 21 TEU on external relations objectives. Hence, third-level coherence is about the quest for a 'greater good' and striving towards an 'overriding purpose'.[248] This means that 'coherence thus implies that norms, actors and instruments are positively aligned towards EU Treaty objectives'.[249]

This understanding of coherence echoes the definition of constitutional objectives used here, ie as codified manifestations of the overall 'common good' to be strived for as the most abstract and basic purpose of any given polity. However, the

[241] Van Vooren (n 52) 65. [242] Poiares Maduro (n 11) 526.
[243] Poiares Maduro (n 11) 527. [244] Curtin and Dekker (n 191) 184.
[245] Cremona (n 61) 89. [246] Van Vooren (n 52) 69; drawing on Hillion (n 61) 17.
[247] Van Vooren (n 52) 69. [248] Van Vooren (n 52) 71.
[249] Van Vooren (n 52) 71; see also A Hatje, *Loyalität als Rechtsprinzip der Europäischen Union* (Nomos, 2001) 51–2.

focus on Union objectives raises the question of what role remains for the objectives of the Member State constitutions as a source of synergy. The duty of cooperation, as the principal expression in the EU Treaties for such synergy, entails for the Union and the Member States general 'solidarity' or 'best efforts' obligations (*obligations de moyen* in French) but also more specific obligations of result (*obligations de résultat*). In the first case, there is indeed scope for the pursuit of national constitutional objectives. In the second case, however, the rallying point for synergy is to be found in EU primary law. Moreover, the latter is judicially enforceable against the Member States, at least in policy fields other than the CFSP.

5.1 Synergy in the vertical relationship

Regarding the relationship between the EU and the Member States, in cases where both are competent to act internationally, the Treaties urge complementarity between their actions. According to the TFEU, '[t]he Union's development cooperation policy and that of the Member States complement and reinforce each other'.[250] Similar formulations can be found for economic, financial, and technical cooperation, as well as for humanitarian aid.[251] In terms of external representation, the Treaties call for 'close cooperation' between Union delegations and Member State diplomatic and consular missions.[252]

Evocations of complementarity, solidarity, or unity are particularly strong in the area of the CFSP. According to Art 24 TEU:

> Within the framework of the principles and objectives of its external action, the Union shall conduct, define and implement a common foreign and security policy, based on the development of mutual political solidarity among Member States, the identification of questions of general interest and the achievement of an ever-increasing degree of convergence of Member States' actions.
>
> The Member States shall support the Union's external and security policy actively and unreservedly in a spirit of loyalty and mutual solidarity and shall comply with the Union's action in this area.
>
> The Member States shall work together to enhance and develop their mutual political solidarity. They shall refrain from any action which is contrary to the interests of the Union or likely to impair its effectiveness as a cohesive force in international relations.[253]

Two observations can be made here. Firstly, the Member States clearly come to the fore as actors (or Schmittian 'polities') in their own right, which is unsurprising in

[250] Art 208(1), first subpara TFEU; also Arts 210(1) and 211 TFEU on EU and Member State coordination in the field of development with third countries and international organizations.

[251] Respectively, Arts 212(1) and 212(3), first subpara TFEU; and Arts 214(1) TFEU and 214(6) TFEU.

[252] Art 212(2) TFEU; also Art 32(3) TEU; and Art 35 TEU.

[253] Art 24(2) and (3) TEU; see also Art 25(c) TEU, which lists as one of the means of the CFSP the 'strengthening systematic cooperation between Member States in the conduct of policy'; and Art 29 TEU, which states that 'Member States shall ensure that their national policies conform to the Union positions' adopted with regard to an EU approach to particular region or thematic subject. See also Eeckhout (n 73) 171–2.

view of the autonomy and control they retain in CFSP/CSDP matters, making this rather a 'cooperative enterprise'[254] of the Union and the Member States. Notions such as 'mutual political solidarity among Member States' underline this. In this regard, a comparison between the new mutual solidarity and assistance clauses is telling. On the one hand, in the face of an act of terrorism or natural or man-made disasters against a Member State, '[t]he Union and its Member States shall act jointly in a spirit of solidarity'.[255] With a view to assistance from the Member States, they 'shall coordinate between themselves in the Council'.[256] On the other hand, when confronted with the existential threat of 'armed aggression' on the territory of a Member State, 'the other Member States shall have towards it an obligation of aid and assistance by all the means in their power'.[257] Here, solidarity only applies among the Member States. The Union is not mentioned, underlining again that security is a core objective that states are reluctant to relinquish.

The second observation to be made is that while the language of these provisions leaves ample room for both the foreign policy objectives of the Union and those of the Member States, numerous references to the principles and objectives of EU external action can be found. As Art 32 TEU puts it, 'Member States shall ensure, through the convergence of their actions, that the Union is able to assert *its* interests and values on the international scene'.[258] Union interests and values thus represent a focal point around which the foreign policies of the Member States are to converge.

In terms of honouring these duties of solidarity, the Member States are called upon to consult and inform each other and the EU institutions within the EU framework.[259] Coordination, consultation, and information are also to take place among the EU and the Member States at international bodies and conferences.[260] This includes explicitly the UN Security Council, albeit with the caveat that the defence of Union positions and interests by the Member States is 'without prejudice to their responsibilities under the provisions of the United Nations Charter'.[261] This reflects again the accommodation of Member State sensitivities in this area, as well as the prerogatives of those that have permanent seats and veto rights at the Security Council (the UK and France).[262] In terms of decision-making, Member States are allowed a form of constructive abstention in CFSP matters.[263] In the CFSP context, it is only possible to find 'best efforts' obligations

[254] Cremona (n 61) 74.

[255] Art 222(1) TFEU. This may involve both CFSP and non-CFSP measures.

[256] Art 222(2) TFEU.

[257] Art 42(7), first subpara TEU.

[258] Art 32(1) TEU (emphasis added).

[259] Art 28(3) and (4) TEU; and Art 32 TEU.

[260] Art 34 TEU.

[261] Art 34(2), second subpara TEU. Note also Declarations No 13 and No 14 attached to the Lisbon Treaty concerning the common foreign and security policy.

[262] Note E Regelsberger and D Kugelmann, 'Art 34 (ex-Art 19 EUV) [Koordiniertes Auftreten auf internationaler Ebene; Unterrichtungspflicht der Sicherheitsratsmitglieder]' in R Streinz (ed), *EUV/AEUV: Vertrag über die Europäische Union und Vertrag über die Arbeitsweise der Europäischen Union*, 2nd edn (C.H. Beck, 2012) 273, who observe that in practice France and the UK tend to rely less frequently on this caveat.

[263] In the case of such a qualified abstention, '[i]n a spirit of mutual solidarity, the Member State concerned shall refrain from any action likely to conflict with or impede Union action based on that decision and the other Member States shall respect its position': Art 31(1), second subpara TEU.

in terms of achieving coherence through synergy. Given that the CFSP is largely excluded from the CJEU's jurisdiction, in most cases 'no EU institution or Member State can be brought before the Court of Justice for non-compliance' with these duties.[264] Instead, supervision and enforcement remain 'merely political'.[265]

This changes when moving to other external policies of the Union—away from the CFSP and back to the rather Arendtian 'constructed' polity. Here, the duty of sincere cooperation, as a justiciable legal principle, plays a central role in achieving unity. Despite the seemingly vague formulation of Art 4(3) TEU (former Art 10 TEC (Nice version)), it has been used repeatedly by the Court in cases within the external relations domain,[266] and consequently received considerable scholarly attention.[267] The provision reads:

> Pursuant to the principle of sincere cooperation, the Union and the Member States shall, in full mutual respect, assist each other in carrying out tasks which flow from the Treaties.
>
> The Member States shall take any appropriate measure, general or particular, to ensure fulfilment of the obligations arising out of the Treaties or resulting from the acts of the institutions of the Union.
>
> The Member States shall facilitate the achievement of the Union's tasks and refrain from any measure which could jeopardise the attainment of the Union's objectives.[268]

The notions of Union 'tasks' and 'objectives' appear prominently in the wording of the provision. The duty of sincere cooperation itself is thus an inherently goal-oriented concept as well. Moreover, in terms of judicially upholding this duty of cooperation, what matters are the *Union's* objectives and not those of the Member States.

The duty of sincere cooperation is often stated together with a related concept, viz the unity of international representation. The latter originated from a transplant of the duty of cooperation found in the EAEC Treaty to the EEC by the Court,[269] and appears in particular in the case law concerning the implementation of mixed agreements.[270] Only as recently as the *PFOS* case has the Court referred to it as a 'principle' rather than a mere 'requirement'.[271] However, doubt may

[264] Eeckhout (n 73) 172. [265] Eeckhout (n 73) 172.

[266] The CJEU had already drawn on this provision early on in its case law: see, in the context of the EAEC, Ruling 1/78 *(Physical Protection of Nuclear Materials, Facilities and Transports)*, EU:C:1978:202, paras 34–6.

[267] See eg F Casolari, 'The Principle of Loyal Co-operation: A "Master Key" for EU External Representation?' in S Blockmans and R Wessel (eds), *Principles and Practices of EU External Representation*, CLEER Working Paper 2012/5; E Neframi, 'The Duty of Loyalty: Rethinking its Scope through its Application in the Field of EU External Relations' (2010) 47 *Common Market Law Review* 323; Hillion (n 41); and M Klamert, *The Principle of Loyalty in EU Law* (OUP, 2014) esp 183–209 on mixed agreements.

[268] Art 4(3) TEU.

[269] Opinion 2/91 *(ILO Convention No 170)*, EU:C:1993:106, para 36. The Court refers explicitly there to Ruling 1/78 *(Physical Protection of Nuclear Materials, Facilities and Transports)* (n 266). See also Hillion (n 41) 89.

[270] Opinion 2/91 *(ILO Convention No 170)* (n 269) para 36; Opinion 1/94 *(WTO)*, EU:C:1994:384, para 106; Opinion 2/00 *(Cartagena Protocol)* (n 200) para 18. See further Van Elsuwege and Merket (n 62) 43.

[271] Case C-246/07 *Commission v Sweden (PFOS)*, EU:C:2010:203, para 104; as noted by A Thies, 'Shared Competence and the EU Member States' Obligation to Refrain from Unilateral External

be cast upon whether it is a self-standing principle. The Court has never made recourse to it in its own right, but always in combination with the duty of cooperation. As the Advocate General emphasized in his Opinion in the *PFOS* case '[t]he unity of international representation of the Community and its Member States does not have an independent value; it is merely an expression of the duty of loyal cooperation under Article 10 EC'.[272]

Considering that the duty of sincere cooperation is not an end in itself but links back to the attainment of the objectives of the Union, the unity of international representation is nothing other than a legal requirement of facilitating the pursuit of Union objectives on the international scene in view of the polyphony and other complexities exhibited by the EU system of external relations. With a view to achieving synergy and bridging divides in terms of competences and policy areas, the principle of unity of international representation harbours potential for the complementary pursuit of objectives.[273]

The pursuit of the constitutional foreign policy objectives of the Member States is constrained by the duty of sincere cooperation in a rather extensive way, especially in comparison with the limited protection which constitutional identity offers the Member States against the pursuit of Union objectives. Here, Union objectives exhibit an interpretive–prohibitive quality vis-à-vis the Member States.

In terms of best efforts obligations, sincere cooperation entails, again, a duty to inform and consult within the Union. This was made clear by the Court in the *Inland Waterway* cases, where it ruled that once 'a concerted [then] Community action at international level'[274] has started, *in casu* to conclude an international agreement with third countries, what is required is:

> if not a duty of abstention on the part of the Member States, at the very least a duty of close cooperation between the latter and the Community institutions in order to facilitate the achievement of the Community tasks and to ensure the coherence and consistency of the action and its international representation.[275]

Accordingly, by ratifying international agreements of their own which covered the same subject matter as the envisaged Community agreements without continuously cooperating and consulting with the Community institutions, the Member States had breached their loyalty obligations.[276] The Court explicitly links the behaviour of the Member States with internal commitments and Treaty objectives, stating

Action: PFOS and Beyond' in J Díez-Hochleitner et al (eds), *Recent Trends in the Case Law of the Court of Justice of the European Union (2008-2011)* (La Ley, 2012) 721.

[272] Case C-246/07 *Commission v Sweden (PFOS)*, Opinion of Advocate General Poiares Maduro, EU:C:2009:589, para 37.

[273] See for an attempt at its practical operationalization, Council of the European Union, *EU Statements in Multilateral Organisations*, Brussels, 24 October 2011, 15901/11. It introduces the term 'EU actor' as a generic designation of the EU organ competent to represent the Union in any given case.

[274] Case C-433/03 *Commission v Germany (Inland Waterway)*, EU:C:2005:462, para 66. Similarly, Case C-266/03 *Commission v Luxembourg (Inland Waterway)*, EU:C:2005:341.

[275] *Commission v Germany (Inland Waterway)* (n 274) para 66

[276] *Commission v Germany (Inland Waterway)* (n 274) para 73.

that the 'Member State jeopardised the implementation of the Council Decision of 7 December 1992 and, *consequently*, the accomplishment of the Community's task and the attainment of the *objectives* of the Treaty'.[277]

Such close cooperation is necessary in particular in the context of mixed agreements, ie where both the Union and Member States are parties and exercise their respective competences.[278] As the Court ruled in *Opinion 1/94*, close cooperation between Union and Member States in such situations is 'essential'.[279] To some extent, the duty of cooperation is complied with by drawing up inter-institutional arrangements regulating the participation of the EU and the Member States in such mixed settings, which concern, for instance, voting rights and representing common positions.[280] While this can create a degree of synergy, the related practice in mixed settings to issue declarations of competence, outlining for which parts of the mixed agreement the Member States or the Union have competence, would seem, on the contrary, to be a matter of delimitation of limited usefulness.[281]

Beyond agreeing on practical arrangements and referring back to competence allocation, sincere cooperation entails further consequences for Members States in terms of Union law obligations in mixed settings. As the CJEU has ruled, there exists a general Union interest that a mixed agreement be implemented in its entirety, including in areas of Member State competence,[282] or those which are only partially covered by Union legislation.[283] In this sense, the duty of cooperation is a device used to ensure the 'strict observance of international law' (Art 3(5) TEU) in the form of mixed agreements by both the Union and its Member States. These latter points indicate that best efforts are not always enough, meaning that in certain situations specific results are required.

According to the case law of the Court of Justice, the political preferences or laws of the Member States cannot stand in the way of achieving such results. This includes the constitutional objectives of the Member States. Instead, the latter become quasi-Union organs mandated to pursue the foreign policy objectives of the Union. They retain their voice on the international stage, but the message to be conveyed is prescribed by the Union. As the Court ruled in the *IMO* case, drawing on *ERTA*, Member States have to 'abstain from any measure which might jeopardise the attainment of the objectives of the Treaty'.[284] This not only covers measures

[277] *Commission v Germany (Inland Waterway)* (n 274) para 69 (emphasis added).

[278] Cremona (n 61) 71; see extensively Hillion (n 41).

[279] Opinion 1/94 *(WTO)* (n 270) para 108.

[280] Case C-25/94 *Commission v Council (FAO)*, EU:C:1996:114, para 49, which states that provisions from the inter-institutional arrangement in question represented 'fulfilment of that duty of cooperation between the Community and its Member States within the [Food and Agricultural Organization]'.

[281] For a recent overview of the practice and criticism on the usefulness of such declarations, see A Delgado Casteleiro, 'EU Declarations of Competence to Multilateral Agreements: A Useful Reference Base?' (2012) 17 *European Foreign Affairs Review* 491.

[282] Case C-13/00 *Commission v Ireland (Berne Convention)*, EU:C:2002:184.

[283] Case C-239/03 *Commission v France (Étang de Berre)*, EU:C:2004:598. See further Neframi (n 267) 331–7.

[284] Case C-45/07 *Commission v Greece (IMO)*, EU:C:2009:81, para 16.

directly opposed to Treaty objectives as such, but also all rules and commitments 'promulgated for the attainment of the objectives of the Treaty'.[285] Hence, the duty of cooperation operates as a vehicle to make the prohibitive function of constitutional objectives felt, at least by the Member States, for the sake of defending the common interest of the European polity.

In a hypothetical case where a national constitutional objective would urge a Member State to speak up on the international stage, the duty of sincere cooperation under the EU Treaties has the power to silence that country nonetheless.[286] Only to the extent that compliance with its Union loyalty would affect its narrowly defined constitutional identity could a Member State arguably still speak up. However, even in such an extreme case, it might be hard to justify why action on the international stage was necessary and why the constitutional objective could not have been pursued *within* the EU framework. Acting through the institutional mechanisms of the Union 'agora', above all the Council as the forum of the Member States, the latter would still be free to pursue their constitutional objectives. The duty of sincere cooperation under EU law would not seem to apply within the internal 'political space' of the Union in the sense that Member States have to reach specific agreements or outcomes there.[287] However, in a case where a Member State is outvoted internally, it is obliged to comply with the resulting acts, including the defence of common positions within international bodies with which it disagrees.[288]

Moreover, as the judgment of the CJEU in *PFOS* shows, the duty of sincere cooperation prohibits Member States from committing certain acts not only in areas of the Union's exclusive competence, but even when exercising their own 'share' of shared competence. This occurs as soon as such exercise is 'likely to compromise the principle of unity in the international representation of the Union and its Member States and weaken their negotiating power' vis-à-vis third parties.[289] The delinquent Member State should have remained silent on the world stage instead of 'dissociat[ing] itself from a concerted common strategy within the Council'[290] and setting in motion a procedure that may have resulted in binding the Union to commitments it was not yet prepared to take internally.[291] This echoes most clearly Post's observations on 'how plurality within an internal agora may require unity in external affairs'.[292] In the pursuit of their national constitutional

[285] *Commission v Greece (IMO)* (n 284) para 17.

[286] On the prohibitive side of the duty of sincere cooperation, see further A Delgado Casteleiro and J Larik, 'The Duty to Remain Silent: Limitless Loyalty in EU External Relations?' (2011) 36 *European Law Review* 522.

[287] In this sense, A von Bogdandy and S Schill, 'Artikel 4 EUV' in E Grabitz, M Hilf, and M Nettesheim (eds), *Das Recht der Europäischen Union*, loose-leaf, 41st supplement (C.H. Beck, 2010) marginal no 105, stressing that the Council is the site for the pursuit of the national interest, from which subsequently a Union position can emerge. However, they regard extreme cases such as obstruction of the functioning of an organ, for instance, through an 'empty chair' policy, as a violation of the duty of cooperation.

[288] See Case C-399/12 *Germany v Council (OIV)*, ECLI:EU:C:2014:2258.

[289] *Commission v Sweden (PFOS)* (n 271) para 104.

[290] *Commission v Sweden (PFOS)* (n 271) para 91.

[291] *Commission v Sweden (PFOS)* (n 271) paras 92–103.

[292] Post (n 2) 239.

objectives, Member States should have confined themselves to acting domestically (in a manner consistent with Union law) or through the Union, ie through the Council and its working parties.[293] According to Cremona, '[t]he Member State may decide to give priority to environmental policy over economic considerations internally, but externally—at least in this context of a mixed agreement—the reconciliation of objectives necessary to policy coherence must be worked out by Union and Member States together'.[294] This also applies to the reconciliation of constitutional objectives in the area of foreign policy.

In addition, Union objectives, via the duty of sincere cooperation, oblige the Member States to actively pursue Union objectives.[295] The clearest expression of this is the situation in which the Union, on the one hand, is barred from an international organization (or from concluding agreements within the framework of such an organization), for instance, due to the membership requirements of that organization, but, on the other hand, the EU has competence in the field in question. According to the CJEU, 'the fact that the European Union did not take part in the international agreement in question does not prevent it from exercising that competence by establishing, through its institutions, a position to be adopted on its behalf in the body set up by that agreement'.[296] In these cases, the Union's 'external competence may, if necessary, be exercised through the medium of the Member States acting jointly in the [then] Community's interest'.[297] Hence, Member States can be regarded in such instances as 'trustees of the Union interest'.[298] In these particular cases, they are also bound to pursue Union objectives at the international level. In other words, while certain international organizations cannot accommodate the single voice of the EU, the foreign policy objectives of the Union and the measures adopted in their pursuit provide the 'sheet music', if you will, for the Member States to perform on the international stage.

From the opposite perspective, the Union organs are equally under a loyalty obligation towards the Member States.[299] However, the Court has been clear in ruling that a potential breach of the duty of sincere cooperation on the part of the Union does not relieve the Member States from fulfilling their obligations in

[293] Note that the Court dismissed the 'minimum standards' argument of the Swedish government that it would have been allowed to act internationally by virtue of the freedom to impose higher domestic environmental standards at home (under ex-Art 176 TEC, now Art 193 TFEU): *Commission v Sweden (PFOS)* (n 271) para 102.

[294] M Cremona, 'Case C-246/07, *Commission v. Sweden (PFOS)*, Judgment of the Court of Justice (Grand Chamber) of 20 April 2010' (2011) 48 *Common Market Law Review* 1639, 1662.

[295] Note Art 4(3), third subpara TEU: 'The Member States shall facilitate the achievement of the Union's tasks.' In this sense also F Reimer, 'Ziele und Zuständigkeiten: Die Funktionen der Unionszielbestimmungen' [2003] *Europarecht* 992, 1005–7.

[296] *Germany v Council (OIV)* (n 288) para 52.

[297] Opinion 2/91 *(ILO Convention No 170)* (n 269) 1076; this was reiterated in the similar setting of the *IMO* case, *Commission v Greece (IMO)* (n 284) para 31.

[298] M Cremona, 'Member States as Trustees of the Union Interest: Participating in International Agreements on Behalf of the European Union' in A Arnull et al (eds), *A Constitutional Order of States: Essays in European Law in Honour of Alan Dashwood* (Hart Publishing, 2011).

[299] Note the post-Lisbon wording of Art 4(3), first subpara TEU: 'Pursuant to the principle of sincere cooperation, the Union and the Member States shall, *in full mutual respect, assist each other in*

this respect.[300] Hence, the loyalty obligation does not operate in an entirely symmetrical fashion. In an instance where a Union organ such as the Commission is in breach of the duty of cooperation, there seems to be no realistic remedy at hand for the Member State. For all practical purposes, the Commission is only under a duty of best endeavours, given the wide discretion it enjoys. Procedurally, as a result of its uncooperative behaviour, there may simply not be a legal act that could be challenged under Art 263 TFEU (ex-Art 230 TEC).[301] Van Vooren thus rightly speaks of a 'pull towards EU powers' despite formal reciprocity.[302] By the same token, it is a pull towards the international pursuit of Union objectives, with a corresponding 'push' of the pursuit of Member State objectives into the internal politics of the EU 'agora'.

However, the legal force of the duty of sincere cooperation may find its limit, at least as far as adjudication is concerned, in the divide between the CFSP and other external policies of the Union. A substantive duty to cooperate is expressed for the CFSP as well, and quite emphatically so. In particular, the formulation stating that the Member States 'shall refrain from any action which is contrary to the interests of the Union or likely to impair its effectiveness as a cohesive force in international relations'[303] seems to restate the constraining force of solidarity incumbent on the Member States to defend the European polity. But the crucial difference here is the exclusion of the jurisdiction of the CJEU from the CFSP.[304]

Yet, the disappearance of a list of designated CFSP objectives weakens the case for total exclusion of the Court of Justice from adjudicating the duty of sincere cooperation in this area. As the Court undoubtedly has jurisdiction over the general duty in Art 4(3) TEU, as well as Arts 3(5) and 21 TEU, an argument could be made that the CJEU could rule on Member State actions which jeopardized Union objectives codified in the latter two provisions.[305] However, this may deprive the explicit exclusion of jurisdiction over the CFSP, and its two specifically mentioned exceptions,[306] of much of their meaning. Thus far, the Court has not pronounced

carrying out tasks which flow from the Treaties' (emphasis added), while Art 10 TEC was addressed to the Member States only.

300 *Commission v Greece (IMO)* (n 284) para 26.

301 M Cremona, 'Extending the Reach of the AETR Principle: Comment on Commission v Greece (C-45/07)' (2009) 34 *European Law Review* 754, 765–6. Note also the rather weak obligation to 'take account' of international commitments binding on the Member States (but which do not bind the Union and do not represent customary international law) in the *Intertanko* case, which did not entail, according to the CJEU, an assessment of the validity of EU legislation in light of such international obligations: Case C-308/06 *Intertanko*, EU:C:2008:312, paras 52 and 66.

302 Van Vooren (n 52) 116; in a similar vein, Van Elsuwege and Merket (n 62) 51–2.

303 Art 24(3), second subpara TEU.

304 Art 24(1), second subpara TEU and Art 275(1) TFEU.

305 Arguing in this direction, C Hillion, 'A Powerless Court? The European Court of Justice and the Common Foreign and Security Policy' in M Cremona and A Thies (eds), *The European Court of Justice and External Relations Law: Constitutional Challenges* (Hart Publishing, 2014); and earlier C Hillion and R Wessel, 'Restraining External Competences of EU Member States under CFSP' in M Cremona and B De Witte (eds), *EU Foreign Relations Law: Constitutional Fundamentals* (Hart Publishing, 2008) 108–12.

306 Art 40 TEU and Art 275(2) TFEU.

itself on this matter. In addition, in the TEU the subparagraph stating that the Member States will refrain from certain actions in this area is followed by this subparagraph: 'The Council and the High Representative shall ensure compliance with these principles.'[307] This could be seen as expressing, *a contrario*, that it is not for the Commission and the Court to enforce coherence and loyalty in the CFSP. Instead, 'the emphasis is on giving effect to CFSP measures and implementation by the Member States themselves rather than enforcement through the Court'.[308] While EU foreign policy objectives are also the substantive rallying point for the CFSP, polyphony remains an inherent feature of this area, as the Member States refuse to be drowned out by supranational institutions in the pursuit of objectives very close to the core of statehood and politics in the Schmittian sense, both internally and externally.

5.2 Synergy in the horizontal relationship

On the horizontal level, synergy is to be achieved through a number of actors and institutions specifically mandated for this purpose. Firstly, the Union as such 'shall ensure consistency between the different areas of its external action and between these and its other policies'.[309] In particular, 'the Council and the Commission, assisted by the High Representative of the Union for Foreign Affairs and Security Policy, shall ensure that consistency and shall cooperate to that effect'.[310] Among the various Council configurations, the Foreign Affairs Council is entrusted with the task of ensuring 'that the Union's action is consistent' in the area of external relations.[311] The High Representative, moreover, is specifically tasked to 'ensure the consistency of the Union's external action'.[312] Within the provisions on the CFSP, it is reiterated that '[t]he Council and the High Representative of the Union for Foreign Affairs and Security Policy shall ensure the unity, consistency and effectiveness of action by the Union'.[313] In this context, there exists among all institutions engaged in the EU's external action a duty to 'practice mutual sincere cooperation'.[314] This applies also to negotiating international agreements, more precisely the relationship and 'institutional balance' between the Union negotiator and the Council, which guides these negotiations through directives and special committees.[315]

The High Representative can be regarded as the main guarantor of coherence. The office, as defined post-Lisbon, combines the former functions of External Relations Commissioner and High Representative for the CFSP, serving as a bridge across the CFSP/non-CFSP divide.[316] Being 'double-hatted', the High Representative

[307] Art 24(3), third subpara TEU. [308] Cremona (n 163) 67.

[309] Art 21(3), second subpara TEU; note also Art 7 TFEU: 'The Union shall ensure consistency between its policies and activities, taking all of its objectives into account and in accordance with the principle of conferral of powers.'

[310] Art 21(3), second subpara TEU. [311] Art 16(6), third subpara TEU.

[312] Art 18(4) TEU. [313] Art 26(2), second subpara TEU. [314] Art 13(2) TEU.

[315] Art 218(4) TFEU. See on this further Case C-425/13 *Commission v Council (Greenhouse gas emissions)*, EU:C:2015:483.

[316] See Eeckhout (n 73) 492; and Van Elsuwege (n 170) 998, who calls the High Representative and the EEAS 'trans-pillar institutions'.

is both Vice President of the Commission and presides over the Foreign Affairs Council.[317] She also takes part in the European Council.[318] Crucially, she is to be assisted in fulfilling her task by the European External Action Service, which itself is a *sui generis* organ composed of assets that used to belong to the external relations departments of the Council and Commission.[319] Hence, regardless of whether the CFSP or non-CFSP policies are concerned, the High Representative and the EEAS always figure as prominent addressees of external relations objectives, with a particular emphasis on ensuring consistency between the different objectives across different policy areas.

In terms of horizontal third-level coherence, Cremona adds certain cross-cutting principles to this, such as combatting discrimination (Art 10 TFEU) and environmental protection (Art 11 TFEU).[320] However, all of these provisions will hardly be enforceable. Rather, they are to be seen as 'guidance to the institutions in the process of policy development, to be read alongside the institutional (and inter-institutional) obligation to ensure consistency'.[321] As practical examples of cross-cutting and coherent external action, one can refer, for instance, to the European Neighbourhood Policy[322] or the so-called 'comprehensive approach' of the EU towards Somalia.[323] Such approaches allow for the simultaneous and balanced pursuit of various, if not most, foreign policy objectives of the EU in a particular area. Given the goal-oriented nature of the concept of coherence, coherence cannot be properly understood without reference to Union objectives. Moreover, given the rather weak legal force of general external relations objectives, harder obligations, such as under Art 40 TEU, may well prevail over them and the quest for synergy,[324] or at least help prioritize among them in any given context. This is not at odds with the understanding of constitutional objectives followed in this book. Indeed, it is one of their defining characteristics that objectives have to be pursued within the existing constitutional structure. To a certain extent, they can help to shape it, but they must not upset it.

[317] Art 18 TEU.

[318] Art 15(2) TEU. Further Kaddous (n 198) 179–80; and Eeckhout (n 73) 493–4.

[319] Art 27(3) TEU; and Council Decision 2010/427/EU of 26 July 2010 establishing the organisation and functioning of the European External Action Service [2010] OJ L 201/30; further S Blockmans and M-L Laatsit, 'The European External Action Service: Enhancing Coherence in EU External Action?' in PJ Cardwell (ed), *EU External Relations Law and Policy in the Post-Lisbon Era* (T.M.C. Asser Press, 2012); and on the peculiar nature of the EEAS in particular, B Van Vooren, 'A Legal–Institutional Perspective on the European Union External Action Service' (2011) 48 *Common Market Law Review* 475.

[320] Cremona (n 61) 89.

[321] Cremona (n 61) 90.

[322] Extensively Van Vooren (n 52); and M Cremona and C Hillion, *L'Union fait la force? Potential and Limitations of the European Neighbourhood Policy as an Integrated EU Foreign and Security Policy*, EUI Working Paper Law 2006/39.

[323] See H-G Ehrhart and K Petretto, 'The EU, the Somalia Challenge, and Counter-piracy: Towards a Comprehensive Approach?' (2012) 17 *European Foreign Affairs Review* 261. See also Joint Communication to the European Parliament and the Council, *The EU's Comprehensive Approach to External Conflict and Crises*, Brussels, 11 December 2013 JOIN(2013) 30 final.

[324] Cremona (n 61) 90.

6. Consequences for the Union and its Member States: The Shifting Bounds of Possibility

As a consequence of the additional complexities of pluralism, external relations polyphony, and the system of EU external relations compared to the situation normally prevalent in states, the question of the 'bounds of possibility', which qualifies the obligatory force of constitutional objectives, must also be revisited. The legal constraints resulting from EU membership that apply to the Member States as international actors have to be balanced against the gains in what can be called the 'shifting bounds of possibility' within the system of EU external relations.

Generally, it was concluded that both in the EU and national legal orders the organs called upon to pursue foreign policy objectives have a wider margin of discretion than they would have in a purely internal situation (Chapter 1, section 5 and Chapter 3, section 4). This is due to the additional factors that have to be taken into account and that lie largely beyond the control of any single state, or of the Union for that matter. With regard to the EU as a polity, it is essential to consider the impact of its own peculiarities as an international actor as well.

On the one hand, where the Member States have joined their capabilities and conferred powers upon the Union, the bounds of what is possible and what is achievable for them on the international stage have widened. Their diversity notwithstanding, which as demonstrated above is accommodated in the Treaties, unity and coherent external action promise greater leverage internationally. As De Witte puts it, there is no reason to pity the Member States for having their powers limited through EU membership 'if one compares their effective space for political and legal maneuver [sic] with that of other European states', such as those in the EEA, which have no seat at the Union institutions,[325] ie which are not part of the EU 'agora'. Instead of having partially relinquished their external relations powers, the Member States 'have rather "pooled" these fragments of sovereignty within the institutional structure of the European Union, so as to enhance their joint capacity for effective international action'.[326] De Witte does not fail to stress their retained control as members of the Council and its working groups, concluding that the 'constraints of EU membership are thus easily outweighed by the increased opportunities for external influence that this membership offers them'[327] and that this 'allows them, most of the time, to act more efficiently in the pursuit of their common interest on the world scene'.[328] Hence, by containing polyphony within the Council, and also by giving the other Union institutions a voice within the internal 'agora' with a view to crafting a coherent message, the EU, as a whole, can subsequently sound this message more loudly and clearly to the outside world.

The latter point relates directly to the operation of constitutional foreign policy objectives of the Member States. As was shown, EU membership often means

[325] De Witte (n 31) 49. [326] De Witte (n 31) 49. [327] De Witte (n 31) 49.
[328] De Witte (n 31) 53.

substituting the pursuit of national with EU objectives on the international scene. However, acting through the Union can reinforce the credibility of the foreign policy objectives of the Member States internally. While external unity can help the pursuit of the foreign policy objectives of both the Member States and the Union, external divisiveness inhibits both the coherence of EU external action as well as the 'effectiveness'[329] of the pursuit of Member State objectives. This applies in particular to smaller Member States with only rather modest material capabilities.

The fact that, internationally, EU objectives have the tendency to overshadow their national counterparts in the Member States only partly qualifies this observation. This is due to the large degree of substantive convergence between them, which allowed the emergence of the European polity in the first place. As the TEU states at the outset, 'the Member States confer competences [upon the Union] to attain objectives *they* have in common'.[330] As was shown above, constitutional pluralism becomes salient in rather extreme cases, where mutual trust within the polity is in question, but as a rule the European constitutional space operates a composite legal order with quasi-federal traits. As a political entity, there is ample opportunity to agree on common causes to be pursued internationally together.

This is what is commonly seen, for example, as one of the merits of a CCP, which has made the EU one of the most important players in world trade negotiations, and where it speaks with a single voice and is represented by a single negotiator.[331] But it is also true for other policy areas, including the intergovernmental CFSP and in particular the CSDP. Civil–military operations within the EU framework offer opportunities, especially to small Member States, which can acquire an international presence that would be unimaginable on an individual basis.

For instance, when Bulgaria sets out to promote 'a just international order',[332] Ireland affirms 'the principle of the pacific settlement of international disputes by international arbitration or judicial determination',[333] Finland embarks on fostering 'international co-operation for the protection of peace and human rights',[334] and Portugal advocates 'the creation of an international order capable of safeguarding peace and justice in relations between peoples',[335] these appear as mutually compatible goals. These can all be pursued more effectively by working together in a coherent fashion than through disparate unilateral actions. Whenever these states have contributions to make on the world stage to give life to their respective constitutional objectives, they can amplify their voice and impact by acting through the Union.

From an EU perspective, the varying degrees of dependency on the political will of the Member States results in additional uncertainty regarding the capacity to

[329] Note that 'goal attainment' is one of the dimensions of 'effectiveness' in international relations scholarship, especially regarding international regimes. See O Young, *International Governance: Protecting the Environment in a Stateless Society* (Cornell University Press, 1994) 144–5.

[330] Art 1(1) TEU (emphasis added).

[331] See, eg S Meunier and K Nicolaïdis, 'The European Union as a Trade Power' in C Hill and M Smith (eds), *International Relations and the European Union*, 2nd edn (OUP, 2011).

[332] Art 24(2) Bulgarian constitution.

[333] Art 29(2) Irish constitution.

[334] Art 1(2) Finnish constitution.

[335] Art 7(2) Portuguese constitution.

effectively pursue its own constitutional foreign policy objectives. It is dependent on the political will being formed within its 'agora' to become internationally active. However, this is a priori no different in other states, especially democratic states where the executive is reined in by other constitutional organs in the conduct of foreign affairs. Constitutional pluralism and 'heterarchy' are not unique to the EU.[336] Nonetheless, where it depends on the unanimous agreement of the Member States, this can hamper the international action of the EU and consequently the effective pursuit of its objectives. More specific to the EU is the polyphonic nature of its external relations, which entails in areas of non-exclusive competence, and where Member States are not pre-empted from acting, the Union having to rely on the willingness of its Member States to act *through* the Union, and on the Member States' self-restraint in not undermining the Union's position. In particular, this applies to the CFSP, where unanimous voting in the Council prevails and the Commission, Court, and Parliament play a diminished role compared to other external relations areas. Moreover, in the case of the CSDP, the Union has to rely on the 'capabilities provided by the Member States' (Art 42(1) TEU), and not its own.

In addition, the EU depends on the willingness of the outside world to interact *with* an actor as unusual as the Union. While both unity internally as well as a willingness to act internationally through the Union may exist, the current state of the international system does not always facilitate such action. Terms such as 'polity' or *sui generis* actor all highlight rather than disguise the fact that, for many practical purposes, the state remains the 'normal person' (*Normalperson*) of the international legal order.[337] Hence, other states might prefer to negotiate international agreements with the Member States directly, or in addition to the Union, which leads again to the complex issue of negotiating and implementing mixed agreements.[338] It should also be recalled that not all international organizations allow the EU to become a member.[339] As a result, it will have to rely on its Member States to represent its interests. This can be seen, for instance, in the context of the United Nations, where the EU experienced protracted difficulties in obtaining enhanced observer status at the General Assembly.[340] It is in these cases that third-level coherence matters most, as even with clear rules of conflict management and unambiguous task allocation within the Union, the international legal order may not always be prepared for the Union to speak with a single voice. The message,

[336] Halberstam (n 8).

[337] V Epping, 'Völkerrechtssubjekte' in K Ipsen (ed), *Völkerrecht*, 6th edn (C.H. Beck, 2014) 49.

[338] See from an American perspective P Olson 'Mixity from the Outside: The Perspective of a Treaty Partner' in C Hillion and P Koutrakos (eds), *Mixed Agreements Revisited: The EU and Its Member States in the World* (Hart Publishing, 2010). Note, for instance, also the US–EU agreement on mutual legal assistance, which makes explicit that future bilateral agreements between the US and EU Member States are not excluded by it: Agreement on mutual legal assistance between the European Union and the United States of America [2003] OJ L 181/34, Art 14.

[339] See I Govaere, J Capiau, and A Vermeersch, 'In-Between Seats: The Participation of the European Union in International Organizations' (2004) 9 *European Foreign Affairs Review* 155; and Eeckhout (n 73) 222–31.

[340] Such status was eventually granted by virtue of United Nations General Assembly Resolution A/RES/65/276, 3 May 2011 on the participation of the Union in the work of the

regardless of its source from within the European constitutional space, can nonetheless be coherent.

7. Conclusion: United in a Common Direction

This chapter brought together the findings from comparative constitutional law and the EU legal order for the analysis of the operation of foreign policy objectives within the European constitutional space. Having scrutinized the operation of these norms in the complex setting marked by both constitutional pluralism and external relations 'polyphony', it becomes clear, first of all, that out of the many parts of the system of EU external relations emerges not *one* 'sole organ';[341] no *E pluribus unum* arises. What emerges instead is something that is coherent despite diversity and plurality: *E pluribus cohaerente*.

Coherence was analysed in different ways, encompassing three dimensions (consistency, task delimitation, and synergy) as well as both the horizontal and vertical relationships within the EU's system of external relations. The different settings and the legal principles that govern these relations have an effect on the pursuit of foreign policy objectives of both the EU and the Member States. In terms of consistency, the constitutional rank of national foreign policy objectives is no excuse for not complying with all the obligations under EU law, unless they form part of the narrow category of a Member State's constitutional identity. However, international actorness of the Member States cannot be eclipsed entirely by the EU. Moreover, particular sensitivities for Member State foreign policies, such as neutrality or NATO membership, have been largely accommodated in the European constitutional space. In the horizontal relationship, EU law and other measures need to be consistent with the constitutional objectives of the Union, ie they can be traced back as being adopted in the pursuit of these objectives.

In terms of task delimitation, the principle of conferral and the requirement for using the correct legal basis condition which actor is allowed to pursue their respective objectives on the international stage. The doctrine of 'implied powers', and in particular the 'necessity' branch of it, serve as a stark illustration of the competence-shaping function of constitutional objectives in the vertical relationship. In the horizontal relationship, foreign policy objectives play an important role when it comes to identifying the correct legal basis, which is of 'constitutional significance'[342] for the EU with important implications for the resulting institutional prerogatives. Hence, these objectives will continue to be drawn on in litigation before the CJEU in cases concerning the EU's external relations.

United Nations. See further P Serrano de Haro, *Participation of the European Union in the Work of the United Nations: General Assembly Resolution 65/276*, CLEER Working Paper 2012/4.

[341] To use the term from the American legal discourse, see L Henkin, *Foreign Affairs and the US Constitution*, 2nd edn (Clarendon Press, 1996) 41–5.

[342] Opinion 2/00 *(Cartagena Protocol)* (n 200) para 5.

Lastly, regarding positive synergy, it becomes apparent that in many situations the EU and the Member States continue to act in parallel on the international stage, pursuing their respective objectives. In these cases, their actions need to complement each other. Vertically, the duty of sincere cooperation and the principle of unity in the international representation, which are inherently goal-oriented concepts, play an important role in bringing about a common direction of these various actors, at least to the extent that they are justiciable. Horizontally, cross-cutting Union organs, above all the High Representative and the EEAS, ensure the coherent pursuit of the EU's foreign policy objectives across different policies.

Whereas the cardinal legal principles governing the European constitutional space and the external relations of the EU entail many constraints—more frequently on the Member States than on the Union institutions—acting together in a coherent fashion expands the bounds of possibility for all of these actors, and consequently can make the pursuit of their respective constitutional foreign policy objectives more effective.

5

'Normative Power' and the Power(lessness) of Norms

Constitutional Foreign Policy Objectives and Theories of International Relations

1. Introduction

In the previous chapter, the analysis of constitutional foreign policy objectives was expanded from within a single legal order to the operation of these norms within the joint constitutional space of the European Union and its Member States. In this final chapter, the analysis looks beyond the strictly legal domain, and surveys the area where law and the study of international relations (IR) overlap. In doing so, it brings together the findings from the comparative and multilevel analysis of constitutional foreign policy objectives with theories of international relations regarding the role of the EU on the international stage.

Just as each constitution exhibits a certain 'world view', each strand of IR theory proposes its own distinctive way of looking at the world, its actors, and the factors that matter in the international order. Consequently, this chapter systematizes cross-disciplinary references and engagements to critically assess their merits. To this end, the chapter revisits the EU Treaties with a view to what they reveal about the tenets of each main theoretical current. It subsequently inverses this perspective, appraising the uses (and abuses) of constitutional foreign policy objectives from the vantage point of the major debates in IR on the EU as global actor.

The role of the European Union in the world has occupied an increasingly prominent place in the study of international relations.[1] Building on the traditional strands of IR theory, each with its own explanatory framework and analytical

[1] This is evidenced by a considerable amount of literature, including numerous edited volumes and monographs dedicated to this topic. See eg O Elgström and M Smith (eds), *The European Union's Roles in International Politics: Concepts and Analysis* (Routledge, 2006); C Bretherton and J Vogler, *The European Union as a Global Actor*, 2nd edn (Routledge, 2006); S Keukeleire and T Delreux, *The Foreign Policy of the European Union*, 2nd edn (Palgrave Macmillan, 2014); F Laursen (ed), *The EU as a Foreign and Security Policy Actor* (Republic of Letters, 2009); R Whitman (ed), *Normative Power Europe: Empirical and Theoretical Perspectives* (Palgrave Macmillan, 2011); C Hill and M Smith (eds), *International Relations and the European Union*, 2nd edn (OUP, 2011).

emphases, these have been applied to the EU and yielded varying assessments of its global performance as well as of the importance of values, norms, and law in its foreign policy. Given the keen interest that both EU legal scholarship and IR exhibit towards the EU in the world, a joint 'conceptual space'[2] becomes visible between the two fields in the area of EU external relations. This goes beyond the mere observation that scholars of IR and EU law happen to be studying the same area. Scholars of both disciplines can already be seen to reach across the disciplinary divide, with lawyers drawing on concepts from the social sciences and IR scholars drawing on legal norms in order to make their arguments.

This disciplinary crossover becomes evident also with regard to constitutional objectives. On the one hand, as the previous chapters have demonstrated, legal scholars regularly evoke the non-legal functions of constitutional objectives. In the Indian context, members of the Indian Constituent Assembly underlined that such principles may serve as 'a body of doctrines to which public opinion can rally'.[3] This dovetails with the idea of constitutional law as an expression of the 'common ideology that governs public life' according to Joseph Raz.[4] With regard to the EU, Franz Reimer contends that next to their legal roles, Union objectives perform 'information' and 'integration' functions, which help to justify the exercise of powers by the EU as a form of 'output legitimacy'.[5] In this sense, EU constitutional law, to use Armin von Bogdandy's term, fulfils a 'manifesto function'.[6] On the other hand, Ian Manners' concept of the EU as a 'normative power' serves as the clearest illustration of the harnessing of law by IR scholarship. Manners bases his argument that the EU possesses a normatively distinct identity as an international actor precisely on its 'political–legal constitution'.[7]

2. Different 'World Views' in International Relations

Assessments of the European Union's place on the international stage abound in the social sciences, and at the same time diverge significantly. Some commentators conclude that the EU is indeed a superpower,[8] which is likely to 'run the 21st

[2] Using the term used by A-M Slaughter, 'International Law in a World of Liberal States' (1995) 6 *European Journal of International Law* 503, 503 with regard to international law and international relations theory; note in this respect also S Ratner, 'Ethics and International Law: Integrating the Global Justice Project(s)' (2013) 5 *International Theory* 1, 34.

[3] G Austin, *The Indian Constitution: Cornerstone of a Nation* (Clarendon Press, 1966) 78.

[4] J Raz, 'On the Authority and Interpretation of Constitutions: Some Preliminaries' in L Alexander (ed), *Constitutionalism: Philosophical Foundations* (CUP, 1998) 154.

[5] F Reimer, 'Ziele und Zuständigkeiten: Die Funktionen der Unionszielbestimmungen' [2003] *Europarecht* 992, 999–1000.

[6] A von Bogdandy, 'The European Constitution and European Identity: Text and Subtext of the Treaty establishing a Constitution for Europe' (2005) 3 *International Journal of Constitutional Law* 295, 308.

[7] I Manners, 'Normative Power Europe: A Contradiction in Terms?' (2002) 40 *Journal of Common Market Studies* 235, 240 (emphasis added).

[8] J McCormick, *The European Superpower* (Palgrave Macmillan, 2007).

century'.[9] Others see it as a 'freakishly oversized "middle power"',[10] or merely a small power,[11] which may be already 'past its peak',[12] facing decline and ultimately irrelevance.[13] In particular, given the distinctive nature of the EU and its legal order, being 'less than a state, but certainly more than a classic international organization'[14] (see Chapter 3, section 2), a debate has emerged concerning the alleged or rejected distinctiveness of the Union as a political actor. This resulted in several conceptual propositions to grasp the Union's nature as an international actor, according to which the EU and its predecessors are successively presented as a 'civilian power',[15] a 'normative power',[16] as an entity employing 'structural foreign policy',[17] and as an 'ethical power'.[18] What all these concepts have in common is the distinction of the Union from a 'classic' power, which follows only its own 'national interest' in the conduct of its foreign policy.[19] The differences between these diverse concepts will be addressed in greater detail below. Before doing so, it must be stressed, as Karen Smith aptly observed, that such assessments of the EU 'depend quite substantially on one's views on the nature of the international system'.[20] Hence, it is worthwhile briefly recalling the core aspects of these different views, which will serve as the backdrop for the subsequent sections.

Traditionally, three major theoretical schools can be distinguished: realism, liberalism, and constructivism, in addition to the theories specifically aimed at explaining European integration.[21] This chapter assumes a bird's eye perspective in contextualizing constitutional foreign policy objectives with the main IR theories, which cannot—and does not claim to—do justice to the depth and wealth of different strands within IR theories. This applies in particular to constructivist and other critical thinking. Constructivism should not be regarded as a homogenous

[9] M Leonard, *Why Europe Will Run the 21st Century* (Fourth Estate, 2005).

[10] A Hyde-Price, 'A Neurotic "Centaur": The Limitations of the EU as a Strategic Actor' in K Engelbrekt and J Hallenberg (eds), *The European Union and Strategy: An Emerging Actor* (Routledge, 2008) 162.

[11] A Toje, *The European Union as a Small Power: After the Post-Cold War* (Palgrave Macmillan, 2010).

[12] C Bretherton and J Vogler, 'Past Its Peak? The European Union as a Global Actor 10 Years after' in F Laursen (ed), *The EU as a Foreign and Security Policy Actor* (Republic of Letters, 2009).

[13] R Youngs, *Europe's Decline and Fall: The Struggle Against Global Irrelevance* (Profile Books, 2010).

[14] H Sjursen, *'Doing Good' in the World? Reconsidering the Basis of the Research Agenda on the EU's Foreign and Security Policy*, RECON Online Working Paper 2007/09, 3; also C Hill and M Smith, 'International Relations and the European Union: Themes and Issues' in C Hill and M Smith (eds), *International Relations and the European Union*, 2nd edn (OUP, 2011) 4.

[15] F Duchêne, 'Europe's Role in World Peace' in R Mayne (ed), *Europe Tomorrow: Sixteen Europeans Look Ahead* (Fontana, 1972).

[16] Manners (n 7).

[17] Keukeleire and Delreux (n 1) 28, which they define as 'a foreign policy which, conducted over the long-term, aims at sustainably influencing or shaping political, legal, economic, social, security or other structures in a given space'.

[18] L Aggestam, 'Introduction: Ethical Power Europe' (2008) 84 *International Affairs* 1.

[19] Sjursen (n 14) 3.

[20] K Smith, *European Union Foreign Policy in a Changing World*, 2nd edn (Cambridge: Polity, 2008) 13.

[21] This distinction follows F Andreatta, 'The European Union's International Relations: A Theoretical View' in C Hill and M Smith (eds), *International Relations and the European Union*, 2nd edn (OUP, 2011).

theory, but represents rather a meta-theoretical approach. Nevertheless, an emphasis on the relevance and explanatory force of norms and ideas, as well as the theorization of rules and law,[22] can be viewed as a feature common to most, if not all, constructivist thinking.[23]

Only rather recently has IR theory begun to address the European Union as a notable phenomenon in international politics. For a long time, it was merely seen as an anomaly that did not fit into paradigms designed around states as the primordial actors.[24] Adding constitutionalism as a characteristic of the integration process did not facilitate the relationship between IR theory and the EU. As JHH Weiler observed, not only has IR scholarship already 'had a fickle relationship with European integration',[25] but in addition, the 'advent of constitutionalism is to international-relations experts in the field what *perestroika* was to Sovietologists'.[26] This already reveals a parallel with an attitude of 'state-centrism' in international law,[27] but also with EU law in respect to the doubts that persist concerning the ability of the Union to boast a 'constitutional' legal order. Traditionally this is considered to be an attribute reserved only for states (see Chapter 3, section 2.4). Anything other than a state, consequently, would have difficulties in presenting itself either as an international actor or as having constitutional credentials.

The EU and its predecessors were therefore first addressed by integration theories. These theories were aimed at providing explanations (or at times, normative prescriptions) for this peculiar regional phenomenon. They can be divided roughly into federalism and functionalism. Federalism was premised on a 'domestic analogy', ie the ultimate formation of a European (federal) state by virtue of a grand design, likely culminating in a fateful 'constitutional moment'. Functionalism envisaged a similar end point, but conceived of the way to reach it as a gradual, incremental process starting with integration in areas of allegedly politically uncontroversial 'low politics', which would proverbially 'spill over' into other policy areas, including the 'high politics' of foreign and defence policy.[28] In both cases, the proclaimed end result was a European 'superstate, eventually with its own security and defence policy'.[29] What role such an integrated Europe would

[22] See A Sinclair, *International Relations Theory and International Law* (CUP, 2010) 7–36.

[23] For an overview see I Hurd, 'Constructivism' in C Reus-Smit and D Snidal (eds), *The Oxford Handbook of International Relations* (OUP, 2010) 299–309.

[24] Andreatta (n 21) 22.

[25] JHH Weiler, *The Constitution of Europe: 'Do the New Clothes Have an Emperor?' and Other Essays on European Integration* (CUP, 1999) 226.

[26] Weiler (n 25) 227 (italics in the original).

[27] See eg S Marks, 'State-Centrism, International Law, and the Anxieties of Influence' (2006) 19 *Leiden Journal of International Law* 339.

[28] Seminally E Haas, *The Uniting of Europe: Political, Social, and Economic Forces 1950–1957* (Stanford University Press, 1958); further W Sandholtz and A Stone Sweet, 'Neofunctionalism and Supranational Governance' in E Jones, A Menon, and S Weatherill (eds), *The Oxford Handbook of the European Union* (OUP, 2012).

[29] Andreatta (n 21) 24. But note also that others argue that statehood need not be the inevitable result of the integration process, eg D Mitrany, 'The Prospect of Integration: Federal or Functional?' in A Groom and P Taylor (eds), *Functionalism: Theory and Practice in International Relations* (University of London Press, 1975). Also historically, unifying and pacifying Europe was not automatically linked to statehood. Rather, as the example of the political thought of Abbé de Saint-Pierre shows, it was

play in the world was another question. While there may have been a vague notion that it might serve as a model for the rest of the world in integration theories, for a long time the Union (or at the time, the Community) was not accounted for within the international system.

In the early 1970s, following the failure of the envisaged European Defence Community and European Political Community, a grand European 'constitutional moment' remained wanting. In addition, instead of a supranational 'spillover' into the area of foreign and defence policy, European Political Cooperation (EPC) developed along intergovernmental lines. Both of these experiences can be said to have paved the way for theoretical approaches 'more in tune with the broader paradigms of international relations theory'.[30] Thus, the two principal schools at the time, realism and liberalism, began to 'come to terms with European integration in general and with the role of European institutions in the world in particular'.[31]

Realism, building on the idea of a Hobbesian 'state of nature', focuses on states as the predominant—if not solely relevant—units of international politics operating in a world characterized by anarchy and the quest for survival rather than mutual trust, rules, norms, or ideals. This view puts an emphasis on power politics (*Realpolitik*), balancing (relative gains as opposed to absolute gains), and the constant prospect and reality of war as the hallmarks of the international system.[32]

Consequently, the EU and its attempts at a common foreign policy, let alone at becoming a world power, were viewed with scepticism.[33] Again, European statehood, or some other form of 'radical change',[34] was deemed necessary for the EU to become a 'true' power in international relations. Should this happen, it too was expected to start balancing other powers, including the United States.[35] Hence, the true international ambitions of the EU, once it would become a great power, would be located somewhere between survival and power maximization.

For some realist scholars, the EU, as it currently operates, represents a disguise for the persisting ambitions and interests of the Member States. Integration was seen as a by-product of the hegemony exercised, and consequent protection offered, by the United States in the West during the Cold War, set against the background of a bipolar system.[36] This is also the underpinning idea of the 'transatlantic bargain',

seen as a way to overcome the rationale of the balance of power as a result of statehood and (absolute) sovereignty. See P Schröder, 'The Holy Roman Empire as a Model for Saint-Pierre's *Projet pour rendre la paix perpétuelle en Europe*' in R Evans and P Wilson (eds), *The Holy Roman Empire, 1495–1806: A European Perspective* (Brill, 2012).

[30] Andreatta (n 21) 26. [31] Andreatta (n 21) 26.

[32] Andreatta (n 21) 27; see in detail W Wohlforth, 'Realism' in C Reus-Smit and D Snidal (eds), *The Oxford Handbook of International Relations* (OUP, 2010); and J Donnelly, *Realism and International Relations* (CUP, 2000).

[33] See, for instance, K Waltz, *Theory of International Politics* (Random House, 1979) 180, stating that for Western Europe, '[u]nity will not come tomorrow, and if it did, Europe would not instantly achieve stardom'.

[34] K Waltz, 'Structural Realism after the Cold War' (2000) 25 *International Security* 5, 32.

[35] B Posen, 'European Union Security and Defense Policy: Response to Unipolarity?' (2006) 15 *Security Studies* 149.

[36] Andreatta (n 21) 29.

meaning 'that the United States would contribute to the defence of Europe and to Europe's economic recovery from the war if the Europeans would organize themselves to help defend against the Soviet threat and use economic aid efficiently'.[37] An integrated Europe is thus part of the security strategy of the Western European states. In the aftermath of the Cold War, realism offered another explanation for integration, including in the area of EU foreign policy, ie attempts by other European countries to constrain Germany.[38]

Liberal theory, employing a less gloomy 'world view', asserts that next to states, other actors exert influence on the international stage, including supranational organizations such as the EU, as well as corporations, individuals, and non-governmental organizations. It also highlights the importance of domestic politics and its links to the international sphere. Consequently, it posits that international anarchy and distrust can be mitigated through cooperation, networks, and institutions, and stresses the importance of economic factors and gains (ie absolute as opposed to relative) instead of focusing solely on pure (military) power politics.[39] In doing so, it reveals the individual ambitions of institutional actors across different levels of governance.

For the European Union, this means that it is perceived as less of an unusual international actor and considered more likely to succeed on the world stage given its economic clout. Furthermore, the continuing importance of states within the Union can be more easily accounted for. According to liberal intergovernmentalism, European integration provides for a sophisticated 'two-level game', in which the executive branches of the Member States, as players on both levels, attempt to maximize their own autonomy.[40] The autonomy that governments traditionally enjoy in the domain of foreign policy is then used to explain the absence of supranational integration in this area.[41] Given the focus on economics, European integration and international actorness are seen as a logical consequence of, and response to, growing 'interdependence'[42] and globalization.[43]

According to more recent criticisms, both realism and liberalism share an excessive focus on positive, exogenous factors (military or otherwise) and the unquestioned assumption of the rationality of actors (state and non-state alike). With a

[37] S Sloan, *NATO, the European Union, and the Atlantic Community: The Transatlantic Bargain Challenged*, 2nd edn (Rowman & Littlefield, 2005) 1.

[38] See eg J Grieco, 'State Interests and Institutional Rule Trajectories: A Neorealist Interpretation of the Maastricht Treaty and European Economic and Monetary Union' (1996) 5 *Security Studies* 261.

[39] Andreatta (n 21) 27; further A Stein, 'Neoliberal Institutionalism' in C Reus-Smit and D Snidal (eds), *The Oxford Handbook of International Relations* (OUP, 2010); and A Moravcsik, 'The New Liberalism' in C Reus-Smit and D Snidal (eds), *The Oxford Handbook of International Relations* (OUP, 2010).

[40] Seminally A Moravcsik, *The Choice for Europe: Social Purpose and State Power from Messina to Maastricht* (UCL Press, 1999).

[41] Andreatta (n 21) 34.

[42] On the concept of interdependence, seminally R Keohane and J Nye, *Power and Interdependence: World Politics in Transition* (Little, Brown, 1977).

[43] See eg M Zürn, 'Democratic Governance Beyond the Nation-State: The EU and Other International Institutions' (2000) 6 *European Journal of International Relations* 183.

view to remedying this overemphasis, constructivist and other critical approaches 'consider actors' motives as an "endogenous" variable dependent on certain cognitive conditions'.[44] They stress the importance of 'the social origins of behaviour' and 'the power of ideational variables'.[45] This means that beyond the mathematical rigidity of balancing finite capabilities or operating sequential games in a payoff matrix, the interaction between different actors changes and gradually aligns their respective 'world views' and ambitions. In other words, the ideas and perceptions that motivate their actions start to change in a process of so-called 'socialization'.[46]

The European Union, consequently, provides a fertile ground for such socialization processes among Member States (and other actors), including in the domain of foreign policy. This has given rise to the term 'Europeanization'.[47] From this point of view, the EU and its Member States would project their integration model developed internally and the ideas that buttress it to the wider world. This would contribute to changing the international order itself, away from an anarchical system towards an 'international society',[48] or, to use Robert Cooper's term, a 'post-modern' world.[49]

This 'post-positivist'[50] turn in the assessment of Europe's role on the international stage was the point of departure for Ian Manners' elaboration of conceiving of the EU as a 'normative power'. Moving beyond the dichotomy of an emphasis on either military or civilian power, he observed that 'both value direct physical power in the form of actual empirical capabilities'.[51] With the demise of the Cold War system of international relations, and reflecting on the reasons for this demise, Manners urged for stronger emphasis 'on the power of ideas and norms rather than the power of empirical force—in other words the role of normative power'.[52] According to Manners, the distinctive power of the European Union resides not in its ability to coerce, but instead in 'its ability to shape conceptions of "normal" international relations',[53] meaning what matters 'is not what it does or what it says, but what it is'.[54]

Subsequently, the passiveness that underpins this concept has been criticized. This is because the concept seems to disregard the fact that the EU has come to

[44] Andreatta (n 21) 36. [45] Andreatta (n 21) 36.

[46] See in detail I Hurd, 'Constructivism' in C Reus-Smit and D Snidal (eds), *The Oxford Handbook of International Relations* (OUP, 2010).

[47] See R Wong, 'The Europeanization of Foreign Policy' in C Hill and M Smith (eds), *International Relations and the European Union*, 2nd edn (OUP, 2011).

[48] Andreatta (n 21) 37. The term 'international society' originates from the English School of International Relations (also known as liberal realism), which was still rather sceptical of cooperation at the international level, and of the EU as a power. See H Bull, *The Anarchical Society: A Study of Order in World Politics* (Macmillan, 1977); and with regard to the EU, H Bull, 'Civilian Power Europe: A Contradiction in Terms?' (1982) 21 *Journal of Common Market Studies* 149.

[49] R Cooper, *The Post-modern State and the World Order* (Demos, 2000).

[50] Andreatta (n 21) 36. [51] Manners (n 7) 238.

[52] Manners (n 7) 238. Note also S Lukes, *Power: A Radical View*, 2nd edn (Palgrave Macmillan, 2004) 108 et seq on the multidimensionality of power including economic/military (coercive) capabilities, agenda setting power, and background conditions that are not always consciously acknowledged but may nevertheless exert significant influence.

[53] Manners (n 7) 239. [54] Manners (n 7) 252.

conduct its external relations not only by civilian means, but also by newly acquired military ones, in particular in view of the emergence of the Common Security and Defence Policy (known pre-Lisbon as the European Security and Defence Policy (ESDP)).[55] Consequently, the notion of the EU as an 'ethical power' was put forward. It asserts that norms, values, and ideals can indeed underpin EU foreign policy, but at the same time that the EU is 'proactively working to change the world in the direction of its vision of the "global common good"',[56] instead of simply 'being' a normative force of attraction.

In sum, the different theories of international relations offer a variety of sophisticated 'world views' with distinct emphases on what constitutes and characterizes the international system, and what drives the actors within it. Looking at the European Union as an international actor through these different theoretical lenses yields contrasting results, ranging from small power to great power, and from military dwarf to normative giant.[57] At the same time, it casts the international ambitions of the EU in rather different shades, ie either as an actor in its own right vying for power, a framework of governance in which institutional actors and groups compete for influence, or as a metaphoric beacon radiating its values into other parts of the world.

The preceding chapters of this book focused on the 'world view' that is codified in European constitutional law. Contextualizing this constitutional 'world view' with theories of international relations raises two main questions. Firstly, how does the 'world view' exhibited by the foreign policy objectives in the EU Treaties cater to these different theories? Secondly, what do these theories have to say about the importance and function of such constitutional norms?

3. Realism

The tenets of realist approaches find some vindication in the constitutional foreign policy objectives of the EU, especially as regards acknowledging the importance of 'interests', as well as security remaining a quintessential state objective. Conversely, realist scholarship is prone to remain highly sceptical of both the EU as a 'normative power' and the importance of its constitutional foreign policy objectives. This is mainly due to realism's focus on states as the basic unit and (military) power as the only solid currency in the international system. From this point of view, the importance of constitutional foreign policy objectives, especially in the case of a non-state entity such as the EU, can only appear as being of negligible significance.

[55] See Manners' reaction and critical stance on the risk of 'militarization' of the EU and its potential for weakening its 'normative power': I Manners, 'Normative Power Europe Reconsidered: Beyond the Crossroads' (2006) 13 *Journal of European Public Policy* 182.

[56] Aggestam (n 18) 1.

[57] To paraphrase Belgian Foreign Minister Mark Eyskens, who in 1991 remarked that the European Community was 'an economic giant, a political dwarf, and a military worm', quoted in J McCormick, *Understanding the European Union: A Concise Introduction*, 6th edn (Palgrave Macmillan, 2014) 196.

3.1 Scope for *Realpolitik* and security as a state objective

Whereas the common criticisms from legal discourse are addressed to the more ambitious and ostensibly normative objectives found in constitutional law (calling them a 'wish list for a better world'[58] or 'motherhood and apple pie'[59]), EU constitutional law in fact leaves ample room for power politics and the defence of 'interests'. Moreover, the set-up of the European constitutional space bolsters rather than refutes the idea of security as a fundamental state objective, which is not readily delegated to the supranational or international levels.

As to the first point, next to the promotion of its values, the TEU mandates the Union to uphold and promote its 'interests'.[60] This is reiterated in the first goal on the list of foreign policy objectives found in Art 21 TEU, which obliges the Union to 'safeguard its values, fundamental interests, security, independence and integrity'.[61]

Since it is rather rare for a national constitution to speak of the national interest in its foreign policy,[62] it may be seen as a matter of course that the state pursues its national interest through foreign policy. However, the different origin and nature of the Union may warrant being more explicit in this respect. The fact that the 'interest' of the Union in the world ranks among its codified objectives brings it closer to the state and its role in the world according to realism. At the same time, it challenges all three concepts of 'civilian', 'normative', and 'ethical power Europe'. The Treaties do not explicate that these interests are to be pursued only through civilian means, but instead provide for the CSDP and the Petersberg Tasks. Moreover, they do not stipulate that EU external action is to be conducted exclusively in the pursuit of normative or ethical ends. In other words, the Treaties condone foreign policy that is self-interested. Nevertheless, there is no clear preference for such an 'egoistic' foreign policy either, as the 'Union interest' has to be pursued in accordance with the overarching principle of coherence.

Furthermore, beyond the textual reference to the defence of the 'Union interest', the limited legal force which applies to all foreign policy objectives (the accentuated caveat of possibility) reserves ample room for *Realpolitik* and the pursuit of its own interests. In a manner similar to the national setting, EU constitutional

[58] In the original: 'Wunschzettel für eine bessere Welt': W Drescher, 'Ziele und Zuständigkeiten' in A Marchetti and C Demesmay (eds), *Der Vertrag von Lissabon: Analyse und Bewertung* (Nomos, 2010) 68.

[59] A Dashwood et al, *Wyatt & Dashwood's European Union Law*, 6th edn (Hart Publishing, 2011) 903.

[60] Art 3(5) TEU.

[61] Art 21(2)(a) TEU. Note also the reference to 'the strategic interests and objectives of the Union', which are to be identified by the European Council: Art 22(1), first subpara TEU.

[62] See for the exceptions from among the constitutions surveyed previously, Art 97(1) Netherlands constitution ('There shall be armed forces for the defence and protection of the interests of the Kingdom, and in order to maintain and promote the international legal order.'); see also Art 89 No 12 Chinese constitution, which refers to the interests of Chinese citizens (listing as one of the functions of the State Council (government) '[t]o protect the legitimate rights and interests of Chinese nationals residing abroad'; and Art 101(1) Swiss constitution ('The Confederation safeguards the interests of the Swiss economy abroad.').

objectives have only a rather limited constraining force, while their main function resides in interpreting the constitution in a way that enlarges public powers. This is especially true in the field of foreign policy. Therefore, depending on the context, any objective codified in the Treaties can be invoked as a justification for the conduct of certain Union policies. For instance, the 'scope for manoeuvre' of the legislative and executive Union organs to conduct a Common Commercial Policy (CCP) can be invoked in order to deny the direct applicability of certain rules of international law.[63] In other instances, compliance with international law or the promotion of human rights and democracy are drawn on by the political branches of the Union to justify restrictions of individual rights within the Union legal order.[64]

However, as elaborated upon in Chapter 4, the 'Union interest' can have a significant constraining effect on the ability of the Member States to pursue their interests internationally. The CJEU stressed in *Opinion 1/75* with reference to the operation of the Common Market that 'for the defence of the common interests of the Community ... the particular interests of the Member States must endeavour to adapt to each other'.[65] In some circumstances this may mean, as the Court ruled in another case, that on the global stage EU competences are to be 'exercised through the medium of the Member States acting jointly in the [then] Community's interest'.[66]

Another tenet of realism is upheld by the enquiry into constitutional foreign policy objectives. This concerns security as a fundamental objective for *states*, as opposed to other objectives and as opposed to other forms of political organizations that could pursue it. There are numerous examples from national constitutions that specifically make security a state objective, including in the area of foreign policy. This includes the protection of citizens abroad. Notably, the only hint at a codified foreign policy objective to be found in the United States constitution of 1787 is to 'provide for the common defence'.[67]

Security also features as a prominent objective in the EU Treaties.[68] The CFSP/CSDP is to cover 'all questions relating to the Union's security'[69] while the Member States are called upon to 'refrain from any action which is contrary to the interests of the Union'.[70] However, this does not include a common defence,[71] and the CSDP remains, also as stipulated clearly in the Treaties, dependent on the assets of the Member States.[72] In all questions of security, the Member States retain a

[63] Case C-149/96 *Portugal v Council*, EU:C:1999:574, para 47; see further A Tancredi, 'EC Practice in the WTO: How Wide is the "Scope for Manoeuvre"?' (2004) 15 *European Journal of International Law* 933.

[64] See, for instance, the measures at stake and arguments used by the Council and Commission in Joined Cases C-402/05 P and C-415/05 P *Kadi and Al Barakaat*, EU:C:2008:461; Case C-376/10 P *Tay Za*, EU:C:2012:138; and Case C-220/14 P *Ahmed Abdelaziz Ezz*, EU:C:2015:147.

[65] Opinion 1/75 *(Local Cost Standard)*, EU:C:1975:145, 1363–4.

[66] Opinion 2/91 *(ILO Convention No 170)*, EU:C:1993:106, 1076.

[67] Preamble, United States constitution.

[68] See Arts 3(5) and 21(2)(a) and (c) TEU.

[69] Art 24(1), first subpara TEU.

[70] Art 24(3), second subpara TEU.

[71] Art 42(2), first subpara TEU.

[72] Art 42(1) TEU.

strong voice within the Union, not least due to unanimity among them being the basic rule, while they remain relatively free to act internationally when compared to other areas of EU external action.

Hence, this confirms Karl-Peter Sommermann's observation of security as the most fundamental objective of the state.[73] Regardless of the criticisms of the other IR theories against 'state-centrism' and an excessive focus on survival, the dynamic internationalization as well as the Europeanization of constitutional law have not changed, but rather confirm, that security represents primarily a state objective.

3.2 The limits of law and the futility of good intentions

The very idea that law would be able to tame an anarchical system is anathema to the core of realism, with (neo)realists being 'generally dismissive of law and ethics'.[74] Both law and norms, consequently, have merely a distinctly secondary role to play.[75] Instead, the proverbial 'law of the jungle'[76] is said to prevail beyond the borders of the state.[77] Even Cooper acknowledges that when dealing with 'modern' as opposed to 'post-modern' states, '[i]n the jungle, one must use the laws of the jungle'.[78] This coincides with the idea that while law may have some function and merit domestically, the same cannot be said for the regulation of foreign affairs. This is because of the widespread perception 'that "it's a jungle out there"', which is said to be inherently 'different' from the domestic arena.[79] Therefore, whatever else may be stipulated in constitutions or elsewhere, the actual functions of the state in its international relations are a given, ie above all self-preservation. For realist scholars, states thus do not differ in terms of their basic objectives. Instead, what matters is the distribution of capabilities among them.[80] Any moral aspirations beyond survival, consequently, must take a back seat.[81]

In the domain of IR, this strict distinction between the foreign and the domestic has been criticized as 'drawing a line in the water'.[82] In the legal domain, the

[73] K-P Sommermann, *Staatsziele und Staatszielbestimmungen* (Mohr Siebeck, 1997) 3; also R Herzog, 'Ziele, Vorbehalte und Grenzen der Staatlichkeit' in J Isensee and P Kirchhof (eds), *Handbuch des Staatsrechts der Bundesrepublik Deutschland. Volume IV: Aufgaben des Staates*, 3rd edn (C.F. Müllller, 2006) 91–2.

[74] Ratner (n 2) 23.

[75] R Gilpin, 'The Richness of the Tradition of Political Realism' in R Keohane (ed), *Neorealism and Its Critics* (Columbia University Press, 1986) 304.

[76] FL Schuman, *International Politics: The Western State System in Transition*, 3rd edn (McGraw-Hill, 1941) 9.

[77] See in particular the useful collection of definitions of realism in Donnelly (n 32) 7–8.

[78] Cooper (n 49) 62.

[79] T Franck, *Political Questions/Judicial Answers: Does the Rule of Law Apply to Foreign Affairs?* (Princeton University Press, 1992) 14; also A-M Slaughter Burley, 'Are Foreign Affairs Different?' (1993) 106 *Harvard Law Review* 1980, 1981; and A Hurrell and T Macdonald, 'Ethics and Norms in International Relations' in W Carlsnaes, T Risse, and B Simmons (eds), *Handbook of International Relations*, 2nd edn (SAGE, 2013) 58.

[80] Waltz (n 33) 96.

[81] In detail Donnelly (n 32) 161–88.

[82] K Goldmann, 'The Line in Water: International and Domestic Politics' (1989) 24 *Cooperation and Conflict* 103, 103.

categorical distinction between an allegedly 'idealized' domestic legal order and an imperfect and deficient international legal order has also been disputed.[83] Constitutional law in particular, as Jack Goldsmith and Daryl Levinson argue, shares many of the key characteristics of international law.[84] Provisions from both tend to be formulated in vague terms and are often not directly enforceable. Nevertheless, this domestic/international distinction remains a central tenet of realism.

As constitutional foreign policy objectives represent the legally codified and entrenched norms concerning state functions in the conduct of its international relations, often with a characteristic moral ring to them, this would already suffice for a realist to discard them. The fact that such norms hail from a non-state entity such as the EU would only reinforce that conclusion. Hence, it is safe to assume that through the eyes of a realist scholar, constitutional foreign policy objectives of the European Union cannot but appear as the ultimate 'dustbin of sentiment',[85] or, at most, as a pretext for the pursuit of core interests.[86]

Indeed, realism turns a deaf ear to the role of both law and 'VIPs' (values, images, and principles)[87] in international relations, especially with regard to the EU. On the one hand, the fact that such constitutional norms leave plenty of leeway and acknowledge the importance of the defence of interests and the safeguarding of security is thus a mere restatement of the 'natural' laws which already govern interstate relations.[88] On the other, the more ambitious, more morally laden objectives would appear as mere hubris. Their pursuit would not be conditioned and limited by, as legal scholarship would have it, 'structural principles' of the respective legal order, but simply by the necessity to cater to 'first-order interests (primarily associated with … security and prosperity)'.[89] As Kenneth Waltz poignantly noted:

[83] M Kumm, 'The Cosmopolitan Turn in Constitutionalism: On the Relationship Between Constitutionalism in and Beyond the State' in J Dunoff and J Trachtman (eds), *Ruling the World? International Law, Global Governance, Constitutionalism* (CUP, 2009).

[84] J Goldsmith and D Levinson, 'Law for States: International Law, Constitutional Law, Public Law' (2009) 122 *Harvard Law Review* 1791. See also on the Schmittian analogy of constitutional and international law as inherently 'political law', L Vinx, 'Carl Schmitt and the Analogy between Constitutional and International Law: Are Constitutional and International Law Inherently Political?' (2013) 2 *Global Constitutionalism* 91.

[85] To use TT Krishnamachari's words at the Indian Constituent Assembly on Indian 'directive principles of state policy', as quoted in O Chinnappa Reddy, *The Court and the Constitution of India: Summits and Shallows* (OUP, 2010) 17.

[86] Realists might still have interest in the use of norms to the extent that they can be instrumentalized to further a state's interests: see WJ Korab-Karpowicz, 'Political Realism in International Relations' in E Zalta (ed), *The Stanford Encyclopedia of Philosophy*, Summer 2013 edn, <http://plato.stanford.edu/archives/sum2013/entries/realism-intl-relations/>.

[87] S Lucarelli, 'Introduction: Values, Principles, Identity and European Union Foreign Policy' in S Lucarelli and I Manners (eds), *Values and Principles in European Union Foreign Policy* (Routledge, 2006) 1.

[88] This is not 'natural law' in the sense of Thomas Aquinas.

[89] A Hyde-Price, 'A "Tragic Actor"? A Realist Perspective on "Ethical Power Europe"' (2008) 84 *International Affairs* 29, 31; see on a similar 'hierarchy of state goals', J Mearsheimer, *The Tragedy of Great Power Politics* (W.W. Norton, 2001) 46–8.

Because states coexist in a self-help system, they are free to do any fool thing they care to, but they are likely to be rewarded for behaviour that is responsive to structural pressures and punished for behaviour that is not.[90]

Thus, both states and the EU are free to put whatever they like into their constitutions in terms of foreign policy goals, but it would be foolish to believe that this would have any bearing on the 'structural pressures' of the international system.

The explanatory force of realism serves as a reminder not to overstate the power of law and ideals in foreign policy, especially in situations of crisis. According to Hans Morgenthau, realism highlights a sharp distinction 'between what is desirable everywhere and at all times and what is possible under the concrete circumstances of time and place'.[91] Therefore, realism bolsters the idea of an accentuated caveat of possibility, which applies to constitutional foreign policy objectives, more than any other IR theory.

This brings to mind also the 'capabilities–expectations gap', from which the EU has been said to suffer.[92] Realism cautions against falling victim to exaggerated expectations of the EU as an international actor through the enticement of fervent constitutional declarations, or any other expression of the global aspirations of the Union. Ultimately, the EU remains dependent on the power structures and the goodwill of other major international players.[93] Rather than a power in its own right, in the words of Adrian Hyde-Price, the EU 'serves as the institutional repository of the second order normative and ethical concerns of its member states'.[94] This, in turn, puts the Treaties and their wealth of ambitious foreign policy objectives in a different light, ie as the legally codified 'repository' of such *second order* concerns rather than the *primary* law it represents for constitutional scholars.

From this point of view, instead of being a distinctive 'normative' or 'ethical power', the EU appears as a secondary option which the Member States only choose when it is desirable. In this vein, realists explain the failure of the EU to act or assert itself in crucial moments of international politics, such as the collapse of Yugoslavia, the 2003 Iraq war, or the 2011 Libyan civil war, and the fact that it lacks a common defence, despite the EU's activism in the 'low politics' of trade and low-intensity crisis management through the CSDP.[95]

[90] K Waltz, 'Evaluating Theories' (1997) 91 *American Political Science Review* 913, 915.

[91] H Morgenthau, *Politics Among Nations: The Struggle for Power and Peace*, 7th edn (McGraw-Hill Higher Education, 2006) 6.

[92] C Hill, 'The Capability-Expectations Gap, or Conceptualising Europe's International Role' (1993) 31 *Journal of Common Market Studies* 305.

[93] As argued by R Kagan, *Of Paradise and Power: America and Europe in the New World Order* (Alfred A. Knopf, 2003); see also Hyde-Price (n 10) 156–7.

[94] Hyde-Price (n 89) 31.

[95] See eg A Hyde-Price, 'Neorealism' in X Kurowska and F Breuer (eds), *Explaining the EU's Common Security and Defence Policy: Theory in Action* (Palgrave Macmillan, 2012); and A Hyde-Price, '"Normative" Power Europe: A Realist Critique' (2008) 13 *Journal of European Public Policy* 217. For a neoclassical realist view, see J-Y Haine, 'The Rise and Fall of the Common Security and Defence Policy: Bringing Strategic Culture Back In' in A Toje and B Kunz (eds), *Neoclassical Realism in European Politics: Bringing Power Back In* (Manchester University Press, 2012). See also A Menon, 'European Defence Policy from Lisbon to Libya' (2011) 53 *Survival* 75.

Scepticism towards the role of law in international relations is by no means foreign to legal scholarship, where warnings of an excessive confidence in international law have also been issued.[96] These criticisms of international law normally refer to the lack of centralized enforcement and the prevailing notion of the national interest. This provides a somewhat different view of constitutionalism in the EU. In essence, because it is seen as fundamentally different to classic international law due to its legal order with supremacy, direct effect, and sophisticated institutional apparatus (Chapter 3, section 2.4), it simply can no longer be international law. By this reasoning, it must be something more akin to the state.

However, the 'dynamic internationalization' of constitutional law poses a challenge to realism in that the scepticism towards international law would need to be applied to *constitutional* law as well. Realism maintains a strict distinction between internally domesticated 'politics' and the anarchical external 'jungle'. In the past, the presence of a constitution could have served as a confirmation for this, as it was concerned precisely and exclusively with governing internal power allocation and dispute resolution. Whatever was governed by the constitution could be considered 'domestic', whereas international law struggled to regulate, with merely moderate success, international relations. The constitution, in this sense, was the 'line in the water'[97] that separated the two spheres. However, today this is no longer the case in view of the 'dynamic internationalization' of constitutional law around the world. On the contrary, constitutions, including the EU Treaties, explicitly demand the 'translation' of internal features to the international 'jungle', which in many cases they also specify, such as the rule of law and peaceful dispute settlement. This leaves realists with a choice of either dismissing constitutional law as well or adopting a more benign view on law in general.

4. Liberalism

EU constitutional law lends credence to three main focus areas of liberalism: democratic peace, the importance of commerce, and the key role of international institutions. At the same time, liberal theory helps to explain the way these constitutional norms are used as justificatory devices in internal two-level politics and litigation.

4.1 Commerce, democratic peace, and the importance of institutions

Regarding both the 'democratic peace' and 'commercial' strands in liberal scholarship, the very outset of European integration and the first external relations objectives that were codified in the founding treaties were indeed about 'peace' and 'free trade' (Chapter 2, section 3.1). The constitutional emphasis on 'the harmonious

[96] J Goldsmith and E Posner, *The Limits of International Law* (OUP, 2005).
[97] Goldmann (n 82) 103.

development of world trade, the progressive abolition of restrictions on international trade',[98] and 'free and fair trade'[99] serve to highlight that balancing and relative power gains are not the only considerations in foreign policy. Absolute gains from trading relationships also matter. The Treaties thus reflect the importance of economic cooperation, both internally through the common market and with the rest of an increasingly interdependent world. Liberal theorists claim that such interdependence has an effect on 'the traditional conception of "national interest" '.[100]

Constitutional objectives are the legal expression of the 'common interest' and 'common good' of a given political community. As the 'internationalization' of such norms shows, the 'common good' can no longer be viewed in isolation from wider, possibly global notions of a *bonum commune*. The evolution of both EU competences and objectives in the area of trade serve as constitutional testimony that the process of interdependence and globalization of the economy, as well as other sectors of transnational interaction, are advancing. Next to the traditional trade in goods, today's Common Commercial Policy also covers trade in services, foreign direct investment, and regulatory aspects,[101] and has to be 'conducted in the context of the principles and objectives of the Union's external action'.[102]

The idea of democratic peace, which has its origin in Kantian republicanism, already finds its expression in EU law in the Treaty establishing the European Coal and Steel Community. Inspired by the Schuman Declaration, the Treaty made peace the prime objective of the project of European integration. A conceptual overlap exists between democratic peace theory and legal scholarship, which highlights the importance of domestic structures and politics for the conduct of foreign policy and legal discourse. Recalling the writings of Hans Kelsen, the 'world view' of the state is engrained in its law and will consequently guide its behaviour internationally.[103] Walter Hallstein, furthermore, stressed the pacificatory function of the 'rule of law'.[104] For liberal scholars, accordingly, 'norms prescribing peaceful conflict resolution' are an integral part of the idea of democratic peace.[105]

It was stressed in the Schuman Declaration and the founding Treaties that European integration was not only about peace in Europe but also a contribution to 'world peace',[106] which is compatible with the idea of democratic peace as a global project. In terms of constitutional objectives, these can today be found in the provisions of the Treaties that are part of its internal values and mandate

[98] Art 206 TFEU. [99] Art 3(5) TEU. [100] Andreatta (n 21) 35.

[101] See the post-Lisbon case law of the CJEU, which confirms that broad scope of the CCP: Case C-414/11 *Daiichi Sankyo*, EU:C:2013:520; and Case C-137/12 *Commission v Council (European Convention on the legal protection of services based on, or consisting of, conditional access)*, EU:C:2013:675.

[102] Art 207(1) TFEU. See further A Dimopoulos, 'The Effects of the Lisbon Treaty on the Principles and Objectives of the Common Commercial Policy' (2010) 15 *European Foreign Affairs Review* 153, 166–7.

[103] H Kelsen, *Essays in Legal and Moral Philosophy* (D. Reidel, 1973) 95–113.

[104] W Hallstein, *Die Europäische Gemeinschaft*, 5th edn (Econ Verlag, 1979) 53.

[105] Andreatta (n 21) 32.

[106] Schuman Declaration, 9 May 1950; and First recital of the preamble, ECSC Treaty.

the Union to promote peace, democracy, and the rule of law through its external action.[107] Constitutional mandates to create and promote structures beyond one's own legal order that are based on the values and principles which are internal to that legal order are referred to here as the 'translation function' of constitutional objectives. The EU Treaties put a particular emphasis on the 'translation' of its internal values into foreign policy (Chapter 2, section 4). The TEU states explicitly that EU 'action on the international scene shall be guided by the principles which have inspired its own creation, development and enlargement'.[108] Democratic peace, against this backdrop, is nothing other than 'translating' the condition of internal peace into the neighbourhood,[109] as well as into the world at large.

It is true that to some extent every great power can be said to pursue its own characteristic foreign policy, which is inspired by internal features.[110] However, comparative analysis shows that constitutions lacking a 'thick'[111] form of constitutionalism do not put a similar emphasis on 'translation' of internal values but rather stress 'peaceful coexistence' and 'non-interference' in the internal affairs, as in the case of the People's Republic of China.[112] This caters to the idea of democratic peace as a global project and the inherent connection between internal structure, values, and foreign policy.

Concerning the strand of liberalism focusing on institutions, the EU Treaties, as well as many national constitutions today, reflect an emphasis on multilateralism and institutionalized international cooperation. From a comparative perspective, it emerges that international cooperation *tout court* is one of the most common foreign policy objectives. In a number of instances, specific international institutions are mentioned in the constitution, such as the International Criminal Court or the European Union itself. The EU Treaties put a strong emphasis on 'multilateral solutions to common problems' through international institutions, especially the United Nations.[113]

Even though such objectives appear at first glance somewhat vacuous, the picture changes in light of the assertion by liberal institutionalism of the potential 'to reinforce the prospect of cooperation by enhancing the commonality of interests among players, by reducing the number of uncertain variables, and by retaining the interaction in a more structured setting'.[114] Therefore, there is an inherent value in such forms of cooperation from the perspective of liberal institutionalism. This coincides conceptually with Stephan de Keukeleire's idea of 'structural foreign policy'[115] and Gráinne de Búrca's concept of a 'governance mode' of EU

[107] Arts 2, 3(5), and 21(1) and (2) TEU.

[108] Art 21(1), first subpara TEU.

[109] Art 8(1) TEU.

[110] A Bradford and E Posner, 'Universal Exceptionalism in International Law' (2011) 52 *Harvard International Law Journal* 3.

[111] Using the definition by Raz (n 4) 153–4.

[112] Preamble, Chinese constitution. See also Chapter 2, section 4.4.

[113] Art 21(1), second subpara TEU; note also Art 220 TFEU on the relations of the EU with international organizations.

[114] Andreatta (n 21) 35.

[115] Keukeleire and Delreux (n 1) 25, but note also their emphasis on 'mental structures' making this at the same time a constructivist approach.

foreign policy, according to which foreign policy pursues not only 'milieu' rather than 'possession goals',[116] but does this through multilateral rather than unilateral means.[117]

4.2 Foreign policy objectives as a justificatory device

While constitutional foreign policy objectives are bound to meet with great scepticism from realists, a more nuanced response can be expected from liberal scholarship. The rule of law is seen as a crucial element of democratic peace and peaceful conflict resolution. However, a more open attitude towards the merits of law in general says little about the usefulness of constitutional foreign policy objectives for liberal approaches. Instead of treating the state as a proverbial 'black box', which realism is often accused of,[118] liberal scholarship pays close attention to interests and processes within the state, as well as to the importance of institutions and bargaining. Such a perspective can serve to highlight the ways in which constitutional objectives are used by different actors and institutions for their own respective purposes. Liberalism puts emphasis on how constitutional objectives, including those in the area of foreign policy, matter domestically, especially in litigation between different actors within a legal order. From this point of view, the Union is not distinctive as an international actor in any 'normative' or 'ethical' sense per se. Rather, it serves as an additional layer of governance, which complicates, but does not fundamentally change, politics in general, as well as the use of constitutional provisions by institutional actors.

In particular, liberal intergovernmentalism and its utilization of the model of multilevel games can be linked to the legal analysis of the European constitutional space (Chapter 4). A central tenet of this school of thought is that international and supranational cooperation have the effect of gradually increasing the powers of the executive within a given domestic political setting, with the result of a 'democracy deficit'.[119] Following this logic, foreign policy is said to have 'undergone less integration than other areas, such as monetary and agricultural affairs, because governments already enjoy a high degree of autonomy in that particular field'.[120] This does not mean, however, that constitutional foreign policy objectives cannot be used for enlarging public powers. The main legal function that such objectives fulfil is exactly that, viz as a device to push the boundaries of public powers through legal interpretation. From the Member State perspective, integration objectives in national constitutions can be used to legally justify the transfer of sovereign powers

[116] De Búrca draws here on the concepts devised by A Wolfers, *Discord and Collaboration: Essays on International Politics* (Johns Hopkins University Press, 1962).

[117] G de Búrca, 'EU External Relations: The Governance Mode of Foreign Policy' in B Van Vooren, S Blockmans, and J Wouters (eds), *The EU's Role in Global Governance: The Legal Dimension* (OUP, 2013).

[118] This is the limitation that neoclassical realism aims to overcome: A Reichwein, 'The Tradition of Neoclassical Realism' in A Toje and B Kunz (eds), *Neoclassical Realism in European Politics: Bringing Power Back In* (Manchester University Press, 2012) 42–4.

[119] Andreatta (n 21) 34.

[120] Andreatta (n 21) 34.

to the supranational level, at which the national executives reassemble within the Council as the 'co-legislator' next to the European Parliament, resulting in what legal scholars have called 'executive federalism'.[121] Here, Member States utilize integration objectives, which are a category of constitutional foreign policy objectives, to enlarge their powers vis-à-vis the other branches at the national level.

However, this leaves the caveat that this would not apply to foreign policy beyond regional integration, being 'high politics', as opposed to 'technical' integration, given the autonomy that the executive already enjoys in the former domain. This is to a certain extent reflected in the EU Treaties by the persisting intergovernmental character of the CFSP, in particular the prevalence of unanimity, the inability to legislate, and the restricted jurisdiction of the Court of Justice in this area.[122] Nevertheless, liberalism can help to explain the system of EU external relations law and the obligations that Union membership entails as a three-level game with shifting dynamics. From this perspective, it becomes evident that all of the objectives of the EU Treaties, including those pertaining to foreign policy, are used by the Union institutions in much the same way, ie for their own benefit vis-à-vis the Member States, other Union institutions, or even individuals.

While the pooling of sovereign powers at the supranational level may enlarge the power of governments within the national domestic setting, the powers of these same governments in the area of foreign affairs are constrained by Union membership. Examining the way that courts deal with foreign policy objectives from a liberal institutional perspective yields the same impression. In a two-level setting (domestic–international), constitutional foreign policy objectives are hardly constraining, but are instead rather permissive regarding government powers by virtue of their legal 'interpretative–permissive' function. In this respect, the famous *Missouri v Holland* decision of the United States Supreme Court can be recalled, which revealed that external treaty-making power and the subsequent need to comply with international legal commitments may be used to seek more room for manoeuvre in the national (federal) legal order.[123]

In the particular three-level game of EU external relations (Member State–EU–international), the previous chapter showed that Union objectives, coupled with principles such as pre-emption, the duty of sincere cooperation, and the principle of unity in the international representation of the Union, serve to push the boundaries of the political branches of the Union. At the same time, these

[121] K Lenaerts, 'Constitutionalism and the Many Faces of Federalism' (1990) 38 *American Journal of Comparative Law* 205, 230; and P Dann, 'European Parliament and Executive Federalism: Approaching a Parliament in a Semi-Parliamentary Democracy' (2003) 9 *European Law Journal* 549.

[122] Art 24(1) TEU.

[123] See the landmark case before the United States Supreme Court concerning the Migratory Bird Treaty Act of 1918: *Missouri v Holland*, decision of 6 March 1920, 252 US 416 (1920), which upheld the power of the federal government to conclude treaties on matters for which it had no enumerated powers domestically; see also *Asakura v City of Seattle*, decision of 26 May 1926, 265 US 332 (1924), 341: 'The treaty-making power of the United States is not limited by any express provision of the Constitution, and, though it does not extend "so far as to authorize what the Constitution forbids," it does extend to all proper subjects of negotiation between our government and other nations.'

objectives restrict the political branches of the governments of the Member States when acting internationally. Within the particular framework of the EU, they have furthermore served as an interpretive device in litigation for the Union institutions to argue for a legal basis which would grant that respective institution more procedural powers. As discussed earlier, the Council and the Commission argued in the *Small arms* case over whether the central purpose of a Council Decision and Joint Action concerning an EU contribution to 'combating the destabilising accumulation and spread of small arms and light weapons' was about international security or development cooperation, respectively.[124] The former interpretation was said to infringe upon the competences of the (then) Community, which at the same time would have adversely impacted on the prerogatives of the Commission. Meanwhile, it was contended that the latter interpretation would infringe upon the competence of the (pre-Lisbon) Union, and at the same time upon the leeway enjoyed by the Council and the Member States in the area of CFSP. While the Council lost this round, it prevailed over the Parliament in the post-Lisbon case *Parliament v Council (Al-Qaeda Sanctions)* concerning the question of whether certain restrictive measures had the fight against terrorism as a matter of internal or international security as their central purpose.

This question was important for the role of the European Parliament in the legislative process, which would be significantly enhanced in case of the former interpretation. The CJEU found against the Parliament, adding that this difference in parliamentary involvement determined by the policy field at hand 'is the result of the choice made by the framers of the Treaty of Lisbon conferring a more limited role on the Parliament with regard to the Union's action under the CFSP'.[125] The 'framers' are none other than the Member States, whose basic choice for more autonomy in the area of international security was confirmed by the CJEU in this case.

The wealth of foreign policy objectives in the Treaties is an important part of the argumentative toolkit for the institutions. Just as individual rights and direct effect serve as useful devices in court for private parties, constitutional objectives usually serve to bolster the case of the political branches at Union level. This re-emphasizes the need for finding the right balance between individual rights and public authority, which features prominently in the Indian and French legal discourses,[126] as

[124] Case C-91/05 *Commission v Council (Small arms and light weapons)*, EU:C:2008:288. See also concerning environmental protection and international trade, eg, Case C-94/03 *Commission v Council (Rotterdam Convention)*, EU:C:2006:2.

[125] Case C-130/10 *Parliament v Council (Al-Qaeda Sanctions)*, EU:C:2012:472, para. 82; but note the duty to keep the Parliament informed during treaty negotiations according to Art 218(10) TFEU, which includes agreements in the area of the CFSP as confirmed in Case C-658/11 *Parliament v Council (EU-Mauritius Agreement)*, EU:C:2014:2025.

[126] Note Justice Chandrachud stressing that the 'harmony and balance between fundamental rights and directive principles is an essential feature of the basic structure of the Constitution': *Minerva Mills Ltd v Union of India and Others*, judgment of 31 July 1980, (1981) 1 SCR 206, 208–9; De Montalivet identified the guaranteeing of the effectiveness of all fundamental rights as the core function of the *objectifs de valeur constitutionnelle*: P De Montalivet, *Les objectifs de valeur constitutionnelle* (Dalloz, 2006) 454.

well as in the case law of the Court of Justice itself ever since *Nold*.[127] The idea that not simply a domestic issue is at hand, but an 'objective of general interest ... fundamental to the international community', serves as justification for at least as much leeway for the political branches as exists in a purely domestic context.[128] However, this argument can be taken only as far as it does not upset the structural principles of a legal order.

The CJEU can be seen as part of this game as well, engaging in what has been called 'judicial activism'.[129] In this vein, the case law of the Court, marked by its 'teleological approach' and reasoning based on *effet utile*, has been interpreted by some legal scholars as a way to enlarge its own powers, together with national courts (of lower instance), by virtue of the preliminary reference procedure.[130] Nonetheless, reliance of judicial institutions on objectives, being constitutional norms, is to be distinguished from unbridled judicial policy-making (*gouvernement des juges*) with no respect for the letter of the law. The fact that different branches rely on opposing interpretations of constitutional law is a rather natural feature in what Daniel Halberstam calls a 'heterarchical system'.[131] Hence, within the EU, the CJEU can be seen as maintaining a 'policy space' in which the different actors formulate EU external action with due regard to international political realities,[132] ie the accentuated caveat of possibility in the foreign affairs domain. The American context reminds us that even where a constitution does not provide for any meaningful constitutional foreign policy objectives, they nevertheless make their way back into these heterarchical contestations, but simply without a proper textual foundation.[133]

[127] Case 4/73 *Nold v Commission*, EU:C:1974:51, para 14.

[128] *Kadi and Al Barakaat* (n 64) para 363. Compare this with the litigation on sanctions autonomously imposed by the EU, where from the outset a stricter standard of judicial review was applied: see Case T-284/08 *People's Mojahedin Organization of Iran*, EU:T:2008:550; and the earlier Case T-228/02 *Organisation des Modjahedines du peuple d'Iran*, EU:T:2006:384, para 101, which distinguishes the case from *Kadi* exactly on the basis of the two different sanctions regimes implemented by the UN Security Council; further T Tridimas, 'Terrorism and the ECJ: Empowerment and Democracy in the EC Legal Order' (2009) 34 *European Law Review* 103; and C Eckes, *EU Counter-Terrorist Policies and Fundamental Rights: The Case of Individual Sanctions* (OUP, 2009) 22 et seq.

[129] See H Rasmussen, *The European Court of Justice* (GadJura, 1998) 27, who, in his critical treatise on the CJEU, defines this is as 'regular judicial policy-making in pursuance of policy-objectives which usurp the rule and policymaking powers of other branches of government'.

[130] Rasmussen (n 129) 31–5 on *effet utile, telos*, and original intent; on the collaborative relationship between the CJEU and national courts, see in particular JHH Weiler, 'A Quiet Revolution: The European Court and Its Interlocutors' (1994) 26 *Comparative Political Studies* 510; and A Stone Sweet and J Caporaso, 'From Free Trade to Supranational Polity: The European Court and Integration' in W Sandholtz and A Stone Sweet (eds), *European Integration and Supranational Governance* (OUP, 1998).

[131] D Halberstam, 'Constitutional Heterarchy: The Centrality of Conflict in the European Union and the United States' in J Dunoff and J Trachtman (eds), *Ruling the World? Constitutionalism, International Law and Global Governance* (CUP, 2009).

[132] M Cremona, 'A Reticent Court? Policy Objectives and the Court of Justice' in M Cremona and A Thies (eds), *The European Court of Justice and External Relations Law: Constitutional Challenges* (Hart Publishing, 2014) 26–31.

[133] See United States Department of Justice, Memorandum Opinion for the Attorney General, Authority to Use Military Force in Libya, 1 April 2011, <http://www.justice.gov/sites/default/files/olc/opinions/2011/04/31/authority-military-use-in-libya.pdf>, 10–12. See also Chapter 1, section 2.

Hence, different foreign policy objectives are more or less useful depending on the actor in whose interest it is to invoke them. For instance, reliance on CFSP objectives, the existence and scope of which is uncertain after Lisbon, would be in the interests of the Council and the Member States. External relations objectives found in the TFEU would be more favourable for the other institutions, including the CJEU, assuming it would want to expand its jurisdiction.[134] Within the European constitutional space, the Member States can also play their national constitutional objectives as a trump card in this game, albeit only to the limited extent that they are part of their constitutional identity (see Chapter 4, section 3.1).

In sum, instead of the unrealistic 'utopia' which realist scholars are likely to consider constitutional foreign policy objectives to portray, liberal theory helps to reveal their—not uncontroversial—potential to serve as an 'apology' for national and supranational institutions to aggrandize their respective powers, for which they can seek confirmation through adjudication.[135] Liberal theory also suggests the addition of a caveat to the general legal definition of constitutional objectives as representing the 'common good' of a polity. While this remains generally valid, it does not stop these norms from being used by institutions to foster their own interests. Here Peter Häberle's words ring true that the notion of the common good in law can serve as nothing other than an 'ideologically embellished instrument of power'.[136] As liberal theory highlights, constitutional foreign policy objectives can indeed serve as such instruments in multilevel games involving the individual, the state, the EU, and the international level. From this point of view, the multilevel constitutional nature of the EU would make it distinctive as a sophisticated site of legal contestation, but not necessarily in any 'normative' or 'ethical' sense. The same 'games' are played, just in a more complex setting.

5. Constructivism

Realism cautions against too much faith in constitutional 'wish lists' and liberalism sheds light on the ways in which constitutional foreign policy objectives can be instrumentalized by institutional actors. Constructivist approaches can be expected to show the greatest interest in, and most favourable disposition towards, constitutional foreign policy objectives given that it can be seen as 'IR theory's best

[134] But note Hillion, who argues that the duty of cooperation may serve to extend the jurisdiction of the Court into the CFSP, as it addresses 'all the objectives of the Union' and not only the non-CFSP ones: C Hillion, 'A Powerless Court? The European Court of Justice and the Common Foreign and Security Policy' in M Cremona and A Thies (eds), *The European Court of Justice and External Relations Law: Constitutional Challenges* (Hart Publishing, 2014) 67.

[135] To draw on the famous dual role of international law as elaborated by M Koskenniemi, *From Apology to Utopia: The Structure of International Legal Argument* (CUP, 2005); see also B De Witte, 'International Law as a Tool for the European Union' (2009) 5 *European Constitutional Law Review* 265.

[136] In the original: 'ideologisch verbrämte[s] Machtinstrument': P Häberle, *Europäische Verfassungslehre*, 7th edn (Nomos, 2011) 372.

effort to understand law'.[137] The proliferation of foreign policy objectives in the EU Treaties and constitutions more generally caters to the idea of law as a reflection of ideas, norms, and identities, including in the areas of foreign policy and global governance. Constructivist scholarship, for its part, transcends the focus on the state as the basic unit of analysis, as well as material factors as the only determinants of the international role of any given actor. Instead, it scrutinizes the role of ideational factors and collective forms of 'identity', which make constitutional documents an interesting source to exploit. It is therefore no surprise that in the writings on 'normative' and 'ethical power Europe', references to the EU Treaties are common for discerning the normative basis of the EU and its foreign policy. In addition to informing the normative basis and identity of the EU as an international actor, constitutional foreign policy objectives also serve as a source of legitimacy and as a driver for socialization.

5.1 The permeation of law by ideas, norms, and identities

A hallmark of constructivist approaches is overcoming the focus on material factors, ie an excessive reliance on a ' "positivist" methodology'[138] employed by both realist and liberal approaches to international relations. Given the emphasis they place instead on norms and ideas 'as helping to form the identity of states rather than merely emanating from the interactions of states expressing predetermined interests',[139]there is an obvious connection between constructivism and constitutional foreign policy objectives. The 'dynamic internationalization' of constitutional law, as a global trend, caters to the proposition that next to other factors such as power and institutional politics, norms matter—so much so they were deemed important enough to be codified into the highest laws of various polities.

Constitutional foreign policy objectives can be seen as 'positive' legal evidence (using the term in the legal sense) for 'post-positivist' approaches (using the term in the sense of IR theory). Sonia Lucarelli uses the terms 'hardware' and 'software' dimensions, with the former meaning 'institutional infrastructure, personnel, and military equipment' and the latter comprising of 'visions, aspirations, worldviews, principles, norms, and beliefs'.[140] Constitutional foreign policy objectives, which are plentiful in the EU Treaties, represent part of the 'software' that feeds into theoretical thinking 'about the way in which the EU is constituted as a political entity by the values, images and principles (VIPs) which shape the discourse and practice of the EU's relations with the rest of the world'.[141]

There is a conceptual overlap between 'identity' as a concept from the social sciences and the use of the constitution as a document that is strongly reflective of the identity of a given political community. This finds an apt illustration in the notion of 'constitutional identity', which serves as a core ingredient of the European constitutional space. Moreover, the findings from comparative constitutional

[137] Sinclair (n 22) 170. [138] Andreatta (n 21) 35. [139] Ratner (n 2) 24.
[140] Lucarelli (n 87) 1. [141] Lucarelli (n 87) 1.

law presented in the preceding chapters show that constitutional objectives, together with constitutionally entrenched values, are considered as the 'soul'[142] or 'souffle'[143] of the constitution. This evokes the understanding of a 'thick' constitution as 'common ideology' according to Joseph Raz, which comprises of principles 'that are generally held to express the common beliefs of the population about the way their society should be governed', serving 'not only as a lawyers' law, but as the people's law'.[144]

Such a wide understanding of the law raised criticisms among some legal scholars. For them, constitutional objectives in general were regarded as not being 'real' constitutional law, which they understand in terms of 'dependable legal guarantees that can be invoked in court'.[145] Otherwise put, this kind of '*soft*ware' fits for some legal scholars uneasily with the idea of '*hard* law'. For IR scholars interested in norms, ideas, and identities, it is no surprise that in the writings on 'normative' and 'ethical power Europe', there are references to the Treaties in attempts to discern the 'normative basis'[146] and international identity of the Union. However, while constitutional norms reign supreme in a given legal order, their importance in any constructivist approach to EU foreign policy is by no means pre-established. In order to address this question, it is necessary to approach this from the inverse point of view, ie revisiting these constitutional provisions through the lens of constructivist approaches.

5.2 Foreign policy objectives as 'normative basis' and 'identity'

Concerning the allegedly exceptional 'normative basis' of EU foreign policy, Ian Manners posits that 'the EU's normative difference comes from its historical context, hybrid polity, and *political-legal constitution*'.[147] Closely related to the idea of this distinctly normative basis is that of the international 'identity' of the Union,[148] for which constitutional law is credited as an important source. For Manners, 'constitutional norms represent crucial constitutive factors determining its international identity'.[149] To some extent, such constitutional norms may be more illuminating regarding a particular actor's identity than international legal norms,[150] seeing that constitutions are specific to a certain polity.

[142] B De Villiers, 'Directive Principles of State Policy and Fundamental Rights: The Indian Experience' (1992) 8 *South African Journal on Human Rights* 29, 33.

[143] A Pilette and E de Poncins, 'Valeurs, objectifs et nature de l'Union' in G Amato, H Bribosia, and B De Witte (eds), *Genesis and Destiny of the European Constitution* (Bruylant, 2007) 309.

[144] Raz (n 4) 153–4.

[145] In the original: 'gerichtlich einlösbare, verläßliche Rechtsgarantien': J Isensee, 'Staatsaufgaben' in J Isensee and P Kirchhof (eds), *Handbuch des Staatsrechts der Bundesrepublik Deutschland. Volume IV: Aufgaben des Staates*, 3rd edn (C.F. Müller, 2006) 144.

[146] Manners (n 7) 242.

[147] Manners (n 7) 240 (emphasis added).

[148] See also Bretherton and Vogler (n 1) 6, who link the concept of 'actorness' to that of 'identity'.

[149] Manners (n 7) 241.

[150] On international law and identity, see J Brunnée and S Toope, 'Constructivism and International Law' in J Dunoff and M Pollack (eds), *Interdisciplinary Perspectives on International Law and International Relations* (CUP, 2013).

This echoes constitutional scholarship, which asserts the broader function of a constitution within a given society. As noted above, according to Raz, the constitution serves as constitutive, enduring, entrenched higher law, which encapsulates a 'common ideology that governs public life'.[151] For Peter Häberle, similarly, 'contemporary ideas are condensed within [constitutions] with particular (also conceptual) "exertion"'.[152] They are made plainly visible and publicly accessible, and difficult to dispose of due to entrenchment.[153]

However, two caveats apply here: Firstly, for IR scholarship, constitutional norms are but one of many sources constitutive of normative basis and international identity; and secondly, such a normative basis is not per se distinctive, exceptional, or reflective of defending universal values and norms.

As to the first caveat, in determining both the normative basis and the international identity of the EU, constructivist scholars use a variety of sources extending beyond constitutional law. On the one hand, in outlining the normative difference of the Union, Manners draws on the Treaties, including their foreign policy objectives.[154] He welcomes the Lisbon Treaty as 'the most recent stage in a process that is constitutive of the EU's normative power in world politics'.[155] Manners dismisses what he calls 'a cynical viewpoint', which may suggest 'that such treaty articles and the policies they drive are at best unimportant, or at worst provide cover for more covert commercial interests'.[156] These perspectives match, respectively, the realist or liberal perceptions of such provisions as outlined above. He contends to the contrary 'that the constitutionalization of these normative principles in the highly contested Lisbon Reform Treaty marks the crystallization and culmination of norms and practices which have been evolving over the past 15 years'.[157] Hence, the constitutional foreign policy objectives of the Union are doubtlessly an important factor in discerning the Union's normative basis.

On the other hand, for Manners these are not the only ingredients for what he calls the normative basis of the Union. Next to references to the Treaties he also considers declarations, speeches, and other sources to be part of this basis. For instance, he points to Romano Prodi's inaugural speech at the European Parliament

[151] Raz (n 4) 154.

[152] In the original: 'sich in ihnen in besonderer (auch begrifflicher) "Anstrengungen" Ideen der Zeit verdichten': P Häberle, 'Das "Weltbild" des Verfassungsstaates—eine Textstufenanalyse zur Menschheit als verfassungsstaatlichem und "letztem" Geltungsgrund des Völkerrechts' in B Ziemske, T Langheid, H Wilms, and G Haverkate (eds), *Staatsphilosophie und Rechtspolitik, Festschrift für Martin Kriele* (C.H. Beck, 1997) 1280.

[153] The distinguishing factor of constitutional law vis-à-vis all other law is its entrenchment (ie its more difficult alteration or abrogation), but also that it binds the exercise of public power in all its forms, and that it possesses supremacy over the other norms of the legal order, P Badura, 'Arten der Verfassungsrechtssätze' in J Isensee and P Kirchhof (eds), *Handbuch des Staatsrechts der Bundesrepublik Deutschland. Volume VII: Normativität und Schutz der Verfassung—Internationale Beziehungen* (C.F. Müller, 1992) 34.

[154] Manners (n 7) 241–2, referring to the Treaties pre-Lisbon, ie Arts 6 and 11 TEU (Nice version) and Art 177 TEC.

[155] I Manners, 'The Normative Ethics of the European Union' (2008) 84 *International Affairs* 45, 48, where he also specifically refers to the codified external relations objectives of the Union.

[156] Manners (n 155) 48. [157] Manners (n 155) 48.

and Commission white papers.[158] Similarly for identity, Sonia Lucarelli defines the 'political identity' of the EU as 'the set of social and political values and principles that Europeans recognise as theirs and give sense to their feeling of belonging to the same political entity'.[159] This may include, but simultaneously goes beyond, legal norms. Lucarelli rejects the idea that identity is a 'given' factor, and contends that it is 'part of processes of self-identification by the individuals in a group, in which foreign policy is particularly important'.[160] She stresses in this respect the need for interpretation through frameworks of '[c]ulture, history, legal practices and institutions'.[161] In this case, constitutional law is but one of a number of factors shaping international identity. Nevertheless, at least for Manners, the Treaties assume a pre-eminent position in establishing the 'normative basis' of the EU in that they represent the 'crystallization and culmination of norms and practices'[162] over time.

Regarding the second caveat, whereas constitutional foreign policy objectives can be regarded as evidence of preferences within that polity regarding international order, having such a normative basis or identity does not automatically make an international actor distinctive, in particular with regard to being an agent for the 'global common good'. Further scrutiny as to the 'global acceptance'[163] of the norms and ideas underpinning such a normative foreign policy are required to determine whether they indeed reflect preferences that are valid beyond the confines of a particular polity.

The unreflective readiness to accept a 'normative' distinctiveness of the EU, buttressed by the codified norms in the EU Treaties, has been criticized by the proponents of 'ethical power' and 'humanitarian power'. Helene Sjursen, for instance, admonishes that 'the "normative power" literature does not discriminate between different types of norms'.[164] Consequently, according to her, 'it does not have a sufficiently nuanced conceptual apparatus to investigate what kind of normative power the EU may be and to substantiate this claim of a particularity to the EU's foreign and security policy'.[165] Such a position vis-à-vis the norms that guide EU foreign policy poses a risk of 'Eurocentric cultural imperialism', and blind reliance on 'the analyst's personal assessment of what is "good", without providing clear reasons or critical standards'.[166] Similarly, Lisbeth Aggestam argues for the consideration of 'the EU's role in a broader international context, rather than simply focussing on the Union's internal characteristics and assuming that these

[158] Manners (n 7) 243. [159] Lucarelli (n 87) 13.

[160] Lucarelli (n 87) 13. Note here also Robert Post's argument of the role of unity in the external relations of the EU as an important factor in consolidating the European 'polity': R Post, 'Constructing the European Polity: ERTA and the Open Skies Judgments' in M Poiares Maduro and L Azoulai (eds), *The Past and Future of EU Law: The Classics of EU Law Revisited on the 50th Anniversary of the Rome Treaty* (Hart Publishing, 2010).

[161] Lucarelli (n 87) 13. [162] Manners (n 155) 48.

[163] R Arnold, 'Reflections on the Universality of Human Rights' in R Arnold (ed), *The Universalism of Human Rights* (Springer, 2013) 1, who defines 'global acceptance' in both vertical terms (acceptance at the national, regional, and international level) and horizontal terms (acceptance 'in all geographical parts of the world).

[164] Sjursen (n 14) 3. [165] Sjursen (n 14) 3. [166] Sjursen (n 14) 4.

determine its role'.[167] This raises the question of how 'normative globalization after the end of the Cold War enabled the EU to assume a more proactive role by drawing on an international ethics largely, but not exclusively, institutionalized within the UN system'.[168] From this point of view, the assumption by proponents of 'normative power Europe' as a distinctive, fundamentally different actor needs to be scrutinized in a more critical manner,[169] factoring in external perspectives of the EU as an international actor as well.[170]

Support for such a critical stance can be found in the scholarship of foreign relations law. Anu Bradford and Eric Posner have argued that every great power has a foreign policy it deems 'exceptional' in one way or the other, which 'typically support[s] a view of international law that embodies their own normative commitments but is presented as a universal set of commitments'.[171] While they address this from the point of view of the claim to 'exceptionalism' of US foreign policy, this can also be applied to the EU. In this vein, Sjursen notes that 'the United States or the former Soviet Union have both in different respects been "normative" powers'.[172] Hence, mere self-assertion does not suffice to establish a form of international distinctiveness as a 'normative' power in the sense of being inclined to defend 'universal values'. This applies also where such assertion takes place through the codification of rather ambitious foreign policy objectives in a constitutional document.

Acceptance beyond one's own polity consequently becomes a crucial factor in overcoming allegations of parochialism or Eurocentrism. As Aggestam notes, 'universal values' should 'exist independently from the specific identity of an actor'.[173] This requires the determination of the universal validity of these norms beyond the specific legal and political context of a given constitution. Manners, in revisiting his 'normative power' concept, concluded that:

> The creative efforts and longer-term vision of EU normative power towards the achievement of a more just, cosmopolitical world which empowers people in the actual conditions of their lives should and must be based on more universally accepted values and principles that can be explained to both Europeans and non-European[s] alike.[174]

Where such links can be made between constitutional norms and norms in other legal orders, as well as in the global discourse, constitutional foreign policy objectives can indeed also be regarded as valid beyond their respective jurisdiction. This is so, according to Manners, because the EU has:

> gone further towards making its external relations informed by, and conditional on, a catalogue of norms which come closer to those of the European Convention on human

[167] Aggestam (n 18) 3–4. [168] Aggestam (n 18) 4. [169] Aggestam (n 18) 4.

[170] See S Lucarelli and L Fioramonti, 'Introduction: The EU in the Eyes of Others—Why Bother?' in S Lucarelli and L Fioramonti (eds), *External Perceptions of the European Union as a Global Actor* (Routledge, 2011); and H Larsen, 'The EU as a Normative Power and the Research on External Perceptions: The Missing Link' (2014) 52 *Journal of Common Market Studies* 896.

[171] Bradford and Posner (n 110) 12. [172] Sjursen (n 14) 3.

[173] Aggestam (n 18) 6. [174] Manners (n 155) 60 (emphasis added).

rights and fundamental freedoms (ECHR) and the universal declaration of human rights (UDHR) than most other actors in world politics.[175]

The findings from comparative constitutional law presented in this book, however, would caution against the alleged uniqueness of the EU. The preceding chapters show that many constitutions today provide for a wide assortment of foreign policy objectives, including the promotion of human rights worldwide (Chapter 2, section 4). While the EU may be in the vanguard of a trend in terms of verbosity in constitutionally exhibiting the norms that guide its external relations, it is by no means a feature unique to the Union. 'Dynamic internationalization' is indeed a global phenomenon in contemporary constitutional law.

In order to draw on constitutional provisions as a source of 'global norms' in foreign policy their universal credentials need to be established beyond the jurisdiction of any particular constitution. This point can also be linked to constitutional scholarship. For instance, Markus Kotzur points to references to 'global law' (*Weltrecht*) found in national constitutions,[176] which to a considerable extent overlap with the trend of 'dynamic internationalization'. The crucial elements then become the reference to external sources with universal credentials and the universalizability of norms. The EU Treaties do provide explicit references to external sources that inform the Union's foreign policy objectives. While the EU is not the only international actor that has cast the 'normative basis' of its foreign policy in constitutional terms, it is certainly at the forefront of a global trend also with regard to intertwining its internal constitutional values with international norms.

The need for universal scope of the foreign policy objectives of the Union was explicitly raised at the Convention on the Future of Europe. In order to avoid any impression of Eurocentrism or of a patronizing foreign policy, one member of the Convention stressed that 'we should underline the *universal* character of the values in Article 2, as well as in Article 3.4 [of the draft text, now Article 3(5) TEU]'.[177] A specific illustration of this is the inclusion of sustainable development among these objectives, on which several members of the Convention insisted in order to reflect its internationally agreed definition (see also Chapter 2, section 3.5).[178]

[175] Manners (n 7) 241.

[176] M Kotzur, 'Weltrechtliche Bezüge in nationalen Verfassungstexten: Die Rezeption verfassungsrechtlicher Normen durch das Völkerrecht' (2008) 39 *Rechtstheorie* 191, 202.

[177] Secretariat of the European Convention, Suggestion for amendment of Article 3.4 by Mr Lennmarker, <http://european-convention.europa.eu/docs/Treaty/pdf/3/Art3-4Lennmarker.pdf> (emphasis in the original).

[178] See eg Secretariat of the European Convention, Suggestion for amendment of Article 1.2: Principles and Objectives by Mr Pat Carey, <http://european-convention.europa.eu/Docs/Treaty/pdf/861/Art1-2CareyEN.pdf>; Secretariat of the European Convention, Suggestion for amendment of Article 1 by Mrs Lena Hjelm-Wallén and Mr Sven-Olof Petersson, government representatives and Mr Sören Lekberg and Mr Kenneth Kvist, national parliament representatives, <http://european-convention.europa.eu/Docs/Treaty/pdf/861/Art1Hjelm-Wall%C3%A9n%20EN.pdf>; and Secretariat of the European Convention, Suggestion for amendment of Article 1.2 by Ms Maria Berger and Mr Caspar Einem, <http://european-convention.europa.eu/Docs/Treaty/pdf/861/Art1-2Berger%20EN.pdf>.

More generally, Marise Cremona conceives of the values of EU foreign policy as a product of iterative processes between the EU, the national, and the international order.[179] For instance, in the area of human rights protection, the EU has been inspired by both the constitutional traditions of the Member States and the European Convention on Human Rights as an external source.[180] At the same time, the Union promotes human rights internationally. It is thereby 'translating' its own structural principles into foreign policy and ultimately into the structures of external partners and the international legal order as a whole. This illustrates, in tune with constructivist thinking, that universal norms are not static, exogenous factors, but in constant flux and prone to change over time. Although constitutional law is entrenched and hence rather static, it can be given different interpretations over time in order to accord with universal norms.

Where such links can be made between constitutional norms and norms in other legal orders to the extent that they can be considered of (quasi-)universal value, constitutional foreign policy objectives can indeed also be regarded as reflecting 'global norms'. Consequently, beyond conformity with one's own legal order and domestic norms, constitutional objectives that meet this additional threshold would serve as the basis and benchmark for a 'normative' foreign policy in the sense of promoting global norms—or the *bonum commune humanitatis*.

5.3 Foreign policy objectives as a source of legitimacy

Considering constitutional foreign policy objectives as part of the 'normative basis' of a polity also lends credence to them as a source of legitimacy. Legitimacy has received a 'recent burgeoning of interest' in both international law and IR scholarship.[181] It has been described as 'the hard currency of future international relations'[182] and the 'new frontier of multilateralism in the twenty-first century'.[183] Helene Sjursen stresses that legitimacy is a crucial component of power, as '[e]ven the world's largest, perhaps only, superpower appears ultimately to be dependent on legitimacy in order to achieve its foreign policy objectives'.[184]

Legitimacy is commonly understood as the justification for exercising political power.[185] For the EU, the legitimizing force of objectives was well captured at the

[179] M Cremona, 'Values in EU Foreign Policy' in M Evans and P Koutrakos (eds), *Beyond the Established Legal Order: Policy Interconnections Between the EU and the Rest of the World* (Hart Publishing, 2011).

[180] Case 4/73 *Nold v Commission*, EU:C:1974:51; see also Case 222/84 *Johnston*, EU:C:1986:206, para 13, stating that the ECHR is of 'particular significance' for its reasoning.

[181] D Bodansky, 'Legitimacy in International Law and International Relations' in J Dunoff and M Pollack (eds), *Interdisciplinary Perspectives on International Law and International Relations* (CUP, 2013) 321.

[182] N Gnesotto and G Grevi, *The New Global Puzzle: What World for the EU in 2025?* (EUISS, 2006) 198.

[183] M Telò, 'Introduction: The EU as a Model, a Global Actor and an Unprecedented Power' in M Telò (ed), *The European Union and Global Governance* (Routledge, 2009) 31.

[184] Sjursen (n 14) 8.

[185] See F Peter, 'Political Legitimacy' in E Zalta (ed), *The Stanford Encyclopedia of Philosophy*, Spring 2014 edn, <http://plato.stanford.edu/archives/spr2014/entries/legitimacy/>.

Convention on the Future of Europe. In the document containing the first set of draft articles for the Draft Constitution, the Præsidium explained the 'philosophy' underlying the provisions on Union objectives to be found therein. According to the Præsidium, these provisions were 'to set out the general objectives justifying the very existence of the Union and its action for its citizens'.[186]

Legitimacy can be broken down into two main facets. In its normative meaning, according to Allen Buchanan and Robert Keohane, legitimacy points to asserting a 'right to rule', while its sociological meaning denotes that an institution 'is widely *believed* to have the right to rule'.[187] Hence, normatively, constitutional objectives in the domain of foreign policy can be seen as an assertion by the constitutional framers to shape the international order. Sociologically, they can be viewed as the expression of a belief within that polity that a foreign policy along these lines would be desirable and appropriate. This dovetails with the distinction between 'input' and 'output' legitimacy,[188] which can also be described as 'consent' to, and 'beneficial consequences' of, policies.[189]

'Input' into such policies through different modes of participation and consultation bolsters the sociological claim that they are 'derived from the authentic preferences of the members of the community'.[190] In any 'thick' constitutional setting, as norms enshrined in a document that has been approved and that are upheld through a democratic procedure, constitutional objectives and the acts adopted in their pursuit indeed possess inherent input legitimacy. With regard to the EU, and in view of the recurring allegations of its democratic deficit, it is worth recalling that the present wealth of foreign policy objectives originated mainly from the Convention on the Future of Europe as a deliberative process including a variety of stakeholders. For the most part, the outcome of this process was later ratified by all of the EU's Member States, according to their constitutional requirements, in the form of the Lisbon Treaty (Chapter 2, sections 3.5 and 3.6).

However, just as the 'normative basis' of foreign policy needs to be contextualized with global standards and perceptions, the input legitimacy of EU external action diminishes insofar as its own foreign policy objectives do not reflect norms and standards which stem from deliberation processes by the international 'community' or which are widely accepted around the world. Therefore, while all constitutional objectives can help bolster the legality of certain acts within a given legal order, they can only bolster their international legitimacy if they fulfil additional criteria of validity beyond one's own legal order.[191]

In the case of the EU, it should be recalled that the foreign policy objectives of the Union, according to the Treaties, are 'guided by the principles which have

186 Secretariat of the European Convention, Draft of Articles 1 to 16 of the Constitutional Treaty, Brussels, 6 February 2003, CONV 528/03, Annex I: *Draft Text of the Articles of the Treaty Establishing a Constitution for Europe*, 12.

187 A Buchanan and R Keohane, 'The Legitimacy of Global Governance Institutions' (2006) 20 *Ethics & International Affairs* 405, 405 (emphasis in the original).

188 On the distinction between 'input' and 'output' legitimacy, see F Scharpf, *Governing Europe: Effective and Legitimate?* (OUP, 1999).

189 Peter (n 185).

190 Sjursen (n 14) 6.

191 See Sjursen (n 14) 8.

inspired its own creation, development and enlargement'[192] and aim to uphold and promote the Union's values,[193] which in turn are 'common to the Member States'.[194] Therefore, there is at least a first step towards legitimacy beyond individual states given that these norms are ostensibly shared by a regional community. Furthermore, these values and codified foreign policy objectives are partially derived from regional or international standards such as the ECHR and also call for respect for international law, putting a special emphasis on the UN and multilateralism. In EU development policy, the Treaties clearly take account of this international dimension. While input legitimacy can be gained internally through pursuing constitutional objectives of the Union,[195] it is externally linked to compliance with commitments 'approved in the context of the United Nations and other competent international organisations'.[196] While this alone certainly does not suffice to legitimize the entirety of foreign policy objectives of the EU as norms of universal value, there are at least clear inroads towards 'universality' as a threshold for their legitimizing potential.[197]

Asserting that particular 'outputs' are beneficial in the sense that they 'promote the common welfare of the constituency in question'[198] is an inherently normative claim. From this point of view, constitutional objectives sketch out ideal conditions to be fashioned by public policy in the pursuit of the 'common welfare' or 'common good'. They represent benchmarks for the output of government action, and consequently for its output legitimacy. Against this backdrop, the EU can 'present and legitimate itself as being more than the sum of its parts',[199] ie it is capable of performing better in delivering beneficial consequences than the individual Member States. This applies to the area of foreign policy, as the Member States may recognize that 'a strong European presence in the world is potentially beneficial to all in increasing individual member states' international influence'.[200] This dovetails with the idea of the 'shifting bounds of possibility'—an understanding that more can be achieved internationally, also with regard to the more effective pursuit of national constitutional objectives through the Union, rather than by relying solely on autonomous national foreign policy (see also Chapter 4, section 6).

[192] Art 21(1), first subpara TEU. [193] Art 3(5) and 21(2)(a) TEU.

[194] Art 2 TEU. But note also Aggestam and Hill who point to the challenge posed by the transnational character of EU politics, which reveals a more complex reality than the Treaties may suggest: L Aggestam and C Hill, 'The Challenge of Multiculturalism in European Foreign Policy' (2008) 84 *International Affairs* 97.

[195] Art 208(1), first subpara TFEU, stating that EU development policy is to be 'conducted within the framework of the principles and objectives of the Union's external action'; and Art 208(1), second subpara TFEU, identifying as 'its primary objective the reduction and, in the long term, the eradication of poverty'.

[196] Art 208(2), second subpara TFEU.

[197] This runs counter to the assertion of Bradford and Posner that they 'have not seen a defense' of the view that 'European norms reflect the universal norms of international law': Bradford and Posner (n 110) 12. Whereas it is certainly misguided to simply assume such universal value, at least at the constitutional level of the EU these links are made evident.

[198] Sjursen (n 14) 6. [199] Manners (n 7) 244. [200] Wong (n 47) 161.

However, in the area of foreign policy and regarding the idea of pursuing the 'global common good', with humankind as the ultimate 'constituency', the matter becomes more complicated. Whereas certain outputs may be domestically legitimated, not least through constitutional sanction, the criterion of universality re-enters the picture with a view to legitimizing the outputs they oblige the constitutional order to strive towards internationally.

To take an example from the CSDP, the EU operation launched in the fight against Somali piracy (EU NAVFOR *Atalanta*) produces 'outputs' which are certainly in the interests of the EU, not least as a major trade power and as an aspiring security actor,[201] which are also reflected in the primary law in the form of constitutional foreign policy objectives.[202] However, the EU did not fail to stress that its actions were also in the interests of the international community at large, as they supported UN Security Council resolutions and protected shipments of humanitarian aid and maritime traffic in general.[203] Such internationally desirable outputs, in turn, are expressly mandated by the EU Treaties. For instance, the operation represents a contribution to a multilateral solution 'to common problems, in particular in the framework of the United Nations',[204] as well as to the 'respect for the principles of the United Nations Charter',[205] and is a means of strengthening 'international security in accordance with the principles of the United Nations Charter'.[206]

In sum, beyond providing the basic framework for legality with a given legal order, constitutional law serves as a source for providing legitimacy for actions of public policy, both in the sociological and normative sense of the terms. Constitutional foreign policy objectives are particularly suited to legitimating the external action of the EU, as long as its action reflects the objectives, shows an added value compared to what individual Member States could achieve, and is consistent with international norms and standards.

However, it should be noted that the long-term perspective has an effect on the legitimacy of constitutional norms. Constitutional entrenchment can become detrimental to legitimating power over the course of time, which is known in constitutional theory as the problematic of the 'dead hand of the past'.[207] Why should

[201] See B Germond and M Smith, 'Re-Thinking European Security Interests and the ESDP: Explaining the EU's Anti-Piracy Operation' (2009) 30 *Contemporary Security Policy* 573, 579–81.

[202] Arts 3(5) and 21(2)(a) and (c) TEU, which refer to security and the interests of the Union.

[203] Council of the European Union, Joint Action 2008/851/CFSP of 10 November 2008 on a European Union military operation to contribute to the deterrence, prevention and repression of acts of piracy and armed robbery off the Somali coast [2008] OJ L 301/33, Art 1. See also M Riddervold, 'Finally Flexing Its Muscles? Atalanta—The European Union's Naval Military Operation against Piracy' (2011) 20 *European Security* 385, 400, who considers the operation an example of the EU behaving as a 'humanitarian actor'.

[204] Art 21(1), first subpara TEU.

[205] Art 3(5) TEU.

[206] Art 41(2) TEU on the tasks of the CSDP.

[207] Raz (n 4) 164–9. See also J Usman, 'Non-Justiciable Directive Principles: A Constitutional Design Effect' (2007) 15 *Michigan State Journal of International Law* 643, who criticizes Indian directive principles mainly for this reason; and for the US context, see A Samaha, 'Dead Hand Arguments and Constitutional Interpretation' (2008) 108 *Columbia Law Review* 606.

current generations adhere to rules enacted by people who are long gone? Over time, such constitutionally expressed preferences thus diminish in their reflecting of the beliefs of the present constituency of members, and may cease to enshrine outcomes which would be seen as beneficial by that community. In the area of foreign policy, codified objectives would amount to this proverbial dead hand remaining at the helm of the ship of state. As Adriana Sinclair stresses in her critical approach, processes of norm formation are in themselves political, and legal codification privileges certain norms over others, creating a constraining structure rather than an apolitical, uncontested space.[208] The 'dead hand of the past' problem as applied to the constitutional objectives on foreign policy could be seen as taking this to the extreme. A certain 'world view' is taken out of the political sphere, placed in a polity's highest laws and becomes entrenched. Although the Lisbon Treaty only entered into force in 2009, Sinclair reminds us of the politics and social structures that produced these laws and then chose to make it harder for not only their contemporaries, but also later generations, to change them.

5.4 Foreign policy objectives and 'Europeanization'

Linked to the issues of identity and legitimacy, which can both be derived from constitutional norms, is that of socialization, and more particularly 'Europeanization'. The evolution of foreign policy objectives in the EU Treaties, as well as their operation within the European constitutional space, can be seen as both the product of, and propellant for, such processes. 'Europeanization' refers generally 'to the political and policy changes caused by the impact of membership of the European Union on the member states'.[209] Reuben Wong argues that foreign policy is by no means excluded from such impact and describes Europeanization in this area as 'a dynamic and increasingly dense interplay between national policies through a complex process of negotiating and coordinating through EU institutions'.[210] Such processes can 'create, reflect, and diffuse inter-subjective normative understandings' and advance 'normative convergence among actors'.[211]

Constitutional foreign policy objectives and their operationalization as legal norms can contribute to the understanding of the different ways in which Europeanization takes place. One way to conceive of Europeanization is as a top-down process of national adaptation to the requirements of EU membership.[212] As shown in Chapter 4, in the quest for coherence in EU external action, legal concepts such as implied powers based on necessity or the duty of sincere cooperation are premised on the need to effectively pursue Union objectives. This

[208] Sinclair (n 22) 23–5, drawing on M Zehfuss, *Constructivism in International Relations* (CUP, 2002) 148.

[209] Wong (n 47) 150 (italics removed).

[210] Wong (n 47) 150.

[211] L Martin and B Simmons, 'International Organizations and Institutions' in W Carlsnaes, T Risse, and B Simmons (eds), *Handbook of International Relations*, 2nd edn (SAGE, 2013) 335.

[212] Wong (n 47) 151; drawing mainly on R Ladrech, 'Europeanisation of Domestic Politics and Institutions: The Case of France' (1994) 32 *Journal of Common Market Studies* 69.

frequently results in constraining Member State behaviour on the international scene. Union objectives (internal and external) hence serve as a constitutional tool to 'Europeanize' the foreign policies of the Member States.

At the same time, the findings of Chapters 2 and 4 also serve as evidence for the 'bottom up' understanding of Europeanization, according to which Member States 'project' or 'upload' 'their national preferences to the EU level'.[213] In this way, the EU is used by the Member States 'as a means and vehicle for the achievement of nationally defined goals'.[214] Such 'nationally defined goals' can be increasingly found in national constitutions, including European integration, participation in the European Union's foreign policy, and particular forms of international cooperation. The Member States, as the 'Masters of the Treaties', have clearly left their mark on the EU Treaties in these respects. A historical example of this is the special reference to the African Caribbean and Pacific (ACP) countries,[215] which was only removed with the Lisbon reform. Other illustrations include the careful formulations in the area of the CFSP/CSDP to safeguard foreign policy preferences of both neutral and strongly Atlanticist Member States or the French insistence on adding the protection of citizens as a Union objective in its relations with the wider world.[216] Member States thus have not only 'uploaded' their national preferences and goals in terms of policy, but also entrenched them in the highest laws of the Union.

Understanding the two above-mentioned processes as interrelated long-term phenomena, it is argued furthermore in the social sciences that a process of 'socialization' occurs in which policies of the Member States begin to converge,[217] developing 'shared senses of legitimate (and illegitimate) choices'.[218] Critically, a distinction is made between 'direct' and 'indirect' Europeanization, similar to that used in Chapter 4, when describing the different legal effects of foreign policy objectives.[219] The former, according to Wong, means that competences have 'passed from the member states to the European Union'.[220] In legal terms, this relates to primacy, exclusivity, and pre-emption, which force Member States to pursue their national constitutional objectives within the Union rather than on the world stage. The latter indicates processes 'where member states begin to emulate one another regarding particular policy choices or policy frameworks'.[221] This dovetails with the concepts of coherence, sincere cooperation, and synergy, which aim to foster a sense of shared direction among the Union and its Member States.

[213] Wong (n 47) 152; drawing, inter alia, on T Börzel, 'Pace-Setting, Foot-Dragging, and Fence-Sitting: Member State Responses to Europeanization' (2002) 40 *Journal of Common Market Studies* 193.

[214] Wong (n 47) 152.

[215] Art 179(3) TEC.

[216] E de Poncins, *Le traité de Lisbonne en 27 clés* (Lignes de repères, 2008) 75–6.

[217] Wong (n 47) 152–4.

[218] Wong (n 47) 154.

[219] Wong (n 47) 153, drawing on C Radaelli, 'How Does Europeanization Produce Domestic Policy Change? Corporate Tax Policy in Italy and the United Kingdom' (1997) 30 *Comparative Political Studies* 553.

[220] Wong (n 47) 153.

[221] Wong (n 47) 153.

In this context, litigation before the CJEU can be seen as a way of establishing principles of what constitute not only legal but also 'legitimate' or 'appropriate' forms of Member State behaviour. As was demonstrated in the previous chapter, the foreign policy objectives of the EU play an important role as a common focal point. For instance, one can learn from the case law of the CJEU that it is inappropriate for Member States to negotiate international agreements with third parties without consulting with the EU organs, and in particular to conclude international agreements while the Union is still negotiating in the same area.[222] As another example, where a Union measure relates to financing and assisting in a disarmament programme carried out by other regional actors, the procedures in the Treaties for development cooperation have to be followed.[223] The procedures of the CFSP apply where the Union itself adopts measures aimed at maintaining international security, for instance, by fighting international terrorism.[224] Once the Court of Justice establishes the principle, by virtue of a judgment, it serves as a guideline for future behaviour. As *res iudicata*, it is not necessary to re-litigate the same issue over and over again. As a matter of policy, a pattern of behaviour to be followed is established. Only when there is no clarity as to the scope of the principle is there occasion to again seek clarification through judicial means.[225]

Eventually, it is argued, through this constant shaping of what is both legal and legitimate in the conduct of foreign policy of the Member States and the Union, Europeanization can lead to 'the redefinition and negotiation of identities'.[226] Over time, through interaction within the framework of the Union and under the guidance of the objectives of the Union, Member States move towards becoming the 'cohesive force in international relations' that the Treaties evoke.[227]

The end result of such a process of Europeanization is not the emergence of a super-state, as functionalism, federalism, and realism would have it.[228] Here, the notion of 'constitutional identity' within the European constitutional space is telling. It operates as a safeguard against pushing European integration to a point where the Member States would be entirely absorbed into such a super-state, and would consequently cease to be actors on the international stage. As the present analysis of the constitutional framework of the system of European foreign policy shows, constitutional objectives can under no circumstances be pursued in a way that would upset the basic structural principles of a given legal order. Within the European constitutional space, safeguarding the constitutional identity

[222] Case C-433/03 *Commission v Germany (Inland Waterway)*, EU:C:2005:462.

[223] At least as the pre-Lisbon case law suggests in *Commission v Council (Small arms and light weapons)* (n 124); for a potentially broader interpretation of CFSP objectives post-Lisbon, note *Ahmed Abdelaziz Ezz* (n 64).

[224] *Parliament v Council (Al-Qaeda Sanctions)* (n 125).

[225] For instance, this was the case with the effects of the duty of cooperation in the contexts of exclusive and shared Union competence. Compare Case C-45/07 *Commission v Greece (IMO)*, EU:C:2009:81; and Case C-246/07 *Commission v Sweden (PFOS)*, EU:C:2010:203.

[226] Wong (n 47) 152, drawing on, among others, L Aggestam, 'Role-identity and the Europeanisation of Foreign Policy: A Political-Cultural Approach' in B Tonra and T Christiansen (eds), *Rethinking European Foreign Policy* (Manchester University Press, 2004).

[227] Art 24(3), second subpara TEU, with regard to the CFSP.

[228] Wong (n 47) 151.

of the Member States is such a structural principle. This is in line with the concern expressed by Aggestam that both the 'civilian' and 'normative power' literature 'consigns to sealed black boxes the underlying dynamics represented by the member states in the constitutive politics and processes of European foreign policy'.[229] The idea of 'ethical power Europe', by contrast, heeds the role the Member States play 'in the dynamics of European foreign policy',[230] as does the pluralist understanding of the European Union.

In sum, according to the constitutional framework of EU external relations, as well as the 'ethical power' concept, even though Europeanization may reshape identities and foster their convergence, it cannot amalgamate them. Here, one can see agreement in legal and IR scholarship as to an understanding of Europeanization, which 'does not mean that the European will simply supplant the national over time'[231] with 'a supranational centre eclipsing the national capitals'.[232] Hence, constitutional foreign policy objectives, both at EU and Member State level, reflect such Europeanization, and serve to advance it further. However, the ultimate aim is convergence and coherence, and not the creation of a super-state as a unitary international actor.

6. Conclusion: A 'Normative Power', in Law and in Theory

This chapter brought together the different disciplinary perspectives of constitutional law and international relations with regard to the EU as an international actor. It assessed what constitutional law has to say about different IR theories, and vice versa, yielding several conclusions. As regards the EU Treaties, they leave ample room for the pursuit of interests next to values. Furthermore, the design of the external relations system of the EU bolsters the idea of security and other 'first-order' interests as central objectives of the state and not of the Union. At the same time, the history of the foreign policy objectives in the EU Treaties fits well into the narratives of European integration as 'democratic peace' and as a commercial project. In addition, the foreign policy objectives present in the EU Treaties put a distinctive emphasis on international norms and institutions. The propensity of the Treaties, especially after the Lisbon reform, to list the various values and principles that are to guide EU foreign policy, as well as the global trend of 'dynamic internationalization' of constitutional law, clearly cater to the central tenet of constructivist approaches that ideas, norms, and values matter more than the classic theories give them credit for.

The reverse perspective paints a more complex picture, asking why the study of IR should take account of constitutional law at all. Here, strongly divergent answers emerge. Given the deep scepticism with which realism regards idealist motivations as well as the role of law in the international arena, foreign policy

229 Aggestam (n 18) 4.
230 Aggestam (n 18) 4.
231 Wong (n 47) 167.
232 Wong (n 47) 168.

objectives as codified in a legal text can only be regarded as virtually devoid of merit. This would appear especially so if these objectives hail from a non-state entity such as the EU. In this sense, realists find themselves on the same side as the detractors of such constitutional objectives among legal scholars. For realist scholars, the function of the state in the world is a given, governed by 'natural laws', which positive law is not capable of altering. Realism thus cautions against overestimating the immediate practical value of such objectives, as all 'good intentions' tend to succumb under pressure to more existential concerns.

Liberal approaches, especially their institutionalist and intergovernmentalist strands, are likely to take such objectives more seriously. This, however, does not mean they would welcome them as normatively desirable. Rather, liberal thinking in terms of multilevel games and institutional politics highlights the ways in which such objectives, their general legal definition as expressions of the 'common good' notwithstanding, can be used by institutional actors for their own good. Hence, even though directed at shaping the international order, liberalism emphasizes the domestic significance of such norms. In the EU context, national constitutional integration objectives serve the interests of Member State governments, while Union objectives serve, in turn, to constrain the Member States. Furthermore, given the continuing division among different EU external policies, different EU foreign policy objectives are used by Union institutions when this is to their advantage.

Lastly, constructivist approaches can draw on constitutional foreign policy objectives in a variety of ways, in particular in view of the role they play in forming identities, to legitimize behaviour, and involve different actors and communities in processes of socialization. However, to what extent such constitutional norms serve to establish the 'normative basis' of EU foreign policy and are reflective of the 'distinctiveness' and global validity of EU foreign policy is a matter of contention. The initial version of the 'normative power' concept devised by Manners seems to accept such norms as proof for both *tout court*. Later reflections on this call for a more nuanced view, requiring a degree of universal appeal for these norms to form not just a source of law, but also of benchmarks for defending the 'global common good', including as perceived from the outside. Similar considerations apply to constitutional foreign policy objectives as a source of legitimacy. While in the intra-EU context, measures in their pursuit benefit from both 'input' and 'output' legitimacy, this is not automatically the case at the international level. There, links to internationally agreed standards and the furtherance of global norms also need to be established in order to benefit from such legitimacy.

While realist approaches tend to discard the immediate usefulness of such norms, and liberalism highlights how they may be instrumentalized in any given case, constructivist scholarship emphasizes their long-term impact. Over time, through European integration and foreign policy coordination, both the Member States and the Union institutions become 'socialized' in a common framework, sharing common understandings as well as a collective identity. Constitutional foreign policy objectives serve as an expression of such processes, but can also be used to advance them further. Both the constructivist view and the idea of a common but pluralist constitutional space, also with regard to the conduct of foreign relations, stress that increasing convergence and coherence do not necessarily lead to the demise of the identities and roles of the constituent parts and their amalgamation into a unitary structure, ie a super-state.

Conclusion

1. European Constitutional Law: Between 'Worldly Ambition' and *spes saeculi*

This book started with the observation that many constitutions today, including the EU Treaties, not only refer to the *salus populi*—the welfare of the people—but have come to display global ambitions. Constitutional foreign policy objectives represent the codified and entrenched aspirations of a political community in the world. However, the term 'global ambition' is marked by an ambiguity that also applies to the appreciation of these as constitutional norms. Global ambition—or 'worldly ambition'—evokes what Saint Augustine, in his work *Confessions*, called *spes saeculi*. For Saint Augustine, it connoted a hedonistic, self-serving lifestyle geared towards 'success in this world'.[1] Eventually, he would cast off his 'worldly ambitions' and instead aspire to greater theological endeavours. A literal translation of the term, however, results in something far less pejorative: 'Hope for the world' or 'hope of our times'.

In an endeavour to move beyond offhand dismissal or unquestioning enthusiasm, this book sought to shed light on constitutional foreign policy objectives as legal norms, their force, and their functions both within a legal order and between the intertwined legal orders of Europe. Having traversed the various chapters from comparative constitutional law, the law of the European Union, the European constitutional space, and finally international relations, it has become evident that these norms cater to both of these aspects. They are at the same time a constitutional expression of the 'hopes' of a political community for the world, but also an instrument that is used by self-interested actors for their very own 'worldly ambitions'.

2. Looking Back: Summary and Main Findings

The book addressed a phenomenon in constitutional law in general and for the European Union in particular, ie the proliferation of norms which appear rather

[1] RSO Tomlin, '*Spes Saeculi*: Augustine's Worldly Ambition and Career' in M Vessey (ed), *A Companion to Augustine* (Wiley-Blackwell, 2012) 57.

peculiar from both the perspective of the traditional charters of international organizations as well as national constitutional documents. These have been given here the generic term 'constitutional foreign policy objectives'. Their peculiarity stems, on the one hand, from the fact that they are not narrowly described technical tasks such as, for instance, ensuring 'a uniform system of administration for the Danube',[2] running a lighthouse on the Moroccan coast,[3] or 'the attainment by all peoples of the highest possible level of health'.[4] On the other hand, they are not among the norms one would traditionally expect in a constitutional text. They are neither individual rights nor norms that distribute power among the different branches and levels of government. Moreover, they are not 'social rights' concerned with the improvement of the living conditions within a particular community, but instead focus on the relations of the polity with the outside world.

These objectives constitutionally commit the state and the EU to pursue certain goals through their foreign policy. These can be rather obvious, such as safeguarding 'national security and independence'[5] and providing 'for the common defence',[6] or overtly self-serving, such as the promotion of the 'interest' of the EU[7] or safeguarding 'the interests of the Swiss economy abroad'.[8] They often evoke rather broad, opaque notions such as the 'devotion to the ideal of peace and friendly co-operation amongst nations founded on international justice and morality'[9] or 'the creation of the international order based on law and justice'.[10] They can be very ambitious, committing the state or the Union to nothing less than the 'the abolition of imperialism, colonialism and any other form of aggression, domination and exploitation in the relations among peoples',[11] 'the alleviation of need and poverty in the world',[12] or the promotion of 'an international system based on stronger multilateral cooperation and good global governance'.[13] They can be reflective of a rather traditional view of the international legal order, stressing the 'principles of mutual respect for sovereignty and territorial integrity, mutual non-aggression, non-interference in each other's internal affairs',[14] or emphasize instead 'the respect for human rights, democracy, the peaceful coexistence of nations, as well as the preservation of natural living conditions'.[15] They can reach out to other countries that share the same language and history,[16] promote regional integration,[17] and

[2] Convention establishing the Definitive Statute of the Danube, Paris, 23 July 1921, League of Nations Treaties Series, Volume XXVI, 173, Art 39.

[3] Convention Concerning the Administration and Upholding of the Lighthouse at Cape Spartel, Tangier, 31 May 1865 (1912) 16 *American Journal of International Law Supplement* 14; see also D Bederman, 'The Souls of International Organizations: Legal Personality and the Lighthouse at Cape Spartel' (1996) 36 *Virginia Journal of International Law* 275.

[4] Constitution of the World Health Organization, Art 2.

[5] Art 24(2) Bulgarian constitution.

[6] Preamble, United States constitution.

[7] Arts 3(5) and 21(2) TEU.

[8] Art 101(1) Swiss constitution.

[9] Art 29(1) Irish constitution.

[10] Art 135(1) Lithuanian constitution.

[11] Art 7(2) Portuguese constitution.

[12] Art 54(2) Swiss constitution.

[13] Art 21(2)(h) TEU.

[14] Preamble, Chinese constitution.

[15] Art 54(2) Swiss constitution.

[16] Art 87 French constitution; Art 7(4) Portuguese constitution.

[17] See the various 'Europe clauses' in the constitutions of the Member States (Chapter 2, section 4.6); and Art 4 (sole paragraph) Brazilian constitution on integration in Latin America.

commit the EU to the goal of 'an area of prosperity and good neighbourliness'.[18] In other cases, however, they can commit a state to refrain from entering into military alliances,[19] or prohibit merging with others to resurrect certain unions deemed undesirable by the constitution.[20]

Motivated by this wealth of constitutional foreign policy objectives, and prompted by the dearth of legal scholarship with regard to their role and function within and across legal orders, the book scrutinized them with the help of insights from comparative constitutional law. Instead of representing constitutional rarities, it was demonstrated how they are increasingly commonplace norms in constitutional law. They reflect the codified expression of two major trends in the evolution of constitutional law, ie the 'internationalization' and 'dynamization' of constitutional law. In addition to drawing a horizontal comparison of national constitutions and a 'transposition', *mutatis mutandis*, to the EU level, the book analysed their role with particular regard to the European constitutional space. This showed how cooperation and integration, also in the pursuit of foreign policy objectives, can produce new sophisticated structures, which in turn obtain objectives of their own to be pursued in the wider world. This introduces a third trend, ie the 'Europeanization' of both law and foreign policy.

While foreign policy objectives are a common feature in many modern constitutions, not every country can boast a consolidated doctrine within which to fit such norms in an abstract sense. The German, French, and Indian concepts of, respectively, *Staatszielbestimmungen, objectifs de valeur constitutionnelle*, and directive principles of state policy, offered a solid and mutually compatible framework for understanding the role and functions of constitutional objectives in general, of which, as it was argued, foreign policy objectives represent a subcategory. As to their position within the constitutional order, foreign policy objectives can best be described as residing at the intersection of constitutional objectives and the foreign affairs constitution (*Außenverfassungsrecht*). This explains why, in the majority of cases, they are located within the part of the constitutional text that deals with international relations, and only rarely within the list of general objectives of the state.

A comparative analysis of these three doctrines yielded a largely uniform idea of what foreign policy objectives can and cannot do within a given legal order. In all three there is general agreement that they represent genuine constitutional norms, despite some criticisms as to the usefulness of their inclusion in a constitutional document. By more enthusiastic commentators, they have been termed part of the 'soul'[21]

[18] Art 8(1) TEU.

[19] Art 9a(1) Austrian constitution and the constitutional law on neutrality (*Neutralitätsgetz*); Art 1(3) Maltese constitution.

[20] Art 150 Lithuanian constitution and the constitutional act 'On the Non-Alignment of the Republic of Lithuania to Post-Soviet Eastern Unions' of 8 June 1992; see also Art 142(2) Croatian constitution.

[21] B De Villiers, 'Directive Principles of State Policy and Fundamental Rights: The Indian Experience' (1992) 8 *South African Journal on Human Rights* 29, 33.

or 'souffle'[22] of the constitution, together with the 'values' enshrined in the constitution. Most explicitly, the Indian constitution proclaims them to be 'fundamental in the governance of the country'.[23] This means that they are binding on all organs of the state. However, in all three doctrines there is similar agreement that their binding force is rather weak, a property which Pierre De Montalivet aptly calls their *normativité limitée*.[24] This resonates strongly with the scepticism that the theory of realism in international relations exhibits towards the role of law and norms in international politics. They neither establish individual rights or duties, nor do they, as such, establish any powers to act. They cannot be pursued in a way that would compromise the structural principles of the legal order. In terms of negative obligations, only the most manifest disregard of constitutional objectives could constitute a justiciable violation of the constitution, if at all. In terms of positive obligations, the full realization of the objective is not required, but instead its active pursuit within the bounds of what is materially possible—the caveat of feasibility. Therefore, similar to social rights, they can be understood as Dworkinian principles or Alexian optimization requirements rather than as rigid rules.

This leads to the third, and arguably most important, legal function, which has been called here the 'interpretive–permissive' function. While there is overall agreement in the three doctrines that constitutional objectives are only marginally justiciable as such, there is at the same time a consensus that they serve as an interpretive device. In view of the way in which constitutional objectives are usually relied upon in adjudication, and given the way they are used by courts in their reasoning, such interpretation usually serves to justify the enhancement of public powers, either vis-à-vis other constitutional organs or with regard to measures which restrict individual rights. However, while the entire constitution and secondary law are to be interpreted in the light of constitutional objectives, such interpretations cannot upset the structural principles and foundations of the legal order.

Regarding constitutional foreign policy objectives, the analysis showed that only the first two functions are affected by the fact that they pertain to this particular policy area. There is an overall consensus that the general caveat of feasibility is accentuated in the area of foreign policy, given the addition of factors which are beyond the control of the state or the EU. The set of solutions that the political branches can furnish to tackle questions of foreign policy, in the words of the *Bundesverfassungsgericht*, is essentially 'narrowed down to what is politically achievable with regard to the external partners'.[25] Therefore, both the obliging and prohibitive force of constitutional objectives in this area is diminished. However, from the point of justiciability and enforceability, constitutional objectives already play

[22] A Pilette and E de Poncins, 'Valeurs, objectifs et nature de l'Union' in G Amato, H Bribosia, and B De Witte (eds), *Genesis and Destiny of the European Constitution* (Bruylant, 2007) 309.

[23] Art 37 Indian constitution.

[24] P De Montalivet, *Les objectifs de valeur constitutionnelle* (Dalloz, 2006) 563.

[25] In the original: 'auf das dem jeweiligen Vertragspartner gegenüber politisch Erreichbare verengt': Decision of 4 May 1955 (*Saarstatut*), BVerfGE 4, 157, para 37.

a marginal role. Hence, the practical relevance of this observation, while theoretically relevant, is of limited practical consequence.

This dilution of their legal force does not apply to the interpretive–permissive function of constitutional foreign policy objectives, which is indeed of tangible practical relevance. By invoking an objective that is 'fundamental to the international community',[26] as opposed to one of mere domestic significance, the opposite picture emerges. Foreign policy objectives appear at least as important as their internal counterparts. Compared to constitutional objectives directed at the internal sphere, foreign policy objectives can serve to enhance public powers even further. The strongest examples of this are arguably 'integration objectives' which help to justify the transfer of sovereign powers to supranational organizations.

As regards the EU Treaties and the wealth of foreign policy objectives they contain, it was shown that they recognized, from the very beginning, that European integration was connected to global governance in the form of a vague notion of 'world peace' and the insertion of specific goals for the Common Commercial Policy. As integration progressed, the codified ambitions of the Union and its predecessors thrived. After milestones such as the Single European Act and the Maastricht Treaty, it was above all through the Convention on the Future of Europe, the results of which were largely integrated into the Lisbon Treaty, that the foreign policy objectives of the Union have been codified in the most extensive and ambitious manner to date.

However, compared to national constitutions, the EU Treaties are by no means special in that they show codified global ambitions. In terms of the substance of constitutional foreign policy objectives present in the constitutions of the twenty-eight EU Member States, as well as the constitutions of a selection of third countries, it emerged that only a few constitutions are either entirely silent or distinctively verbose in this regard. In the vast majority of cases, at least one provision exhibiting the objectives for the foreign policy of a state was included. The examples found could be organized according to six basic substantive categories, ie the prohibition of war, collective security and defence, respect for international law, promotion of human rights, integration, and international solidarity. The EU Treaties address all of these categories with their objectives, but also add additional themes, ie free and fair trade, and promoting the rule of law and democracy. Whereas the former was present from the beginning as the external dimension of the common market, the latter represent an innovation compared to most constitutions. Consequently, it can be concluded that while the EU Treaties are not unique, they certainly are in the vanguard in terms of constitutionally codifying an explicit and wide-ranging foreign policy agenda.

On the basis of the common vocabulary derived from comparative constitutional law to understand the legal functions of foreign policy objectives as well as common themes in terms of substance, the analysis turned to the constitutional credentials of the EU and its codified objectives. Instead of a simple one-by-one

[26] Joined Cases C-402/05 P and C-415/05 P *Kadi and Al Barakaat*, EU:C:2008:461, para 363.

transfer, the particular nature of the EU and its legal order had to be carefully accounted for. This first required an assessment of the claim of the 'constitutionalization' of the Union. The book subscribes to the view that constitutionalism in the 'thick' sense is not restricted to states. Instead, it is more useful to conceive of it as a possibility for all forms of political community, given that they fulfil a certain threshold. This threshold, although hard to define in absolute terms, would include the presence of a normative order, ie a set of broad values underpinning the legal order that go beyond limited and technical functions which characterize classic international organizations. In addition to this normative element, a sophisticated and balanced institutional apparatus is necessary which legislates, administers, and adjudicates within this order on the basis of its normative grounding. This includes the protection of individual rights in a comprehensive and effective manner. Revisiting the historical evolution of the European Union, including the widening of its competences and objectives, confirmed that despite its lack of statehood, the Union meets such a standard.

This preliminary conclusion required special attention to be paid to the idea of *finalité* of the Union. From the point of view of constitutional objectives, it is difficult to view it as an objective in its own right, much less as a 'substantive' objective. As the President of the European Commission José Manuel Barroso noted in his 2012 Nobel Peace Prize lecture, the 'quest for European unity' is 'not an end in itself, but a means to higher ends'.[27] Thus, deeper integration and the idea of an 'ever closer Union' can be understood rather as a rationale for the more effective pursuit of substantive objectives. It has to be balanced, however, with other constitutional principles of the EU, above all conferral, subsidiarity, and preservation of the 'constitutional identity' of the Member States.

Having accepted the constitutional credentials of the EU legal order, the analysis then scrutinized the role and place of constitutional objectives within the Union legal order. It was shown that in a manner very similar to the national sphere, Union objectives, including those pertaining to its external action, are indeed part and parcel of the primary law. They bind all Union organs to the active pursuit of these goals at home and abroad. However, they also operate for all practical purposes as an interpretive–permissive device for the benefit of enhancing public powers, and in this vein, as a way to justify measures adopted which restrict individual rights.

Following the analysis of the national and Union spheres individually, it was imperative to bring them together within the shared European constitutional space. Here, the reasons for selecting Europe and the EU for the present enquiry became most evident. Instead of simply comparing the operation of certain constitutional norms by juxtaposition or by transferring national concepts to the European level, the interaction of constitutional norms in a pluralistic and multilevel context was

[27] H Van Rompuy and J Durão Barroso, *From War to Peace: A European Tale*, Nobel Peace Prize Lecture on behalf of the European Union, Oslo, 10 December 2012, <http://consilium.europa.eu/uedocs/cms_data/docs/pressdata/en/ec/134126.pdf>, 6.

explored. This context is above all marked by the dual challenge of fostering unity in the European polity while maintaining diversity between legal orders. The area of foreign policy and the pursuit of foreign policy objectives from various constitutional sources only serve to stress this challenge further. Whereas the idea of a joint constitutional space already highlights the presence of a multitude of constitutional sources and legal orders, the focus on foreign policy adds the multiplicity of actors on the international stage. Both the EU and its Member States all pursue their own goals but are bound together through their common adherence to the rules of this constitutional space.

Generally, viewing the substance of foreign policy objectives present in this space, a large degree of convergence becomes evident. Nonetheless, there are identifiable areas of tension, especially in the area of security and defence policy. In order to grasp the management of this intricate balance in all its different aspects in the double context of constitutional pluralism and foreign affairs 'polyphony', the book embraced a three-level conception of coherence and connected it to the concept of pluralism in the European constitutional space. Given that constitutional foreign policy objectives reside precisely at the intersection of constitutional law and foreign relations law, only such a combined approach promises to elucidate fully their role and function within the constitutional space.

Firstly, in terms of consistency, the primacy of EU law over national law needs to be balanced with the protection of the constitutional identity of the Member States. Accordingly, the foreign policy objectives of the EU Treaties, or indeed any EU law, reign supreme over their national counterparts. Hence, the pursuit of national foreign policy objectives cannot be used as an excuse not to comply with the obligations of EU membership or in order to defect from rules that the Member States helped to bring about at the Union level. Nevertheless, even though specific Member State policy concerns, such as neutrality, do not always have constitutional status, the constitutional framework for EU external relations accommodates these sensitivities to a large extent. Moreover, the general rule of primacy does not apply when obligations would compromise the narrowly defined constitutional identity of the Member States, including their statehood and consequently their status as actors on the international stage. However, constitutional foreign policy objectives do not a priori form part of this identity, and would thus in most cases not benefit from protection thereunder.

Secondly, concerning coherence understood as the delimitation of tasks, it was shown that Member States are barred from pursuing their own objectives independently where the Union has exclusive competence or where the former are pre-empted due to common rules of Union law. Furthermore, it revealed how Union objectives help to shape external powers of the EU, which may in turn restrict the scope of action of the Member States. However, this does not result in the Member States having to abandon the objectives enshrined in their respective constitutions altogether. Instead, the pursuit of these may be channelled through the Union and no longer through autonomous actions on the international stage. As a particularity of the EU, any action must be based on the proper legal basis in EU law, which determines the procedures to be followed and the institutional prerogatives that these entail. In ascertaining this, objectives play a crucial role as well, thus making them an important reference point in inter-institutional litigation.

Thirdly, when conceiving of coherence as synergy, the role of the EU's foreign policy objectives as a common focal point for the external action of both the Member States and the EU became evident. The legal principles that are to bring about such synergy, above all the duty of sincere cooperation and the unity of international representation, ultimately rely on the need for Union objectives to be pursued effectively and not to be jeopardized by the Member States. Without reference to Union objectives, these principles would be ends in themselves, devoid of any substance. However, a similar function for national objectives in the European constitutional space does not exist. The vanishing point for coherent external action of the EU and its Member States are the objectives codified in the EU Treaties. This does not mean that Member States can no longer pursue their own constitutional objectives, to which they remain bound as a matter of national law. In cases where their loyalty obligations towards the Union prohibit them to speak up internationally, they are to pursue them within the Union framework. The national constitutional objectives thus still serve as guidance for each Member State to act within the Union, and to the extent that it is compatible with the obligations of Union membership, also for its international action.

It is important not to consider Union membership solely as a constraining factor. One of the underlying motivations of European integration from the very outset was the insight that more could be achieved better together rather than individually. In the terminology used here, this entails a shift in the 'bounds of possibility' for both the Union and the Member States. On the one hand, for the Member States, especially the smaller ones, more can be attained if they harness the potential of the Union, including in terms of the more effective pursuit of their own constitutional objectives. On the other hand, the EU, especially in the field of foreign, security, and defence policy, is dependent on the Member States, their political willingness, and capabilities, which in turn may limit the extent to which it is feasible for the Union to act internationally. This appears to be the price to be paid in a polity that is deeply rooted in both the preservation of diversity and the quest for unity.

While the legal orders of the EU and the Member States are joined within a common constitutional space, the disciplines of law and international relations also share a joint space of themes, issues, and concepts. The legal analysis of constitutional foreign policy objectives focused on their properties as legal norms and their relations amongst each other and with other constitutional norms. Taking the analysis beyond the disciplinary boundaries of law, the final chapter of the book linked these legal findings to the debates in international relations on the role of the EU as an international actor, and in particular the importance ascribed to law and values, ideas, and norms in its foreign policy. Just as the 'dynamic internationalization' of constitutional law makes explicit the 'world view' that underlies a constitutional document, different theories of international relations present sophisticated frames of thought on the principal actors and the main factors that matter on the global stage. This chapter revisited both constitutional law and the main schools of international relations, each from the vantage point of the other. Whereas the various references in the EU Treaties to values and norms to be promoted internationally may suggest a predisposition towards constructivist approaches, the focus on the pursuit of interests and security, as well as on trade, peace, and multilateral institutional cooperation also dovetail with tenets of realist and liberal thinking, respectively. Inversing the perspective, it was shown how the different aspects emphasized by each school with regard to the role of law and the importance of norms and values in international politics help to bolster the main legal findings of the book, and open up ways to gain a deeper understanding of them.

Firstly, realist approaches stress the weak force of both law and norms in international politics whenever more existential concerns are at stake. Whatever 'normative' or 'ethical' approach actors may afford themselves when they can, ultimately the rules of survival and power struggles prevail. Realism equips the sceptics among legal scholars with additional arguments on the undesirability of the inclusion of foreign policy objectives into a constitutional document. As the more altruistic aspirations can only ever be 'second order' concerns, they should not be part of the highest laws either. Regarding the EU in particular, the fact that its founding Treaties contain so many 'ethical' goals does not mean it is in fact a 'normative' or 'ethical' power, or in fact any power at all. Whenever lawyers wish to point to the weakness and limited practical relevance of constitutional foreign policy objectives regarding any case of perceived (short-term) failure of EU foreign policy, realist scholarship can likely furnish a structural explanation.

Secondly, liberal approaches help to emphasize the internal effects that such objectives can produce. Breaking up the 'black box' of the state or the Union, they provide explanations for power struggles between different branches and levels of government. In such struggles, constitutional foreign policy objectives can serve as useful legal or rhetorical weapons. On the one hand, drawing on the logic of two-level games, integration objectives of the Member States can be used to justify the transfer of legislative powers to the European level, with the effect of enhancing the powers of the national executive. On the other hand, Union objectives, including the ones in the area of foreign policy, serve to bolster the powers of the Union vis-à-vis the Member States, the institutions vis-à-vis each other, and vis-à-vis individuals and their rights. The case law before the Court of Justice of the EU revealed that the Commission can use them to frame legal arguments in terms of Union loyalty in order to have Member States condemned for actions carried out internationally; the Council and the Commission draw on them to face off in disputes on the proper legal basis, but can also join forces to justify restrictions of individual rights. Liberal scholarship reminds us that while the EU may wield law as its 'weapon of choice'[28] in its international dealings, in fact every institution may avail itself of constitutional foreign policy objectives whenever this serves its own interests. For this reason, it is imperative to integrate constitutional policy objectives within the overall constitutional framework and to recall one of their basic

[28] M Leonard, *Why Europe Will Run the 21st Century* (Fourth Estate, 2005) 36.

characteristics, ie that they cannot be pursued in a manner that would upset the basic structure of the legal order.

Thirdly, constructivist approaches shift the focus away from crises, emergencies, and other existential moments, as well as from institutional politics and power mongering, towards long-term processes of socialization, identity formation, evolving understandings of roles, legitimacy, and the emergence of 'normative power' in international relations. As Ian Manners graphically put it, 'the long-term diffusion of ideas in a normatively sustainable way works like water on stone, not like napalm in the morning'.[29] From this point of view, constitutional foreign policy objectives are both the product of, and propellant for, such processes.

The debate on 'normative' and 'ethical power Europe' sheds light on the potential of constitutional foreign policy objectives in serving as the codified 'normative basis' for EU foreign policy and as a source of legitimacy. Ian Manners' concept of 'normative power' refers directly to the EU Treaties and their foreign policy objectives as the 'crystallization and culmination of norms and practices'.[30] However, subsequent examinations of this concept stressed that to serve as norms, the pursuit of which would be in the service of the global common good, other criteria must be met, such as the universal character of norms beyond their own legal order. Such a global common good cannot be simply promulgated by any localized document, including constitutions. Due to the inspiration that many of the EU's foreign policy objectives draw from international sources and given the emphasis the Treaties put on multilateral cooperation, there is indeed scope to consider at least part of these goals as reflecting the 'normative power' of the EU in the world at large. To the extent that actions of the EU on the international scene can be construed as pursuing such ends, they can also find legitimacy beyond the Union's borders.

Lastly, the role of constitutional law in socialization processes highlighted the third trend from which emerged, and which characterizes, the foreign policy objectives found in the EU Treaties, ie 'Europeanization'. Constructivist scholarship helps to better understand the legally peculiar European constitutional space and polyphonic system of EU external relations. It does so by stressing that identities and roles can be shared without having to result in the amalgamation of different actors. The fact that the Union and the Member States share common purposes codified in the Treaties, and that these serve as a common point of reference for their respective foreign policies, is not an absurdity, but the logical product of the integration process.

3. Looking Ahead: Trajectories of Future Research

What has this book revealed which was not known before, and how can future scholarship draw on its findings? Firstly, the research conducted here demonstrated that

[29] I Manners, 'The Normative Ethics of the European Union' (2008) 84 *International Affairs* 45, 60.

[30] Manners (n 29) 48.

foreign policy objectives are by no means a rarity in constitutional documents. This arguably says more about the concept of the state than about the EU. The EU always had a 'need for objectives' (Ipsen's *Zielbedarf*),[31] even though its goals over time moved far away from the narrowly defined ones of classic international organizations. States, on the contrary, are traditionally regarded as the 'normal' subjects of international law,[32] and as entities possessing the ultimate power to allocate all the powers within their legal order (*Kompetenz-Kompetenz*). Hence, they do not have to justify themselves by reference to any explicitly stated purposes. And yet, the modern national constitution contains exactly that. Internally, this was already captured by the proliferation of codified objectives of the state (and arguable social rights) in constitutional documents. By adding these legal norms to its highest laws, the state can be said to legitimate itself towards its citizens by virtue of constitutional promises that it will deliver through its public policy. By extending the codification of objectives to the domain of foreign policy, the state promises its citizens even more, ie a better international order and better global governance. Beyond that, it can also be seen as a means of legitimation towards the outside world, as a constitutional attestation of being a 'good international citizen'.[33] In this sense, constitutional foreign policy objectives truly become expressions of the 'higher ends'[34] which the state, the EU, or indeed any form of organized public authority are to serve as 'purposes beyond themselves'[35] and within an ever closer international environment.

Given that these norms are not the exception but are becoming the rule, it is increasingly inappropriate to simply brush them away as a 'wish list for a better world'[36] or ridicule them as 'redolent of motherhood and apple pie'.[37] At the same time, it would be unwise, and unscholarly, to have oneself enchanted by them, at which point the constitutional 'souffle' risks turning into a Siren's call. Instead of falling prey to either of these extremes, it becomes incumbent on legal scholarship to acknowledge these norms as a phenomenon of comparative constitutional law, in the national, the EU, and possibly other legal orders. This entails understanding their legal functions, their relation to other legal norms, and their role within and across legal orders. This book has put forward such a common understanding, highlighting what such norms can and cannot do. Beyond the strictly legal, these developments are also of relevance for related disciplines, a number of the links to which the book systematized.

Looking ahead, there are several directions in which further research can be conducted and for which the present work can serve as a point of departure. Three potential avenues include: Firstly, delving more deeply into the 'dynamic

[31] HP Ipsen, *Europäisches Gemeinschaftsrecht* (Mohr Siebeck, 1972) 995.

[32] V Epping, 'Völkerrechtssubjekte' in K Ipsen (ed), *Völkerrecht*, 6th edn (C.H. Beck, 2014) 49, who calls the state the 'Normalperson des Völkerrechts'.

[33] T Dunne, 'Good Citizen Europe' (2008) 84 *International Affairs* 13.

[34] Van Rompuy and Barroso (n 27) 6.

[35] Dunne (n 33) 13.

[36] In the original: 'Wunschzettel für eine bessere Welt': W Drescher, 'Ziele und Zuständigkeiten' in A Marchetti and C Demesmay (eds), *Der Vertrag von Lissabon: Analyse und Bewertung* (Nomos, 2010) 68.

[37] A Dashwood et al, *Wyatt & Dashwood's European Union Law*, 6th edn (Hart Publishing, 2011) 903.

internationalization' of constitutional law in a comparative context and analysing the consequences this has for the concepts of constitution and constitutionalism; secondly, more profound reflections on the blurring of borderlines between national, EU, and international law towards common parameters and purposes for the legitimate exercise of public authority that transcend legal orders; and, thirdly, a more thorough exploration of the shared conceptual space of law and international relations and the ensuing potentials and risks associated more generally with the 'legalization' of world politics,[38] which has acquired a distinctly constitutional dimension.

For the foreseeable future, and all crises in Europe and beyond notwithstanding, the trend of codifying foreign policy objectives into constitutions is bound to continue, as a look at the constitutions of the five most recently independent states suggests.[39] The constitution of Timor Leste from 2002 is a case in point, as it contains both an article on 'objectives of the state'[40] and an article on the country's international relations with specific foreign policy objectives.[41] In the latter, Timor Leste commits:

> to govern itself by the principles of national independence, the right of the Peoples to self-determination and independence, the permanent sovereignty of the peoples over their wealth and natural resources, the protection of human rights, the mutual respect for sovereignty, territorial integrity and equality among States and the non-interference in domestic affairs of other States.[42]

Other more recent constitutions, such as those of Montenegro, Serbia, and Kosovo, are less detailed in this respect. Nonetheless, they express, for example, that '[t]he foreign policy of the Republic of Serbia shall be based on generally accepted principles and rules of international law'[43] or that 'Montenegro shall cooperate and develop friendly relations with other states, regional and international organizations, based on the principles and rules of international law'.[44] The constitution of Kosovo includes the familiar objectives to 'respect international law',[45] to participate 'in international cooperation for promotion and protection of peace, security and human rights',[46] and to 'delegate state powers for specific matters to international organizations'.[47] Lastly, the transitional constitution of the Republic of South

[38] See J Goldstein, M Kahler, R Keohane, and A-M Slaughter, 'Introduction: Legalization and World Politics' (2000) 54 *International Organization* 385.

[39] It should be noted that not all of them have been generally recognized by the international community, especially Kosovo. This survey serves simply to illustrate this trend in contemporary constitutional drafting.

[40] Art 6 constitution of Timor Leste; see (a) and (h) specifically on foreign policy.

[41] Art 8 constitution of Timor Leste.

[42] Art 8(1) constitution of Timor Leste; note also Art 8(3) on ties with Portuguese-speaking countries and (4) on its relations with neighbouring countries and in the region.

[43] Art 16(1) Serbian constitution.

[44] Art 15(1) Montenegrin constitution; note also Art 15(3) on accession to the EU and (4) on a prohibition to 'enter into a union with another state by which it loses its independence and full international personality'.

[45] Art 16(3) Kosovar constitution.

[46] Art 17(2) Kosovar constitution.

[47] Art 20(1) Kosovar constitution.

Sudan, in force since 9 July 2011, contains a list of foreign policy objectives that is highly reminiscent of Art 21 TEU, and is worthwhile quoting in full. Article 43 of the transitional constitution on the foreign policy of South Sudan states:

> Foreign policy of the Republic of South Sudan shall serve the national interest and shall be conducted independently and transparently with the view to achieving the following:
> (a) promotion of international cooperation, specially within the United Nations family, African Union and other international and regional organizations, for the purposes of consolidating universal peace and security, respect for international law, treaty obligations and fostering a just world economic order;
> (b) achievement of African economic integration, within the ongoing regional plans and fora as well as promoting African unity and co-operation as foreseen in those plans;
> (c) enhancement of respect for human rights and fundamental freedoms regionally and internationally;
> (d) promotion of dialogue among civilizations and establishment of international order based on justice and common human destiny;
> (e) respect for international law and treaty obligations, as well as the seeking of the peaceful settlement of international disputes by negotiation, mediation, conciliation, arbitration and adjudication;
> (f) enhancement of economic cooperation among countries of the region;
> (g) non-interference in the affairs of other States, promotion of goodneighbourliness and mutual cooperation with all neighbours and maintaining amicable and balanced relations with other countries; and
> (h) combating international and trans-national organized crime, piracy and terrorism.[48]

It was the principal goal of this book to contribute to a better understanding of what it means when constitutions 'acknowledge inviolable and inalienable human rights as the foundation of every community, of peace and justice in the world',[49] when they invoke 'cooperation among people for the progress of humanity',[50] and commit 'to the reinforcement of the European identity'[51] or other regional undertakings. It endeavoured to shed light on both the potential and the fallacies that lie in the remarkable fact that both the European Union, which encapsulates twenty-eight sovereign states and which is one of the richest parts of the world, and South Sudan, as a country which is new as it is poor and ridden with conflict, call in their highest laws for similar, internationally oriented goals. These goals are as ambitious as, respectively, the promotion of 'an international system based on stronger multilateral cooperation and good global governance'[52] and the 'promotion of dialogue among civilizations and establishment of international order based on justice and common human destiny'.[53]

In sum, such constitutional expressions of global ambitions lead back to the two different ways of translating the term as used by Saint Augustine. On the one hand, the analogous translation, 'worldly ambition', coincides with the way

[48] Art 43 of the transitional constitution of the Republic of South Sudan, 7 July 2011, <http://www.wipo.int/wipolex/en/text.jsp?file_id=250715>.

[49] Art 1(2) German constitution.

[50] Art 4 (principle IX) Brazilian constitution.

[51] Art 7(5) Portuguese constitution.

[52] Art 21(2)(h) TEU.

[53] Art 43(d) transitional constitution of the Republic of South Sudan.

these norms are being used by institutional actors. They serve to bolster arguments which enhance the respective powers of these actors, vis-à-vis other branches of government, across different levels of governance, or vis-à-vis individuals and their rights. They are invoked when it is in the interest of these actors to pursue their very own ambitions. As TT Krishnamachari remarked at the Indian Constituent Assembly, such aspirational norms have the potential to be instrumentalized by public authorities to entrench certain 'hobby horse[s]',[54] or to serve, to use Peter Häberle's words, as an 'ideologically embellished instrument of power'.[55] This is no different when these norms concern foreign affairs or when they are applied in the context of the European Union.

On the other hand, such uses do not deprive these norms of their quality as genuine expressions of *spes saeculi*—translated as 'hope for the world'—or what Jack Balkin calls 'constitutional redemption'[56] with a global outlook. They show that the domestic legal order acknowledges that welfare at home and the global common good, in other words the 'perfectionnement de l'ordre social'[57] and the *perfectionnement de l'ordre mondial*, exist in a mutually dependent relationship. Hence, whenever public powers, either at the national, supranational, or international level, seek a constitutional basis for their own endeavours, they will have to convincingly argue, in court as well as in the proverbial 'court of world opinion', that their 'worldly ambitions' are indeed conducive to the global aspirations enshrined in their highest laws.

[54] As quoted in G Austin, *The Indian Constitution: Cornerstone of a Nation* (Clarendon Press, 1966) 76.

[55] In the original: 'ideologisch verbrämte[s] Machtinstrument': P Häberle, *Europäische Verfassungslehre*, 7th edn (Nomos, 2011) 372.

[56] J Balkin, *Constitutional Redemption: Political Faith in an Unjust World* (Harvard University Press, 2011).

[57] B Faure, 'Les objectifs de valeur constitutionnelle: une nouvelle catégorie juridique?' (1995) No. 21 *Revue française de Droit Constitutionnel* 47, 59–60.

Bibliography

Adamovich, L and Funk, B, *Österreichisches Verfassungsrecht*, 3rd edn (Springer, 1985).

Aggestam, L and Hill, C, 'The Challenge of Multiculturalism in European Foreign Policy' (2008) 84 *International Affairs* 97.

Aggestam, L, 'Introduction: Ethical Power Europe' (2008) 84 *International Affairs* 1.

Aggestam, L, 'Role-identity and the Europeanisation of Foreign Policy: A Political-Cultural Approach' in B Tonra and T Christiansen (eds), *Rethinking European Foreign Policy* (Manchester University Press, 2004) 81–98.

Alecu de Flers, N, *EU Foreign Policy and the Europeanization of Neutral States: Comparing Irish and Austrian Foreign Policy* (Routledge, 2012).

Alexy, R, *A Theory of Constitutional Rights* (OUP, 2002).

Amtenbrink, F and Kochenov, D (eds), *The European Union's Shaping of the International Legal Order* (CUP, 2013).

Amtenbrink, F and Kochenov, D, 'The Active Paradigm of the Study of the EU's Place in the World: An Introduction' in F Amtenbrink and D Kochenov (eds), *The European Union's Shaping of the International Legal Order* (CUP, 2013) 1–18.

Andreatta, F, 'The European Union's International Relations: A Theoretical View' in C Hill and M Smith (eds), *International Relations and the European Union*, 2nd edn (OUP, 2011) 21–43.

Aoi, C, 'Asserting Civilian Power or Risking Irrelevance? Japan's Post-Cold War Policy Concerning the Use of Force' in S Katada, H Maull, and T Inoguchi (eds), *Global Governance: Germany and Japan in the International System* (Ashgate, 2004) 111–28.

Aquinas, T, *Treatise on Law*, trans R Thomas (Hackett Publishing, 2000).

Arnold, R, 'Reflections on the Universality of Human Rights' in R Arnold (ed), *The Universalism of Human Rights* (Springer, 2013) 1–12.

Austin, G, *The Indian Constitution: Cornerstone of a Nation* (Clarendon Press, 1966).

Avbelj, M and Komárek, J (eds), *Constitutional Pluralism in the European Union and Beyond* (Hart, 2012).

Avbelj, M and Komárek, J, 'Introduction' in M Avbelj and J Komárek (eds), *Constitutional Pluralism in the European Union and Beyond* (Hart, 2012) 1–15.

Avbelj, M, 'Questioning EU Constitutionalisms' (2008) 9 *German Law Journal* 1.

Ávila, H, *Theory of Legal Principles* (Springer, 2007).

Azoulai, L, 'Article I-3' in L Burgorgue-Larsen, A Levade, and F Picod (eds), *Traité établissant une Constitution pour l'Europe. Volume I* (Bruyalt, 2007) 60–77.

Azoulai, L, '"Euro-Bonds" The Ruiz Zambrano judgment or the Real Invention of EU Citizenship' (2011) 3 *Perspectives on Federalism* 31.

Azoulai, L, 'Introduction: The Question of Competence' in L Azoulai (ed), *The Question of Competence in the European Union* (OUP, 2014) 1–16.

Badura, P, 'Arten der Verfassungsrechtssätze' in J Isensee and P Kirchhof (eds), *Handbuch des Staatsrechts der Bundesrepublik Deutschland. Volume VII: Normativität und Schutz der Verfassung—Internationale Beziehungen* (C.F. Müller, 1992) 33–55.

Balkin, J, 'Original Meaning and Constitutional Redemption' (2007) 24 *Constitutional Commentary* 427.

Balkin, J, *Constitutional Redemption: Political Faith in an Unjust World* (Harvard University Press, 2011).

Barents, R, *Het Verdrag van Lissabon: Achtergronden en commentaar* (Kluwer, 2008).

Barnard, C, 'Introduction: The Constitutional Treaty, the Constitutional Debate and the Constitutional Process' in C Barnard (ed), *The Fundamentals of EU Law Revisited: Assessing the Impact of the Constitutional Debate* (OUP, 2007) 1–11.

Bartels, L, 'Trade and Development Policy of the European Union' in M Cremona (ed), *Developments in EU External Relations Law* (OUP, 2008) 128–71.

Bartels, L, *Human Rights Conditionality in the EU's International Agreements* (OUP, 2005).

Bartents, R, *Het Verdrag van Lissabon: Achtergronden en Commentaar* (Kluwer, 2008).

Basedow, J, 'Zielkonflikte und Zielhierarchien im Vertrag über die europäische Gemeinschaft' in O Due, M Lutter, and J Schwarze (eds), *Festschrift für Ulrich Everling* (Nomos, 1995) 19–68.

Bederman, D, 'The Souls of International Organizations: Legal Personality and the Lighthouse at Cape Spartel' (1996) 36 *Virginia Journal of International Law* 275.

Bennett, R and Solum, L, *Constitutional Originalism: A Debate* (Cornell University Press, 2011).

Berlin, I, *Liberty: Incorporating Four Essays on Liberty* (OUP, 2002).

Berman, P, 'From Laeken to Lisbon: The Origins and Negotiation of the Lisbon Treaty' in A Biondi, P Eeckhout, and S Ripley (eds), *EU Law After Lisbon* (OUP, 2012) 3–39.

Besselink, L, 'The Notion and Nature of the European Constitution After the Lisbon Treaty' in J Wouters, L Verhey, and P Kiiver (eds), *European Constitutionalism Beyond Lisbon* (Intersentia, 2009) 261–81.

Bieber, R and Widmer, P (eds), *L'espace constitutionnel europeen/Der Europäische Verfassungsraum/The European Constitutional Area* (Schulthess, 1995).

Biscop, S, 'The European Security Strategy in Context: A Comprehensive Trend' in S Biscop and J Andersson (eds), *The EU and the European Security Strategy: Forging a Global Europe* (Routledge, 2008) 5–20.

Blanke, H-J, 'Art. 2 (ex-Art. B)' in C Calliess and M Ruffert (eds), *EUV/EGV: Das Verfassungsrecht der Europäischen Union mit Europäischer Grundrechtecharta*, 3rd edn (C.H. Beck, 2007) 27–37.

Blockmans, S and Laatsit, M-L 'The European External Action Service: Enhancing Coherence in EU External Action?' in PJ Cardwell (ed), *EU External Relations Law and Policy in the Post-Lisbon Era* (T.M.C. Asser Press, 2012) 135–59.

Blockmans, S, 'Friend or Foe? Reviewing EU Relations with Its Neighbours Post Lisbon' in P Koutrakos (ed), *The European Union's External Relations a Year after Lisbon*, CLEER Working Paper 2011/3 113–24.

Blumann, C, 'Objectifs et principes en droit communautaire' in *Le droit de l'Union européenne en principes: Liber amicorum en l'honneur de Jean Raux* (Apogée, 2006) 39–67.

Bodansky, D, 'Legitimacy in International Law and International Relations' in J Dunoff and M Pollack (eds), *Interdisciplinary Perspectives on International Law and International Relations* (CUP, 2013) 321–41.

Börzel, T and Panke, D, 'Europeanization' in M Cini and N Pérez-Solórzano Borragán (eds), *European Union Politics*, 4th edn (OUP, 2013) 405–17.

Börzel, T, 'Pace-Setting, Foot-Dragging, and Fence-Sitting: Member State Responses to Europeanization' (2002) 40 *Journal of Common Market Studies* 193.

Bosse-Platière, I, *L'article 3 TEU: Recherche sur une exigence de cohérence de l'action extérieure de l'Union européenne* (Bruylant, 2009).

Bossuyt, M and Wouters, J, *Grondlijnen van internationaal recht* (Intersentia, 2005).

Bradford, A and Posner, E, 'Universal Exceptionalism in International Law' (2011) 52 *Harvard International Law Journal* 3.

Bradley, C and Goldsmith, J, *Foreign Relations Law: Cases & Materials*, 4th edn (Wolters Kluwer Law & Business, 2011).

Breiter, U, *Staatszielbestimmungen als Problem des schweizerischen Bundesverfassungsrechts* (Schulthess, 1980).

Bretherton, C and Vogler, J, 'Past Its Peak? The European Union as a Global Actor 10 Years After' in F Laursen (ed), *The EU as a Foreign and Security Policy Actor* (Republic of Letters, 2009) 23–43.

Bretherton, C and Vogler, J, *The European Union as a Global Actor*, 2nd edn (Routledge, 2006).

Brkan, M, 'The Role of the European Court of Justice in the Field of Common Foreign Security Policy After the Treaty of Lisbon: New Challenges for the Future' in PJ Cardwell (ed), *EU External Relations Law and Policy in the Post-Lisbon Era* (T.M.C. Asser Press, 2012) 97–115.

Bronckers, M and Kuijper, PJ, 'WTO Law in the European Court of Justice' (2005) 42 *Common Market Law Review* 1313.

Bronckers, M, 'From "Direct Effect" to "Muted Dialogue"' (2008) 11 *Journal of International Economic Law* 885.

Brosig, M, 'The Emerging Peace and Security Regime in Africa: The Role of the EU' (2011) 16 *European Foreign Affairs Review* 107.

Brunnée, J and Toope, S, 'Constructivism and International Law' in J Dunoff and M Pollack (eds), *Interdisciplinary Perspectives on International Law and International Relations* (CUP, 2013) 119–45.

Buchanan, A and Keohane, R, 'The Legitimacy of Global Governance Institutions' (2006) 20 *Ethics & International Affairs* 405.

Bull, H, 'Civilian Power Europe: A Contradiction in Terms?' (1982) 21 *Journal of Common Market Studies* 149.

Bull, H, *The Anarchical Society: A Study of Order in World Politics* (Macmillan, 1977).

Calliess, C, 'Art. 1 (ex-Art. 1 EUV) [Gründung der Europäischen Union; Grundlagen]' in C Calliess and M Ruffert (eds), *EUV/AEUV Kommentar*, 4th edn (C.H. Beck, 2011) 3–29.

Calliess, C, 'Art. 2 [Die Werte der Union]' in C Calliess and M Ruffert (eds), *EUV/AEUV Kommentar*, 4th edn (C.H. Beck, 2011) 29–41.

Calliess, C, 'Art. 5 (ex-Art. 5 EGV) [Grundsatz der begrenzten Einzelermächtigung, Subsidiarität und Verhältnismäßigkeit]' in C Calliess and M Ruffert (eds), *EUV/AEUV Kommentar*, 4th edn (C.H. Beck, 2011) 121–42.

Calliess, C, 'Art. 13 [Die Organe der Union]' in C Calliess and M Ruffert (eds), *EUV/AEUV Kommentar*, 4th edn (C.H. Beck, 2011) 211–29.

Calliess, C, 'Auswärtige Gewalt' in J Isensee and P Kirchhof (eds), *Handbuch des Staatsrechts der Bundesrepublik Deutschland. Volume IV: Aufgaben des Staates*, 3rd edn (C.F. Müller, 2006) 589–632.

Calliess, C, 'Gemeinwohl in der Europäischen Union—Über den Staaten- und Verfassungsverbund zum Gemeinwohlverbund' in W Brugger, S Kirste, and M Anderheiden (eds), *Gemeinwohl in Deutschland, Europa und der Welt* (Nomos, 2002) 172–214.

Calliess, C, 'Kollektive Ziele und Prinzipien im Verfassungsrecht der EU—Bestandsaufnahme, Wirkungen und Perspektiven' (2003) 92 *Archiv für Rechts- und Sozialphilosophie-Beiheft* 85.

Campbell, A, 'The Limits of the Powers of International Organisations' (1983) 32 *International & Comparative Law Quarterly* 532.

Canelas de Castro, PJ, 'Portugal's World Outlook in the Constitution of 1976' (1995) 71 *Boletim da Faculdade de Direito da Universidade de Coimbra* 489.

Cannizzaro, E, 'Unity and Pluralism in the EU's Foreign Relations Power' in C Barnard (ed), *The Fundamentals of EU Law Revisited: Assessing the Impact of the Constitutional Debate* (OUP, 2007) 193–234.

Cannizzaro, E, Palchetti, P, and Wessel, R (eds), *International Law as Law of the European Union* (Martinus Nijhoff, 2012).

Cappelletti, M, Seccombe, M, and Weiler, JHH, 'Integration Through Law: Europe and the American Federal Experience—A General Introduction' in M Cappelletti, M Seccombe, and JHH Weiler (eds), *Integration Through Law: Europe and the American Federal Experience. Volume I, Book 1* (Walter de Gruyter, 1986) 3–68.

Cardwell, PJ (ed), *EU External Relations Law and Policy in the Post-Lisbon Era* (T.M.C. Asser Press, 2012).

Casolari, F, 'Giving Indirect Effect to International Law within the EU Legal Order: The Doctrine of Consistent Interpretation' in E Cannizzaro, P Palchetti, and R Wessel (eds), *International Law as Law of the European Union* (Martinus Nijhoff, 2012) 395–415.

Casolari, F, 'The Principle of Loyal Co-operation: A "Master Key" for EU External Representation?' in S Blockmans and R Wessel (eds), *Principles and Practices of EU External Representation*, CLEER Working Paper 2012/5 11–35.

Chandrasekhara Rao, P, *The Indian Constitution and International Law* (Martinus Nijhoff/Taxmann, 1994).

Chinnappa Reddy, O, *The Court and the Constitution of India: Summits and Shallows* (OUP, 2010).

Chiti, E and Teixeira, PG, 'The Constitutional Implications of the European Responses to the Financial and Public Debt Crisis' (2013) 50 *Common Market Law Review* 683.

Church, C and Phinnemore, D, *Understanding the European Constitution: An Introduction to the EU Constitutional Treaty* (Routledge, 2006).

Claes, M and de Visser, M, 'Reflection on Comparative Method in European Constitutional Law' in M Adams and J Bomhoff (eds), *Practice and Theory in Comparative Law* (CUP, 2012) 143–69.

Closa, C, 'The Convention Method and the Transformation of EU Constitutional Politics' in E Eriksen, J Fossum, and A Menéndez (eds), *Developing a Constitution for Europe* (Routledge, 2004) 183–206.

Cooper, R, *The Post-modern State and the World Order* (Demos, 2000).

Craig, P and de Búrca, G, *EU Law: Text, Cases and Materials*, 4th edn (OUP, 2008).

Craig, P and de Búrca, G, *EU Law: Text, Cases and Materials*, 6th edn (OUP, 2015).

Craig, P, 'Constitutions, Constitutionalism, and the European Union' (2001) 7 *European Law Journal* 125.

Craig, P, 'The ECJ and ultra vires Action: A Conceptual Analysis' (2011) 48 *Common Market Law Review* 495.

Craig, P, *The Lisbon Treaty: Law, Politics, and Treaty Reform* (OUP, 2010).

Cremona, M and De Witte, B (eds), *EU Foreign Relations Law: Constitutional Fundamentals* (Hart Publishing, 2008).

Cremona, M and De Witte, B, 'Introduction' in M Cremona and B De Witte (eds), *EU Foreign Relations Law: Constitutional Fundamentals* (Hart Publishing, 2008) xi–xv.

Cremona, M and Hillion, C, *L'Union fait la force? Potential and Limitations of the European Neighbourhood Policy as an Integrated EU Foreign and Security Policy*, EUI Working Paper Law 2006/39.

Cremona, M and Thies, A, 'Introduction' in M Cremona and A Thies (eds), *The European Court of Justice and External Relations Law: Constitutional Challenges* (Hart Publishing, 2014) 1–11.

Cremona, M, 'A Reticent Court? Policy Objectives and the Court of Justice' in M Cremona and A Thies (eds), *The European Court of Justice and External Relations Law: Constitutional Challenges* (Hart Publishing, 2014) 15–32.

Cremona, M, 'Coherence in European Union Foreign Relations Law' in P Koutrakos (ed), *European Foreign Policy: Legal and Political Perspectives* (Edward Elgar, 2011) 55–92.

Cremona, M, 'Defending the Community Interest: The Duties of Cooperation and Compliance' in M Cremona and B De Witte (eds), *EU Foreign Relations Law: Constitutional Fundamentals* (Hart Publishing, 2008) 125–69.

Cremona, M, 'Defining Competence in EU External Relations: Lessons from the Treaty Reform Process' in A Dashwood and M Maresceau (eds), *Law and Practice of EU External Relations: Salient Features of a Changing Landscape* (CUP, 2008) 34–69.

Cremona, M, 'Extending the Reach of the AETR Principle: Comment on Commission v Greece (C- 45/07)' (2009) 34 *European Law Review* 754.

Cremona, M, 'External Relations and External Competence of the European Union: The Emergence of an Integrated Policy' in P Craig and G de Búrca (eds), *The Evolution of EU Law*, 2nd edn (OUP, 2011) 217–68.

Cremona, M, 'Member States as Trustees of the Union Interest: Participating in International Agreements on Behalf of the European Union' in A Arnull et al (eds), *A Constitutional Order of States: Essays in European Law in Honour of Alan Dashwood* (Hart Publishing, 2011) 435–57.

Cremona, M, 'The Common Foreign and Security Policy of the European Union and the External Relations Powers of the European Community' in D O'Keeffe and P Twomey (eds), *Legal Issues of the Maastricht Treaty* (Wiley Chancery, 1994) 247–58.

Cremona, M, 'The Draft Constitutional Treaty: External Relations and External Action' (2003) 40 *Common Market Law Review* 1347.

Cremona, M, 'The European Neighbourhood Policy: More than a Partnership?' in M Cremona (ed), *Developments in EU External Relations Law* (OUP, 2008) 244–99.

Cremona, M, 'The Two (or Three) Treaty Solution: The New Treaty Structure of the EU' in A Biondi, P Eeckhout, and S Ripley (eds), *EU Law After Lisbon* (OUP, 2012) 40–61.

Cremona, M, 'The Union's External Action: Constitutional Perspectives' in G Amato, H Bribosia, and B De Witte (eds), *Genesis and Destiny of the European Constitution* (Bruylant, 2007) 1173–217.

Cremona, M, 'Values in EU Foreign Policy' in M Evans and P Koutrakos (eds), *Beyond the Established Legal Orders: Policy Interconnections Between the EU and the Rest of the World* (Hart Publishing, 2011) 275–315.

Cremona, M, 'Case C-246/07, *Commission v. Sweden (PFOS)*, Judgment of the Court of Justice (Grand Chamber) of 20 April 2010' (2011) 48 *Common Market Law Review* 1639.

Curtin, D and Dekker, I, 'The European Union from Maastricht to Lisbon: Institutional and Legal Unity out of the Shadows' in P Craig and G de Búrca (eds), *The Evolution of EU Law*, 2nd edn (OUP, 2011) 155–85.

d'Aspremont, J and Dopagne, F, 'Two Constitutionalisms in Europe: Pursuing an Articulation of the European and International Legal Orders' (2008) 68 *Zeitschrift für ausländisches öffentliches Recht und Völkerrecht* 939.

Dann, P, 'European Parliament and Executive Federalism: Approaching a Parliament in a Semi-Parliamentary Democracy' (2003) 9 *European Law Journal* 549.

Dashwood, A et al, *Wyatt & Dashwood's European Union Law*, 6th edn (Hart Publishing, 2011).

Dashwood, A, 'Article 47 TEU and the Relationship between First and Second Pillar Competences' in A Dashwood and M Maresceau (eds), *Law and Practice of EU External Relations: Salient Features of a Changing Landscape* (CUP, 2008) 70–103.

Dashwood, A, 'External Relations Provisions of the Amsterdam Treaty' in D O'Keeffe and P Twomey (eds), *Legal Issues of the Amsterdam Treaty* (Hart Publishing, 1999) 201–24.

Dashwood, A, 'The Continuing Bipolarity of EU External Action' in I Govaere et al, *The European Union in the World: Essays in Honour of Marc Maresceau* (Martinus Nijhoff, 2014) 3–16.

De Baere, G, *Constitutional Principles of EU External Relations* (OUP, 2008).

de Búrca, G and Weiler, JHH (eds), *The Worlds of European Constitutionalism* (CUP, 2011).

de Búrca, G, 'EU External Relations: The Governance Mode of Foreign Policy' in B Van Vooren, S Blockmans, and J Wouters (eds), *The EU's Role in Global Governance: The Legal Dimension* (OUP, 2013) 39–58.

de Búrca, G, 'Europe's *raison d'être*' in D Kochenov and F Amtenbrink (eds), *The European Union's Shaping of the International Legal Order* (CUP, 2013) 21–37.

de Búrca, G, *The EU on the Road from the Constitutional Treaty to the Lisbon Treaty*, Jean Monnet Working Paper 03/08.

De Montalivet, P, *Les objectifs de valeur constitutionnelle* (Dalloz, 2006).

de Poncins, E, *Le traité de Lisbonne en 27 clés* (Lignes de repères, 2008).

De Villiers, B, 'Directive Principles of State Policy and Fundamental Rights: The Indian Experience' (1992) 8 *South African Journal on Human Rights* 29.

De Visscher, P, 'Les tendances internationales des constitutions modernes' (1952) 1 *Recueil de Cours* 511.

De Witte, B and Thies, A, 'Why Choose Europe? The Place of the European Union in the Architecture of International Legal Cooperation' in B Van Vooren, S Blockmans, and J Wouters (eds), *The EU's Role in Global Governance: The Legal Dimension* (OUP, 2013) 24–38.

De Witte, B, 'A Selfish Court? The Court of Justice and the Design of International Dispute Settlement beyond the European Union' in M Cremona and A Thies (eds), *The European Court of Justice and External Relations Law: Constitutional Challenges* (Hart Publishing, 2014) 33–46.

De Witte, B, 'Direct Effect, Primacy, and the Nature of the Legal Order' in P Craig and G de Búrca, *The Evolution of EU Law*, 2nd edn (OUP, 2011) 323–62.

De Witte, B, 'International Law as a Tool for the European Union' (2009) 5 *European Constitutional Law Review* 265.

De Witte, B, 'The Emergence of a European System of Public International Law: The EU and its Member States as Strange Subjects' in J Wouters, A Nollkaemper, and E de Wet (eds), *The Europeanisation of International Law: The Status of International Law in the EU and its Member States* (T.M.C. Asser Press, 2008) 39–54.

De Witte, B, 'The European Union as an International Legal Experiment' in G de Búrca and JHH Weiler (eds), *The Worlds of European Constitutionalism* (CUP, 2011) 19–56.

De Witte, B, 'The Pillar Structure and the Nature of the European Union: Greek Temple or French Gothic Cathedral' in T Heukels, N Blokker, and M Brus (eds), *The European Union after Amsterdam: A Legal Analysis* (Kluwer Law International, 1998) 51–68.

De Witte, B, 'Too Much Constitutional Law in the European Union's Foreign Relations' in M Cremona and B De Witte (eds), *EU Foreign Relations Law: Constitutional Fundamentals* (Hart Publishing, 2008) 3–15.

De Witte, F, *Justice in the EU: The Emergence of Transnational Solidarity* (OUP, 2015).

Delgado Casteleiro, A and Larik, J, 'The Duty to Remain Silent: Limitless Loyalty in EU External Relations?' (2011) 36 *European Law Review* 522.

Delgado Casteleiro, A, 'EU Declarations of Competence to Multilateral Agreements: A Useful Reference Base?' (2012) 17 *European Foreign Affairs Review* 491.

Deutsch, K et al, *Political Community and the North Atlantic Area: International Organization in the Light of Historical Experience* (Princeton University Press, 1957).

Di Fabio, U, 'Some Remarks on the Allocation of Competences Between the EU and its Member States' (2002) 39 *Common Market Law Review* 1289.

Dicey, AV, *Introduction to the Study of the Law of the Constitution*, 10th edn (Macmillan, 1961).

Dimopoulos, A, 'The Effects of the Lisbon Treaty on the Principles and Objectives of the Common Commercial Policy' (2010) 15 *European Foreign Affairs Review* 153.

Doherty, R, *Ireland, Neutrality and European Security Integration* (Ashgate, 2002).

Dollat, P, *Droit européen et droit de l'Union européenne*, 3rd edn (Sirey, 2010).

Donnelly, J, *Realism and International Relations* (CUP, 2000).

Dorf, M, 'The Aspirational Constitution' (2009) 77 *The George Washington Law Review* 1631.

Douglas-Scott, S, *Constitutional Law of the European Union* (Longman, 2002).

Drago, G and Molfessis, N, 'Justice constitutionnelle' (1996) No 3 *Justices: Revue générale de droit processuel* 308.

Drago, G, *Contentieux constitutionnel français*, 2nd edn (Presses universitaires de France, 2006).

Drescher, W, 'Ziele und Zuständigkeiten' in A Marchetti and C Demesmay (eds), *Der Vertrag von Lissabon: Analyse und Bewertung* (Nomos, 2010) 59–71.

Duchêne, F, 'Europe's Role in World Peace' in R Mayne (ed), *Europe Tomorrow: Sixteen Europeans Look Ahead* (Fontana, 1972) 32–47.

Dunne, T, 'Good Citizen Europe' (2008) 84 *International Affairs* 13.

Dworkin, R, 'The Model of Rules' (1967) 35 *University of Chicago Law Review* 14.

Dworkin, R, *Taking Rights Seriously* (Duckworth, 1978).

Dyck, A, *A Commentary on Cicero, De Legibus* (The University of Michigan Press, 2004).

Eckes, C, *EU Counter-Terrorist Policies and Fundamental Rights: The Case of Individual Sanctions* (OUP, 2009).

Eeckhout, P, *EU External Relations Law*, 2nd edn (OUP, 2011).

Ehrhart, H-G and Petretto, K, 'The EU, the Somalia Challenge, and Counter-piracy: Towards a Comprehensive Approach?' (2012) 17 *European Foreign Affairs Review* 261.

Elgström, O and Smith, M (eds), *The European Union's Roles in International Politics: Concepts and Analysis* (Routledge, 2006).

Epping, V, 'Völkerrechtssubjekte' in K Ipsen (ed), *Völkerrecht*, 6th edn (C.H. Beck, 2014) 46–386.

Fabbrini, F, *Economic Governance in Europe: Comparative Paradoxes, Constitutional Challenges* (OUP, 2016).

Fassbender, B, 'Rediscovering a Forgotten Constitution: Notes on the Place of the UN Charter in the International Legal Order' in J Dunhoff and J Trachtman (eds), *Ruling the World? Constitutionalism, International Law, and Global Governance* (CUP, 2009) 133–48.

Fassbender, B, *Der offene Bundesstaat* (Mohr Siebeck, 2007).

Fastenrath, U, *Kompetenzverteilung im Bereich der ausgewärtigen Gewalt* (C.H. Beck, 1986).

Faure, B, 'Les objectifs de valeur constitutionnelle: une nouvelle catégorie juridique?' (1995) No 21 *Revue française de Droit Constitutionnel* 47.

Finer, SE, Bogdanor, V, and Rudden, B, *Comparing Constitutions* (Clarendon Press, 1995).

Fischer, PC, *Staatszielbestimmungen in den Verfassungen und Verfassungsentwürfen der neuen Bundesländer* (VVF, 1994).

Fisler Damrosch, L, 'Constitutional Control of Military Actions: A Comparative Dimension' (1991) 85 *American Journal of International Law* 92.

Fletcher, G, *Basic Concepts of Legal Thought* (OUP, 1996).

Follesdal, A, 'Towards a Stable *finalité* with Federal Features? The Balancing Acts of the Constitutional Treaty for Europe' (2005) 12 *Journal of European Public Policy* 572.

Franck, T, *Political Questions/Judicial Answers: Does the Rule of Law Apply to Foreign Affairs?* (Princeton University Press, 1992).

Frankenberg, G, 'Comparative Constitutional Law' in M Bussani and U Mattei (eds), *The Cambridge Companion to Comparative Law* (CUP, 2012) 171–90.

Galtung, J, 'Violence, Peace and Peace Research' 6 *Journal of Peace Research* 167 (1969).

García-Dobarco González, G, 'Unión Europea, política exterior y Constitución. Apuntas de un viaje a Itaca' in E Álvarez Conde and V Garrido Mayol (eds), *Comentarios a la Constitución Europea. Libro III* (Tirant lo Blanch, 2004) 1297–330.

Geiger, R, *Grundgesetz und Völkerrecht: Die Bezüge des Staatsrechts zum Völkerrecht und Europarecht*, 3rd edn (C.H. Beck, 2002).

Genevois, B, *La jurisprudence du Conseil constitutionnel: Principes Directeurs* (STH, 1988).

Germond, B and Smith, M, 'Re-Thinking European Security Interests and the ESDP: Explaining the EU's Anti-Piracy Operation' (2009) 30 *Contemporary Security Policy* 573.

Gicquel, J and Gicquel, J-E, *Droit constitutionnel et institutions politiques*, 24th edn (Montchrestien, 2010).

Gilpin, R, 'The Richness of the Tradition of Political Realism' in R Keohane (ed), *Neorealism and Its Critics* (Columbia University Press, 1986) 301–21.

Ginsburg, T, Chernykh, S, and Elkins, Z, 'Commitment and Diffusion: How and Why National Constitutions Incorporate International Law' (2008) *University of Illinois Law Review* 201.

Glaesner, H-J, 'Les objectifs de la Communauté économique européenne: origine et développements' in *L'Europe et le droit: Mélanges en hommage à Jean Boulouis* (Dalloz, 1991) 285–95.

Gnesotto, N and Grevi, G, *The New Global Puzzle: What World for the EU in 2025?* (EUISS, 2006).

Goldmann, K, 'The Line in Water: International and Domestic Politics' (1989) 24 *Cooperation and Conflict* 103.

Goldsmith, J and Levinson, D, 'Law for States: International Law, Constitutional Law, Public Law' (2009) 122 *Harvard Law Review* 1791.

Goldsmith, J and Posner, E, *The Limits of International Law* (OUP, 2005).

Goldstein, J, Kahler, M, Keohane, R, and Slaughter, A-M, 'Introduction: Legalization and World Politics' (2000) 54 *International Organization* 385.

Götz, V, 'Innere Sicherheit' in J Isensee and P Kirchhof (eds), *Handbuch des Staatsrechts der Bundesrepublik Deutschland. Volume IV: Aufgaben des Staates*, 3rd edn (C.F. Müller, 2006) 671–99.

Govaere, I, Capiau, J, and Vermeersch, A, 'In-Between Seats: The Participation of the European Union in International Organizations' (2004) 9 *European Foreign Affairs Review* 155.

Grabenwarter, C, 'National Constitutional Law Relating to the European Union' in A von Bogdandy and J Bast (eds), *Principles of European Constitutional Law*, 2nd edn (Hart Publishing/C.H. Beck, 2011) 83–129.

Grevi, G, Helly, D, and Keohane, D (eds), *European Security and Defence Policy: The First 10 Years (1999–2009)* (EUISS, 2009).

Grewe, W, 'Die Auswärtige Gewalt der Bundesrepublik' (1954) 12 *Veröffentlichungen der Vereinigung der Deutschen Staatsrechtslehrer* 129.

Grieco, J, 'State Interests and Institutional Rule Trajectories: A Neorealist Interpretation of the Maastricht Treaty and European Economic and Monetary Union' (1996) 5 *Security Studies* 261.

Griller, S, 'Is this a Constitution? Remarks on a Contested Concept' in S Griller and J Ziller (eds), *The Lisbon Treaty: EU Constitutionalism without a Constitutional Treaty?* (Springer, 2008) 21–56.

Griller, S, 'The Reform's Typology: Treaty or Constitution?' in I Pernice and E Tanchev (eds), *Ceci n'est pas une Constitution—Constitutionalisation without a Constitution?* (Nomos, 2009) 44–55.

Grimm, D, 'Ursprung und Wandel der Verfassung' in J Isensee and P Kirchhof (eds), *Handbuch des Staatsrechts der Bundesrepublik Deutschland. Volume I: Historische Grundlagen*, 3rd edn (C.F. Müller, 2003) 3–43.

Haas, E, *The Uniting of Europe: Political, Social, and Economic Forces 1950–1957* (Stanford University Press, 1968)

Häberle, P, 'Das "Weltbild" des Verfassungsstaates—eine Textstufenanalyse zur Menschheit als verfassungsstaatlichem und "letztem" Geltungsgrund des Völkerrechts' in B Ziemske, T Langheid, H Wilms, and G Haverkate (eds), *Staatsphilosophie und Rechtspolitik, Festschrift für Martin Kriele* (C.H. Beck, 1997) 1277–306.

Häberle, P, 'Die Verfassungsbewegung in den fünf neuen Bundesländern Deutschlands 1991 bis 1992' (1994) 42 *Jahrbuch des öffentlichen Rechts der Gegenwart* 149.

Häberle, P, *Europäische Verfassungslehre*, 7th edn (Nomos, 2011).

Häferlin, U, Haller, W, and Keller, H, *Schweizerisches Bundesstaatsrecht*, 8th edn (Schulthess, 2012).

Haine, J-Y, 'The Rise and Fall of the Common Security and Defence Policy: Bringing Strategic Culture Back In' in A Toje and B Kunz (eds), *Neoclassical Realism in European Politics: Bringing Power Back In* (Manchester University Press, 2012) 182–213.

Halberstam, D and Stein, E, 'The United Nations, the European Union, and the King of Sweden: Economic Sanctions and Individual Rights in a Plural World Order' (2009) 46 *Common Market Law Review* 13.

Halberstam, D, 'Constitutional Heterarchy: The Centrality of Conflict in the European Union and the United States' in J Dunoff and J Trachtman (eds), *Ruling the World? Constitutionalism, International Law and Global Governance* (CUP, 2009) 326–55.

Halberstam, D, 'Systems Pluralism and Institutional Pluralism in Constitutional Law: National, Supranational and Global Governance' in M Avbelj and J Komárek (eds), *Constitutional Pluralism in the European Union and Beyond* (Hart Publishing, 2012) 85–125.

Hallstein, W, *Die Europäische Gemeinschaft*, 5th edn (Econ Verlag, 1979).

Hart, HLA, *The Concept of Law*, 2nd edn (OUP, 1997).

Hatje, A, 'Artikel 2 [Gemeinschaftsaufgabe]' in J Schwarze (ed), *EU-Kommentar*, 2nd edn (Nomos, 2008) 262–7.

Hatje, A, *Loyalität als Rechtsprinzip der Europäischen Union* (Nomos, 2001).

Hay, P, *Federalism and Supranational Organisations: Patterns for New Legal Structures* (University of Illinois Press, 1966).

Hedge, SK, 'Directive Principles of State Policy in the Constitution of India' (1971) 5 *Journal of Constitutional and Parliamentary Studies* 129.

Henderson, J, *The Constitution of the Russian Federation* (Hart Publishing, 2011).

Henkin, L, *Constitutionalism, Democracy and Foreign Affairs* (Columbia University Press, 1990).

Henkin, L, *Foreign Affairs and the US Constitution*, 2nd edn (Clarendon Press, 1996).

Henkin, L, *The Rights of Man Today* (Stevens, 1979).

Herrmann, C, 'Much Ado about Pluto? The "Unity of the Legal Order of the European Union" Revisited' in M Cremona and B De Witte (eds), *EU Foreign Relations Law: Constitutional Fundamentals* (Hart Publishing, 2008) 19–51.

Herzog, R, 'Ziele, Vorbehalte und Grenzen der Staatlichkeit' in J Isensee and P Kirchhof (eds), *Handbuch des Staatsrechts der Bundesrepublik Deutschland. Volume IV: Aufgaben des Staates*, 3rd edn (C.F. Müller, 2006) 81–116.

Hesse,K, *Grundzüge des Verfassungsrechts der Bundesrepublik Deutschland*, 20th edn (C.F. Müller, 1995).

Hill, C and Smith, M (eds), *International Relations and the European Union*, 2nd edn (OUP 2011).

Hill, C and Smith, M, 'International Relations and the European Union: Themes and Issues' in C Hill and M Smith (eds), *International Relations and the European Union*, 2nd edn (OUP, 2011) 3–20.

Hill, C, 'The Capability-Expectations Gap, or Conceptualising Europe's International Role' (1993) 31 *Journal of Common Market Studies* 305.

Hillion, C and Wessel, R, 'Restraining External Competences of EU Member States under CFSP' in M Cremona and B De Witte (eds), *EU Foreign Relations Law: Constitutional Fundamentals* (Hart Publishing, 2008) 79–121.

Hillion, C, 'A Powerless Court? The European Court of Justice and the Common Foreign and Security Policy' in M Cremona and A Thies (eds), *The European Court of Justice and External Relations Law: Constitutional Challenges* (Hart Publishing, 2014) 47–70.

Hillion, C, 'Mixity and Coherence in EU External Relations: The Significance of the "Duty of Cooperation"' in C Hillion and P Koutrakos (eds), *Mixed Agreements Revisited: The EU and its Member States in the World* (Hart Publishing, 2010) 87–115.

Hillion, C, 'The EU's Neighbourhood Policy towards Eastern Europe' in A Dashwood and M Maresceau (eds), *Law and Practice of EU External Relations: Salient Features of a Changing Landscape* (CUP, 2008) 309–33.

Hillion, C, '*Tous pour un, un pour tous!* Coherence in the External Relations of the European Union' in M Cremona (ed), *Developments in EU External Relations Law* (OUP, 2008) 10–36.

Hinarejos, A, *The Euro Area Crisis in Constitutional Perspective* (OUP, 2015).

Hoffmeister, F, 'Outsider or Frontrunner? Recent Developments under International and European Law on the Status of the European Union in International Organizations and Treaty Bodies' (2007) 44 *Common Market Law Review* 41.

Hoffmeister, F, 'The Contribution of EU Practice to International Law' in M Cremona (ed), *Developments in EU External Relations Law* (OUP, 2008) 37–127.

Hoffmeister, F, *Menschenrechts- und Demokratieklauseln in den vertraglichen Aussenbeziehungen der Europäischen Gemeinschaft* (Springer, 1998).

Hogan, G and Whyte, G, *J.M. Kelly: The Irish Constitution*, 4th edn (LexisNexis, 2003).

Holdgaard, R, *External Relations Law of the European Community: Legal Reasoning and Legal Discourses* (Kluwer Law International, 2008).

Howorth, J, *Security and Defence Policy in the European Union*, 1st edn (Palgrave Macmillan, 2007).

Howorth, J, *Security and Defence Policy in the European Union*, 2nd edn (Palgrave Macmillan 2014).

Hurd, I, 'Constructivism' in C Reus-Smit and D Snidal (eds), *The Oxford Handbook of International Relations* (OUP, 2010) 298–316.

Hurrell, A and Macdonald, T, 'Ethics and Norms in International Relations' in W Carlsnaes, T Risse, and B Simmons (eds), *Handbook of International Relations*, 2nd edn (SAGE, 2013).

Hyde-Price, A, '"Normative" Power Europe: A Realist Critique' (2008) 13 *Journal of European Public Policy* 217.

Hyde-Price, A, 'A "Tragic Actor"? A Realist Perspective on "Ethical Power Europe"' (2008) 84 *International Affairs* 29.

Hyde-Price, A, 'A Neurotic "Centaur": The Limitations of the EU as a Strategic Actor' in K Engelbrekt and J Hallenberg (eds), *The European Union and Strategy: An Emerging Actor* (Routledge, 2008) 153–66.

Hyde-Price, A, 'Neorealism' in X Kurowska and F Breuer (eds), *Explaining the EU's Common Security and Defence Policy: Theory in Action* (Palgrave Macmillan, 2012) 16–40.

Ianniello Saliceti, A, 'The Protection of EU Citizens Abroad: Accountability, Rule of Law, Role of Consular and Diplomatic Services' (2011) 17 *European Public Law* 91.

Ipsen, HP, *Europäisches Gemeinschaftsrecht* (Mohr Siebeck, 1972).

Isensee, J, 'Gemeinwohl im Verfassungsstaat' in J Isensee and P Kirchhof (eds), *Handbuch des Staatsrechts der Bundesrepublik Deutschland. Volume IV: Aufgaben des Staates*, 3rd edn (C.F. Müller, 2006) 3–79.

Isensee, J, 'Staatsaufgaben' in J Isensee and P Kirchhof (eds), *Handbuch des Staatsrechts der Bundesrepublik Deutschland. Volume IV: Aufgaben des Staates*, 3rd edn (C.F. Müller, 2006) 117–60.

Isensee, J, 'Vorbehalt der Verfassung' in J Isensee and H Lechler (eds), *Freiheit und Eigentum, Festschrift für Walter Leisner* (Duncker & Humblot, 1999) 359–99.

Jacobs, F, 'Direct Effect and Interpretation of International Agreements in the Recent Case Law of the European Court of Justice' in A Dashwood and M Maresceau (eds), *Law and Practice of EU External Relations: Salient Features in a Changing Landscape* (CUP, 2008) 13–33.

Jaklic, K, *Constitutional Pluralism in the EU* (OUP, 2014).

Jellinek, G, *Allgemeine Staatslehre*, 3rd edn (Hähring, 1914).

Joerges, C, Meny, Y, and Weiler, JHH (eds), *What Kind of Constitution for What Kind of Polity? Responses to Joschka Fischer* (EUI, 2000).

Kaddous, C, 'External Action under the Lisbon Treaty' in I Pernice and E Tanchev (eds), *Ceci n'est pas une Constitution—Constitutionalisation without a Constitution?* (Nomos, 2009) 172–87.

Kadelbach, S and Kleinlein, T, 'Überstaatliches Verfassungsrecht: Zur Konstiutionalisierung im Völkerrecht' (2006) 44 *Archiv des Völkerrechts* 236.

Kagan, R, *Of Paradise and Power: America and Europe in the New World Order* (Alfred A. Knopf, 2003).

Kelsen, H, *Essays in Legal and Moral Philosophy* (D. Reidel, 1973).

Keohane, R and Nye, J, *Power and Interdependence: World Politics in Transition* (Little, Brown, 1977).

Keukeleire, S and Delreux, T, *The Foreign Policy of the European Union*, 2nd edn (Palgrave Macmillan, 2014).

Kirchhof, F, 'Verteidigung und Bundeswehr' in J Isensee and P Kirchhof (eds), *Handbuch des Staatsrechts der Bundesrepublik Deutschland. Volume IV: Aufgaben des Staates*, 3rd edn (C.F. Müller, 2006) 633–69.

Klabbers, J, 'Presumptive Personality: The European Union in International Law' in M Koskenniemi (ed), *International Law Aspects of the European Union* (Kluwer Law International, 1998) 231–53.

Klamert, M, *The Principle of Loyalty in EU Law* (OUP, 2014).

Klein, E, 'Die Internationalen und die Supranationalen Organisationen' in W Graf Vitzthum (ed), *Völkerrecht*, 5th edn (De Gruyter, 2010) 263–87.

Klein, H, 'Staatszielbestimmungen—Die Verfassung als politischer Wunschzettel?' (1992) 29 *Zeitschrift zur politischen Bildung* 78.

Klug, H, *The Constitution of South Africa: A Contextual Analysis* (Hart Publishing, 2010).

Knowles, R, 'American Hegemony and the Foreign Affairs Constitution' (2009) 47 *Arizona State Law Journal* 87.

Kochenov, D, 'The Essence of EU Citizenship Emerging from the Last Ten Years of Academic Debate: Beyond the Cherry Blossoms and The Moon?' (2013) 62 *International & Comparative Law Quarterly* 97.

Kokott, J, 'From Reception and Transplantation to Convergence of Constitutional Models in the Age of Globalization' in C Starck (ed), *Constitutionalism, Universalism and Democracy—a Comparative Analysis: The German Contributions to the Fifth World Congress of the International Association of Constitutional Law* (Nomos, 1999) 71–134.

Kokott, J, 'Kontrolle der Auswärtigen Gewalt' (1996) 111 *Deutsches Verwaltungsblatt* 937.

Komárek, J and Avbelj, M, *Four Visions of Constitutional Pluralism*, EUI Working Paper Law 2008/21.

Komesar, N, *Imperfect Alternatives—Choosing Institutions in Law, Economics and Public Policy* (Chicago University Press, 1994).

Kommers, D, 'Comparative Constitutional Law: Its Increasing Relevance' in V Jackson and M Tushnet (eds), *Defining the Field of Comparative Constitutional Law* (Praeger, 2002) 61–70.

Korab-Karpowicz, WJ, 'Political Realism in International Relations' in E Zalta (ed), *The Stanford Encyclopedia of Philosophy*, Summer 2013 edn, <http://plato.stanford.edu/archives/sum2013/entries/realism-intl-relations/>.

Kortmann, C and Bovend'Eert, P, *Constitutional Law of the Netherlands: An Introduction* (Kluwer Law International, 2007).

Koskenniemi, M, *From Apology to Utopia: The Structure of International Legal Argument* (CUP, 2005).

Kotzian, P, Knodt, M, and Urdze, S, 'Instruments of the EU's External Democracy Promotion' (2011) 49 *Journal of Common Market Studies* 995.

Kotzur, M, 'Die Ziele der Union: Verfassungsidentität und Gemeinschaftsidee' (2005) 58 *Die Öffentliche Verwaltung* 313.

Kotzur, M, 'Weltrechtliche Bezüge in nationalen Verfassungstexten: Die Rezeption verfassungsrechtlicher Normen durch das Völkerrecht' (2008) 39 *Rechtstheorie* 191.

Koutrakos, P, 'Legal Basis Delimitation of Competence in EU External Relations' in M Cremona and B De Witte (eds), *EU Foreign Relations Law: Constitutional Fundamentals* (Hart Publishing, 2008) 171–98.

Koutrakos, P, 'The European Union's External Relations a Year After Lisbon—Introduction' in P Koutrakos (ed), *The European Union's External Relations a Year after Lisbon*, CLEER Working Paper 2011/3 7–10.

Koutrakos, P, 'The Role of Law in Common Security and Defence Policy: Functions, Limitations and Perceptions' in P Koutrakos (ed), *European Foreign Policy: Legal and Political Perspectives* (Edward Elgar, 2011) 235–58.

Koutrakos, P, *EU International Relations Law*, 2nd edn (Hart Publishing, 2015).

Krämer, L, *EC Environmental Law*, 6th edn (Sweet & Maxwell, 2007).

Kraußer, H-P, *Das Prinzip begrenzter Ermächtigung im Gemeinschaftsrecht als Strukturprinzip des EWG-Vertrages* (Duncker & Humblot, 1991).

Kühling, J, 'Fundamental Rights' in A von Bogdandy and J Bast (eds), *Principles of European Constitutional Law*, 2nd edn (Hart Publishing/C.H. Beck, 2011) 479–514.

Kuijper, PJ, 'Customary International Law, Decisions of International Organisations and Other Techniques for Ensuring Respect for International Legal Rules in European Community Law' in J Wouters, A Nollkaemper, and E de Wet (eds), *The Europeanisation of International Law: The Status of International Law in the EU and Its Member States* (T.M.C. Asser Press, 2008) 96–102.

Kuijper, PJ, 'The Case Law of the Court of Justice of the EU and the Allocation of External Relations Powers: Whither the Traditional Role of the Executive in EU Foreign Relations?' in M Cremona and A Thies (eds), *The European Court of Justice and External Relations Law: Constitutional Challenges* (Hart Publishing, 2014) 95–114.

Kuijper, PJ, Wouters, J, Hoffmeister, F, and Ramopoulos, T, *The Law of EU External Relations: Cases, Materials, and Commentary on the EU as an International Legal Actor*, 2nd edn (OUP, 2015).

Kumar, N, *Judiciary on Goals of Governance: Directive Principles of State Policy* (Anamika Publishers, 2005).

Kumm, M, 'The Cosmopolitan Turn in Constitutionalism: On the Relationship Between Constitutionalism in and Beyond the State' in J Dunoff and J Trachtman (eds), *Ruling the World? International Law, Global Governance, Constitutionalism* (CUP, 2009) 258–326.

Ladrech, R, 'Europeanisation of Domestic Politics and Institutions: The Case of France' (1994) 32 *Journal of Common Market Studies* 69.

Larik, J, 'From Speciality to a Constitutional Sense of Purpose: On the Changing Role of the Objectives of the European Union' (2014) 63 *International & Comparative Law Quarterly* 935.

Larik, J, 'Operation Atalanta and Protection of EU Citizens: Civis Europaeus Unheeded?' (2011) 3 *Perspectives on Federalism* 40.

Larik, J, 'Two Ships in the Night or in the Same Boat Together: How the ECJ Squared the Circle and Foreshadowed Lisbon in its Kadi Judgment' (2010) 13 *Yearbook of Polish European Studies* 149.

Larsen, H, 'The EU as a Normative Power and the Research on External Perceptions: The Missing Link' (2014) 52 *Journal of Common Market Studies* 896.

Laursen, F (ed), *The EU as a Foreign and Security Policy Actor* (Republic of Letters, 2009).

Lavranos, N, 'Protecting European Law from International Law' (2010) 15 *European Foreign Affairs Review* 265.

Lenaerts, K and Van Nuffel, P, *European Union Law*, 3rd edn (Sweet & Maxwell, 2011).

Lenaerts, K, 'Constitutionalism and the Many Faces of Federalism' (1990) 38 *American Journal of Comparative Law* 205.

Leonard, M, *Why Europe Will Run the 21st Century* (Fourth Estate, 2005).

Leyland, P, *The Constitution of the United Kingdom: A Contextual Analysis* (Hart Publishing, 2012).

Lienbacher, G, 'Ausgewählte Rechtsfragen der Anwendung des Vertrages von Lissabon in Österreich' in W Hummer and W Obwexer (eds), *Der Vertrag von Lissabon* (Nomos, 2009) 427–48.

Loughlin, M, *Foundations of Public Law* (OUP, 2010).

Loveland, I, *Constitutional Law, Administrative Law, and Human Rights: A Critical Introduction*, 7th edn (OUP, 2015).

Lucarelli, S and Fioramonti, L, 'Introduction: The EU in the Eyes of Others—Why Bother?' in S Lucarelli and L Fioramonti (eds), *External Perceptions of the European Union as a Global Actor* (Routledge, 2011) 1–9.

Lucarelli, S, 'Introduction: Values, Principles, Identity and European Union Foreign Policy' in S Lucarelli and I Manners (eds), *Values and Principles in European Union Foreign Policy* (Routledge, 2006) 1–18.

Luchaire, F, 'Brèves remarques sur une création du Conseil constitutionnel: l'objectif de valeur constitutionnelle' (2005) No 64 *Revue française de Droit Constitutionnel* 675.

Lukes, S, *Power: A Radical View*, 2nd edn (Palgrave Macmillan, 2004).

Lysén, G, 'Some Views on Neutrality and Membership of the European Communities: The Case of Sweden' (1992) 29 *Common Market Law Review* 229.

Manin, P, *Droit constitutionnel de l'Union européenne* (Pedone, 2004).

Manners, I, 'Normative Power Europe Reconsidered: Beyond the Crossroads' (2006) 13 *Journal of European Public Policy* 182.

Manners, I, 'Normative Power Europe: A Contradiction in Terms?' (2002) 40 *Journal of Common Market Studies* 235.

Manners, I, 'The Normative Ethics of the European Union' (2008) 84 *International Affairs* 45.

Marchetti, A, 'Die Gemeinsame Sicherheits- und Verteidigungspolitik' in A Marchetti and C Demesmay (eds), *Der Vertrag von Lissabon: Analyse und Bewertung* (Nomos, 2010) 251–65.

Marks, S, 'State-Centrism, International Law, and the Anxieties of Influence' (2006) 19 *Leiden Journal of International Law* 339.

Marmor, A, *Law in the Age of Pluralism* (OUP, 2007).

Martin, L and Simmons, B, 'International Organizations and Institutions' in W Carlsnaes, T Risse, and B Simmons (eds), *Handbook of International Relations*, 2nd edn (SAGE, 2013) 326–51.

Martinico, G, *The Tangled Complexity of the EU Constitutional Process: The Frustrating Knot of Europe* (Routledge, 2014).

Mathieu, B and Verpeaux, M, *Contentieux constitutionnel des droits fondamentaux* (L.G.D.J., 2002).

Maurer, H, *Staatsrecht I: Grundlagen, Verfassungsorgane, Staatsfunktionen*, 3rd edn (C.H. Beck, 2002).

Mayer, F and Wendel, M, 'Multilevel Constitutionalism and Constitutional Pluralism: Querelle Allemande or Querelle d'Allemand?' in M Avbelj and J Komárek (eds), *Constitutional Pluralism in the European Union and Beyond* (Hart Publishing, 2012) 128–51.

Mayer, F, 'Die Bedeutung der Rechts- und Verfassungsvergleichung im Europäischen Verfassungsverbund' in C Calliess (ed), *Verfassungswandel im europäischen Staaten- und Verfassungsverbund* (Mohr Siebeck, 2007) 167–85.

McCormick, J, *The European Superpower* (Palgrave Macmillan, 2007).

McCormick, J, *Understanding the European Union: A Concise Introduction*, 6th edn (Palgrave Macmillan, 2014).

Mearsheimer, J, *The Tragedy of Great Power Politics* (W.W. Norton, 2001).

Menon, A, 'European Defence Policy from Lisbon to Libya' (2011) 53 *Survival* 75.

Merten, D, 'Über Staatsziele' (1993) 46 *Die Öffentliche Verwaltung* 368.

Meunier, S and Nicolaïdis, K, 'The European Union as a Trade Power' in C Hill and M Smith (eds), *International Relations and the European Union*, 2nd edn (OUP, 2011) 275–98.

Millet, F-X, *L'Union européenne et l'identité constitutionnelle des États membres* (L.G.D.J., 2013).

Mitrany, D, 'The Prospect of Integration: Federal or Functional?' in A Groom and P Taylor (eds), *Functionalism: Theory and Practice in International Relations* (University of London Press, 1975) 53–78.

Mögele, R, 'Art. 218 (ex-Art. 300 EGV) [Vertragsabschlussverfahren; Gutachten des EuGH]' in R Streinz (ed), *EUV/AEUV: Vertrag über die Europäische Union und Vertrag über die Arbeitsweise der Europäischen Union*, 2nd edn (C.H. Beck, 2012) 2073–87.

Moraru, M, 'Protection of EU Citizens Abroad: A Legal Assessment of the EU Citizen's Right to Consular and Diplomatic Protection' (2011) 3 *Perspectives on Federalism* 67.

Moravcsik, A, 'The New Liberalism' in C Reus-Smit and D Snidal (eds), *The Oxford Handbook of International Relations* (OUP, 2010) 234–54.

Moravcsik, A, *The Choice for Europe: Social Purpose and State Power from Messina to Maastricht* (UCL Press, 1999).

Morgenthau, H, *Politics Among Nations: The Struggle for Power and Peace*, 7th edn (McGraw-Hill Higher Education, 2006).

Müller-Graff, P-C, 'Verfassungsziele der EG/EU' in M Dauses (ed), *Handbuch des EU-Wirtschaftsrechts*, loose-leaf, 27th supplement (C.H. Beck, 2010).

Müllerson, R, Fitzmaurice, M, and Andenas, M (eds), *Constitutional Reforms and International Law in Central and Eastern Europe* (Kluwer Law International, 1998).

Neframi, E, 'The Duty of Loyalty: Rethinking its Scope through its Application in the Field of EU External Relations' (2010) 47 *Common Market Law Review* 323.

Neframi, E, *L'action extérieure de l'Union européenne: fondements, moyens, principes* (L.G.D.J., 2010).

Norman, P, *The Accidental Constitution: The Story of the European Convention*, 2nd edn (EuroComment, 2005).

Nugent, N, *The Government and Politics of the European Union*, 7th edn (Palgrave Macmillan, 2010).

Nuttall, S, 'Coherence and Consistency' in C Hill and M Smith (eds), *International Relations and the European Union*, 1st edn (OUP, 2005) 91–112.

O'Keeffe, D, 'Exclusive, Concurrent and Shared Competence' in A Dashwood and C Hillion (eds), *The General Law of E.C. External Relations* (Sweet & Maxwell, 2000) 179–99.

Oda, H, *Japanese Law*, 2nd edn (OUP, 1999).

Öhlinger, T, *Verfassungsrecht*, 9th edn (Facultas, 2012).

Olson, P, 'Mixity from the Outside: The Perspective of a Treaty Partner' in C Hillion and P Koutrakos (eds), *Mixed Agreements Revisited: The EU and its Member States in the World* (Hart Publishing, 2010) 331–48.

'Oxford Constitutions of the World', <http://oxcon.ouplaw.com/home/OCW>, formerly the Oceana Law® database 'Constitutions of the Countries of the World Online'.

Pactet, P, 'La désacralisation progressive de la Constitution de 1958' in *La République: Mélanges en l'honneur de Pierre Avril* (Montchrestien, 2001) 389–99.

Pech, L, '"A Union Founded on the Rule of Law": Meaning and Reality of the Rule of Law as a Constitutional Principle of EU Law' (2010) 6 *European Constitutional Law Review* 359.

Pech, L, *Rule of Law as a Guiding Principle of the European Union's External Action*, CLEER Working Paper 2012/03.

Pechstein, M, 'Art. 1 (ex-Art. 1 EUV) [Gründung der Europäischen Union; Grundlagen]' in R Streinz (ed), *EUV/AEUV: Vertrag über die Europäische Union und Vertrag über die Arbeitsweise der Europäischen Union*, 2nd edn (C.H. Beck, 2012) 7–15.

Pechstein, M, 'Art. 3 (ex-Art. 2 EUV) [Ziele der Union]' in R Streinz (ed), *EUV/AEUV: Vertrag über die Europäische Union und Vertrag über die Arbeitsweise der Europäischen Union*, 2nd edn (C.H. Beck, 2012) 18–20.

Pernice, I, 'The Treaty of Lisbon: Multilevel Constitutionalism in Action' (2009) 15 *Columbia Journal of European Law* 349.

Pernice, I, 'Theorie und Praxis des europäischen Verfassungsverbundes' in C Calliess (ed), *Verfassungswandel im europäischen Staaten- und Verfassungsverbund* (Mohr Siebeck, 2007) 61–92.

Pescatore, P, 'Les objectifs de la Communauté européenne comme principes d'interprétation dans la jurisprudence de la Cour de justice' in *Miscellanea W. J. Ganshof van der Meersch: Studia ab discipulis amicisque in honorem egregii professoris edita* (Bruylant, 1972) 325–63.

Peter, F, 'Political Legitimacy' in E Zalta (ed), *The Stanford Encyclopedia of Philosophy*, Spring 2014 edn, <http://plato.stanford.edu/archives/spr2014/entries/legitimacy/>.

Pilette, A and de Poncins, E, 'Valeurs, objectifs et nature de l'Union' in G Amato, H Bribosia, and B De Witte (eds), *Genesis and Destiny of the European Constitution* (Bruylant, 2007) 287–310.

Piris, J-C, *The Lisbon Treaty: A Legal and Political Analysis* (CUP, 2010).

Plecher-Hochstraßer, B, *Zielbestimmungen im Mehrebenensystem: Die Verzahnung der Staatszielbestimmungen im GG mit den Zielbestimmungen im EUV, EGV, EuratomV und EUVV* (Meidenbauer, 2006).

Podstawa, K, *EU External Human Rights Policy in Search for a Framework of Evaluation*, PhD Thesis defended at the European University Institute (September 2014).

Poiares Maduro, M, 'Contrapunctual Law: Europe's Constitutional Pluralism in Action' in N Walker (ed), *Sovereignty in Transition* (Hart Publishing, 2003) 502–37.

Poiares Maduro, M, 'Courts and Pluralism: Essay on a Theory of Judicial Adjudication in the Context of Legal and Constitutional Pluralism' in J Dunoff and J Trachtman (eds), *Ruling the World: Constitutionalism, International Law, and Global Governance* (CUP, 2009) 356–79.

Poiares Maduro, M, 'Three Claims of Constitutional Pluralism' in M Avbelj and J Komárek (eds), *Constitutional Pluralism in the European Union and Beyond* (Hart Publishing, 2012) 67–84.

Pollack, M, *The Engines of European Integration: Delegation, Agency, and Agenda Setting in the EU* (OUP, 2003).

Posen, B, 'European Union Security and Defense Policy: Response to Unipolarity?' (2006) 15 *Security Studies* 149.

Post, R, 'Constructing the European Polity: ERTA and the Open Skies Judgments' in M Poiares Maduro and L Azoulai (eds), *The Past and Future of EU Law: The Classics of EU Law Revisited on the 50th Anniversary of the Rome Treaty* (Hart Publishing, 2010) 234–47.

Prechal, S, de Vries, S, and van Eijken, H, 'The Principle of Attributed Powers and the "Scope of EU Law"' in L Besselink, F Pennings, and S Perchal (eds), *The Eclipse of the Legality Principle in the European Union* (Kluwer Law International, 2011) 213–47.

Priollaud, F-X and Siritzky, D, *Le Traité de Lisbonne: Texte et commentaire article par article des nouveaux traités Européens (TUE-TFUE)* (La Documentation Française, 2008).

Quoc Dinh, N et al, *Droit International Public*, 8th edn (L.G.D.J. 2009).

Radaelli, C, 'How Does Europeanization Produce Domestic Policy Change? Corporate Tax Policy in Italy and the United Kingdom' (1997) 30 *Comparative Political Studies* 553.

Rasmussen, H, *The European Court of Justice* (GadJura, 1998).

Ratner, S, 'Ethics and International Law: Integrating the Global Justice Project(s)' (2013) 5 *International Theory* 1.

Raube, K, 'Democratic Accountability and EU Diplomacy: The EEAS and the Role of the European Parliament' in D Spence and J Batora (eds), *The European External Action Service: European Diplomacy Post-Westphalia* (Palgrave Macmillan, 2015) 140–156.

Raz, J, 'On the Authority and Interpretation of Constitutions: Some Preliminaries' in L Alexander (ed), *Constitutionalism: Philosophical Foundations* (CUP, 1998) 152–93.

Redmond, J and Pace, R, 'European Security in the 1990s and Beyond: The Implications of the Accession of Cyprus and Malta to the European Union' (1996) 17 *Contemporary Security Policy* 430.

Regelsberger, E and Kugelmann, D, 'Art 21 EUV' in R Streinz (ed), *EUV/AEUV: Vertrag über die Europäische Union und Vertrag über die Arbeitsweise der Europäischen Union*, 2nd edn (C.H. Beck, 2012) 231–40.

Regelsberger, E and Kugelmann, D, 'Art 34 (ex-Art 19 EUV) [Koordiniertes Auftreten auf internationaler Ebene; Unterrichtungspflicht der Sicherheitsratsmitglieder' in R Streinz (ed), *EUV/AEUV: Vertrag über die Europäische Union und Vertrag über die Arbeitsweise der Europäischen Union*, 2nd edn (C.H. Beck, 2012) 271–3.

Reichard, M, *The EU-NATO Relationship: A Legal and Political Perspective* (Ashgate, 2006).

Reichwein, A, 'The Tradition of Neoclassical Realism' in A Toje and B Kunz (eds), *Neoclassical Realism in European Politics: Bringing Power Back In* (Manchester University Press, 2012) 30–60.

Reimer, F, 'Wertegemeinschaft durch Wertenormierung? Die Grundwerteklausel im europäischen Verfassungsvertrag' (2003) 18 *Zeitschrift für Gesetzgebung* 208.

Reimer, F, 'Ziele und Zuständigkeiten: Die Funktionen der Unionszielbestimmungen' [2003] *Europarecht* 992.

Riddervold, M, 'Finally Flexing Its Muscles? Atalanta—The European Union's Naval Military Operation against Piracy' (2011) 20 *European Security* 385.

Röben, V, *Außenverfassungsrecht* (Mohr Siebeck, 2007).

Robinson, P, *Dictionary of International Security* (Polity Press, 2008).

Rosamond, B, *Theories of European Integration* (Macmillan, 2000).

Rosas, A and Armati, L, *EU Constitutional Law: An Introduction*, 2nd edn (Hart Publishing, 2012).

Rousseau, D, *Droit du contentieux constitutionnel*, 8th edn (Montchrestien, 2008).

Roussillon, H, *Le Conseil constitutionnel*, 5th edn (Dalloz, 2004).

Ruffert, M, 'Art. 3 (ex-Art. 2 EUV) [Ziele der EU]' in C Calliess and M Ruffert (eds), *EUV/AEUV Kommentar*, 4th edn (C.H. Beck, 2011) 41–54.

Sachs, M, 'Normtypen im deutschen Verfassungsrecht' (1991) 6 *Zeitschrift für Gesetzgebung* 1.

Samaha, A, 'Dead Hand Arguments and Constitutional Interpretation' (2008) 108 *Columbia Law Review* 606.

Sandholtz, W and Stone Sweet, A, 'Neofunctionalism and Supranational Governance' in E Jones, A Menon, and S Weatherill (eds), *The Oxford Handbook of the European Union* (OUP, 2012) 18–33.

Sands, P and Klein, P, *Bowett's Law of International Institutions*, 6th edn (Sweet & Maxwell, 2009).

Sari, A, 'Between Legalization and Organizational Development: Explaining the Evolution of EU Competence in the Field of Foreign Policy' in PJ Cardwell (ed), *EU External Relations Law and Policy in the Post-Lisbon Era* (T.M.C. Asser Press, 2012) 59–95.

Sarkar, RS, *The Constitution of India* (National Publishing House, 1991).

Sartori, G, *Comparative Constitutional Engineering*, 2nd edn (Macmillan Press, 1997).

Sauron, J-L, *Comprendre le Traité de Lisbonne: Texte consolidé intégral des traités* (Gualino, 2007).

Scharpf, F, *Governing Europe: Effective and Legitimate?* (OUP, 1999).

Schermers, H and Blokker, N, *International Institutional Law*, 5th edn (Martinus Nijhoff, 2011).

Scheuner, U, *Staatstheorie und Staatsrecht—Gesammelte Schriften* (Duncker & Humblot, 1978).

Schmidt-Aßmann, E, 'Der Rechtsstaat' in J Isensee and P Kirchhof (eds), *Handbuch des Staatsrechts der Bundesrepublik Deutschland. Volume II: Verfassungsstaat*, 3rd edn (C.F. Müller, 2004) 541–612.

Schmitt, C, *The Concept of the Political*, trans G Schwab (University of Chicago Press, 2007).

Schröder, P, 'The Holy Roman Empire as a Model for Saint-Pierre's *Projet pour rendre la paix perpétuelle en Europe*' in R Evans and P Wilson, *The Holy Roman Empire, 1495–1806: A European Perspective* (Brill, 2012) 35–50.

Schuman, FL, *International Politics: The Western State System in Transition*, 3rd edn (McGraw-Hill, 1941).

Schütze, R, 'Federalism and Foreign Affairs: Mixity as an (Inter)national Phenomenon' in C Hillion and P Koutrakos (eds), *Mixed Agreements Revisited: The EU and Its Member States in the World* (Hart Publishing, 2010) 57–86.

Schütze, R, 'Lisbon and the Federal Order of Competences: A Prospective Analysis' (2008) 33 *European Law Review* 709.

Schütze, R, *European Constitutional Law* (CUP, 2012).

Schütze, R, *From Dual to Cooperative Federalism: The Changing Structure of European Law* (OUP, 2009).

Seervai, HM, *Constitutional Law of India: A Critical Commentary. Volume II*, 4th edn (N.M. Tripathi, 1993).

Serrano de Haro, P, *Participation of the European Union in the Work of the United Nations: General Assembly Resolution 65/276*, CLEER Working Paper 2012/4.

Shaw, M, *International Law*, 7th edn (CUP, 2014).

Shiva Rao, B, *The Framing of India's Constitution, Select Documents. Volume II* (Indian Institute of Public Administration, 1967).

Sinclair, A, *International Relations Theory and International Law* (CUP, 2010).

Singh, DK, *V.N. Shukla's Constitution of India*, 6th edn (Eastern Book Company, 1975).

Sjursen, H, *'Doing Good' in the World? Reconsidering the Basis of the Research Agenda on the EU's Foreign and Security Policy*, RECON Online Working Paper 2007/09.

Slaughter Burley, A-M, 'Are Foreign Affairs Different?' (1993) 106 *Harvard Law Review* 1980.

Slaughter, A-M, 'International Law in a World of Liberal States' (1995) 6 *European Journal of International Law* 503.

Sloan, S, *NATO, the European Union, and the Atlantic Community: The Transatlantic Bargain Challenged*, 2nd edn (Rowman & Littlefield, 2005).

Smith, K, *European Union Foreign Policy in a Changing World*, 2nd edn (Cambridge: Polity, 2008).

Snyder, F (ed), *The Europeanisation of Law: The Legal Effects of European Integration* (Hart Publishing, 2000).

Söderbaum, F, 'African Regionalism and EU-African Interregionalism' in M Telò (ed), *European Union and New Regionalism: Regional Actors and Global Governance in a Post-Hegemonic Era*, 2nd edn (Ashgate, 2007) 185–202.

Sommermann, K-P, 'Die Diskussion über die Normierung von Staatszielen' (1993) 32 *Der Staat* 430.

Sommermann, K-P, *Staatsziele und Staatszielbestimmungen* (Mohr Siebeck, 1997).

Sorrentino, F, 'The Purposes of the European Union According to the Constitutional Treaty' in HJ Blanke and S Mangiameli (eds), *Governing Europe under a Constitution: The Hard Road from the European Treaties to a European Constitutional Treaty* (Springer, 2006) 123–31.

Stein, A, 'Neoliberal Institutionalism' in C Reus-Smit and D Snidal (eds), *The Oxford Handbook of International Relations* (OUP, 2010) 200–20.

Stein, E, 'Lawyers, Judges, and the Making of a Transnational Constitution' (1981) 75 *American Journal of International Law* 1.

Stein, E, 'Towards a European Foreign Policy? The European Foreign Affairs System from the Perspective of the United States Constitution' in M Cappelletti, M Seccombe, and JHH Weiler (eds), *Integration Through Law: Europe and the American Federal Experience. Volume I, Book 3* (Walter de Gruyter, 1986) 3–82.

Stelzer, M, *The Constitution of the Republic of Austria: A Contextual Analysis* (Hart Publishing, 2011).

Stone Sweet, A and Caporaso, J, 'From Free Trade to Supranational Polity: The European Court and Integration' in W Sandholtz and A Stone Sweet (eds), *European Integration and Supranational Governance* (OUP, 1998) 92–133.

Streinz, R and Kruis, T, 'Art. 209 AEUV' in R Streinz (ed), *EUV/AEUV: Vertrag über die Europäische Union und Vertrag über die Arbeitsweise der Europäischen Union*, 2nd edn (C.H. Beck, 2012) 1998–2010.

Streinz, R, 'Art. 4 [Beziehungen zwischen der Union und den Mitgliedstaaten]' in R Streinz (ed), *EUV/AEUV: Vertrag über die Europäische Union und Vertrag über die Arbeitsweise der Europäischen Union*, 2nd edn (C.H. Beck, 2012) 20–46.

Streinz, R, 'European Integration through Constitutional Law' in H-J Blanke and S Mangiameli (eds), *Governing Europe under a Constitution: The Hard Road from the European Treaties to a European Constitutional Treaty* (Springer, 2006) 1–22.

Streinz, R, Ohler, C, and Herrmann, C, *Der Vertrag von Lissabon zur Reform der EU: Einführung mit Synopse*, 3rd edn (C.H. Beck, 2010).

Stumpf, C, 'Artikel 2 [Ziele]' in J Schwarze (ed), *EU-Kommentar*, 2nd edn (Nomos, 2008) 70–6.

Sunstein, C, 'Why Does the American Constitution Lack Social and Economic Guarantees?' (2005) 56 *Syracuse Law Review* 1.

Tamanaha, B, 'A Concise Guide to the Rule of Law' in G Palombella and N Walker (eds), *Relocating the Rule of Law* (Hart Publishing, 2009) 139–69.

Tanchev, E, 'The Lisbon Treaty within and without Constitutional Orthodoxy' in I Pernice and E Tanchev (eds), *Ceci n'est pas une Constitution—Constitutionalisation without a Constitution?* (Nomos, 2009) 22–43.

Tancredi, A, 'EC Practice in the WTO: How Wide is the "Scope for Manoeuvre"?' (2004) 15 *European Journal of International Law* 933.

Telò, M, 'Introduction: The EU as a Model, a Global Actor and an Unprecedented Power' in M Telò (ed), *The European Union and Global Governance* (Routledge, 2009) 1–39.

Terhechte, J, 'Kommentierung zum Art. 3 EUV (Ziele der Union)' in E Grabitz, M Hilf, and M Nettesheim (eds), *Das Recht der Europäischen Union*, loose-leaf, 41st supplement (C.H. Beck, 2010).

Thies, A, 'Shared Competence and the EU Member States' Obligation to Refrain from Unilateral External Action: *PFOS* and Beyond' in J Díez-Hochleitner et al (eds), *Recent Trends in the Case Law of the Court of Justice of the European Union (2008–2011)* (La Ley, 2012) 703–28.

Thym, D, 'Foreign Affairs' in A von Bogdandy and J Bast (eds), *Principles of European Constitutional Law*, 2nd edn (Hart Publishing/C.H. Beck, 2011) 309–43.

Thym, D, 'Parliamentary Involvement in European International Relations' in M Cremona and B De Witte (eds), *EU Foreign Relations Law: Constitutional Fundamentals* (Hart Publishing, 2008) 201–32.

Thym, D, 'The Intergovernmental Constitution of the EU's Foreign, Security & Defence Executive' (2011) 7 *European Constitutional Law Review* 453.

Tietje, C, 'The Status of International Law in the European Legal Order: The Case of International Treaties and Non-Binding International Agreements' in J Wouters,

A Nollkaemper, and E de Wet (eds), *The Europeanisation of International Law: The Status of International Law in the EU and Its Member States* (T.M.C. Asser Press, 2008) 55–69.

Tizzano, A, 'Der italienische Verfassungsgerichtshof (Corte costituzionale) und der Gerichtshof der Europäischen Union' (2010) 37 *Europäische Grundrechte Zeitschrift* 1.

Toje, A, *The European Union as a Small Power: After the Post-Cold War* (Palgrave Macmillan, 2010).

Tomlin, RSO, '*Spes Saeculi*: Augustine's Worldly Ambition and Career' in M Vessey (ed), *A Companion to Augustine* (Wiley-Blackwell, 2012) 57–68.

Tomuschat, C, 'Der Verfassungsstaat im Geflecht der internationalen Beziehungen' (1978) *Veröffentlichungen der Vereinigung deutscher Staatsrechtslehrer* 7.

Tope, TK, *Constitutional Law of India*, 2nd edn (Eastern Book Company, 1992).

Tourard, H, *L'internationalisation des constitutions nationales* (L.D.G.J., 2000).

Tridimas, T, 'Terrorism and the ECJ: Empowerment and Democracy in the EC Legal Order' (2009) 34 *European Law Review* 103.

Tsakaloyannis, P, *The European Union as a Security Community: Problems and Prospects* (Nomos, 1996).

Tuori, K and Tuori, K, *The Eurozone Crisis: A Constitutional Analysis* (CUP, 2014).

Tupiassu, L, 'Le droit constitutionnel: Les institutions politiques' in D Païva de Almeida (ed), *Introduction au droit brésilien* (Harmattan, 2006) 15–46.

Tushnet, M, 'Social Welfare Rights and the Forms of Judicial Review' (2003) 82 *Texas Law Review* 1895.

Uerpmann-Wittzack, R, 'Rechtsfragen und Rechtsfolgen des Beitritts der Europäischen Union zur EMRK' [2012] *Europarecht (Beiheft 2)* 167.

Uitz, R, 'Can You Tell When an Illiberal Democracy is in the Making? An Appeal to Comparative Constitutional Scholarship from Hungary' (2015) 13 *International Journal of Constitutional Law* 279.

Usman, J, 'Non-Justiciable Directive Principles: A Constitutional Design Effect' (2007) 15 *Michigan State Journal of International Law* 643.

Van Elsuwege, P and Merket, H, 'The Role of the Court of Justice in Ensuring the Unity of the EU's External Representation' in S Blockmans and R Wessel (eds), *Principles and Practices of EU External Representation*, CLEER Working Paper 2012/5, 37–57.

Van Elsuwege, P, 'EU External Action after the Collapse of the Pillar Structure: In Search of a New Balance between Delimitation and Consistency' (2010) 47 *Common Market Law Review* 987.

Van Vooren, B and Wessel, R, *EU External Relations Law: Text, Cases and Materials* (CUP, 2014).

Van Vooren, B, 'A Legal–Institutional Perspective on the European Union External Action Service' (2011) 48 *Common Market Law Review* 475.

Van Vooren, B, *EU External Relations Law and the European Neighbourhood Policy: A Paradigm for Coherence* (Routledge, 2012).

Vasconcelos, A, 'European Union and MERCOSUR' in M Telò, *European Union and New Regionalism: Regional Actors and Global Governance in a Post-Hegemonic Era*, 2nd edn (Ashgate, 2007) 165–83.

Verdroß, A, 'Vom Gemeinwohl der Staatsbürger zum Gemeinwohl der Menschheit' in H Kelsen, H Klecatsky, R Marcic, and H Schambeck (eds), *Die Wiener Rechtstheoretische Schule. Volume I* (Franz Steiner Verlag, 2010) 663–6.

Vereshchetin, V, 'New Constitutions and the Old Problem of the Relationship between International Law and National Law' (1996) 7 *European Journal of International Law* 1.

Vespaziani, A, 'Comparison, Translation and the Making of a Common European Constitutional Culture' (2008) 9 *German Law Journal* 547.

Vigni, P, 'The Protection of EU Citizens: The Perspective of International Law' in J Larik and M Moraru (eds), *Ever-Closer in Brussels—Ever-Closer in the World? EU External Action after the Lisbon Treaty*, EUI Working Paper Law 2011/10, 91–106.

Vimbert, C, 'L'ordre public dans la jurisprudence du Conseil constitutionnel' (1994) No 3 *Revue du droit public et de la science politique en France et à l'étranger* 693.

Vinx, L, 'Carl Schmitt and the Analogy between Constitutional and International Law: Are Constitutional and International Law Inherently Political?' (2013) 2 *Global Constitutionalism* 91.

Vogel, K, *Verfassungsentscheidung des Grundgesetzes für eine internationale Zusammenarbeit* (Mohr Siebeck, 1964).

von Bogdandy, A and Bast, J, 'The Constitutional Approach to EU Law' in A von Bogdandy and J Bast (eds), *Principles of European Constitutional Law*, 2nd edn (Hart Publishing/ C.H. Beck 2011) 1–7.

von Bogdandy, A and Bast, J, 'The Federal Order of Competences' in A von Bogdandy and J Bast (eds), *Principles of European Constitutional Law*, 2nd edn (Hart Publishing/ C.H. Beck, 2011) 275–307.

von Bogdandy, A and Schill, S, 'Artikel 4 EUV' in E Grabitz, M Hilf, and M Nettesheim (eds), *Das Recht der Europäischen Union*, loose-leaf, 41st supplement (C.H. Beck, 2010).

von Bogdandy, A and Schill, S, 'Overcoming Absolute Primacy: Respect for National Identity under the Lisbon Treaty' (2011) 48 *Common Market Law Review* 1417.

von Bogdandy, A, 'Constitutional Principles for Europe' in E Riedel and R Wolfrum (eds), *Recent Trends in German and European Constitutional Law* (Springer, 2006) 1–35.

von Bogdandy, A, Cruz Villalón, P, and Huber, P, 'Vorwort' in A von Bogdandy, P Cruz Villalón and P Huber (eds), *Handbuch Ius Publicum Europaeum. Volume I: Grundlagen und Grundzüge staatlichen Verfassungsrechts* (C.F. Müller, 2007) v–vi.

von Bogdandy, A, 'Founding Principles of EU Law: A Theoretical and Doctrinal Sketch' (2009) 16 *European Law Journal* 95.

von Bogdandy, A, 'Founding Principles' in A von Bogdandy and J Bast (eds), *Principles of European Constitutional Law*, 2nd edn (Hart Publishing/C.H. Beck, 2011) 11–54.

von Bogdandy, A, 'The European Constitution and European identity: Text and Subtext of the Treaty establishing a Constitution for Europe' (2005) 3 *International Journal of Constitutional Law* 295.

von Bogdandy, A, 'Zur Übertragbarkeit staatsrechtlicher Figuren auf die Europäische Union' in M Brenner, P Huber, and M Möstl (eds), *Der Staat des Grundgesetzes—Kontinuität und Wandel. Festschrift für Peter Badura zum siebzigsten Geburtstag* (Mohr Siebeck, 2004) 1033–52.

von Jhering, R, *Law as a Means to an End*, trans I Husik (The Boston Book Company, 1913).

Walker, N, 'After *Finalité*? The Future of the European Constitutional Idea' in G Amato, H Bribosia, and B De Witte (eds), *Genesis and Destiny of the European Constitution* (Bruylant, 2007) 1245–70.

Walker, N and Tierney, S, 'Introduction: A Constitutional Mosaic? Exploring the New Frontiers of Europe's Constitutionalism' in N Walker, J Shaw, and S Tierney (eds), *Europe's Constitutional Mosaic* (Hart Publishing, 2011) 1–18.

Walker, N, 'Late Sovereignty in the European Union' in N Walker (ed), *Sovereignty in Transition* (Hart Publishing, 2003) 3–32.

Walker, N, 'Post-national Constitutionalism and the Problem of Translation' in JHH Weiler and M Wind (eds), *European Constitutionalism Beyond the State* (CUP, 2003) 27–54.

Walker, N, 'The Idea of Constitutional Pluralism' (2002) 68 *Modern Law Review* 317.

Walker, N, 'The Rule of Law and the EU: Necessity's Mixed Virtue' in G Palombella and N Walker (eds), *Relocating the Rule of Law* (Hart Publishing, 2009) 119–38.

Walker, N, 'The Place of European Law' in G de Búrca and JHH Weiler (eds), *The Worlds of European Constitutionalism* (CUP, 2011) 57–104.

Walker, N, Shaw, J, and Tierney, S (eds), *Europe's Constitutional Mosaic* (Hart Publishing, 2011).

Walter, R and Mayer, H, *Grundriß des österreichischen Bundesverfassungsrechts*, 9th edn (Manz, 2000).

Waltz, K, 'Evaluating Theories' (1997) 91 *American Political Science Review* 913.

Waltz, K, 'Structural Realism after the Cold War' (2000) 25 *International Security* 5.

Waltz, K, *Theory of International Politics* (Random House, 1979).

Webber, M, 'The Common Security and Defence Policy in a Multilateral World' in P Koutrakos (ed), *European Foreign Policy: Legal and Political Perspectives* (Edward Elgar, 2011) 205–34.

Weiler, JHH, 'A Quiet Revolution: The European Court and Its Interlocutors' (1994) 26 *Comparative Political Studies* 510.

Weiler, JHH, 'Does Europe Need a Constitution? Demos, Telos and the German Maastricht Decision' (1995) 1 *European Law Journal* 219.

Weiler, JHH, 'The Transformation of Europe' (1991) 100 *Yale Law Journal* 2403.

Weiler, JHH, *The Constitution of Europe: 'Do the New Clothes Have an Emperor?' and Other Essays on European Integration* (CUP, 1999).

Wessel, R, 'The EU as Black Widow: Devouring the WEU to Give Birth to a European Security and Defence Policy' in V Kronenberger (ed), *The EU and the International Legal Order: Discord or Harmony?* (T.M.C. Asser Press, 2001) 405–34.

West, R, 'The Aspirational Constitution' (1993) 88 *Northwestern University Law Review* 241.

Wetzel, A and Orbie, J, 'Promoting Embedded Democracy? Researching the Substance of EU Democracy Promotion' (2011) 16 *European Foreign Affairs Review* 565.

Whitman, R (ed), *Normative Power Europe: Empirical and Theoretical Perspectives* (Palgrave Macmillan, 2011).

Wilson, R, 'International Law in New National Constitutions' (1964) 58 *American Journal of International Law* 432.

Wivel, A, 'The Security Challenge of Small EU Member States: Interests, Identity and the Development of the EU as a Security Actor' (2005) 43 *Journal of Common Market Studies* 393.

Wohlforth, W, 'Realism' in C Reus-Smit and D Snidal (eds), *The Oxford Handbook of International Relations* (OUP, 2010) 405–34.

Wolfers, A, *Discord and Collaboration: Essays on International Politics* (Johns Hopkins University Press, 1962).

Wong, R and Hill, C (eds), *National and European Foreign Policy: Towards Europeanization* (Routledge, 2011).

Wong, R, 'The Europeanization of Foreign Policy' in C Hill and M Smith (eds), *International Relations and the European Union*, 2nd edn (OUP, 2011) 149–71.

Wouters, J and Basu, S, 'The Creation of a Global Criminal Justice System: The European Union and the International Criminal Court' in C Ryngaert (ed), *The Effectiveness of International Criminal Justice* (Intersentia, 2009) 117–44.

Wouters, J, 'National Constitutions and the European Union' (2000) 27 *Legal Issues of Economic Integration* 25.

Wouters, J, 'The Tormented Relationship between International Law and EU Law' in P Bekker, R Dolzer, and M Waibel (eds), *Making Transnational Law Work in the Global Economy: Essays in Honour of Detlev Vagts* (CUP, 2010) 198–221.

Wouters, J, Coppens, D, and De Meester, B, 'The European Union's External Relations After the Lisbon Treaty' in S Griller and J Ziller (eds), *The Lisbon Treaty: EU Constitutionalism without a Constitutional Treaty?* (Springer, 2008) 143–203.

Wouters, J, Nollkaemper, A, and de Wet, E (eds), *The Europeanisation of International Law: The Status of International Law in the EU and Its Member States* (T.M.C. Asser Press, 2008).

Wouters, J, Verhey, L, and Kiiver, P (eds), *European Constitutionalism Beyond Lisbon* (Intersentia, 2009).

Wyatt, D, 'Is the European Union an Organization of Limited Powers?' in A Arnull et al (eds), *A Constitutional Order of States? Essays in EU Law in Honour of Alan Dashwood* (Hart Publishing, 2011) 3–23.

Young, O, *International Governance: Protecting the Environment in a Stateless Society* (Cornell University Press, 1994).

Youngs, R, *Europe's Decline and Fall: The Struggle Against Global Irrelevance* (Profile Books, 2010).

Zacher, H, 'Das soziale Staatsziel' in J Isensee and P Kirchhof (eds), *Handbuch des Staatsrechts der Bundesrepublik Deutschland. Volume IV: Aufgaben des Staates*, 3rd edn (C.F. Müller, 2006) 659–784.

Zehfuss, M, *Constructivism in International Relations* (CUP, 2002).

Zhang, Q, 'A Constitution without Constitutionalism? The Paths of Constitutional Development in China' (2010) 8 *International Journal of Constitutional Law* 950.

Ziller, J (ed), *L'européanisation des droits constitutionnels à la lumière de la constitution pour l'Europe/The Europeanisation of Constitutional Law in the Light of the Constitution for Europe* (L'Harmattan, 2003).

Zürn, M, 'Democratic Governance Beyond the Nation-State: The EU and Other International Institutions' (2000) 6 *European Journal of International Relations* 183.

Index

Introductory Note

References such as '178–9' indicate (not necessarily continuous) discussion of a topic across a range of pages. As the entire work concerns 'foreign policy objectives' and 'constitutional law', with a particular focus on the European Union, the use of these terms (and certain others which occur very frequently throughout the book) as an entry point has been restricted. Information will be found under the corresponding detailed topics.

The manufacturer's authorised representative in the EU for product safety is Oxford University Press España S.A. of el Parque Empresarial San Fernando de Henares, Avenida de Castilla, 2 – 28830 Madrid (www.oup.es/en or product.safety@oup.com). OUP España S.A. also acts as importer into Spain of products made by the manufacturer.

www.ingramcontent.com/pod-product-compliance
Lightning Source LLC
LaVergne TN
LVHW011910200926
848484LV00002B/580
* 9 7 8 0 1 9 8 7 3 6 3 9 4 *